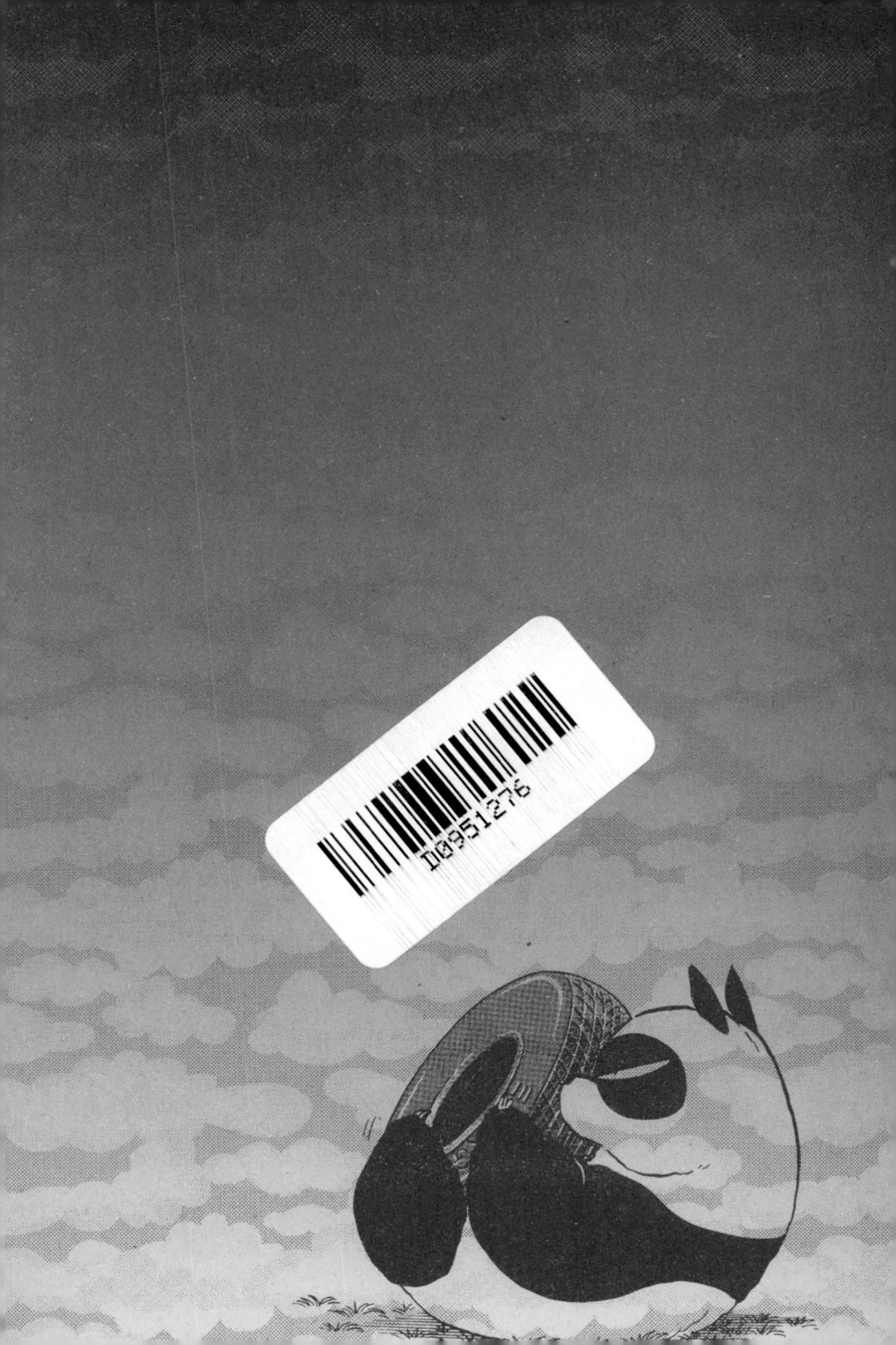

Ranma 1/2

VOL. 1
Action Edition (2nd Edition)

Story and Art by
RUMIKO TAKAHASHI

English Adaptation/Gerard Jones and Matt Thorn
Touch-Up Art & Lettering/Wayne Truman
Cover Design/Hidemi Sahara
Graphics & Design/Sean Lee
Editors (1st Edition)/Satoru Fujii and Trish Ledoux
Editor (Action Edition)/Julie Davis

Managing Editor/Annette Roman
Director of Production /Noboru Watanabe
VP of Publishing/Alvin Lu
Sr. Director of Acquisitions/Rika Inouye
VP of Sales & Marketing/Liza Coppola
Publisher/Hyoe Narita

Published by VIZ Media, LLC
P.O. Box 77010
San Francisco, CA 94107

1st Edition published 1993

Action Edition (2nd Edition)
10 9 8 7
First printing, April 2003
Sixth printing, October 2004
Seventh printing, January 2006

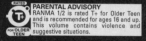

www.viz.com

store.viz.com

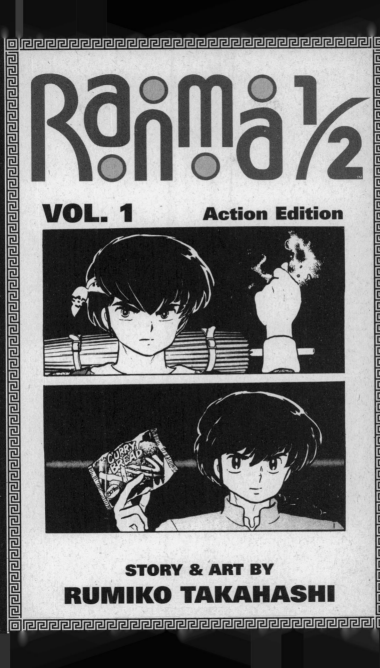

Ranma 1/2

VOL. 1   Action Edition

STORY & ART BY
RUMIKO TAKAHASHI

CONTENTS

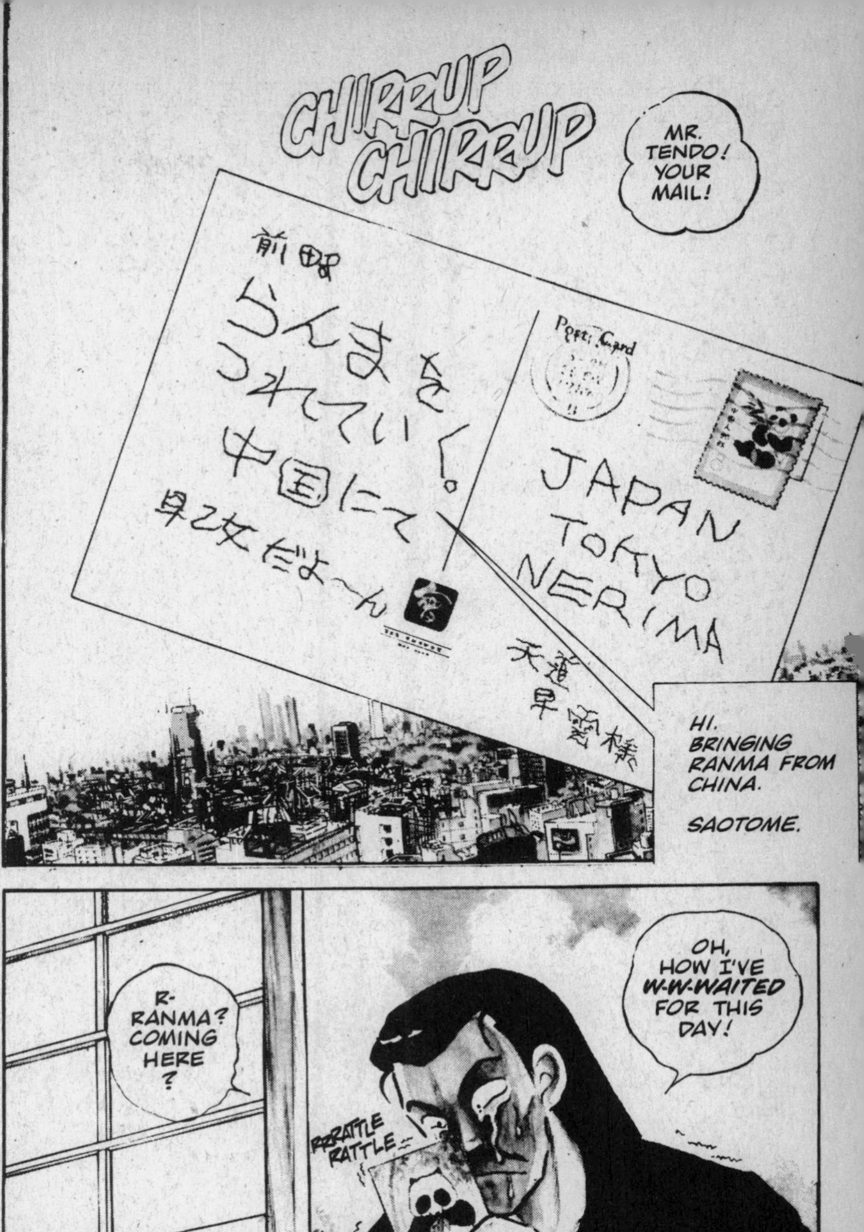
CHIRRUP CHIRRUP
MR. TENDO! YOUR MAIL!
前略
らんまをつれていく。
中国にて
早乙女だよ〜ん
Post Card
JAPAN TOKYO NERIMA
天道早雲様
HI. BRINGING RANMA FROM CHINA.
SAOTOME.
R- RANMA? COMING HERE?
RRRATTLE RATTLE
OH, HOW I'VE W-W-WAITED FOR THIS DAY!

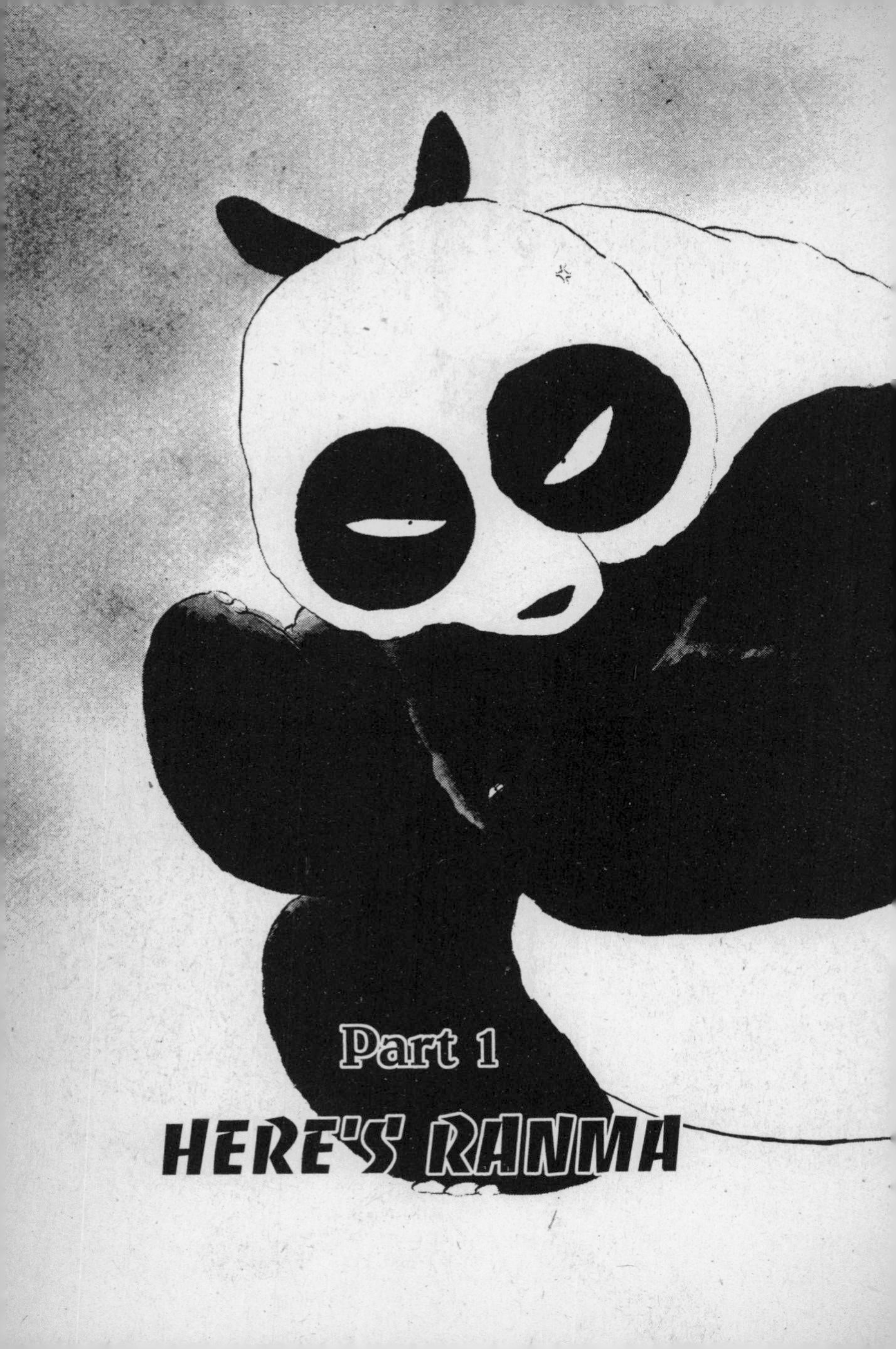

Part 1

HERE'S RANMA

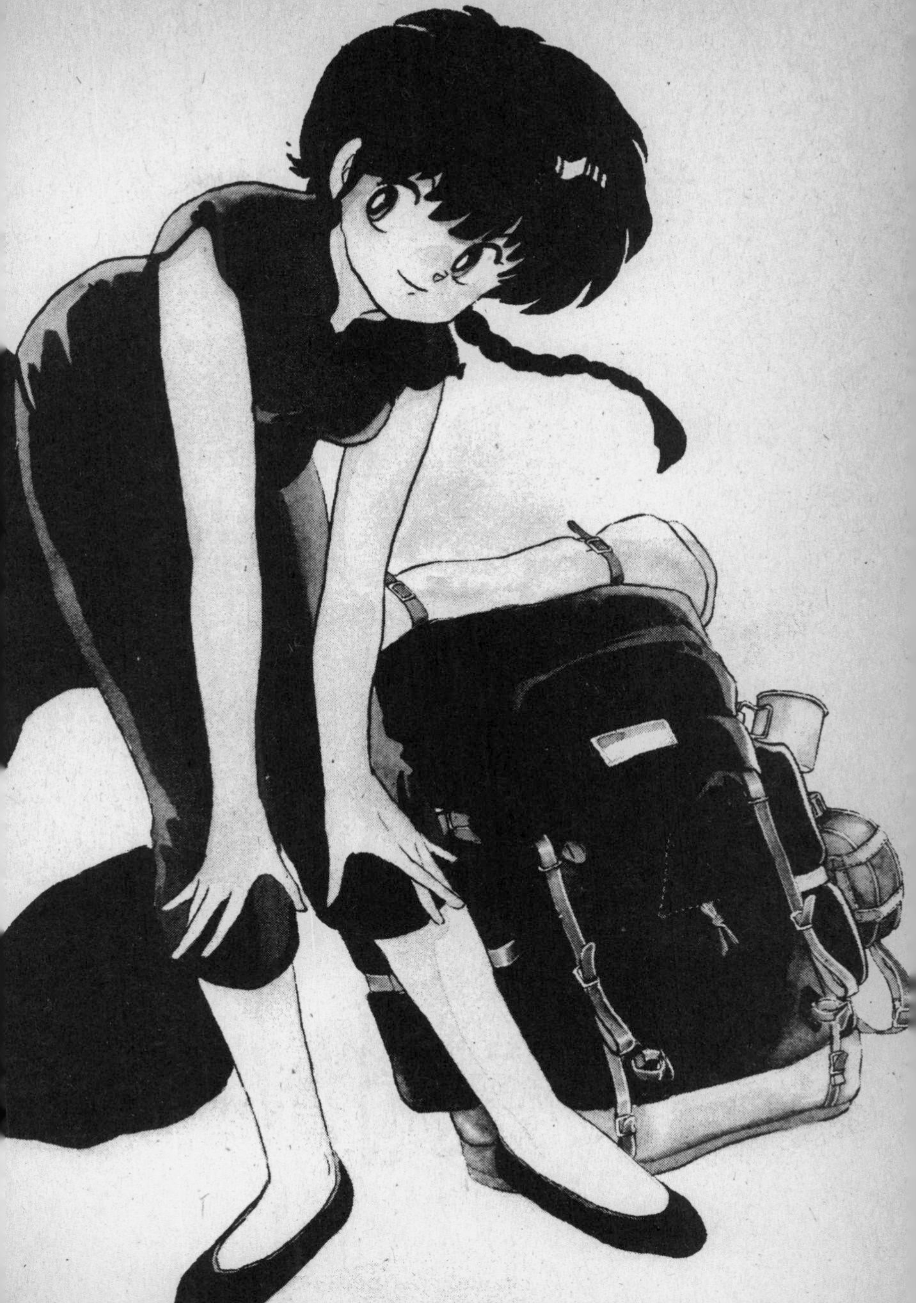

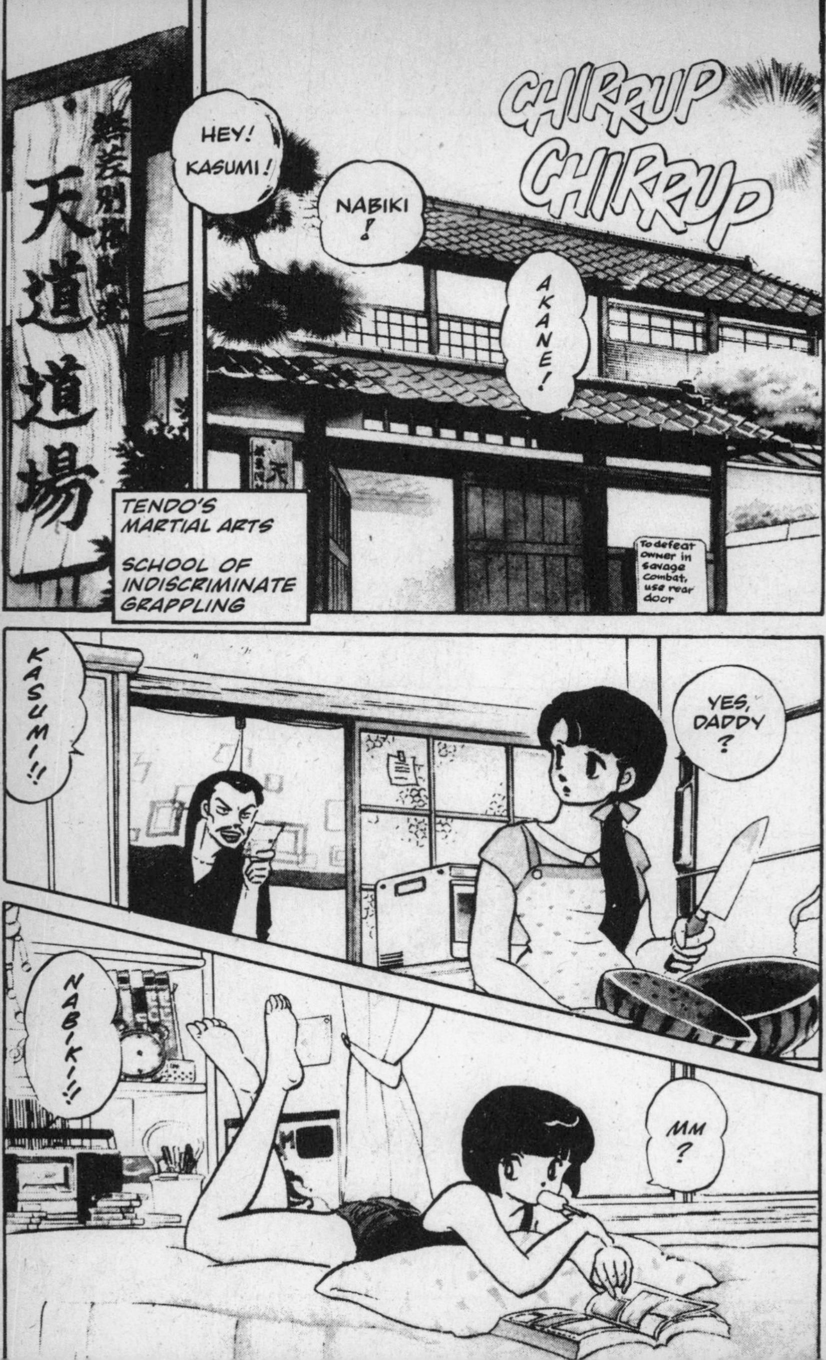
天道道場
HEY! KASUMI!
NABIKI!
CHIRRUP
CHIRRUP
AKANE!
TENDO'S MARTIAL ARTS
SCHOOL OF INDISCRIMINATE GRAPPLING
To defeat owner in savage combat, use rear door
KASUMI!!
YES, DADDY?
NABIKI!!!
MM?

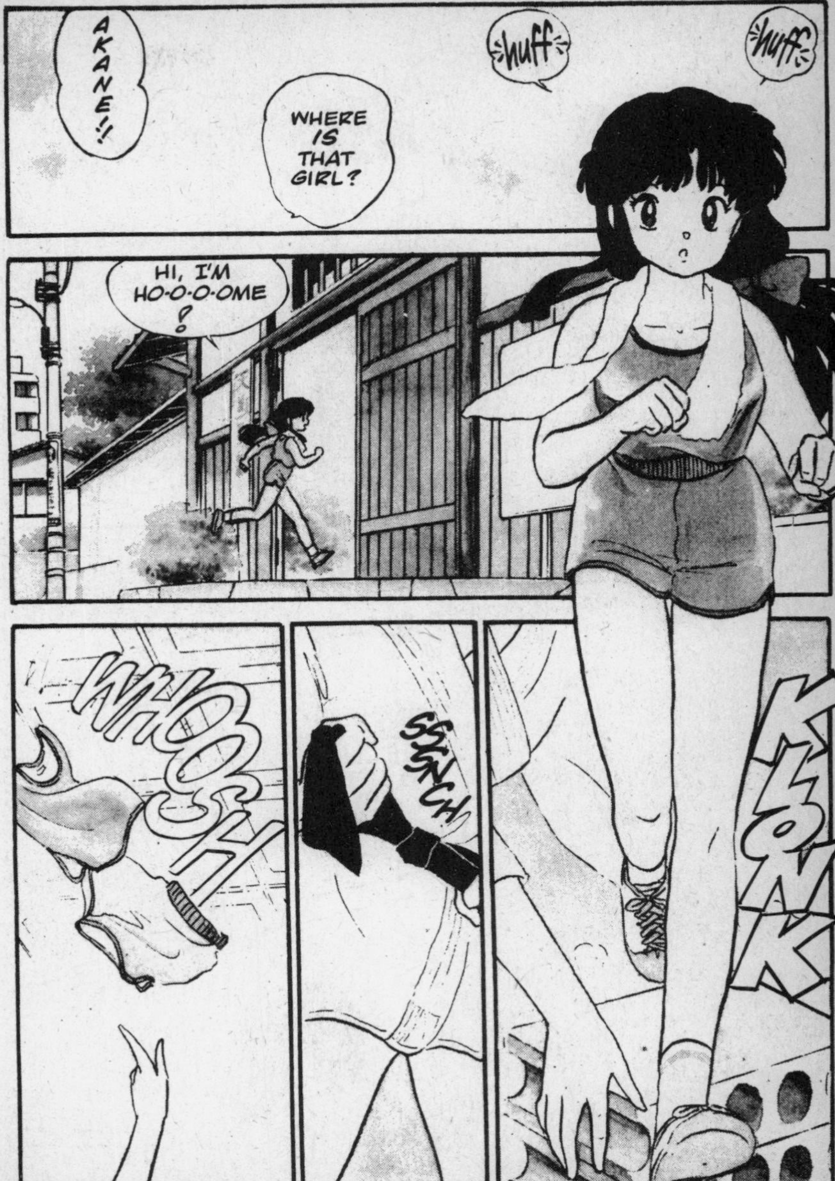
AKANE!!
WHERE IS THAT GIRL?
huff
huff
HI, I'M HO-O-O-OME!
WHOOSH
SSSNCH
KLONK

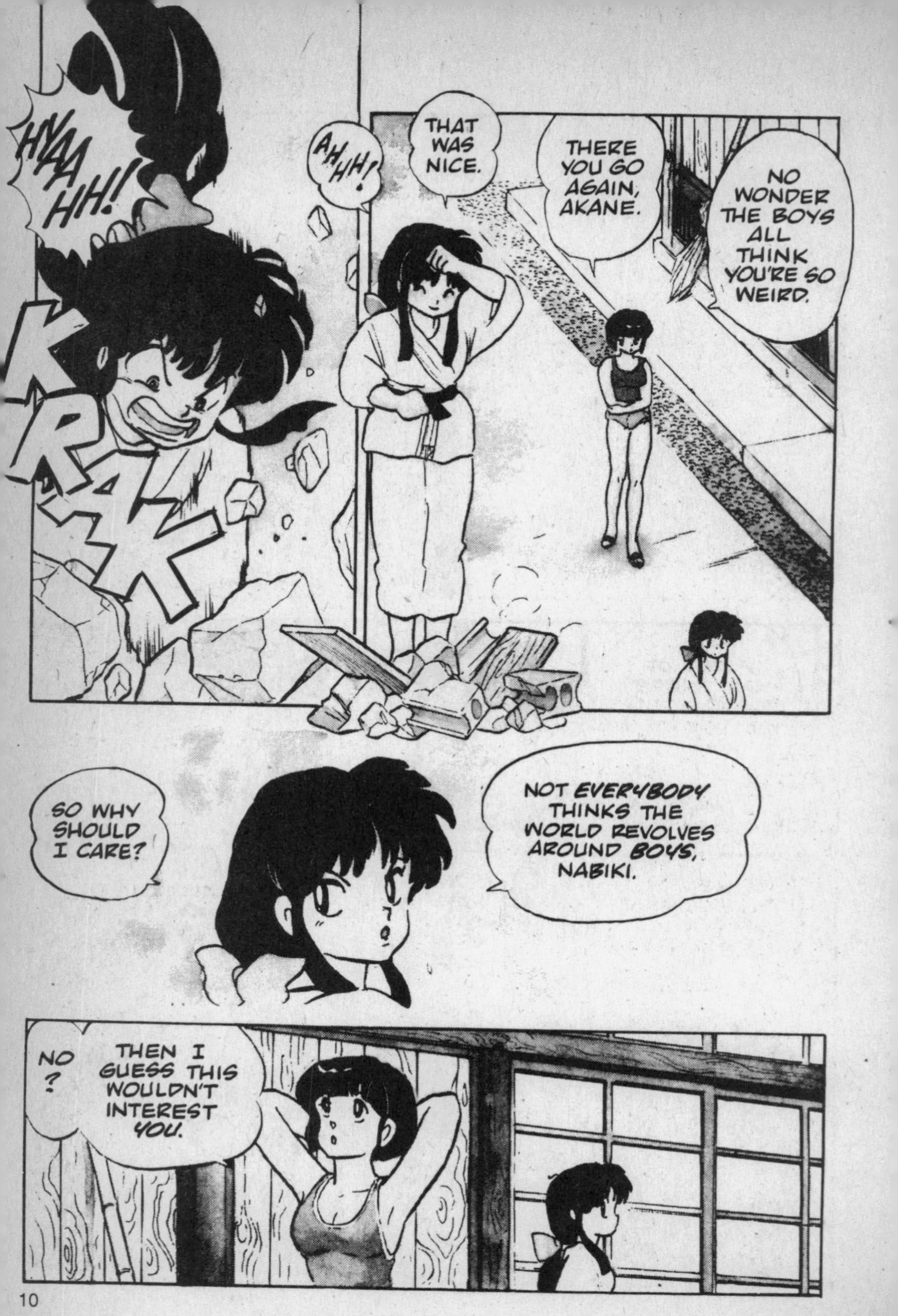

HYAAAHH!
KRAK
AHHH!
THAT WAS NICE.
THERE YOU GO AGAIN, AKANE.
NO WONDER THE BOYS ALL THINK YOU'RE SO WEIRD.
SO WHY SHOULD I CARE?
NOT *EVERYBODY* THINKS THE WORLD REVOLVES AROUND *BOYS*, NABIKI.
NO?
THEN I GUESS THIS WOULDN'T INTEREST *YOU*.

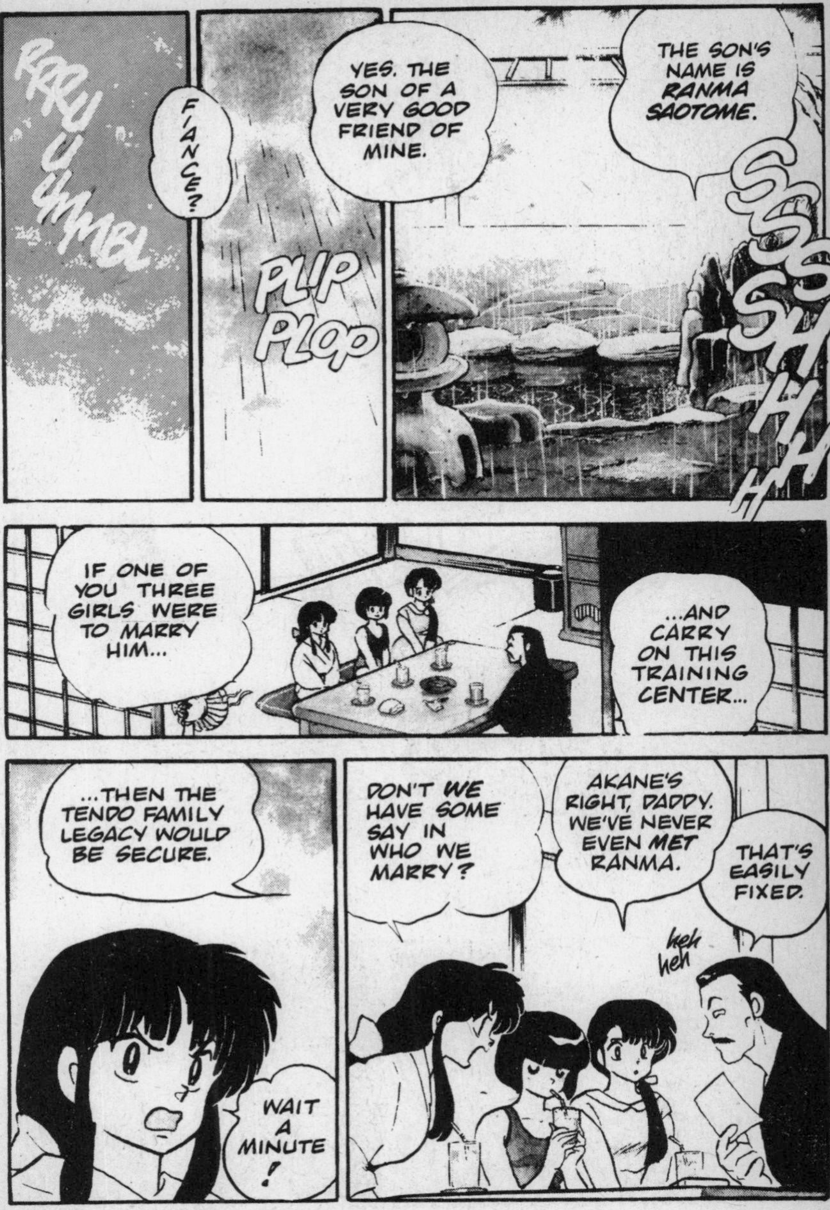
RRRUUMMBL
FIANCE?
YES. THE SON OF A VERY GOOD FRIEND OF MINE.
PLIP PLOP
THE SON'S NAME IS RANMA SAOTOME.
SSSSHHHH
IF ONE OF YOU THREE GIRLS WERE TO MARRY HIM...
...AND CARRY ON THIS TRAINING CENTER...
...THEN THE TENDO FAMILY LEGACY WOULD BE SECURE.
WAIT A MINUTE!
DON'T WE HAVE SOME SAY IN WHO WE MARRY?
AKANE'S RIGHT, DADDY. WE'VE NEVER EVEN MET RANMA.
THAT'S EASILY FIXED.
keh heh

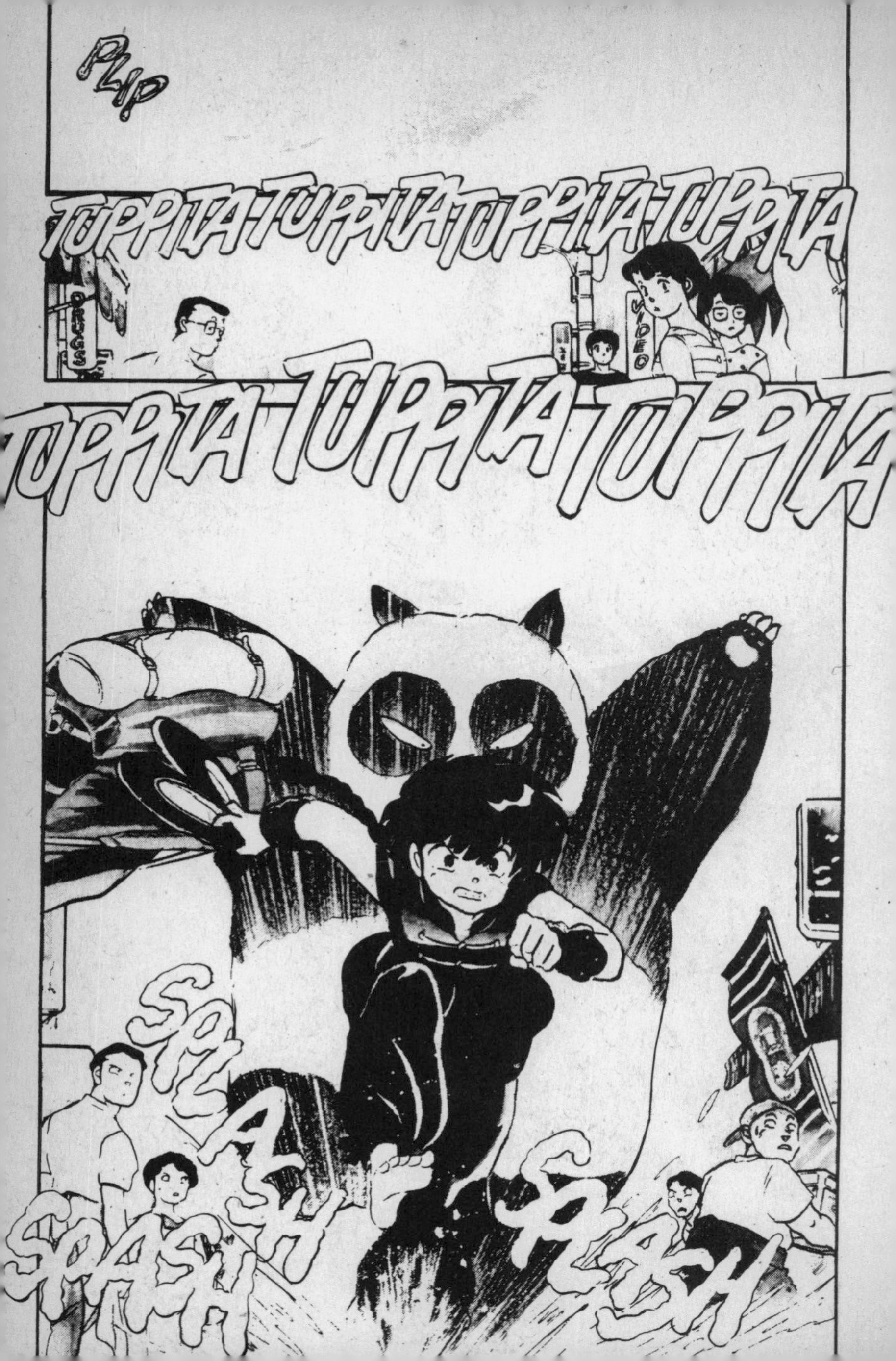
PLIP
TUPPITA TUPPITA TUPPITA TUPPITA
DRUGS
VIDEO
TUPPITA TUPPITA TUPPITA
SPLASH
SPLASH
SPLASH

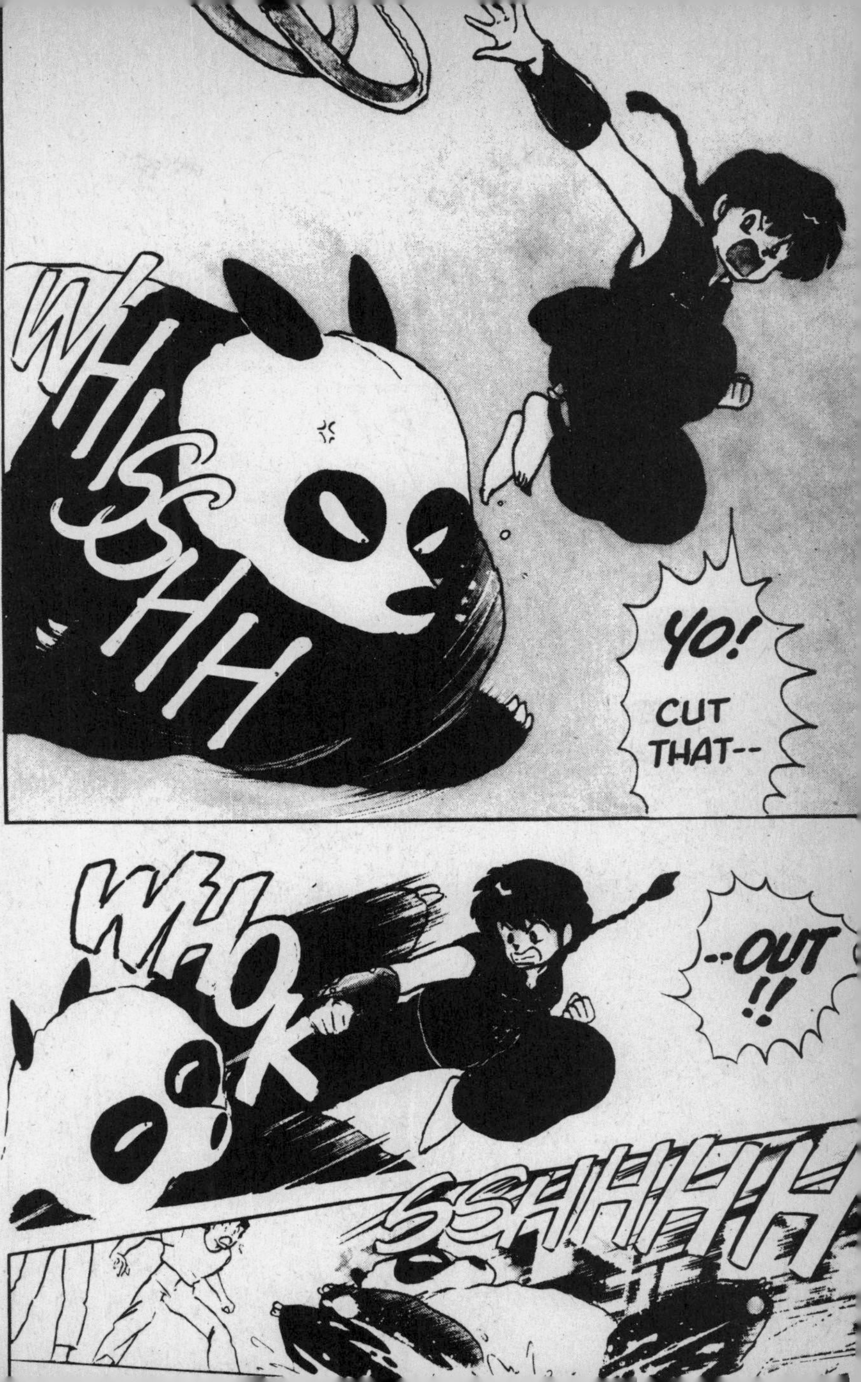
WHISSHH
YO! CUT THAT--
WHOK
--OUT !!
SSHHHHH

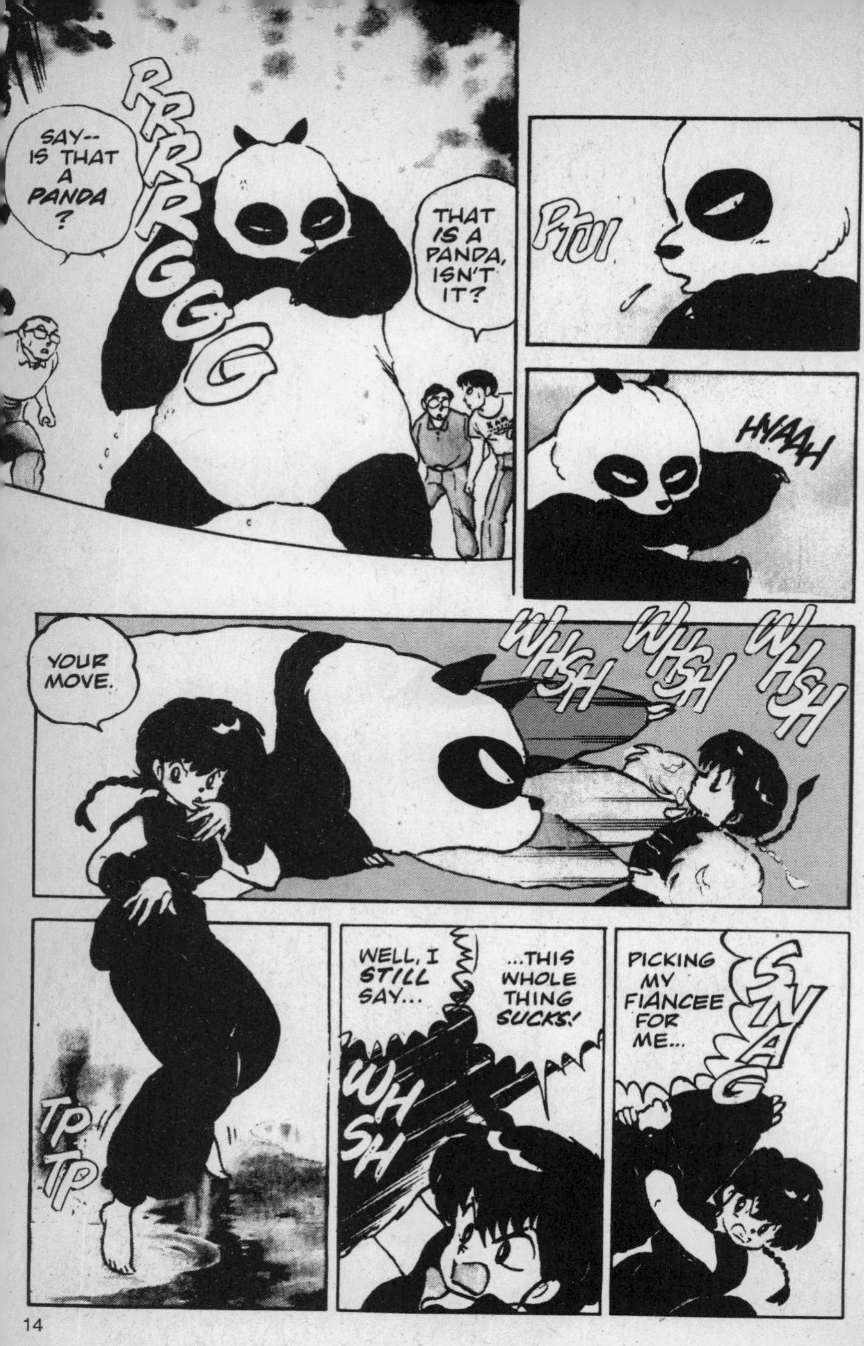
SAY-- IS THAT A PANDA ?
RRRRGGG
THAT IS A PANDA, ISN'T IT?
PTUI
HYAAAH
YOUR MOVE.
WHSH
WHSH
WHSH
TP TP
WELL, I STILL SAY...
...THIS WHOLE THING SUCKS!
WHSH
PICKING MY FIANCEE FOR ME...
SNAG

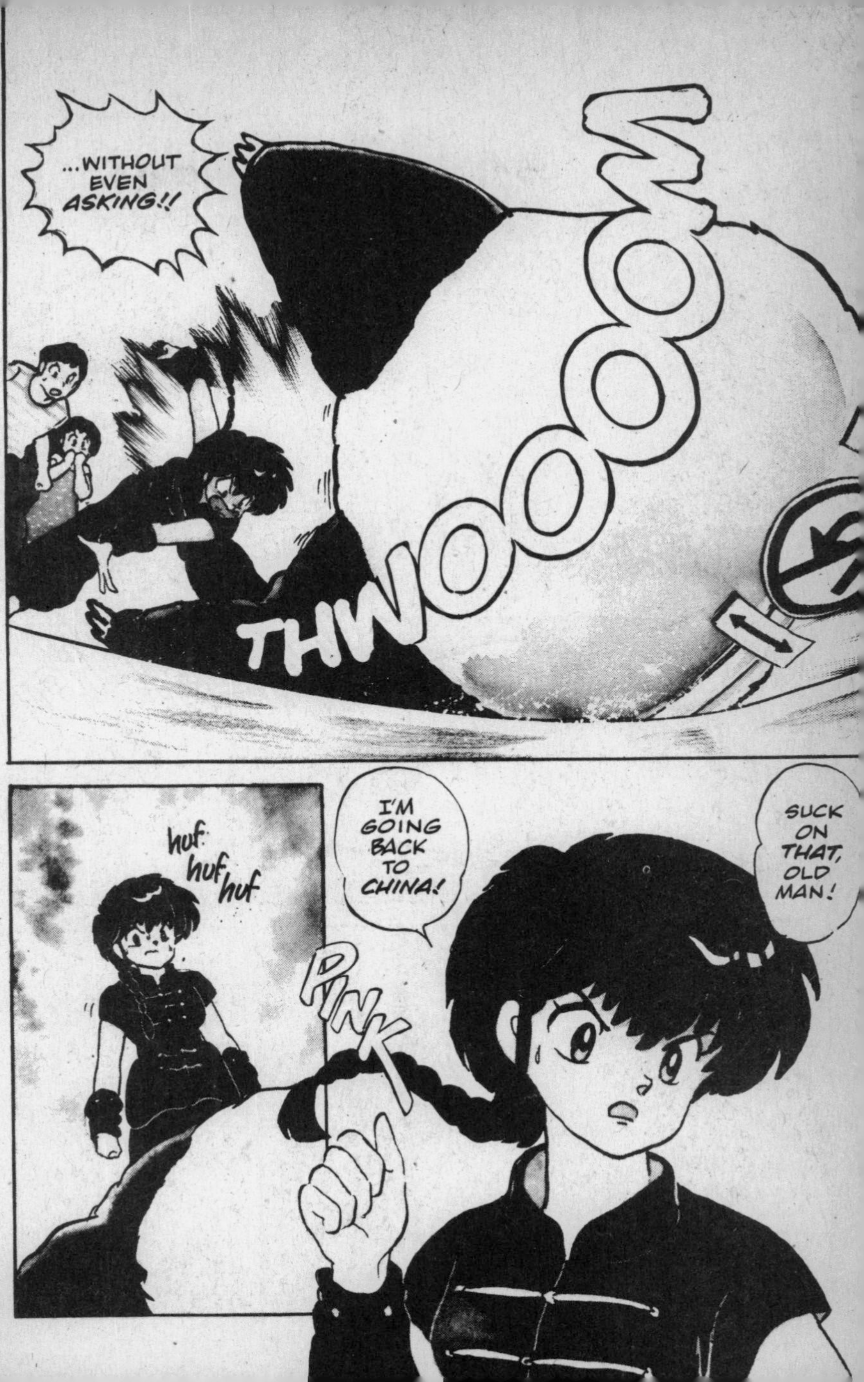
...WITHOUT EVEN ASKING!!
THWOOOOOOM
huf huf huf
I'M GOING BACK TO CHINA!
PINK
SUCK ON THAT, OLD MAN!

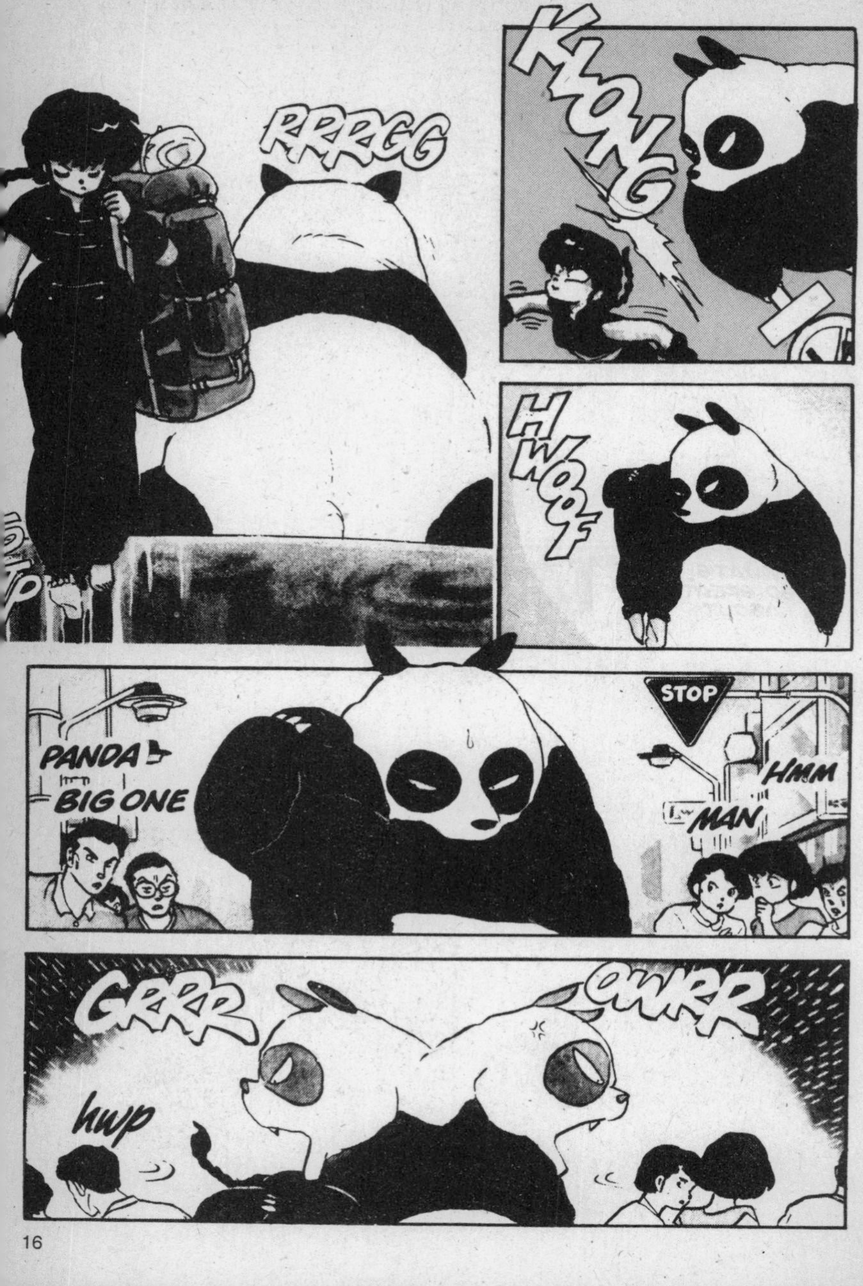
RRRGG
KLONG
HWOOF
PANDA
BIG ONE
STOP
HMM
MAN
GRRR
hwp
OWRR

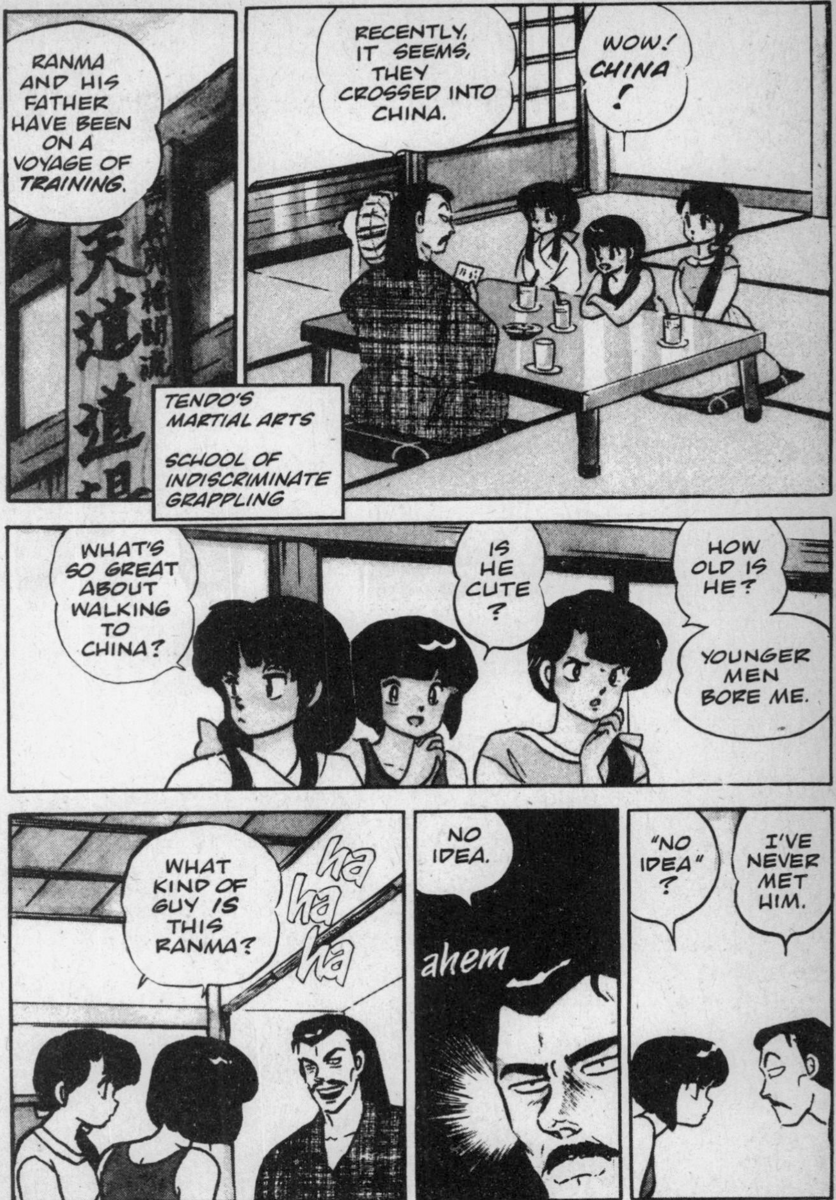
RANMA AND HIS FATHER HAVE BEEN ON A VOYAGE OF *TRAINING.*
RECENTLY, IT SEEMS, THEY CROSSED INTO CHINA.
WOW! CHINA!
TENDO'S MARTIAL ARTS
SCHOOL OF INDISCRIMINATE GRAPPLING
WHAT'S SO GREAT ABOUT WALKING TO CHINA?
IS HE CUTE?
HOW OLD IS HE?
YOUNGER MEN BORE ME.
WHAT KIND OF GUY *IS* THIS RANMA?
ha ha ha
NO IDEA.
ahem
"NO IDEA"?
I'VE NEVER MET HIM.

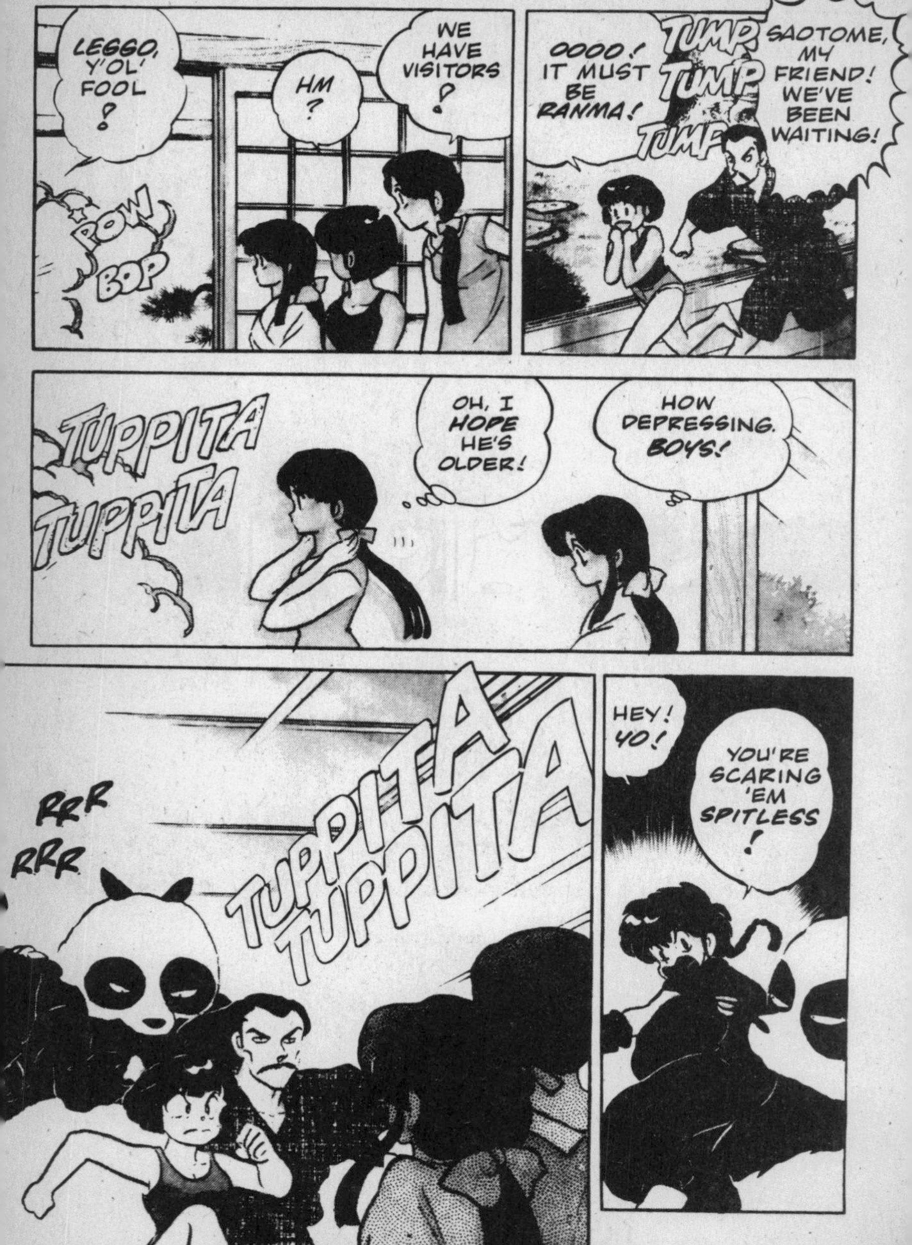
LEGGO, Y'OL' FOOL!
POW
BOP
HM?
WE HAVE VISITORS!
OOOO! IT MUST BE RANMA!
TUMP TUMP TUMP
SAOTOME, MY FRIEND! WE'VE BEEN WAITING!
TUPPITA TUPPITA
OH, I HOPE HE'S OLDER!
HOW DEPRESSING. BOYS!
RRR RRR
TUPPITA TUPPITA
HEY! YO!
YOU'RE SCARING 'EM SPITLESS!

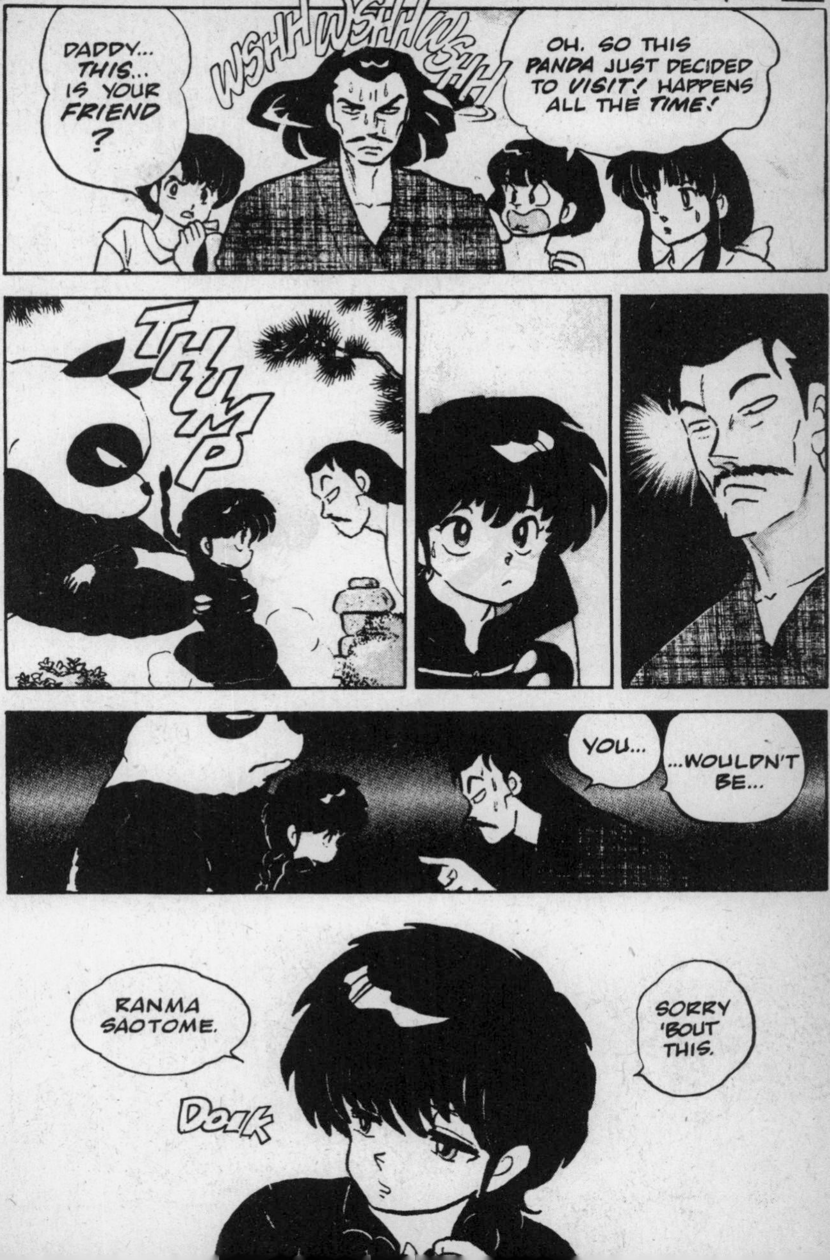
DADDY... THIS... IS YOUR FRIEND ?
WSHH WSHH WSHH
OH. SO THIS PANDA JUST DECIDED TO VISIT! HAPPENS ALL THE TIME!
THUMP
YOU...
...WOULDN'T BE...
RANMA SAOTOME.
SORRY 'BOUT THIS.
DONK

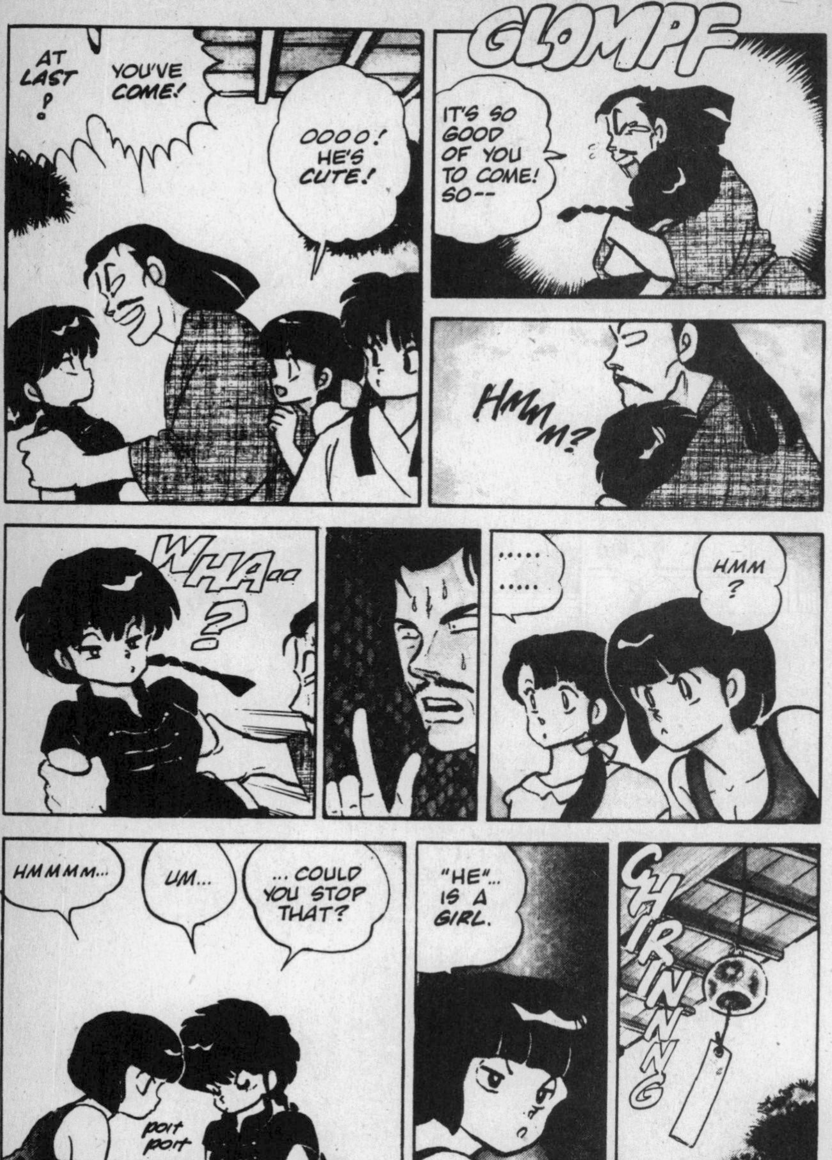
AT LAST !
YOU'VE COME!
OOOO! HE'S CUTE!
GLOMPF
IT'S SO GOOD OF YOU TO COME! SO--
HMMM?
WHAaa ?
......
......
HMM ?
HMMMM...
UM...
... COULD YOU STOP THAT?
poit poit
"HE"... IS A GIRL.
CHIRINNNG

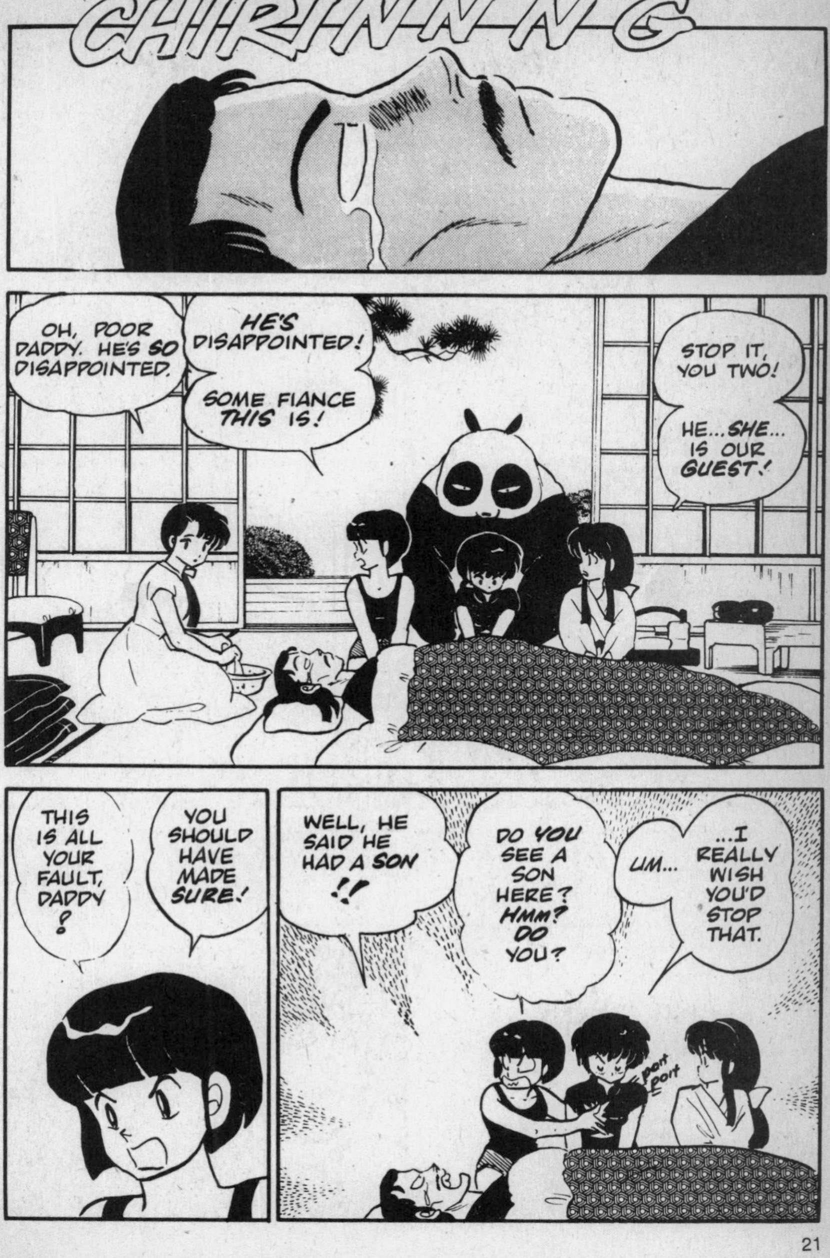
CHIRINNNG
OH, POOR DADDY. HE'S SO DISAPPOINTED.
HE'S DISAPPOINTED!
SOME FIANCE THIS IS!
STOP IT, YOU TWO!
HE...SHE... IS OUR GUEST!
THIS IS ALL YOUR FAULT, DADDY!
YOU SHOULD HAVE MADE SURE!
WELL, HE SAID HE HAD A SON!!
DO YOU SEE A SON HERE? HMM? DO YOU?
UM...
...I REALLY WISH YOU'D STOP THAT.
port port

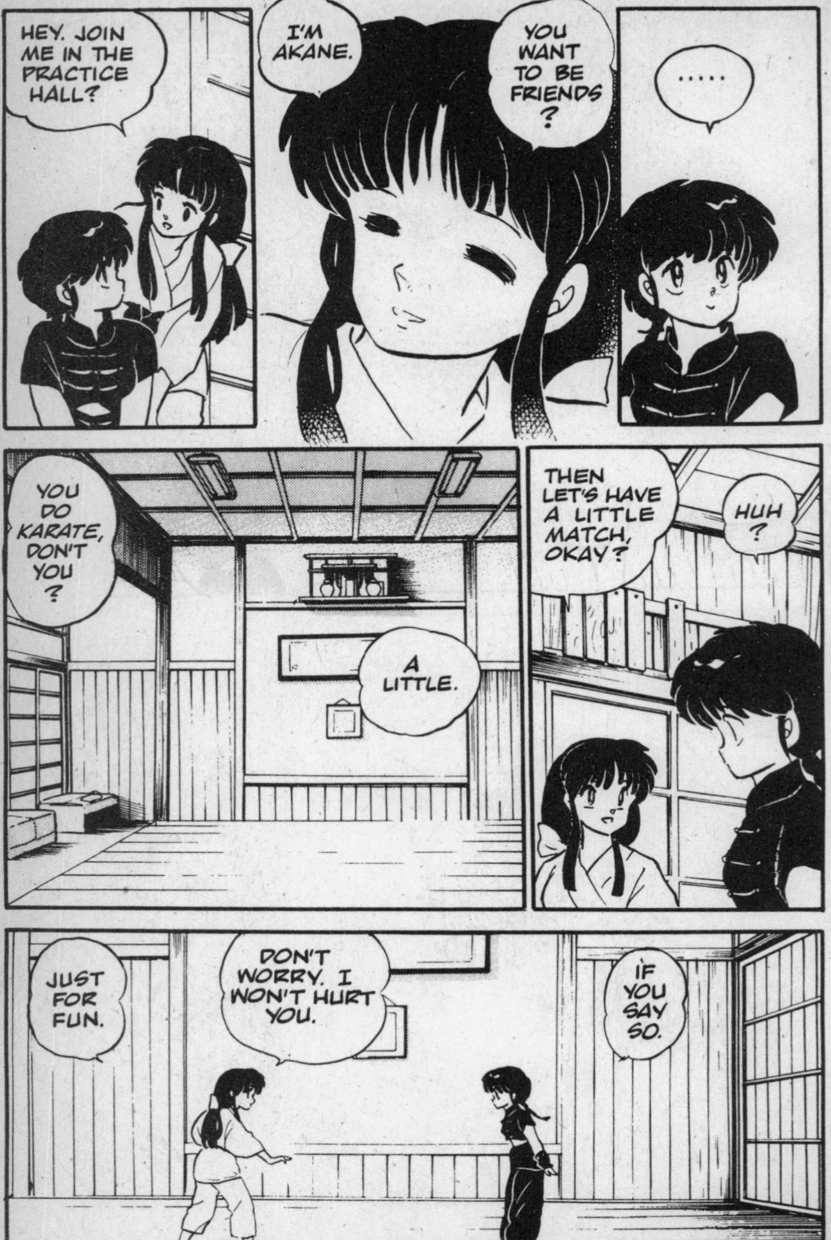
HEY. JOIN ME IN THE PRACTICE HALL?
I'M AKANE.
YOU WANT TO BE FRIENDS?
.....
YOU DO KARATE, DON'T YOU?
A LITTLE.
THEN LET'S HAVE A LITTLE MATCH, OKAY?
HUH?
JUST FOR FUN.
DON'T WORRY. I WON'T HURT YOU.
IF YOU SAY SO.

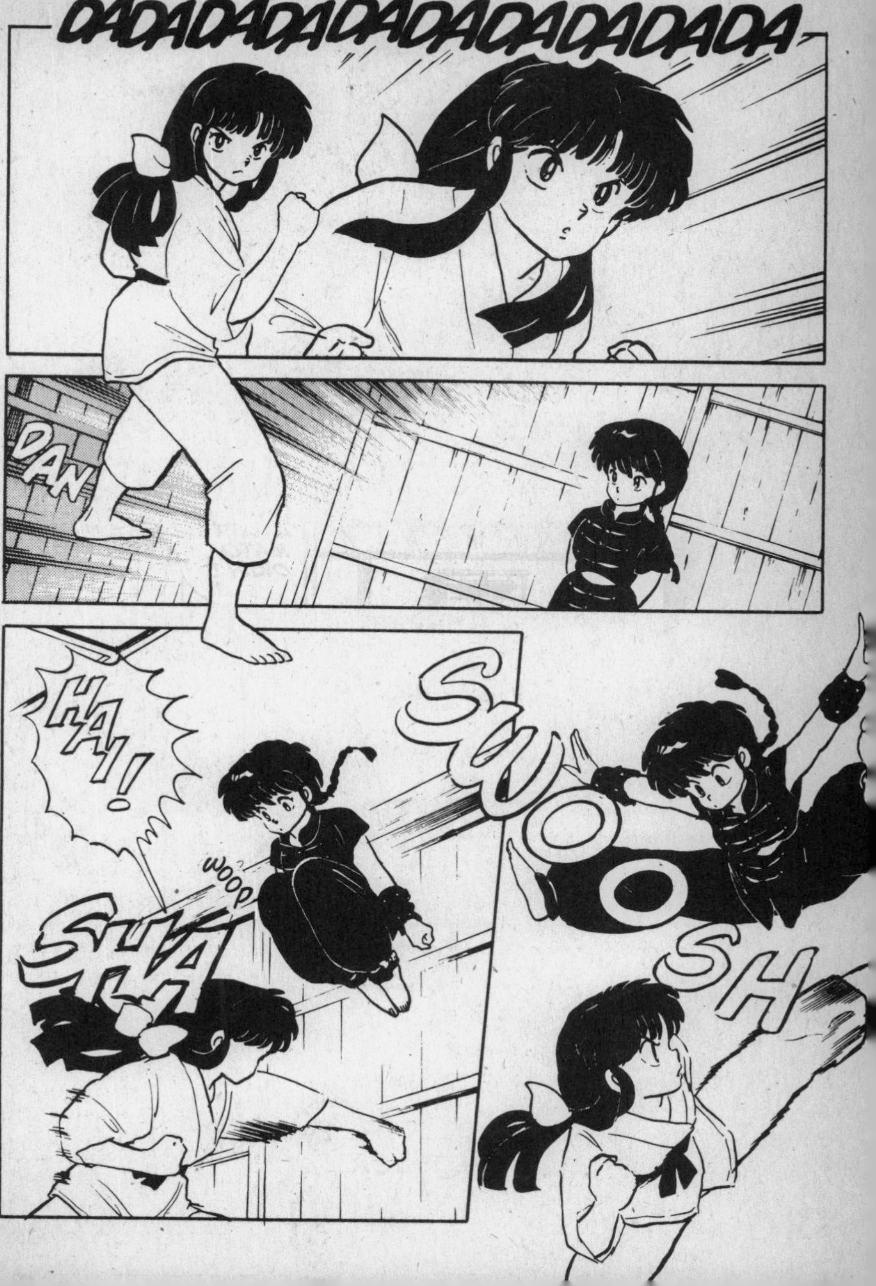
DADADADADADADADADADADADADA
DAN
HAI!
WOOP
SHA
SWOOOSH

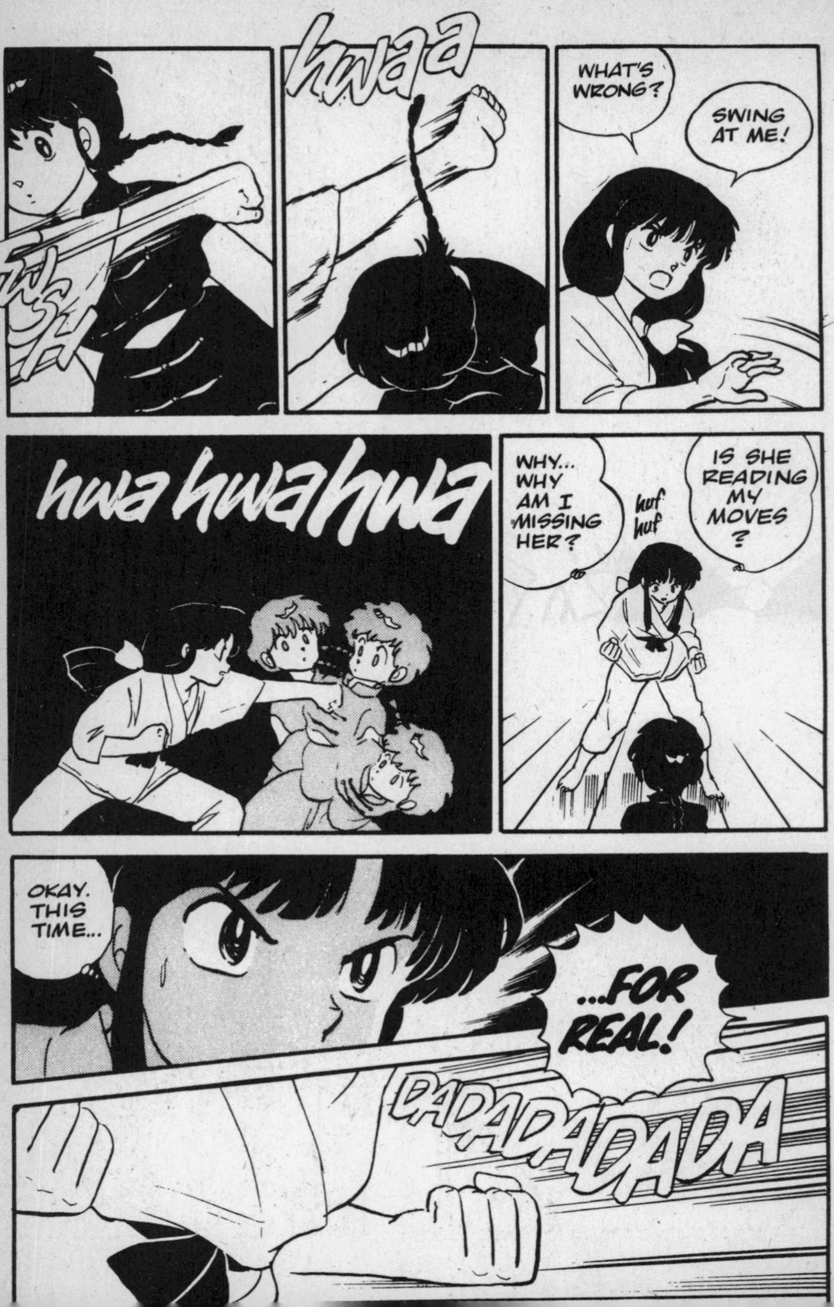
FWSH
hwaa
WHAT'S WRONG?
SWING AT ME!
hwa hwa hwa
WHY... WHY AM I MISSING HER?
huf huf
IS SHE READING MY MOVES?
OKAY. THIS TIME...
...FOR REAL!
DADADADADADA

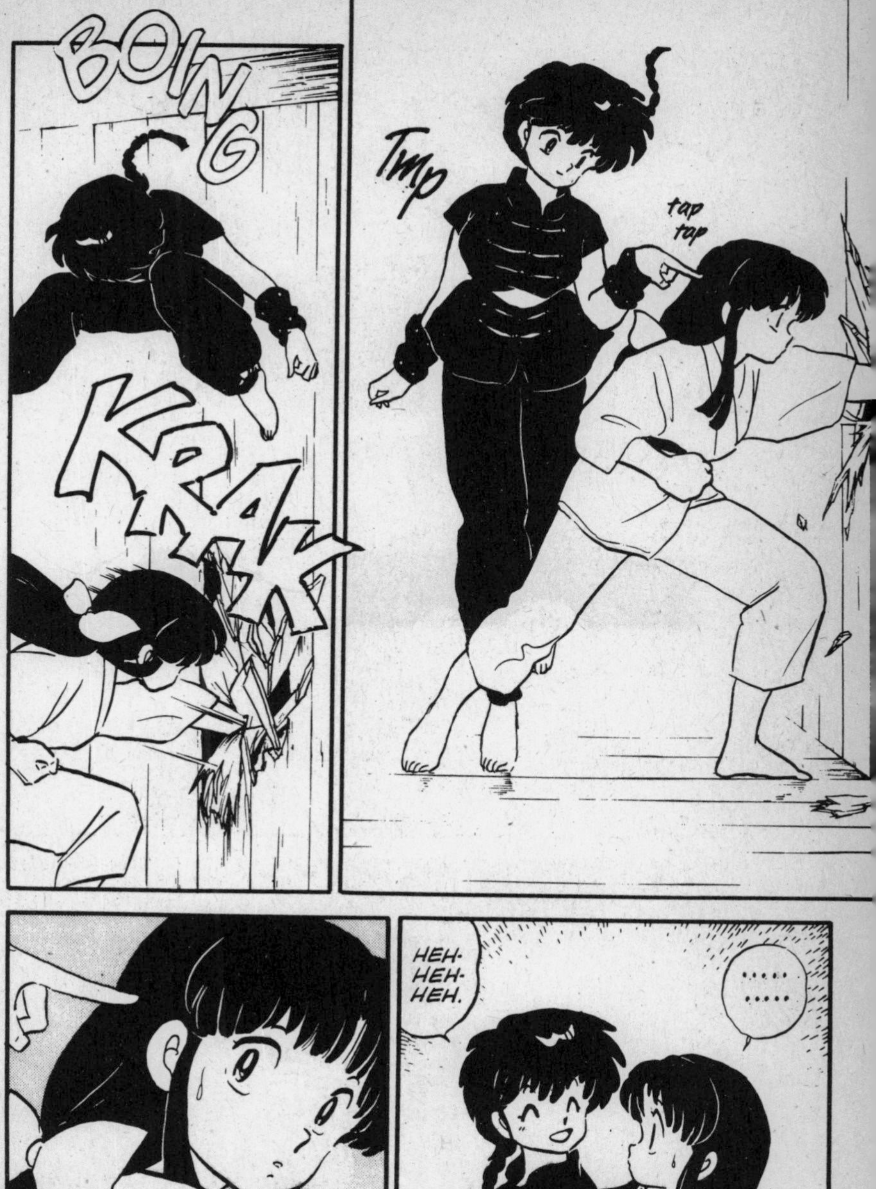
BOING
KRAKK
Tmp
tap tap
HEH-HEH-HEH.
.....
.....

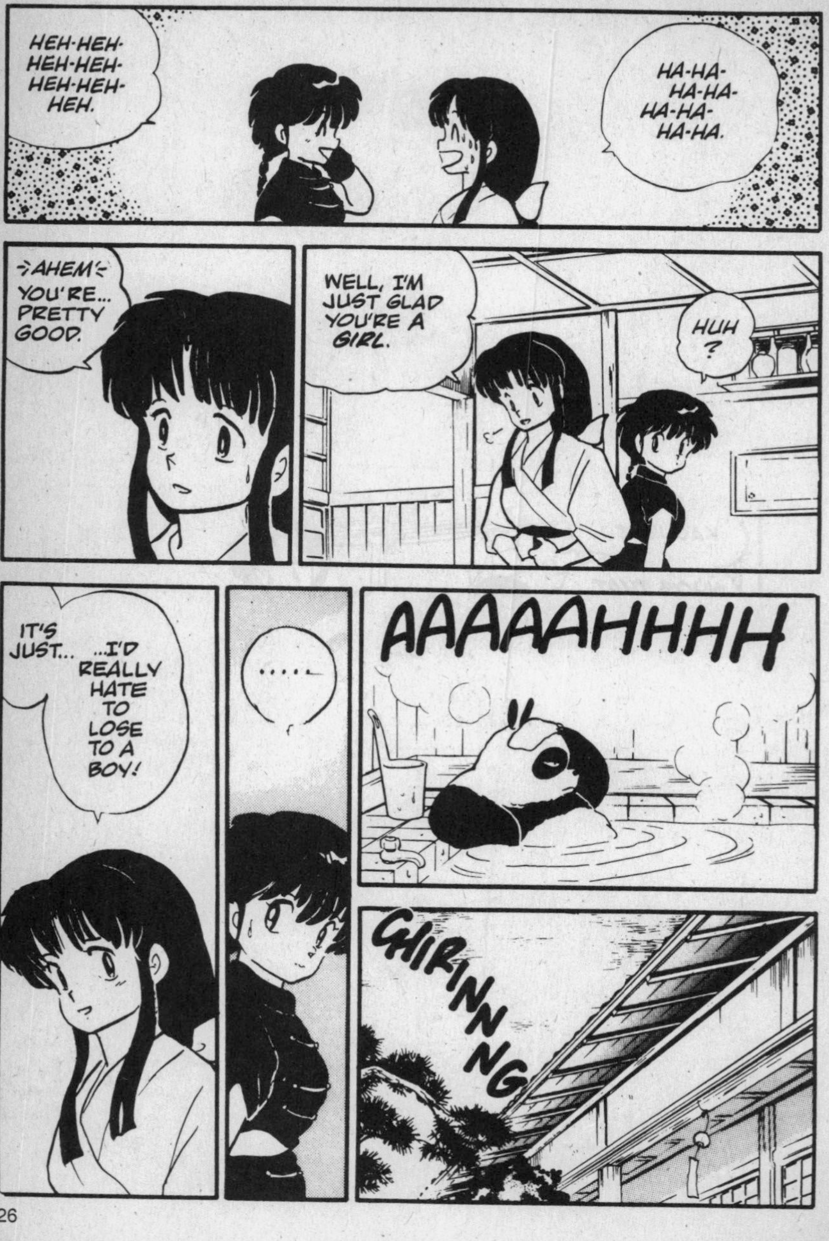
HEH-HEH-HEH-HEH-HEH-HEH-HEH.
HA-HA-HA-HA-HA-HA-HA-HA.
~AHEM~ YOU'RE... PRETTY GOOD.
WELL, I'M JUST GLAD YOU'RE A GIRL.
HUH?
IT'S JUST... ...I'D REALLY HATE TO LOSE TO A BOY!
.....
AAAAAHHHH
CHIRINNNG

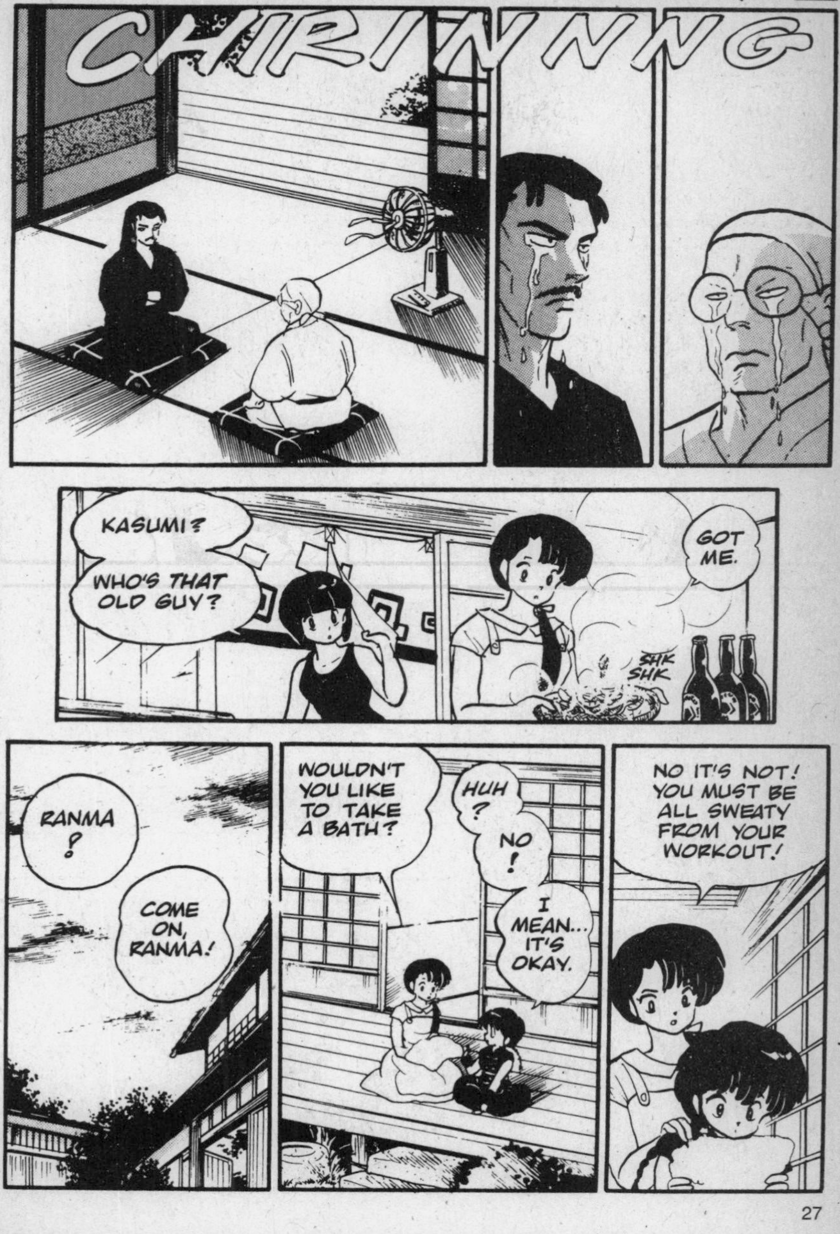
CHIRINNNG
KASUMI?
WHO'S THAT OLD GUY?
GOT ME.
SHK SHK
RANMA?
COME ON, RANMA!
WOULDN'T YOU LIKE TO TAKE A BATH?
HUH?
NO!
I MEAN... IT'S OKAY.
NO IT'S NOT! YOU MUST BE ALL SWEATY FROM YOUR WORKOUT!

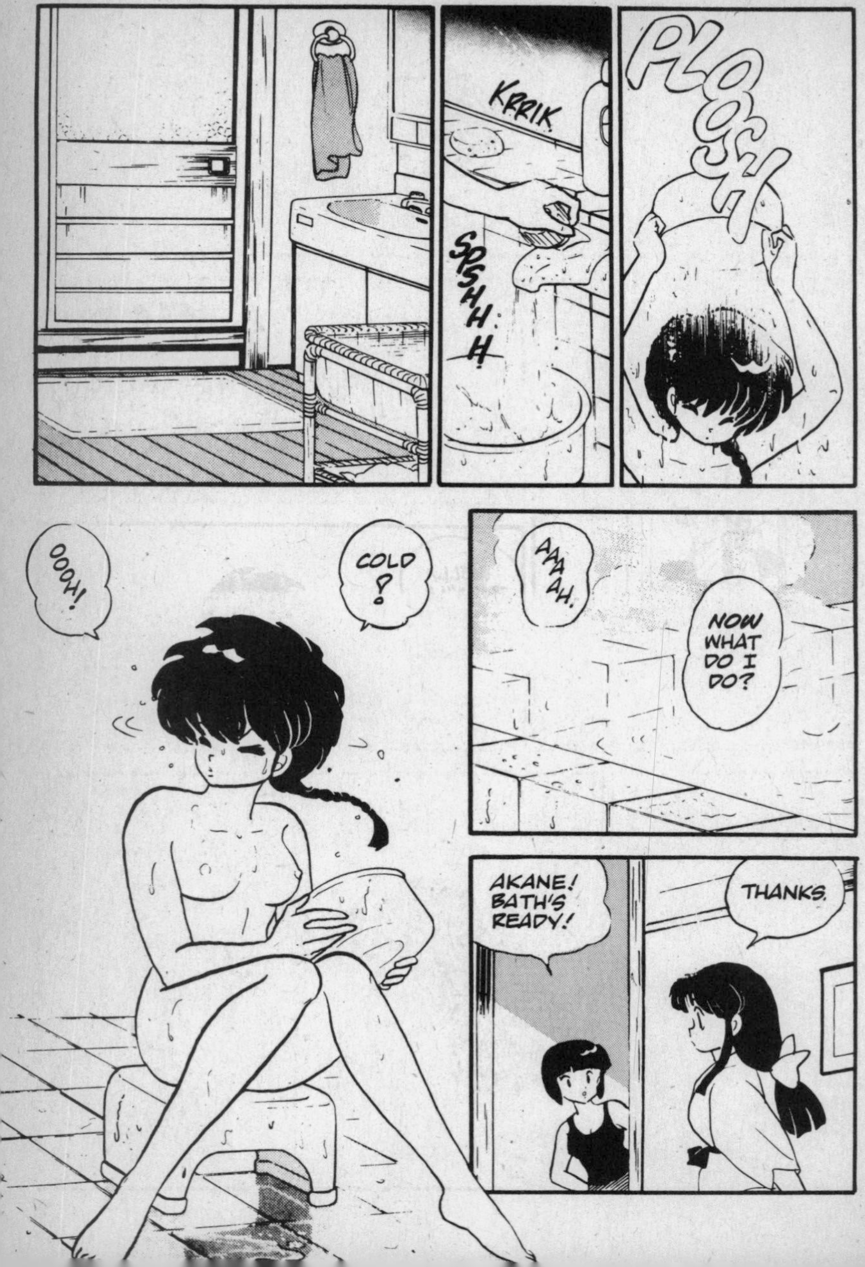
KRRIK
SPSHHH
PLOSH
OOOH!
COLD?
AAAAAH.
NOW WHAT DO I DO?
AKANE! BATH'S READY!
THANKS.

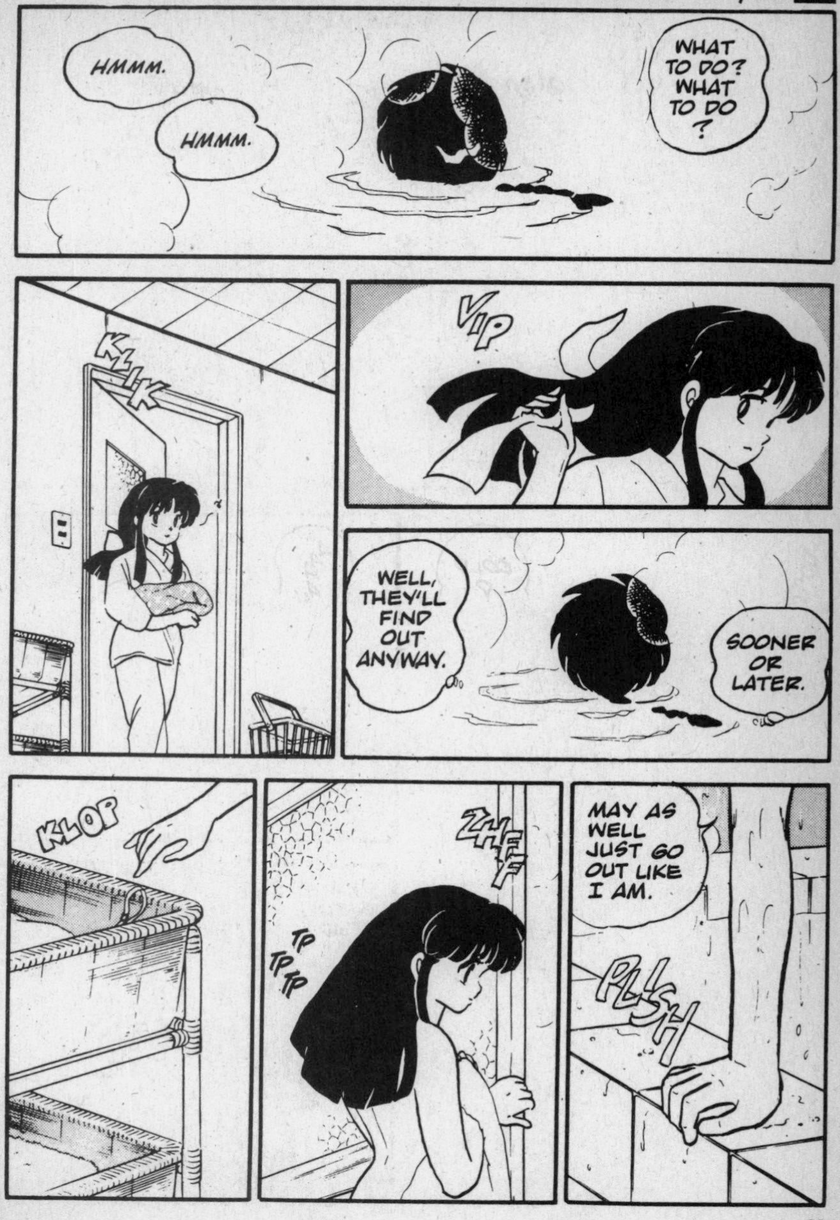
HMMM.
HMMM.
WHAT TO DO? WHAT TO DO?
KLIK
VIP
WELL, THEY'LL FIND OUT ANYWAY.
SOONER OR LATER.
KLOP
ZHFF
TP TP TP
MAY AS WELL JUST GO OUT LIKE I AM.
PLISH

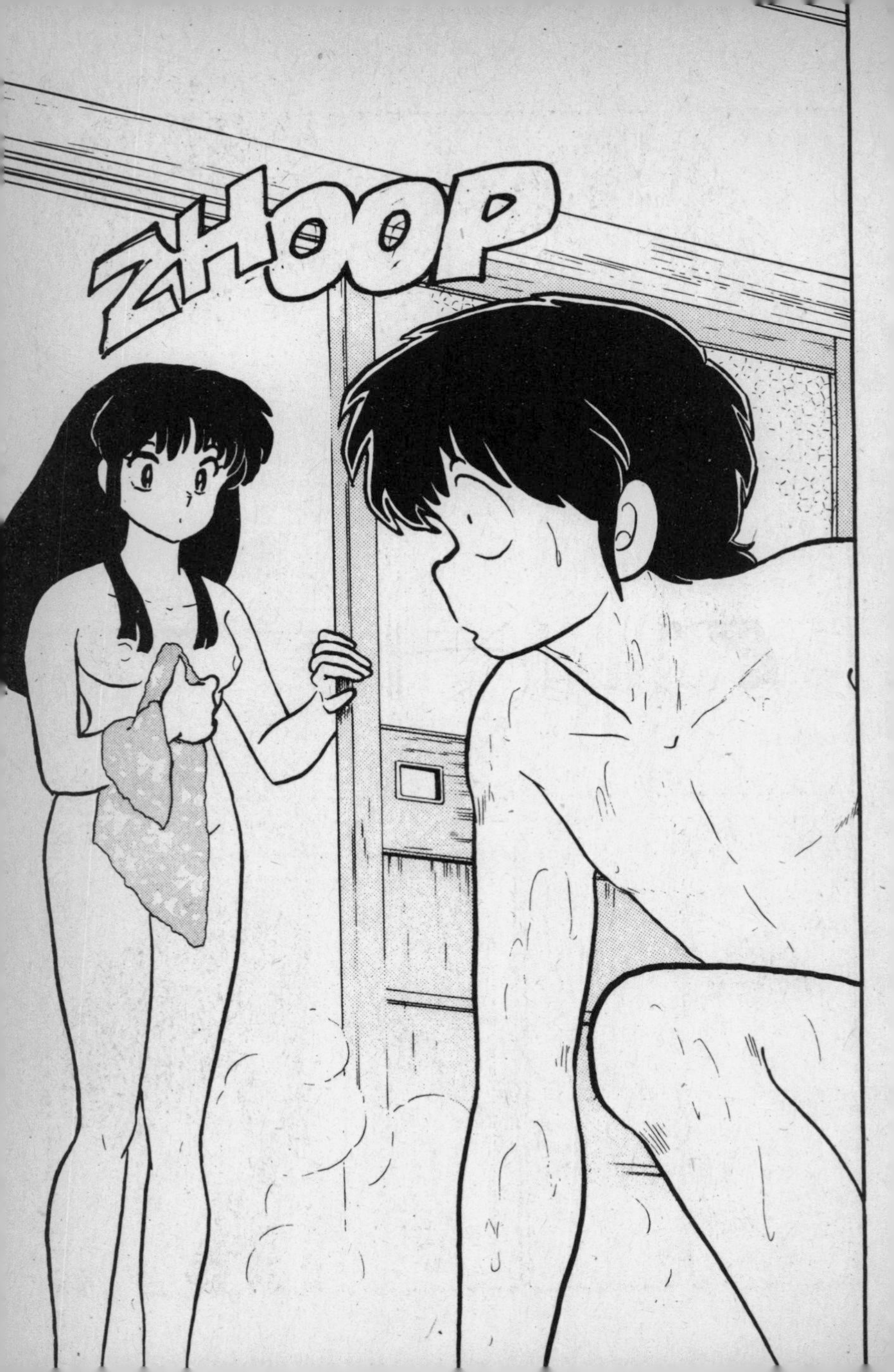
ZHOOP

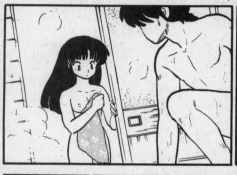

ZHOOP..PP

SHFF
SHFF

SQUIK..

KLIK

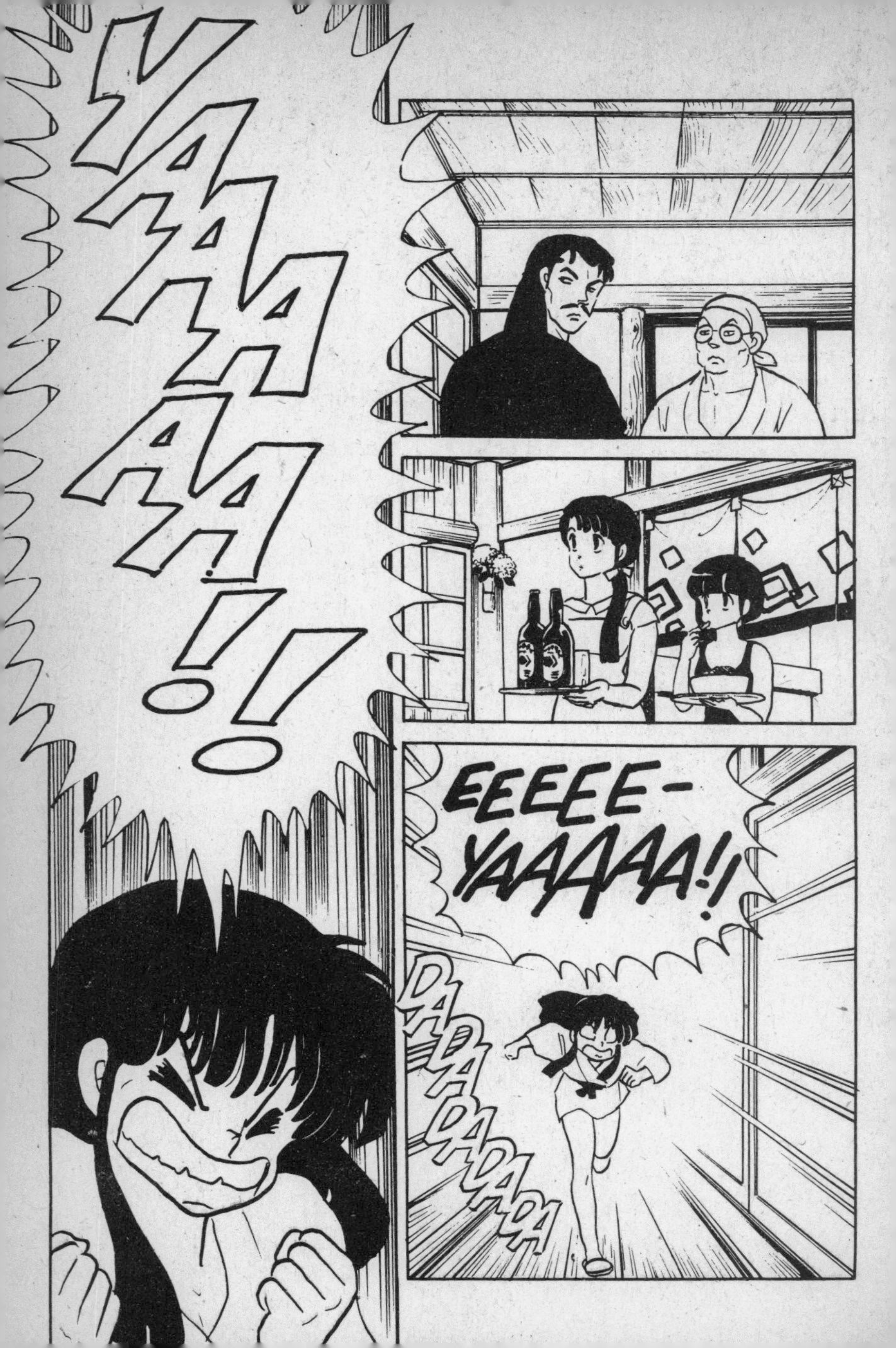
YAAAAA!!
EEEEE-
YAAAAA!!
DADADADADADA

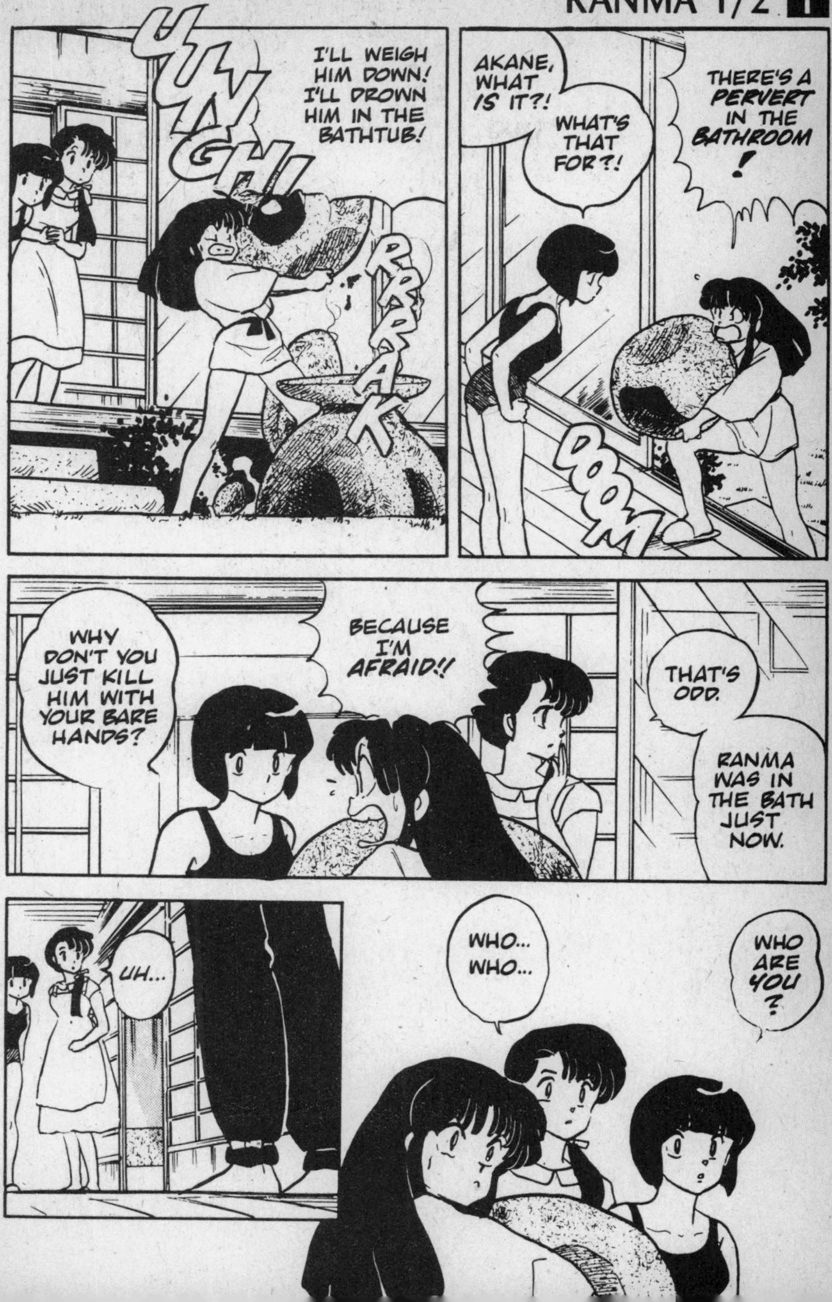
UUNGH!
I'LL WEIGH HIM DOWN! I'LL DROWN HIM IN THE BATHTUB!
RRRAK
AKANE, WHAT IS IT?!
WHAT'S THAT FOR?!
THERE'S A PERVERT IN THE BATHROOM!
DOOM
WHY DON'T YOU JUST KILL HIM WITH YOUR BARE HANDS?
BECAUSE I'M AFRAID!!
THAT'S ODD.
RANMA WAS IN THE BATH JUST NOW.
UH...
WHO... WHO...
WHO ARE YOU?

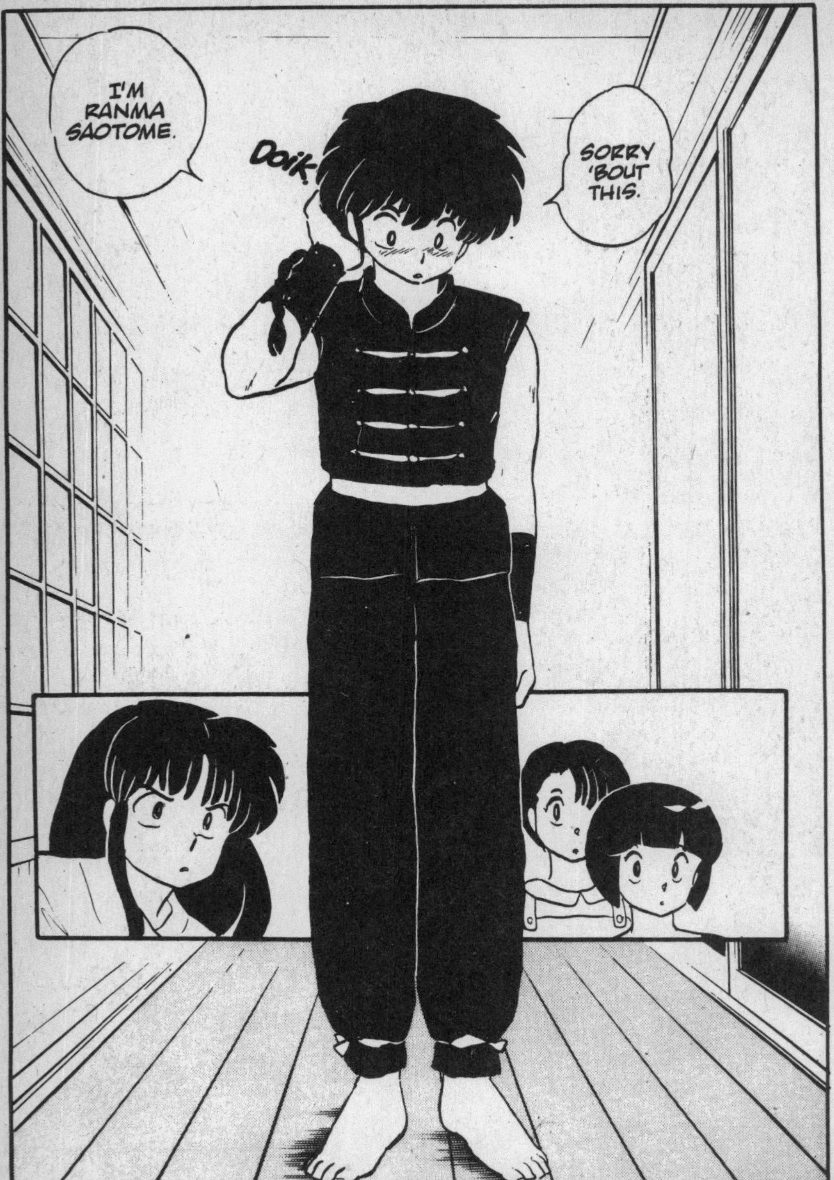
I'M RANMA SAOTOME.
DOIK
SORRY 'BOUT THIS.

Part 2 RANMA'S SECRET

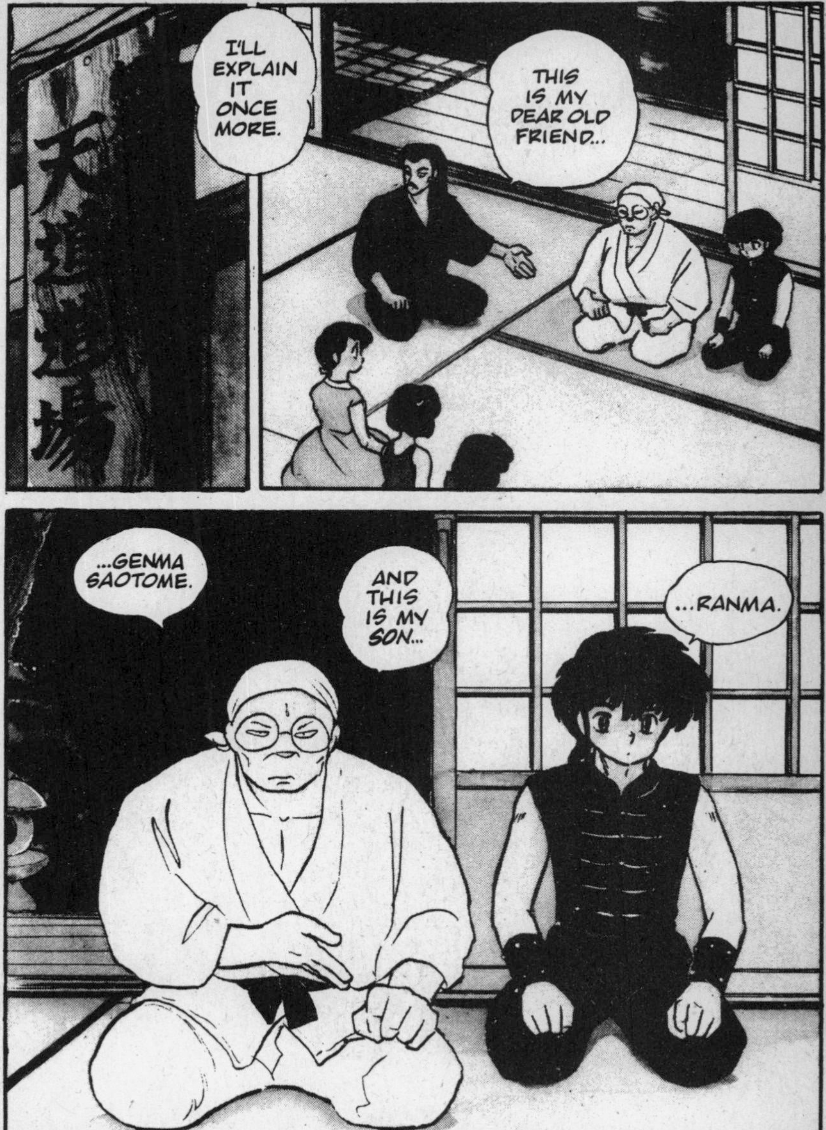
天道道場
I'LL EXPLAIN IT ONCE MORE.
THIS IS MY DEAR OLD FRIEND...
...GENMA SAOTOME.
AND THIS IS MY SON...
...RANMA.

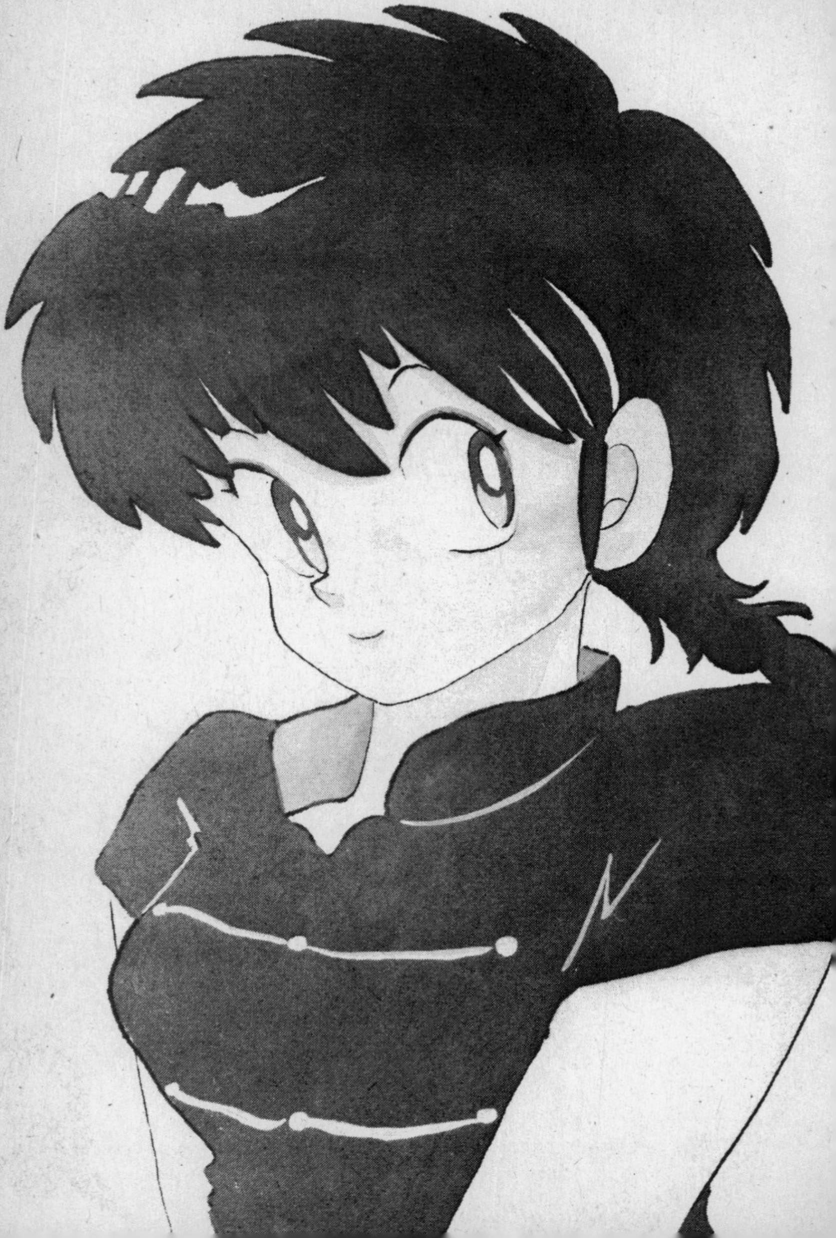

Part 2
RANMA'S SECRET

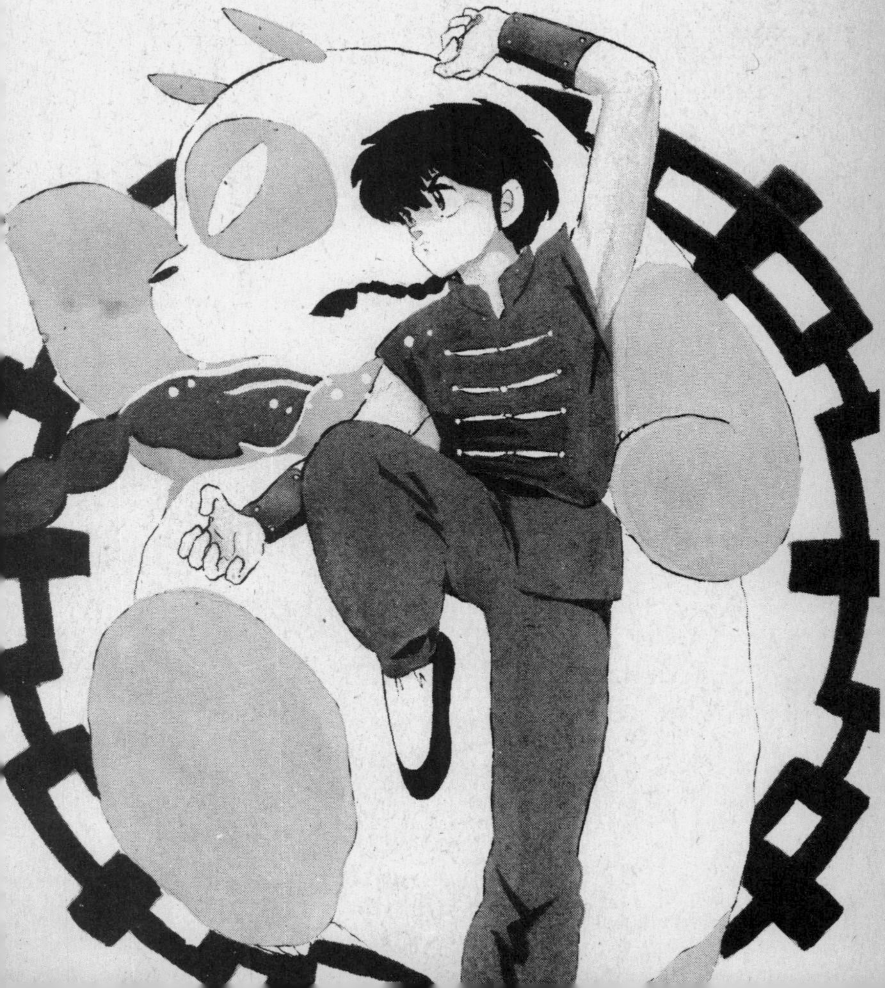

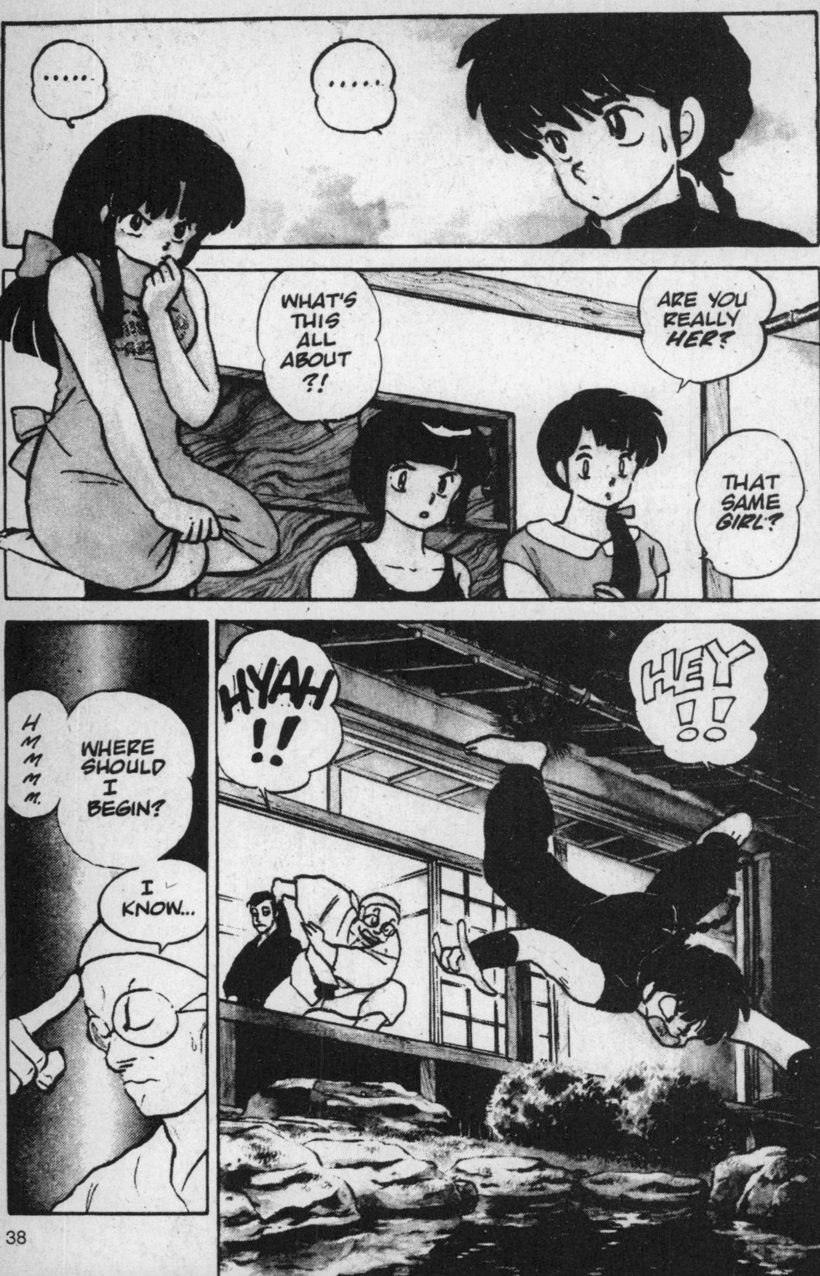

......
......
WHAT'S THIS ALL ABOUT ?!
ARE YOU REALLY HER?
THAT SAME GIRL?
HMMMM.
WHERE SHOULD I BEGIN?
I KNOW...
HYAH !!
HEY !!

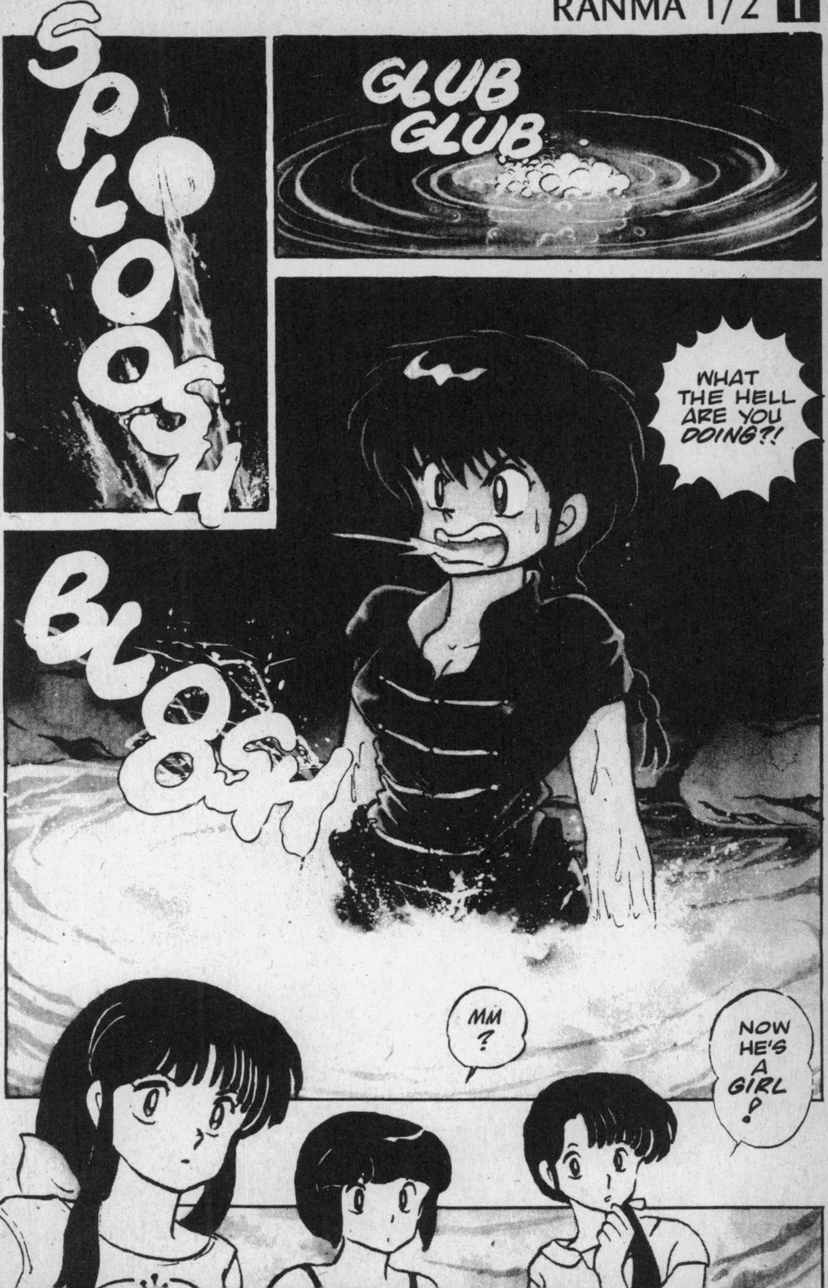
SPLOOSH
GLUB GLUB
BLOOSH
WHAT THE HELL ARE YOU DOING?!
MM ?
NOW HE'S A GIRL ?

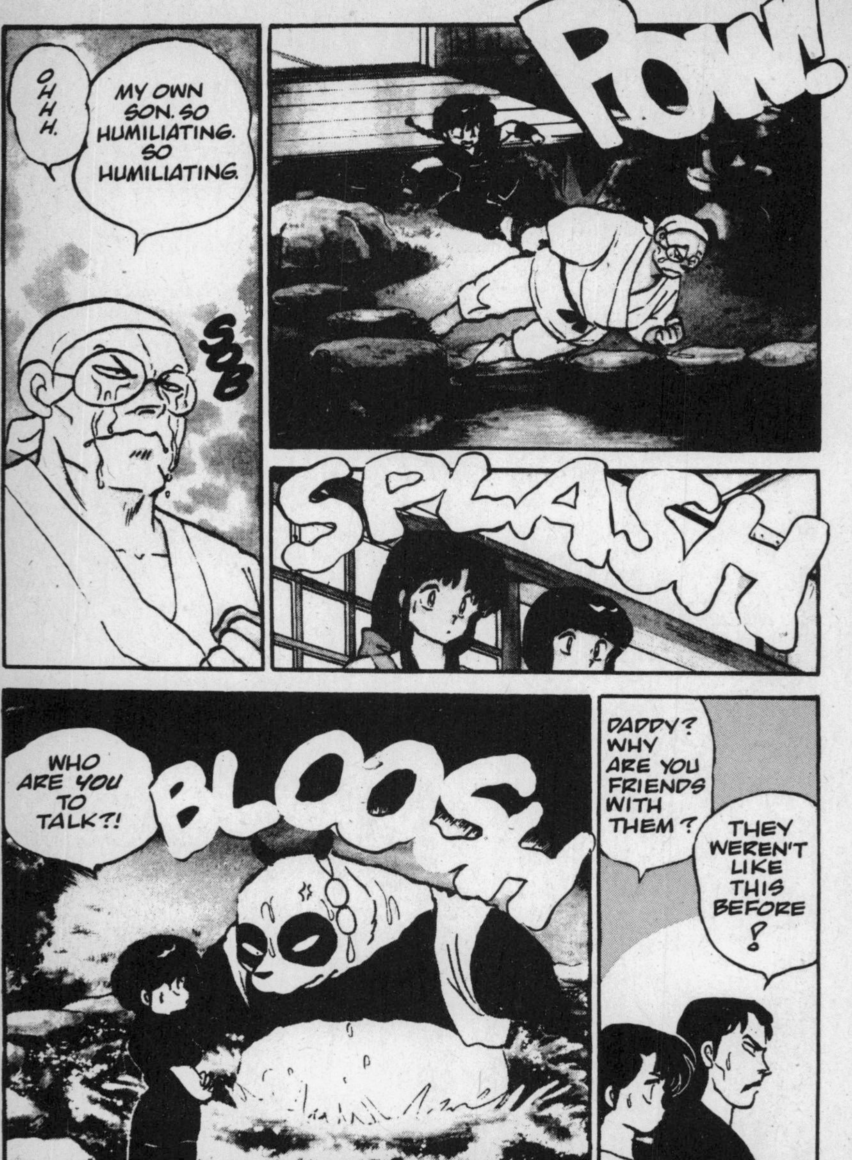
OHHH.
MY OWN SON. SO HUMILIATING. SO HUMILIATING.
SOB
POW!
SPLASH
WHO ARE YOU TO TALK?!
BLOOSH
DADDY? WHY ARE YOU FRIENDS WITH THEM?
THEY WEREN'T LIKE THIS BEFORE?

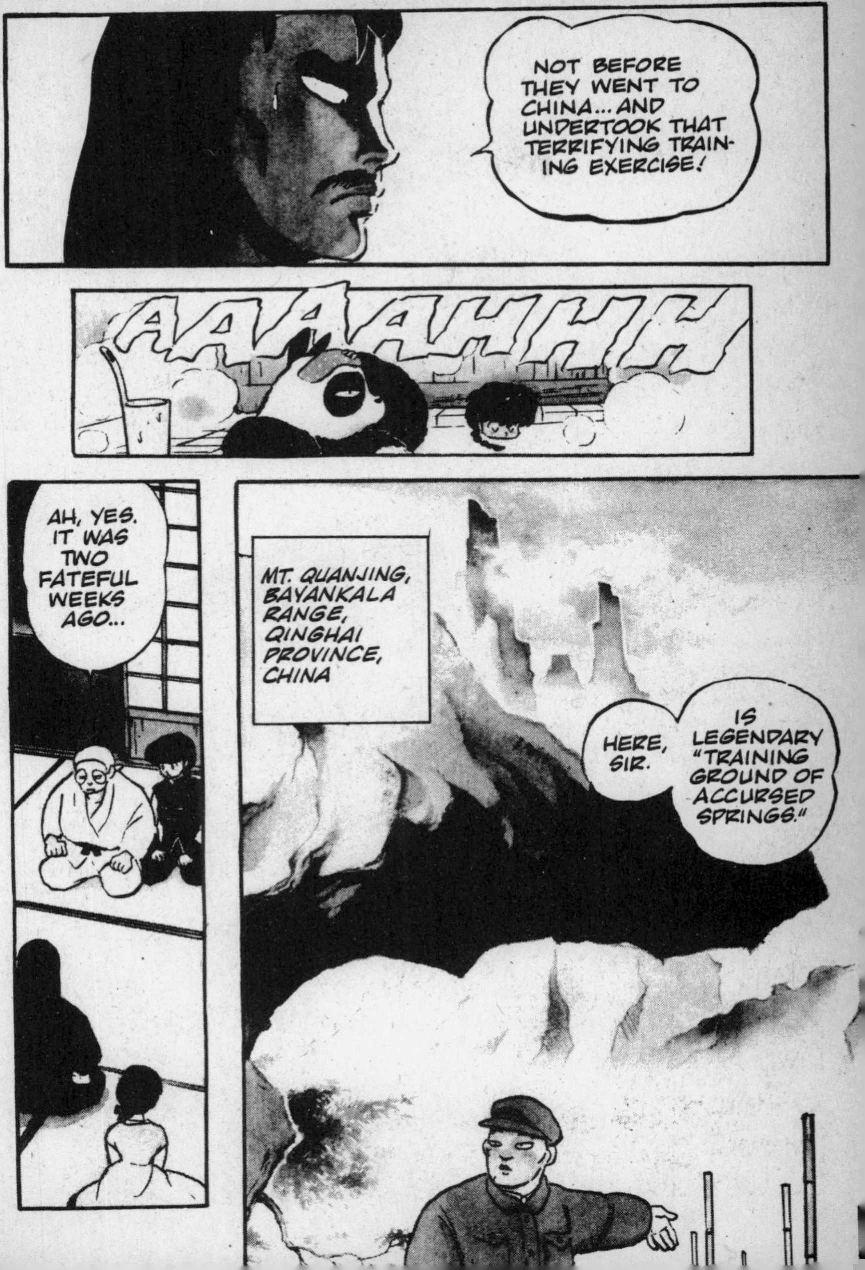
NOT BEFORE THEY WENT TO CHINA... AND UNDERTOOK THAT TERRIFYING TRAINING EXERCISE!
AAAAHHH
AH, YES. IT WAS TWO FATEFUL WEEKS AGO...
MT. QUANJING, BAYANKALA RANGE, QINGHAI PROVINCE, CHINA
HERE, SIR.
IS LEGENDARY "TRAINING GROUND OF ACCURSED SPRINGS."

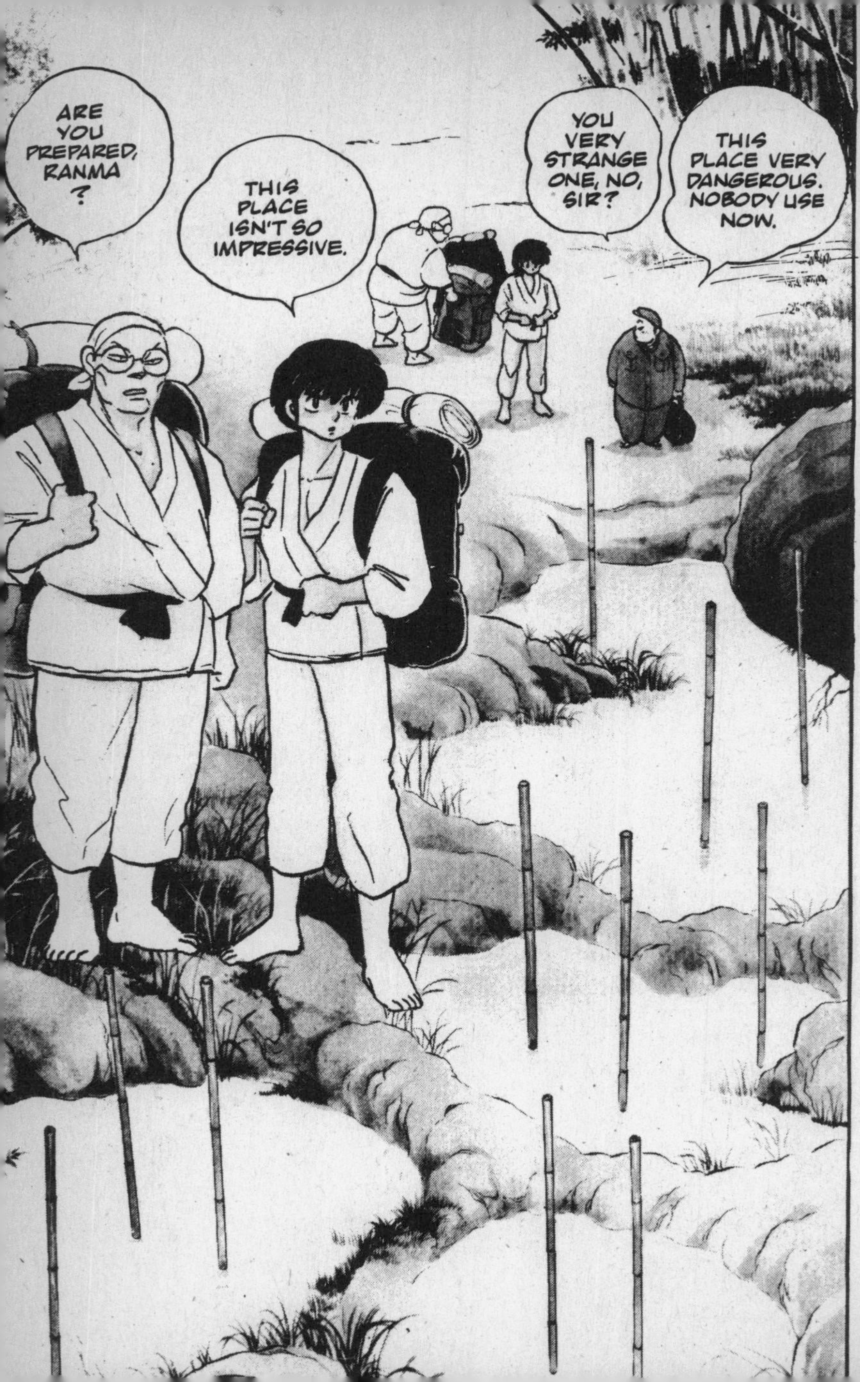
ARE YOU PREPARED, RANMA?
THIS PLACE ISN'T SO IMPRESSIVE.
YOU VERY STRANGE ONE, NO, SIR?
THIS PLACE VERY DANGEROUS. NOBODY USE NOW.

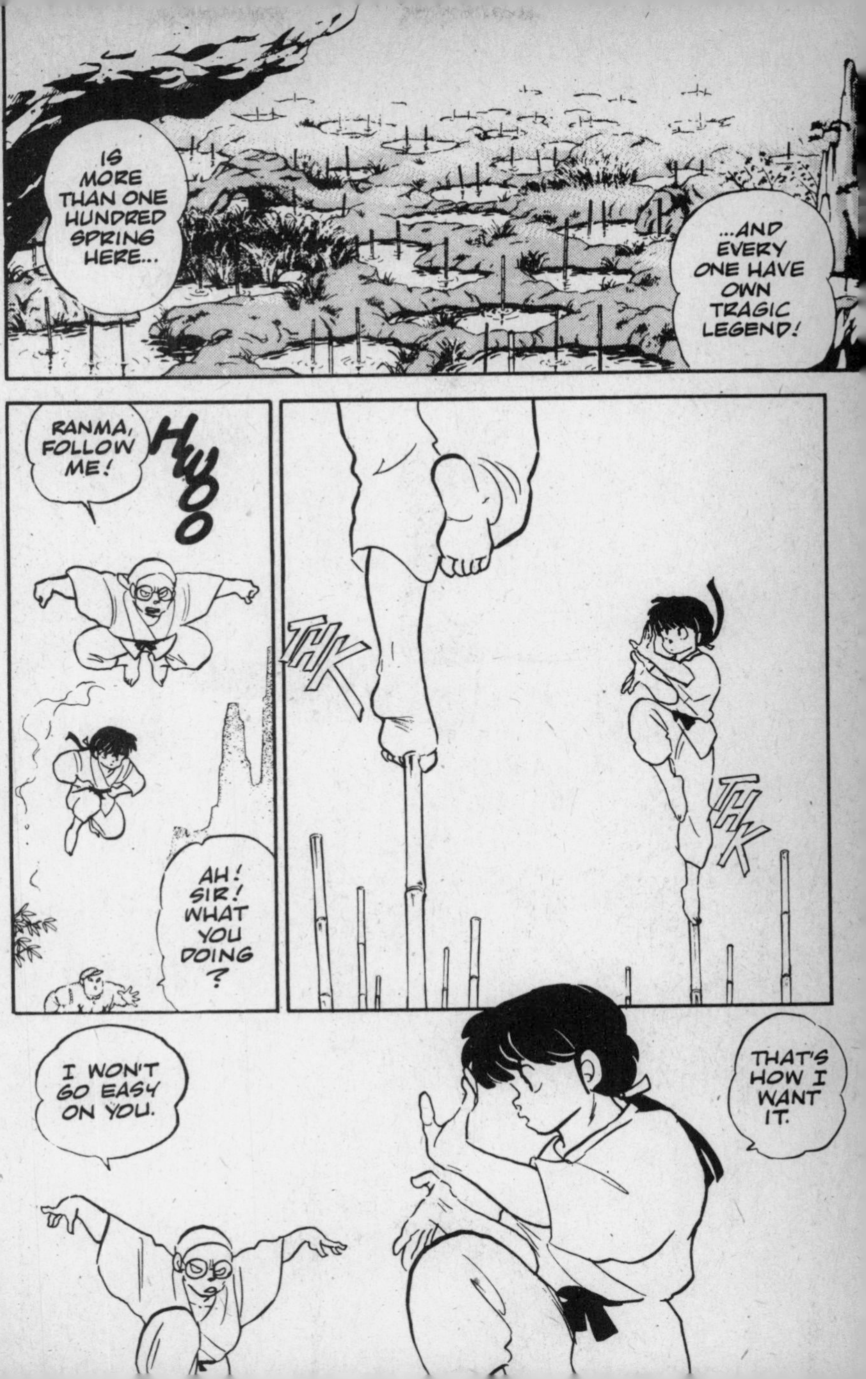
IS MORE THAN ONE HUNDRED SPRING HERE...
...AND EVERY ONE HAVE OWN TRAGIC LEGEND!
RANMA, FOLLOW ME!
HWOO
AH! SIR! WHAT YOU DOING ?
THK
THK
I WON'T GO EASY ON YOU.
THAT'S HOW I WANT IT.

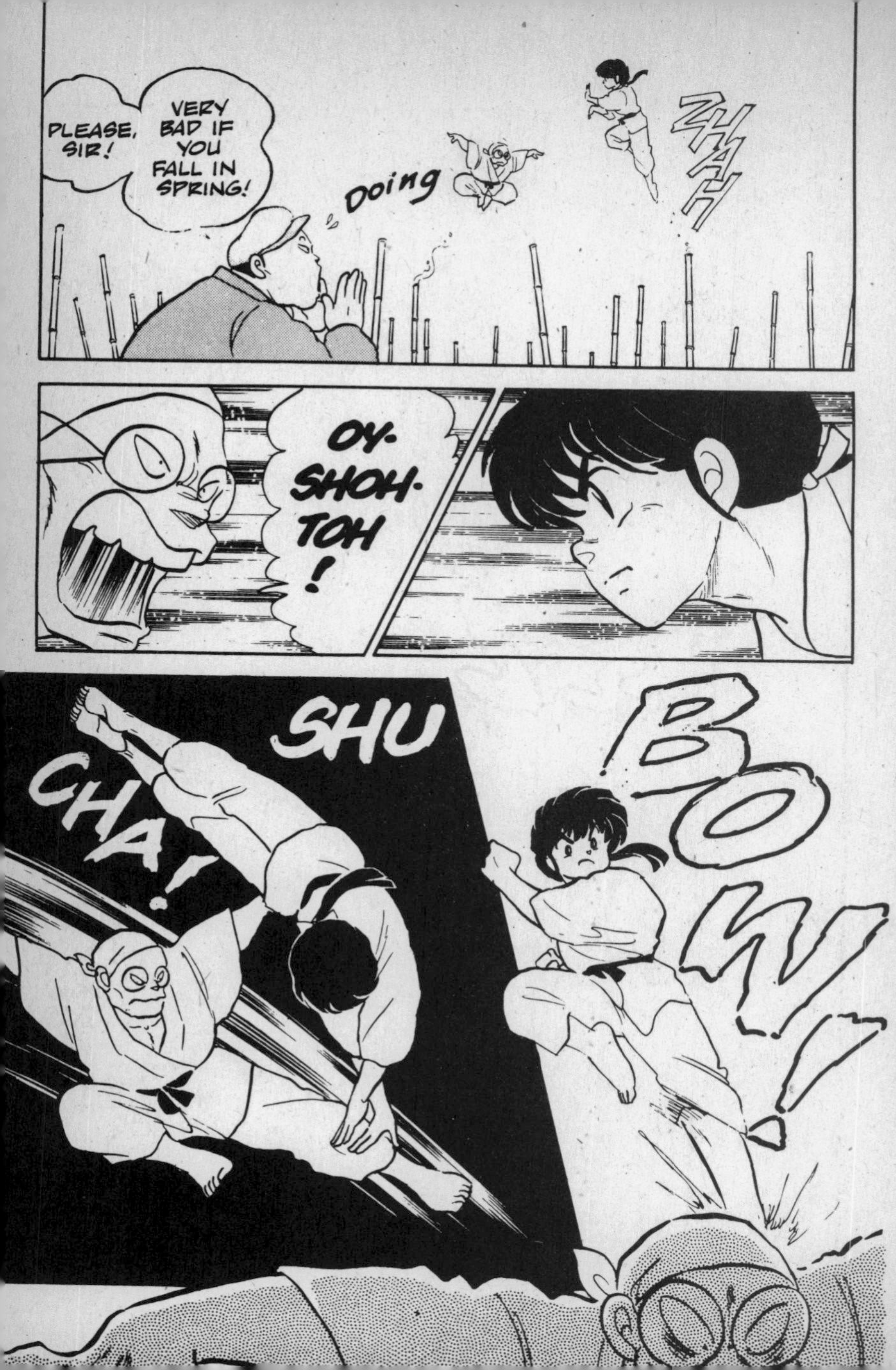
PLEASE, SIR!
VERY BAD IF YOU FALL IN SPRING!
Doing
ZHAH
OY-SHOH-TOH!
SHU CHA!
BOW!

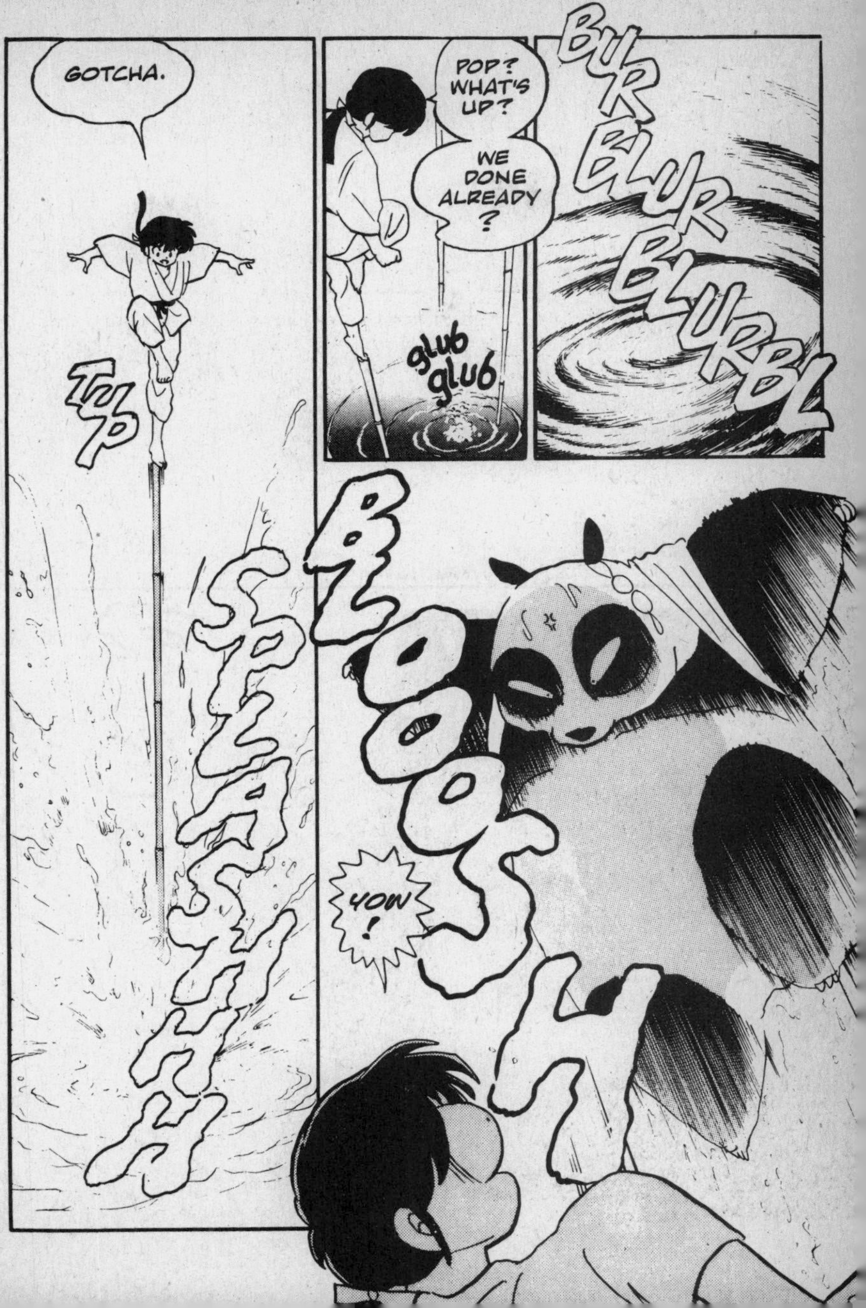
GOTCHA.
TUP
POP? WHAT'S UP?
WE DONE ALREADY?
glub glub
BURBLURBLURBLURBL
SPLASHHH
BLOOOSH
YOW!

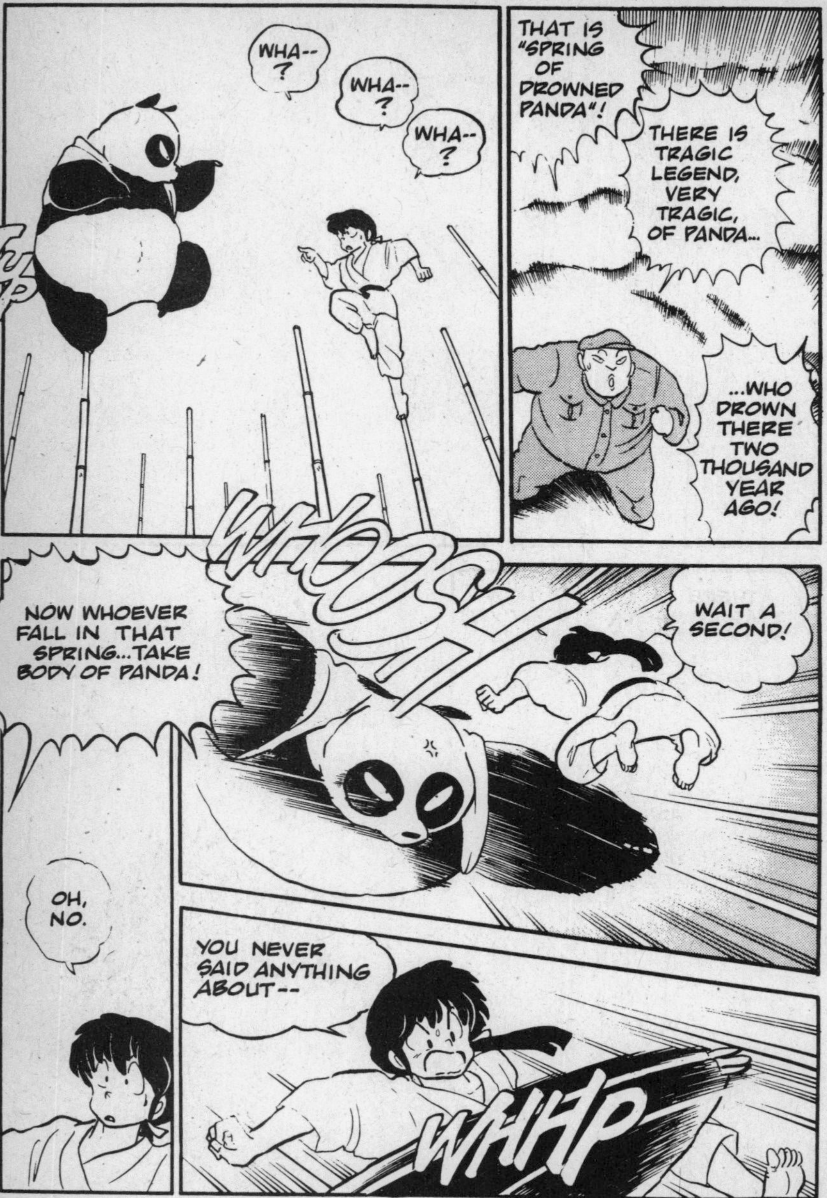

TUP
WHA-- ?
WHA-- ?
WHA-- ?
THAT IS "SPRING OF DROWNED PANDA"!
THERE IS TRAGIC LEGEND, VERY TRAGIC, OF PANDA...
...WHO DROWN THERE TWO THOUSAND YEAR AGO!
NOW WHOEVER FALL IN THAT SPRING...TAKE BODY OF PANDA!
OH, NO.
WHOOSH
WAIT A SECOND!
YOU NEVER SAID ANYTHING ABOUT--
WHHP

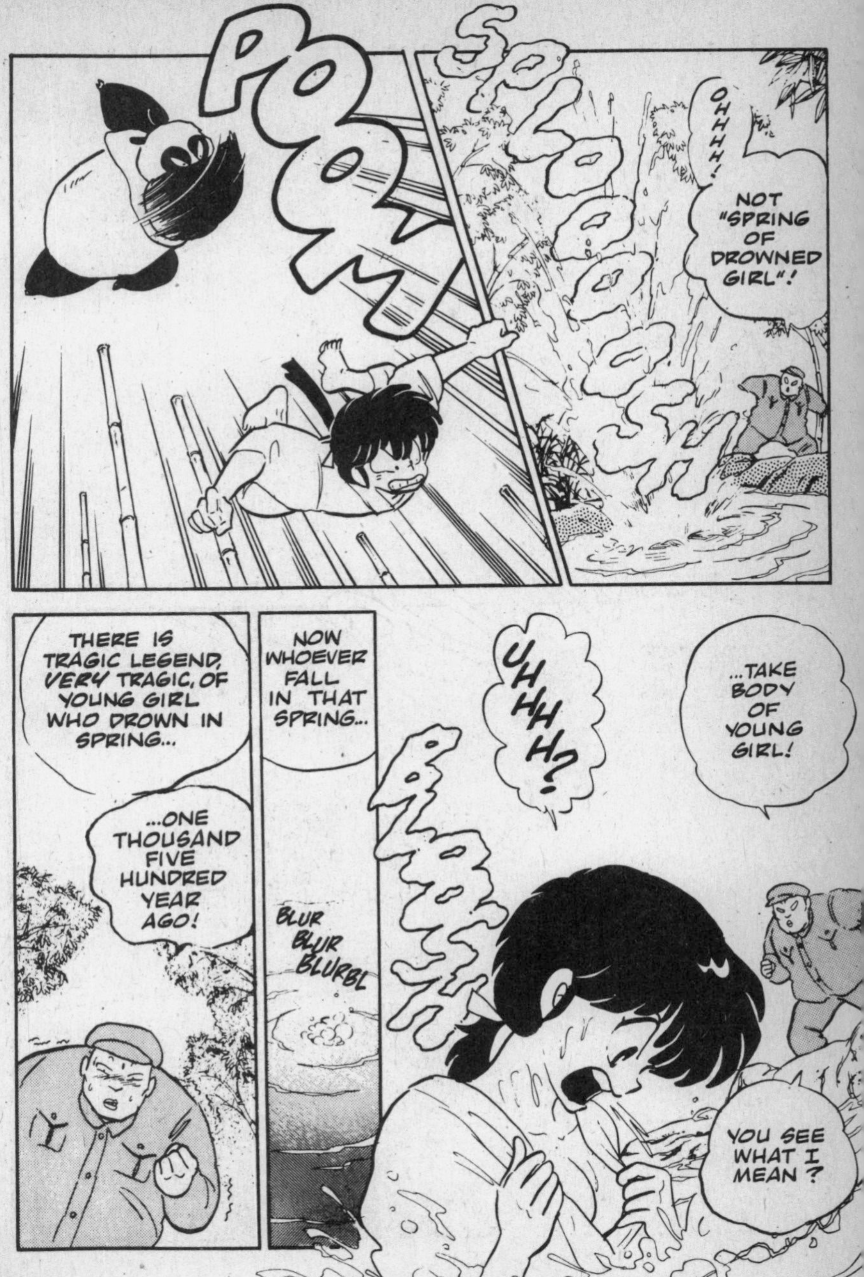
POOOM!
SPLOOOOSH
OHHHH!
NOT "SPRING OF DROWNED GIRL"!
THERE IS TRAGIC LEGEND, VERY TRAGIC, OF YOUNG GIRL WHO DROWN IN SPRING...
...ONE THOUSAND FIVE HUNDRED YEAR AGO!
NOW WHOEVER FALL IN THAT SPRING...
BLUR BLUR BLURBL
UHHHH?
PLOOSH
...TAKE BODY OF YOUNG GIRL!
YOU SEE WHAT I MEAN?

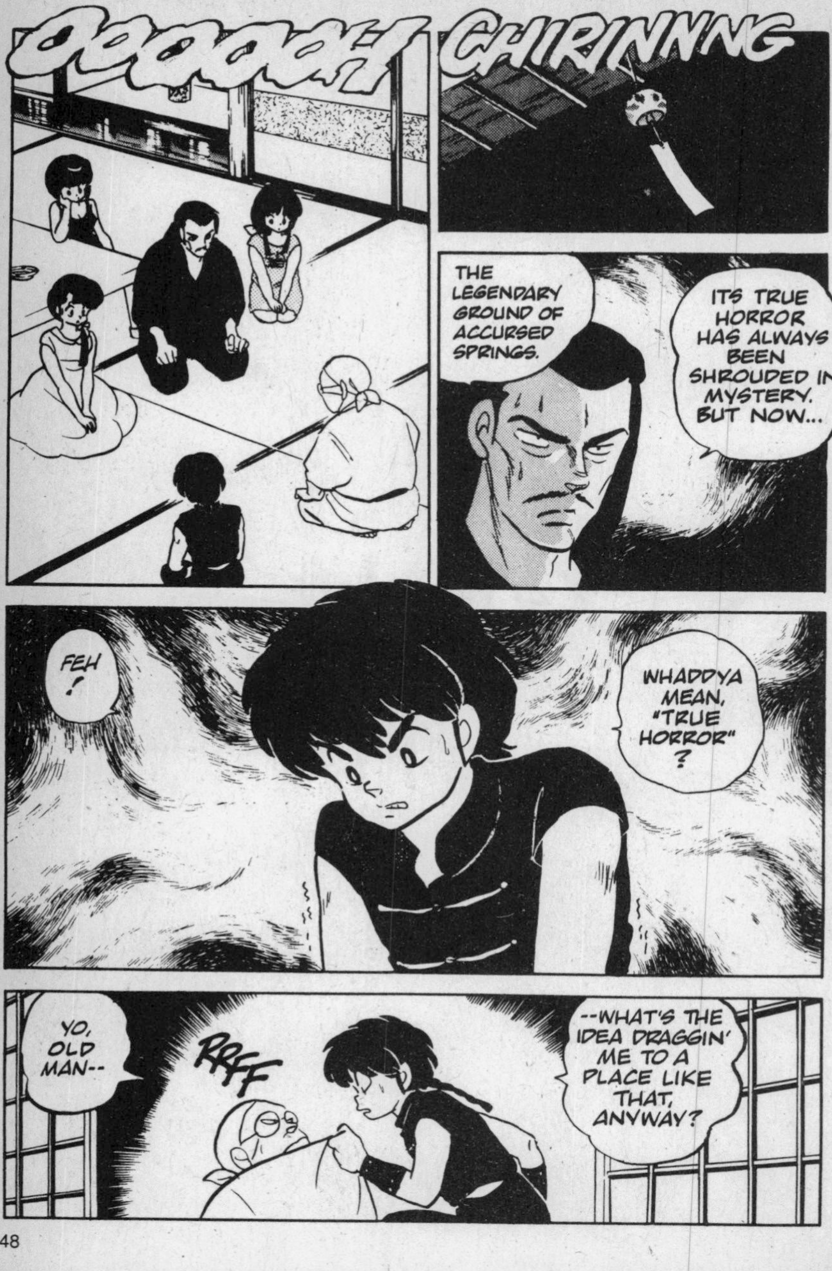
OOOOOOH
CHIRINNNG
THE LEGENDARY GROUND OF ACCURSED SPRINGS.
ITS TRUE HORROR HAS ALWAYS BEEN SHROUDED IN MYSTERY. BUT NOW...
FEH!
WHADDYA MEAN, "TRUE HORROR"?
YO, OLD MAN--
RRFF
--WHAT'S THE IDEA DRAGGIN' ME TO A PLACE LIKE THAT, ANYWAY?

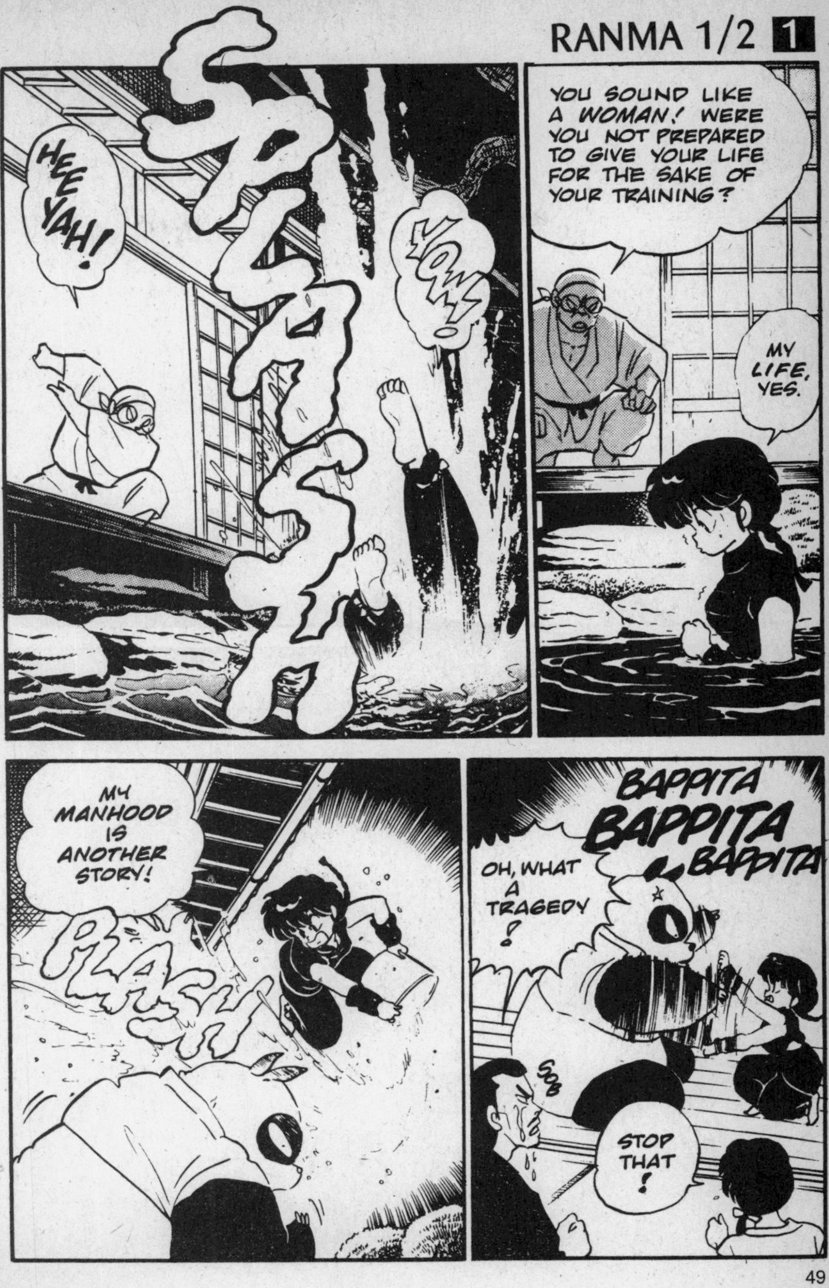
HEEYAH!
SPLASH
YOW!
YOU SOUND LIKE A *WOMAN!* WERE YOU NOT PREPARED TO GIVE YOUR LIFE FOR THE SAKE OF YOUR TRAINING?
MY *LIFE,* YES.
MY MANHOOD IS ANOTHER STORY!
PLASH!
BAPPITA
BAPPITA
BAPPITA
OH, WHAT A TRAGEDY!
SOB
STOP THAT!

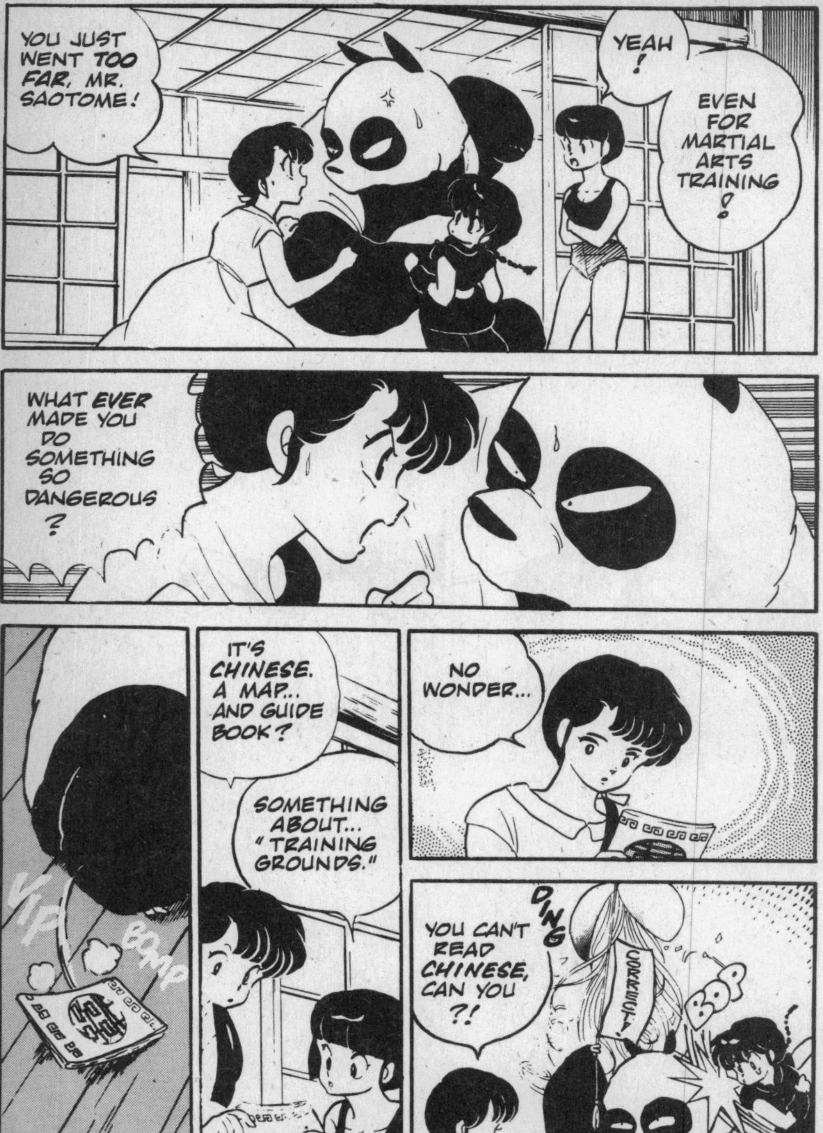

YOU JUST WENT TOO FAR, MR. SAOTOME!
YEAH!
EVEN FOR MARTIAL ARTS TRAINING!
WHAT EVER MADE YOU DO SOMETHING SO DANGEROUS?
VIP
BOMP
IT'S CHINESE. A MAP... AND GUIDE BOOK?
SOMETHING ABOUT... "TRAINING GROUNDS."
NO WONDER...
YOU CAN'T READ CHINESE, CAN YOU?!
DING
CORRECT!
BOP

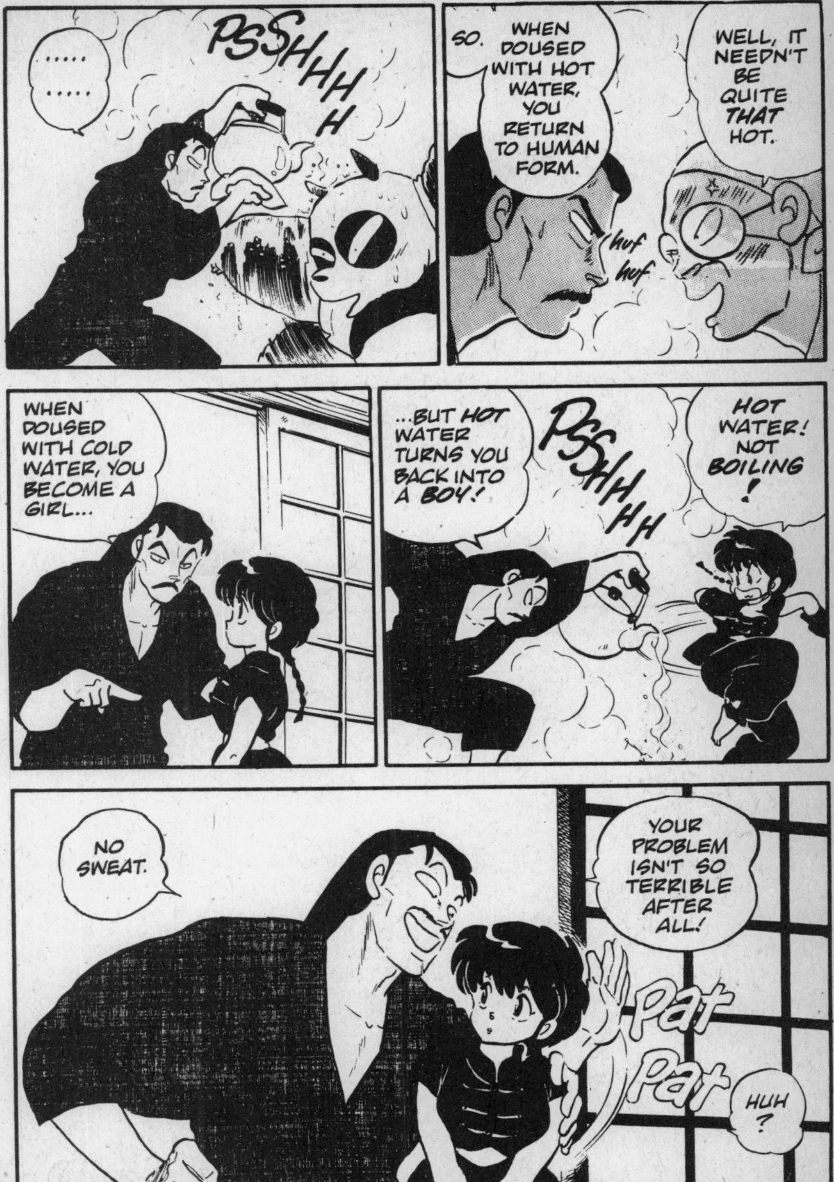
......
......
PSSHHHH
SO.
WHEN DOUSED WITH HOT WATER, YOU RETURN TO HUMAN FORM.
WELL, IT NEEDN'T BE QUITE THAT HOT.
huf huf
WHEN DOUSED WITH COLD WATER, YOU BECOME A GIRL...
...BUT HOT WATER TURNS YOU BACK INTO A BOY!
PSSHHHH
HOT WATER! NOT BOILING!
NO SWEAT.
YOUR PROBLEM ISN'T SO TERRIBLE AFTER ALL!
Pat Pat
HUH?

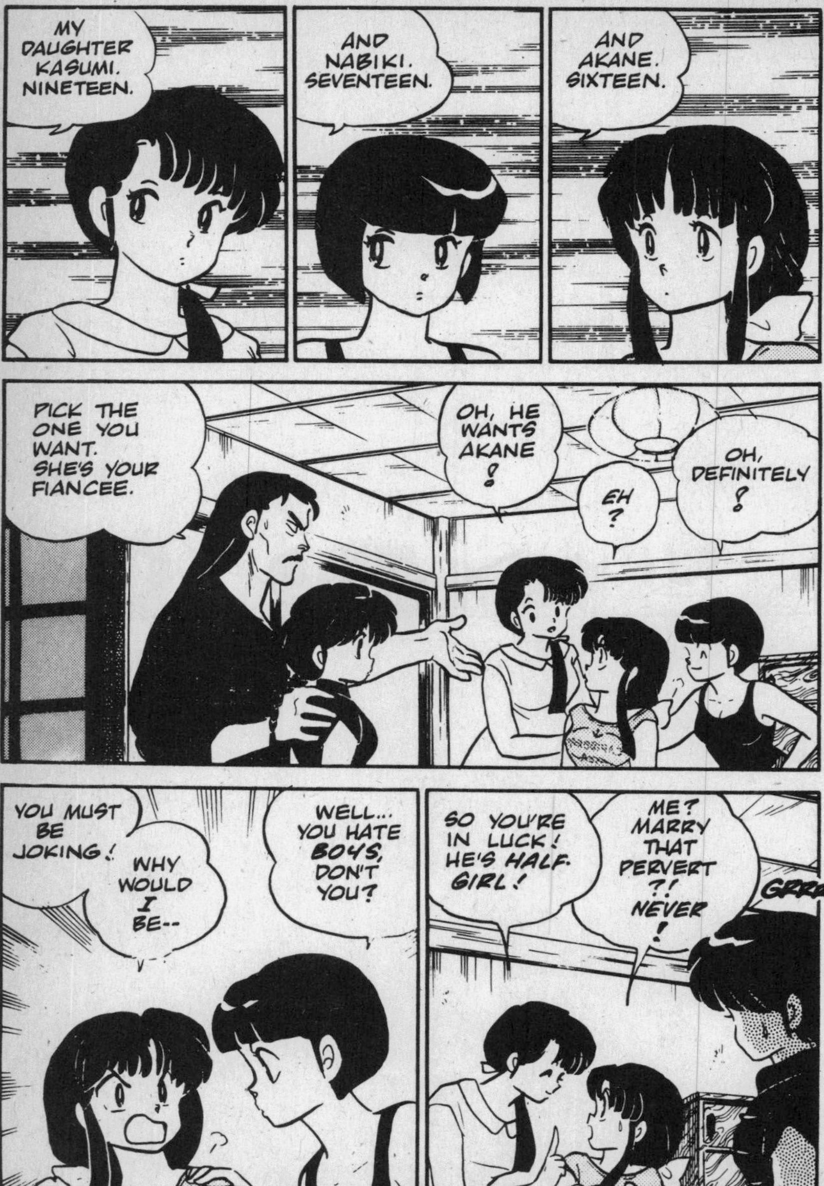
MY DAUGHTER KASUMI. NINETEEN.
AND NABIKI. SEVENTEEN.
AND AKANE. SIXTEEN.
PICK THE ONE YOU WANT. SHE'S YOUR FIANCEE.
OH, HE WANTS AKANE!
EH?
OH, DEFINITELY!
YOU MUST BE JOKING!
WHY WOULD I BE--
WELL... YOU HATE BOYS, DON'T YOU?
SO YOU'RE IN LUCK! HE'S HALF GIRL!
ME? MARRY THAT PERVERT?! NEVER!
GRRR

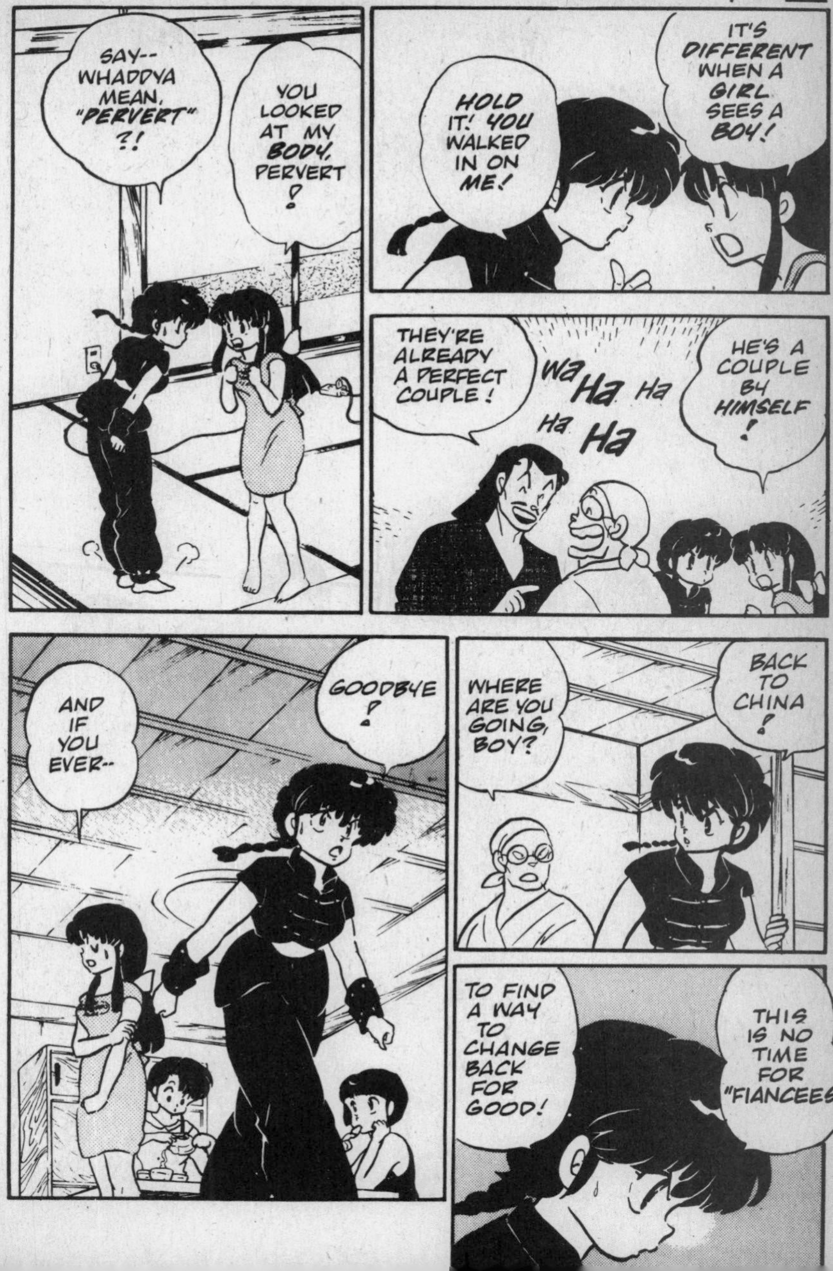
SAY-- WHADDYA MEAN, "PERVERT" ?!
YOU LOOKED AT MY BODY, PERVERT !
HOLD IT! YOU WALKED IN ON ME!
IT'S DIFFERENT WHEN A GIRL SEES A BOY!
THEY'RE ALREADY A PERFECT COUPLE!
WA HA HA HA HA
HE'S A COUPLE BY HIMSELF!
AND IF YOU EVER--
GOODBYE !
WHERE ARE YOU GOING, BOY?
BACK TO CHINA!
TO FIND A WAY TO CHANGE BACK FOR GOOD!
THIS IS NO TIME FOR "FIANCEES."

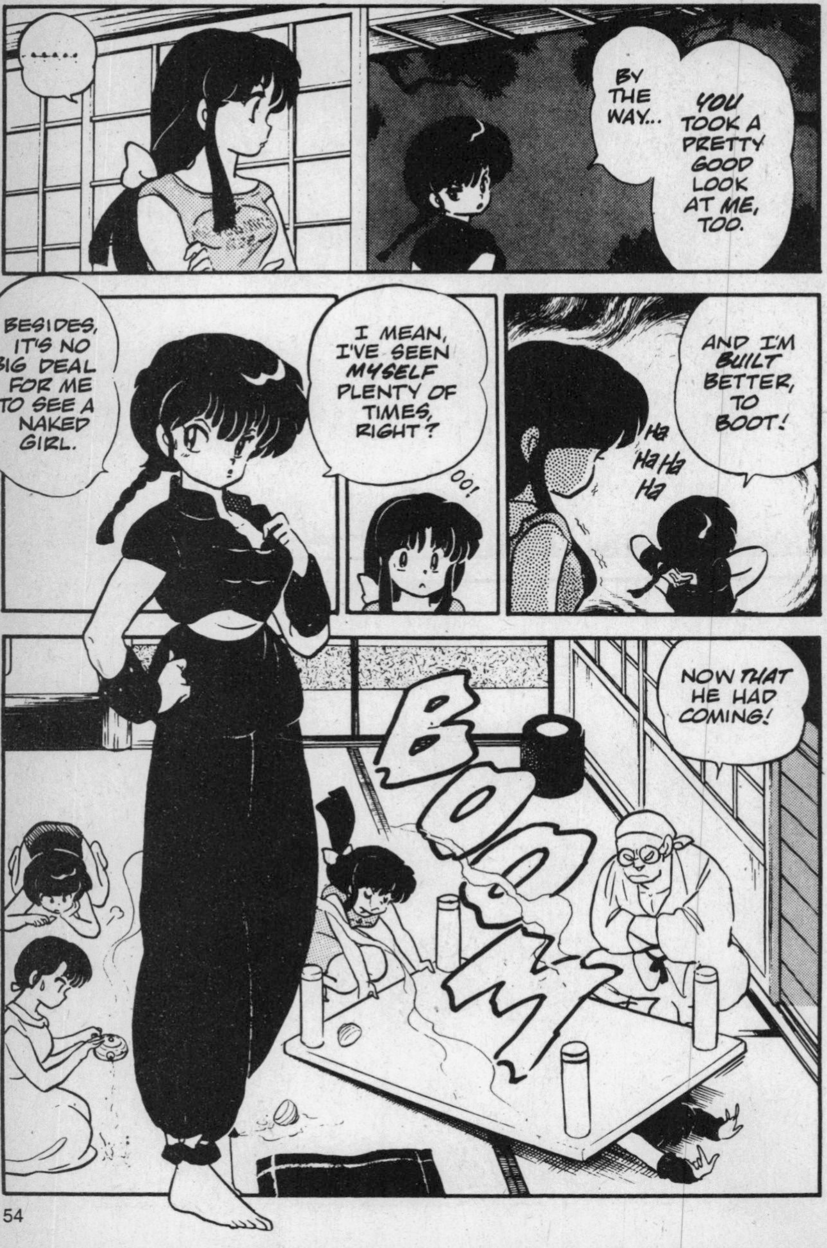
......
BY THE WAY...
YOU TOOK A PRETTY GOOD LOOK AT ME, TOO.
BESIDES, IT'S NO BIG DEAL FOR ME TO SEE A NAKED GIRL.
I MEAN, I'VE SEEN MYSELF PLENTY OF TIMES, RIGHT?
OO!
AND I'M BUILT BETTER, TO BOOT!
Ha Ha Ha Ha
NOW THAT HE HAD COMING!
BOOM

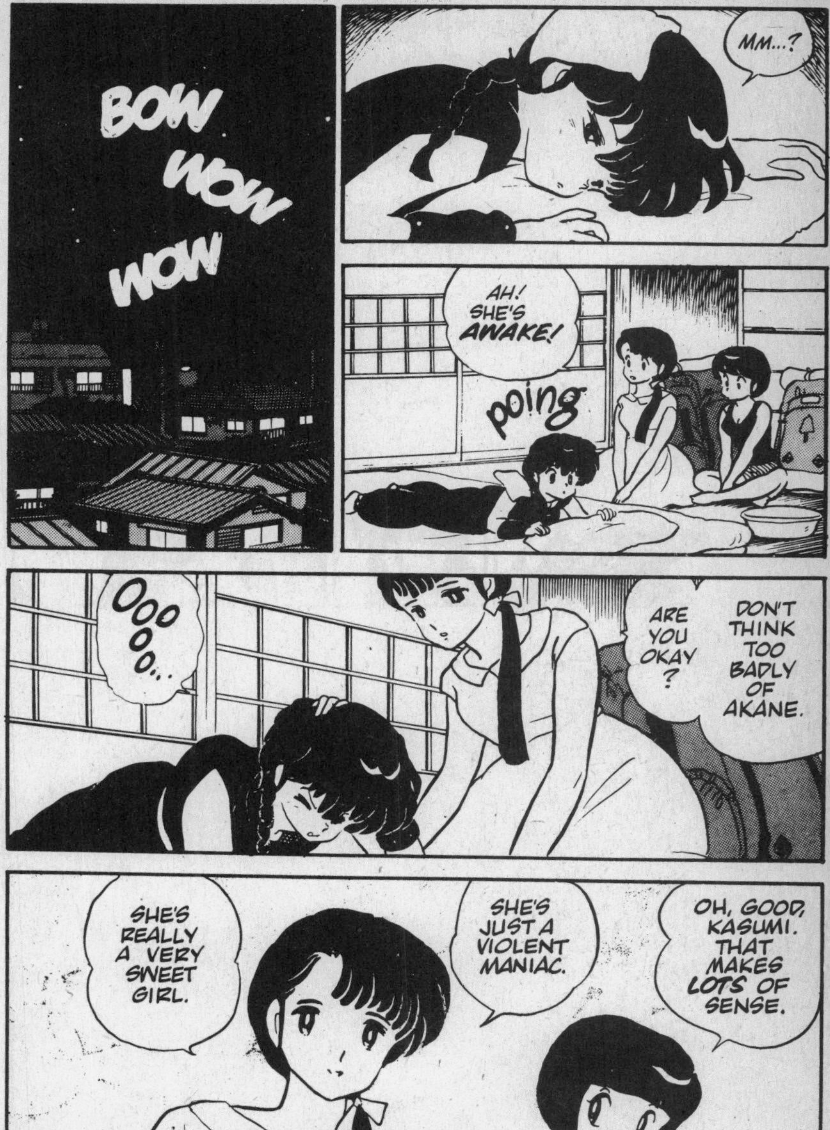
BOW WOW WOW
MM...?
AH! SHE'S AWAKE!
poing
OOO OOO...
ARE YOU OKAY?
DON'T THINK TOO BADLY OF AKANE.
SHE'S REALLY A VERY SWEET GIRL.
SHE'S JUST A VIOLENT MANIAC.
OH, GOOD, KASUMI. THAT MAKES LOTS OF SENSE.

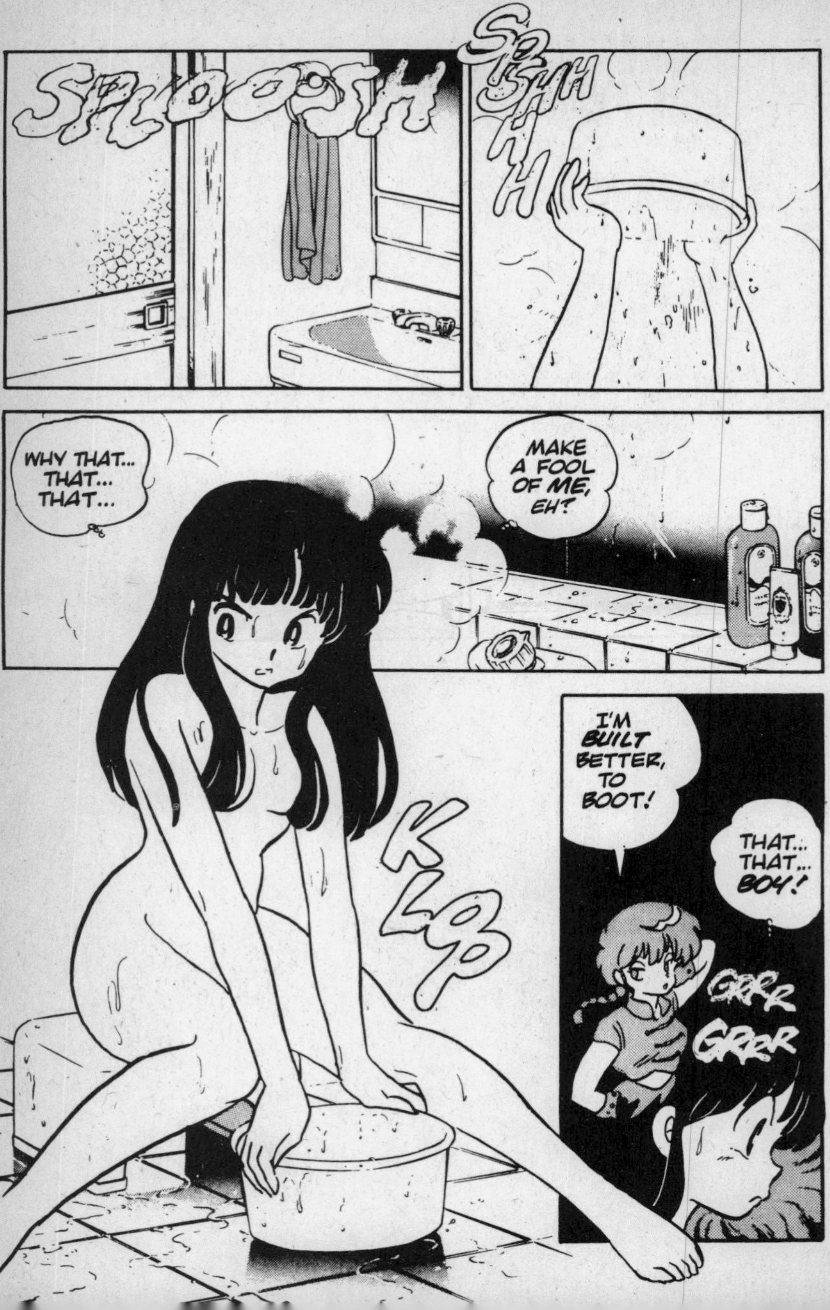

SPLOOSH
SPSHHHH
WHY THAT... THAT... THAT...
MAKE A FOOL OF ME, EH?
KLOP
I'M BUILT BETTER, TO BOOT!
THAT... THAT... BOY!
GRRR
GRRR

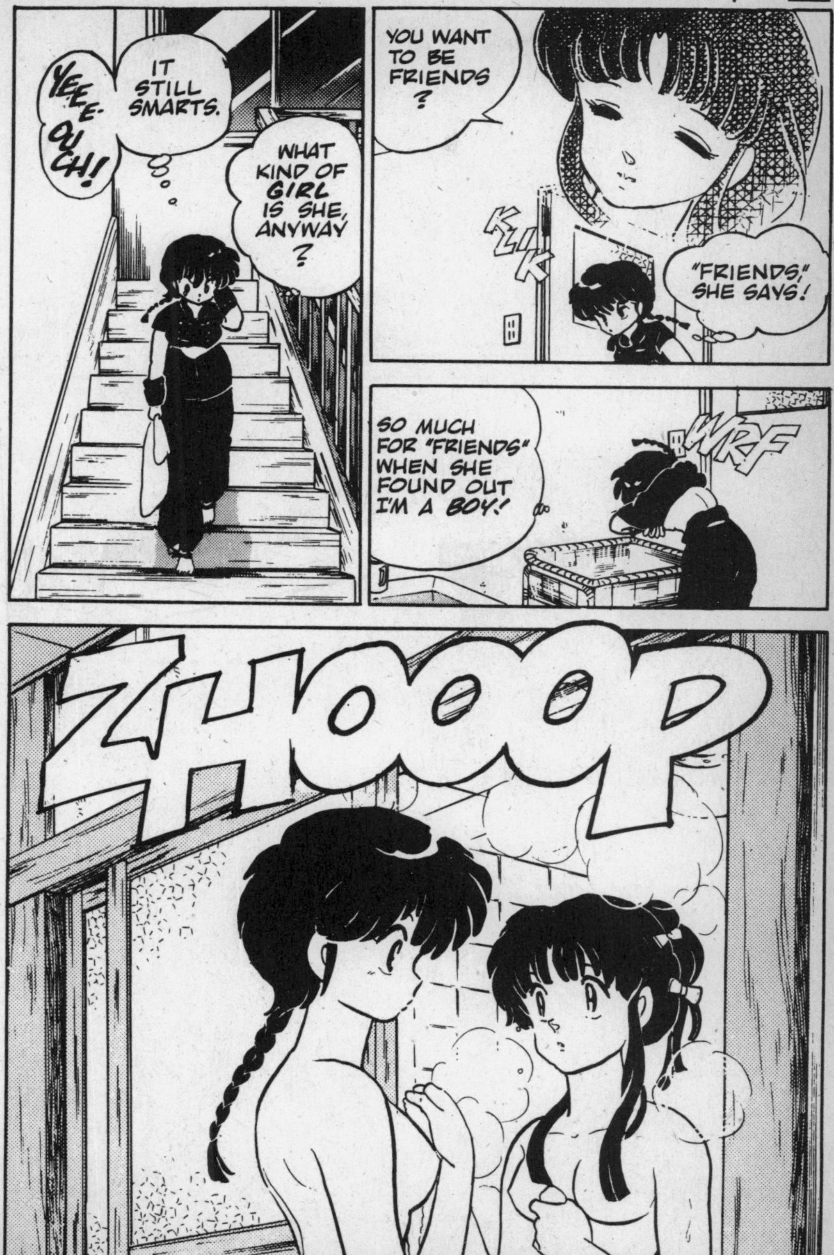
YEEEE-OUCH!
IT STILL SMARTS.
WHAT KIND OF GIRL IS SHE, ANYWAY?
YOU WANT TO BE FRIENDS?
KLIK
"FRIENDS," SHE SAYS!
SO MUCH FOR "FRIENDS" WHEN SHE FOUND OUT I'M A BOY!
WRF
ZHOOOP

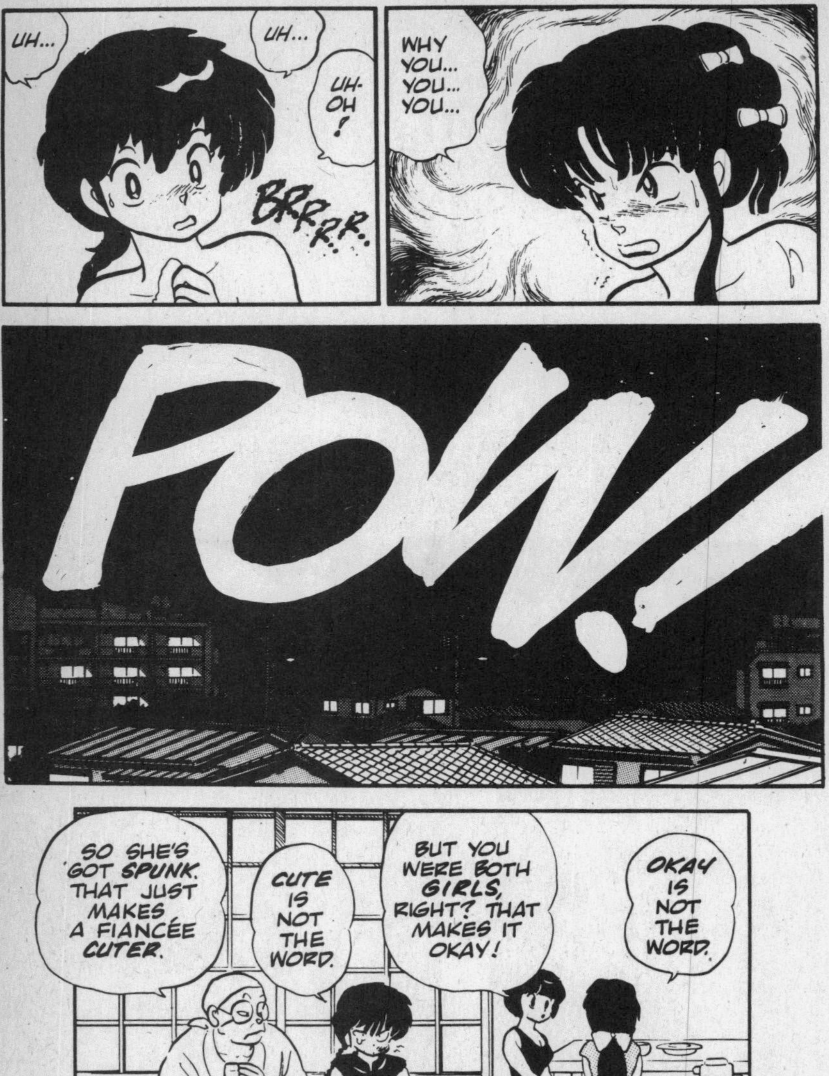
UH...
UH...
UH-OH!
BRRRRR...
WHY YOU... YOU... YOU...
POW!
SO SHE'S GOT SPUNK. THAT JUST MAKES A FIANCÉE CUTER.
CUTE IS NOT THE WORD.
BUT YOU WERE BOTH GIRLS, RIGHT? THAT MAKES IT OKAY!
OKAY IS NOT THE WORD.

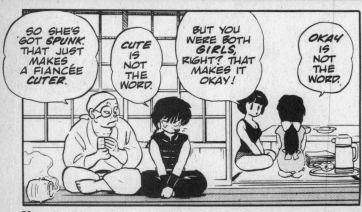

Part 3

I HATE MEN!

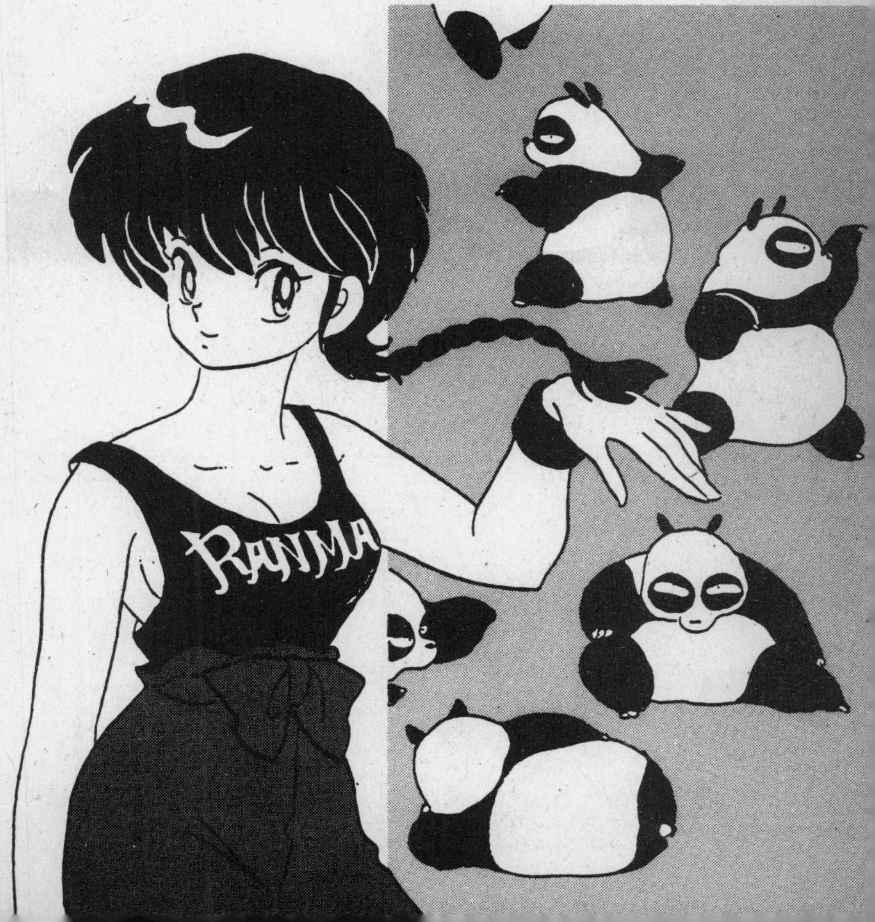
RANMA

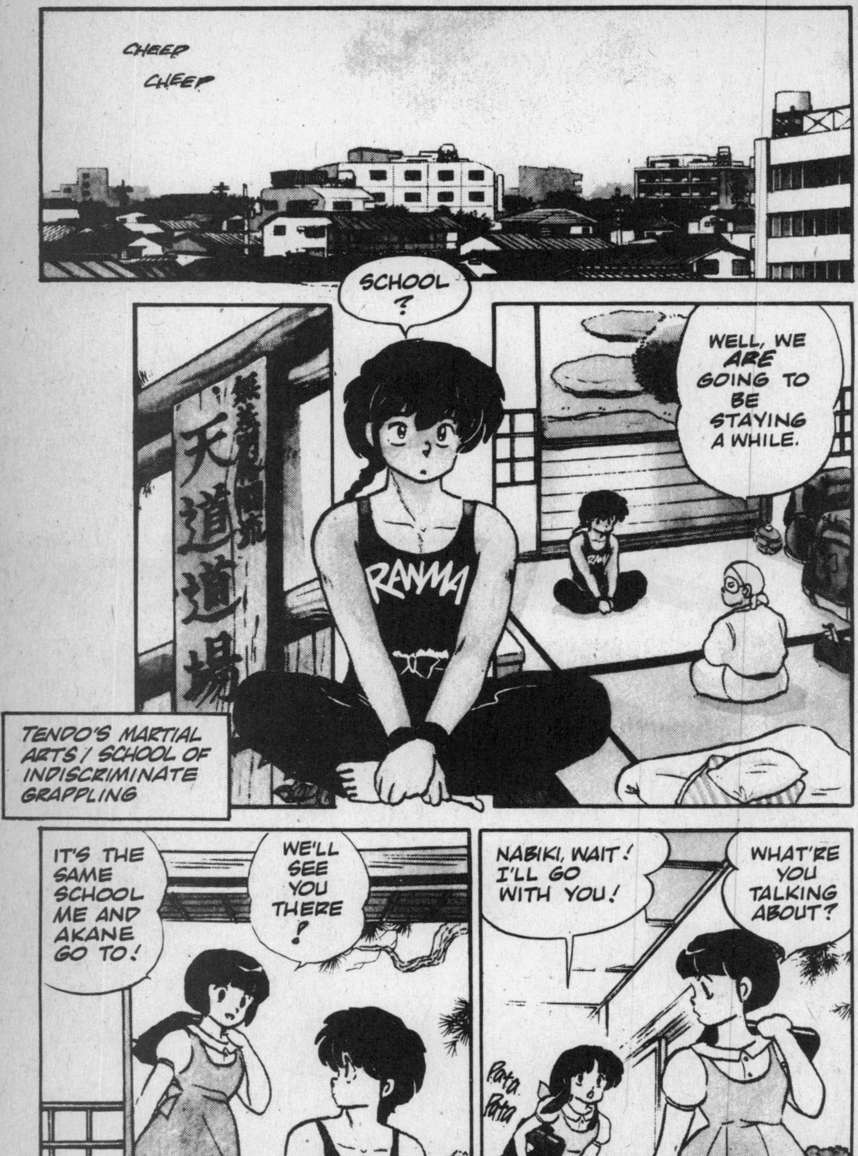

CHEEP
CHEEP
SCHOOL?
天道道場
TENDO'S MARTIAL ARTS / SCHOOL OF INDISCRIMINATE GRAPPLING
WELL, WE ARE GOING TO BE STAYING A WHILE.
RANMA
IT'S THE SAME SCHOOL ME AND AKANE GO TO!
WE'LL SEE YOU THERE!
RANMA
NABIKI, WAIT! I'LL GO WITH YOU!
WHAT'RE YOU TALKING ABOUT?
Pata Pata

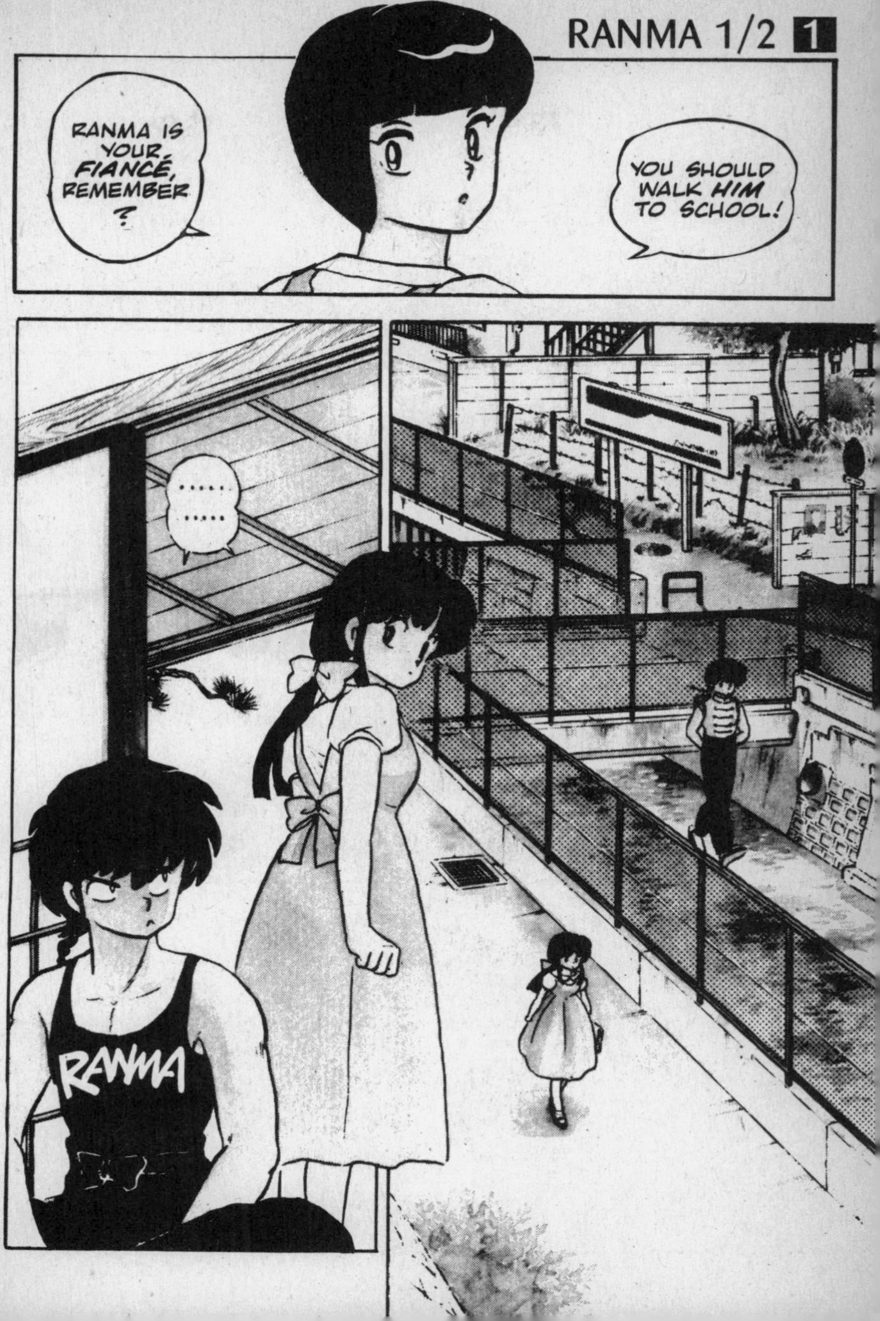
RANMA IS YOUR *FIANCÉ*, REMEMBER?
YOU SHOULD WALK *HIM* TO SCHOOL!
....
RANMA

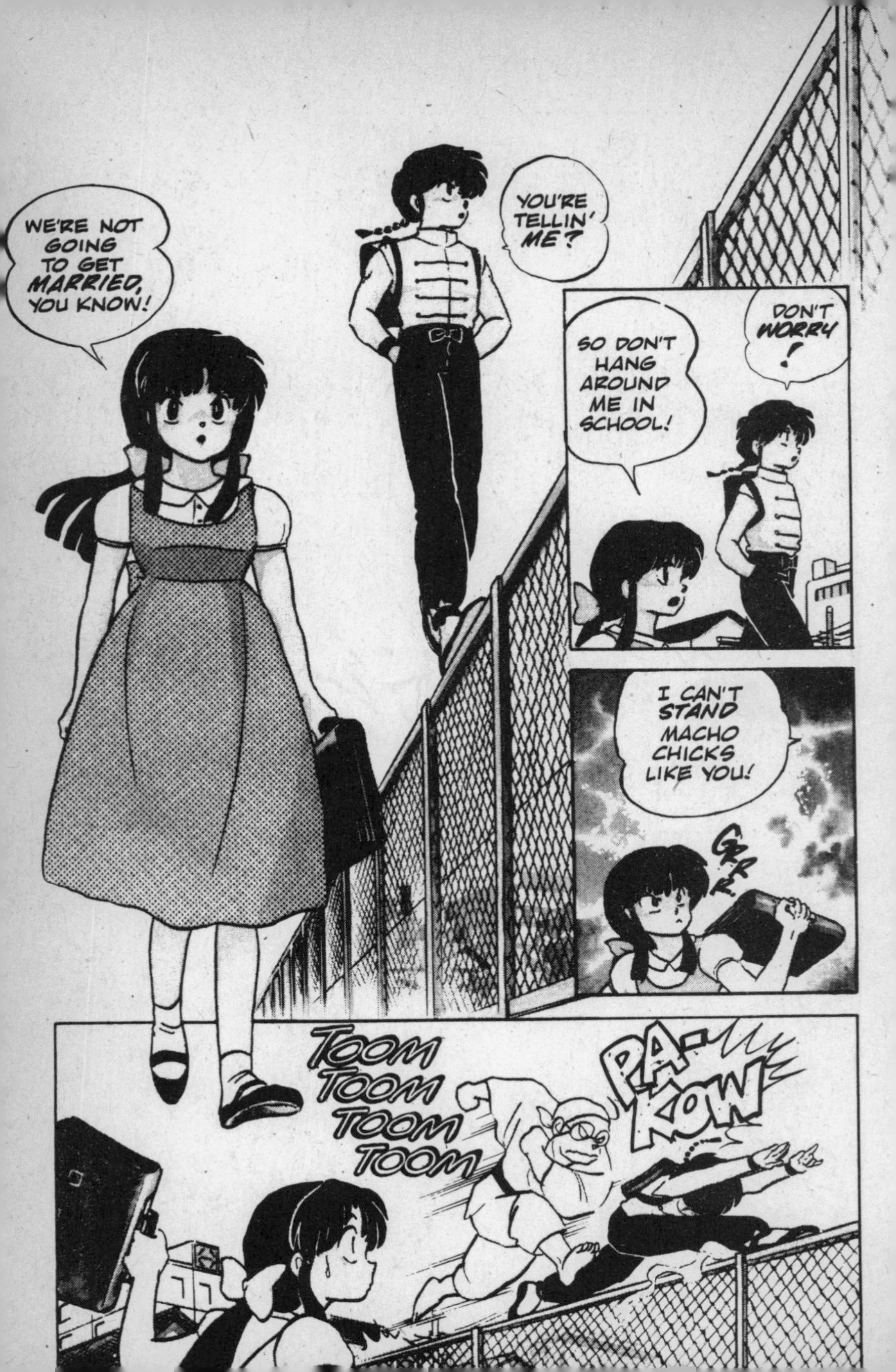
WE'RE NOT GOING TO GET MARRIED, YOU KNOW!
YOU'RE TELLIN' ME?
SO DON'T HANG AROUND ME IN SCHOOL!
DON'T WORRY!
I CAN'T STAND MACHO CHICKS LIKE YOU!
GRRR
TOOM TOOM TOOM TOOM
PA-KOW

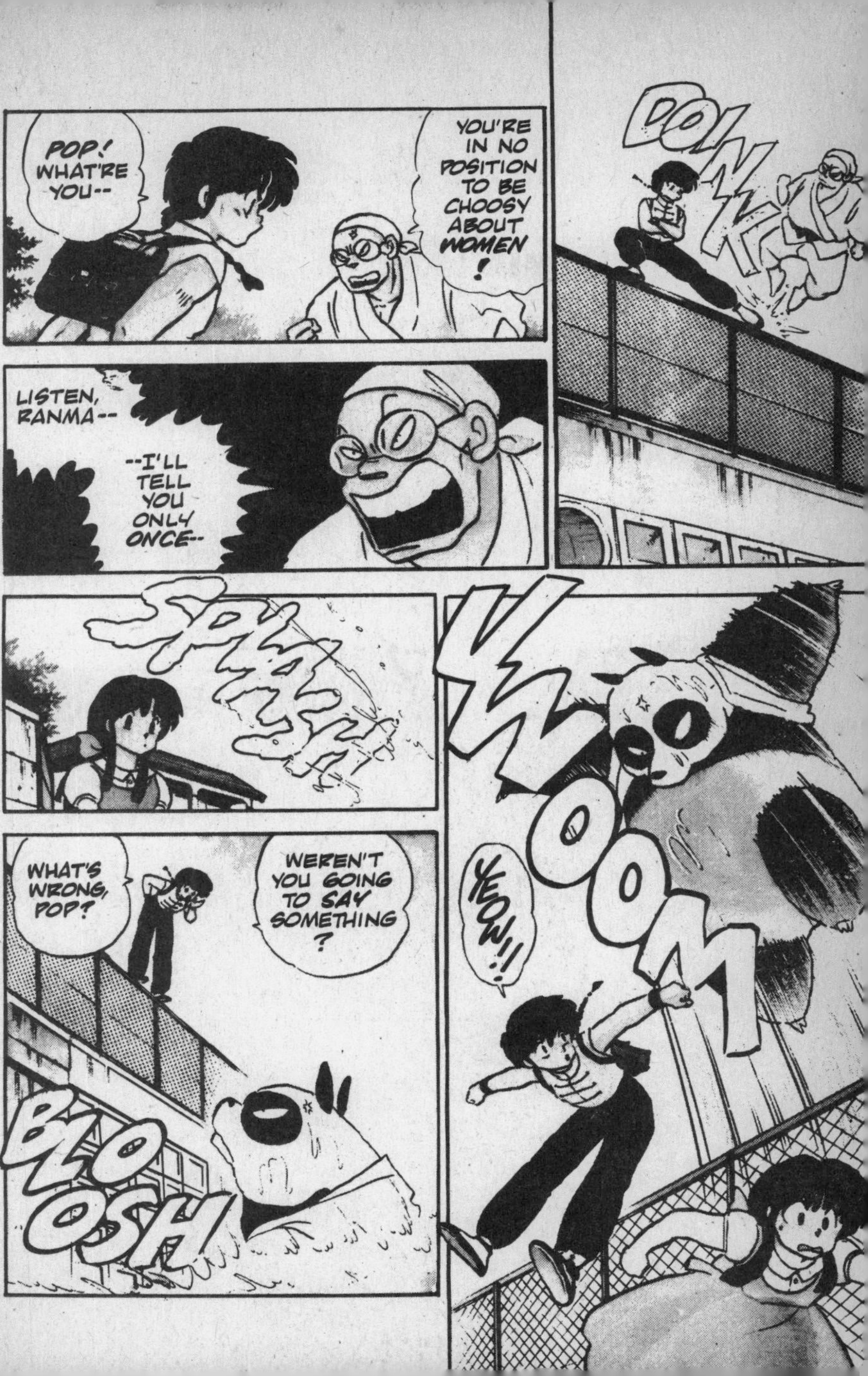
POP! WHAT'RE YOU--
YOU'RE IN NO POSITION TO BE CHOOSY ABOUT WOMEN!
LISTEN, RANMA--
--I'LL TELL YOU ONLY ONCE--
DOINK
SPLASH
WHAT'S WRONG, POP?
WEREN'T YOU GOING TO SAY SOMETHING?
BLOOSH
WHOOM
YEOW!!

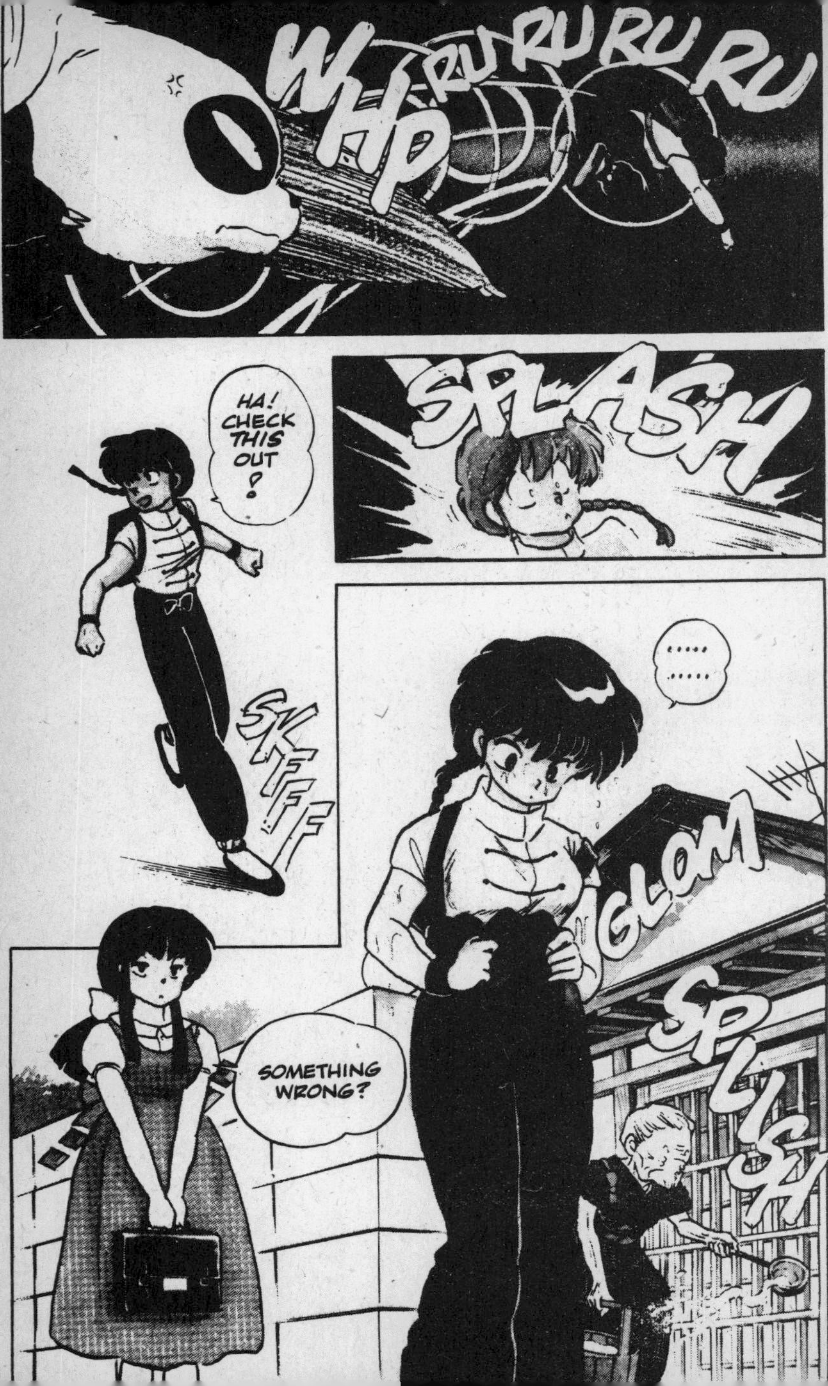
WHIP
RURURURURURU
HA! CHECK THIS OUT!
SKFFF
SPLASH
......
......
GLOM
SPLISH
SOMETHING WRONG?

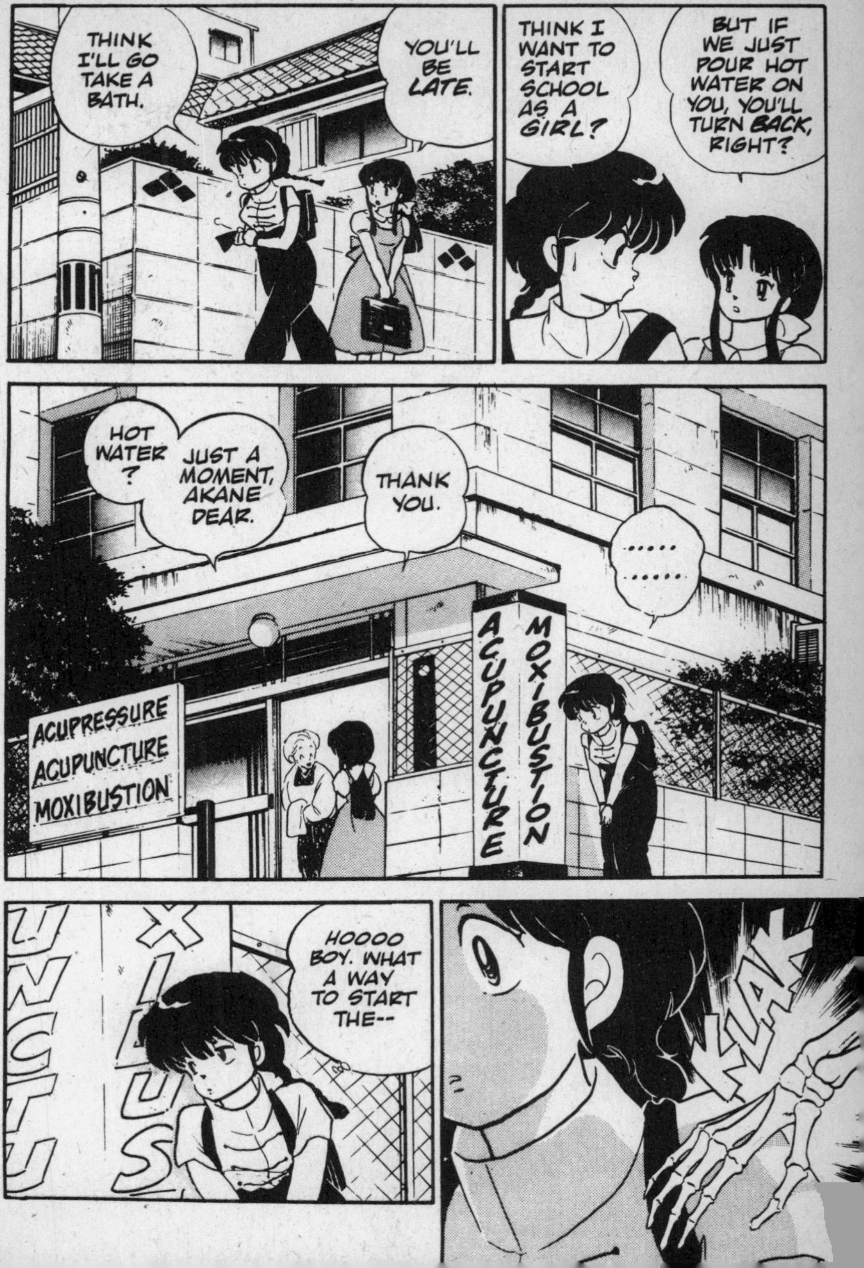
THINK I'LL GO TAKE A BATH.
YOU'LL BE LATE.
THINK I WANT TO START SCHOOL AS A GIRL?
BUT IF WE JUST POUR HOT WATER ON YOU, YOU'LL TURN BACK, RIGHT?
HOT WATER?
JUST A MOMENT, AKANE DEAR.
THANK YOU.
....
ACUPRESSURE
ACUPUNCTURE
MOXIBUSTION
ACUPUNCTURE
MOXIBUSTION
HOOOO BOY. WHAT A WAY TO START THE--
KLAK

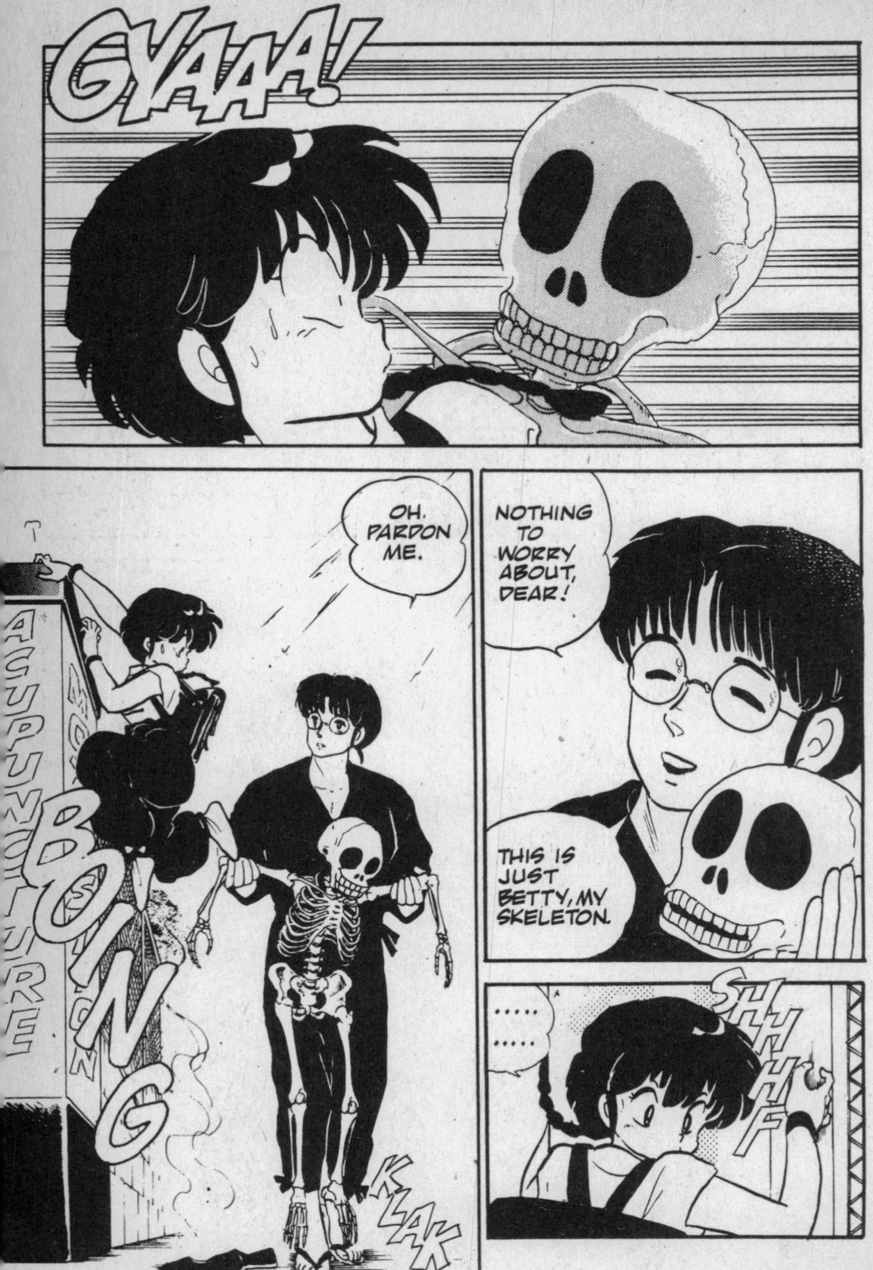
GYAAA!
OH. PARDON ME.
BOING
ACUPUNCTURE
MOXIBUSTION
KLAK
NOTHING TO WORRY ABOUT, DEAR!
THIS IS JUST BETTY, MY SKELETON.
.....
.....
SHHHF

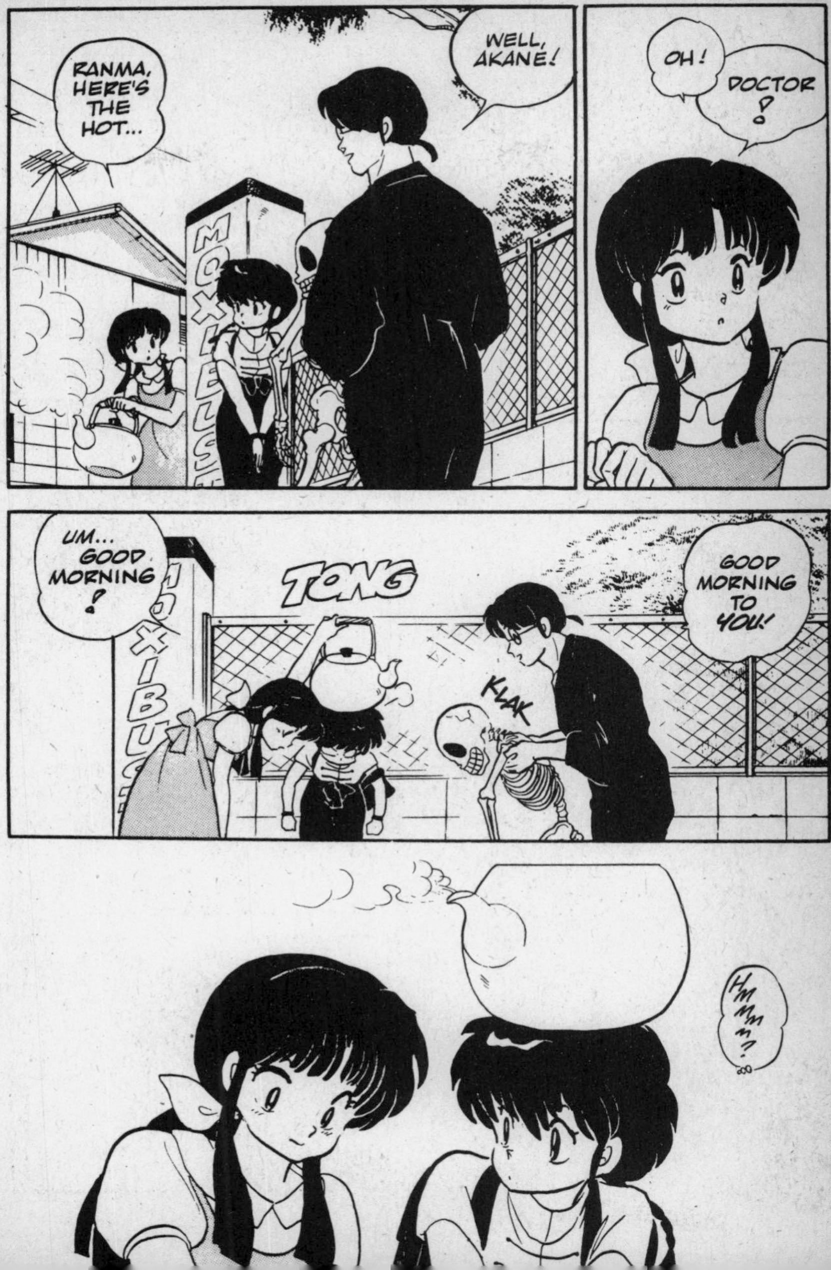
RANMA, HERE'S THE HOT...
MOXIBUST
WELL, AKANE!
OH!
DOCTOR?
UM... GOOD MORNING!
TONG
MOXIBUST
GOOD MORNING TO YOU!
KLAK
HMMMM?

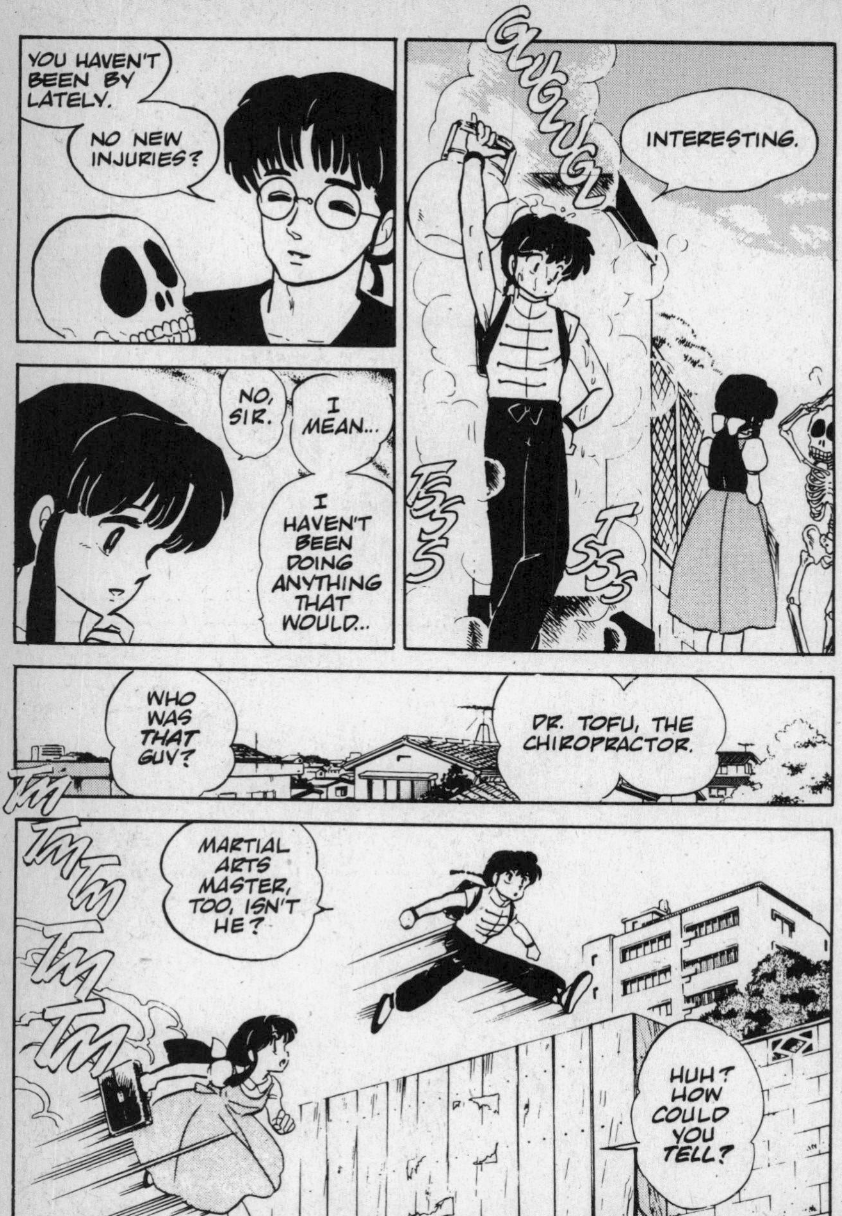
YOU HAVEN'T BEEN BY LATELY.
NO NEW INJURIES?
GLUGLUGL
INTERESTING.
NO, SIR.
I MEAN...
I HAVEN'T BEEN DOING ANYTHING THAT WOULD...
TSSS
TSSS
WHO WAS THAT GUY?
DR. TOFU, THE CHIROPRACTOR.
TM
TMTMTM
TM TM
TM TM
MARTIAL ARTS MASTER, TOO, ISN'T HE?
HUH? HOW COULD YOU TELL?

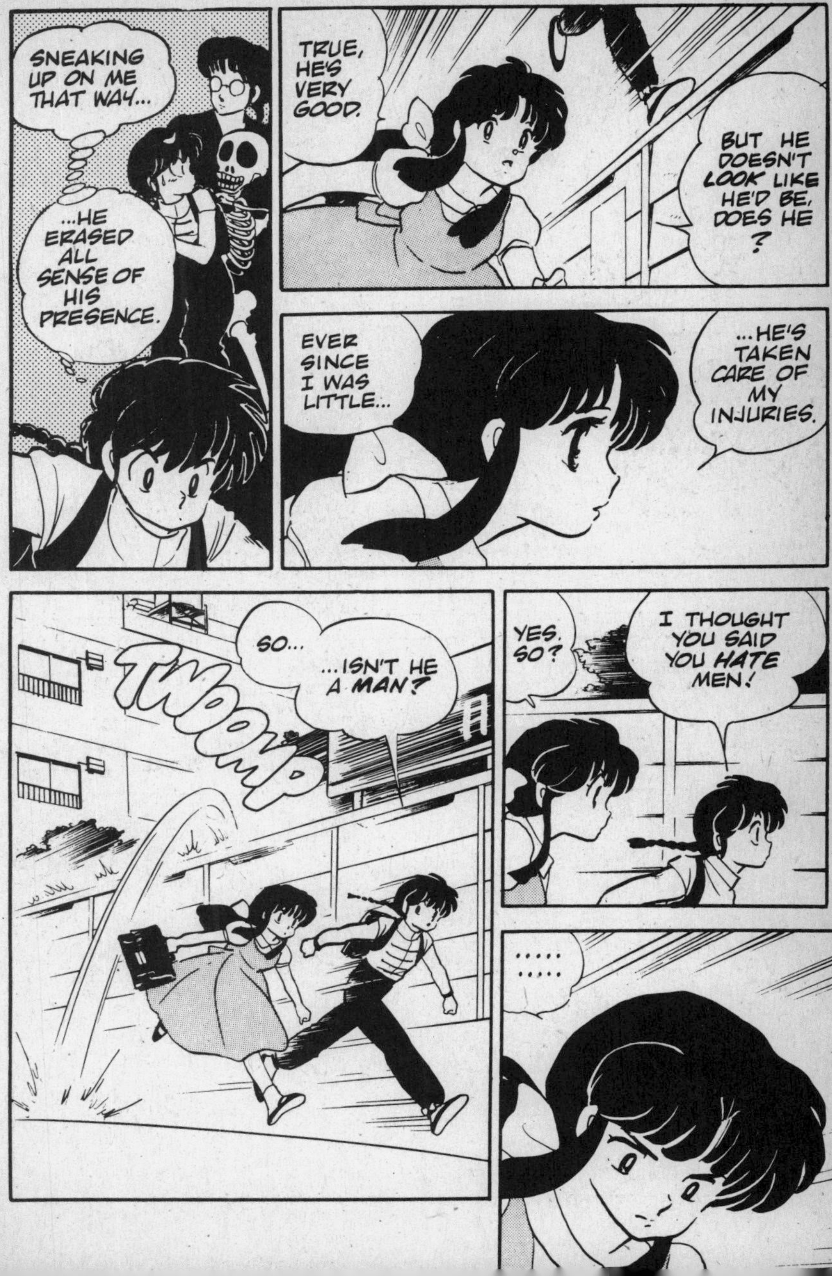
SNEAKING UP ON ME THAT WAY...
...HE ERASED ALL SENSE OF HIS PRESENCE.
TRUE, HE'S VERY GOOD.
BUT HE DOESN'T *LOOK* LIKE HE'D BE, DOES HE?
EVER SINCE I WAS LITTLE...
...HE'S TAKEN CARE OF MY INJURIES.
SO...
...ISN'T HE A *MAN?*
TWOMP
YES. SO?
I THOUGHT YOU SAID YOU *HATE* MEN!
.....
.....

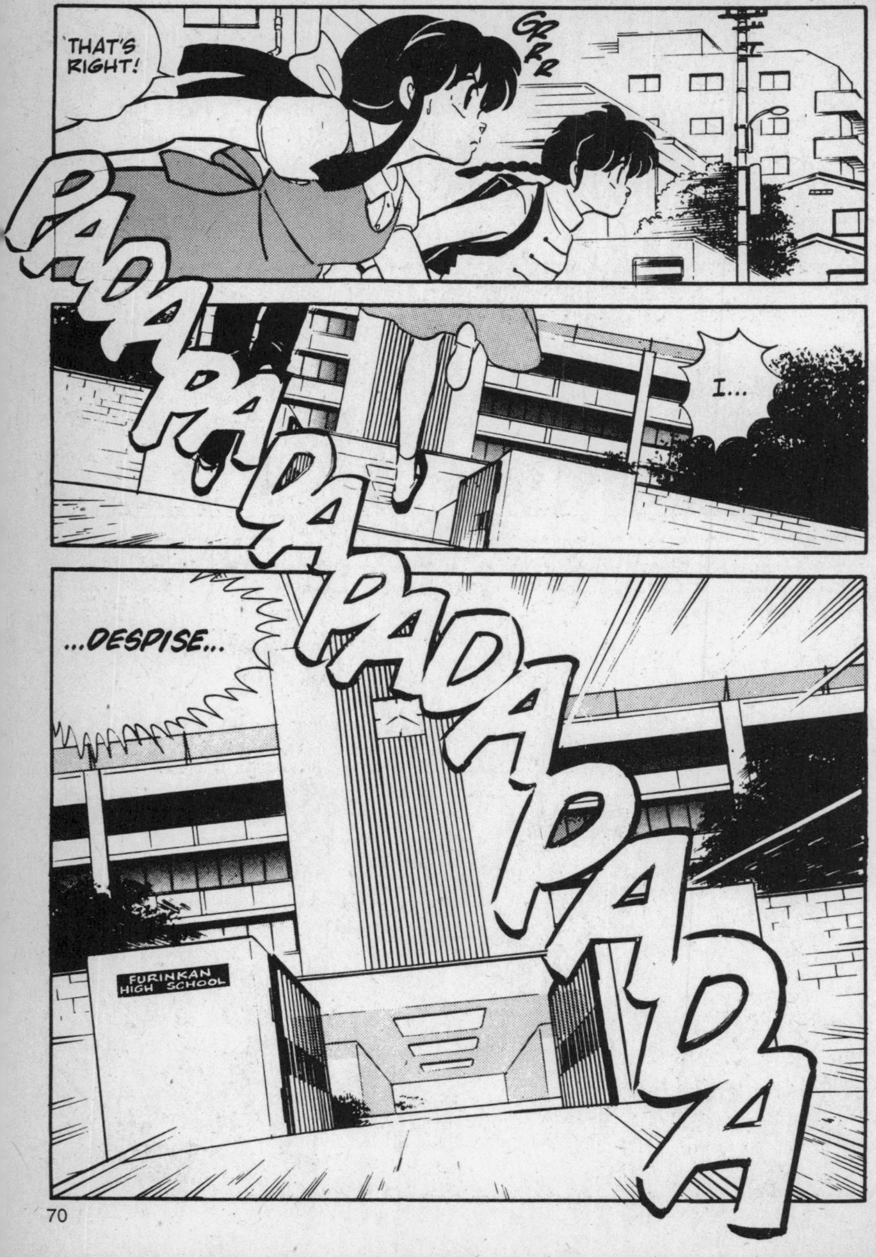
THAT'S RIGHT!
GRRR
PADAPADAPADAPADAPADA
I...
...DESPISE...
FURINKAN HIGH SCHOOL

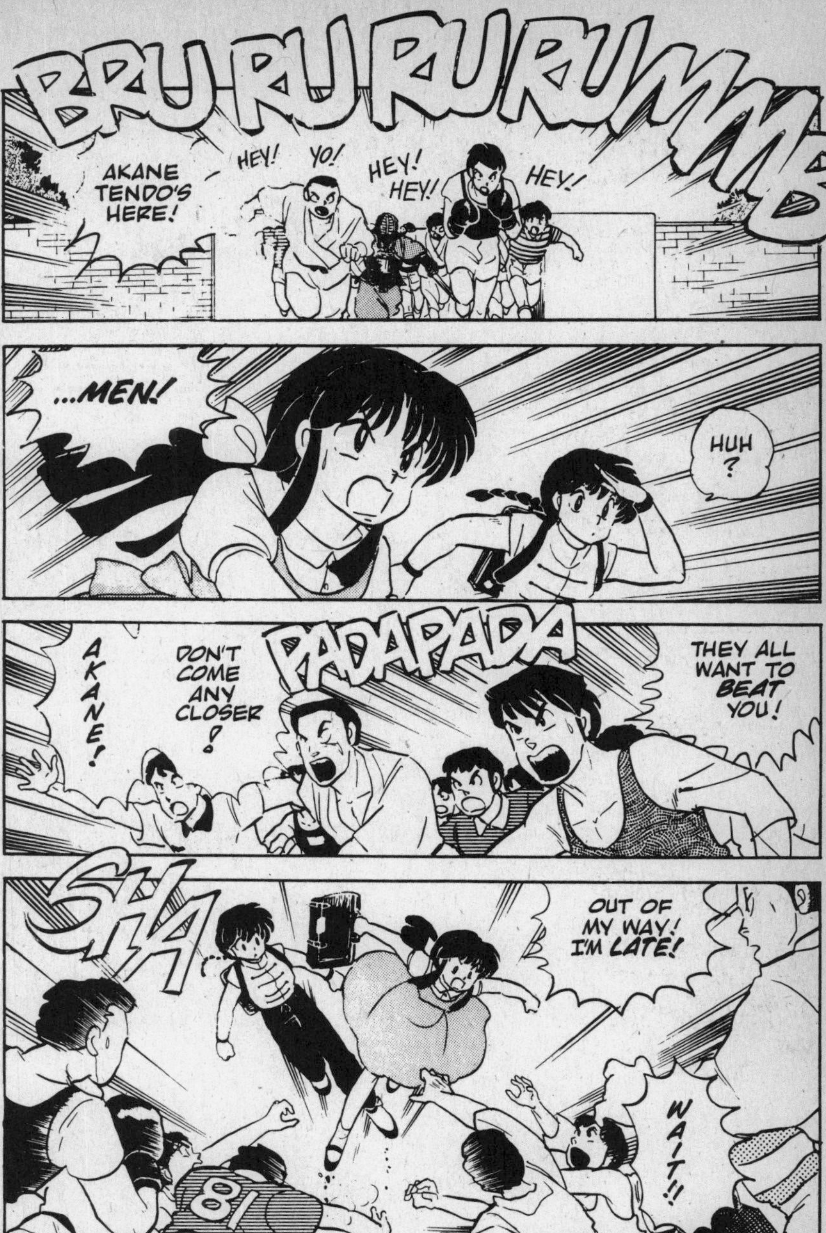
BRURURURUMMB
AKANE TENDO'S HERE!
HEY!
YO!
HEY! HEY!
HEY!
...MEN!
HUH?
PADAPADA
AKANE!
DON'T COME ANY CLOSER!
THEY ALL WANT TO BEAT YOU!
SHA
OUT OF MY WAY! I'M LATE!
WAIT!!

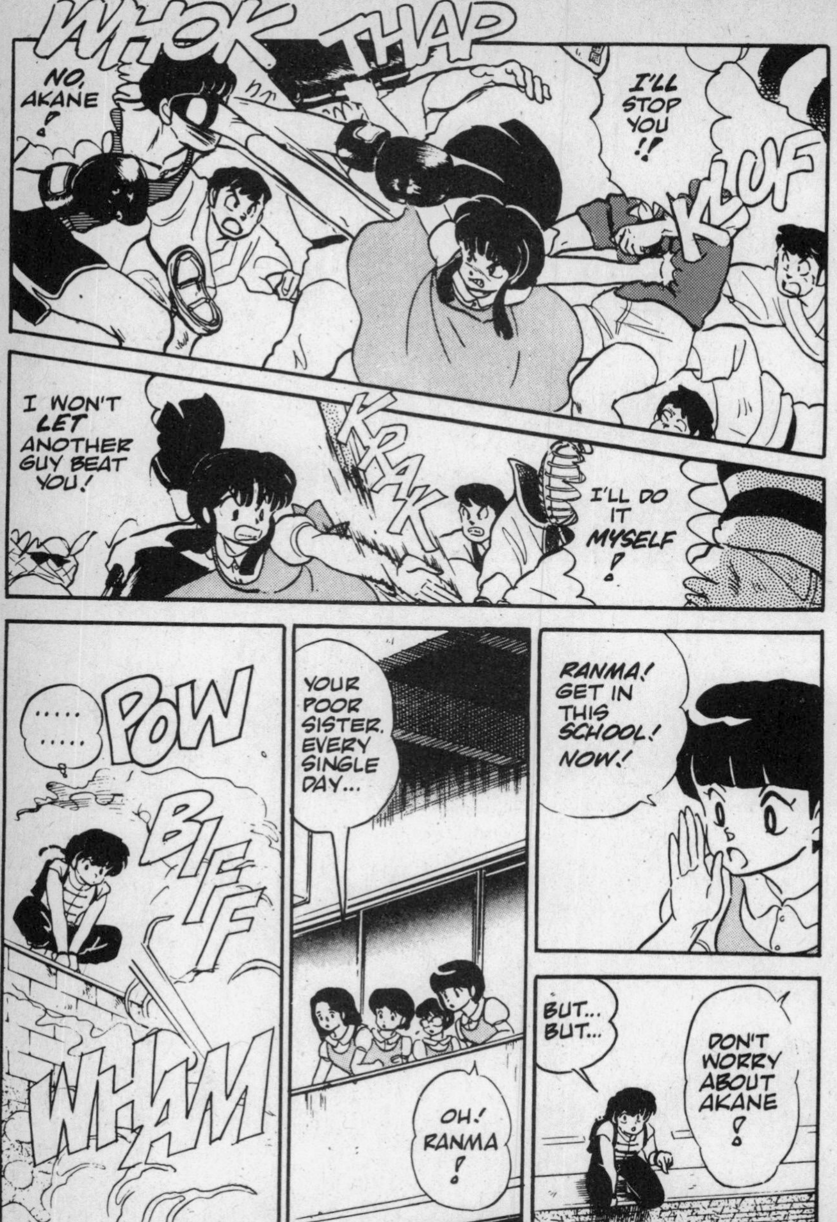
WHOK
THAP
NO, AKANE!
I'LL STOP YOU!!
KLUF
I WON'T LET ANOTHER GUY BEAT YOU!
KRAK
I'LL DO IT MYSELF!
....
POW
BIFF
WHAM
YOUR POOR SISTER. EVERY SINGLE DAY...
OH! RANMA!
RANMA! GET IN THIS SCHOOL! NOW!
BUT... BUT...
DON'T WORRY ABOUT AKANE!

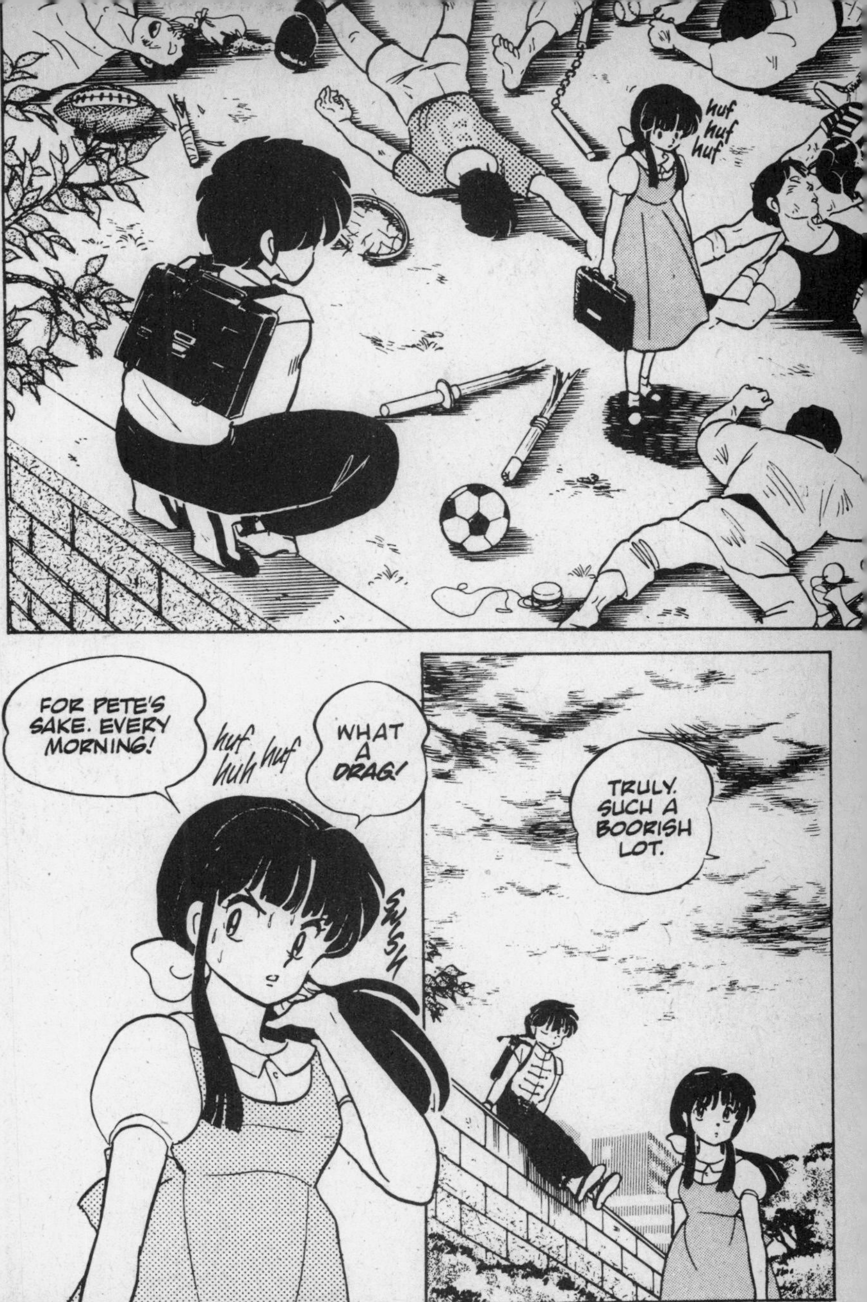
huf
huf
huf
FOR PETE'S SAKE. EVERY MORNING!
huf huh huf
WHAT A DRAG!
SWISH
TRULY. SUCH A BOORISH LOT.

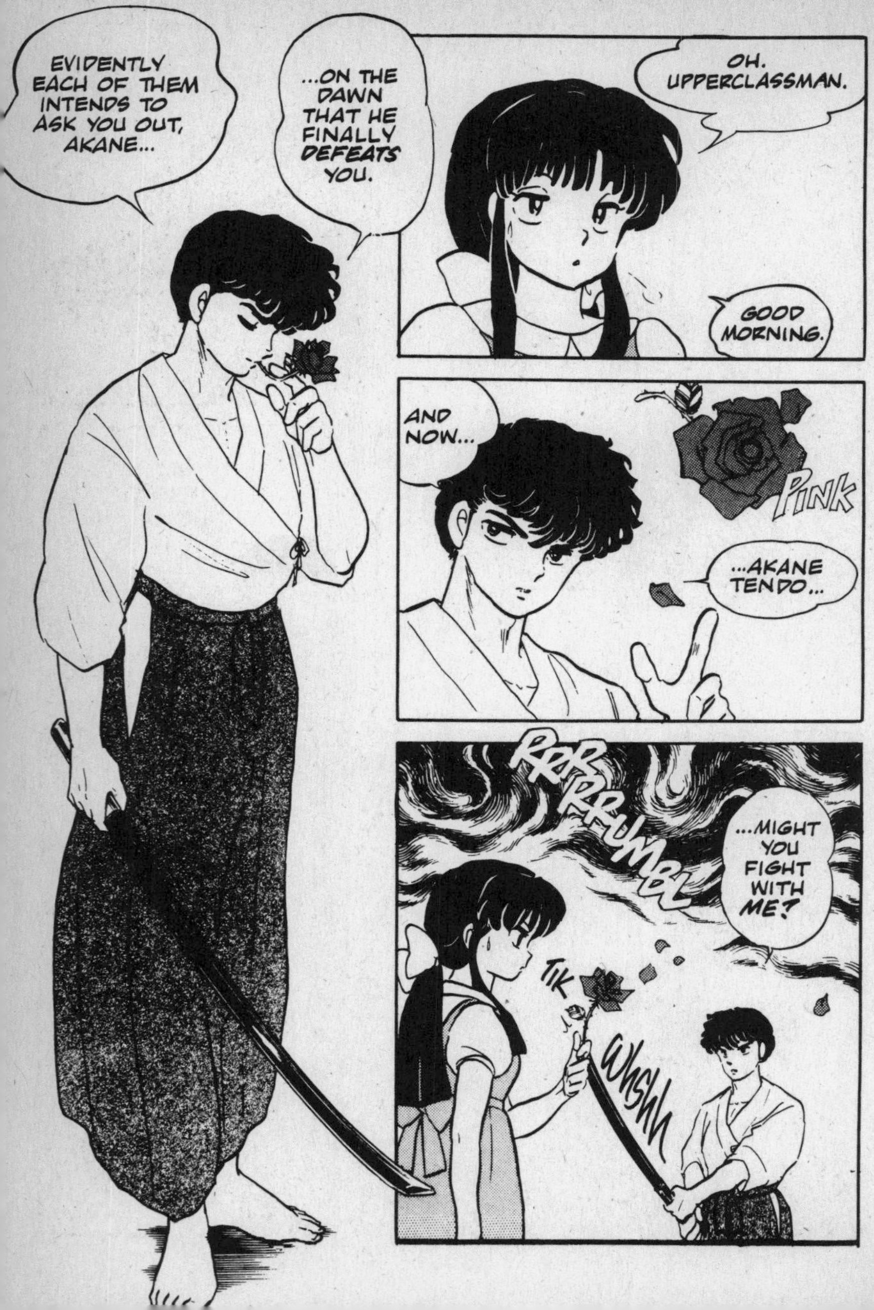
EVIDENTLY EACH OF THEM INTENDS TO ASK YOU OUT, AKANE...
...ON THE DAWN THAT HE FINALLY DEFEATS YOU.
OH. UPPERCLASSMAN.
GOOD MORNING.
AND NOW...
PINK
...AKANE TENDO...
RRRRRRUMBL
...MIGHT YOU FIGHT WITH ME?
TIK
WHSHH

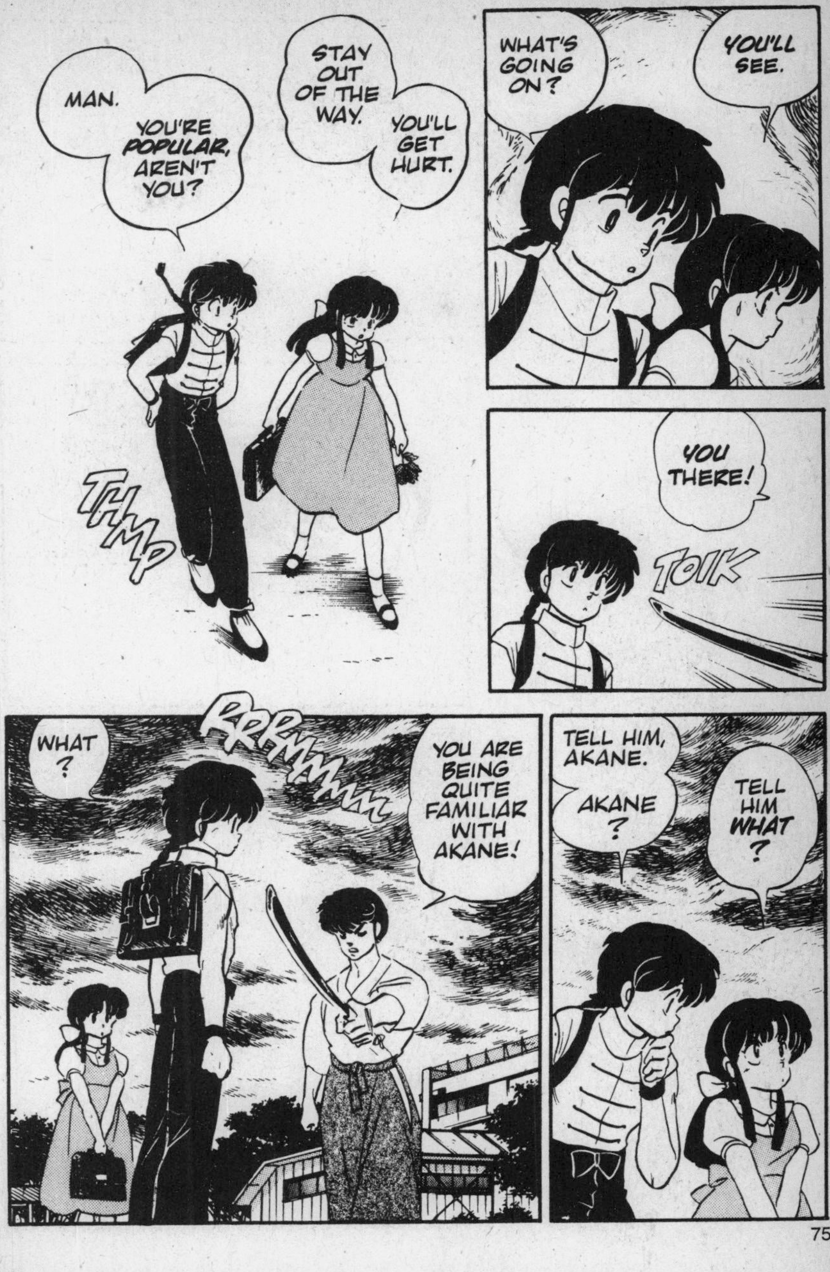
MAN.
YOU'RE POPULAR, AREN'T YOU?
STAY OUT OF THE WAY.
YOU'LL GET HURT.
THMP
WHAT'S GOING ON?
YOU'LL SEE.
YOU THERE!
TOIK
WHAT?
RRRMMMM
YOU ARE BEING QUITE FAMILIAR WITH AKANE!
TELL HIM, AKANE.
AKANE?
TELL HIM WHAT?

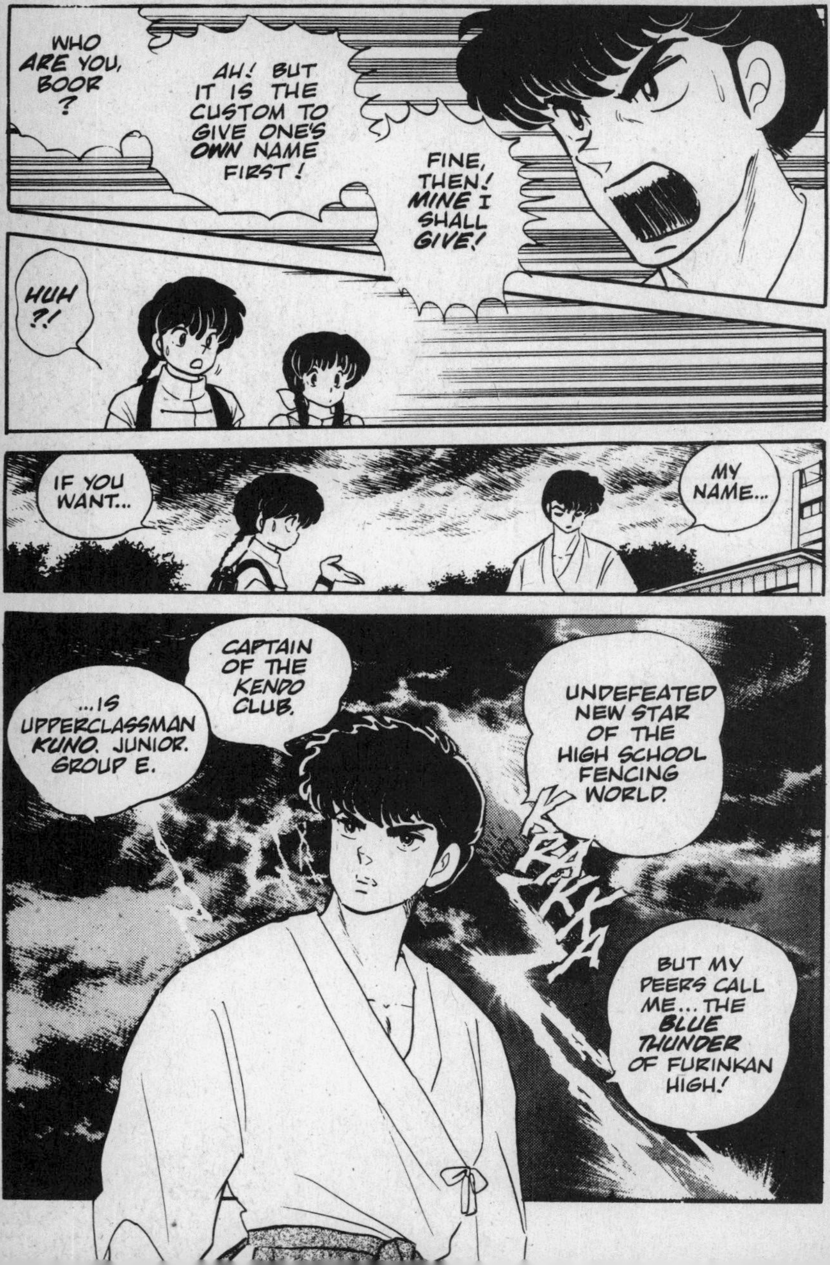
WHO ARE YOU, BOOR ?
AH! BUT IT IS THE CUSTOM TO GIVE ONE'S OWN NAME FIRST!
FINE, THEN! MINE I SHALL GIVE!
HUH ?!
IF YOU WANT...
MY NAME...
...IS UPPERCLASSMAN KUNO. JUNIOR. GROUP E.
CAPTAIN OF THE KENDO CLUB.
UNDEFEATED NEW STAR OF THE HIGH SCHOOL FENCING WORLD.
BUT MY PEERS CALL ME... THE BLUE THUNDER OF FURINKAN HIGH!

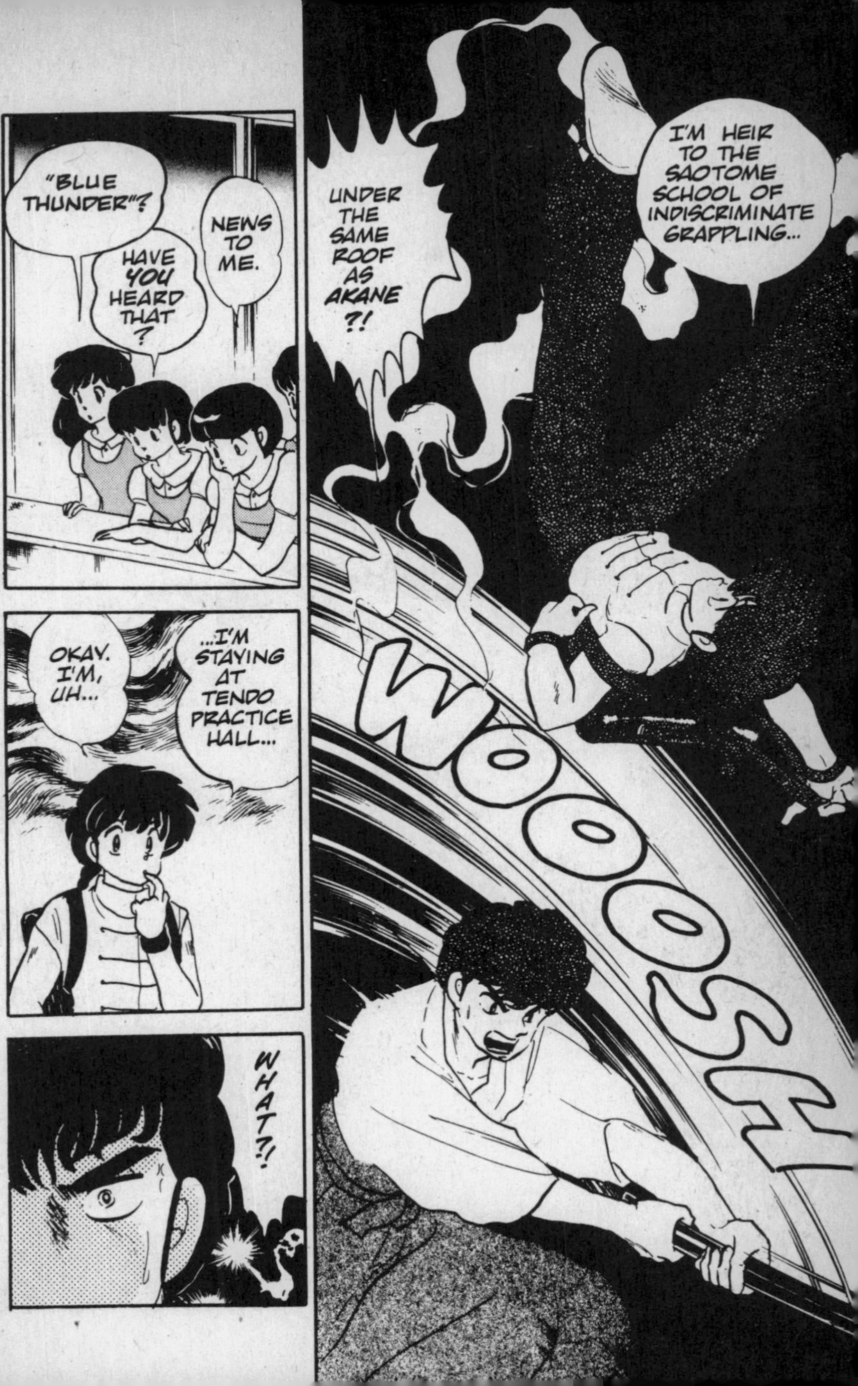
"BLUE THUNDER"?
HAVE YOU HEARD THAT?
NEWS TO ME.
OKAY. I'M, UH...
...I'M STAYING AT TENDO PRACTICE HALL...
WHAT?!
UNDER THE SAME ROOF AS AKANE?!
I'M HEIR TO THE SAOTOME SCHOOL OF INDISCRIMINATE GRAPPLING...
WOOOOSH

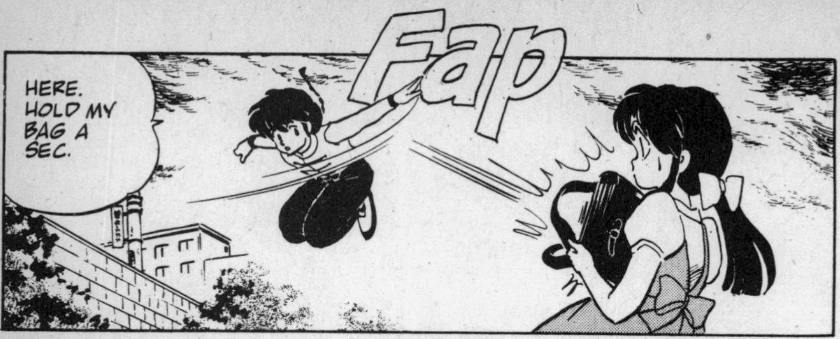
HERE. HOLD MY BAG A SEC.
Fap

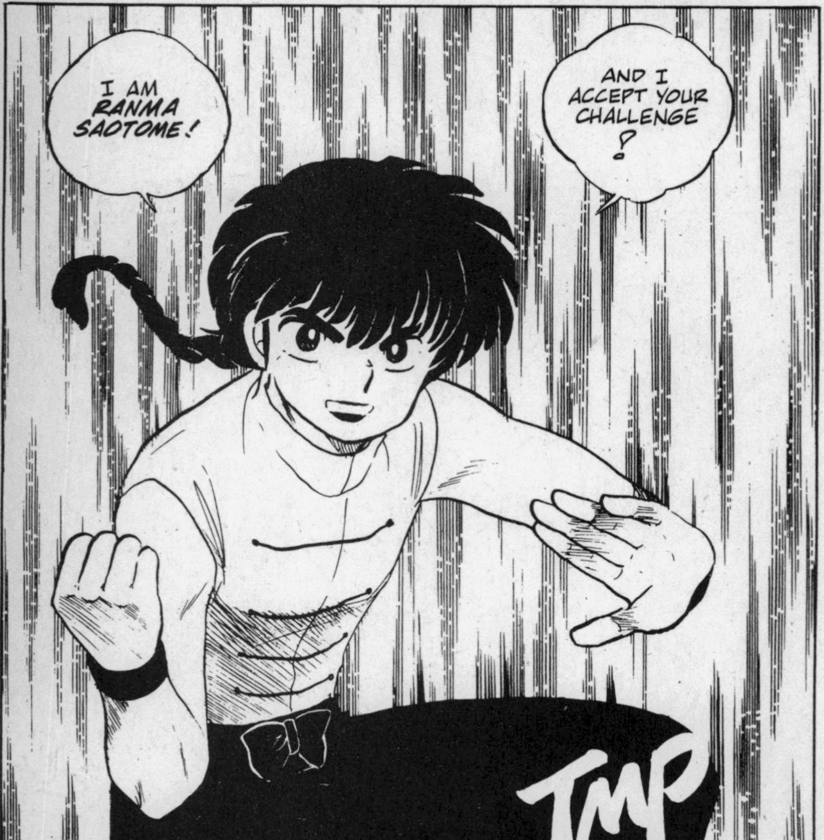
I AM RANMA SAOTOME!
AND I ACCEPT YOUR CHALLENGE!
TMP

Part 4
NEVER, NEVER, NEVER

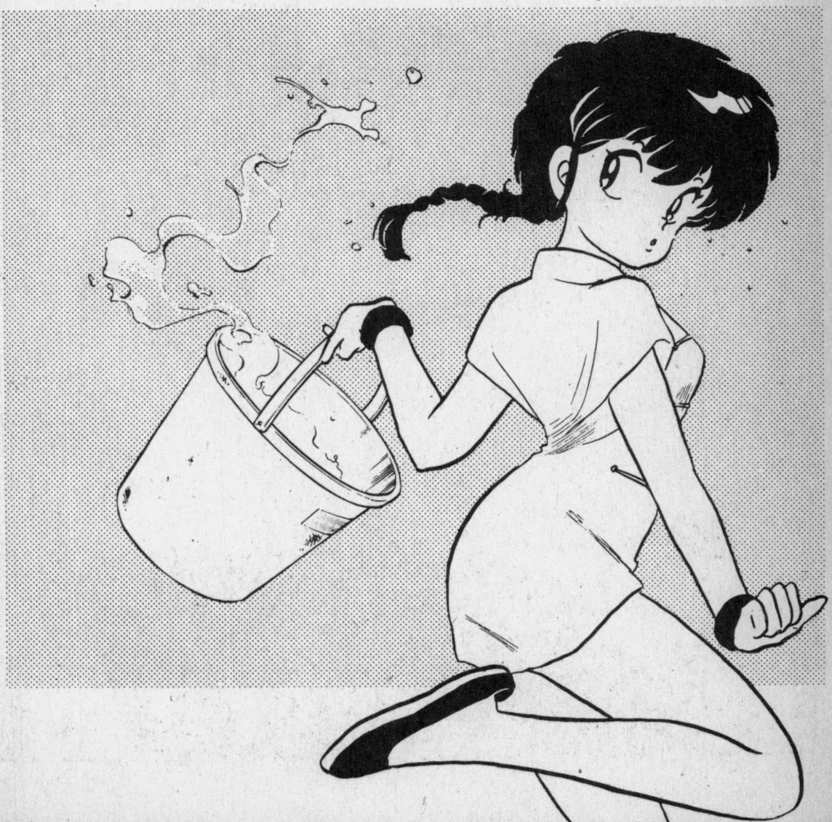

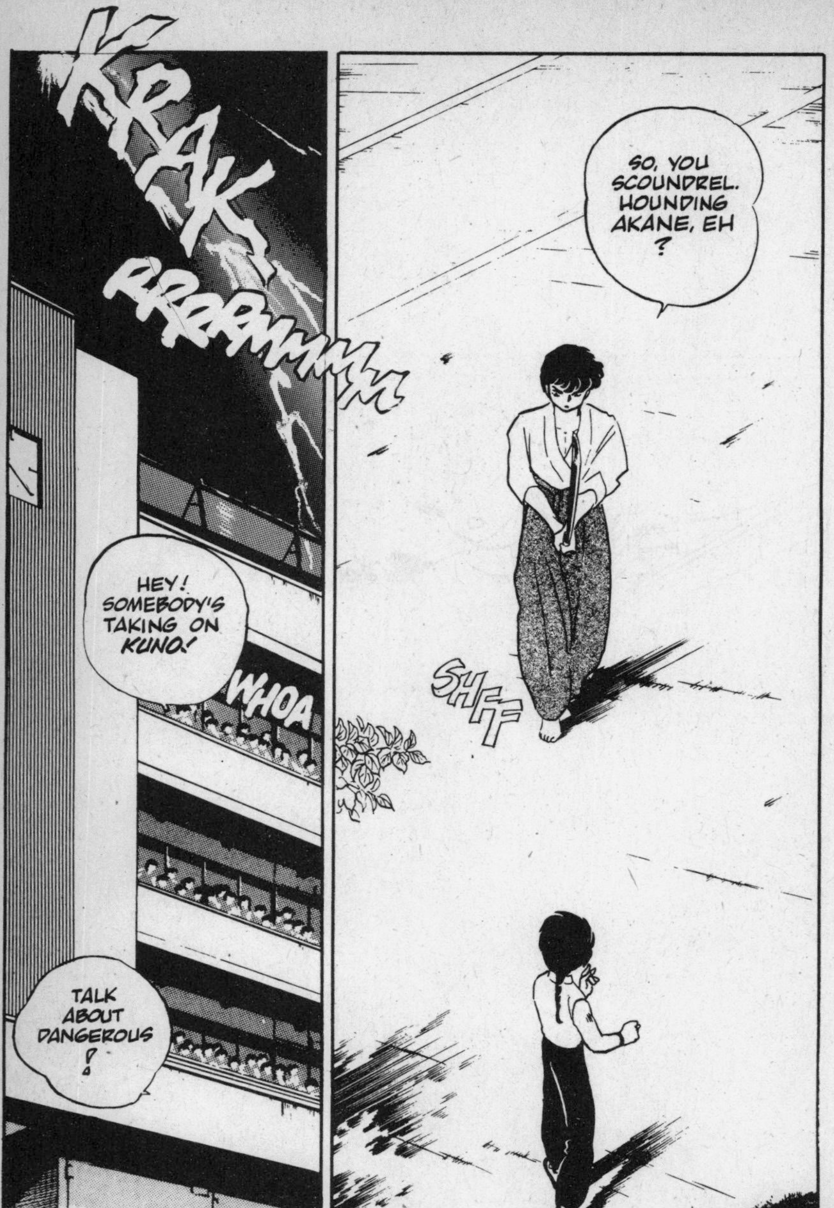
KRAK
HEY! SOMEBODY'S TAKING ON KUNO!
WHOA
TALK ABOUT DANGEROUS?!
SO, YOU SCOUNDREL. HOUNDING AKANE, EH?
SHFF

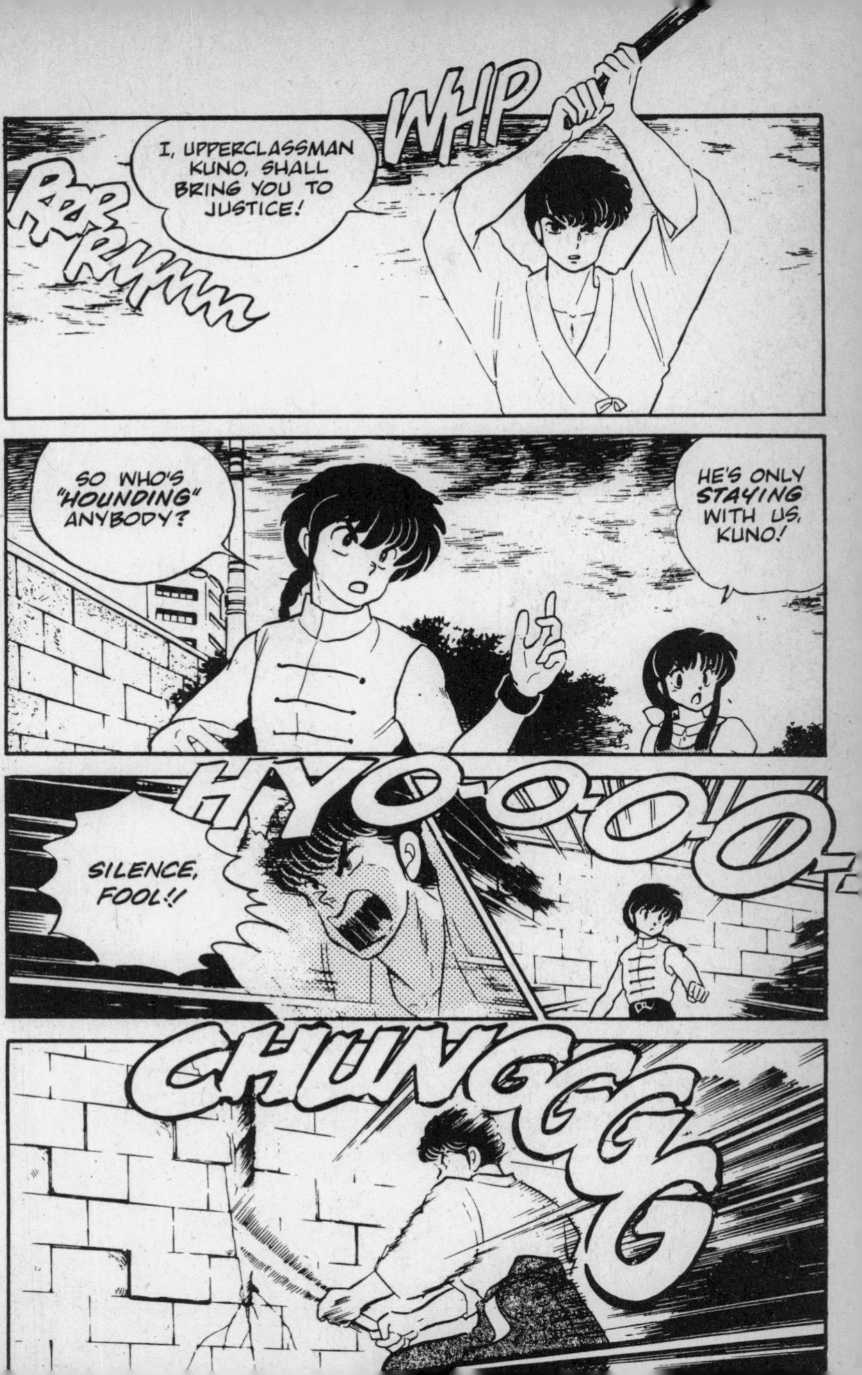
WHP
RRRRRMMMM
I, UPPERCLASSMAN KUNO, SHALL BRING YOU TO JUSTICE!
SO WHO'S "HOUNDING" ANYBODY?
HE'S ONLY STAYING WITH US, KUNO!
HYO-O-O-O
SILENCE, FOOL!!
CHUNGGG

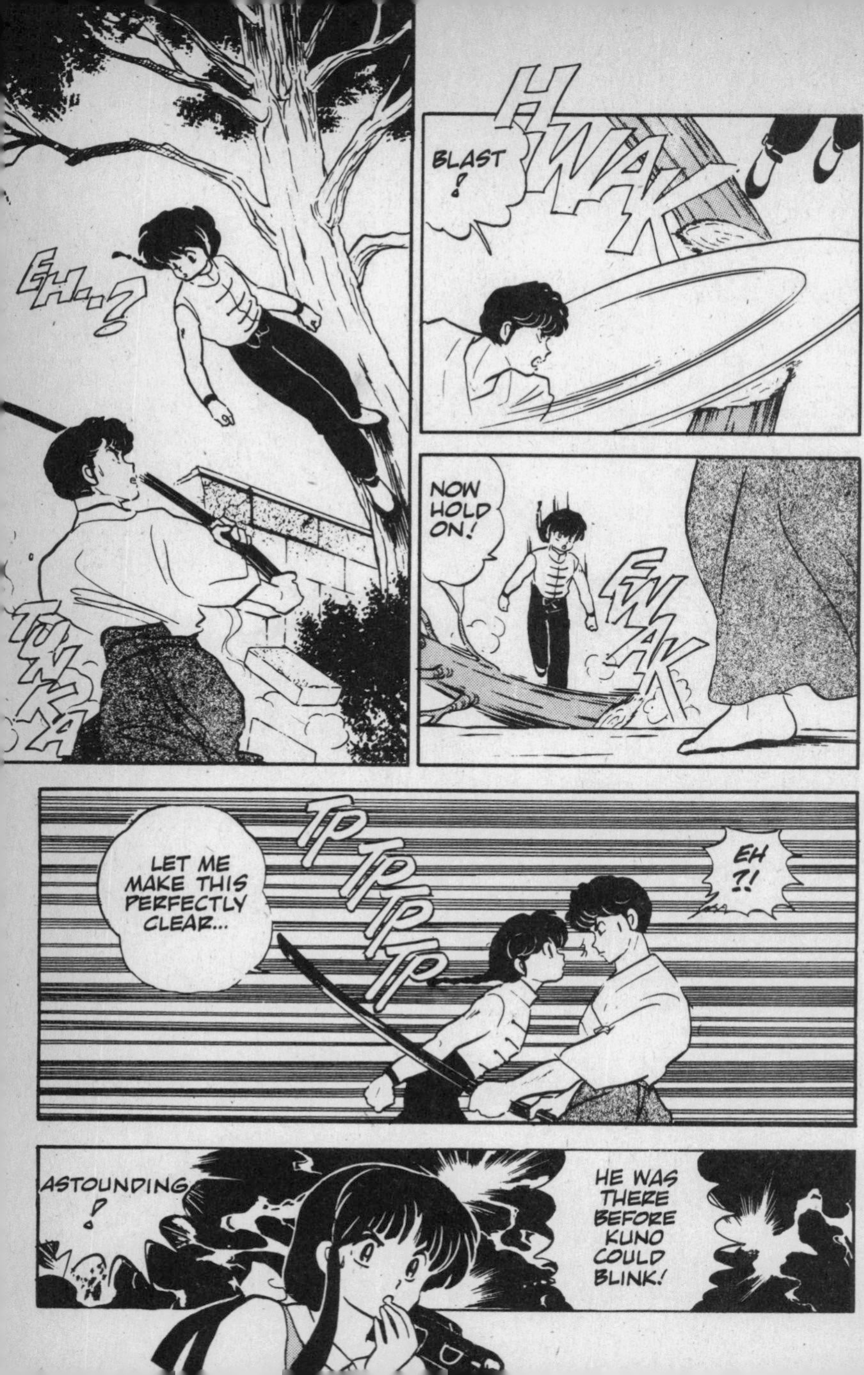

EH..?
TUNKA
HWAK
BLAST!
NOW HOLD ON!
FWAK
LET ME MAKE THIS PERFECTLY CLEAR...
TP TP TP TP
EH ?!
ASTOUNDING!
HE WAS THERE BEFORE KUNO COULD BLINK!

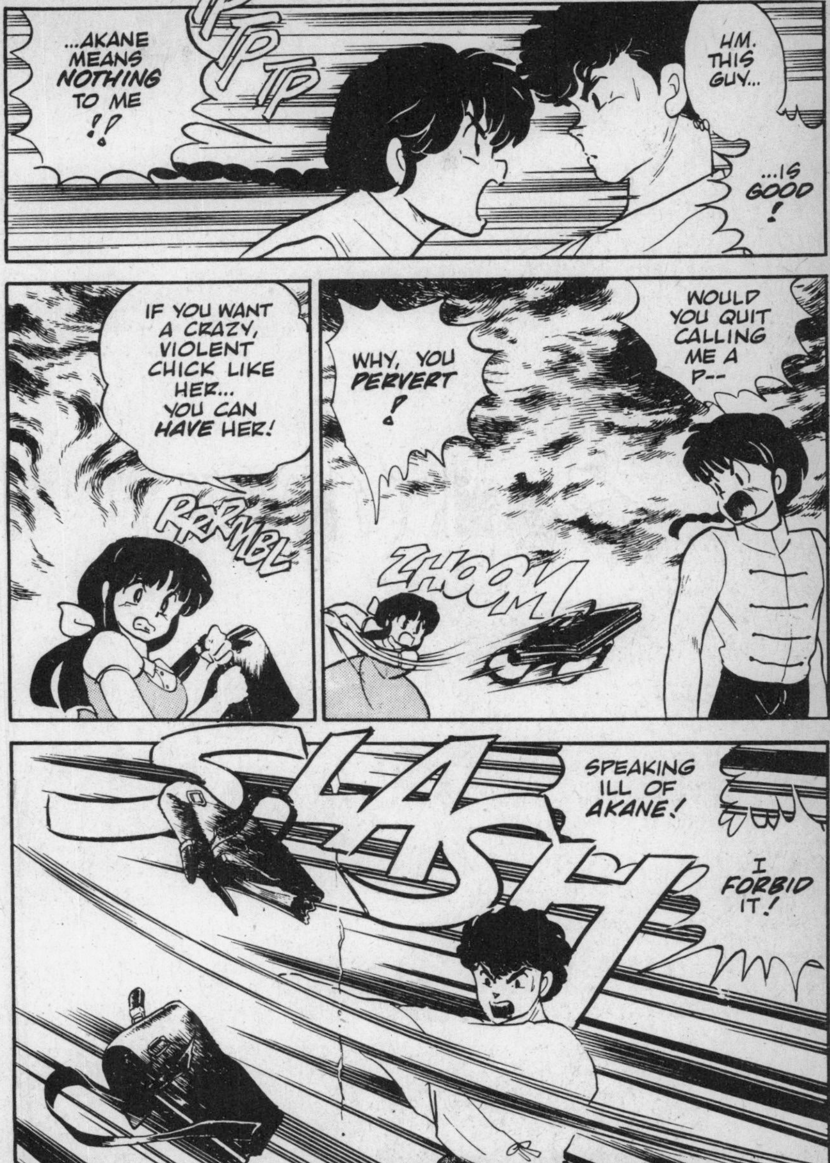
TP TP TP TP
...AKANE MEANS NOTHING TO ME !!
HM. THIS GUY...
...IS GOOD!
IF YOU WANT A CRAZY, VIOLENT CHICK LIKE HER... YOU CAN HAVE HER!
RRRMBL
WHY, YOU PERVERT!
WOULD YOU QUIT CALLING ME A P--
ZHOOM
SLASH
SPEAKING ILL OF AKANE!
I FORBID IT!

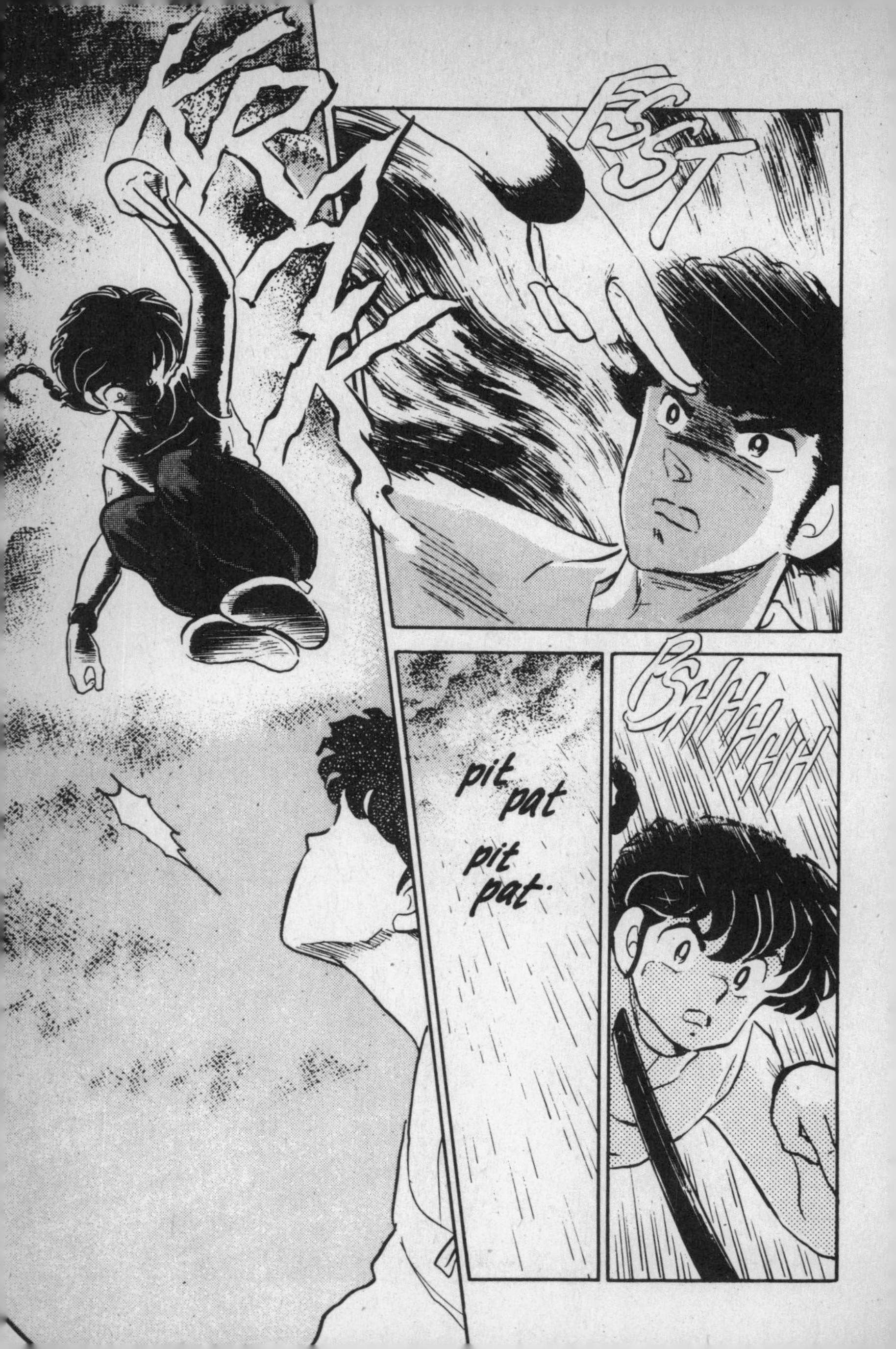
FSST
pit pat
pit pat
PSHHHHH

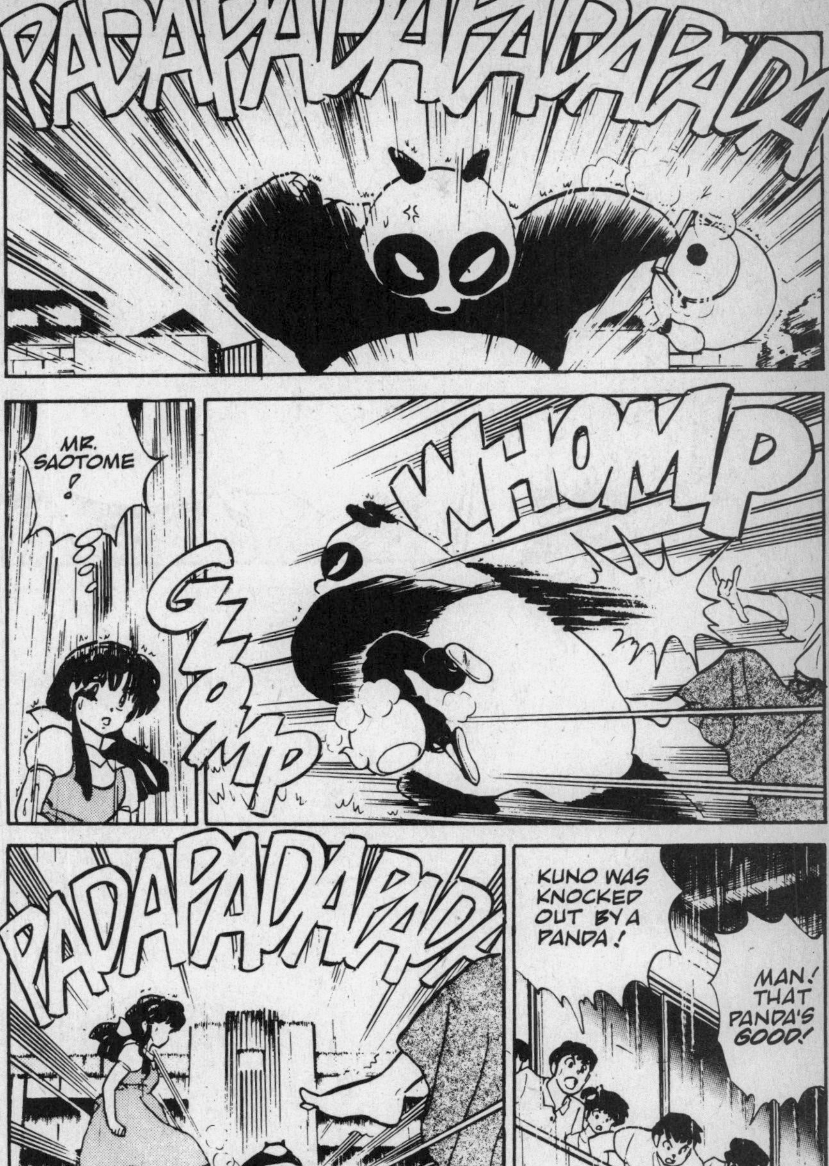
PADAPADAPADAPADAPADA
MR. SAOTOME!
WHOMP
GLOMP
PADAPADAPADA
KUNO WAS KNOCKED OUT BY A PANDA!
MAN! THAT PANDA'S GOOD!

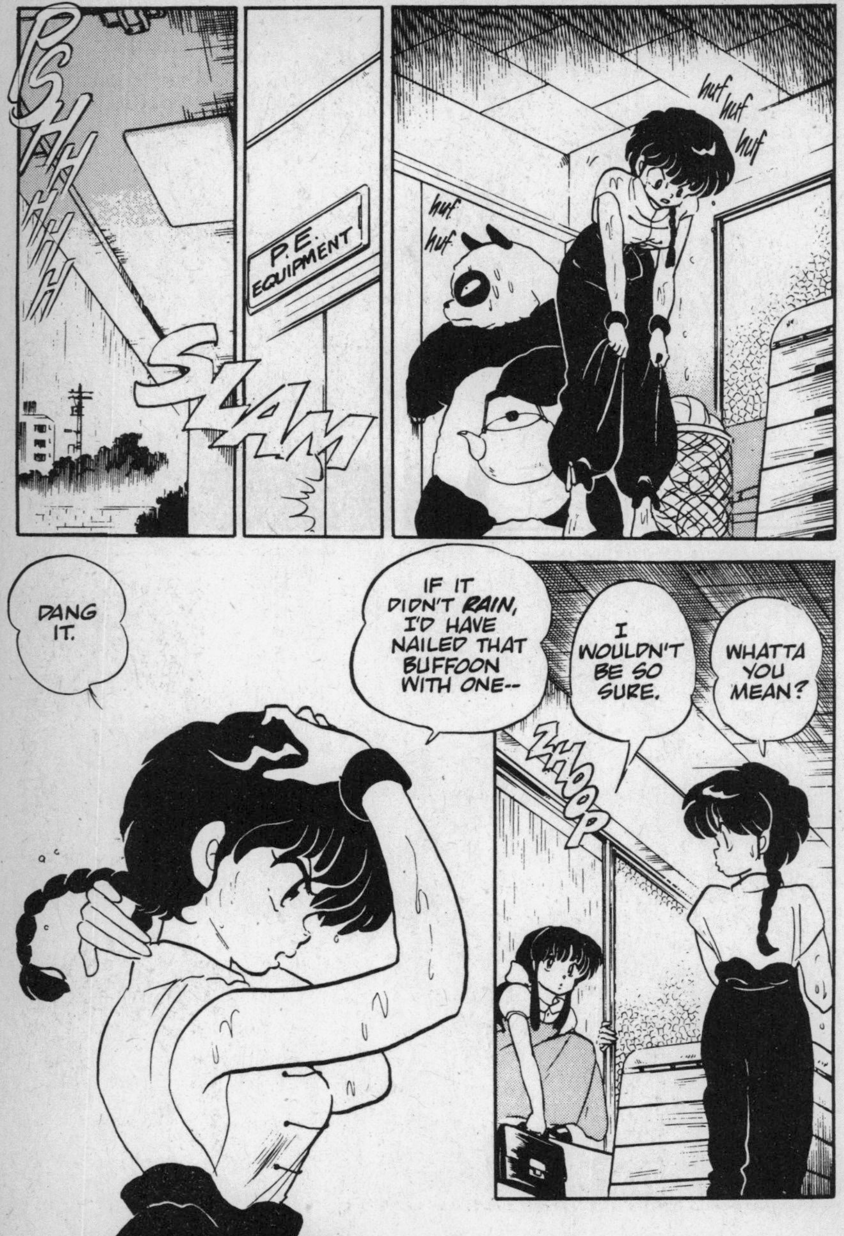
PSHHHHHH
SLAM
P.E. EQUIPMENT
huf huf huf
huf huf
DANG IT.
IF IT DIDN'T RAIN, I'D HAVE NAILED THAT BUFFOON WITH ONE--
I WOULDN'T BE SO SURE.
WHATTA YOU MEAN?
ZHOOP

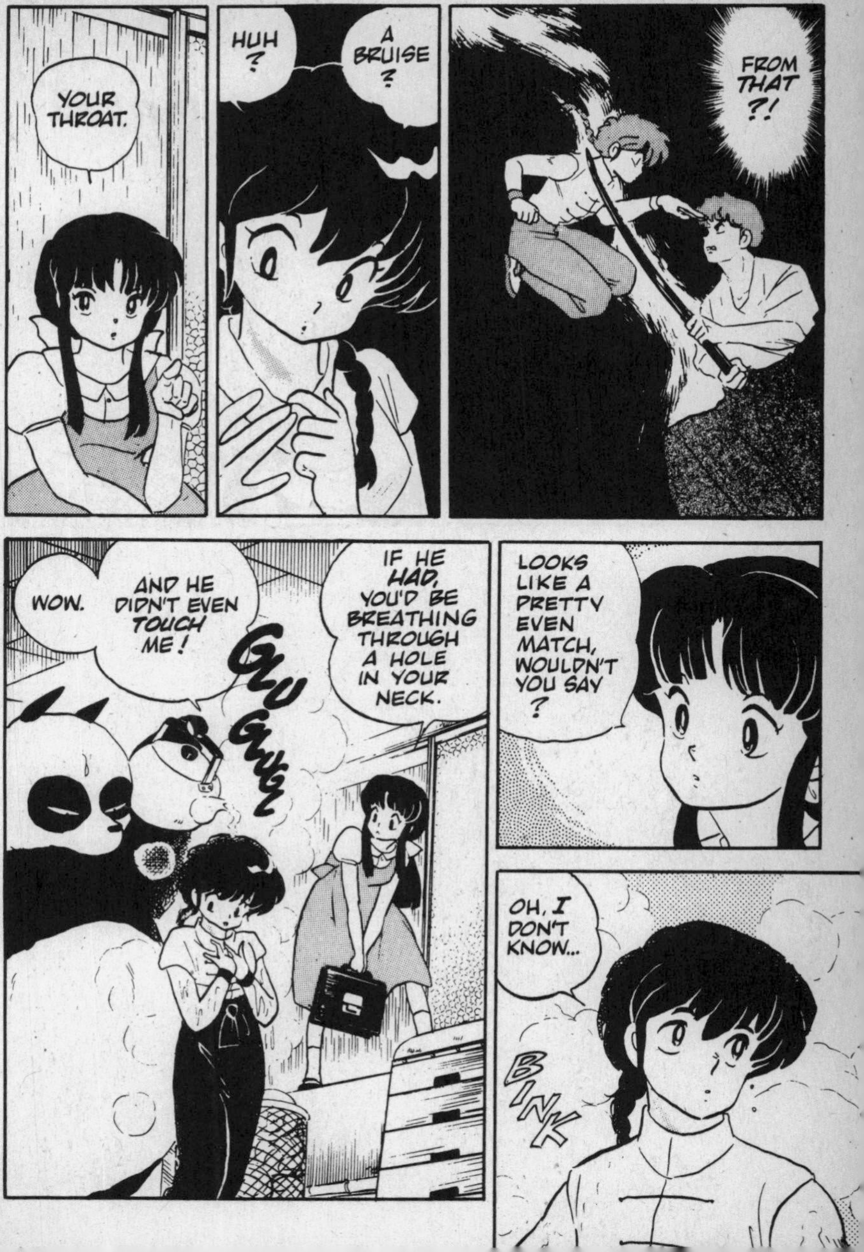
YOUR THROAT.
HUH?
A BRUISE?
FROM THAT?!
WOW.
AND HE DIDN'T EVEN TOUCH ME!
GLUG GLUG
IF HE HAD, YOU'D BE BREATHING THROUGH A HOLE IN YOUR NECK.
LOOKS LIKE A PRETTY EVEN MATCH, WOULDN'T YOU SAY?
OH, I DON'T KNOW...
BLINK

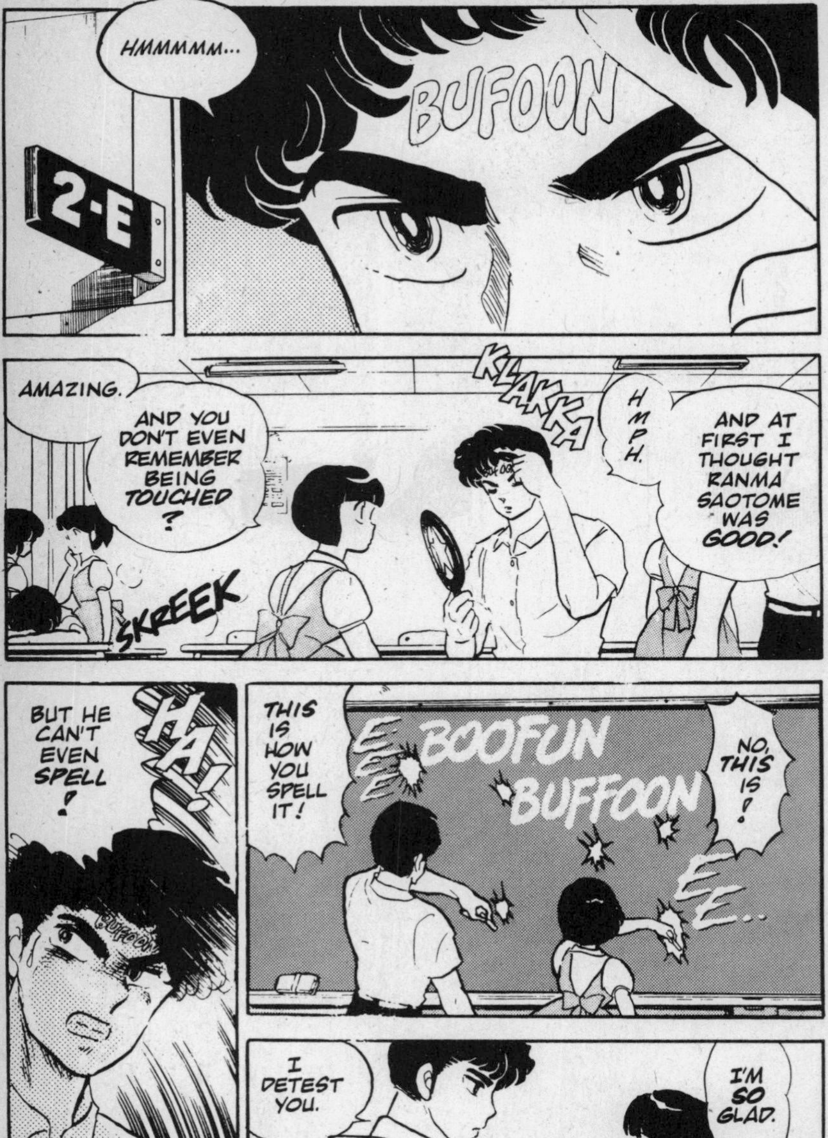

HMMMMM...
BUFOON
2-E
AMAZING.
AND YOU DON'T EVEN REMEMBER BEING TOUCHED?
KLAKKA
HMPH.
AND AT FIRST I THOUGHT RANMA SAOTOME WAS GOOD!
SKREEK
BUT HE CAN'T EVEN SPELL!
HA!
BUFOON
THIS IS HOW YOU SPELL IT!
EEE
BOOFUN
BUFFOON
NO, THIS IS!
EEE...
I DETEST YOU.
I'M SO GLAD.

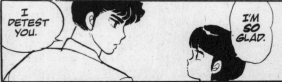

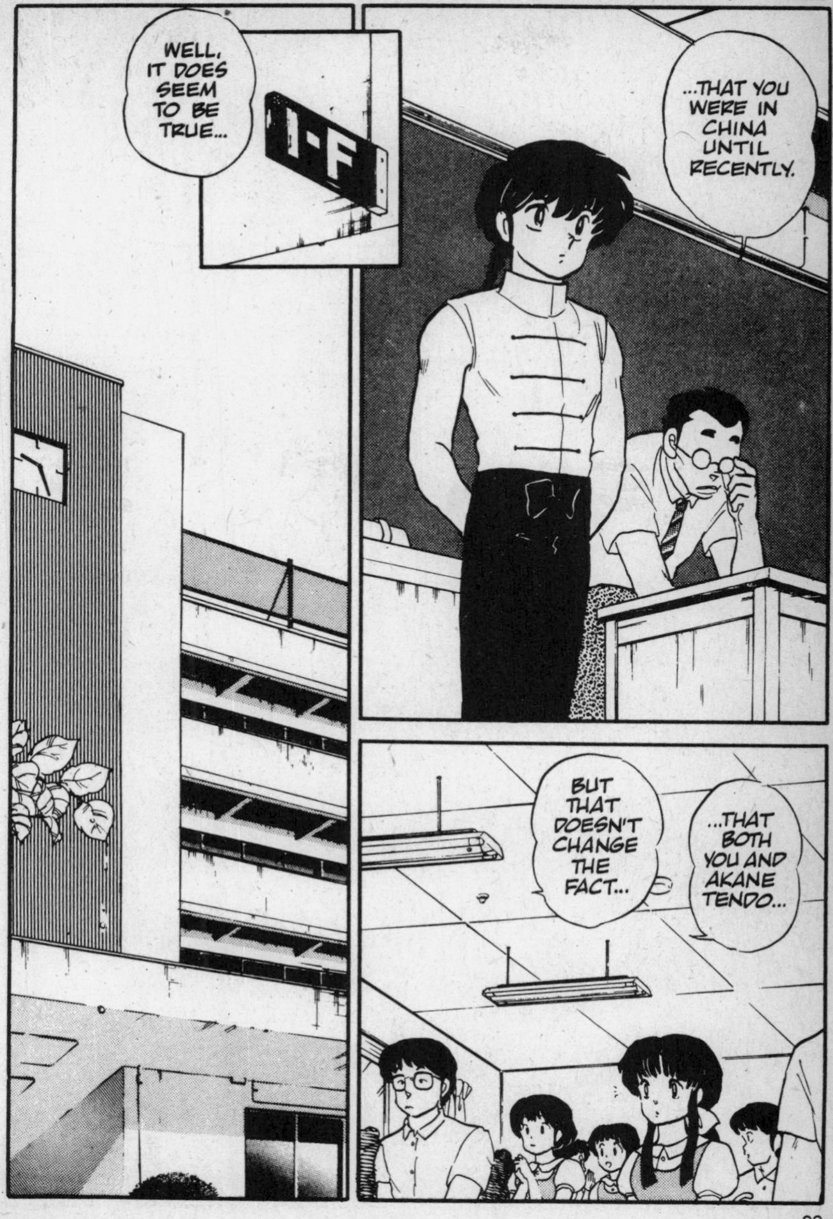
WELL, IT DOES SEEM TO BE TRUE...
1-F
...THAT YOU WERE IN CHINA UNTIL RECENTLY.
BUT THAT DOESN'T CHANGE THE FACT...
...THAT BOTH YOU AND AKANE TENDO...

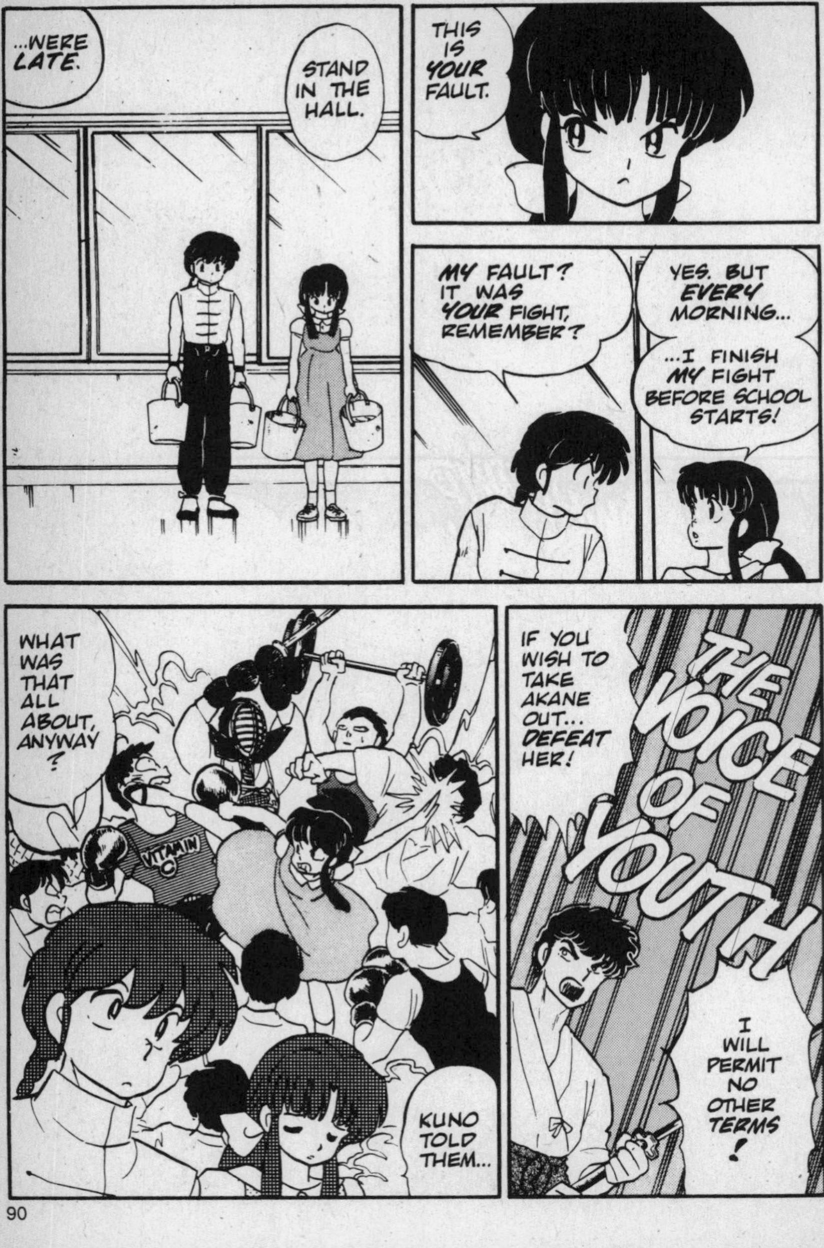

...WERE LATE.
STAND IN THE HALL.
THIS IS YOUR FAULT.
MY FAULT? IT WAS YOUR FIGHT, REMEMBER?
YES. BUT EVERY MORNING...
...I FINISH MY FIGHT BEFORE SCHOOL STARTS!
WHAT WAS THAT ALL ABOUT, ANYWAY?
VITAMIN C
KUNO TOLD THEM...
IF YOU WISH TO TAKE AKANE OUT... DEFEAT HER!
THE VOICE OF YOUTH
I WILL PERMIT NO OTHER TERMS!

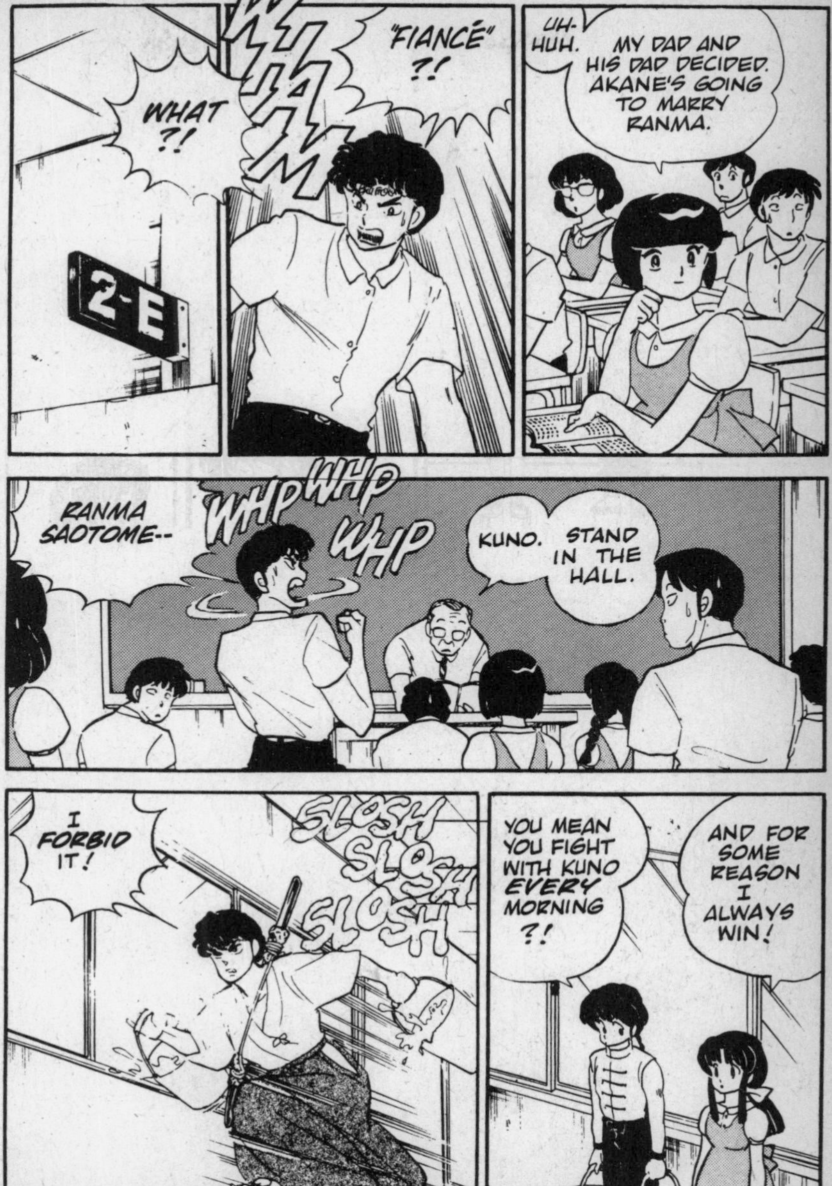
WHAT ?!
WHAM
"FIANCÉ" ?!
UH-HUH.
MY DAD AND HIS DAD DECIDED. AKANE'S GOING TO MARRY RANMA.
2-E
RANMA SAOTOME--
WHP WHP WHP WHP
KUNO. STAND IN THE HALL.
I FORBID IT!
SLOSH SLOSH SLOSH SLOSH
YOU MEAN YOU FIGHT WITH KUNO EVERY MORNING ?!
AND FOR SOME REASON I ALWAYS WIN!

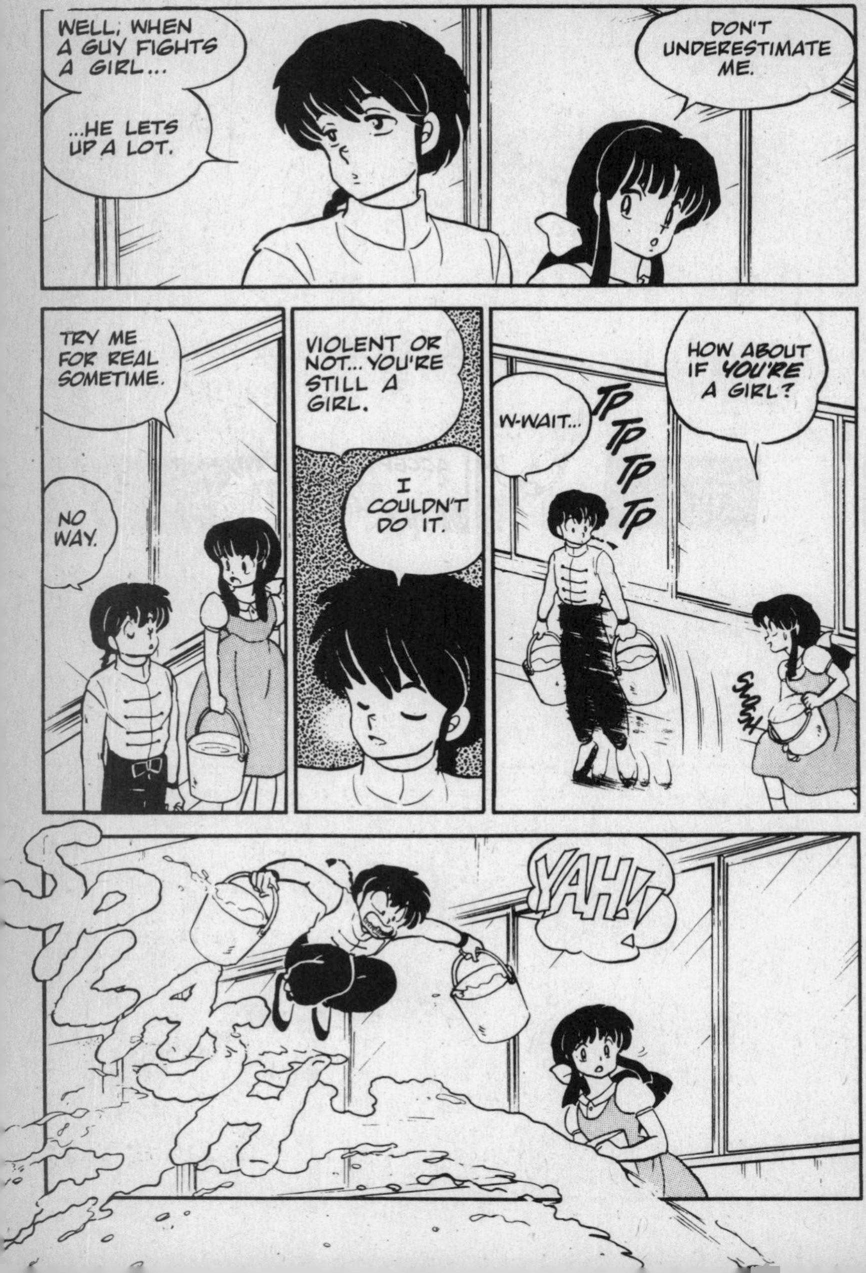
WELL, WHEN A GUY FIGHTS A GIRL...
...HE LETS UP A LOT.
DON'T UNDERESTIMATE ME.
TRY ME FOR REAL SOMETIME.
NO WAY.
VIOLENT OR NOT... YOU'RE STILL A GIRL.
I COULDN'T DO IT.
W-WAIT...
TP TP TP TP
HOW ABOUT IF YOU'RE A GIRL?
YAH!!

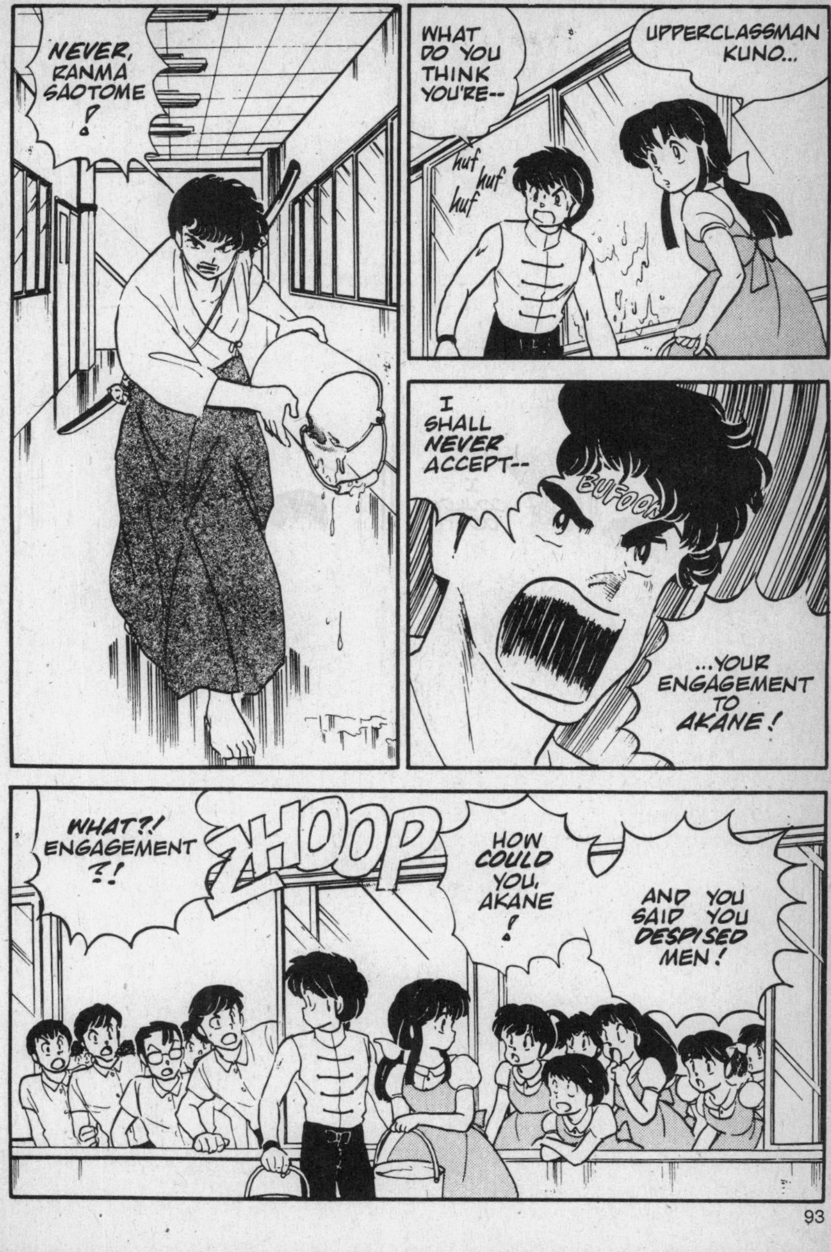
NEVER, RANMA SAOTOME !
WHAT DO YOU THINK YOU'RE--
UPPERCLASSMAN KUNO...
huf huf huf
I SHALL NEVER ACCEPT--
...YOUR ENGAGEMENT TO AKANE!
WHAT?! ENGAGEMENT ?!
ZHOOP
HOW COULD YOU, AKANE !
AND YOU SAID YOU DESPISED MEN!

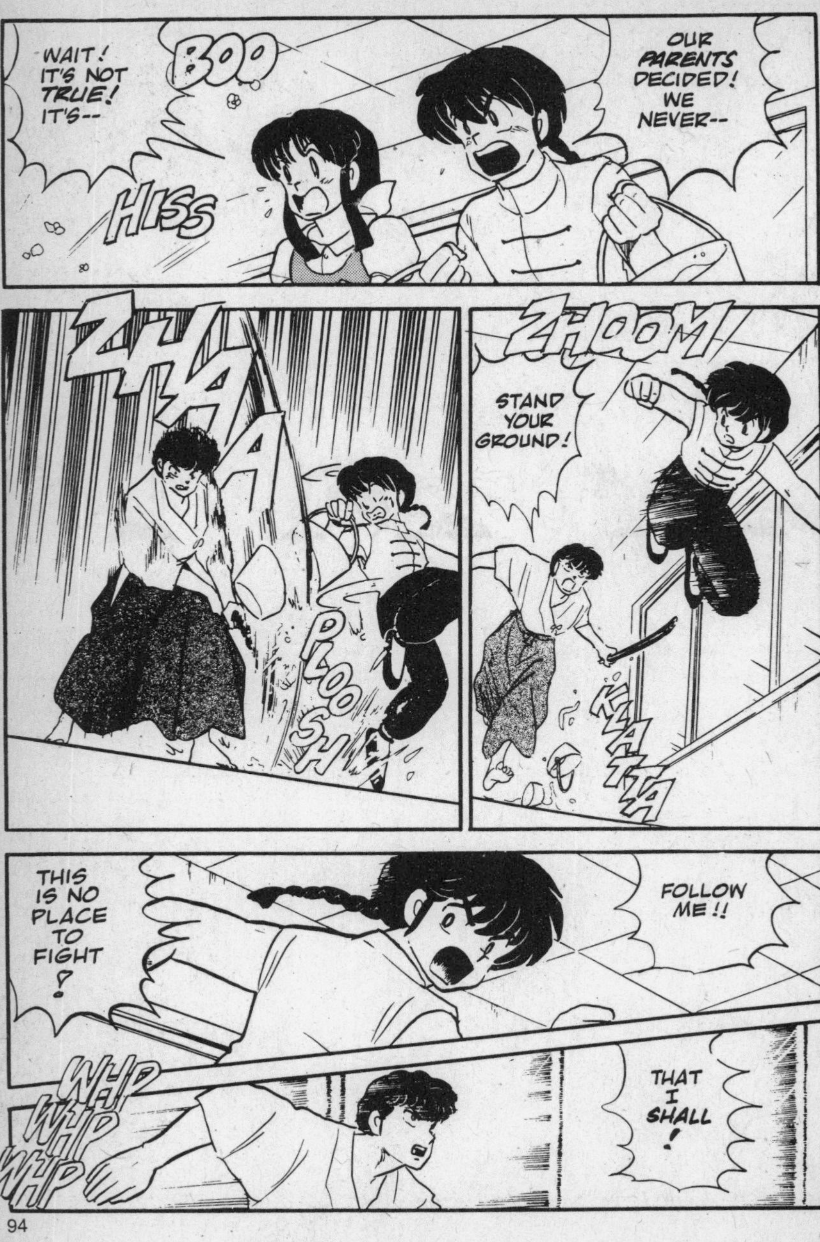
WAIT! IT'S NOT TRUE! IT'S--
BOO
HISS
OUR PARENTS DECIDED! WE NEVER--
ZHAA
PLOOSH
ZHOOM
STAND YOUR GROUND!
KLATTA
THIS IS NO PLACE TO FIGHT!
FOLLOW ME!!
WHP WHP WHP
THAT I SHALL!

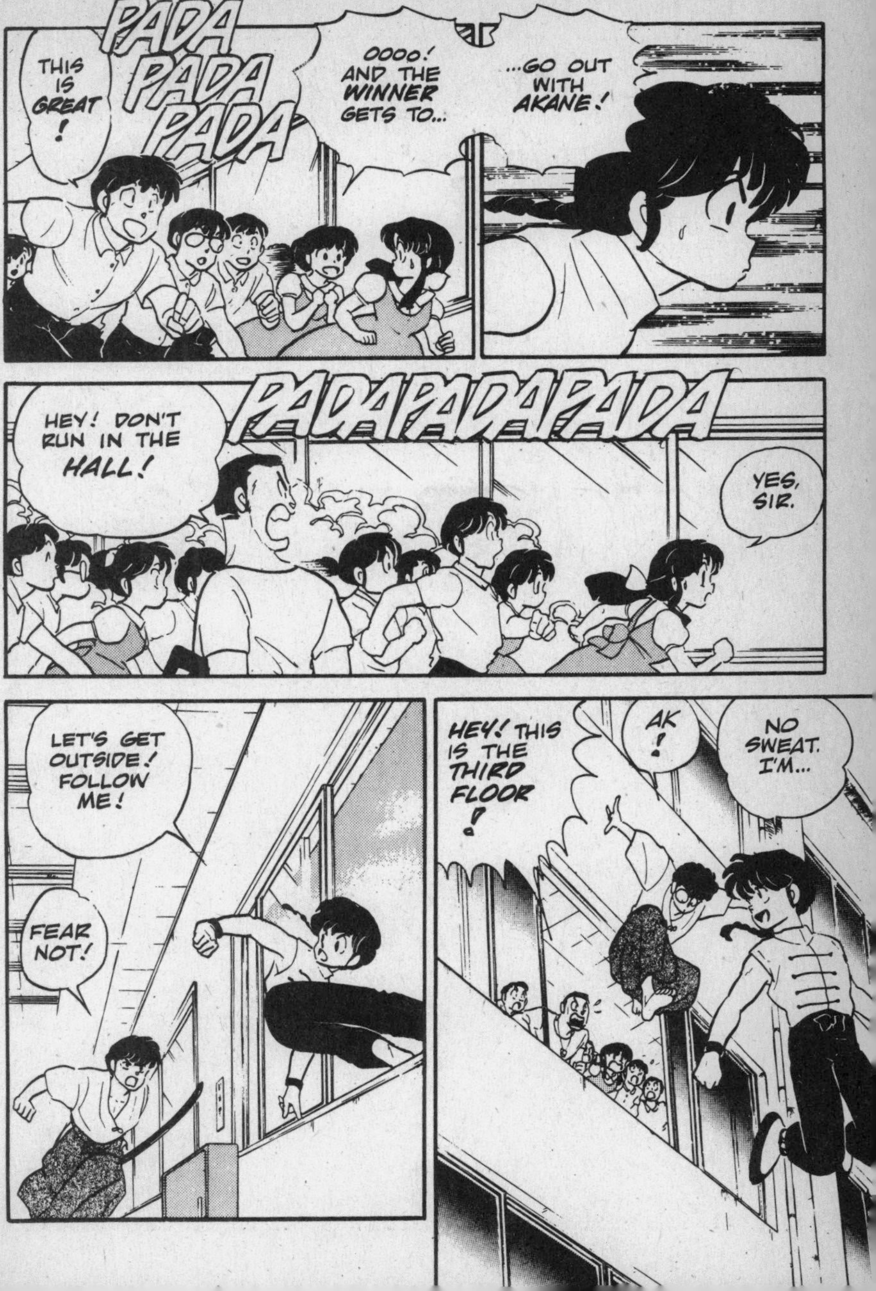
THIS IS GREAT!
PADA PADA PADA
OOOO! AND THE WINNER GETS TO...
...GO OUT WITH AKANE!
HEY! DON'T RUN IN THE HALL!
PADAPADAPADA
YES, SIR.
LET'S GET OUTSIDE! FOLLOW ME!
FEAR NOT!
HEY! THIS IS THE THIRD FLOOR!
AK!
NO SWEAT. I'M...

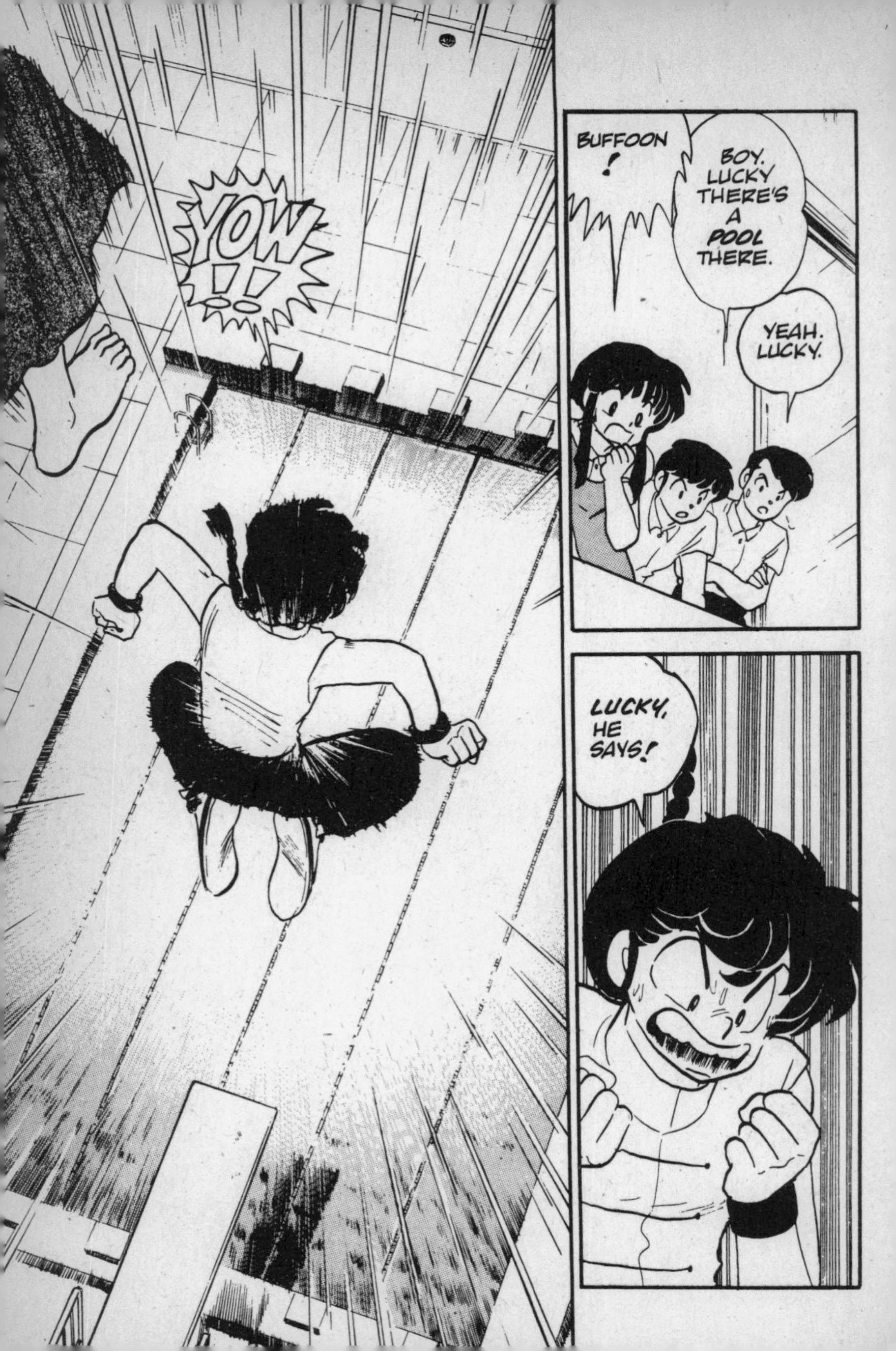
YOW !!
BUFFOON!
BOY. LUCKY THERE'S A POOL THERE.
YEAH. LUCKY.
LUCKY, HE SAYS!

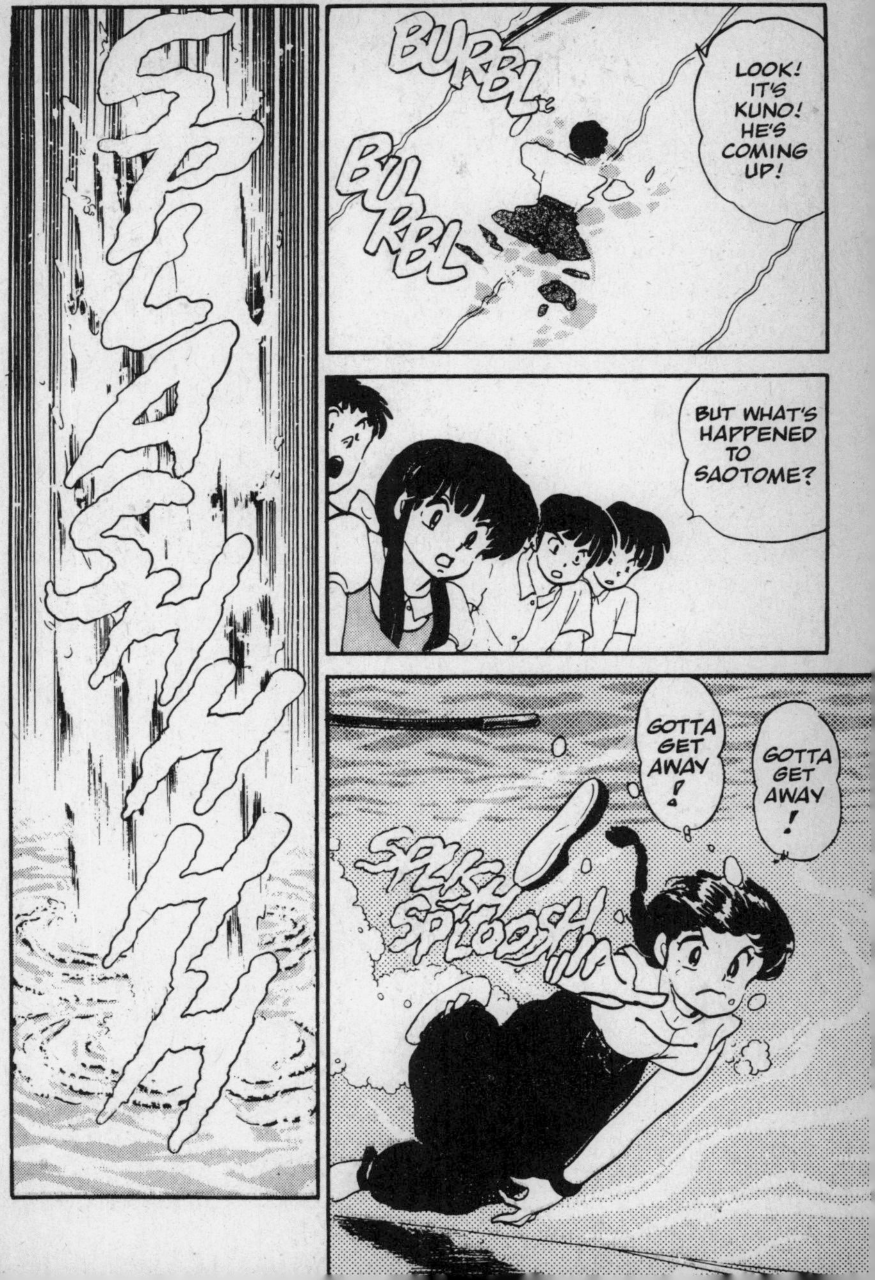
BURBL
BURBL
LOOK! IT'S KUNO! HE'S COMING UP!
BUT WHAT'S HAPPENED TO SAOTOME?
GOTTA GET AWAY!
GOTTA GET AWAY!
SPLISH SPLOOSH

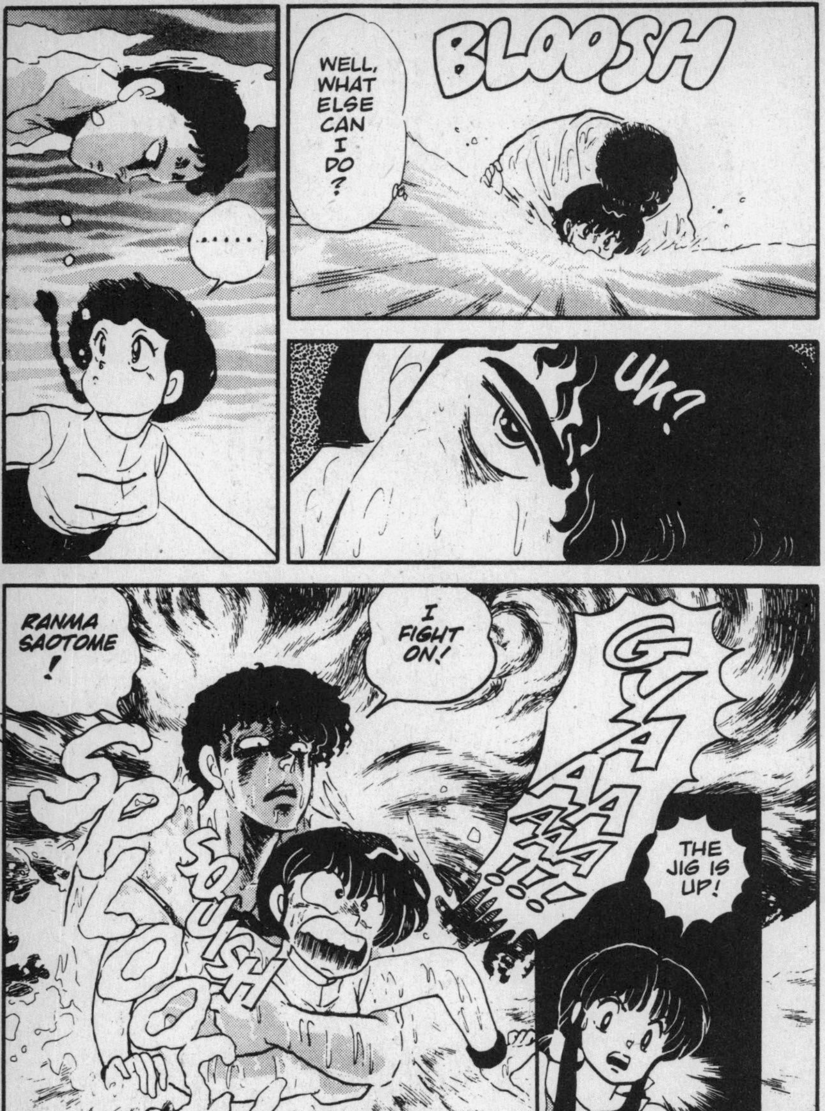
......
WELL, WHAT ELSE CAN I DO?
BLOOSH
UK?!
RANMA SAOTOME!
I FIGHT ON!
GUAAAAAAA!!!
SPLOOSH
SQUISH
THE JIG IS UP!

Part 5
TO THE TREE-BORNE KETTLE-GIRL

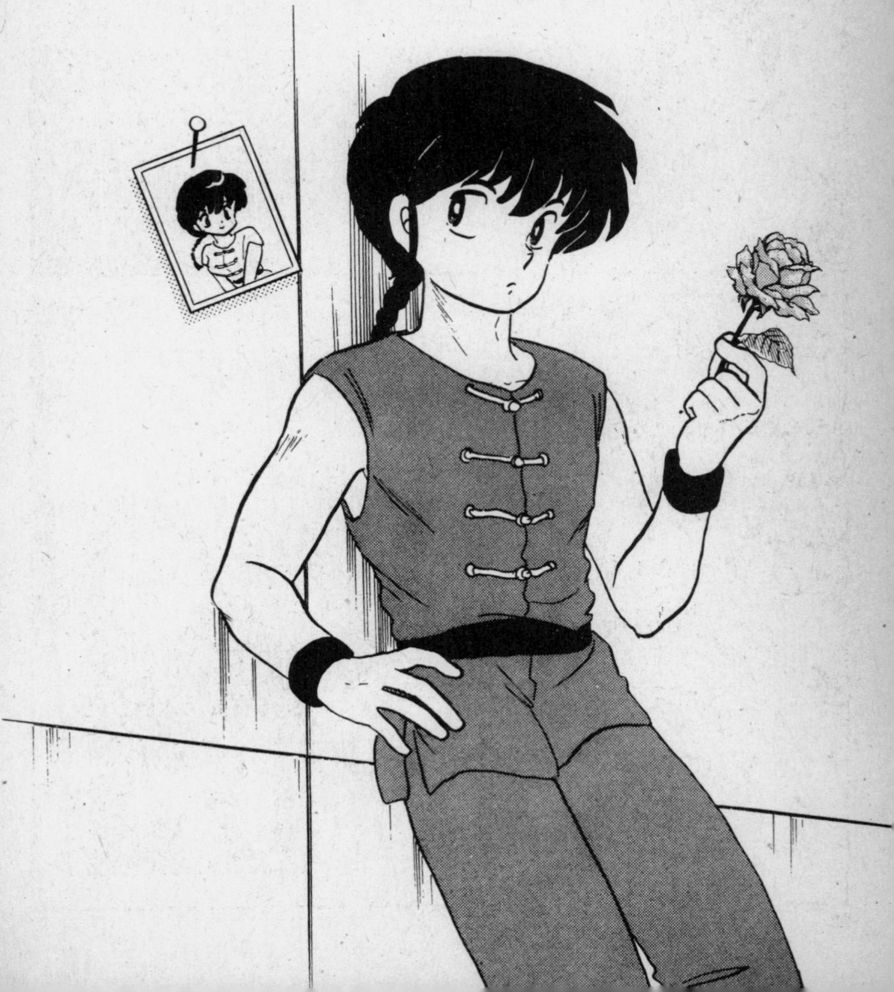

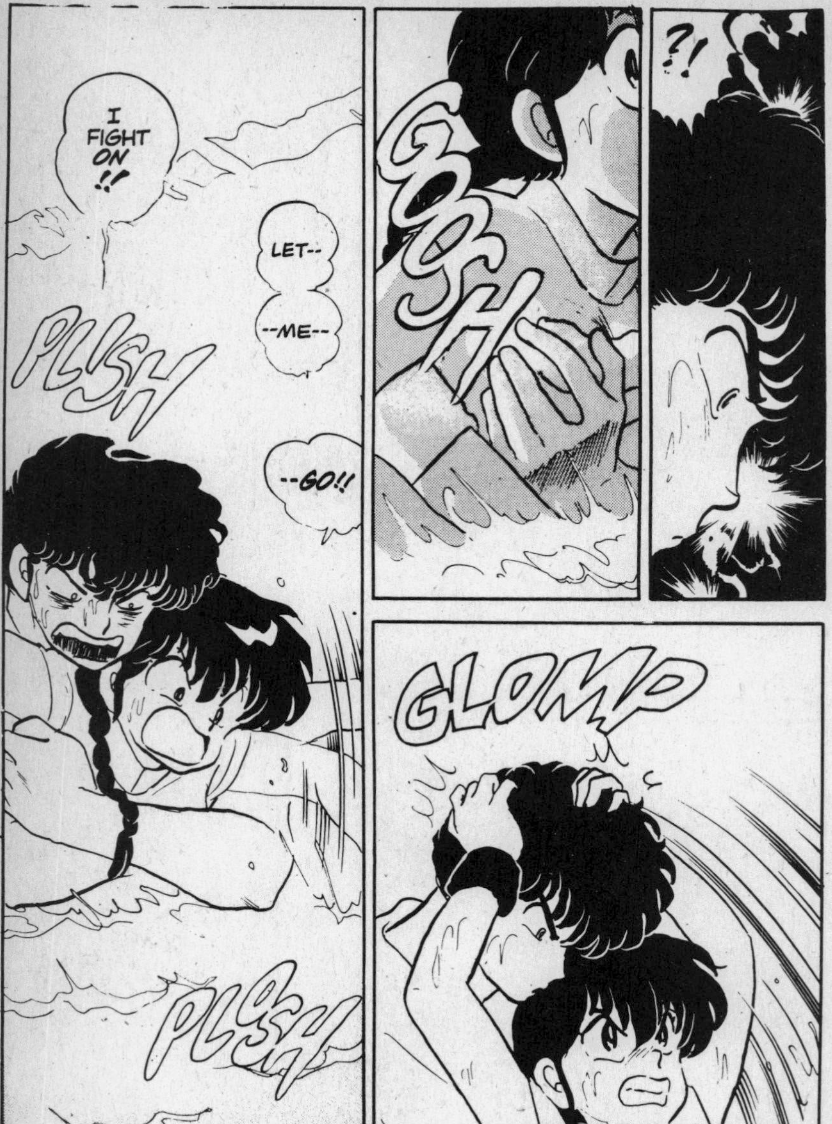
I FIGHT ON !!
LET--
--ME--
--GO!!
PLUSH
PLOSH
GOOSH
?!
GLOMP

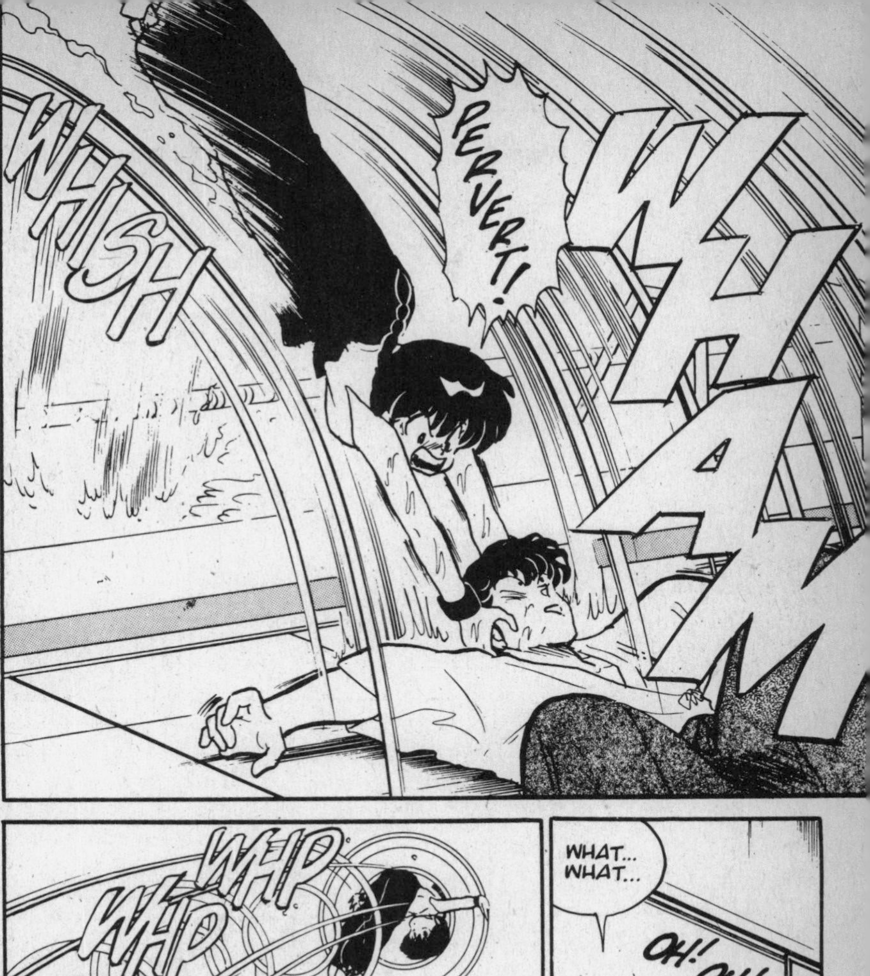
WHISH
PERVERT!!
WHAM
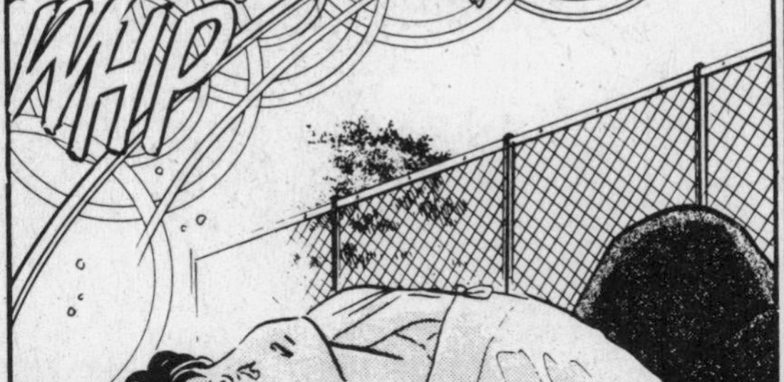
WHP
WHP
WHP
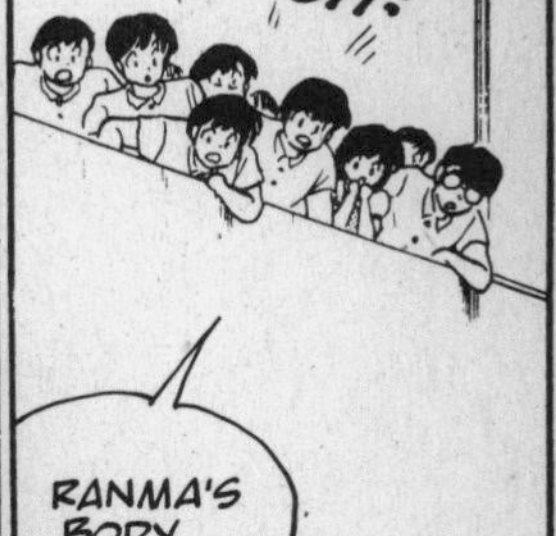
WHAT... WHAT...
OH! OH!
RANMA'S BODY...

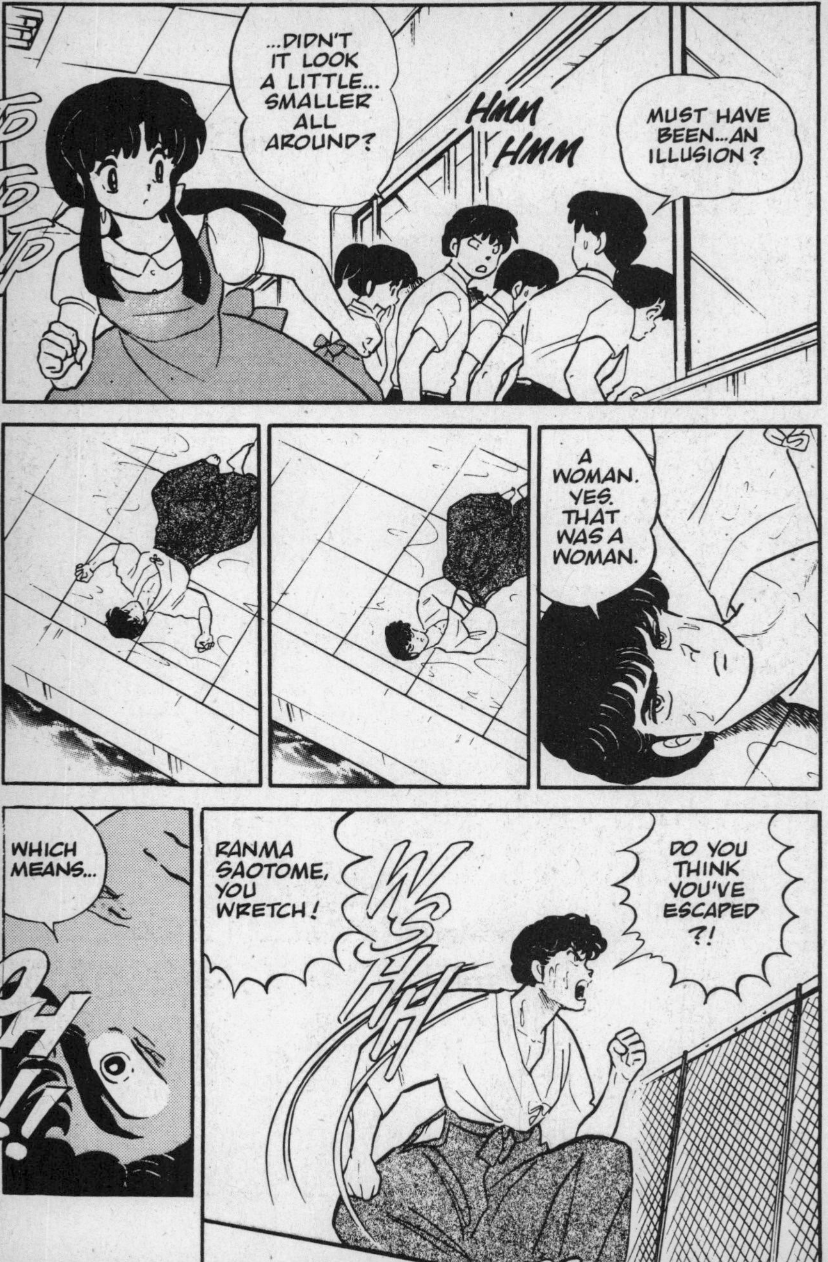
TP TP TP
...DIDN'T IT LOOK A LITTLE... SMALLER ALL AROUND?
HMM HMM
MUST HAVE BEEN...AN ILLUSION?
A WOMAN. YES. THAT WAS A WOMAN.
WHICH MEANS...
OH!!
RANMA SAOTOME, YOU WRETCH!
WSHH
DO YOU THINK YOU'VE ESCAPED ?!

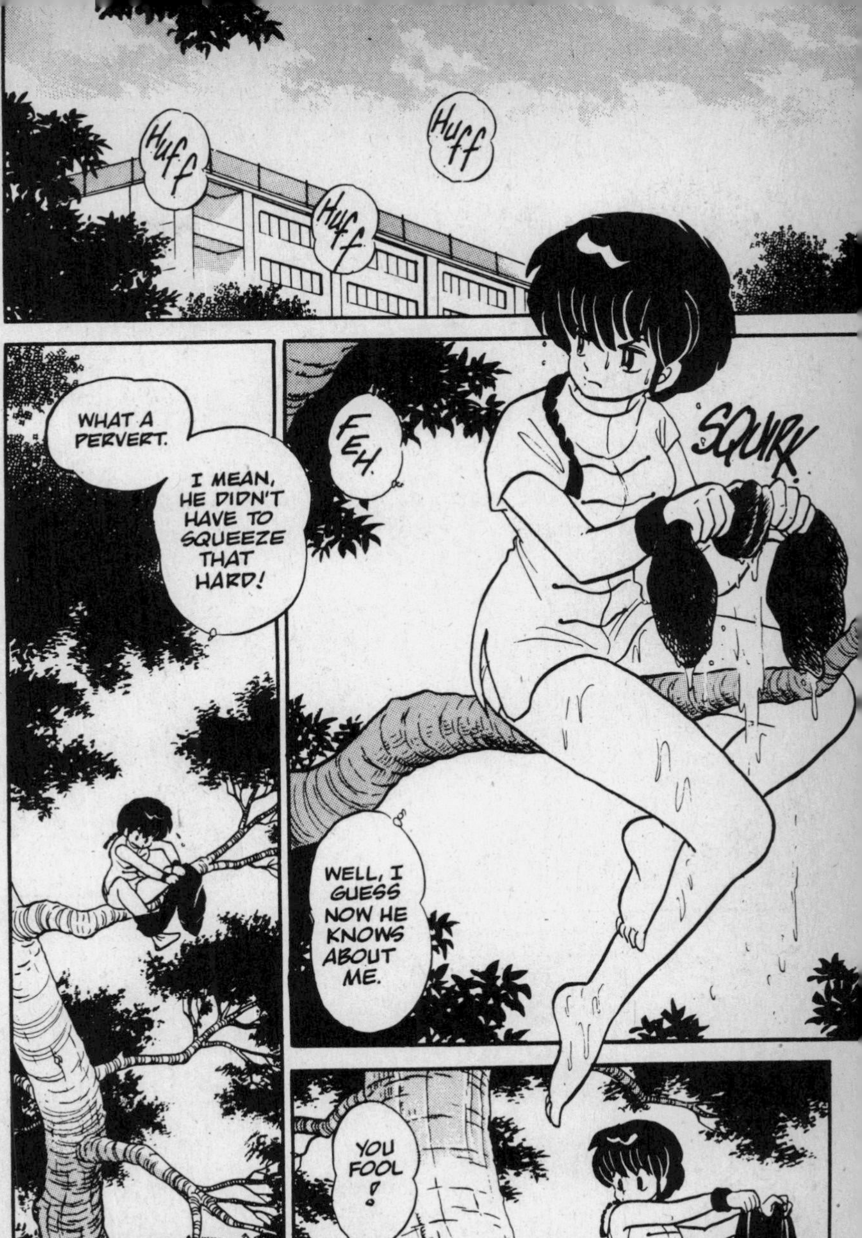
Huff
Huff
Huff
WHAT A PERVERT.
I MEAN, HE DIDN'T HAVE TO SQUEEZE THAT HARD!
FEH.
SQUIRK
WELL, I GUESS NOW HE KNOWS ABOUT ME.
YOU FOOL!

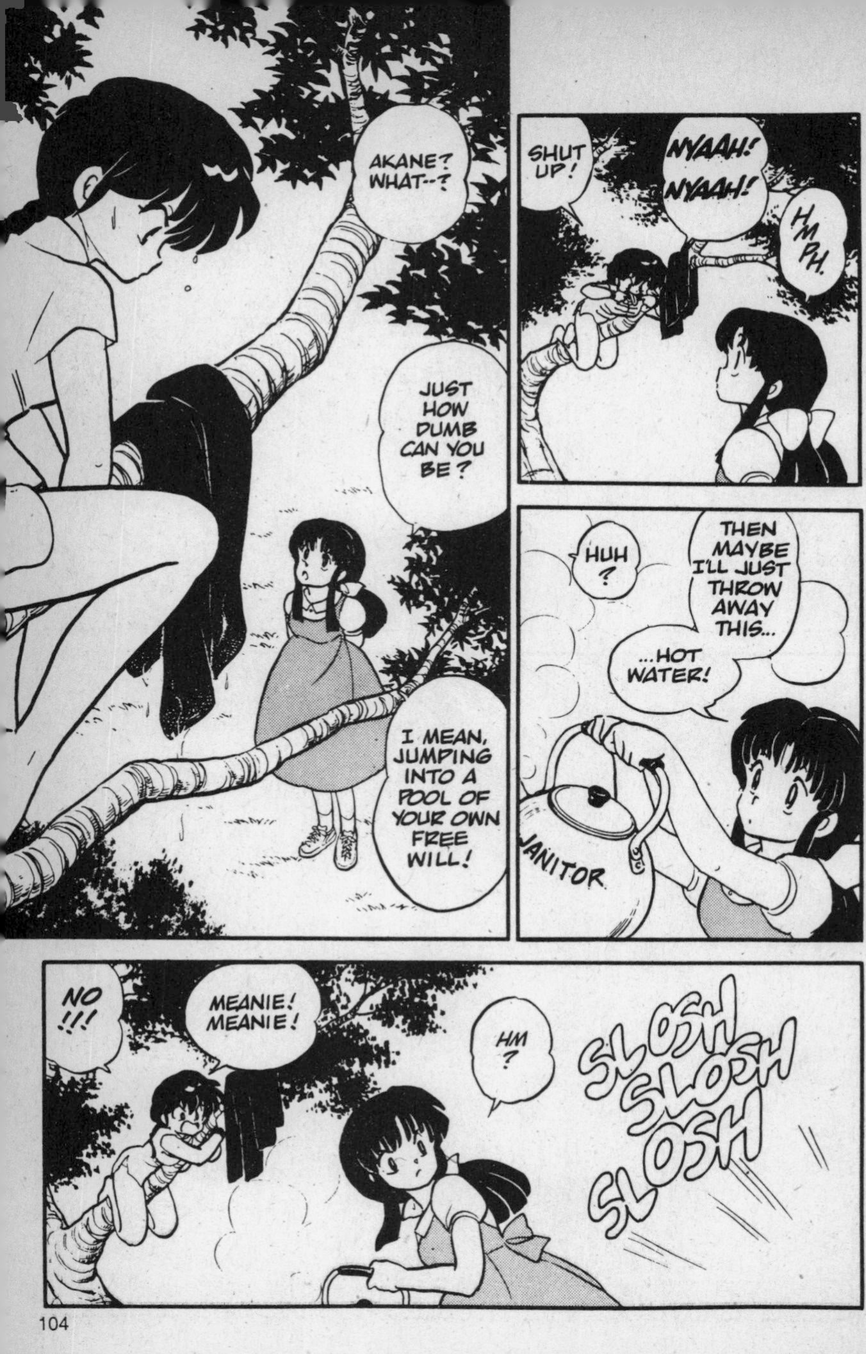
AKANE? WHAT--?
JUST HOW DUMB CAN YOU BE?
I MEAN, JUMPING INTO A POOL OF YOUR OWN FREE WILL!
SHUT UP!
NYAAH! NYAAH!
HMPH.
HUH?
THEN MAYBE I'LL JUST THROW AWAY THIS...
...HOT WATER!
JANITOR
NO!!!
MEANIE! MEANIE!
HM?
SLOSH SLOSH SLOSH SLOSH

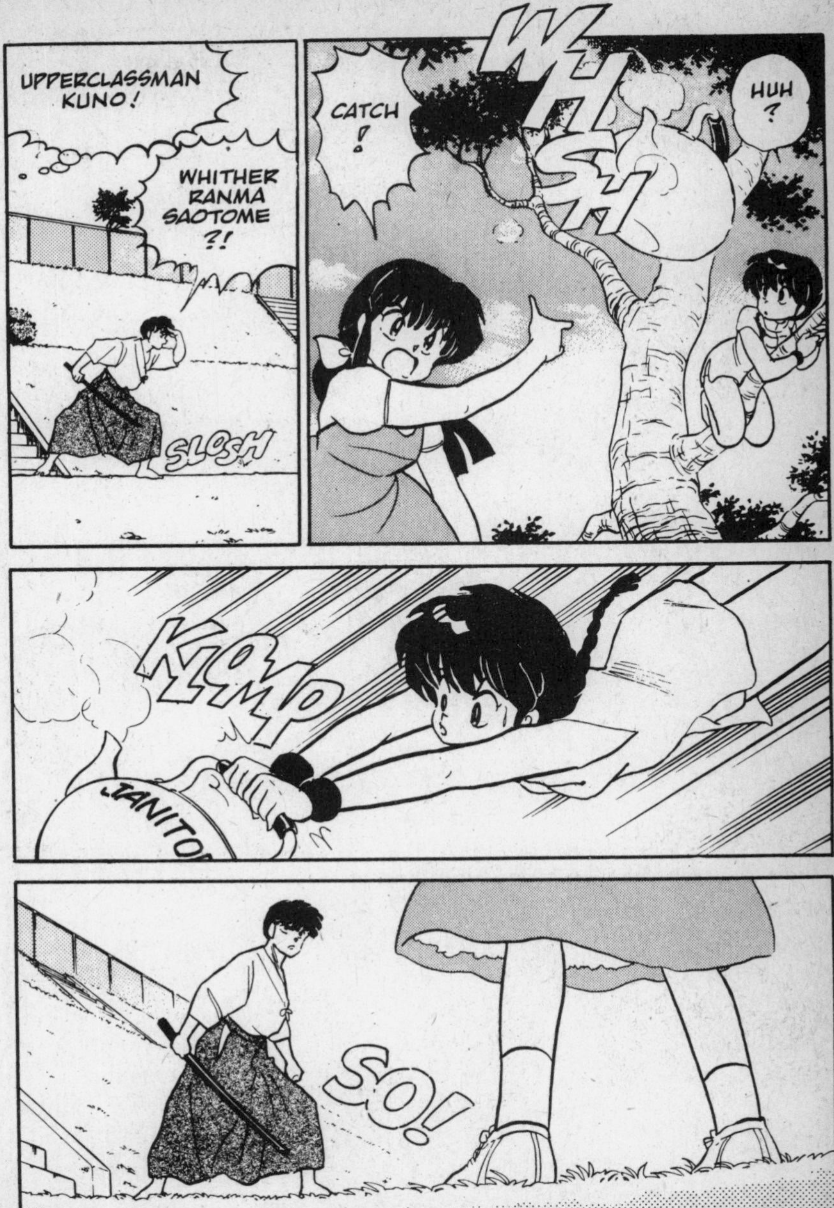
UPPERCLASSMAN KUNO!
WHITHER RANMA SAOTOME ?!
SLOSH
CATCH!
WHSH
HUH?
KLOMP
JANITOR
SO!

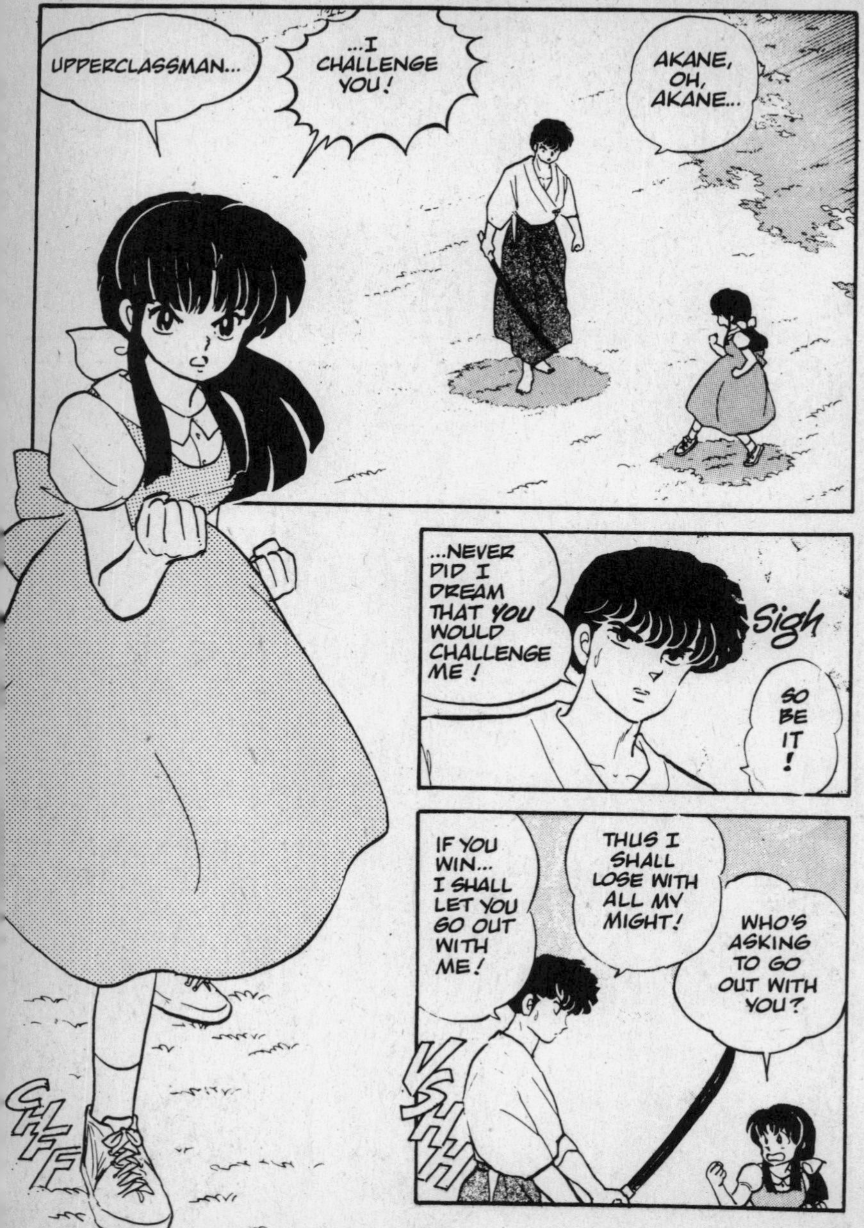
UPPERCLASSMAN...
...I CHALLENGE YOU!
AKANE, OH, AKANE...
...NEVER DID I DREAM THAT YOU WOULD CHALLENGE ME!
Sigh
SO BE IT!
IF YOU WIN... I SHALL LET YOU GO OUT WITH ME!
THUS I SHALL LOSE WITH ALL MY MIGHT!
WHO'S ASKING TO GO OUT WITH YOU?
VSHH
CHFF

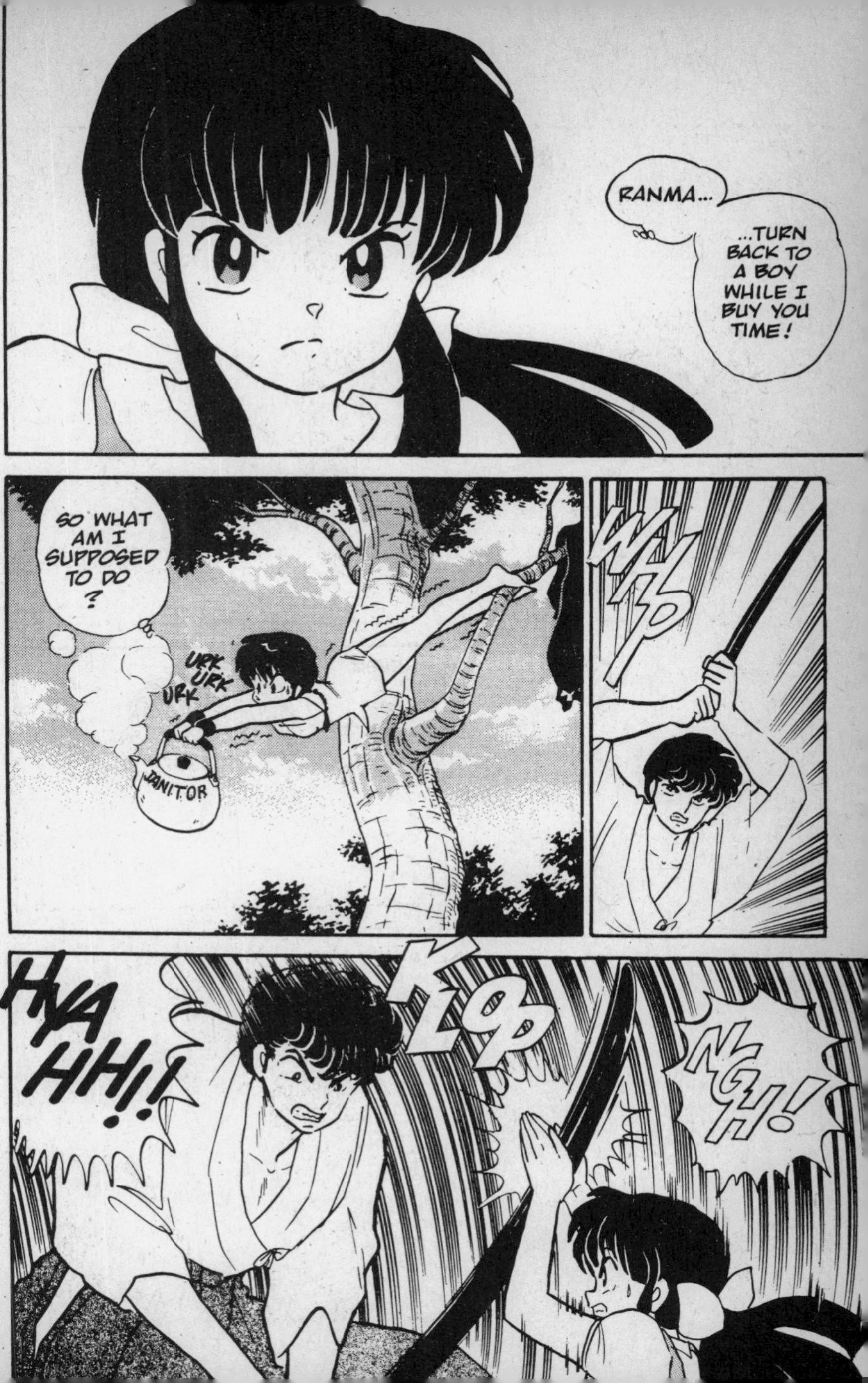
RANMA...
...TURN BACK TO A BOY WHILE I BUY YOU TIME!
SO WHAT AM I SUPPOSED TO DO ?
URK URK URK
JANITOR
WHIP
HYAHHI!!
KLOP
NGH!

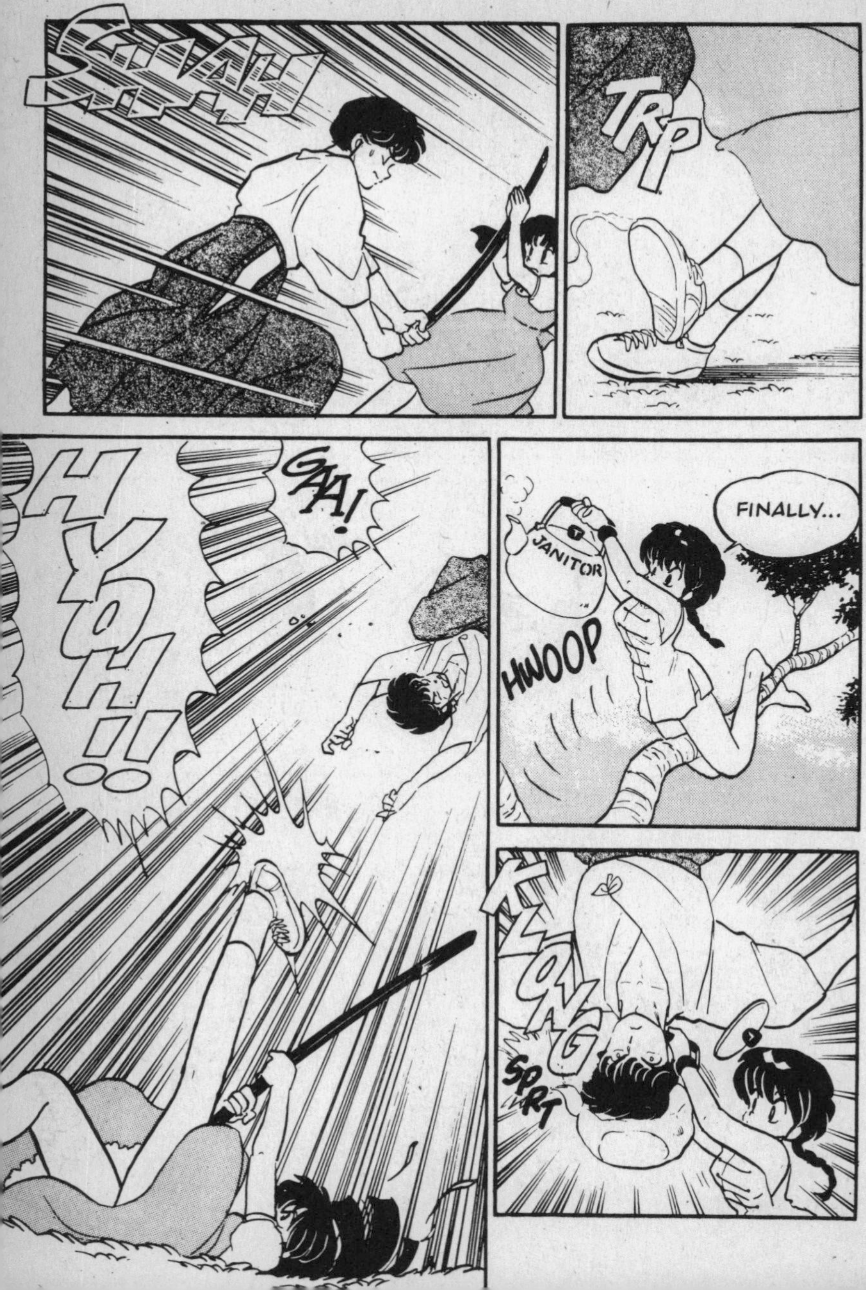
TRP
GAAA!
HYOOH!!
JANITOR
FINALLY...
HWOOP
KLONG
SPRT

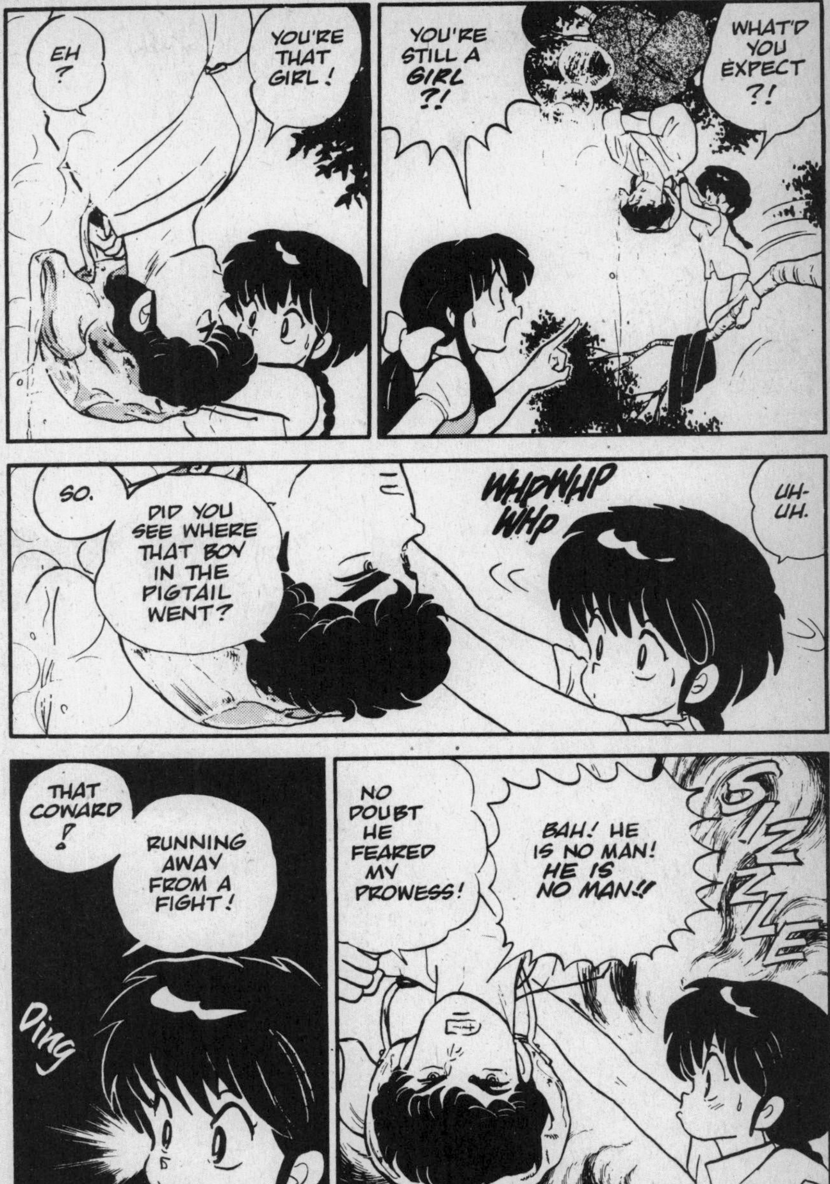
EH ?
YOU'RE THAT GIRL !
YOU'RE STILL A GIRL ?!
WHAT'D YOU EXPECT ?!
SO.
DID YOU SEE WHERE THAT BOY IN THE PIGTAIL WENT?
WHPWHP WHP
UH-UH.
THAT COWARD !
RUNNING AWAY FROM A FIGHT !
Ding
NO DOUBT HE FEARED MY PROWESS!
BAH! HE IS NO MAN! HE IS NO MAN!!
SIZZLE

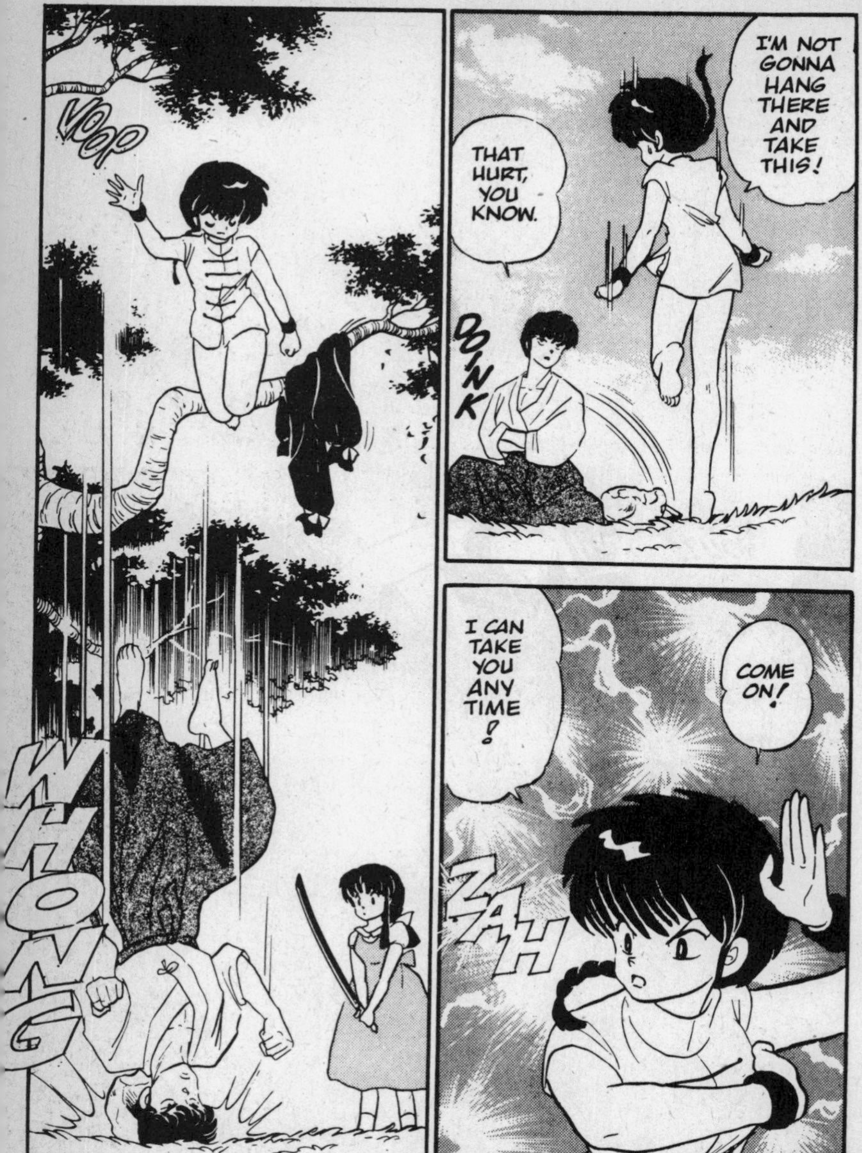
VOOP
WHONG
THAT HURT, YOU KNOW.
DOINK
I'M NOT GONNA HANG THERE AND TAKE THIS!
I CAN TAKE YOU ANY TIME!
COME ON!
ZAAH

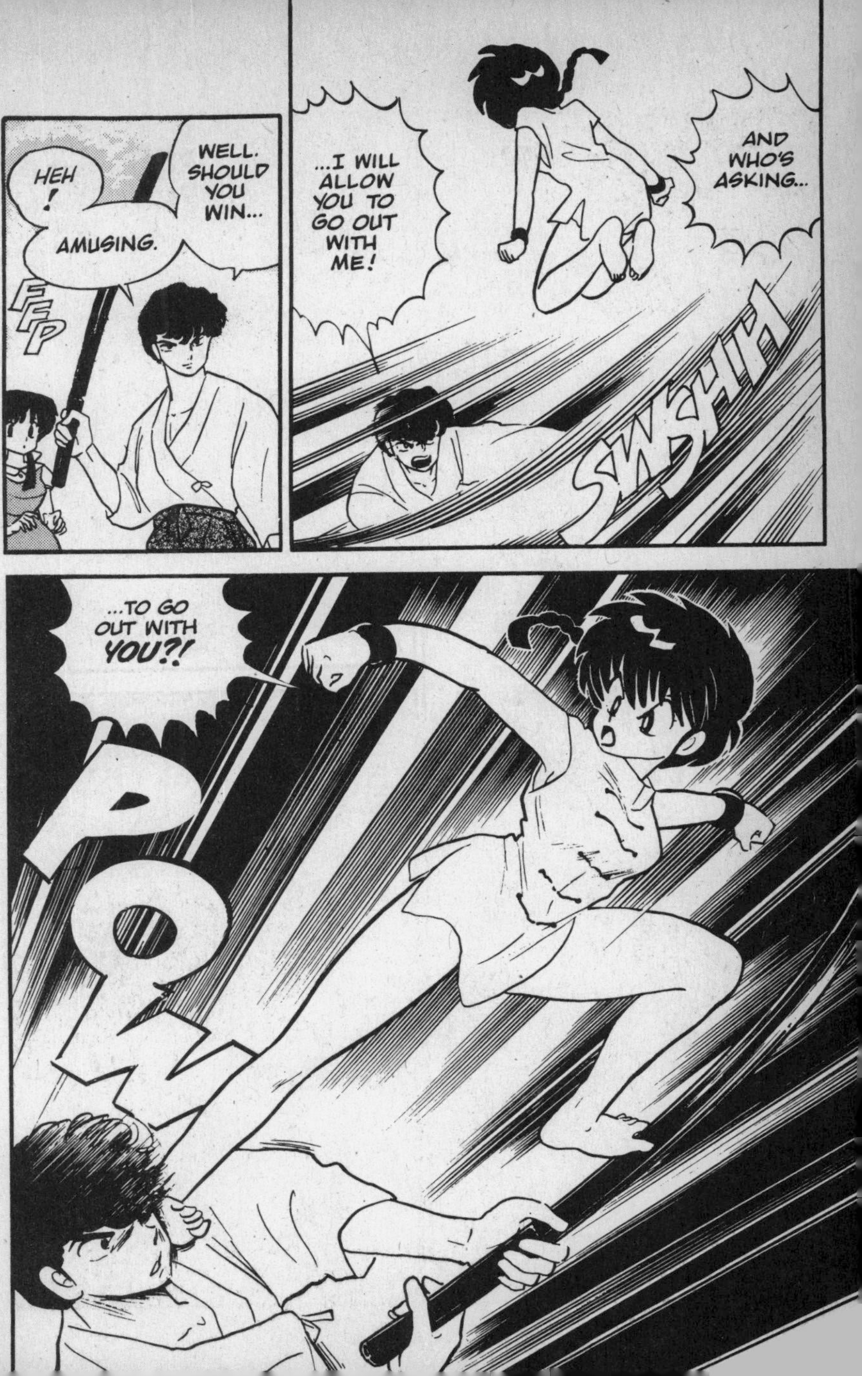
HEH! AMUSING.
WELL. SHOULD YOU WIN...
FFP
...I WILL ALLOW YOU TO GO OUT WITH ME!
AND WHO'S ASKING...
SWSHHH
...TO GO OUT WITH YOU?!
POW

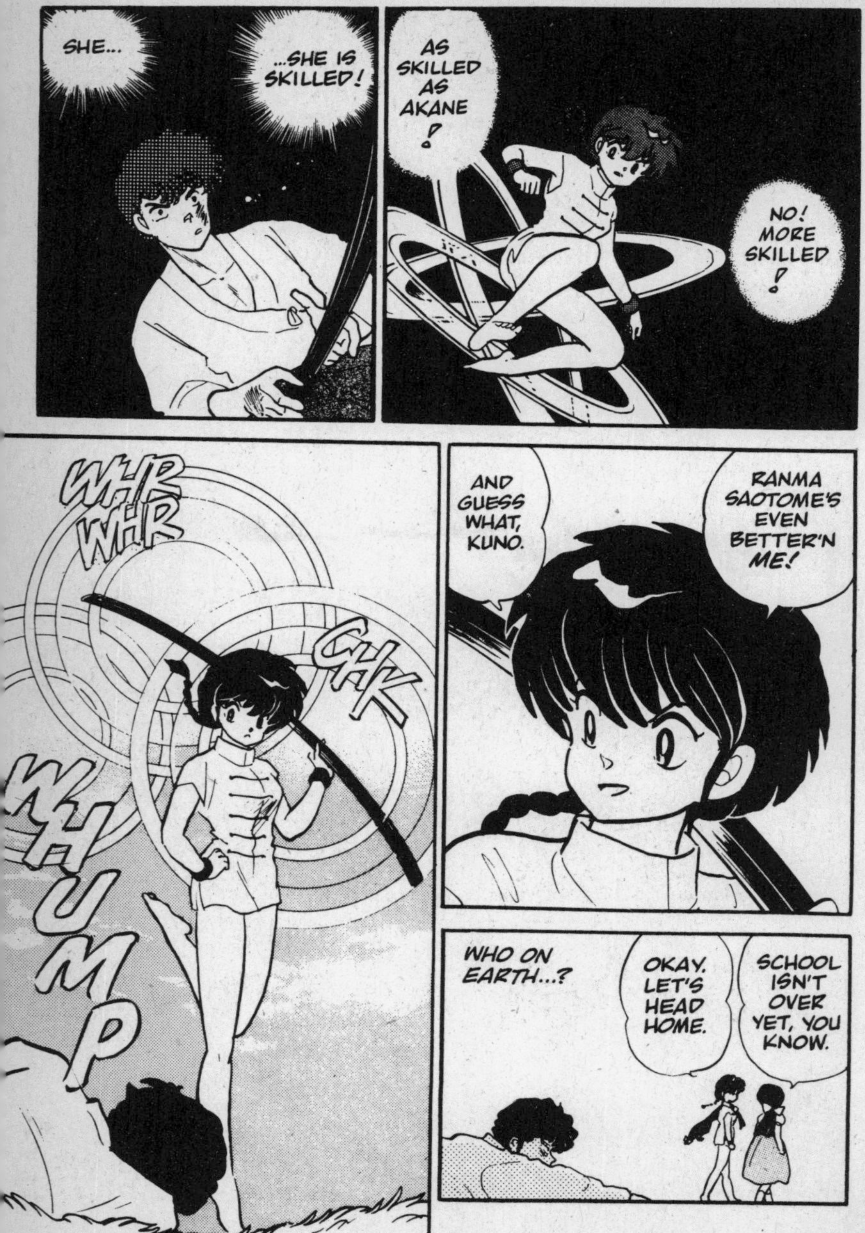
SHE...
...SHE IS SKILLED!
AS SKILLED AS AKANE!
NO! MORE SKILLED!
WHR WHR
CHK
WHUMP
AND GUESS WHAT, KUNO.
RANMA SAOTOME'S EVEN BETTER'N ME!
WHO ON EARTH...?
OKAY. LET'S HEAD HOME.
SCHOOL ISN'T OVER YET, YOU KNOW.

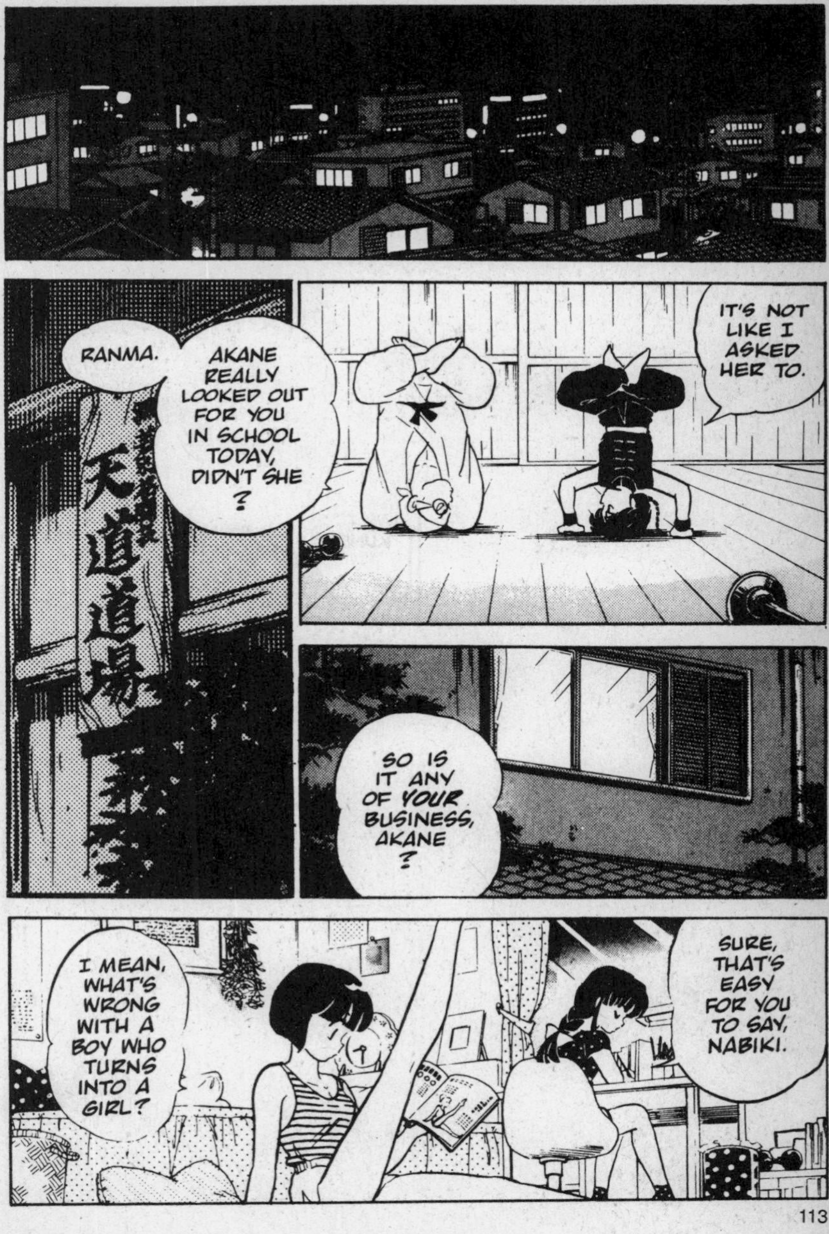
天道道場
RANMA.
AKANE REALLY LOOKED OUT FOR YOU IN SCHOOL TODAY, DIDN'T SHE?
IT'S NOT LIKE I ASKED HER TO.
SO IS IT ANY OF YOUR BUSINESS, AKANE?
I MEAN, WHAT'S WRONG WITH A BOY WHO TURNS INTO A GIRL?
SURE, THAT'S EASY FOR YOU TO SAY, NABIKI.

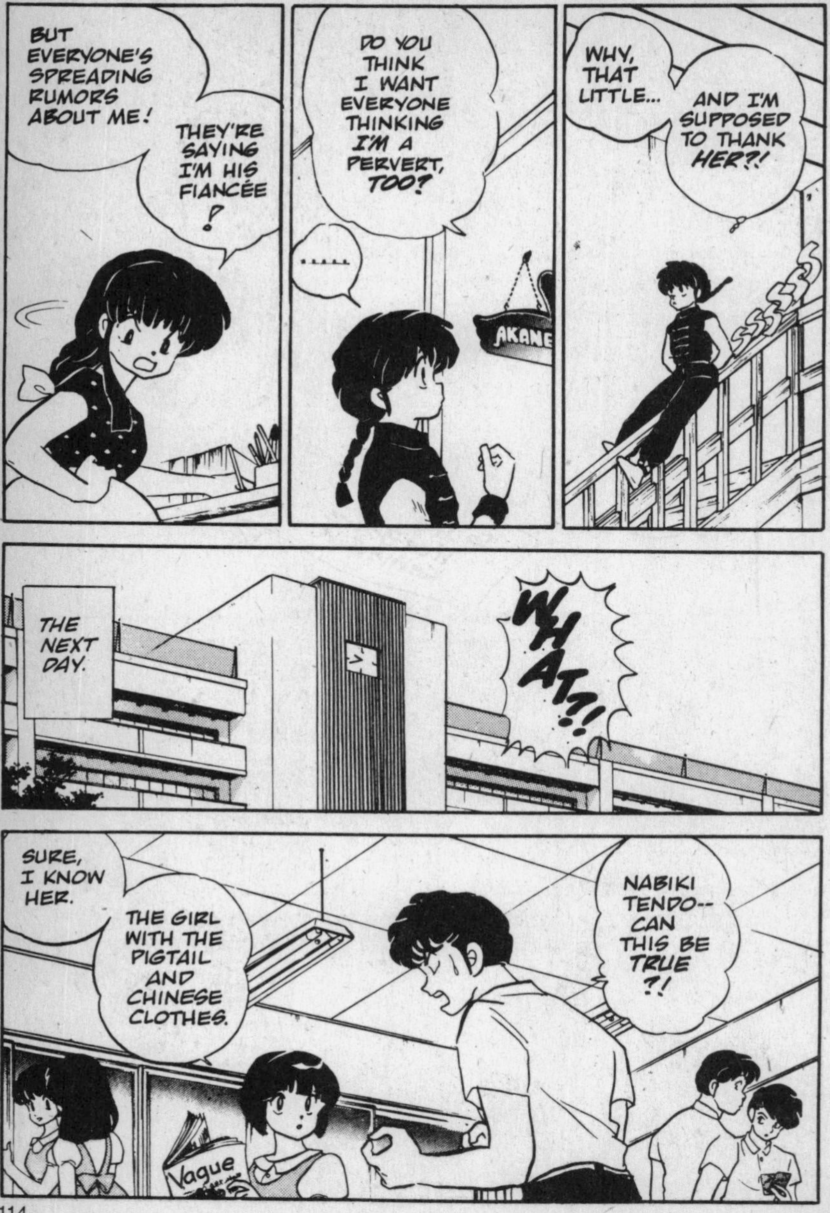
BUT EVERYONE'S SPREADING RUMORS ABOUT ME!
THEY'RE SAYING I'M HIS FIANCÉE?
DO YOU THINK I WANT EVERYONE THINKING I'M A PERVERT, TOO?
.....
AKANE
WHY, THAT LITTLE...
AND I'M SUPPOSED TO THANK HER?!
SSSSS
THE NEXT DAY.
WHAT?!!
SURE, I KNOW HER.
THE GIRL WITH THE PIGTAIL AND CHINESE CLOTHES.
NABIKI TENDO-- CAN THIS BE TRUE?!
Vague

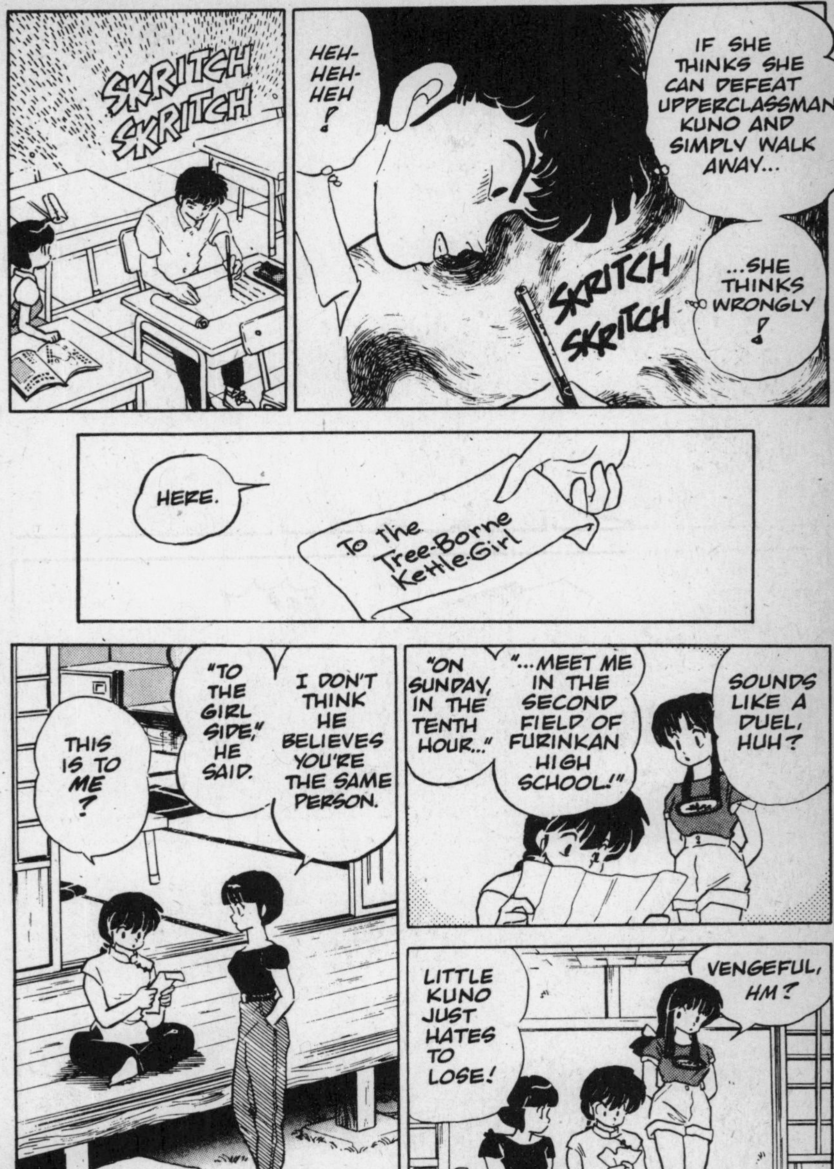
SKRITCH SKRITCH
HEH-HEH-HEH!
IF SHE THINKS SHE CAN DEFEAT UPPERCLASSMAN KUNO AND SIMPLY WALK AWAY...
SKRITCH SKRITCH
...SHE THINKS WRONGLY!
HERE.
To the Tree-Borne Kettle-Girl
THIS IS TO ME?
"TO THE GIRL SIDE," HE SAID.
I DON'T THINK HE BELIEVES YOU'RE THE SAME PERSON.
"ON SUNDAY, IN THE TENTH HOUR..."
"...MEET ME IN THE SECOND FIELD OF FURINKAN HIGH SCHOOL!"
SOUNDS LIKE A DUEL, HUH?
LITTLE KUNO JUST HATES TO LOSE!
VENGEFUL, HM?

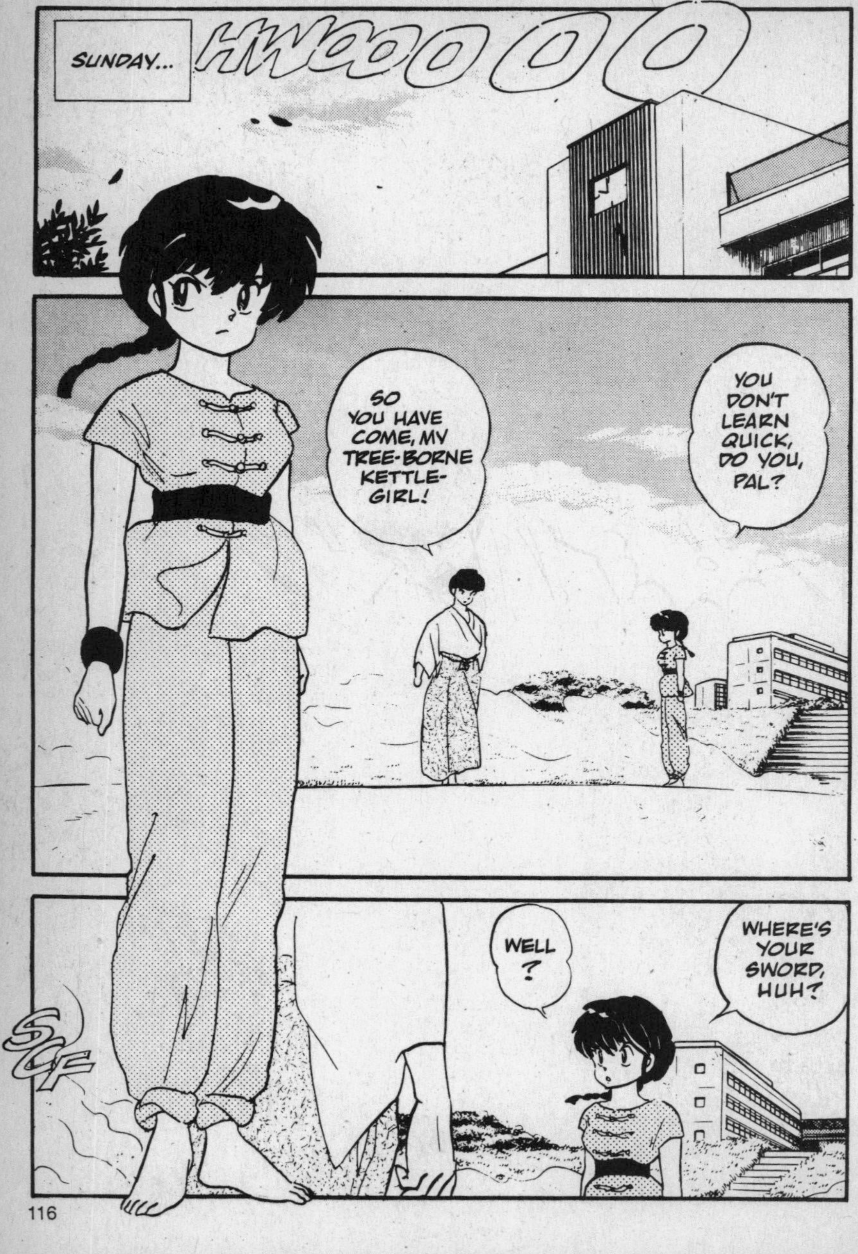
SUNDAY...
HWOOOOOO
SO YOU HAVE COME, MY TREE-BORNE KETTLE-GIRL!
YOU DON'T LEARN QUICK, DO YOU, PAL?
SCF
WELL?
WHERE'S YOUR SWORD, HUH?

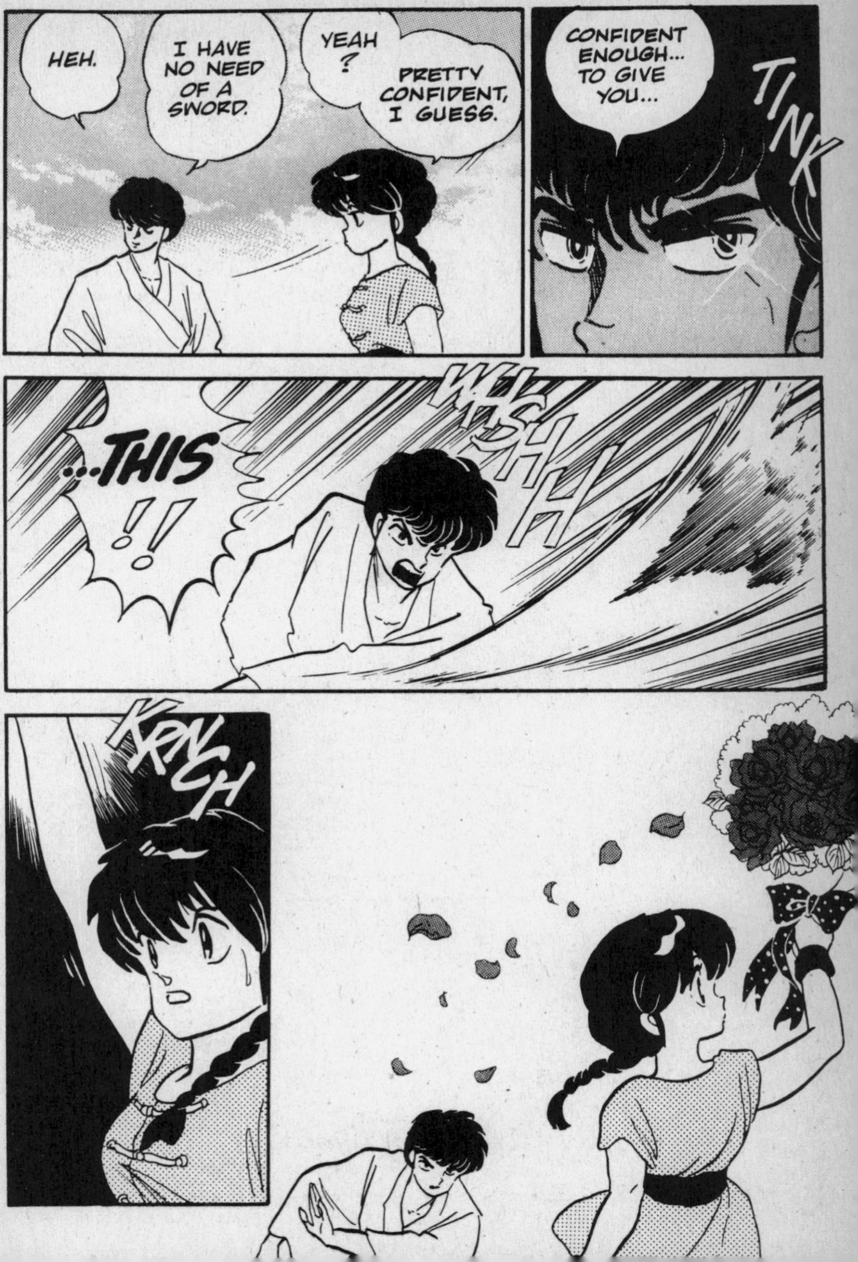
HEH.
I HAVE NO NEED OF A SWORD.
YEAH?
PRETTY CONFIDENT, I GUESS.
CONFIDENT ENOUGH... TO GIVE YOU...
TINK
...THIS!!
WHSSHH
KRNCH

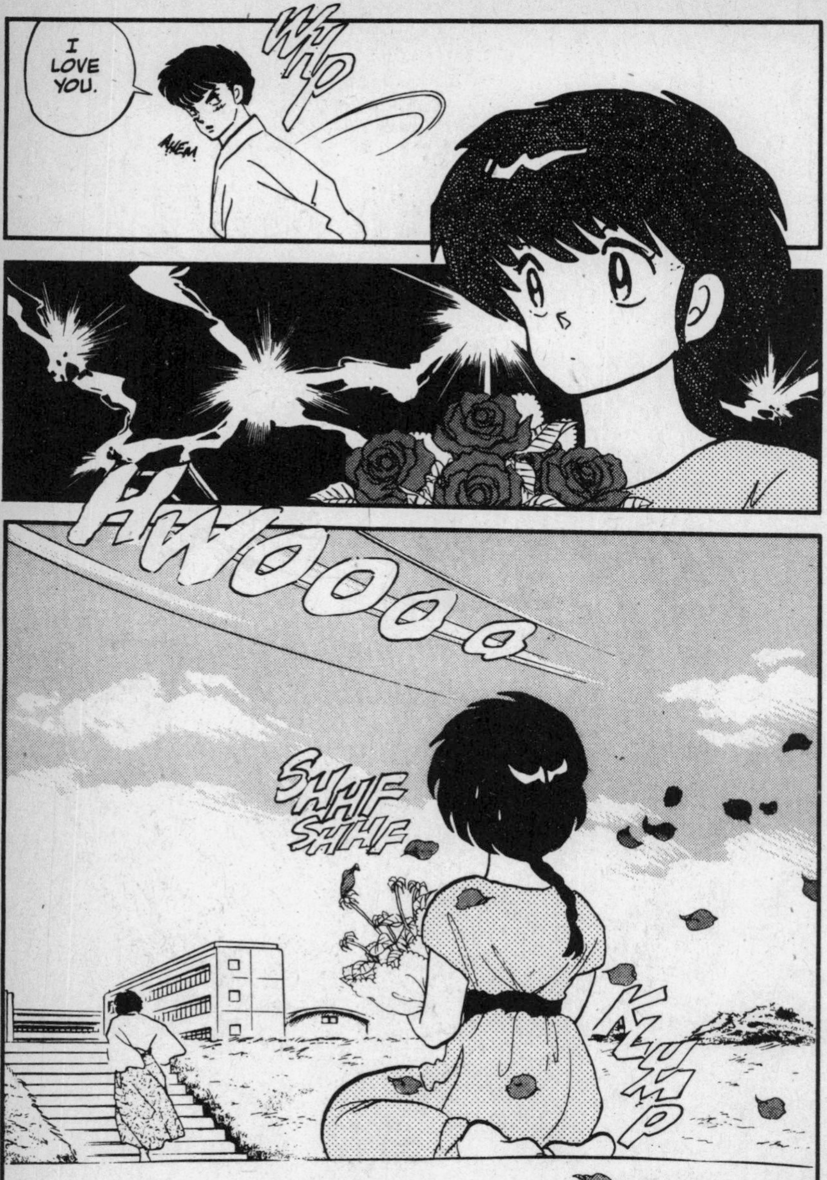
I LOVE YOU.
AHEM
WHP
HWOOOO
SHHF SHHF
KLUMP

Part 6
BODY AND SOUL

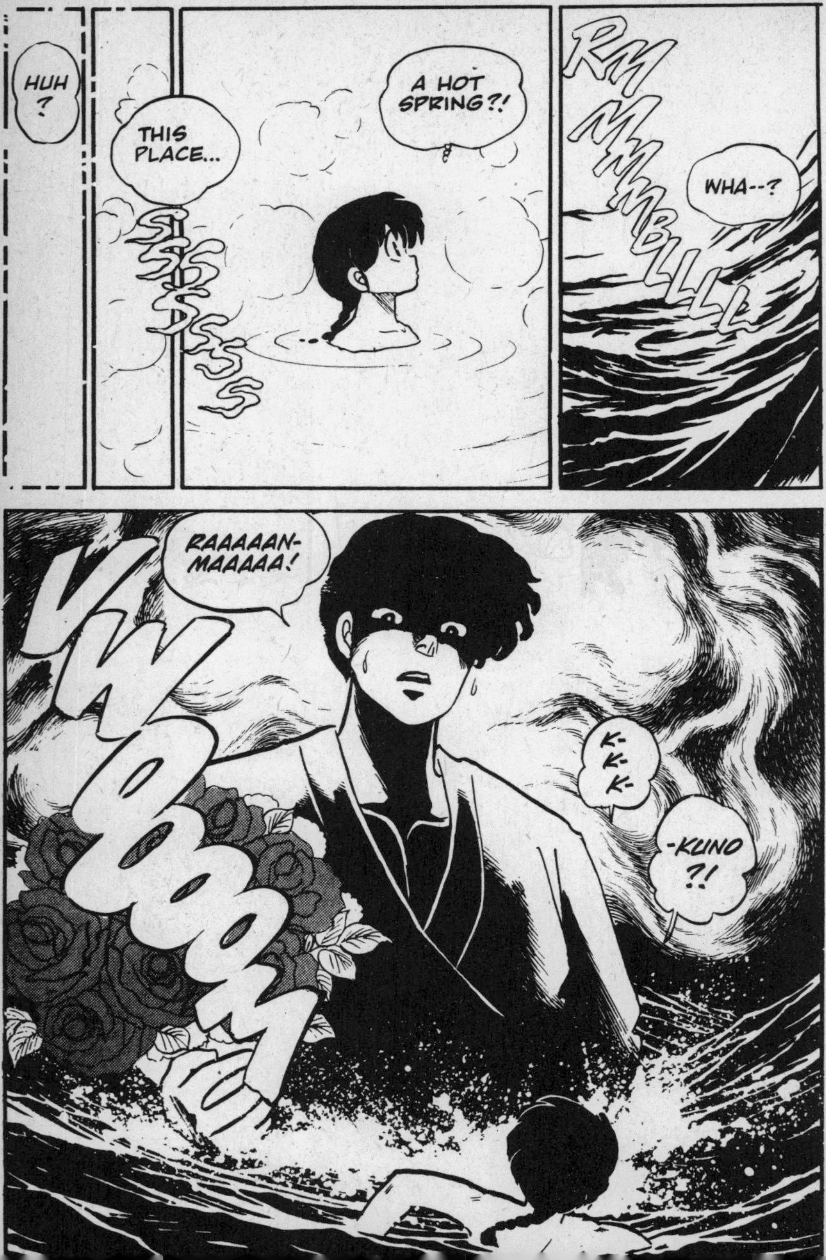
HUH?
THIS PLACE...
SSSSSSSS
A HOT SPRING?!
RMMMMBLLLL
WHA--?
RAAAAAN-MAAAAA!
VWOOOM
K-K-K-
-KUNO?!

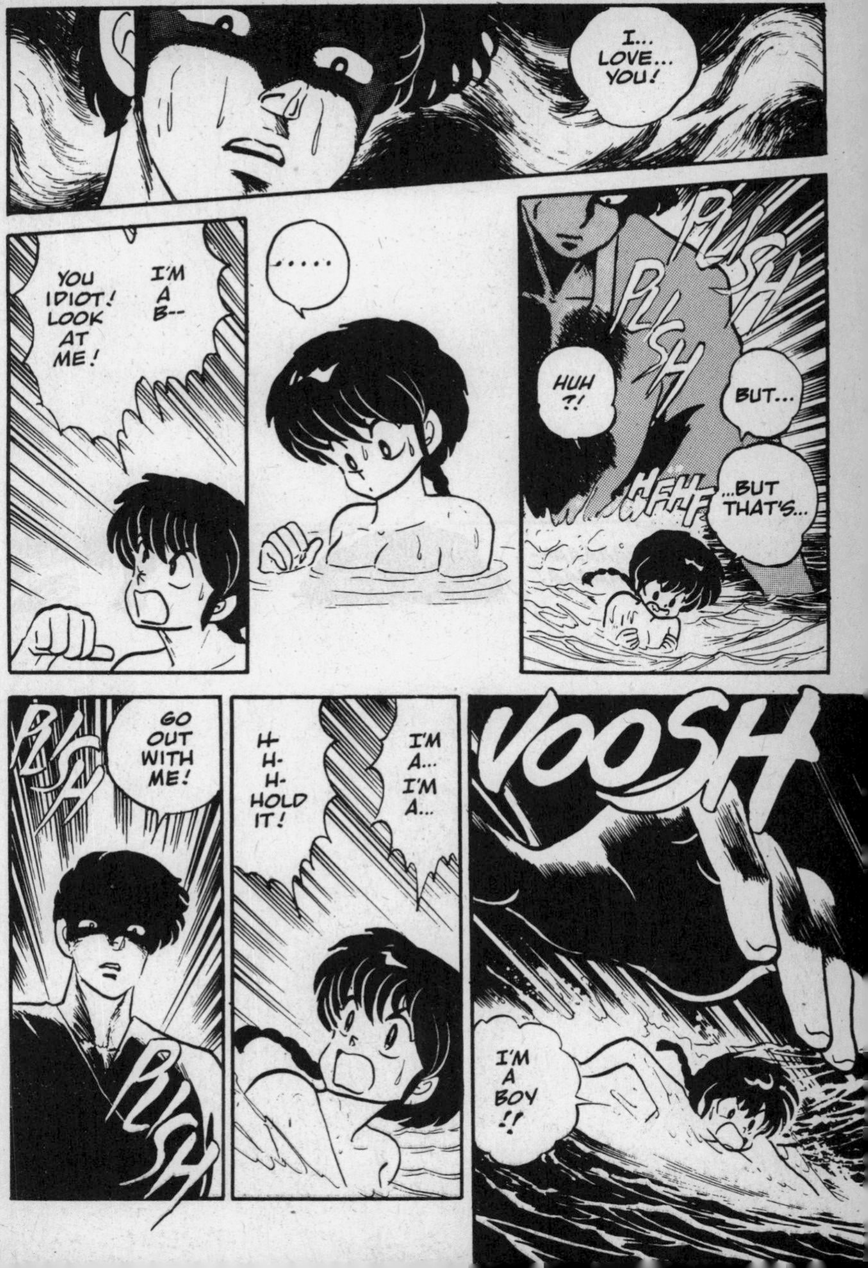
I... LOVE... YOU!
YOU IDIOT! LOOK AT ME!
I'M A B--
.....
PUSH
PUSH
HUH?!
BUT...
HFHF
...BUT THAT'S...
PUSH
GO OUT WITH ME!
PUSH
H-H-H-HOLD IT!
I'M A... I'M A...
VOOSH
I'M A BOY!!

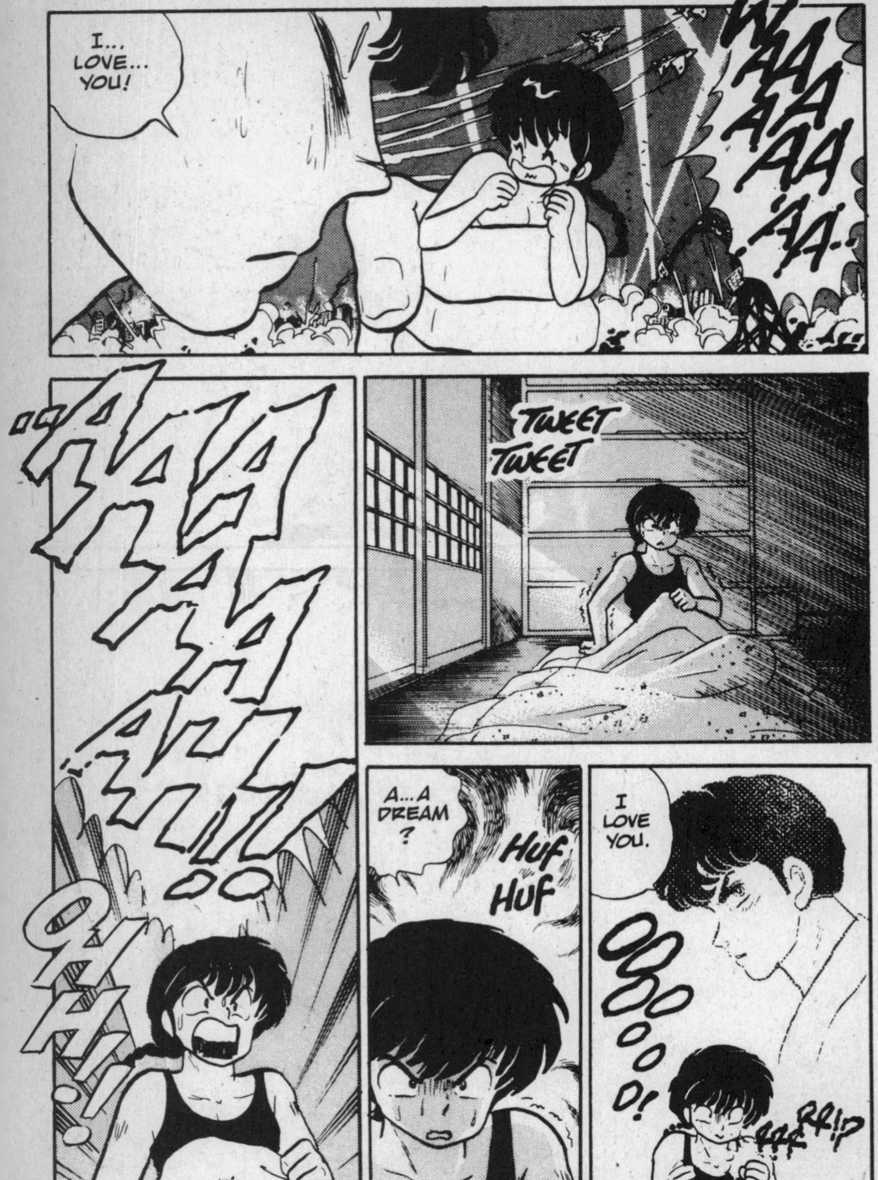
I... LOVE... YOU!
WAAAAAAAAAA...
..AAAAAAAHHH..
OHH!..
TWEET TWEET
A...A DREAM?
HUF HUF
I LOVE YOU.
OOOOOOOO!
RRRRR!?

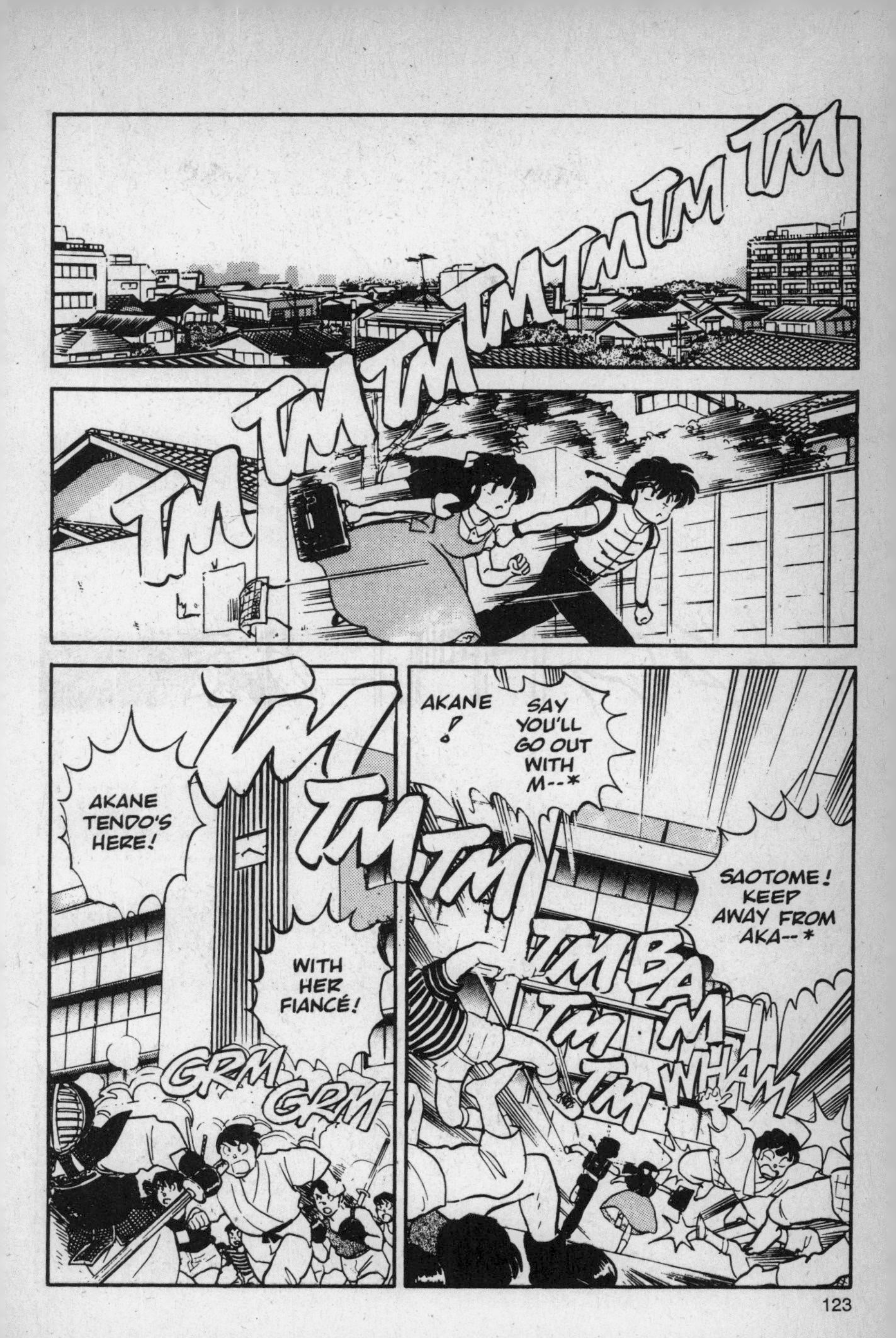
TM TM TM TM TM TM TM TM TM
TM TM TM
AKANE TENDO'S HERE!
TM TM·TM
WITH HER FIANCÉ!
GRM GRM
AKANE!
SAY YOU'LL GO OUT WITH M--*
SAOTOME! KEEP AWAY FROM AKA--*
TM TM TM
BAM
WHAM

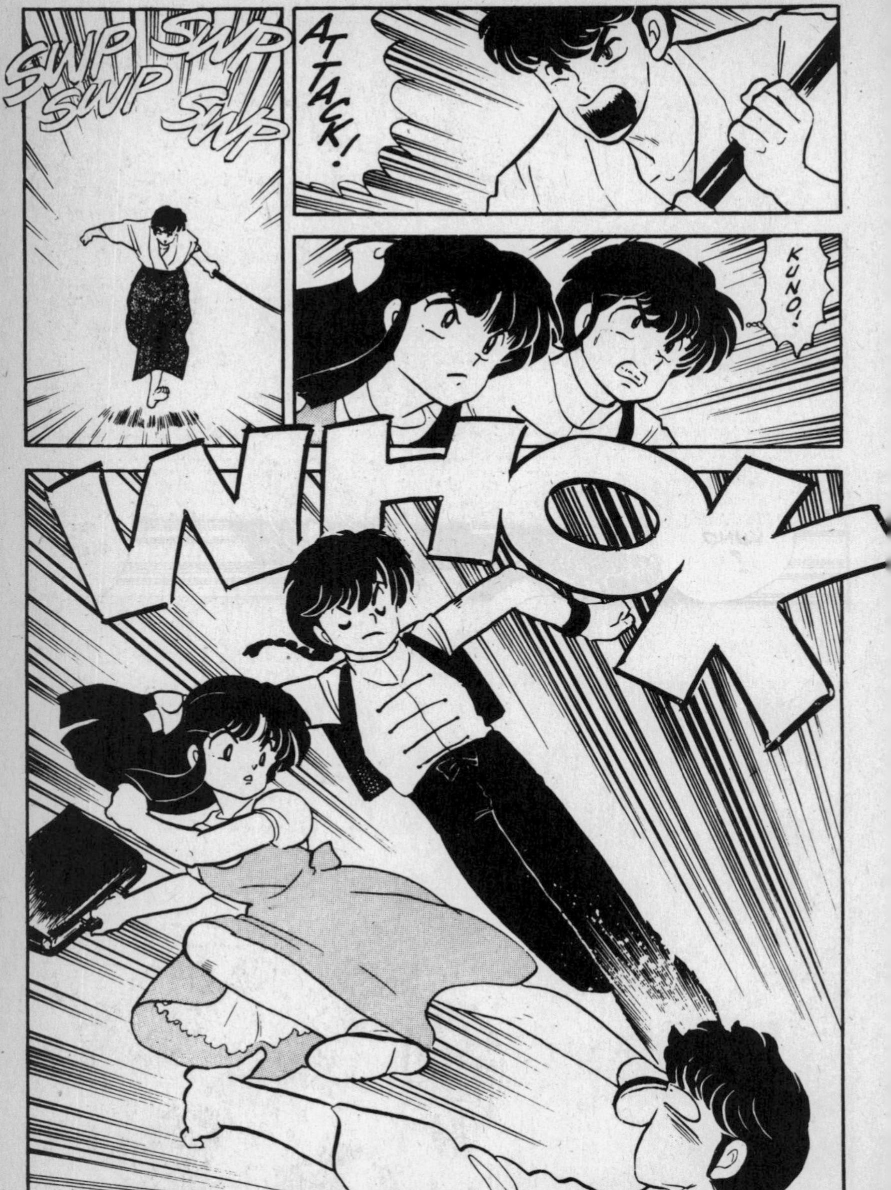
SWP SWP
SWP SWP
ATTACK!
KUNO!
WHOK

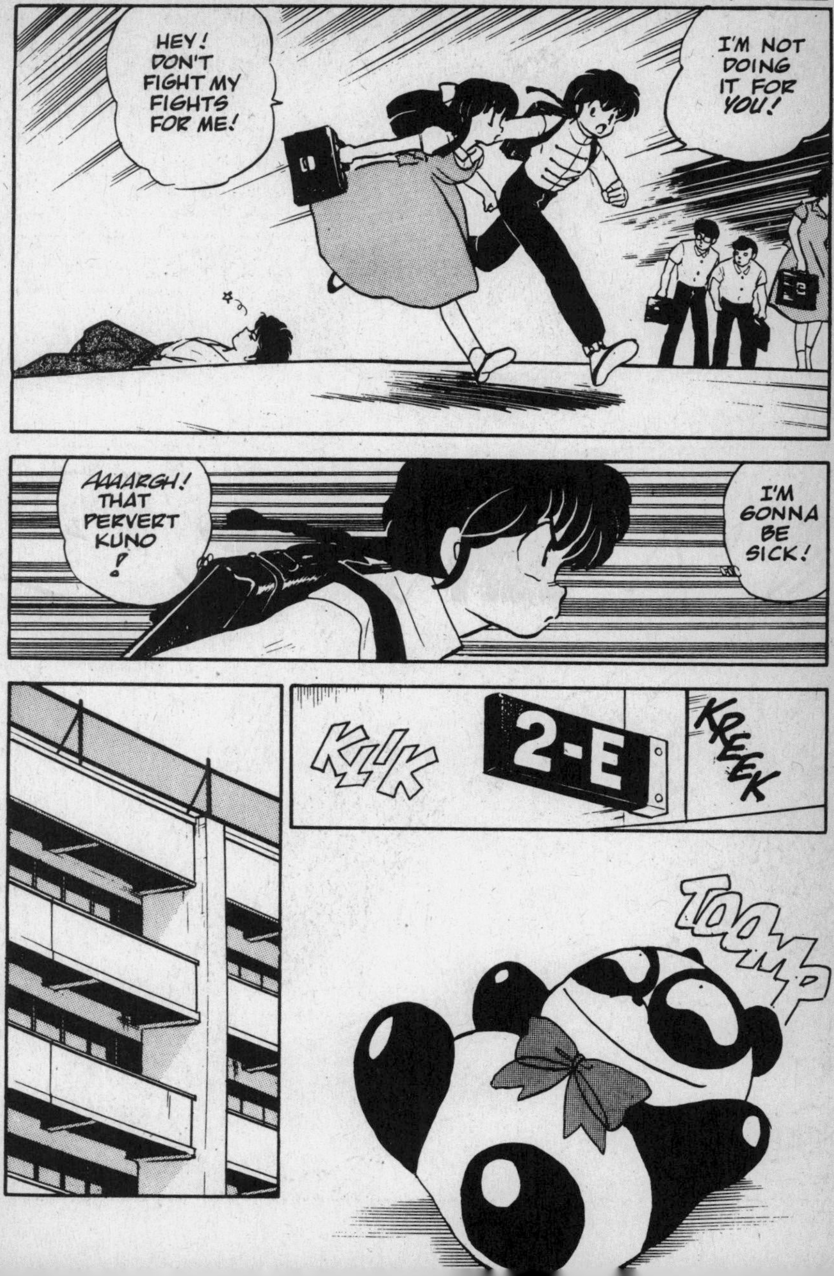
HEY! DON'T FIGHT MY FIGHTS FOR ME!
I'M NOT DOING IT FOR YOU!
AAAARGH! THAT PERVERT KUNO!
I'M GONNA BE SICK!
KLIK
2-E
KREEEK
TOOMP

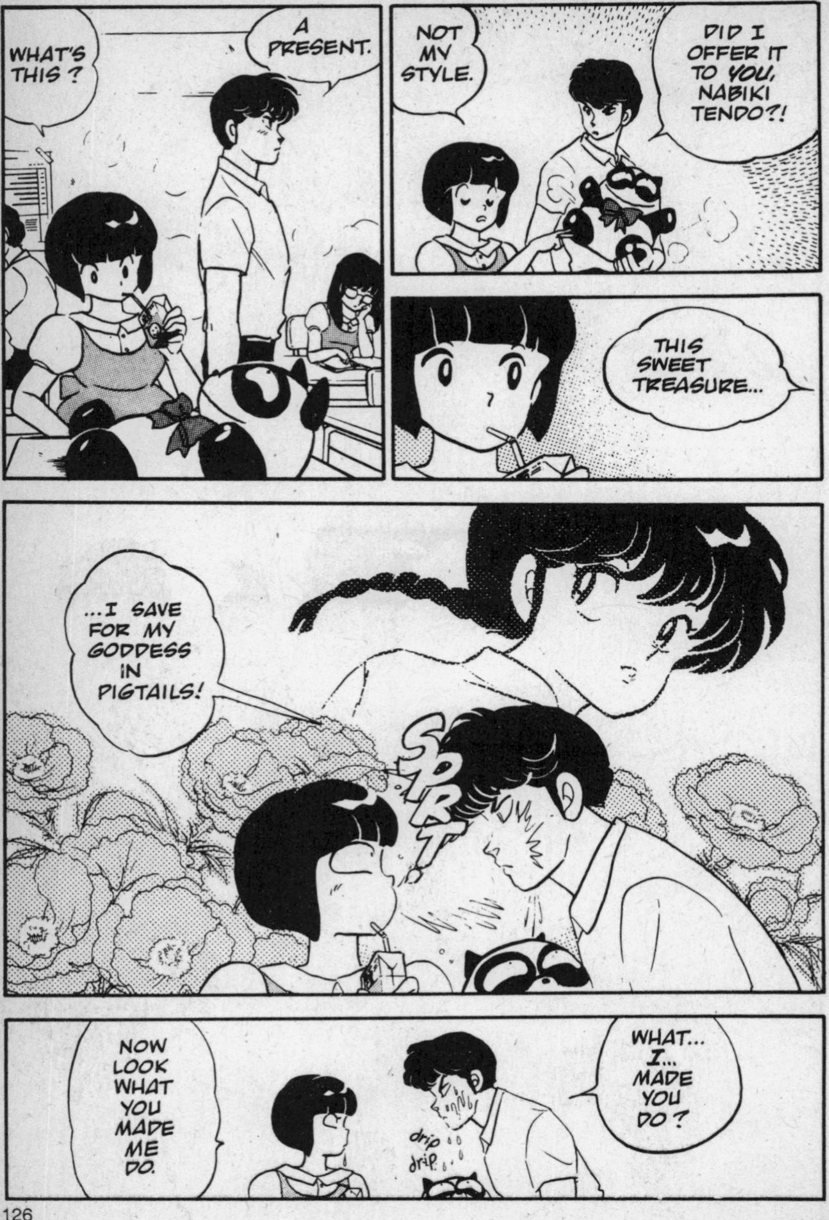
WHAT'S THIS?
A PRESENT.
NOT MY STYLE.
DID I OFFER IT TO YOU, NABIKI TENDO?!
THIS SWEET TREASURE...
...I SAVE FOR MY GODDESS IN PIGTAILS!
SPRT
NOW LOOK WHAT YOU MADE ME DO.
drip drip
WHAT... I... MADE YOU DO?

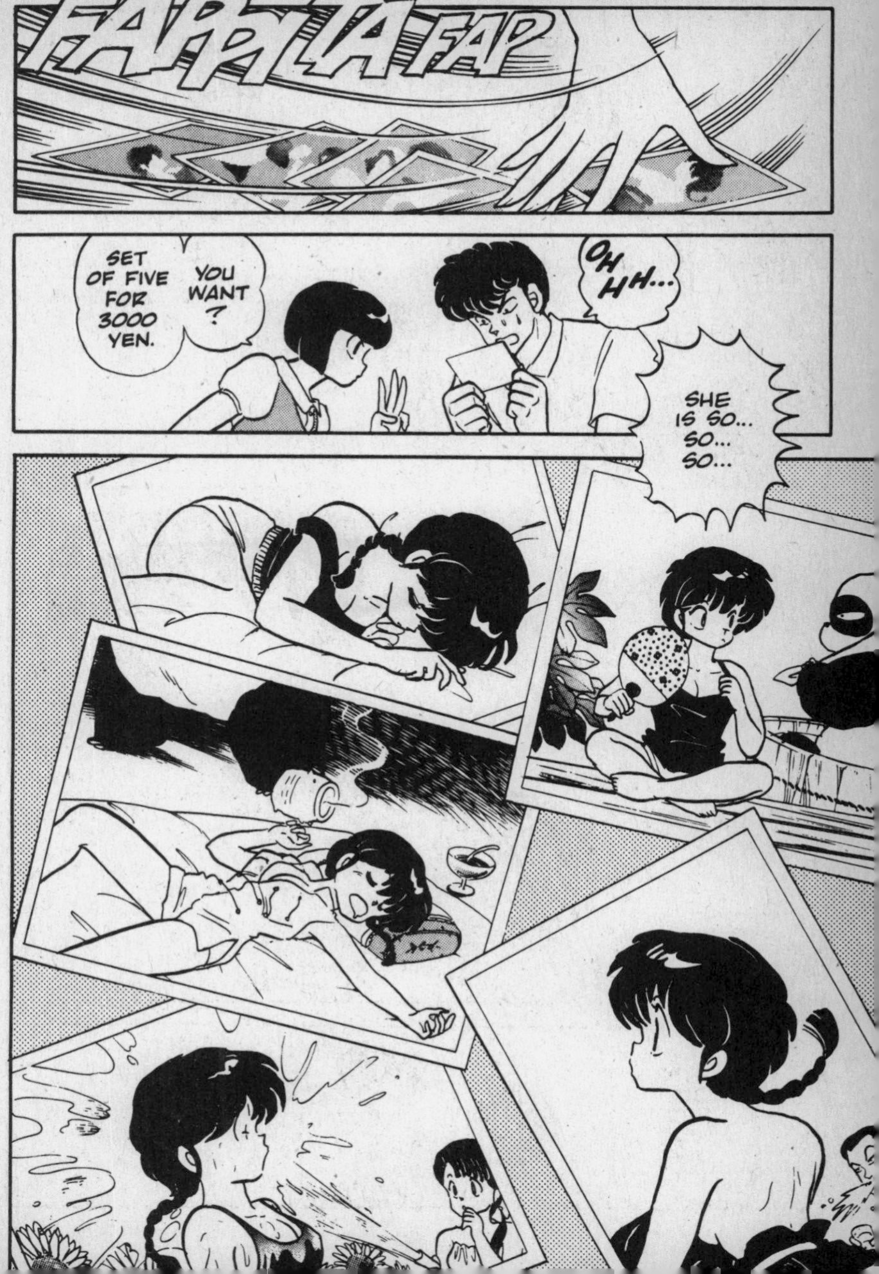
FAP PA LA FAP
SET OF FIVE FOR 3000 YEN.
YOU WANT ?
OHHH...
SHE IS SO... SO... SO...

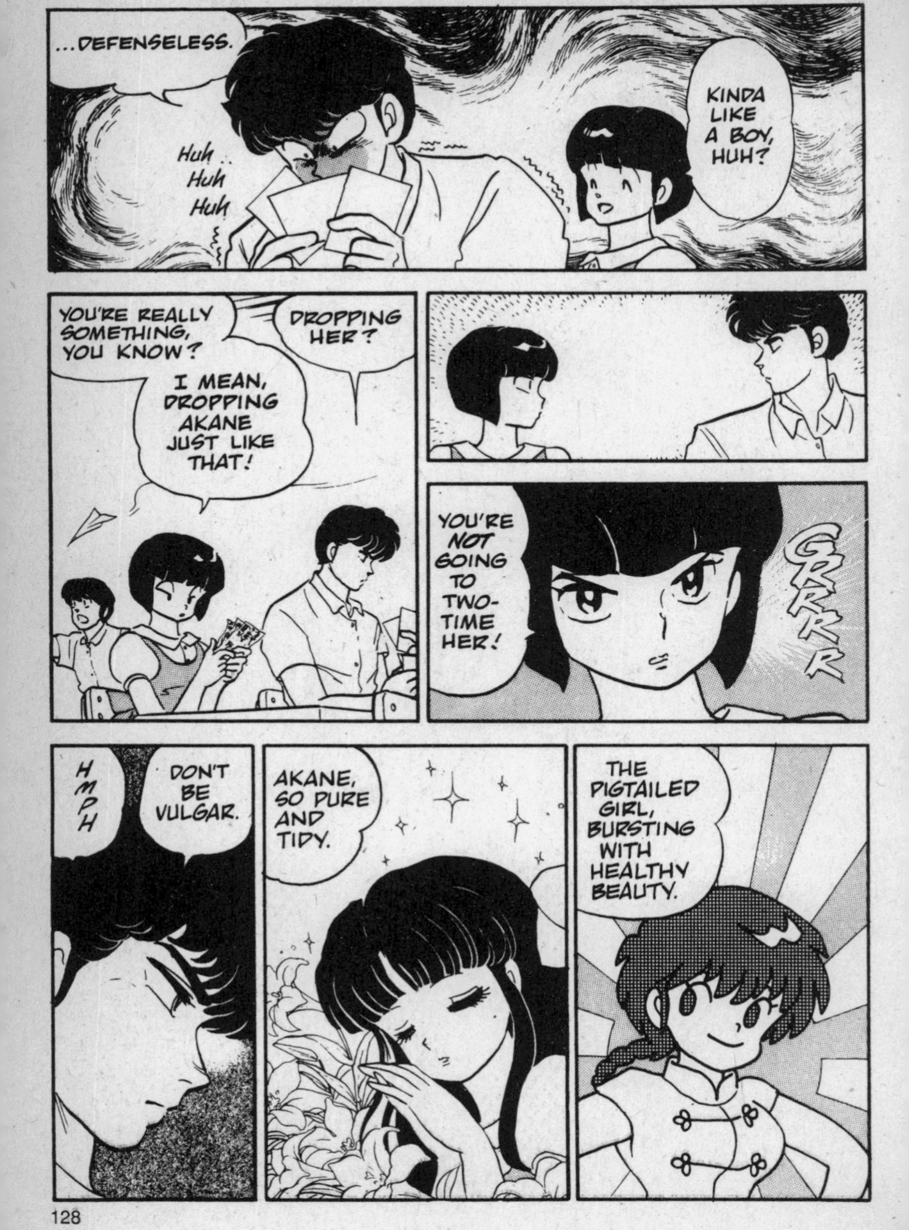
...DEFENSELESS.
Huh.. Huh Huh
KINDA LIKE A BOY, HUH?
YOU'RE REALLY SOMETHING, YOU KNOW?
I MEAN, DROPPING AKANE JUST LIKE THAT!
DROPPING HER?
YOU'RE NOT GOING TO TWO-TIME HER!
GRRRR
HMPH
DON'T BE VULGAR.
AKANE, SO PURE AND TIDY.
THE PIGTAILED GIRL, BURSTING WITH HEALTHY BEAUTY.

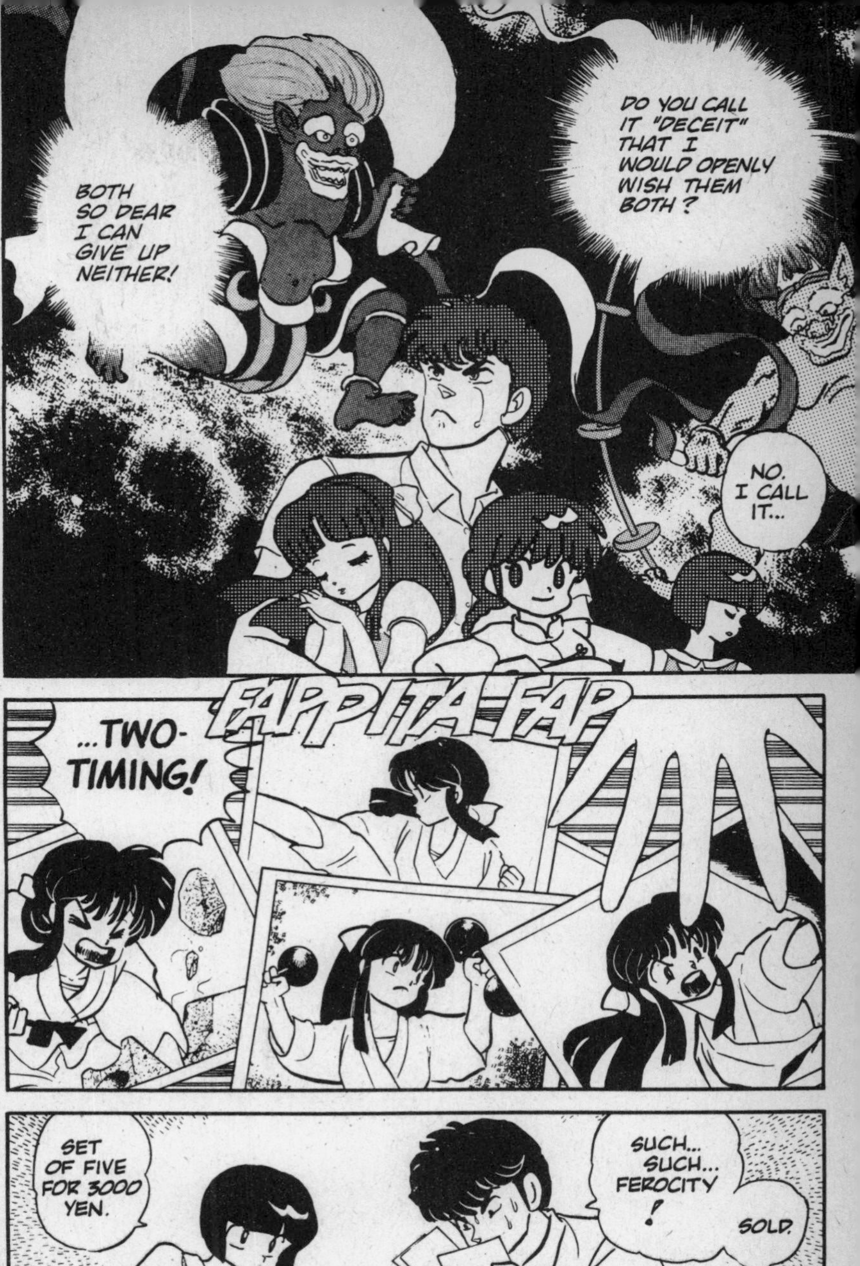
BOTH SO DEAR I CAN GIVE UP NEITHER!
DO YOU CALL IT "DECEIT" THAT I WOULD OPENLY WISH THEM BOTH?
NO. I CALL IT...
...TWO-TIMING!
FAPPITA FAP
SET OF FIVE FOR 3000 YEN.
SUCH... SUCH... FEROCITY!
SOLD.

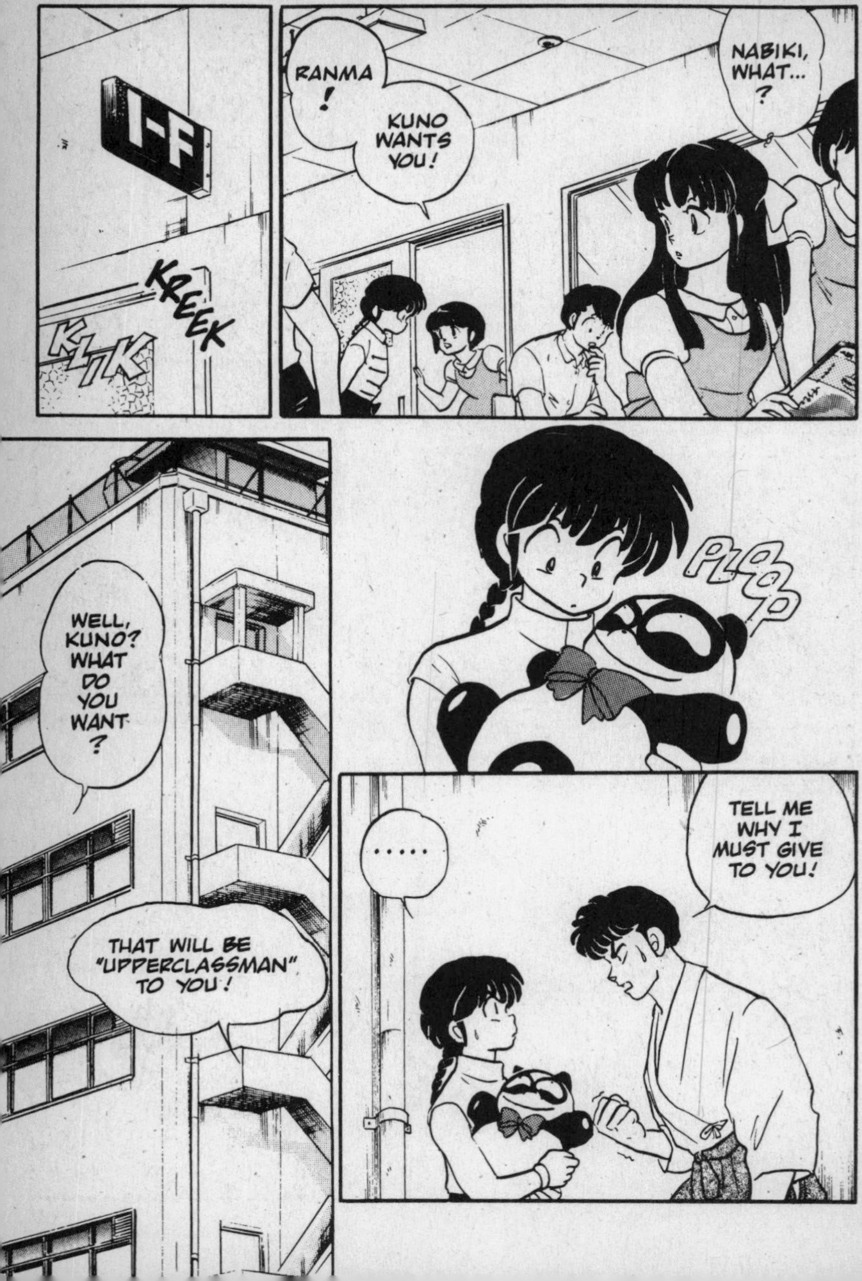
I-F
KREEK
KLIK
RANMA!
KUNO WANTS YOU!
NABIKI, WHAT...?
WELL, KUNO? WHAT DO YOU WANT?
THAT WILL BE "UPPERCLASSMAN" TO YOU!
PLOOP
.....
TELL ME WHY I MUST GIVE TO YOU!

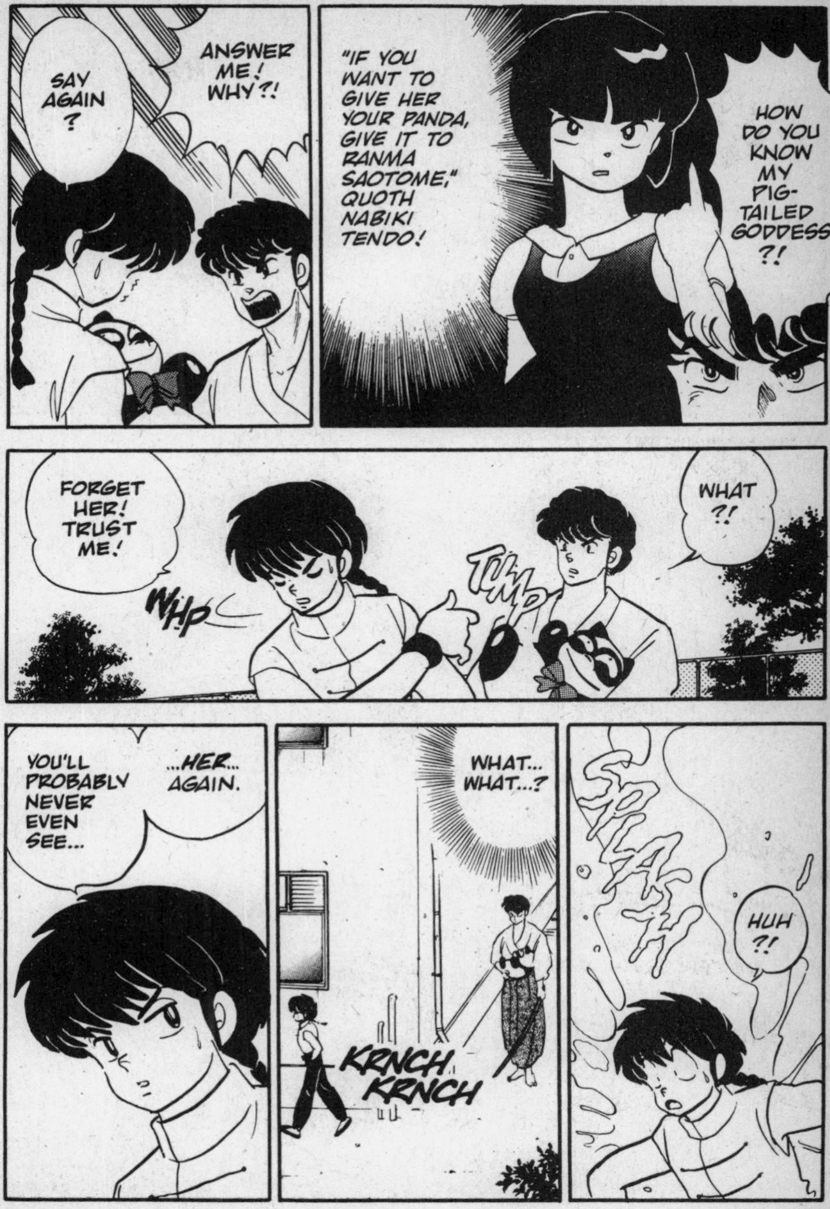
SAY AGAIN ?
ANSWER ME! WHY?!
"IF YOU WANT TO GIVE HER YOUR PANDA, GIVE IT TO RANMA SAOTOME," QUOTH NABIKI TENDO!
HOW DO YOU KNOW MY PIG-TAILED GODDESS ?!
FORGET HER! TRUST ME!
WHP
TMP
WHAT ?!
YOU'LL PROBABLY NEVER EVEN SEE...
...HER... AGAIN.
WHAT... WHAT...?
KRNCH KRNCH
SPLASH
HUH ?!

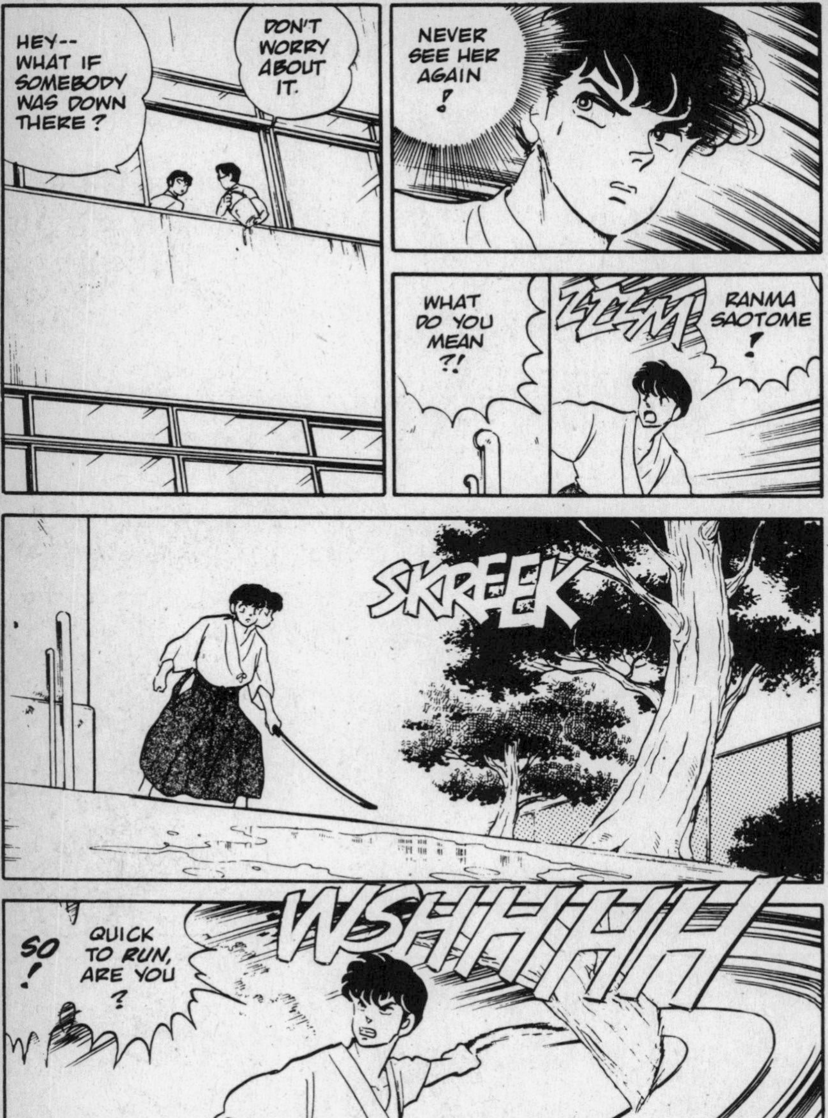
HEY-- WHAT IF SOMEBODY WAS DOWN THERE?
DON'T WORRY ABOUT IT.
NEVER SEE HER AGAIN!
WHAT DO YOU MEAN?!
ZZZM
RANMA SAOTOME!
SKREEK
WSHHHHH
SO!
QUICK TO RUN, ARE YOU?

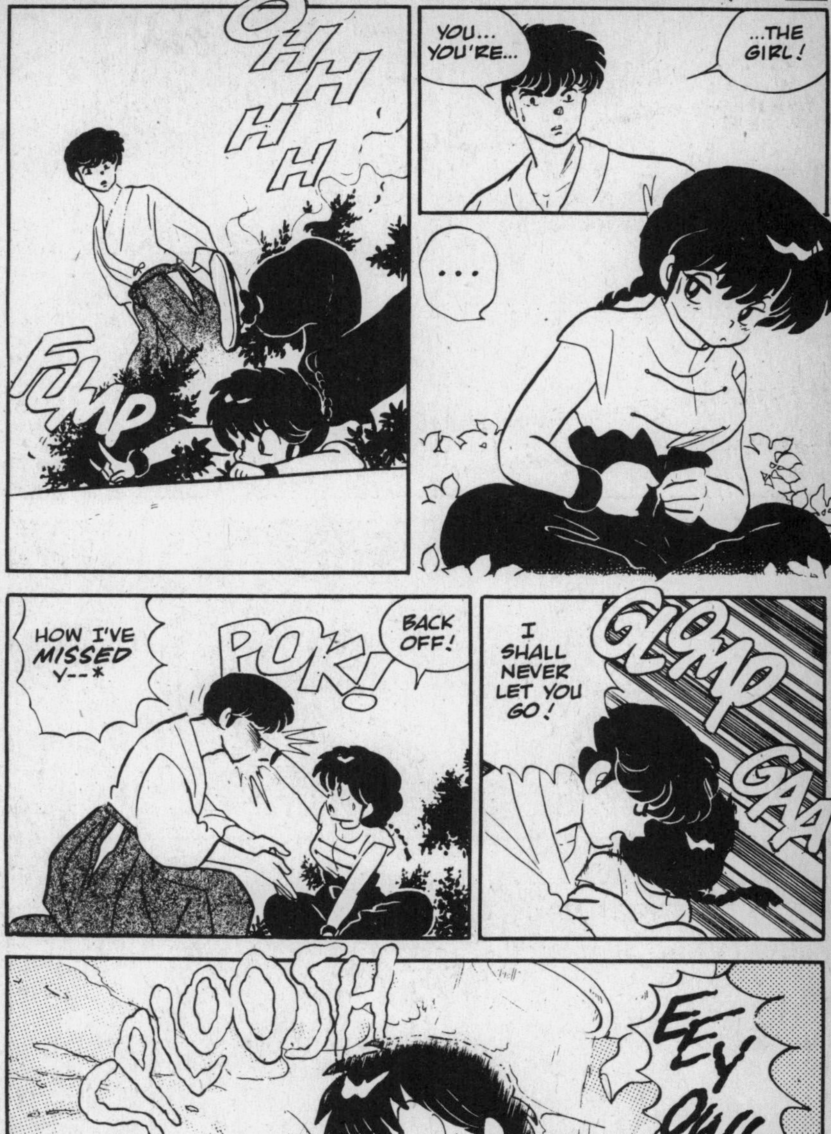
OHHHHH
FUMP
YOU... YOU'RE...
...THE GIRL!
...
HOW I'VE MISSED Y--*
POK!
BACK OFF!
I SHALL NEVER LET YOU GO!
GLOMP
GAA
SPLOOSH
EEEYOW!!!

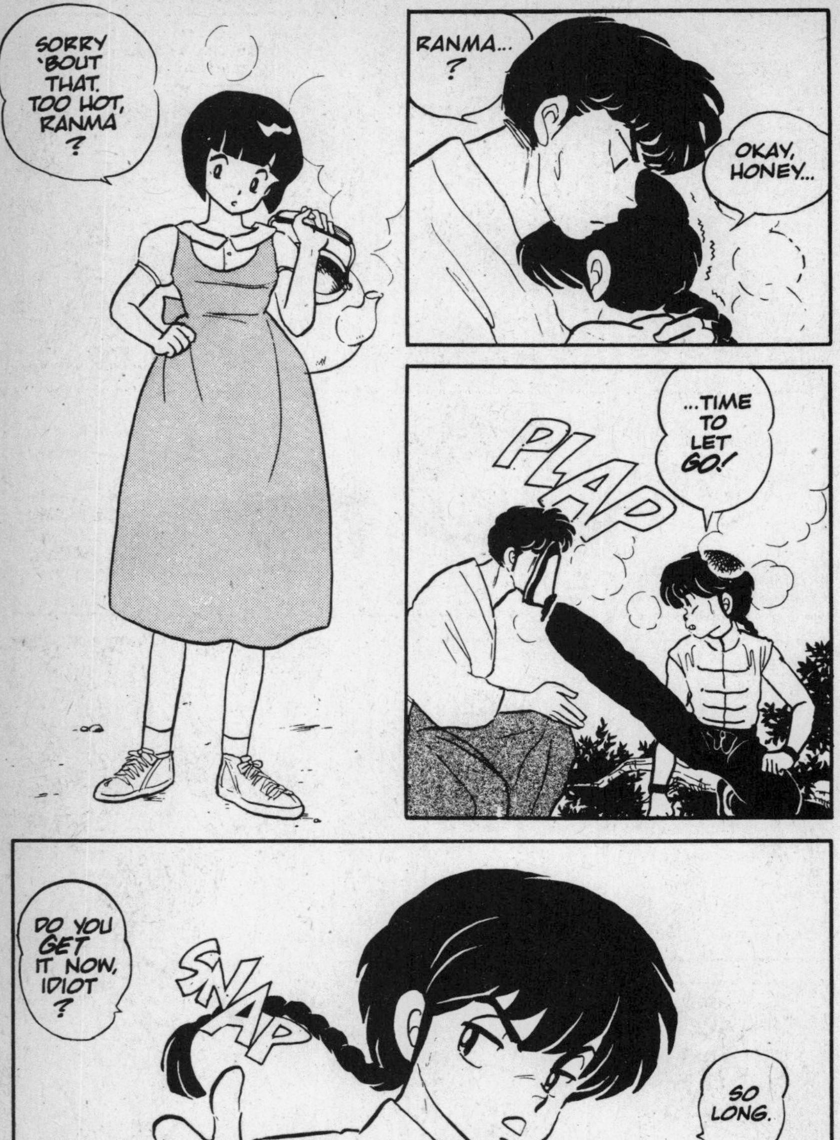
SORRY 'BOUT THAT. TOO HOT, RANMA?
RANMA...?
OKAY, HONEY...
PLAP
...TIME TO LET GO!
SNAP
DO YOU GET IT NOW, IDIOT?
SO LONG.

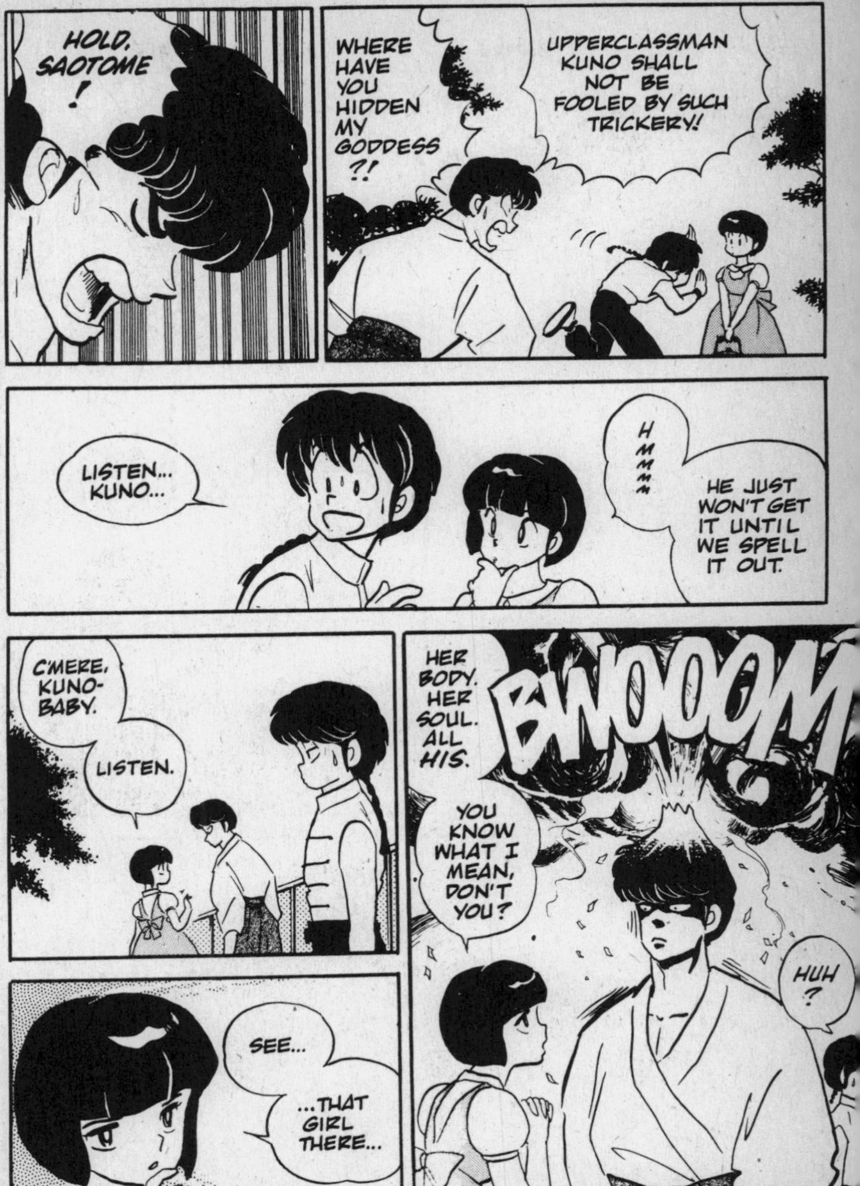
HOLD, SAOTOME!
WHERE HAVE YOU HIDDEN MY GODDESS?!
UPPERCLASSMAN KUNO SHALL NOT BE FOOLED BY SUCH TRICKERY!
LISTEN... KUNO...
HMMMM
HE JUST WON'T GET IT UNTIL WE SPELL IT OUT.
C'MERE, KUNO-BABY.
LISTEN.
SEE...
...THAT GIRL THERE...
HER BODY. HER SOUL. ALL HIS.
BWOOOM
YOU KNOW WHAT I MEAN, DON'T YOU?
HUH?

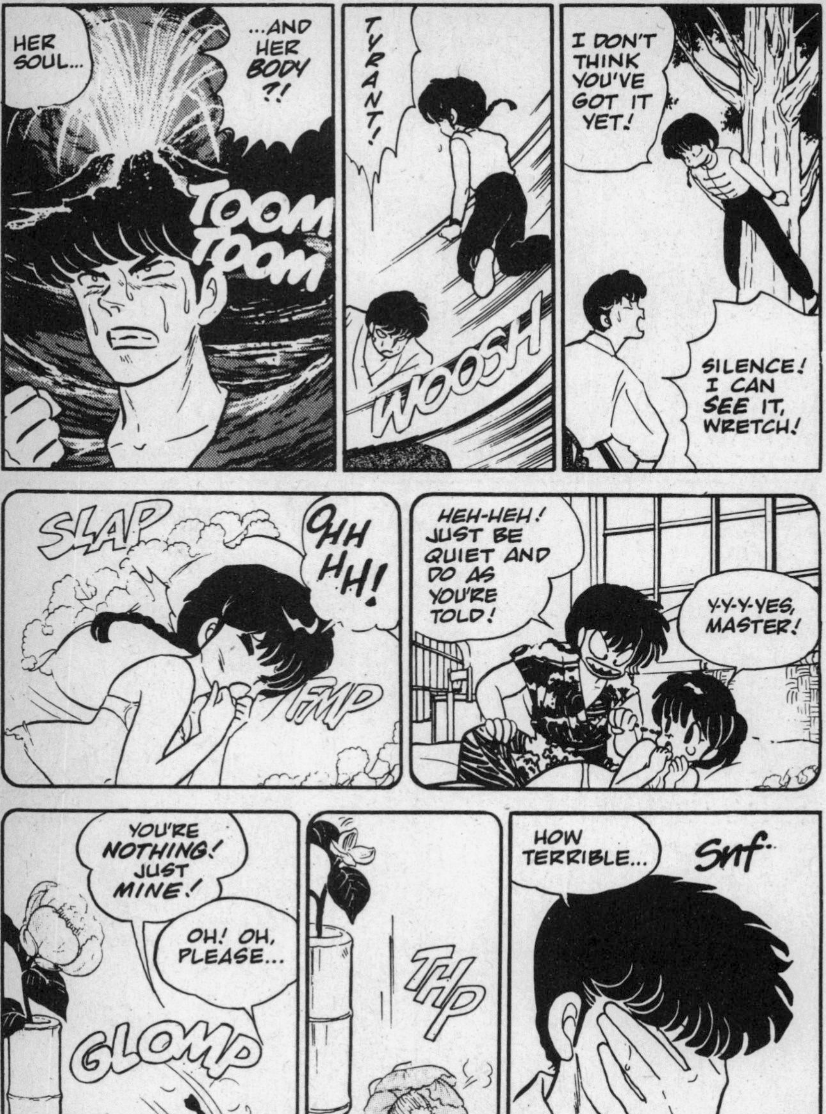
HER SOUL...
...AND HER BODY ?!
TOOM TOOM
TYRANT!
WOOSH
I DON'T THINK YOU'VE GOT IT YET!
SILENCE! I CAN SEE IT, WRETCH!
SLAP
OHHHH!
FMP
HEH-HEH! JUST BE QUIET AND DO AS YOU'RE TOLD!
Y-Y-Y-YES, MASTER!
YOU'RE NOTHING! JUST MINE!
OH! OH, PLEASE...
GLOMP
THP
HOW TERRIBLE...
Snf..

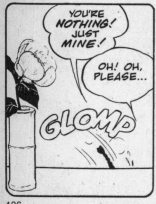

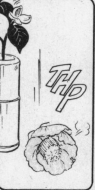

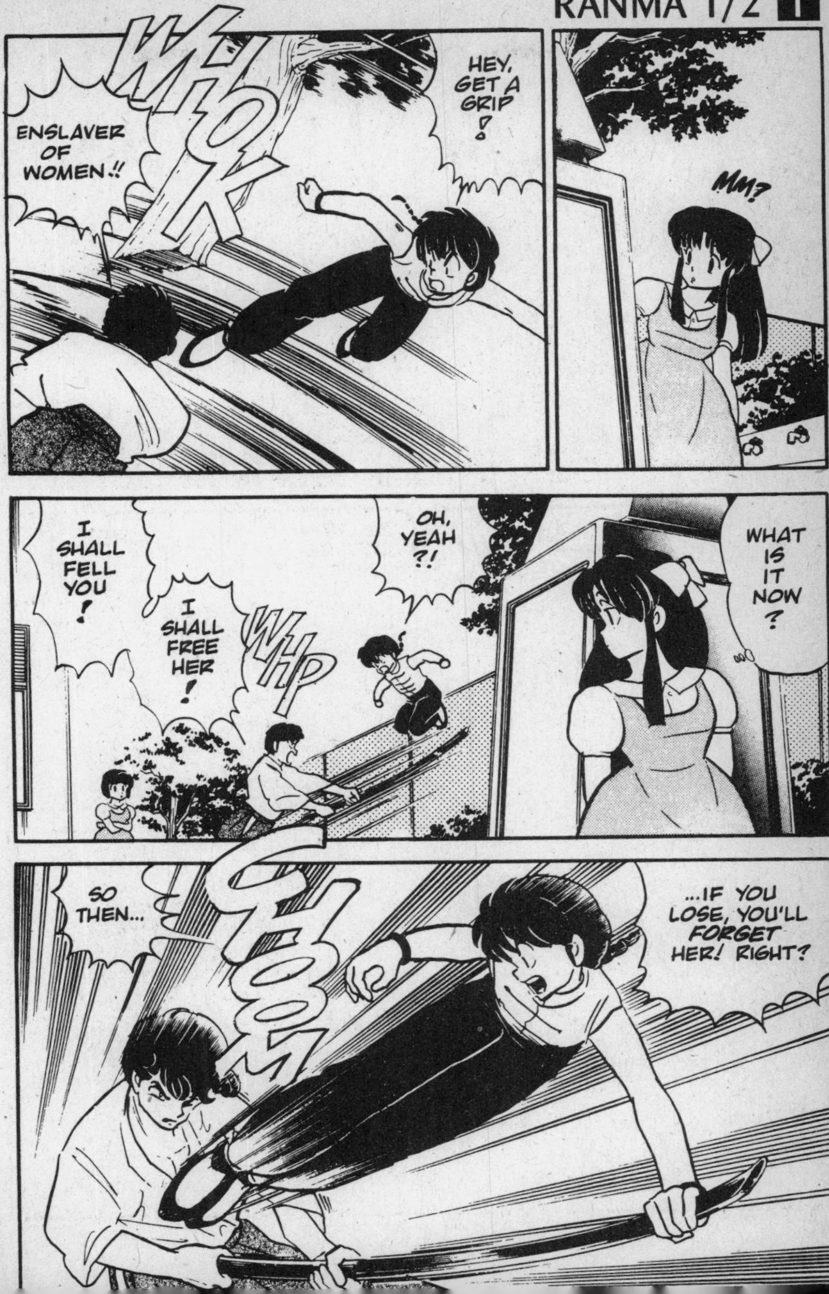
WHOK
ENSLAVER OF WOMEN!!
HEY, GET A GRIP!
MM?
I SHALL FELL YOU!
I SHALL FREE HER!
WHP
OH, YEAH?!
WHAT IS IT NOW?
SO THEN...
CHOOOM
...IF YOU LOSE, YOU'LL FORGET HER! RIGHT?

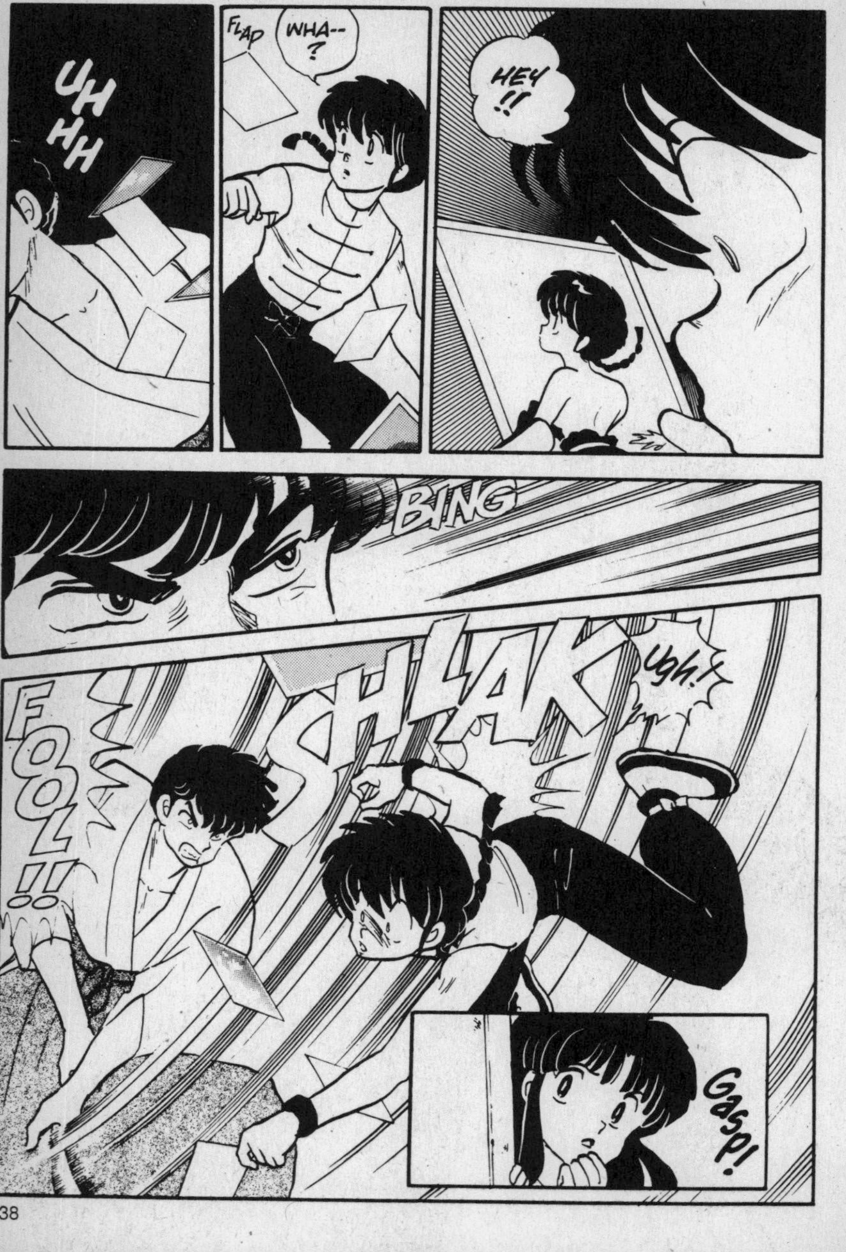

UHHHH
FLAP
WHA-- ?
HEY !!
BING
SHLAK
Ugh!
FOOL!!
Gasp!

Part 7
YOU'LL UNDERSTAND SOON ENOUGH

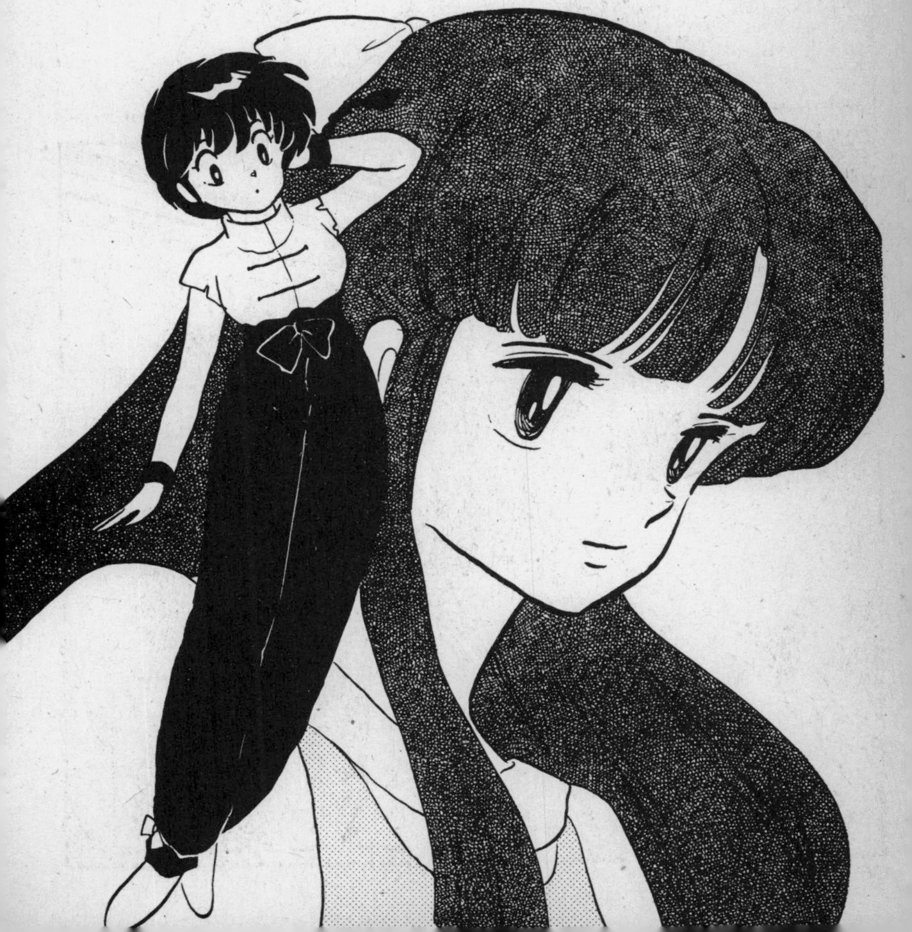

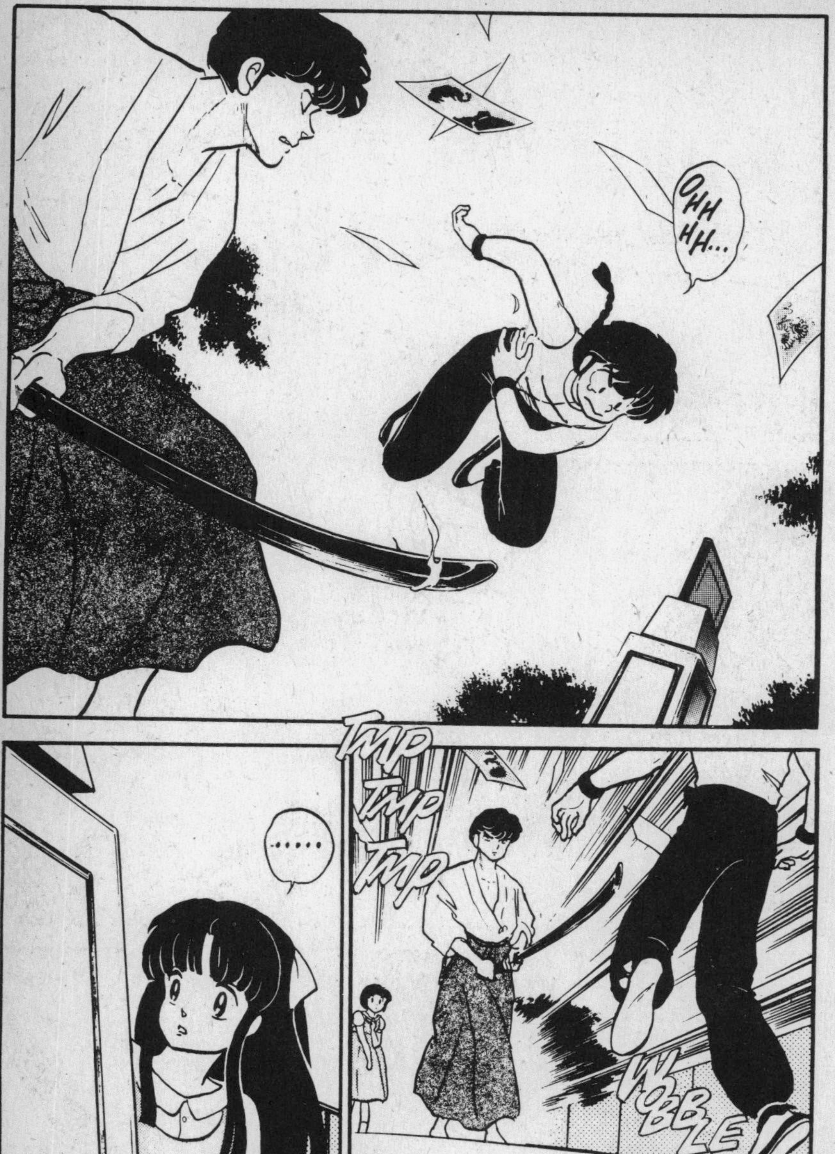
OHHHH...
......
TMP TMP TMP
WOBBLE

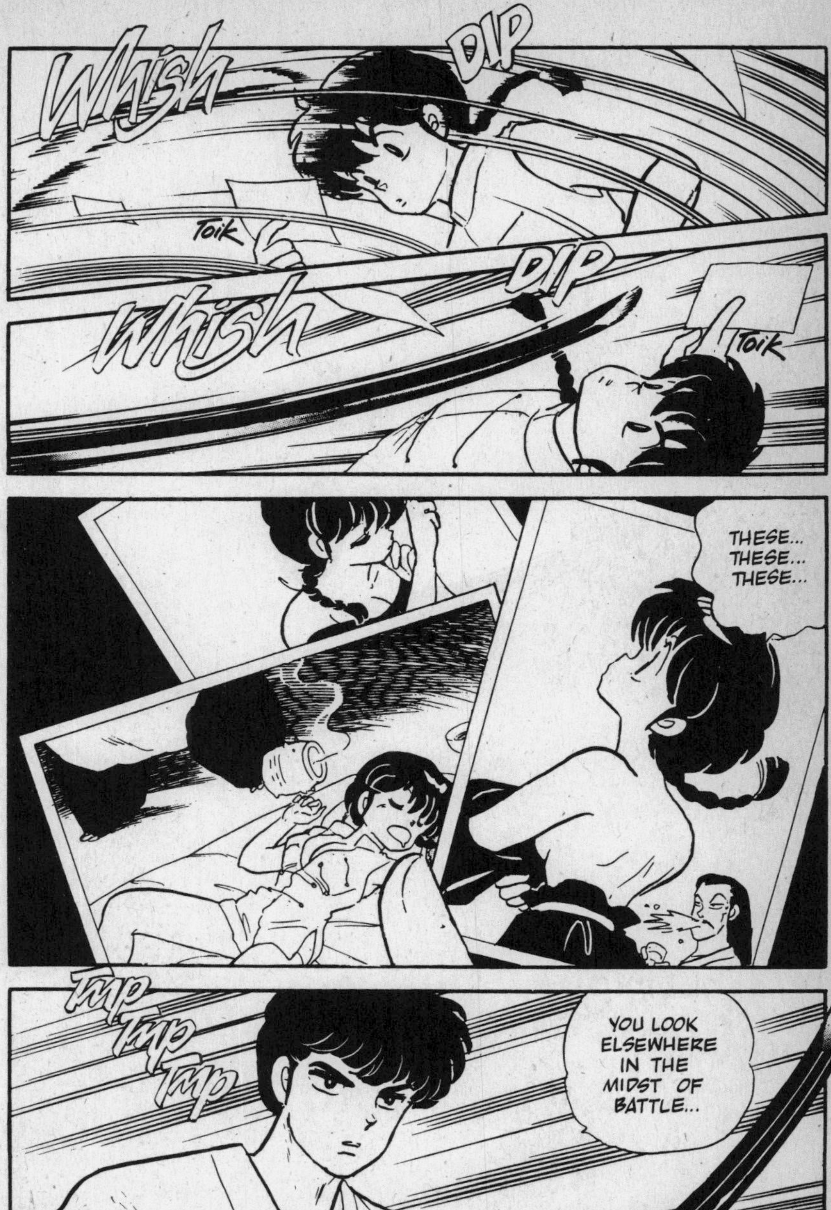
Whish
DIP
Toik
Whish
DIP
Toik
THESE... THESE... THESE...
Tmp Tmp Tmp
YOU LOOK ELSEWHERE IN THE MIDST OF BATTLE...

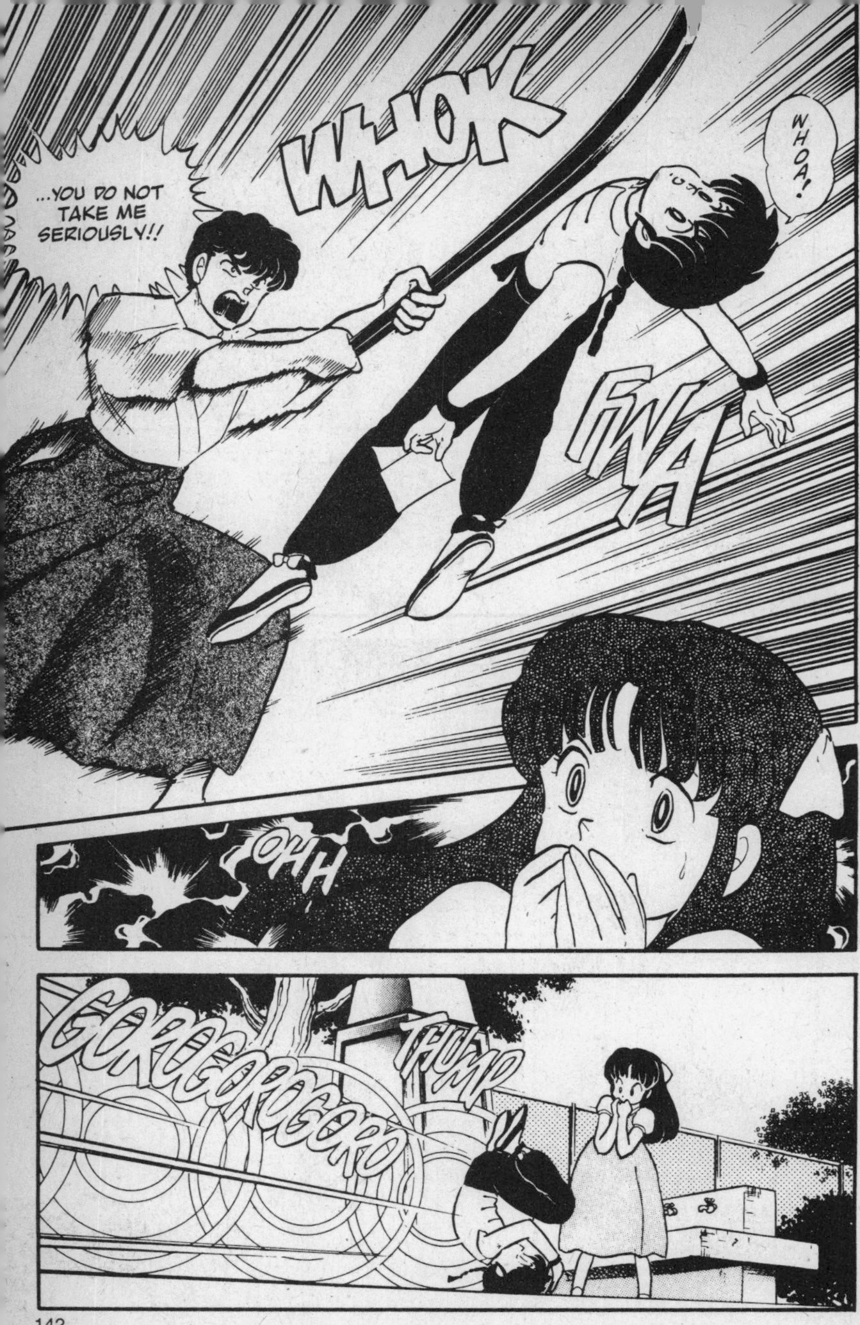

...YOU DO NOT TAKE ME SERIOUSLY!!
WHOK
WHOA!
FWA
OHH
GOROGOROGORO
THUMP

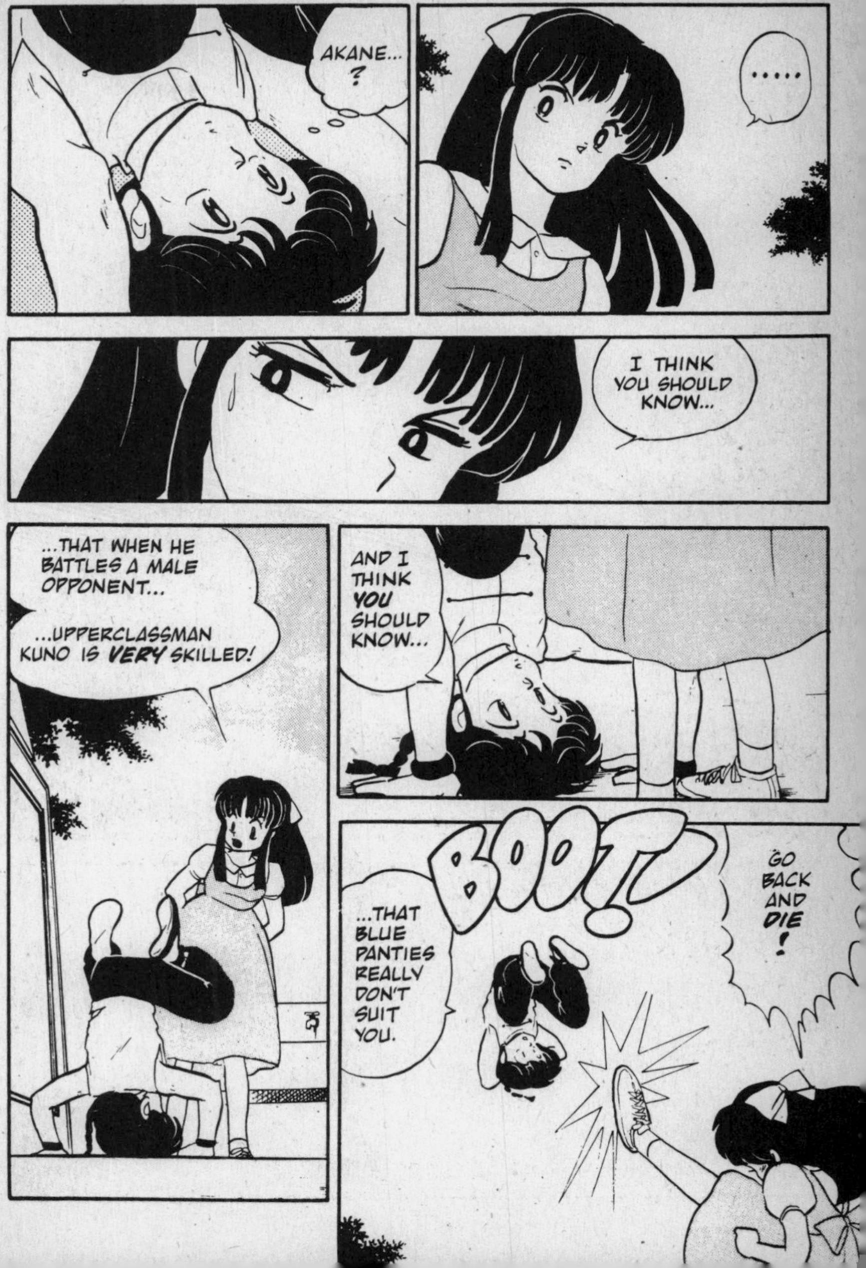
AKANE...
?
.....
I THINK YOU SHOULD KNOW...
...THAT WHEN HE BATTLES A MALE OPPONENT...
...UPPERCLASSMAN KUNO IS **VERY** SKILLED!
AND I THINK **YOU** SHOULD KNOW...
BOOT!
...THAT BLUE PANTIES REALLY DON'T SUIT YOU.
GO BACK AND **DIE**!

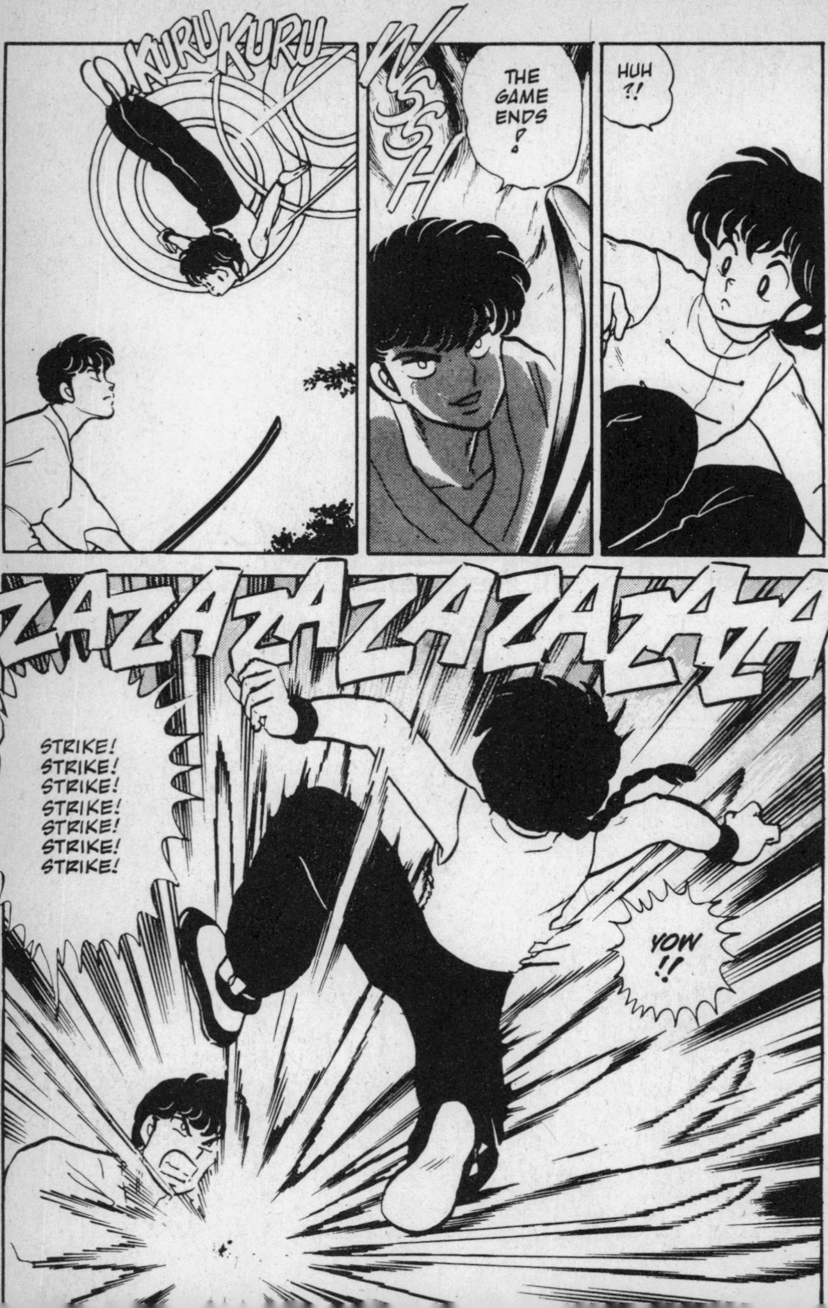
KURU KURU
WHSSH
THE GAME ENDS!
HUH ?!
ZAZAZAZAZAZAZAA
STRIKE! STRIKE! STRIKE! STRIKE! STRIKE! STRIKE! STRIKE!
YOW !!

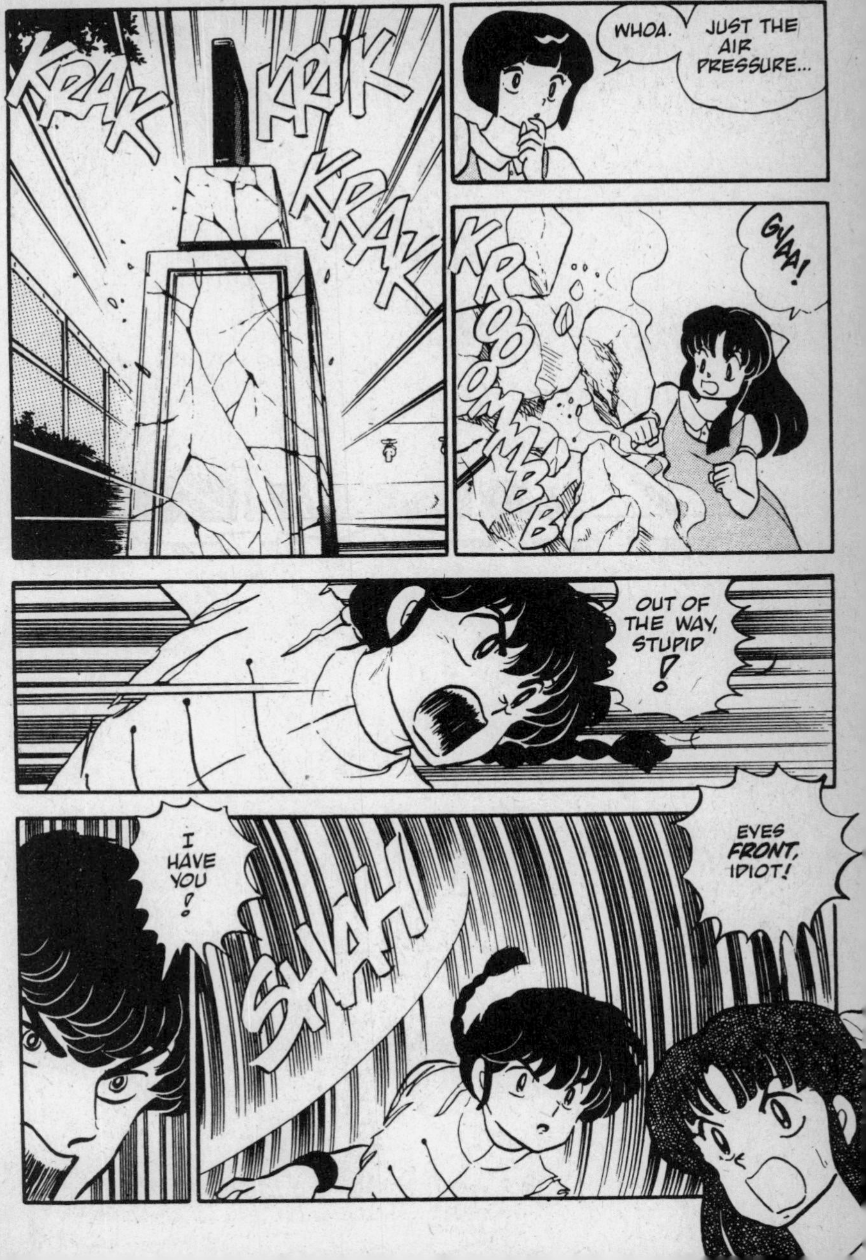
KRAK
KRIK
KRAK
KRAK
WHOA.
JUST THE AIR PRESSURE...
KRROOOMMBB
GYAAA!
OUT OF THE WAY, STUPID!
I HAVE YOU!
SHAH
EYES FRONT, IDIOT!

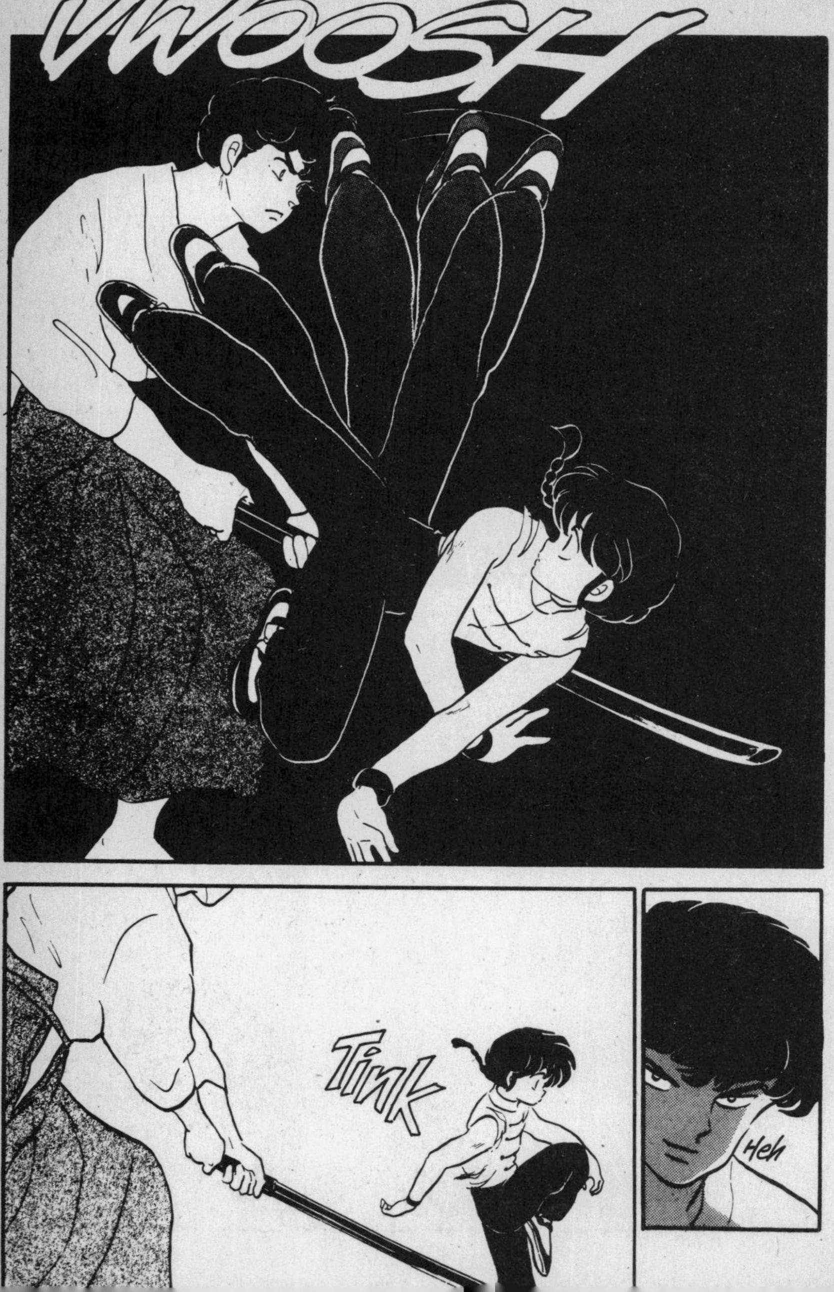
VVWOOSH
Tink
Heh

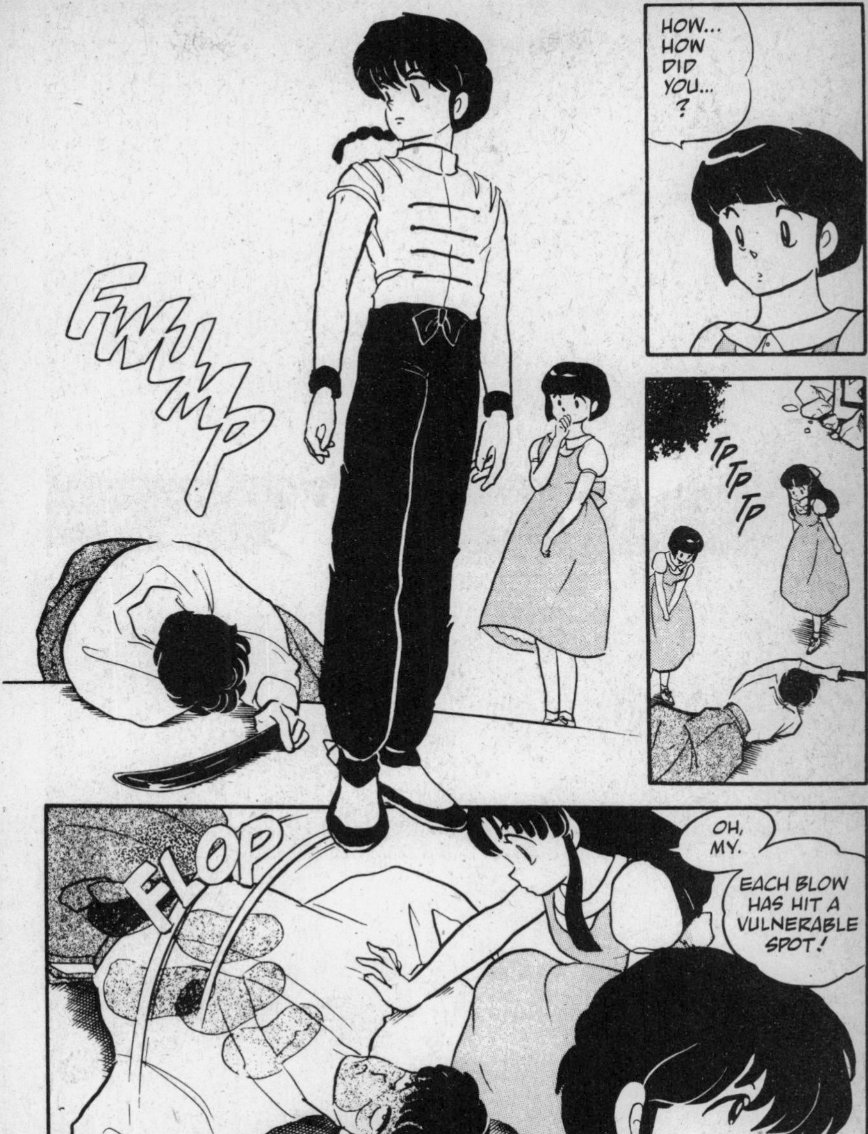
FWUMP
HOW... HOW DID YOU... ?
TP TP TP TP
FLOP
OH, MY.
EACH BLOW HAS HIT A VULNERABLE SPOT!

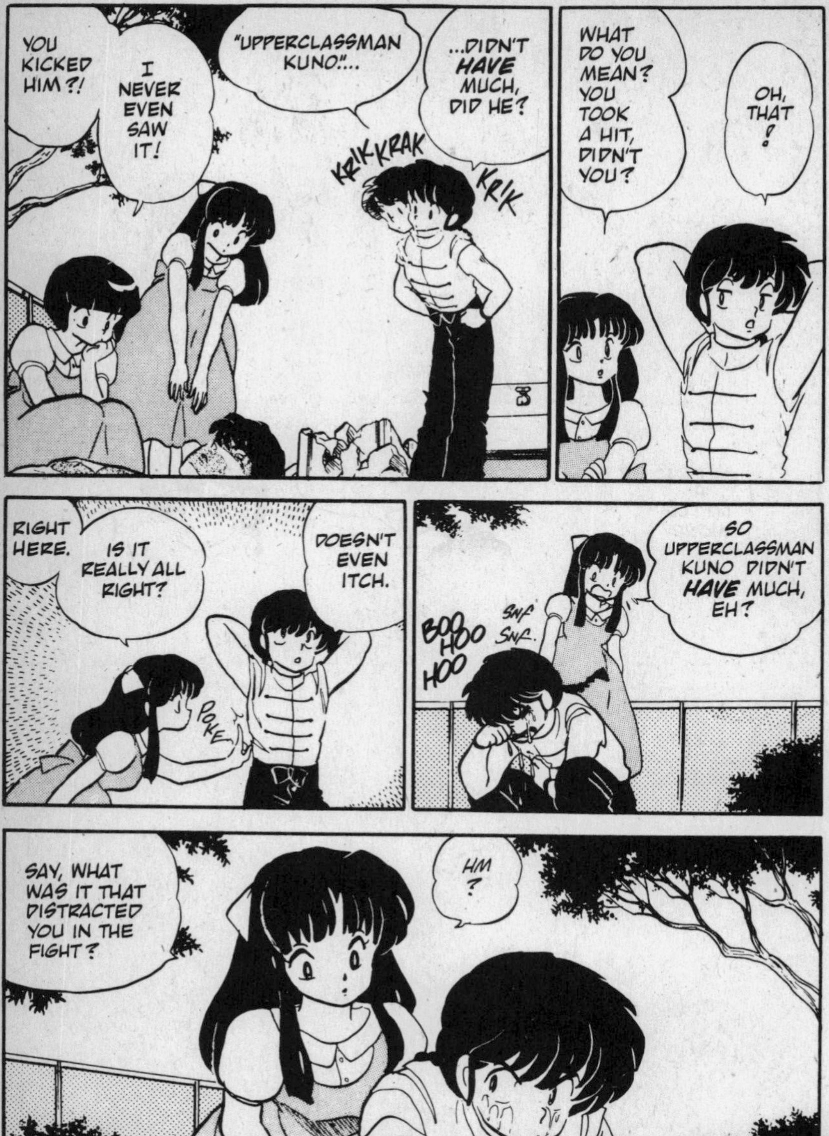
YOU KICKED HIM?!
I NEVER EVEN SAW IT!
"UPPERCLASSMAN KUNO"...
...DIDN'T HAVE MUCH, DID HE?
KRIK-KRAK
KRIK
WHAT DO YOU MEAN? YOU TOOK A HIT, DIDN'T YOU?
OH, THAT!
RIGHT HERE.
IS IT REALLY ALL RIGHT?
DOESN'T EVEN ITCH.
POKE
BOO HOO HOO
SNF SNF.
SO UPPERCLASSMAN KUNO DIDN'T HAVE MUCH, EH?
SAY, WHAT WAS IT THAT DISTRACTED YOU IN THE FIGHT?
HM?

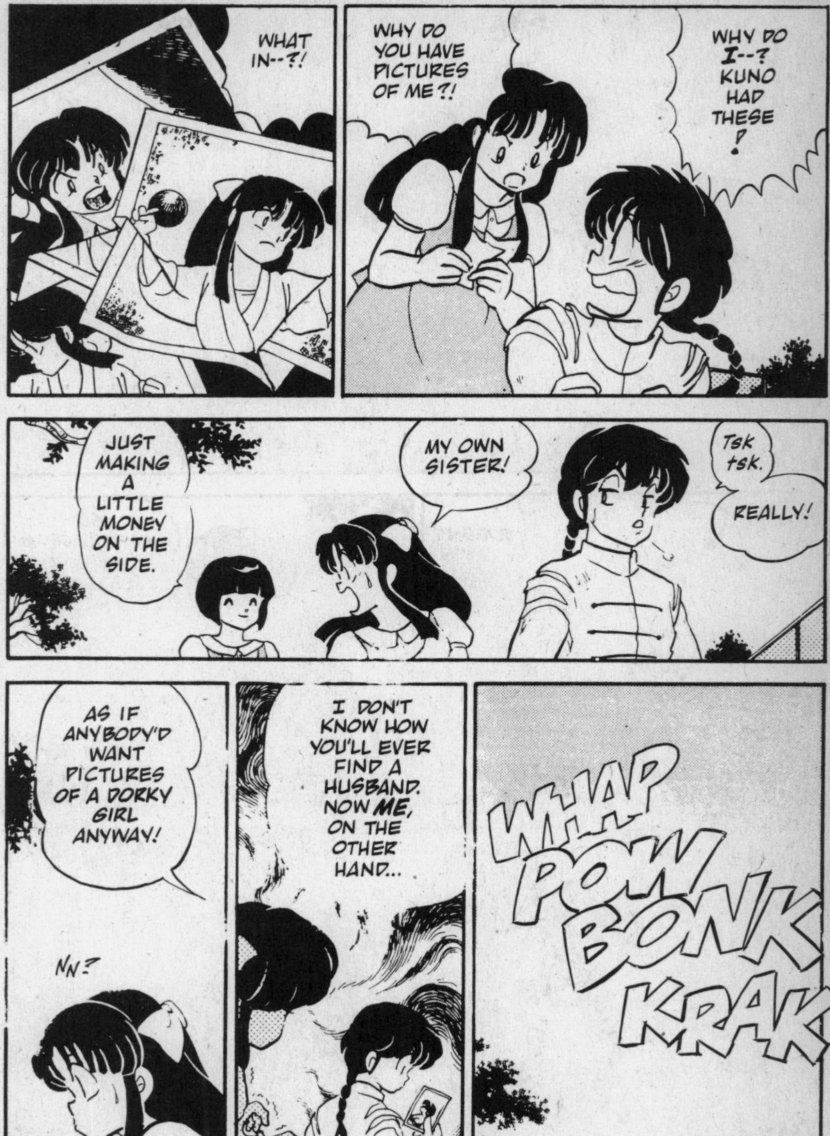
WHAT IN--?!
WHY DO YOU HAVE PICTURES OF ME?!
WHY DO I--? KUNO HAD THESE!
JUST MAKING A LITTLE MONEY ON THE SIDE.
MY OWN SISTER!
Tsk tsk.
REALLY!
AS IF ANYBODY'D WANT PICTURES OF A DORKY GIRL ANYWAY!
NN?
I DON'T KNOW HOW YOU'LL EVER FIND A HUSBAND. NOW ME, ON THE OTHER HAND...
WHAP
POW
BONK
KRAK

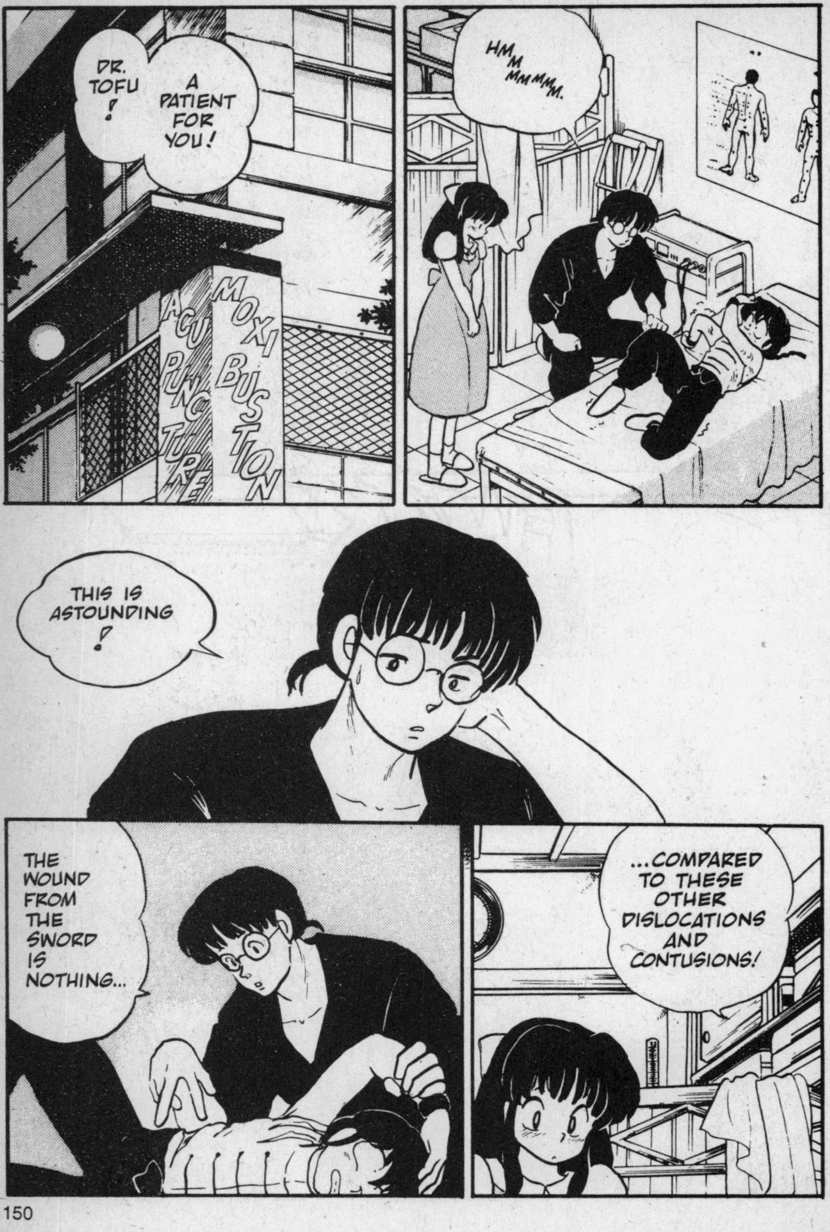
DR. TOFU!
A PATIENT FOR YOU!
ACUPUNCTURE
MOXIBUSTION
HMMMMMMM.
THIS IS ASTOUNDING!
THE WOUND FROM THE SWORD IS NOTHING...
...COMPARED TO THESE OTHER DISLOCATIONS AND CONTUSIONS!

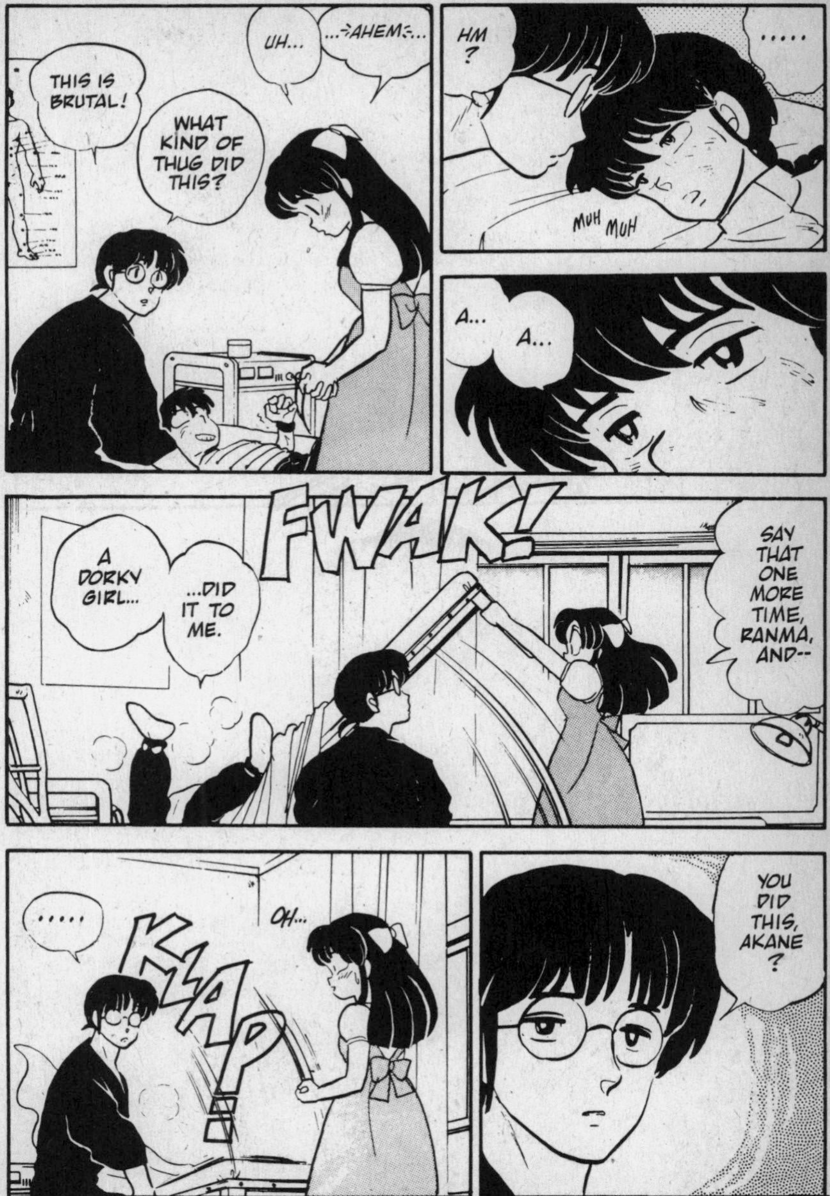
THIS IS BRUTAL!
WHAT KIND OF THUG DID THIS?
UH...
...AHEM...
HM ?
.....
MUH MUH
A...
A...
FWAK!
A DORKY GIRL...
...DID IT TO ME.
SAY THAT ONE MORE TIME, RANMA, AND--
.....
KLAP
OH...
YOU DID THIS, AKANE ?

UM... WELL...

...THAT IS...

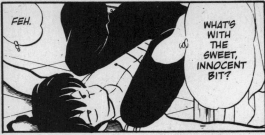

FEH.

WHAT'S WITH THE SWEET, INNOCENT BIT?

WHAP

MM?

WELL, IT FIGURES!

I HAD A FEELING!

HA HA HA HA HA HA HA HA HA HA!

THE WAY THIS JOINT'S TWISTED BACKWARDS, FOR INSTANCE...

POP

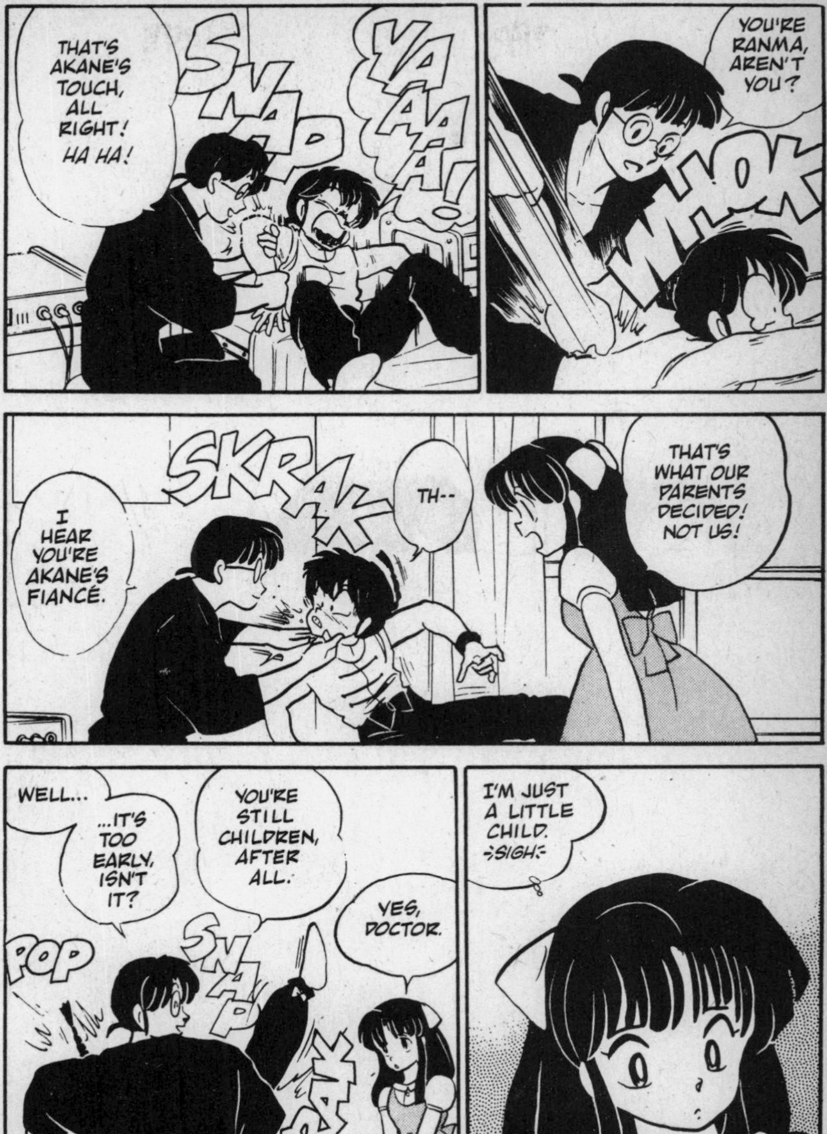
THAT'S AKANE'S TOUCH, ALL RIGHT! HA HA!
SNAP
YAAAA!
YOU'RE RANMA, AREN'T YOU?
WHOK
SKRAK
I HEAR YOU'RE AKANE'S FIANCÉ.
TH--
THAT'S WHAT OUR PARENTS DECIDED! NOT US!
WELL...
...IT'S TOO EARLY, ISN'T IT?
YOU'RE STILL CHILDREN, AFTER ALL.
POP
SNAP
YES, DOCTOR.
KRAK
I'M JUST A LITTLE CHILD.
SIGH

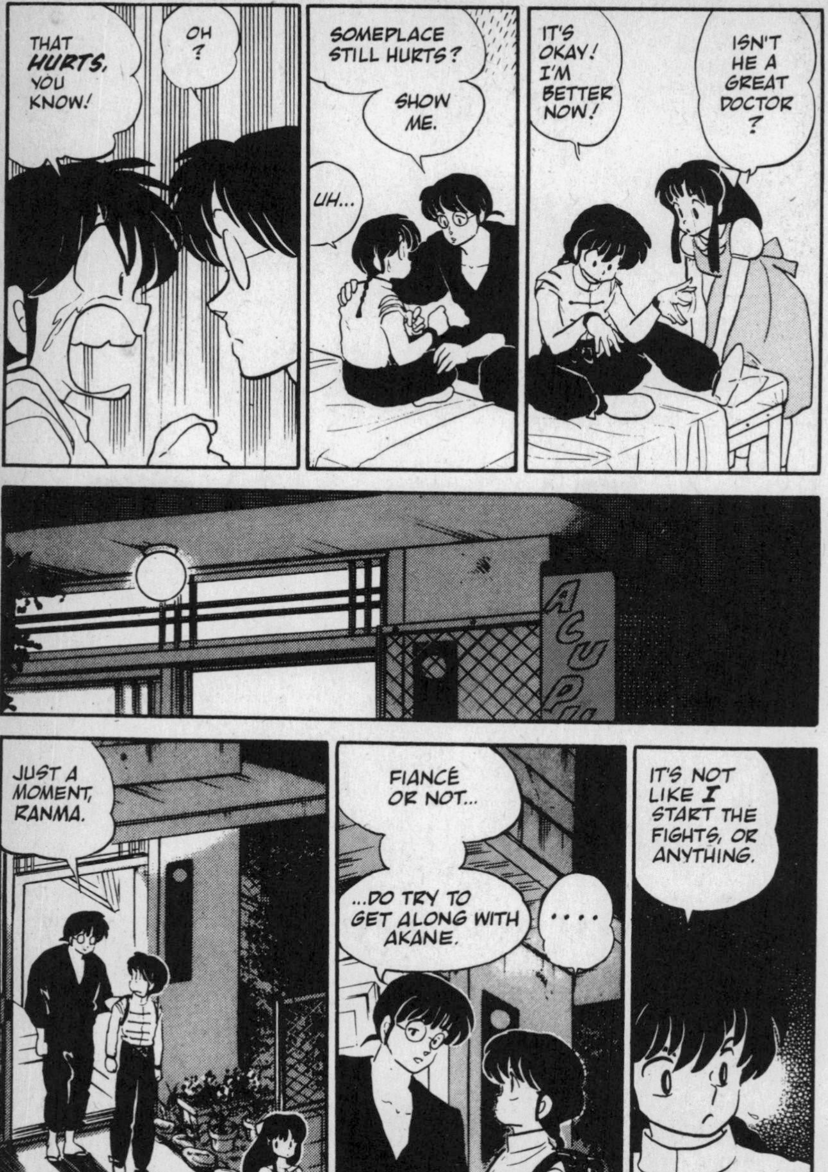
THAT **HURTS,** YOU KNOW!
OH ?
SOMEPLACE STILL HURTS?
SHOW ME.
UH...
IT'S OKAY! I'M BETTER NOW!
ISN'T HE A GREAT DOCTOR ?
JUST A MOMENT, RANMA.
FIANCÉ OR NOT...
...DO TRY TO GET ALONG WITH AKANE.
....
IT'S NOT LIKE **I** START THE FIGHTS, OR ANYTHING.

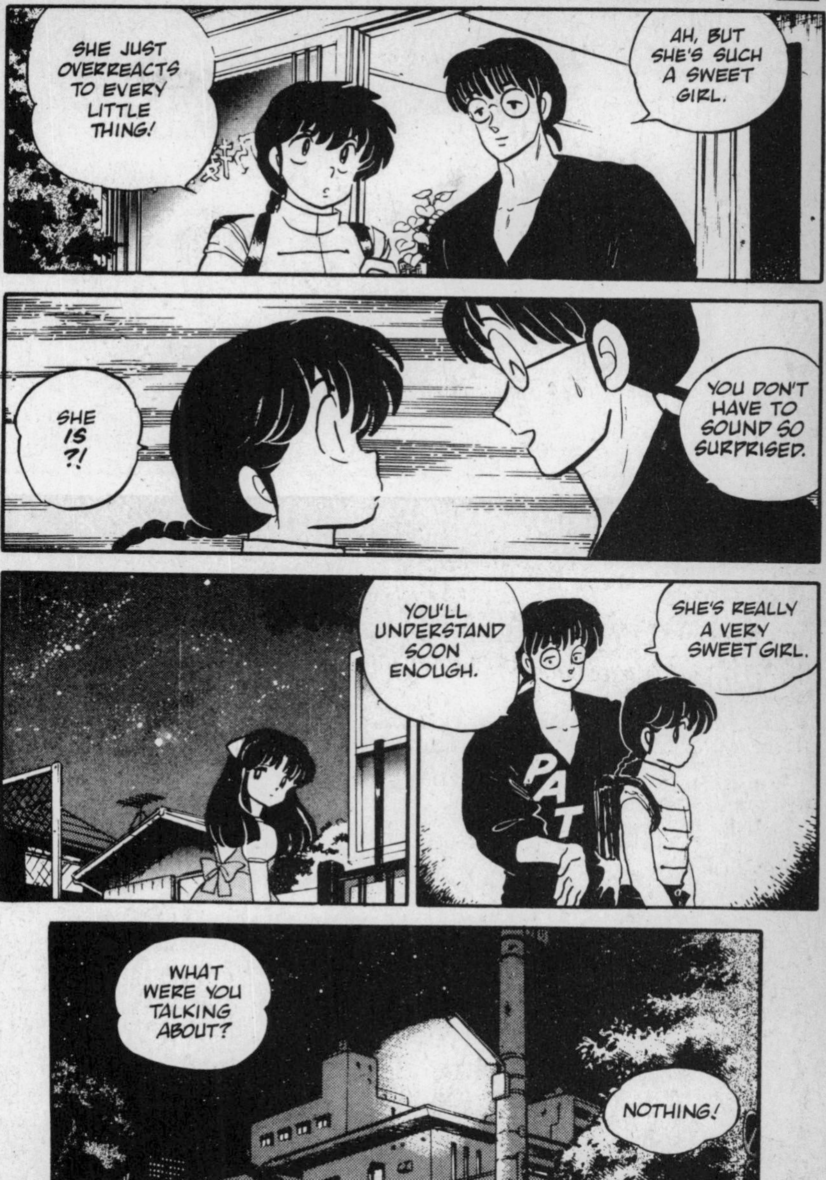
SHE JUST OVERREACTS TO EVERY LITTLE THING!
AH, BUT SHE'S SUCH A SWEET GIRL.
SHE IS ?!
YOU DON'T HAVE TO SOUND SO SURPRISED.
YOU'LL UNDERSTAND SOON ENOUGH.
SHE'S REALLY A VERY SWEET GIRL.
PAT
WHAT WERE YOU TALKING ABOUT?
NOTHING!

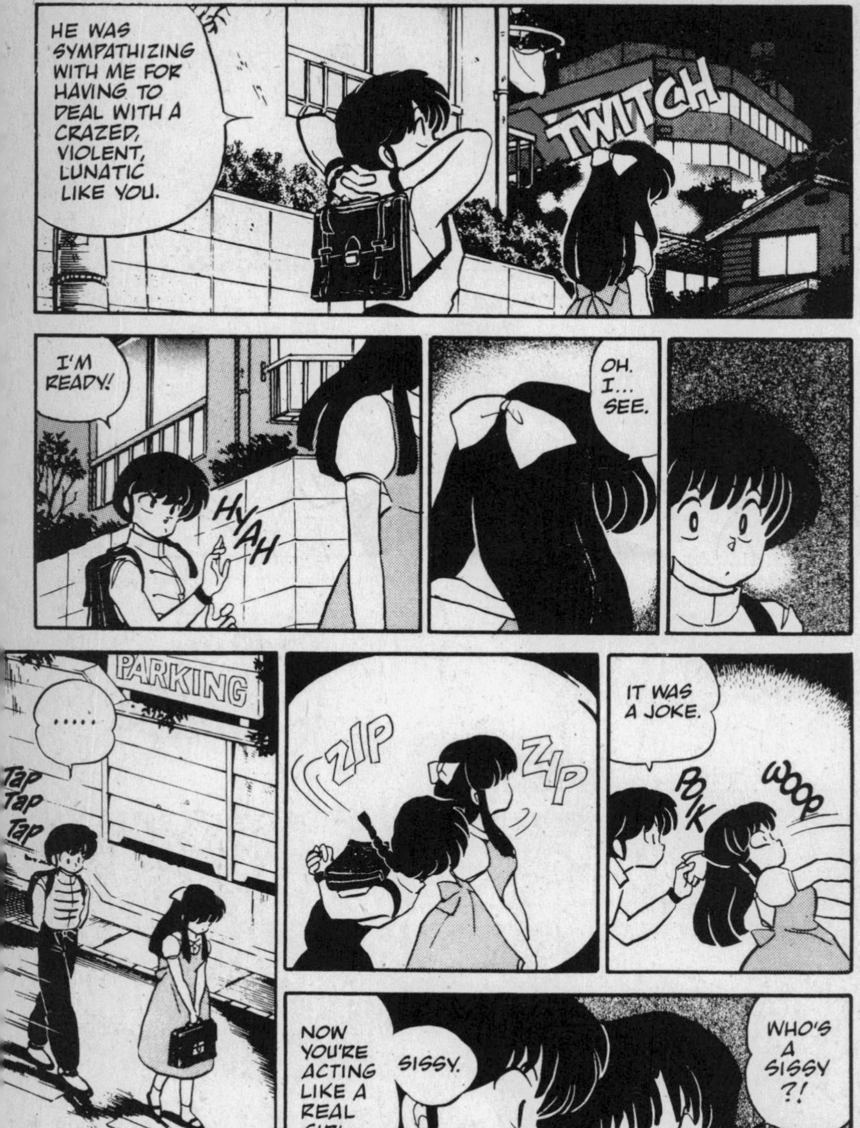
HE WAS SYMPATHIZING WITH ME FOR HAVING TO DEAL WITH A CRAZED, VIOLENT, LUNATIC LIKE YOU.
TWITCH
I'M READY!
HYAH
OH. I... SEE.
PARKING
.....
Tap Tap Tap
ZIP
ZIP
IT WAS A JOKE.
POIK
WOOP
NOW YOU'RE ACTING LIKE A REAL GIRL.
SISSY.
WHO'S A SISSY ?!

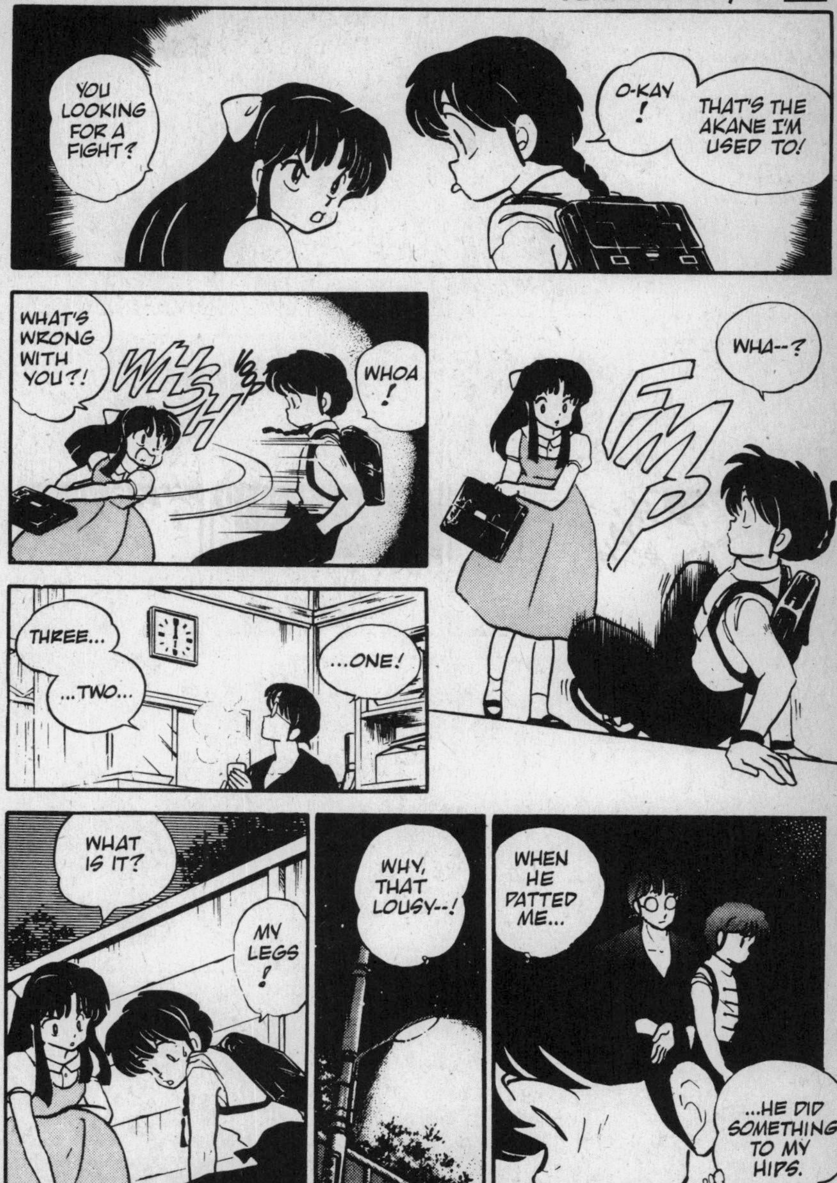
YOU LOOKING FOR A FIGHT?
O-KAY!
THAT'S THE AKANE I'M USED TO!
WHAT'S WRONG WITH YOU?!
WHSH
WHOA!
THREE...
...TWO...
...ONE!
WHA--?
FMP
WHAT IS IT?
MY LEGS!
WHY, THAT LOUSY--!
WHEN HE PATTED ME...
...HE DID SOMETHING TO MY HIPS.

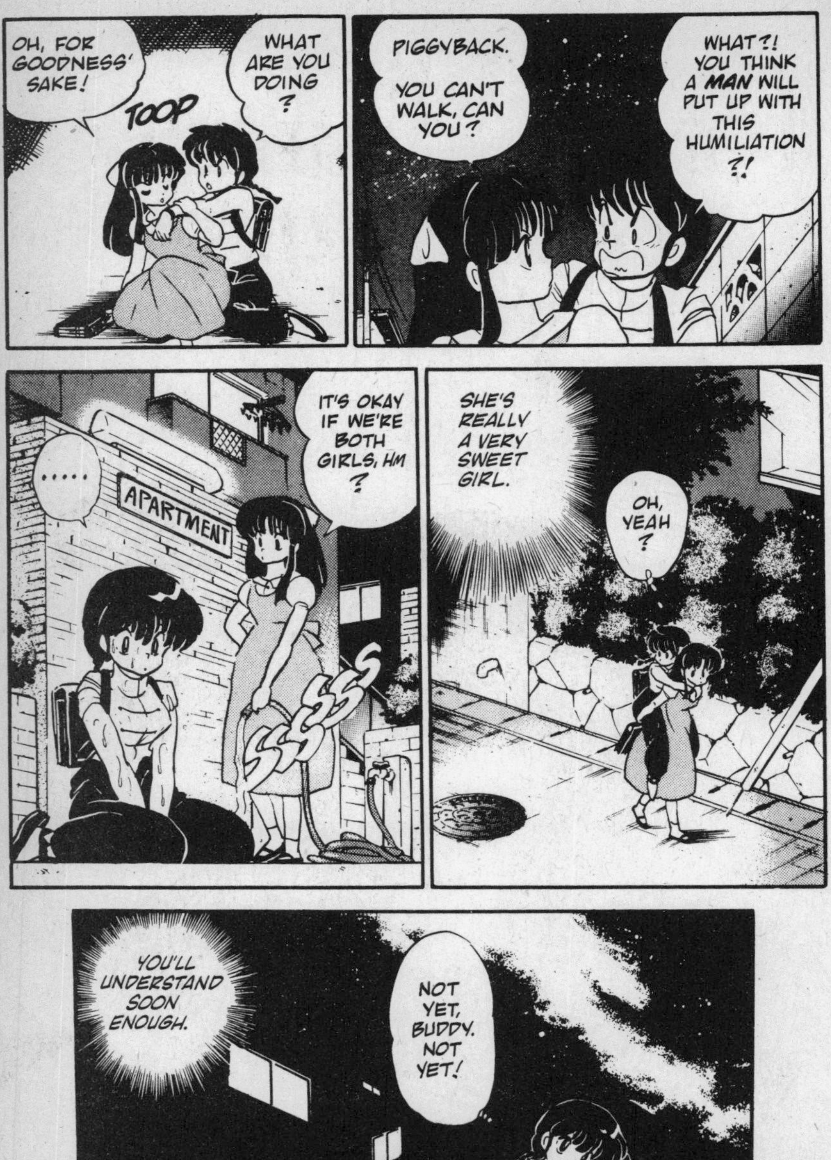
OH, FOR GOODNESS' SAKE!
TOOP
WHAT ARE YOU DOING?
PIGGYBACK.
YOU CAN'T WALK, CAN YOU?
WHAT?! YOU THINK A **MAN** WILL PUT UP WITH THIS HUMILIATION?!
.....
APARTMENT
IT'S OKAY IF WE'RE BOTH GIRLS, HM?
SSSSS
SHE'S REALLY A VERY SWEET GIRL.
OH, YEAH?
YOU'LL UNDERSTAND SOON ENOUGH.
NOT YET, BUDDY. NOT YET!

Part 8
BECAUSE THERE'S A GIRL HE LIKES

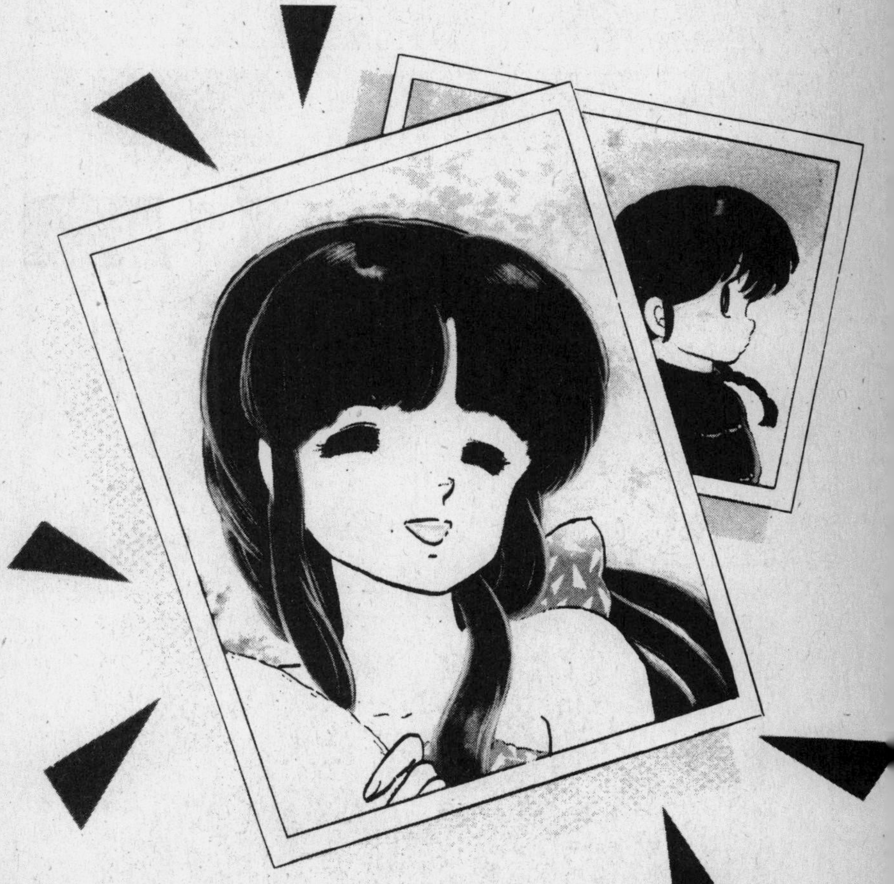

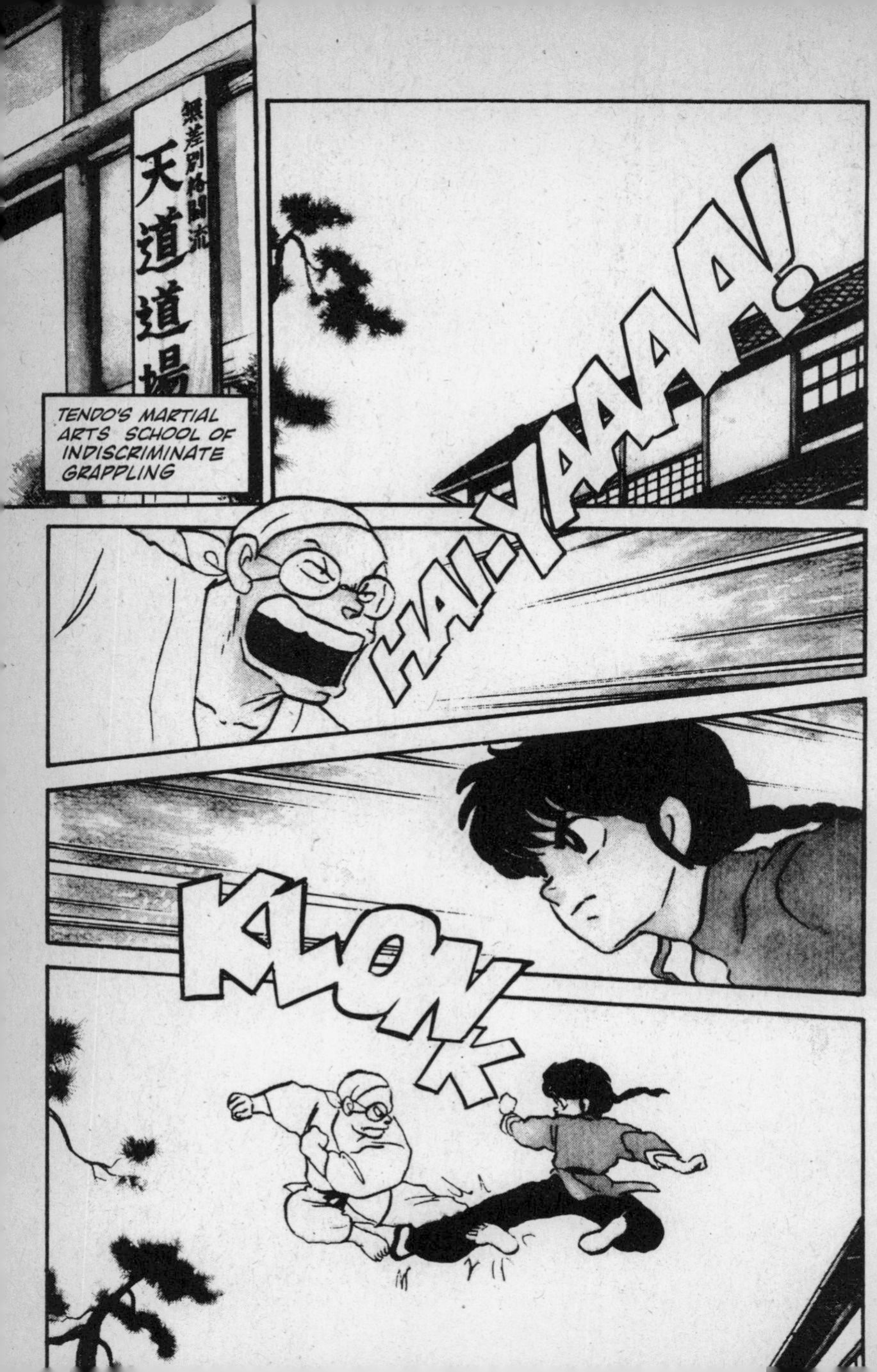
無差別格闘流
天道道場
TENDO'S MARTIAL ARTS SCHOOL OF INDISCRIMINATE GRAPPLING
HAI-YAAAA!
KLONK

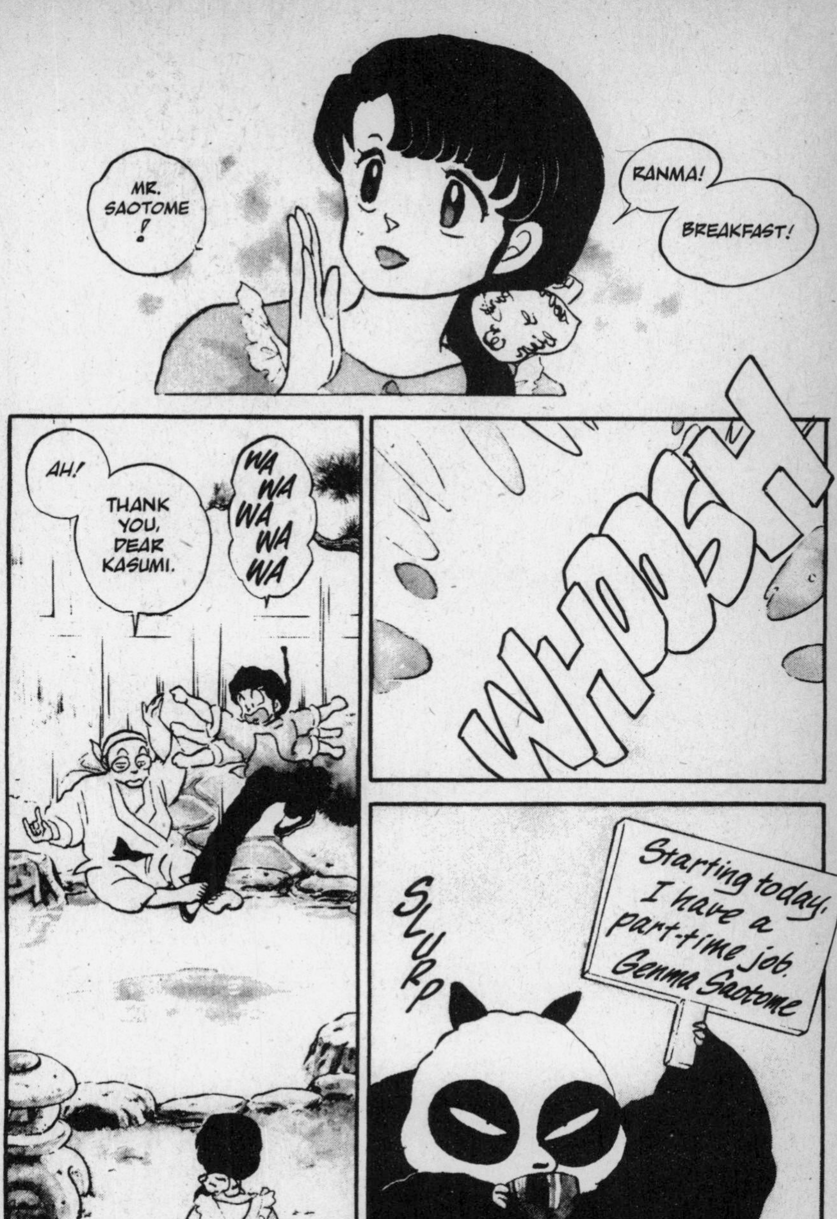
MR. SAOTOME!
RANMA!
BREAKFAST!
AH!
THANK YOU, DEAR KASUMI.
WA WA WA WA WA WA
WHOOSH!
SLURP
Starting today, I have a part-time job. Genma Saotome

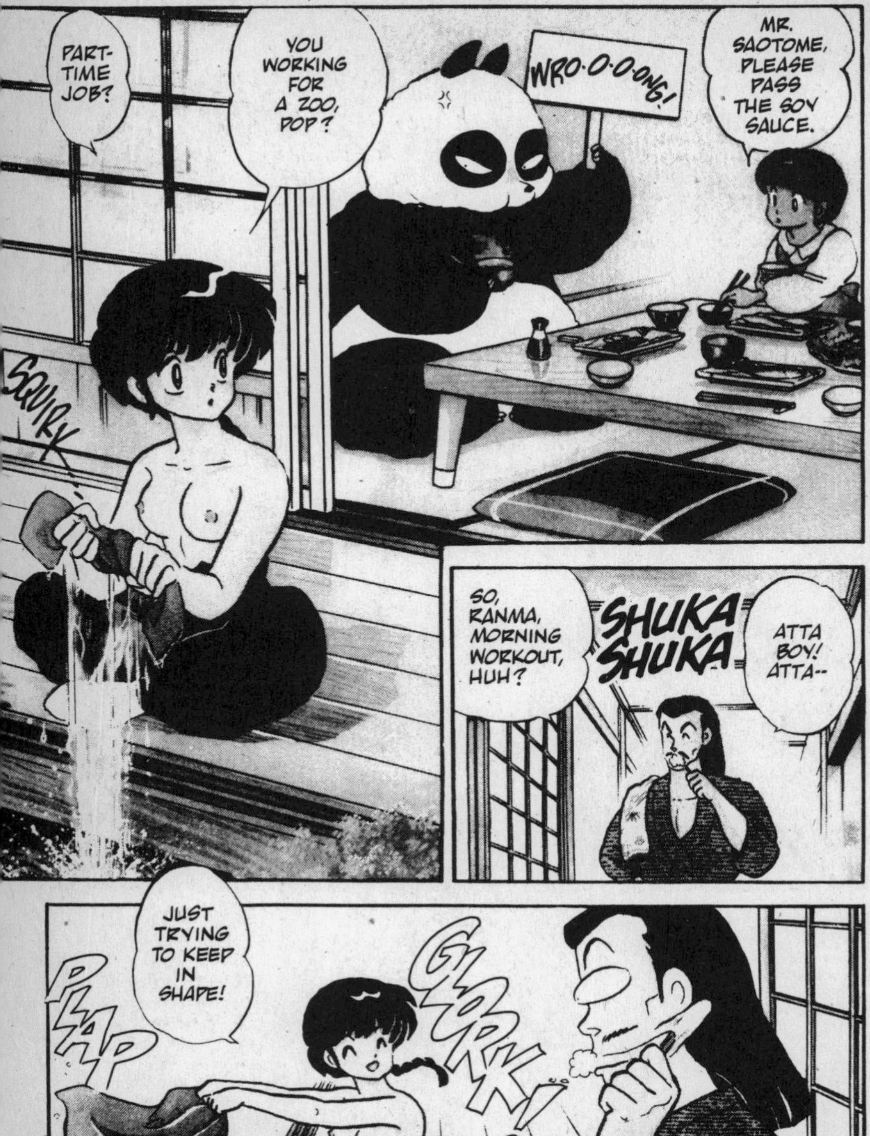
PART-TIME JOB?
YOU WORKING FOR A ZOO, POP?
WRO-O-O-ONG!
MR. SAOTOME, PLEASE PASS THE SOY SAUCE.
SQUIRK
SO, RANMA, MORNING WORKOUT, HUH?
SHUKA SHUKA
ATTA BOY! ATTA--
JUST TRYING TO KEEP IN SHAPE!
PLAP
GLORK!

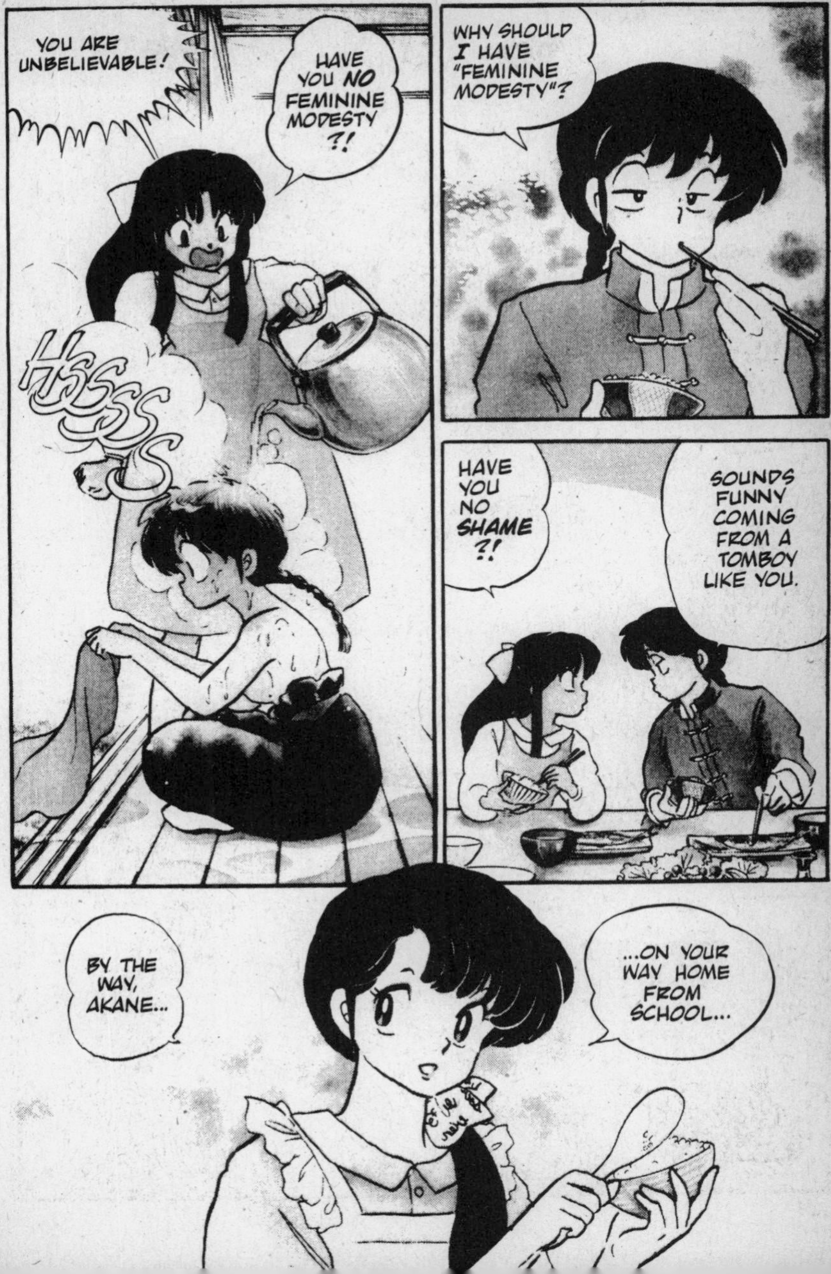
YOU ARE UNBELIEVABLE!
HAVE YOU NO FEMININE MODESTY ?!
HSSSSS
WHY SHOULD I HAVE "FEMININE MODESTY"?
HAVE YOU NO SHAME ?!
SOUNDS FUNNY COMING FROM A TOMBOY LIKE YOU.
BY THE WAY, AKANE...
...ON YOUR WAY HOME FROM SCHOOL...

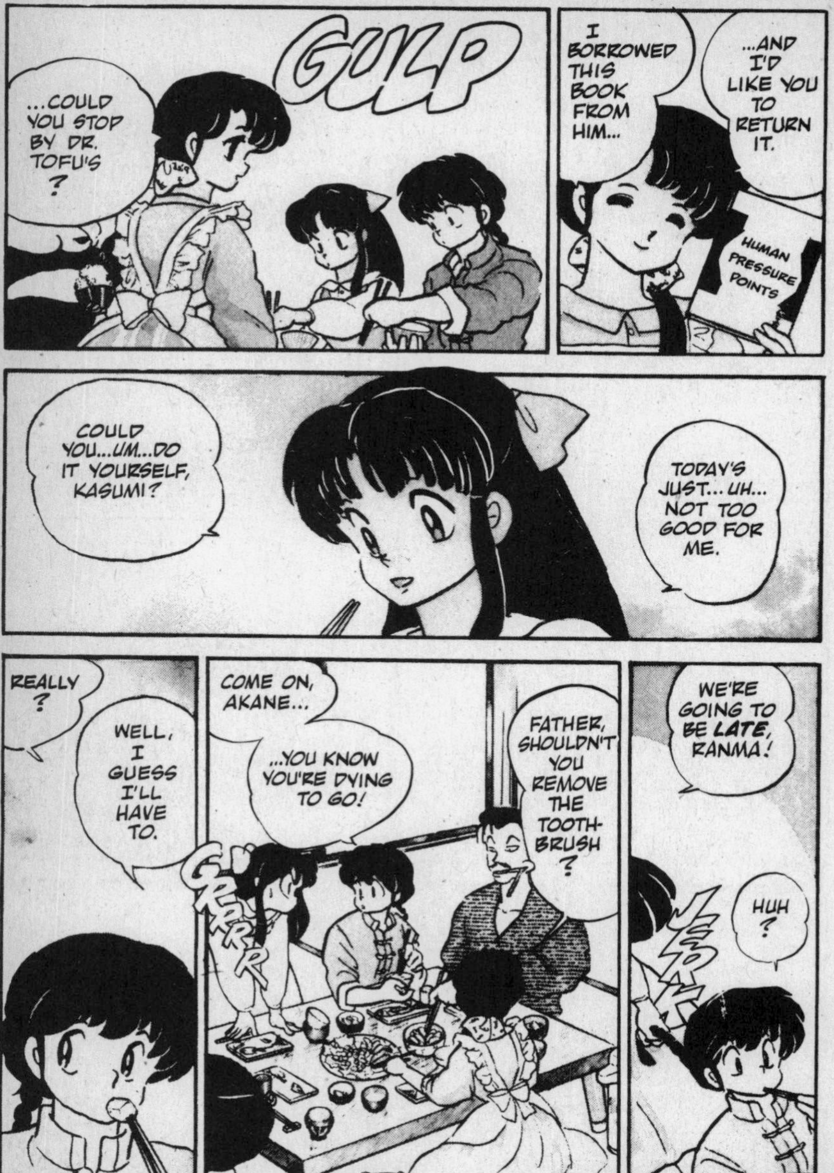
...COULD YOU STOP BY DR. TOFU'S?
GULP
I BORROWED THIS BOOK FROM HIM...
...AND I'D LIKE YOU TO RETURN IT.
HUMAN PRESSURE POINTS
COULD YOU...UM...DO IT YOURSELF, KASUMI?
TODAY'S JUST... UH... NOT TOO GOOD FOR ME.
REALLY?
WELL, I GUESS I'LL HAVE TO.
COME ON, AKANE...
...YOU KNOW YOU'RE DYING TO GO!
FATHER, SHOULDN'T YOU REMOVE THE TOOTH-BRUSH?
GRRR
WE'RE GOING TO BE *LATE*, RANMA!
HUH?

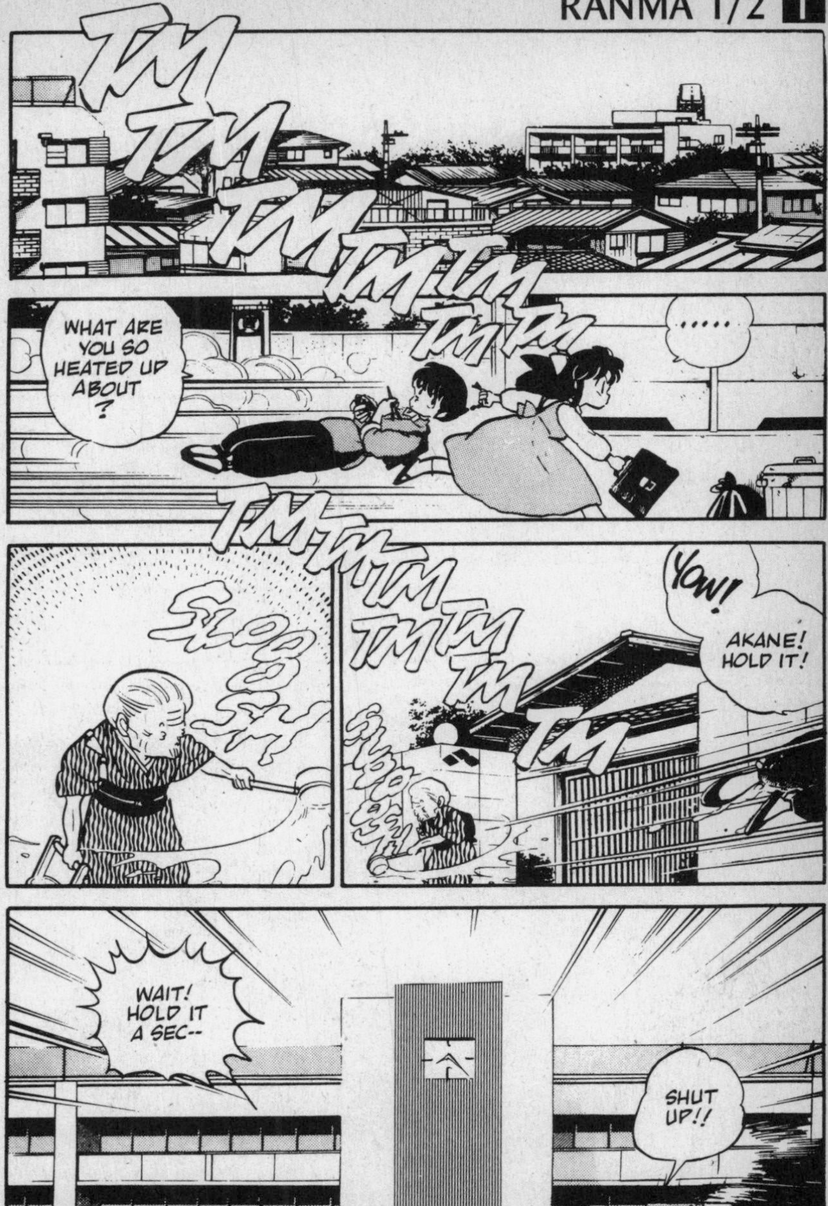
TM TM TM TM TM TM TM TM
WHAT ARE YOU SO HEATED UP ABOUT?
......
TM TM TM
SLOOSH
TM TM TM TM
SLOOSH
YOW!
AKANE! HOLD IT!
WAIT! HOLD IT A SEC--
SHUT UP!!

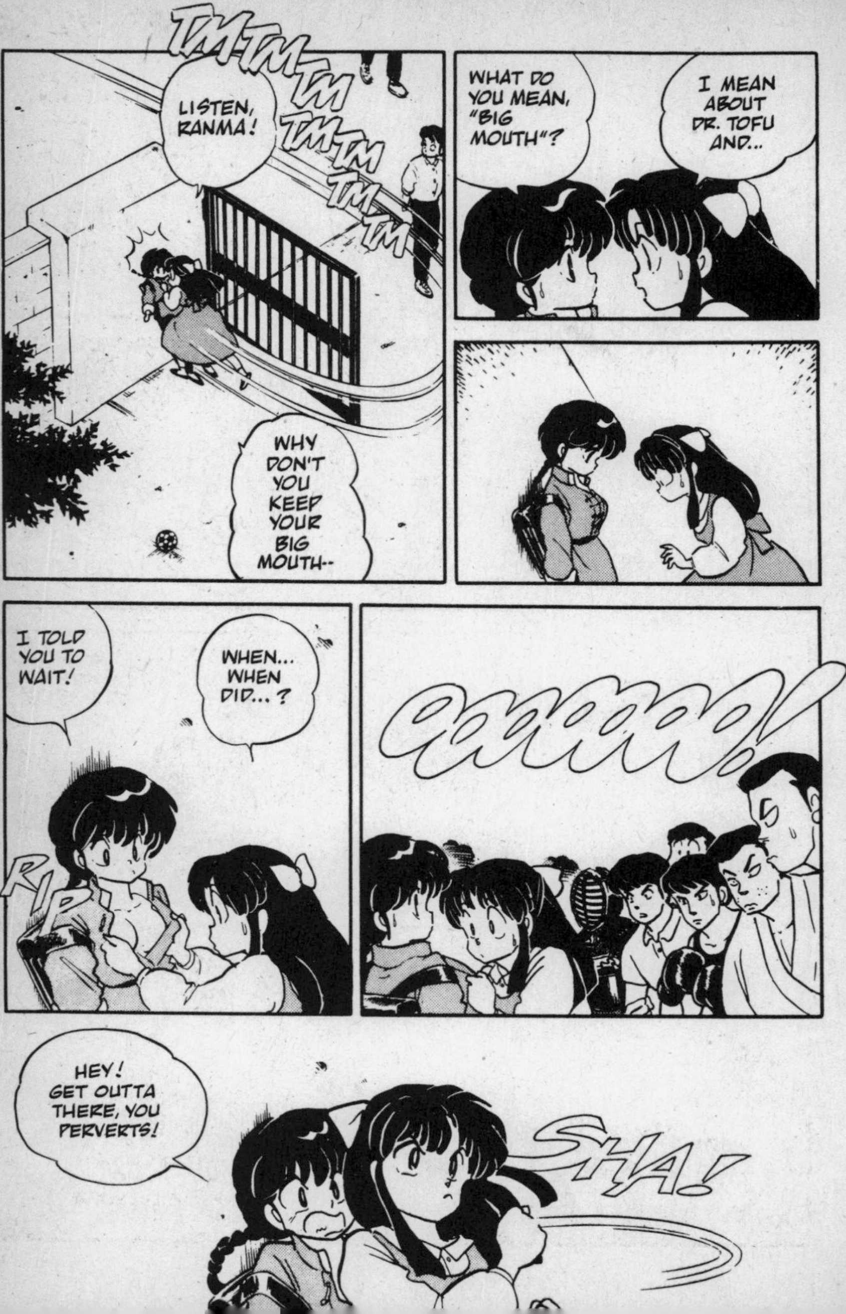
TM TM TM TM TM TM TM TM TM
LISTEN, RANMA!
WHY DON'T YOU KEEP YOUR BIG MOUTH--
WHAT DO YOU MEAN, "BIG MOUTH"?
I MEAN ABOUT DR. TOFU AND...
I TOLD YOU TO WAIT!
WHEN... WHEN DID...?
RIP
OOOOOO!
HEY! GET OUTTA THERE, YOU PERVERTS!
SHA!

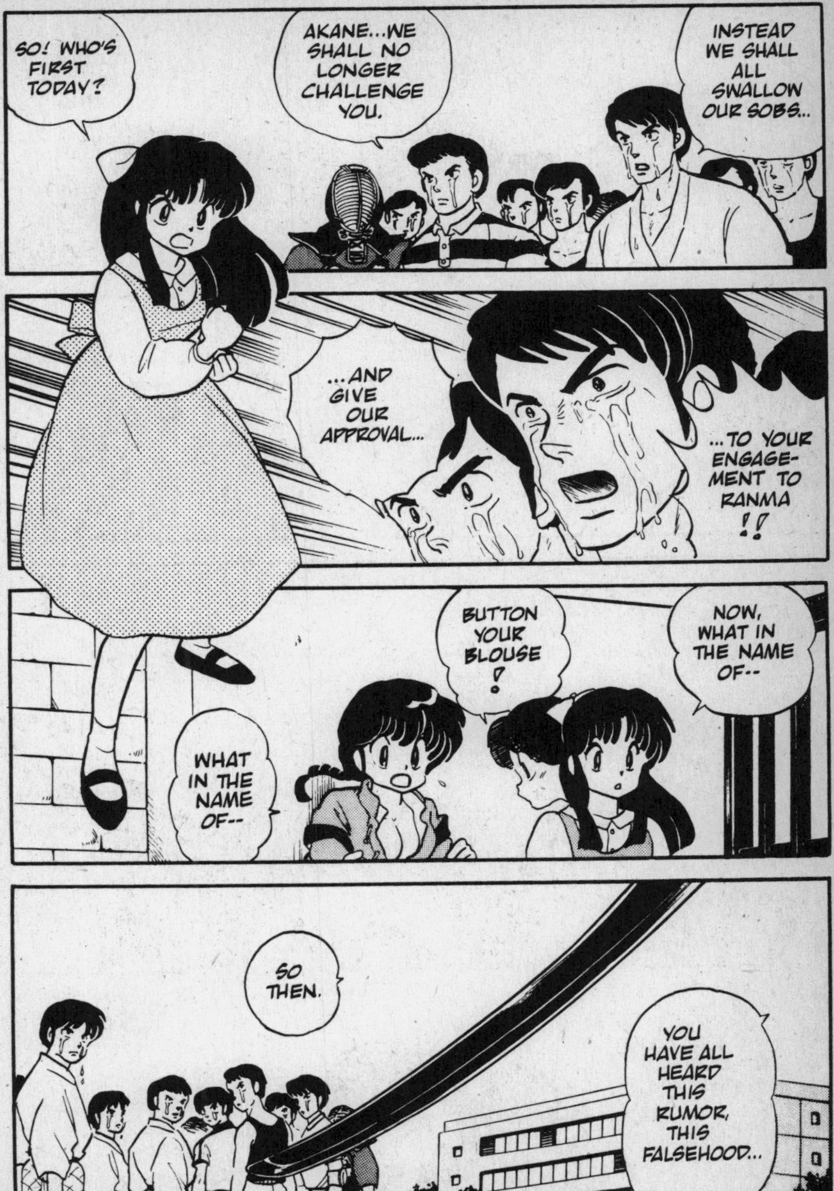
SO! WHO'S FIRST TODAY?
AKANE...WE SHALL NO LONGER CHALLENGE YOU.
INSTEAD WE SHALL ALL SWALLOW OUR SOBS...
...AND GIVE OUR APPROVAL...
...TO YOUR ENGAGEMENT TO RANMA!!
BUTTON YOUR BLOUSE!
NOW, WHAT IN THE NAME OF--
WHAT IN THE NAME OF--
SO THEN.
YOU HAVE ALL HEARD THIS RUMOR, THIS FALSEHOOD...

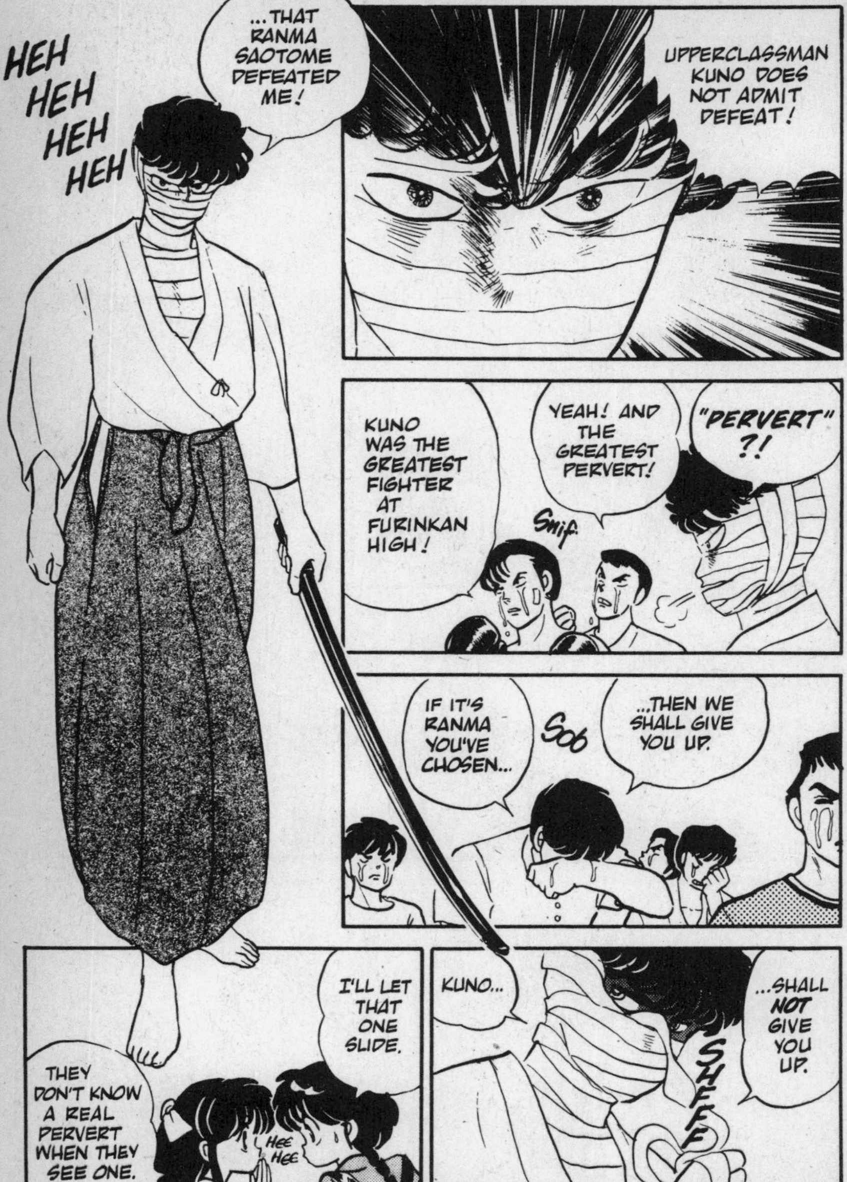
HEH HEH HEH HEH
...THAT RANMA SAOTOME DEFEATED ME!
UPPERCLASSMAN KUNO DOES NOT ADMIT DEFEAT!
KUNO WAS THE GREATEST FIGHTER AT FURINKAN HIGH!
YEAH! AND THE GREATEST PERVERT!
Snif.
"PERVERT" ?!
IF IT'S RANMA YOU'VE CHOSEN...
Sob
...THEN WE SHALL GIVE YOU UP.
I'LL LET THAT ONE SLIDE.
THEY DON'T KNOW A REAL PERVERT WHEN THEY SEE ONE.
HEE HEE
KUNO...
...SHALL NOT GIVE YOU UP.
SHFFF

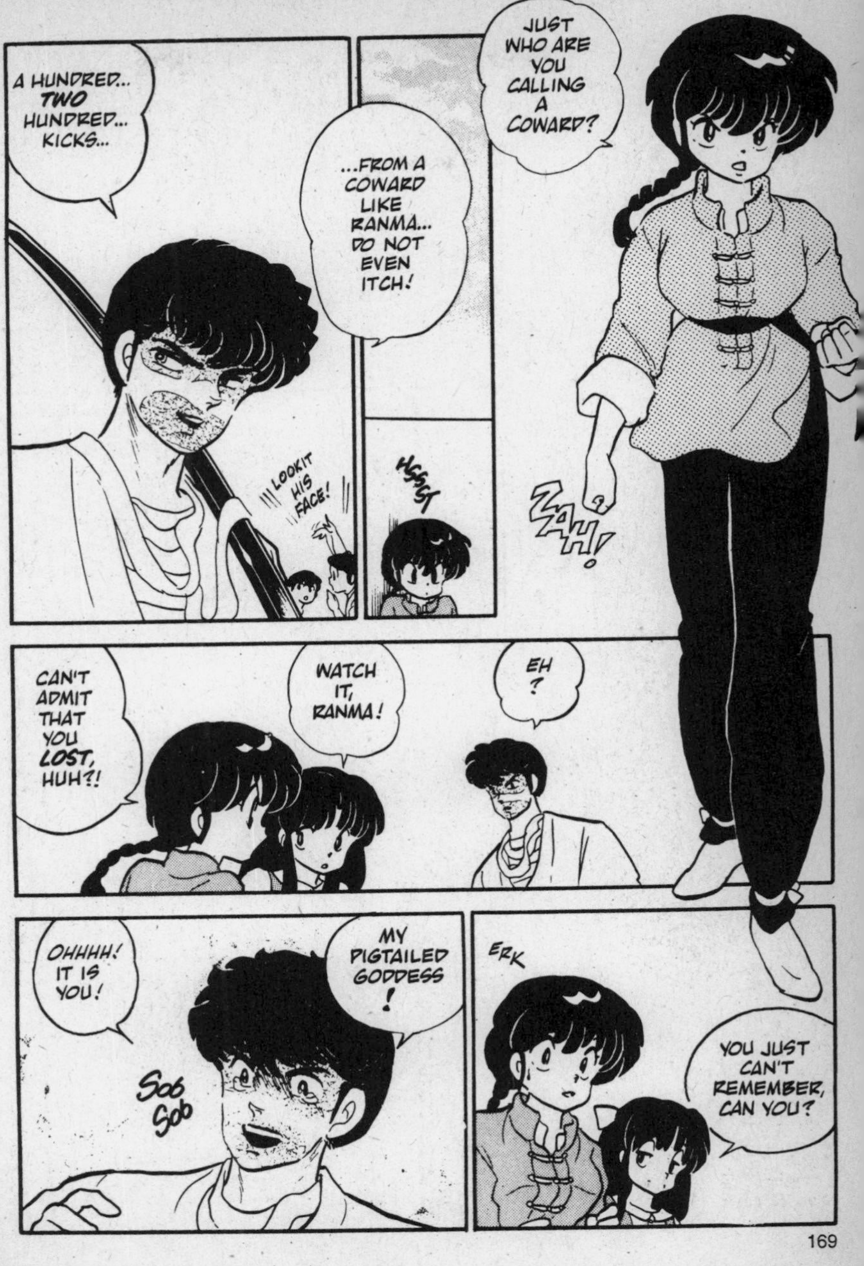
A HUNDRED... TWO HUNDRED... KICKS...
LOOKIT HIS FACE!
...FROM A COWARD LIKE RANMA... DO NOT EVEN ITCH!
HSSST
JUST WHO ARE YOU CALLING A COWARD?
ZAAH!
CAN'T ADMIT THAT YOU LOST, HUH?!
WATCH IT, RANMA!
EH?
OHHHH! IT IS YOU!
MY PIGTAILED GODDESS!
Sob Sob
ERK
YOU JUST CAN'T REMEMBER, CAN YOU?

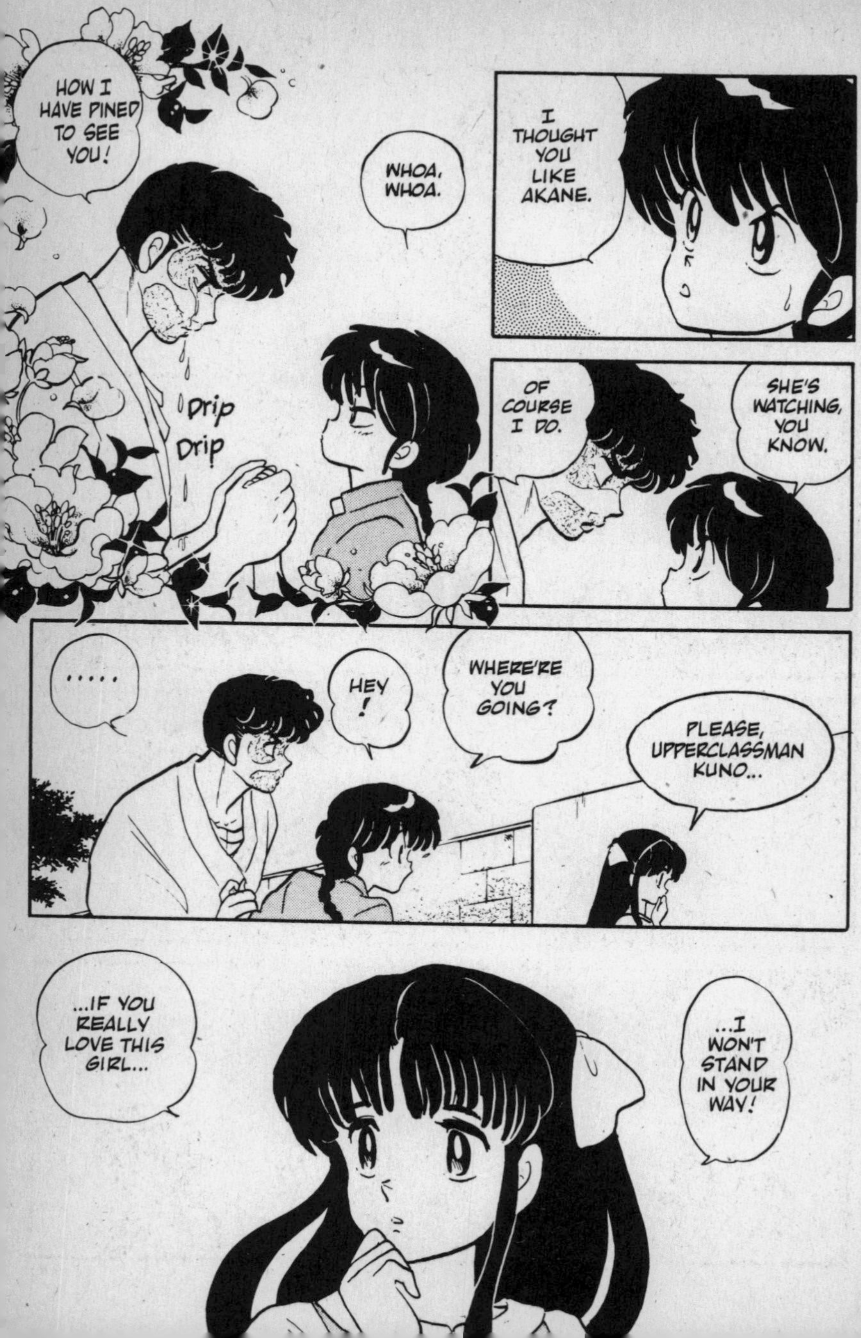
HOW I HAVE PINED TO SEE YOU!
WHOA, WHOA.
Drip
Drip
I THOUGHT YOU LIKE AKANE.
OF COURSE I DO.
SHE'S WATCHING, YOU KNOW.
.....
HEY!
WHERE'RE YOU GOING?
PLEASE, UPPERCLASSMAN KUNO...
...IF YOU REALLY LOVE THIS GIRL...
...I WON'T STAND IN YOUR WAY!

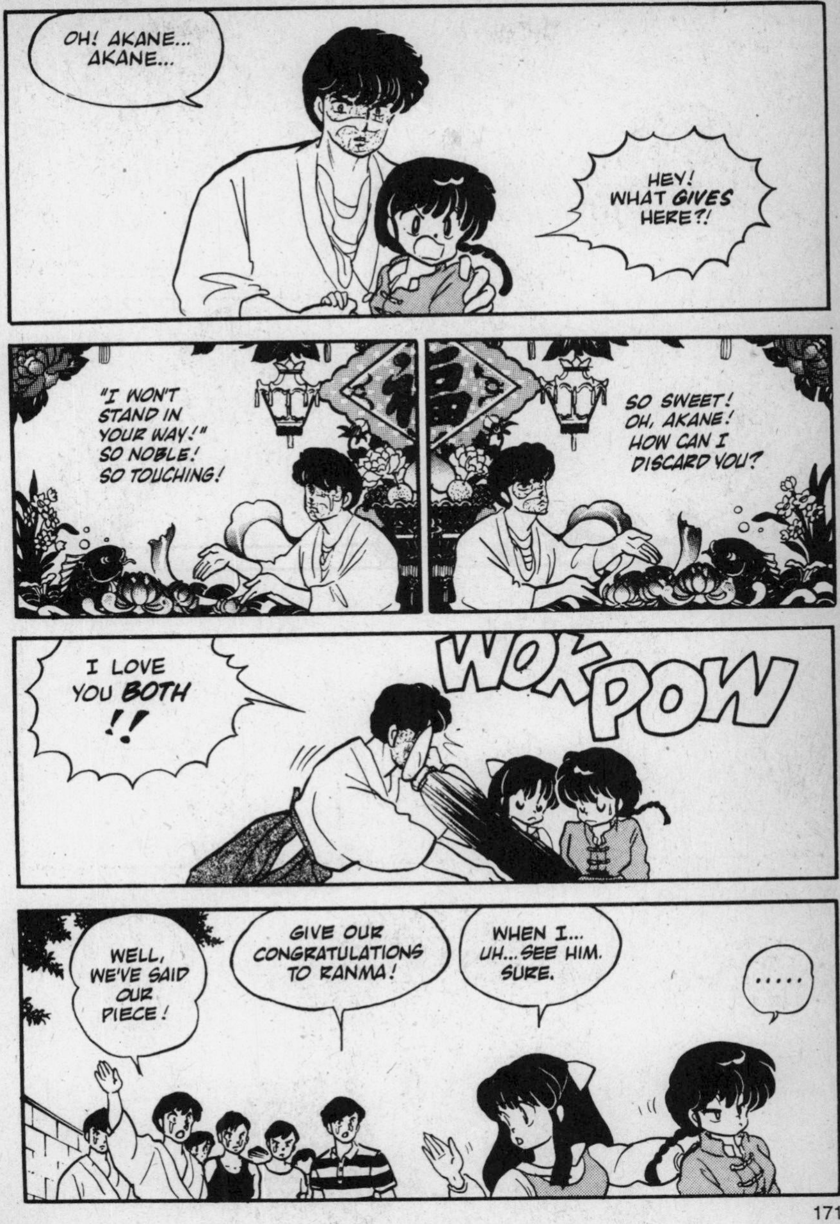
OH! AKANE... AKANE...
HEY! WHAT GIVES HERE?!
"I WON'T STAND IN YOUR WAY!" SO NOBLE! SO TOUCHING!
SO SWEET! OH, AKANE! HOW CAN I DISCARD YOU?
I LOVE YOU BOTH !!
WOK POW
WELL, WE'VE SAID OUR PIECE!
GIVE OUR CONGRATULATIONS TO RANMA!
WHEN I... UH... SEE HIM. SURE.
.....

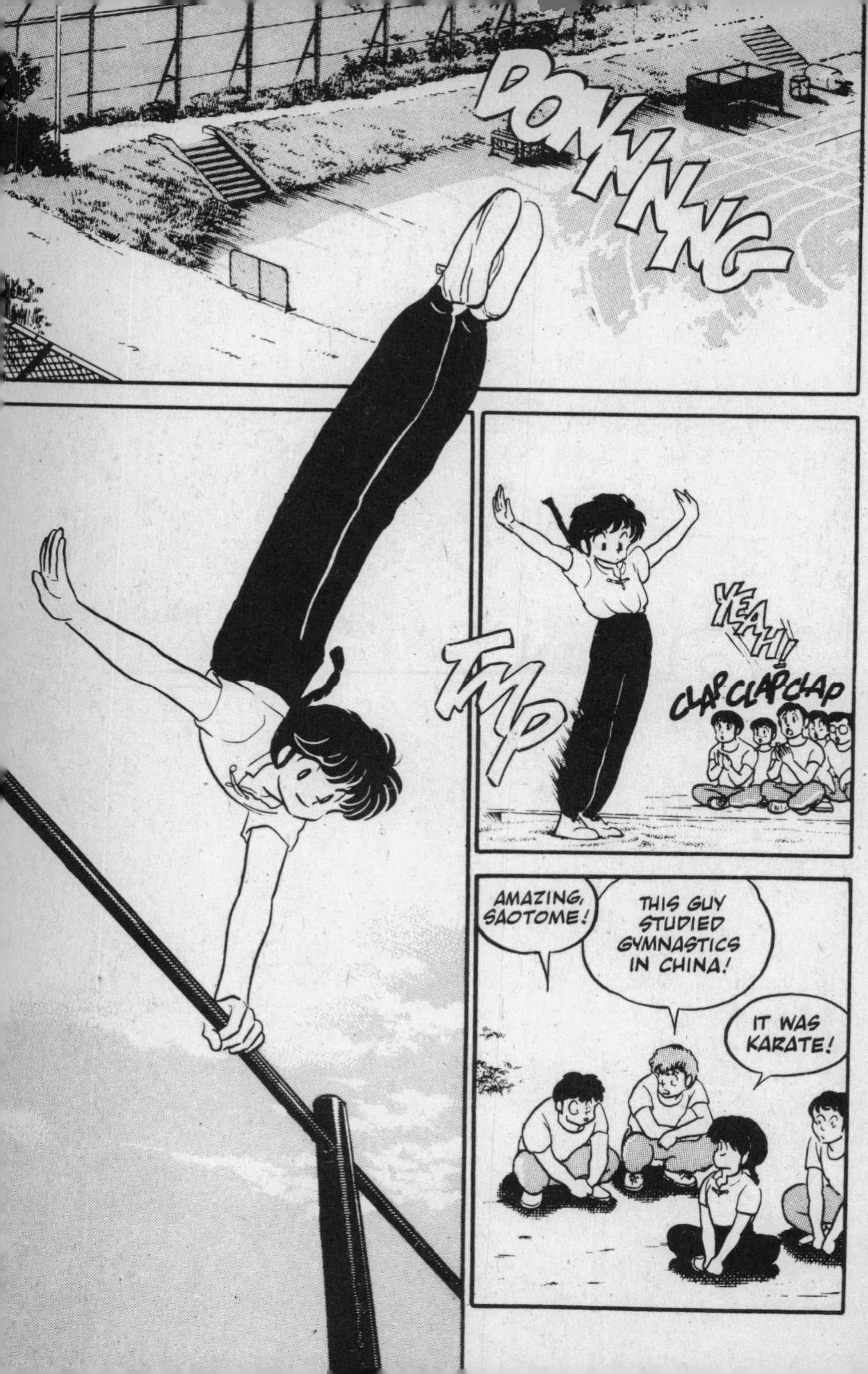
DOINNNG
TMP
YEAH!!
CLAP CLAP CLAP
AMAZING, SAOTOME!
THIS GUY STUDIED GYMNASTICS IN CHINA!
IT WAS KARATE!

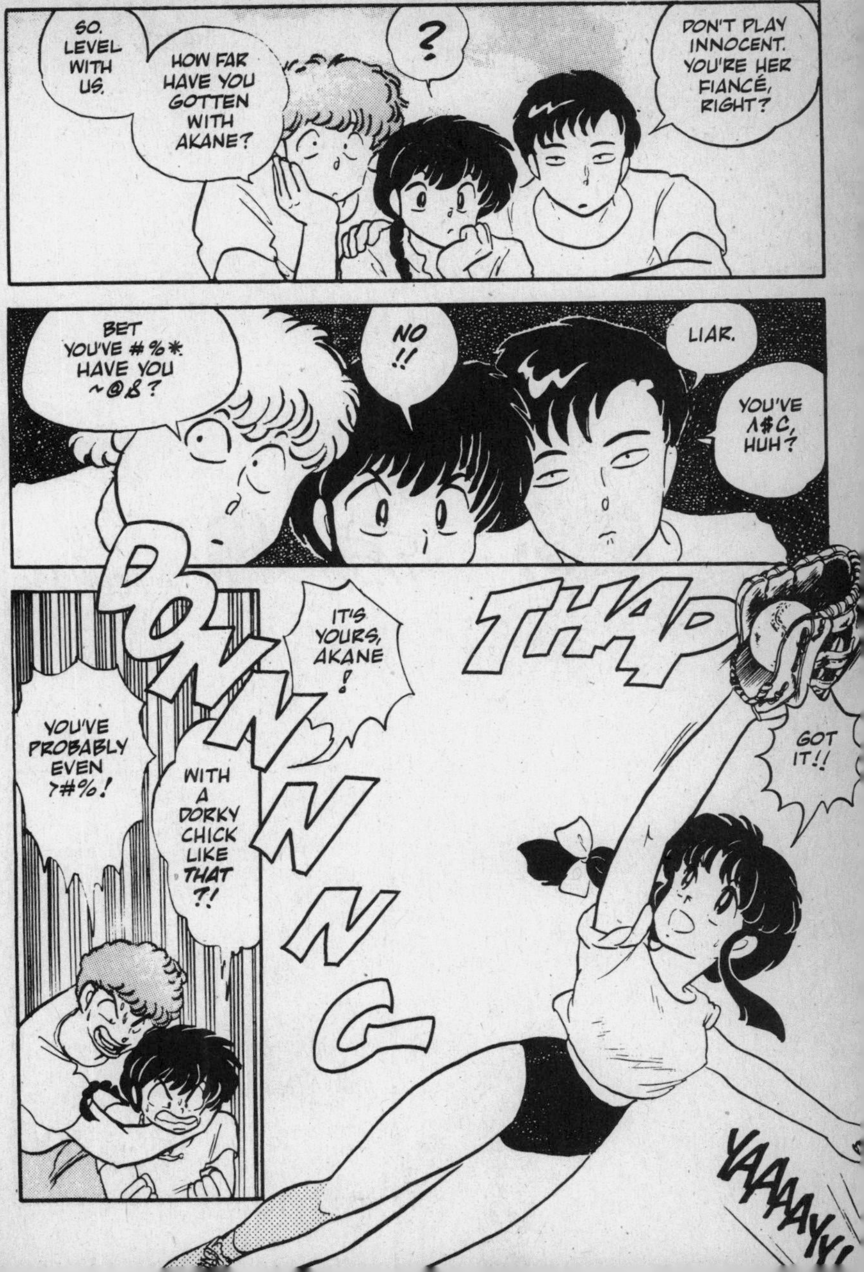
SO. LEVEL WITH US.
HOW FAR HAVE YOU GOTTEN WITH AKANE?
?
DON'T PLAY INNOCENT. YOU'RE HER FIANCÉ, RIGHT?
BET YOU'VE #%*. HAVE YOU ~@&?
NO !!
LIAR.
YOU'VE ^$C, HUH?
DONNNNG
YOU'VE PROBABLY EVEN ?#%!
IT'S YOURS, AKANE!
WITH A DORKY CHICK LIKE THAT?!
THAP
GOT IT!!
YAAAAYY!

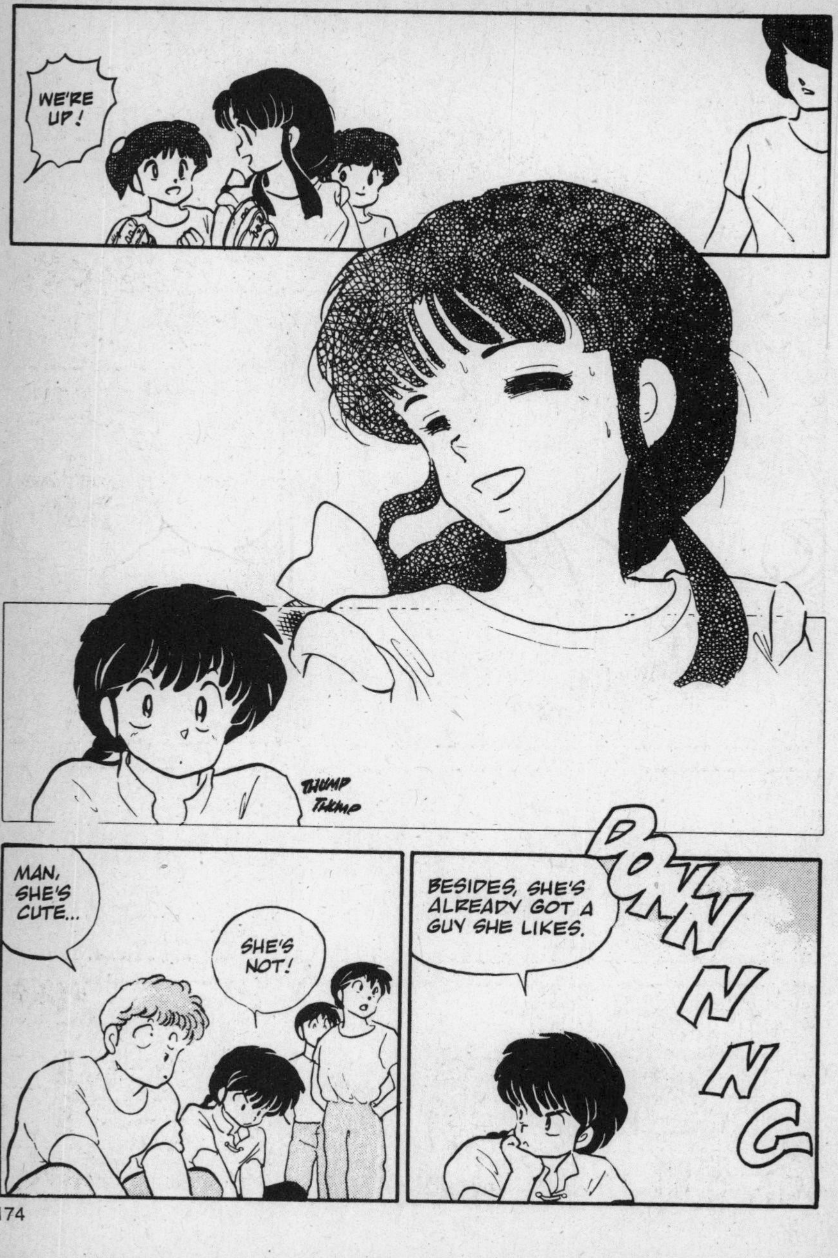
WE'RE UP!
THUMP THUMP
MAN, SHE'S CUTE...
SHE'S NOT!
BESIDES, SHE'S ALREADY GOT A GUY SHE LIKES.
DOWNNNNG

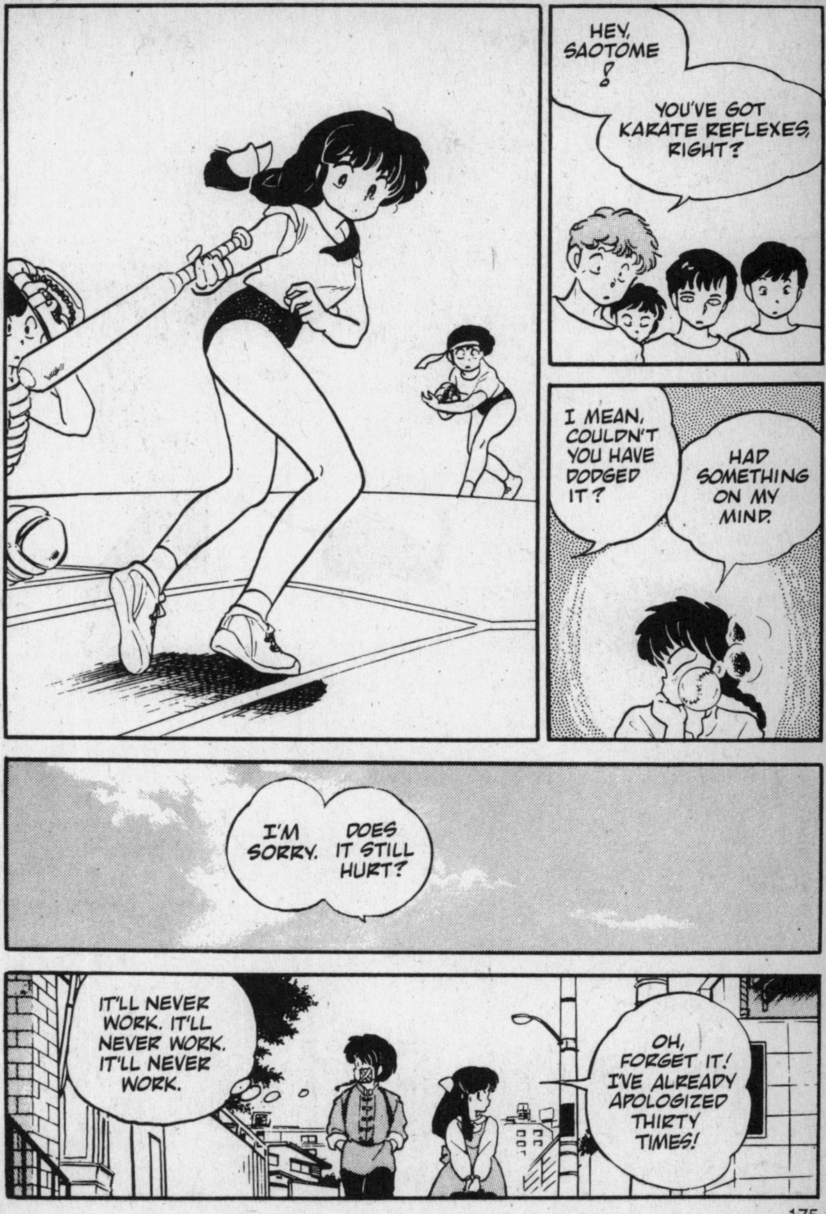
HEY, SAOTOME!
YOU'VE GOT KARATE REFLEXES, RIGHT?
I MEAN, COULDN'T YOU HAVE DODGED IT?
HAD SOMETHING ON MY MIND.
I'M SORRY.
DOES IT STILL HURT?
IT'LL NEVER WORK. IT'LL NEVER WORK. IT'LL NEVER WORK.
OH, FORGET IT! I'VE ALREADY APOLOGIZED THIRTY TIMES!

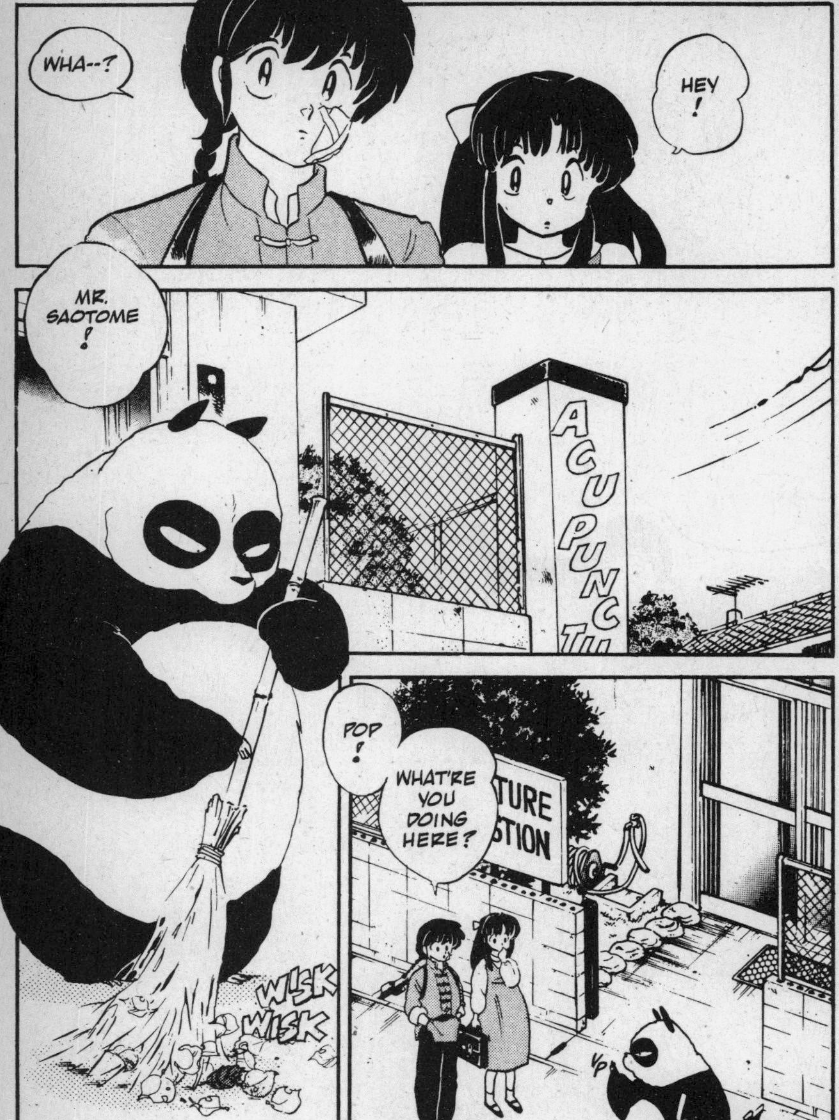
WHA--?
HEY!
MR. SAOTOME!
WISK
WISK
ACUPUNC
POP!
WHAT'RE YOU DOING HERE?
TURE
STION

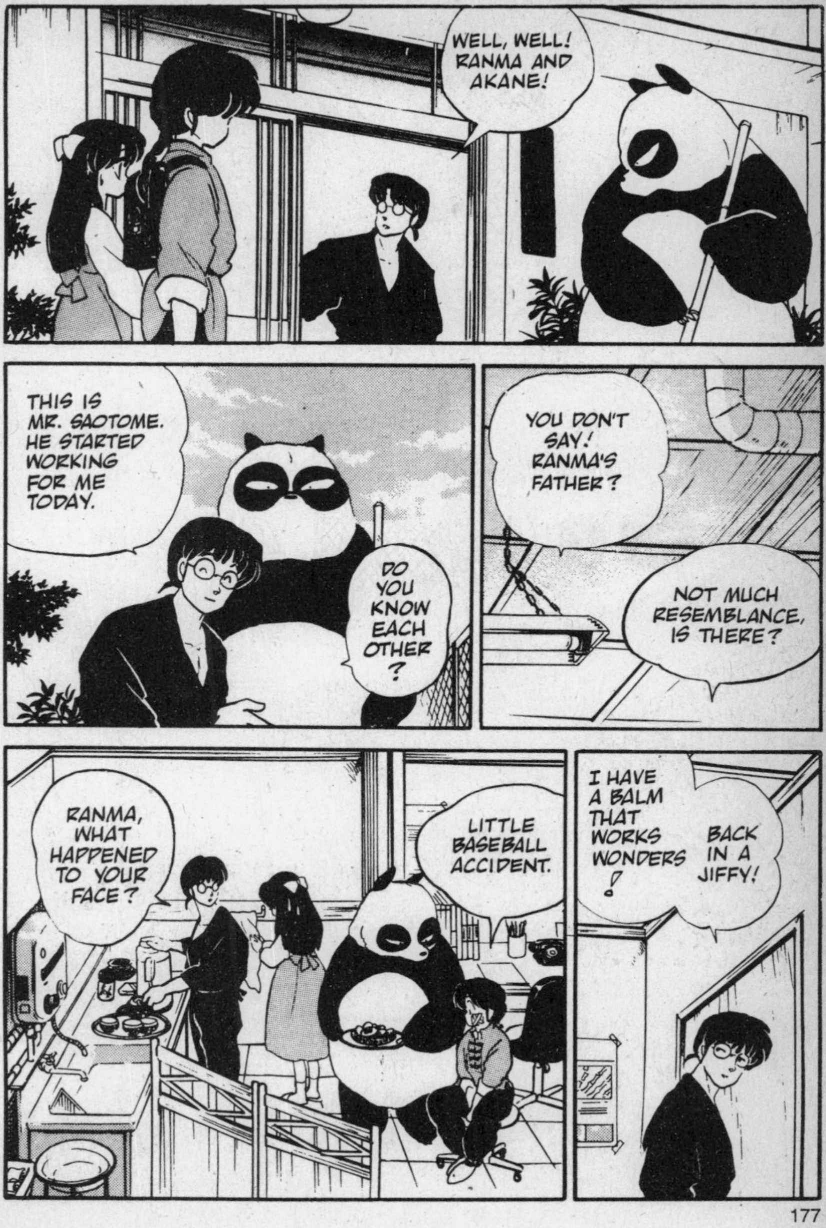
WELL, WELL! RANMA AND AKANE!
THIS IS MR. SAOTOME. HE STARTED WORKING FOR ME TODAY.
DO YOU KNOW EACH OTHER?
YOU DON'T SAY! RANMA'S FATHER?
NOT MUCH RESEMBLANCE, IS THERE?
RANMA, WHAT HAPPENED TO YOUR FACE?
LITTLE BASEBALL ACCIDENT.
I HAVE A BALM THAT WORKS WONDERS!
BACK IN A JIFFY!

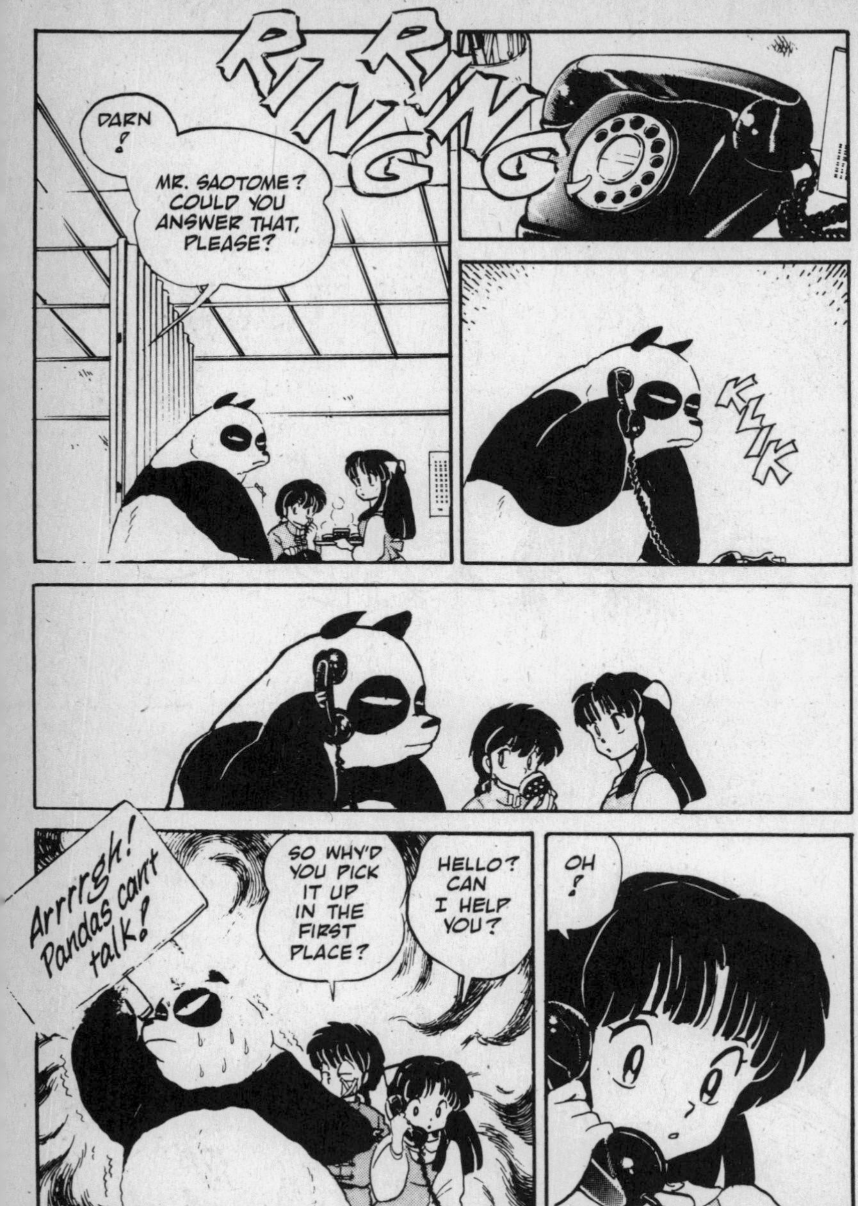
RRING RING
DARN!
MR. SAOTOME? COULD YOU ANSWER THAT, PLEASE?
KLIK
Arrrrgh! Pandas can't talk!
SO WHY'D YOU PICK IT UP IN THE FIRST PLACE?
HELLO? CAN I HELP YOU?
OH!

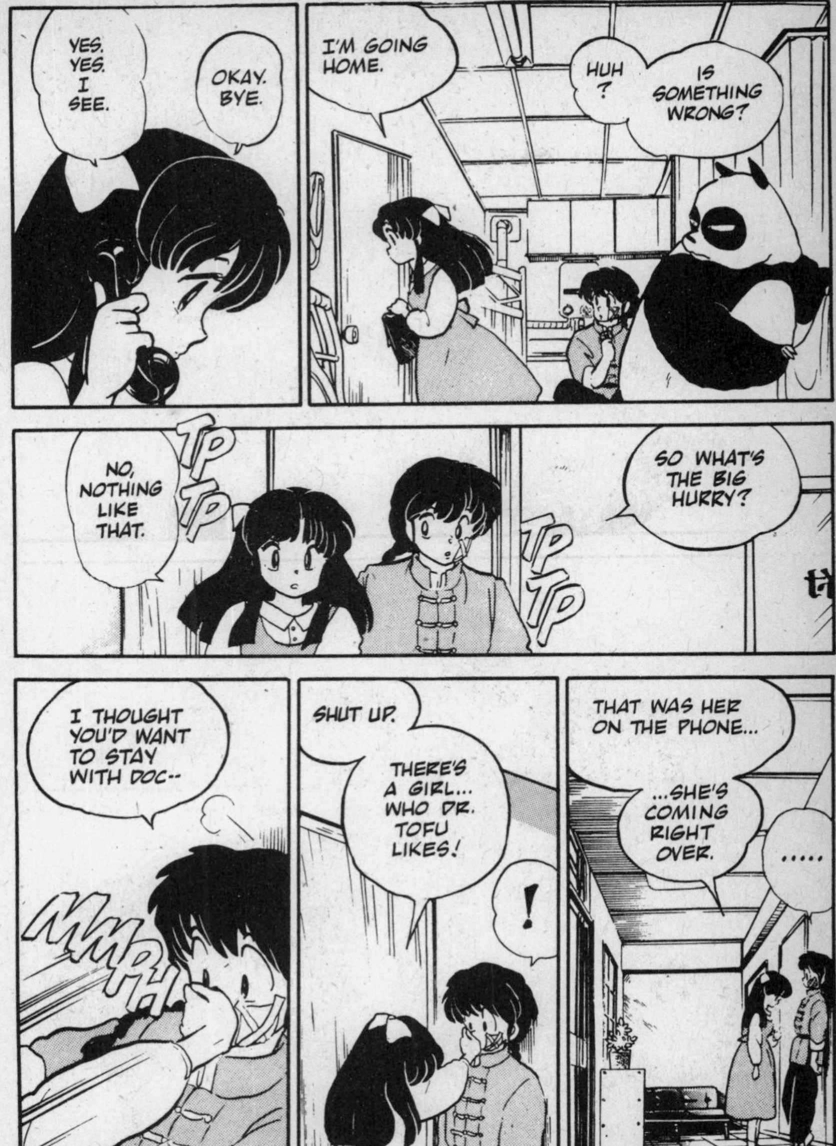
YES. YES. I SEE.
OKAY. BYE.
I'M GOING HOME.
HUH?
IS SOMETHING WRONG?
NO, NOTHING LIKE THAT.
TP TP
TP TP
SO WHAT'S THE BIG HURRY?
I THOUGHT YOU'D WANT TO STAY WITH DOC--
MMPH
SHUT UP.
THERE'S A GIRL... WHO DR. TOFU LIKES!
!
THAT WAS HER ON THE PHONE...
...SHE'S COMING RIGHT OVER.
.....

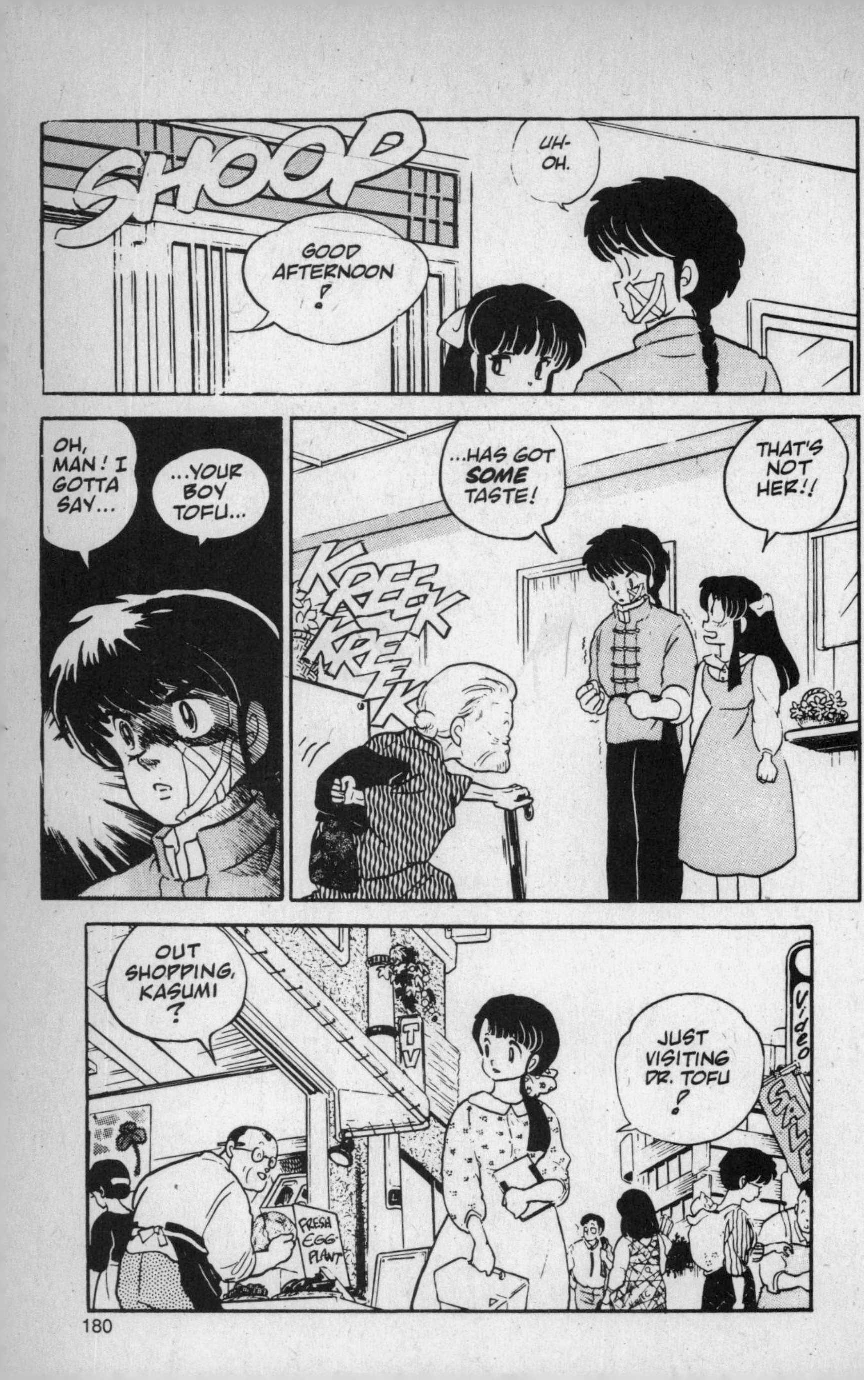
SHOOP
GOOD AFTERNOON!
UH-OH.
OH, MAN! I GOTTA SAY...
...YOUR BOY TOFU...
...HAS GOT SOME TASTE!
KREEK KREEK
THAT'S NOT HER!!
OUT SHOPPING, KASUMI?
TV
FRESH EGG-PLANT
Video
JUST VISITING DR. TOFU!

Part 9

YOU'RE CUTE WHEN YOU SMILE

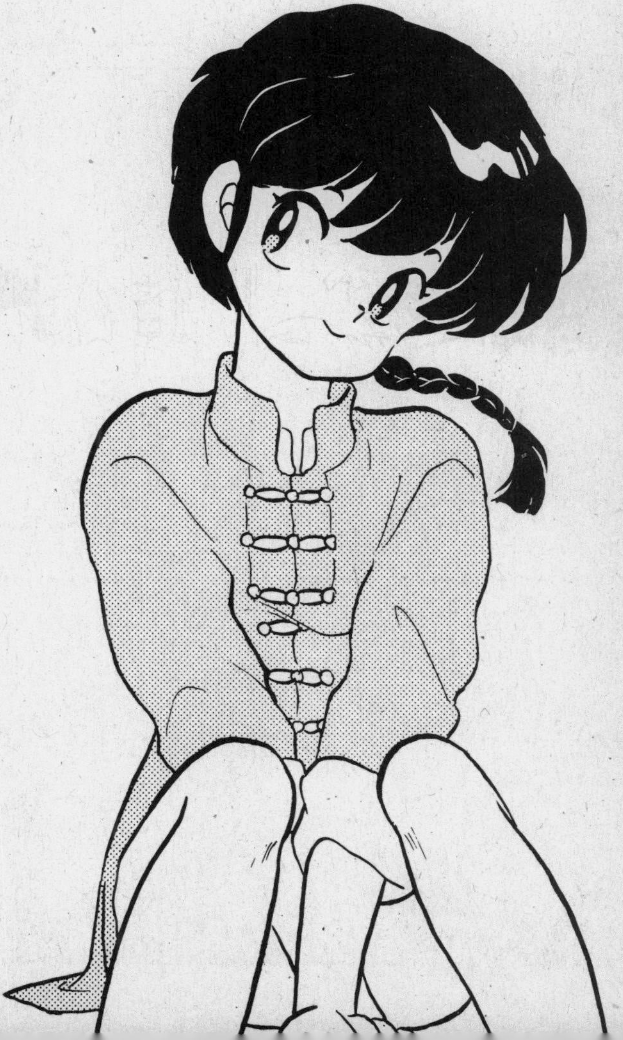

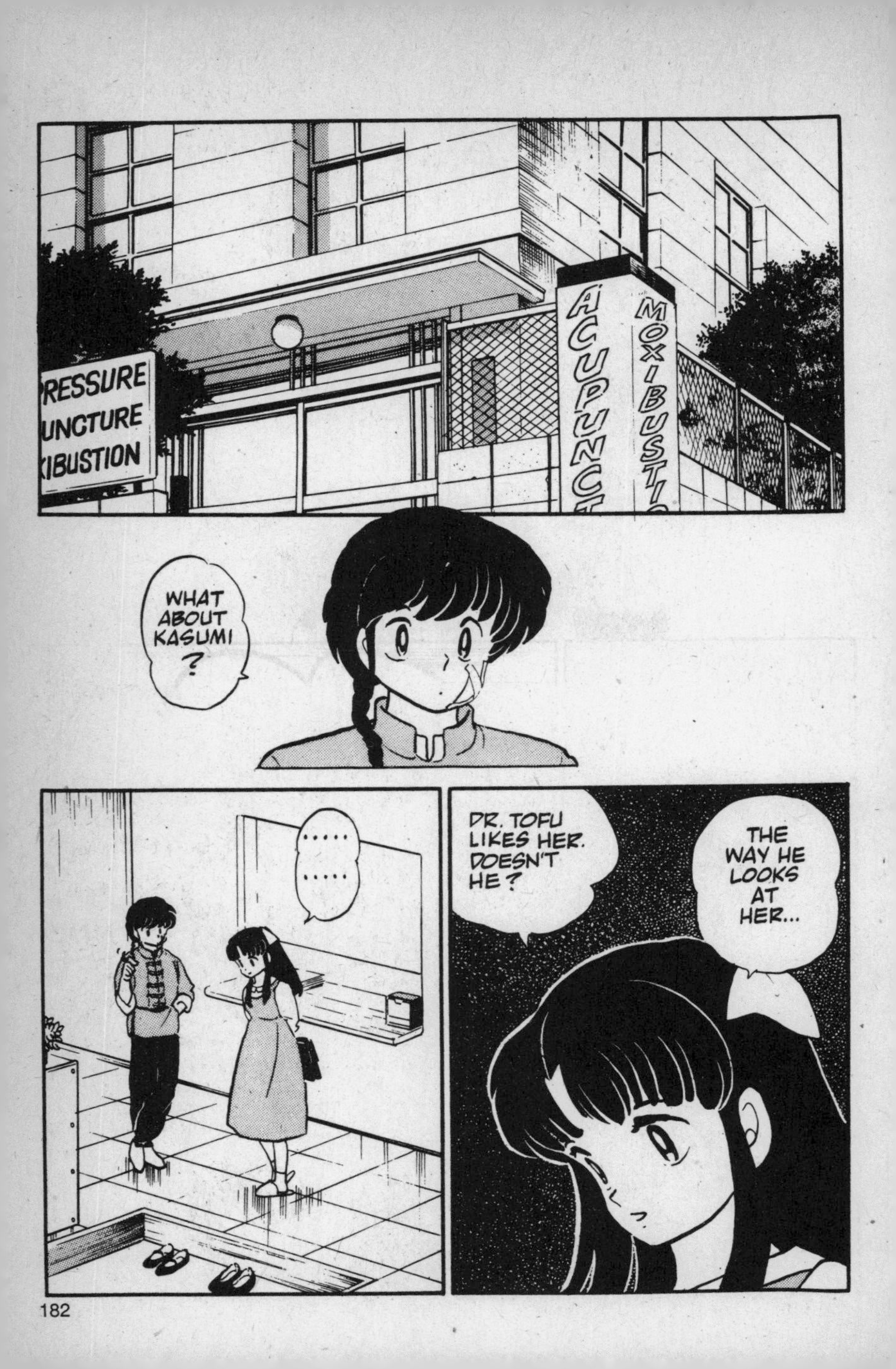
PRESSURE
UNCTURE
XIBUSTION
ACUPUNC
MOXIBUSTI
WHAT ABOUT KASUMI?
.....
.....
DR. TOFU LIKES HER. DOESN'T HE?
THE WAY HE LOOKS AT HER...

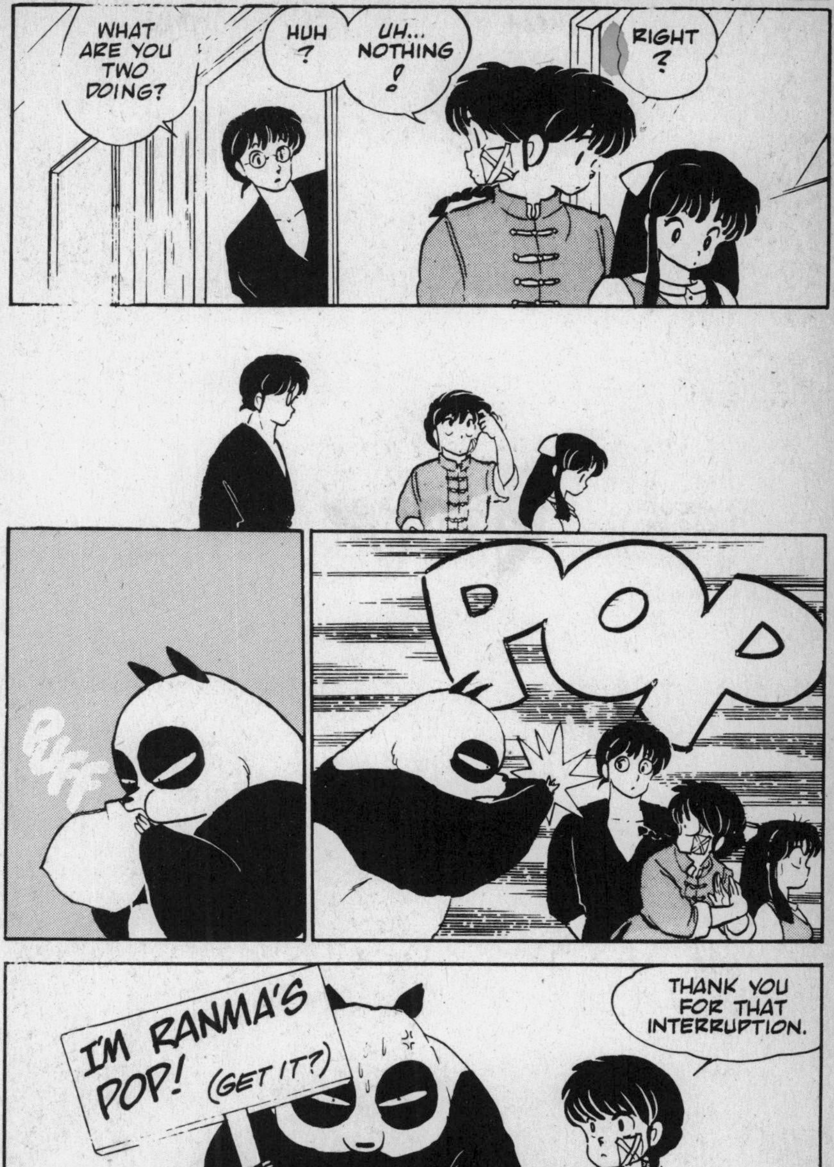
WHAT ARE YOU TWO DOING?
HUH ?
UH... NOTHING !
RIGHT ?
PUFF
POP
I'M RANMA'S POP! (GET IT?)
THANK YOU FOR THAT INTERRUPTION.

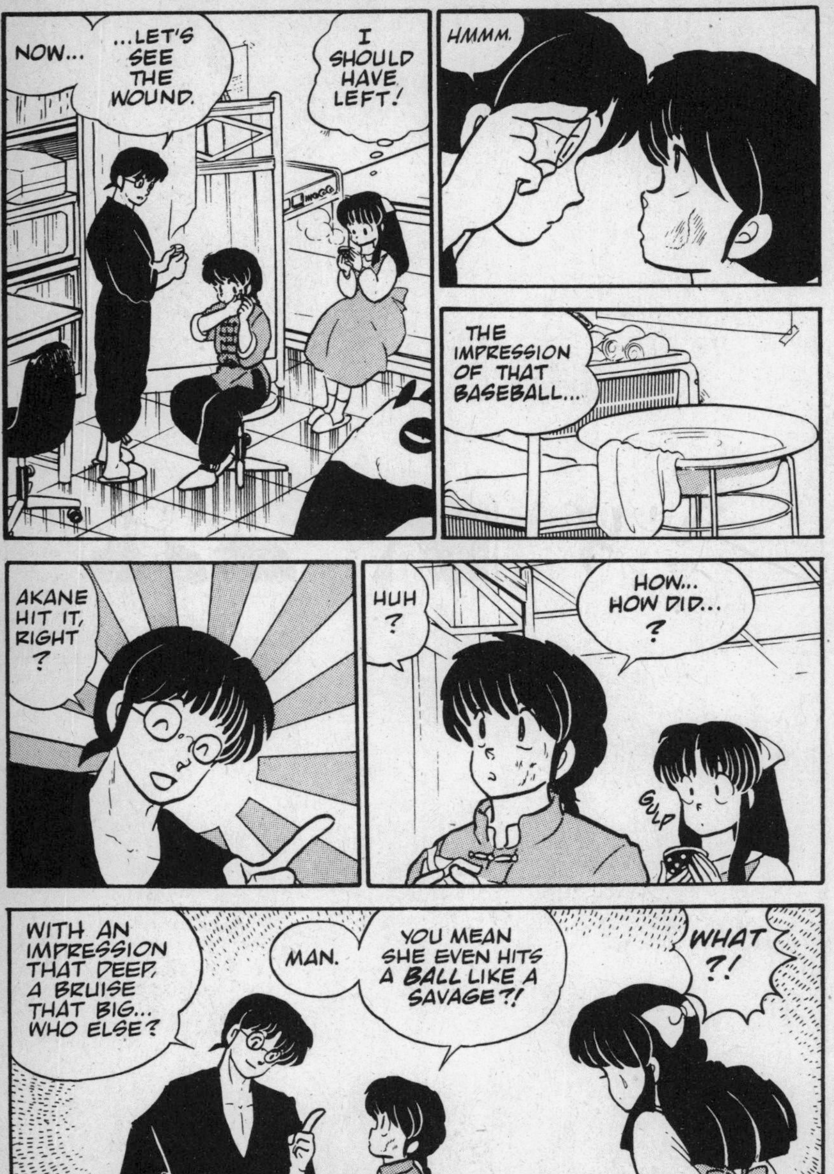
NOW...
...LET'S SEE THE WOUND.
I SHOULD HAVE LEFT!
HMMM.
THE IMPRESSION OF THAT BASEBALL...
AKANE HIT IT, RIGHT?
HUH?
HOW... HOW DID...?
GULP
WITH AN IMPRESSION THAT DEEP, A BRUISE THAT BIG... WHO ELSE?
MAN.
YOU MEAN SHE EVEN HITS A BALL LIKE A SAVAGE?!
WHAT?!

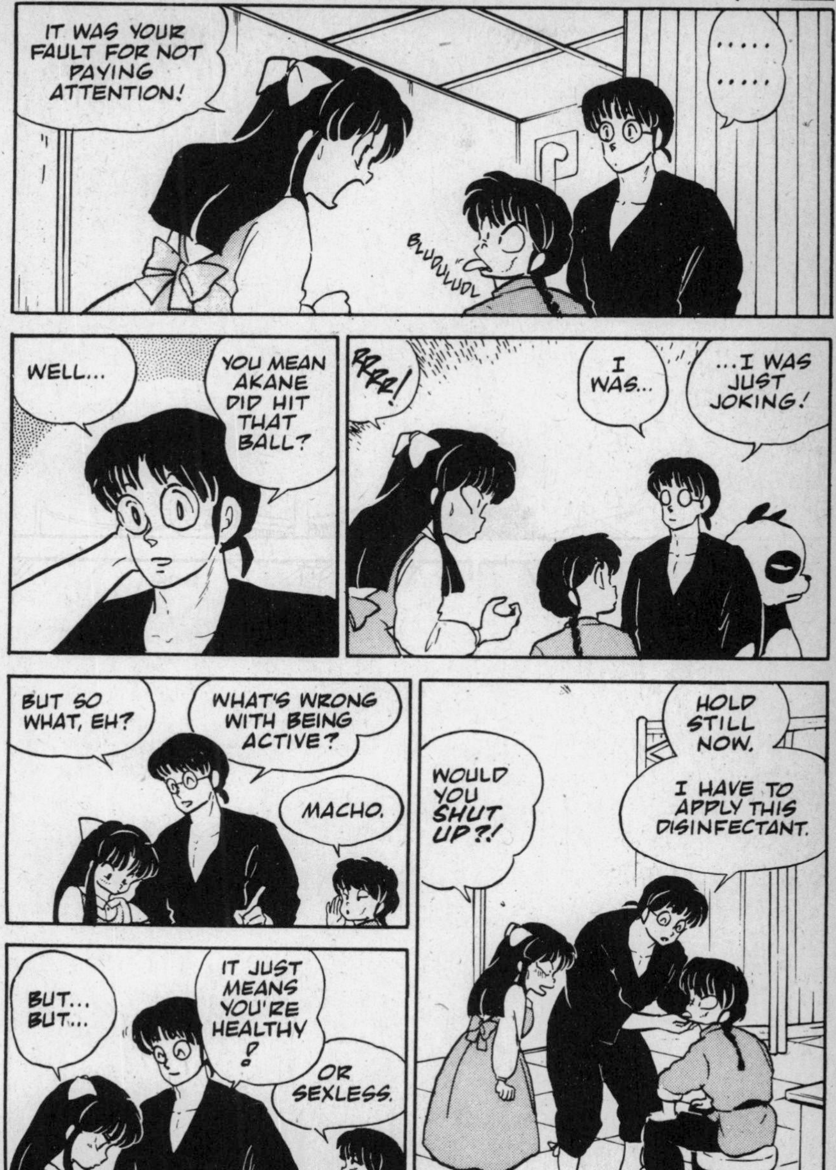
IT WAS YOUR FAULT FOR NOT PAYING ATTENTION!
BLUDULUDL
.....
.....
WELL...
YOU MEAN AKANE DID HIT THAT BALL?
RRRR!
I WAS...
...I WAS JUST JOKING!
BUT SO WHAT, EH?
WHAT'S WRONG WITH BEING ACTIVE?
MACHO.
BUT... BUT...
IT JUST MEANS YOU'RE HEALTHY!
OR SEXLESS.
HOLD STILL NOW.
I HAVE TO APPLY THIS DISINFECTANT.
WOULD YOU SHUT UP?!

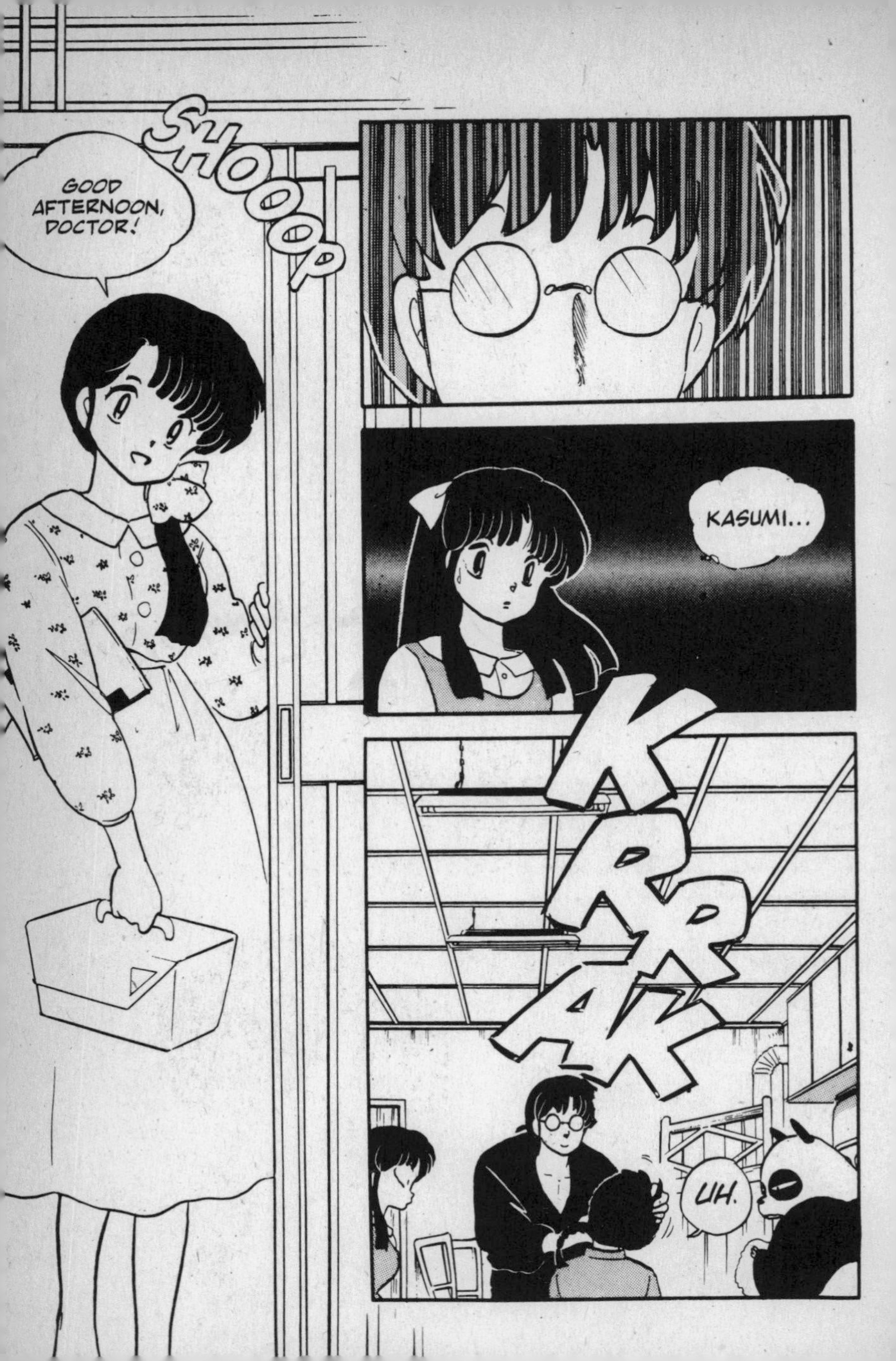
SHOOOP
GOOD AFTERNOON, DOCTOR!
KASUMI...
KRRAK
UH.

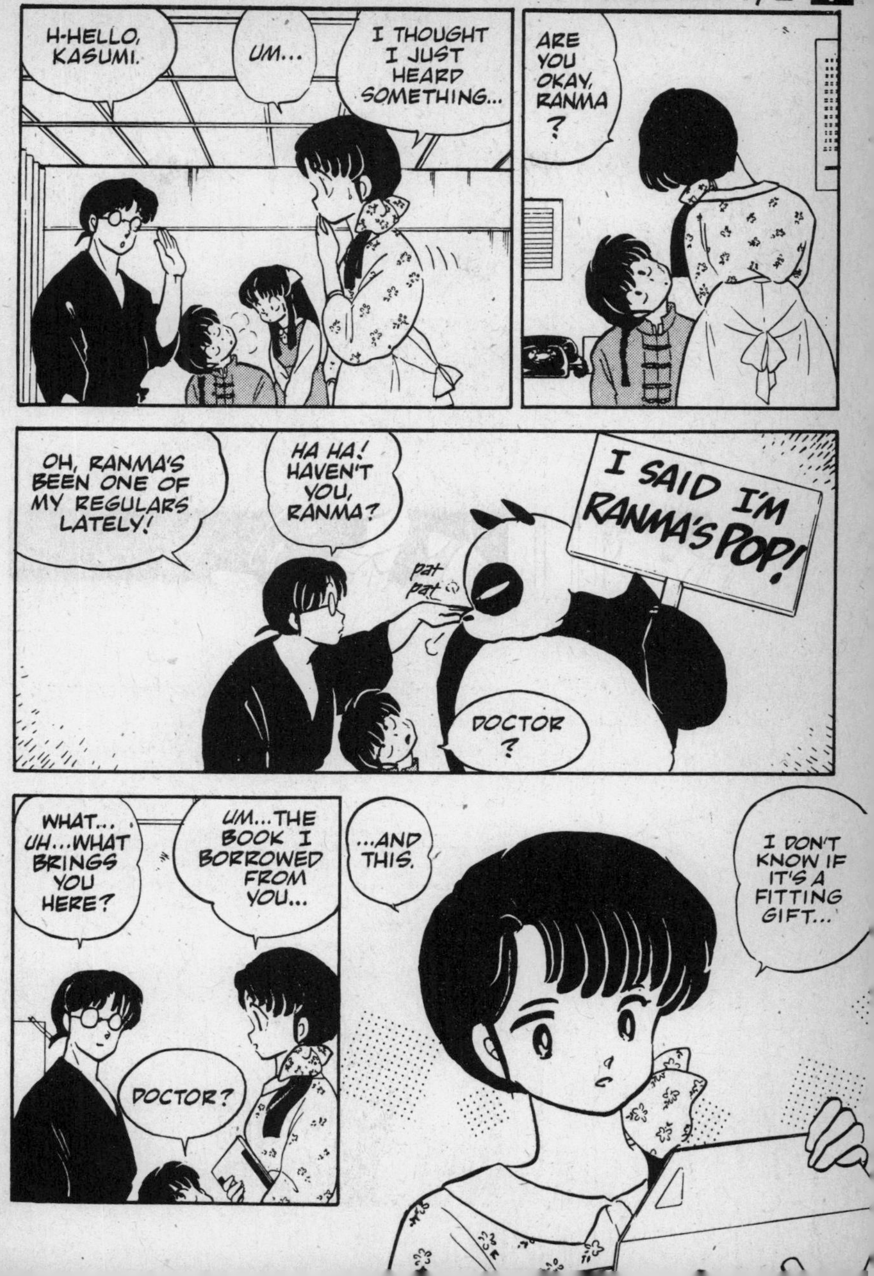
H-HELLO, KASUMI.
UM...
I THOUGHT I JUST HEARD SOMETHING...
ARE YOU OKAY, RANMA?
OH, RANMA'S BEEN ONE OF MY REGULARS LATELY!
HA HA! HAVEN'T YOU, RANMA?
pat pat
I SAID I'M RANMA'S POP!
DOCTOR?
WHAT... UH...WHAT BRINGS YOU HERE?
UM...THE BOOK I BORROWED FROM YOU...
...AND THIS.
DOCTOR?
I DON'T KNOW IF IT'S A FITTING GIFT...

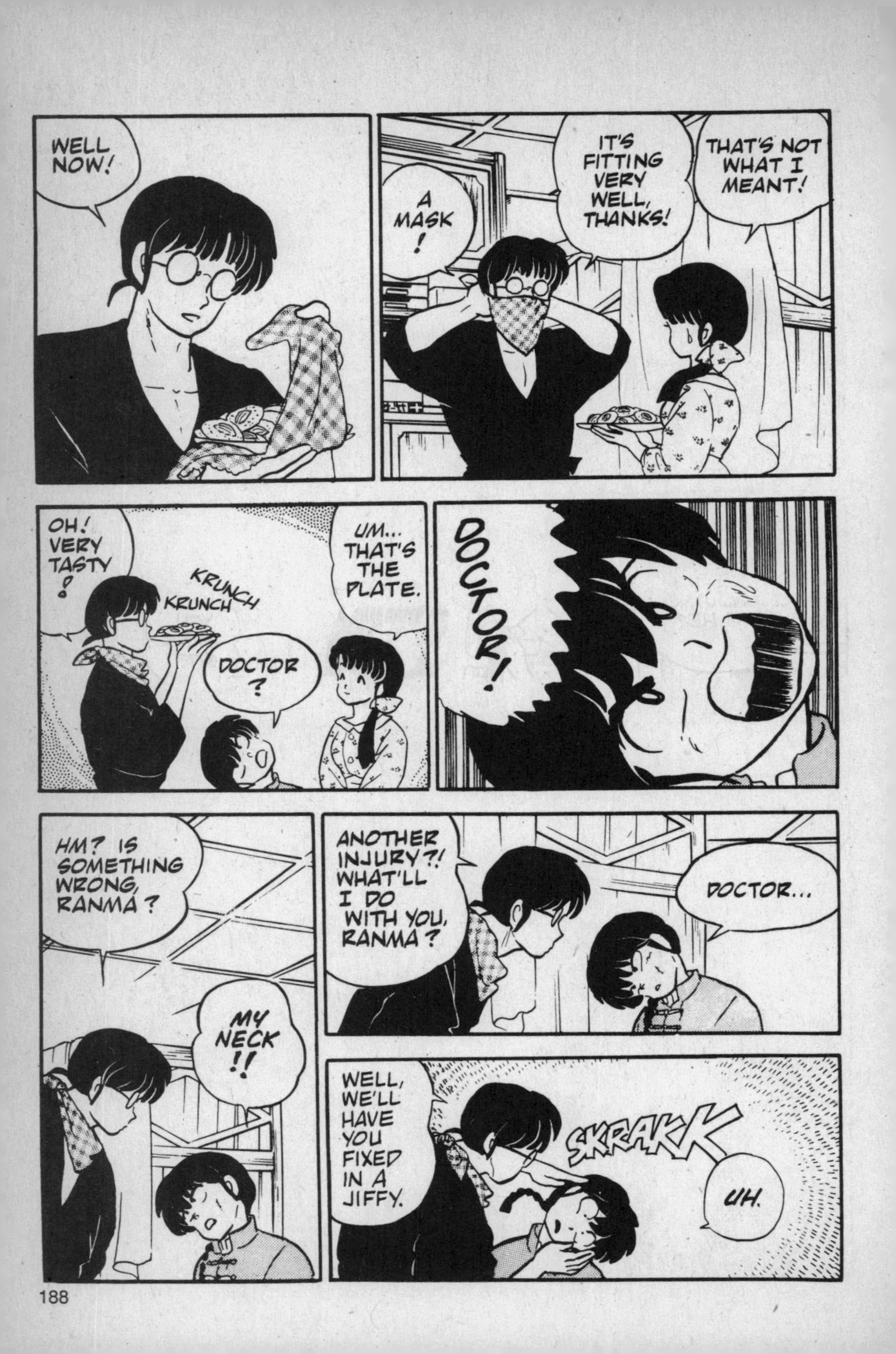
WELL NOW!
A MASK!
IT'S FITTING VERY WELL, THANKS!
THAT'S NOT WHAT I MEANT!
OH! VERY TASTY!
KRUNCH
KRUNCH
UM... THAT'S THE PLATE.
DOCTOR?
DOCTOR!
HM? IS SOMETHING WRONG, RANMA?
MY NECK!!
ANOTHER INJURY?! WHAT'LL I DO WITH YOU, RANMA?
DOCTOR...
WELL, WE'LL HAVE YOU FIXED IN A JIFFY.
SKRAKK
UH.

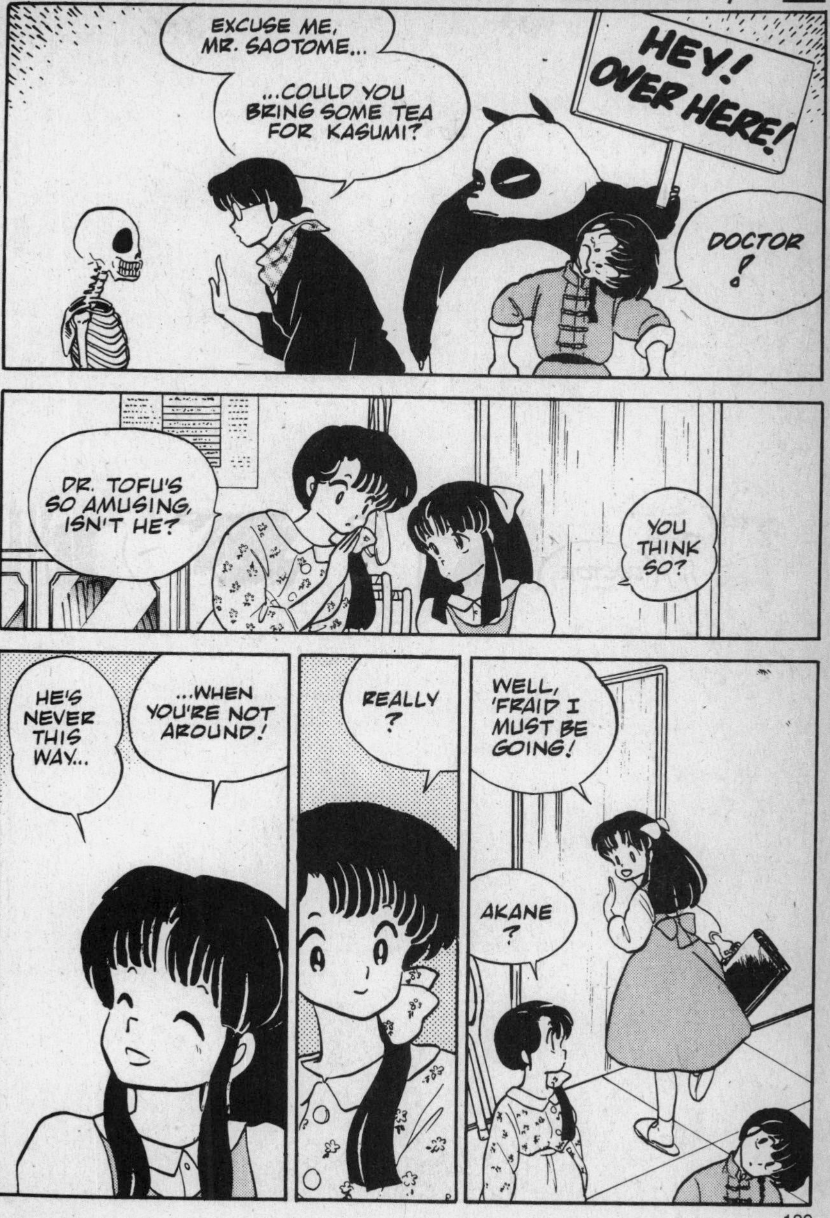
EXCUSE ME, MR. SAOTOME...
...COULD YOU BRING SOME TEA FOR KASUMI?
HEY! OVER HERE!
DOCTOR?
DR. TOFU'S SO AMUSING, ISN'T HE?
YOU THINK SO?
HE'S NEVER THIS WAY...
...WHEN YOU'RE NOT AROUND!
REALLY?
WELL, 'FRAID I MUST BE GOING!
AKANE?

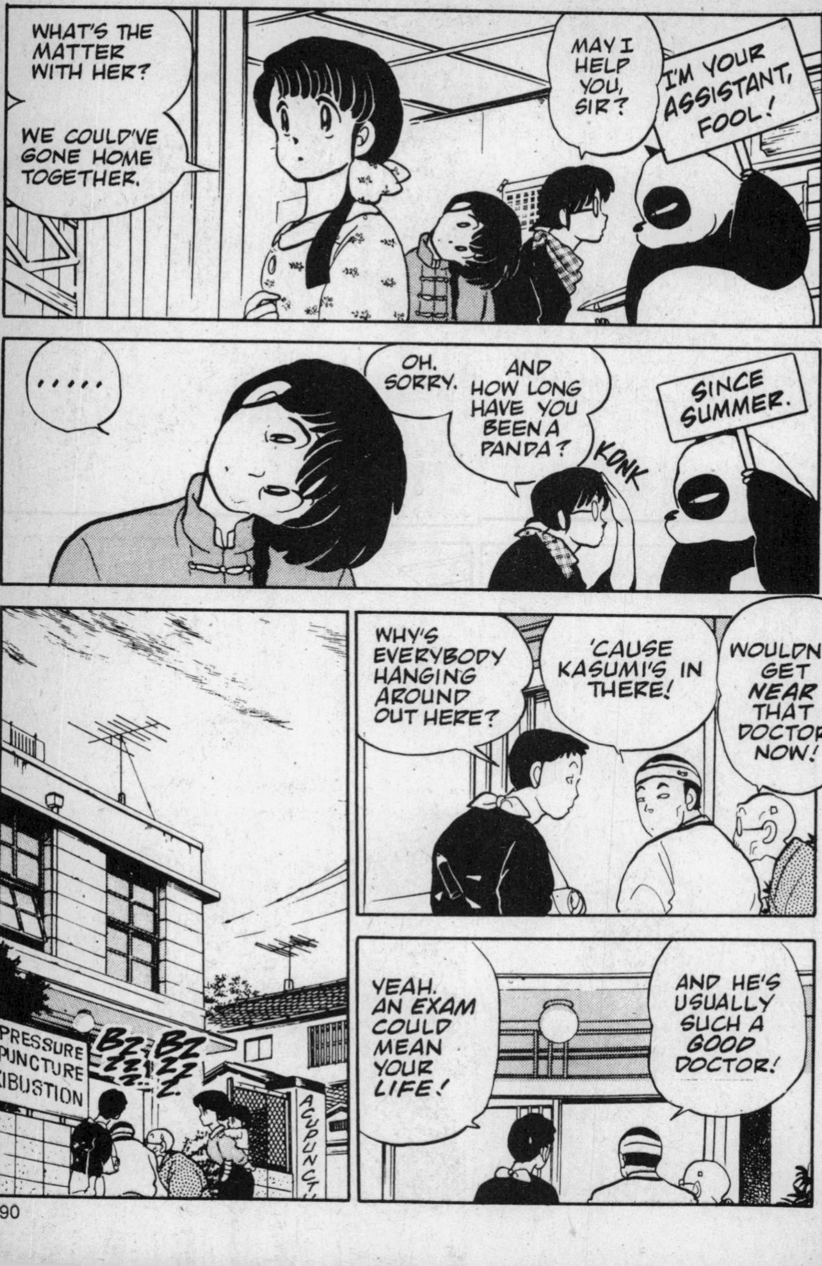
WHAT'S THE MATTER WITH HER?
WE COULD'VE GONE HOME TOGETHER.
MAY I HELP YOU, SIR?
I'M YOUR ASSISTANT, FOOL!
.....
OH. SORRY.
AND HOW LONG HAVE YOU BEEN A PANDA?
KONK
SINCE SUMMER.
PRESSURE
PUNCTURE
XIBUSTION
BZZZZ... BZZZ.
ACUPUNCT
WHY'S EVERYBODY HANGING AROUND OUT HERE?
'CAUSE KASUMI'S IN THERE!
WOULDN'T GET NEAR THAT DOCTOR NOW!
YEAH. AN EXAM COULD MEAN YOUR LIFE!
AND HE'S USUALLY SUCH A GOOD DOCTOR!

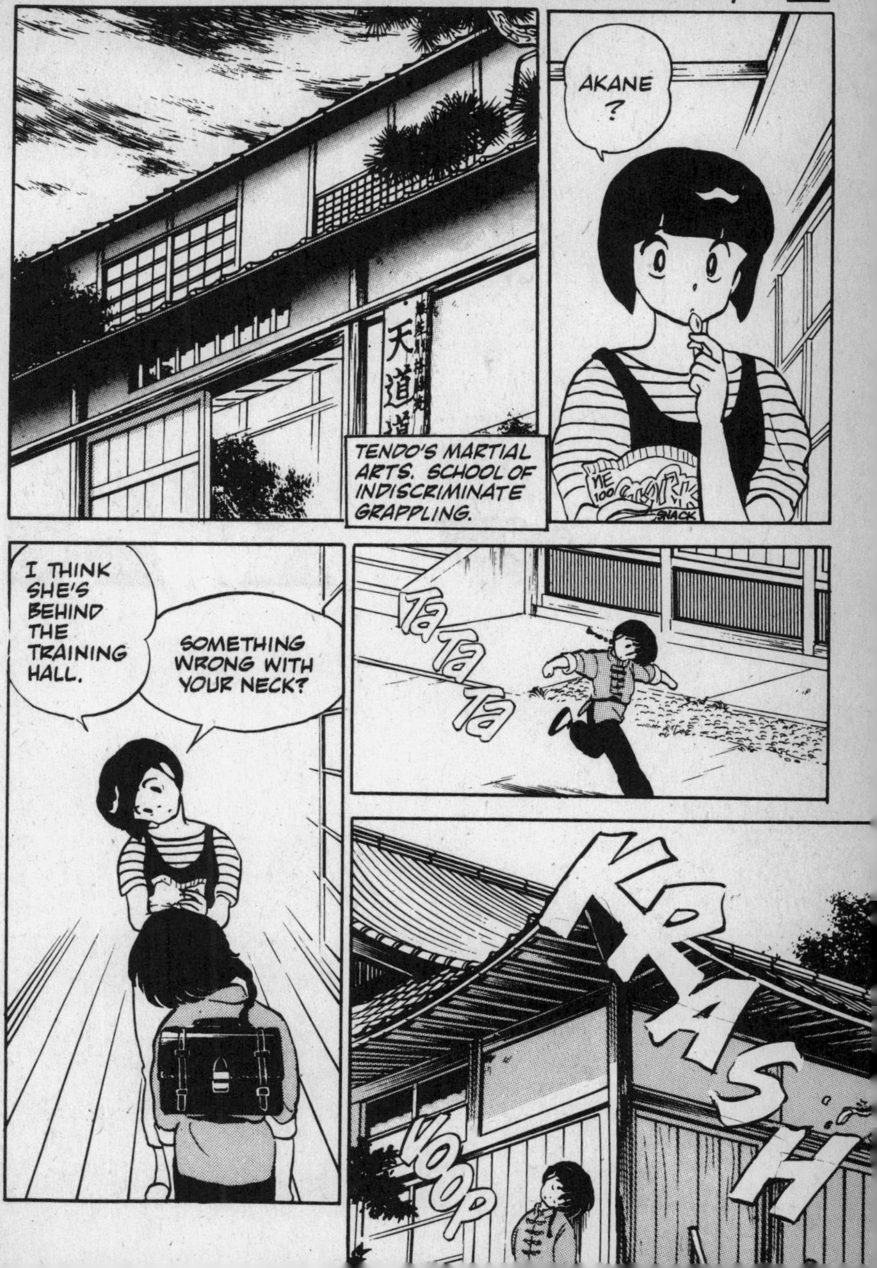
天道道
TENDO'S MARTIAL ARTS. SCHOOL OF INDISCRIMINATE GRAPPLING.
AKANE ?
SNACK
I THINK SHE'S BEHIND THE TRAINING HALL.
SOMETHING WRONG WITH YOUR NECK?
TA TA TA
KRASH
VOOP

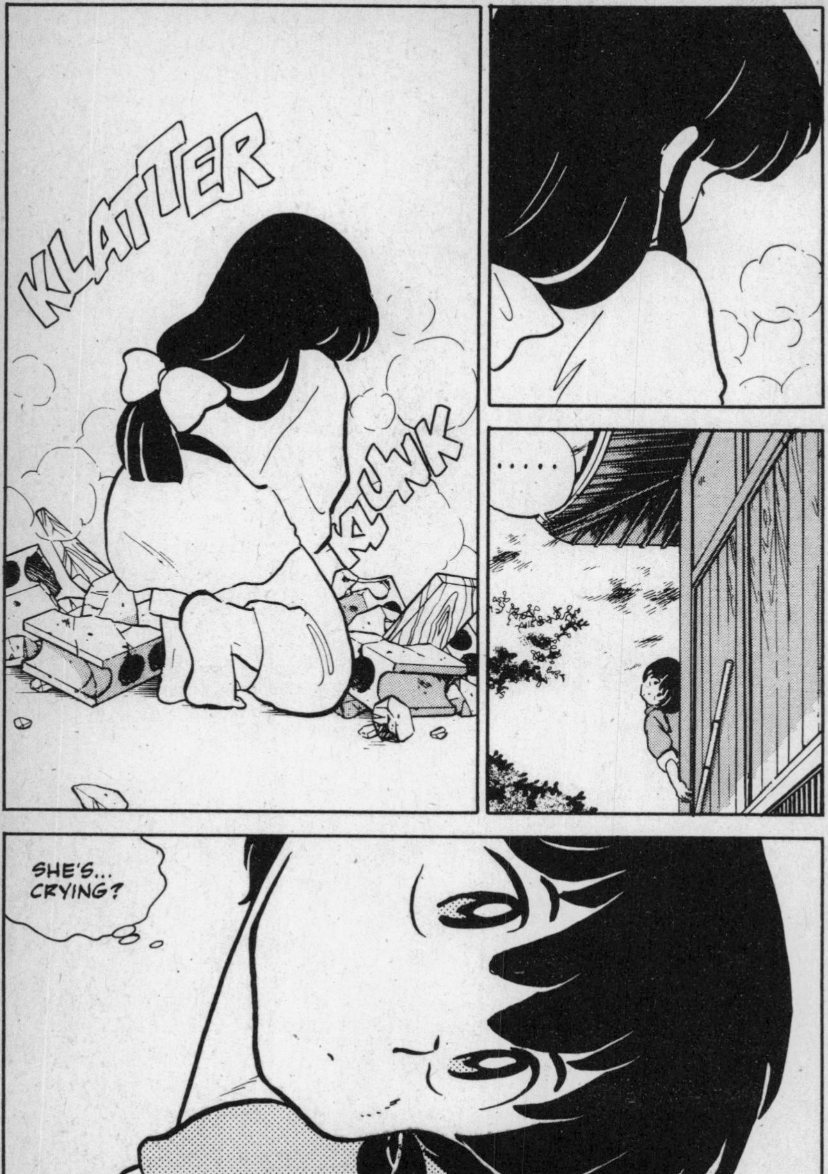
KLATTER
KLUNK
......
SHE'S... CRYING?

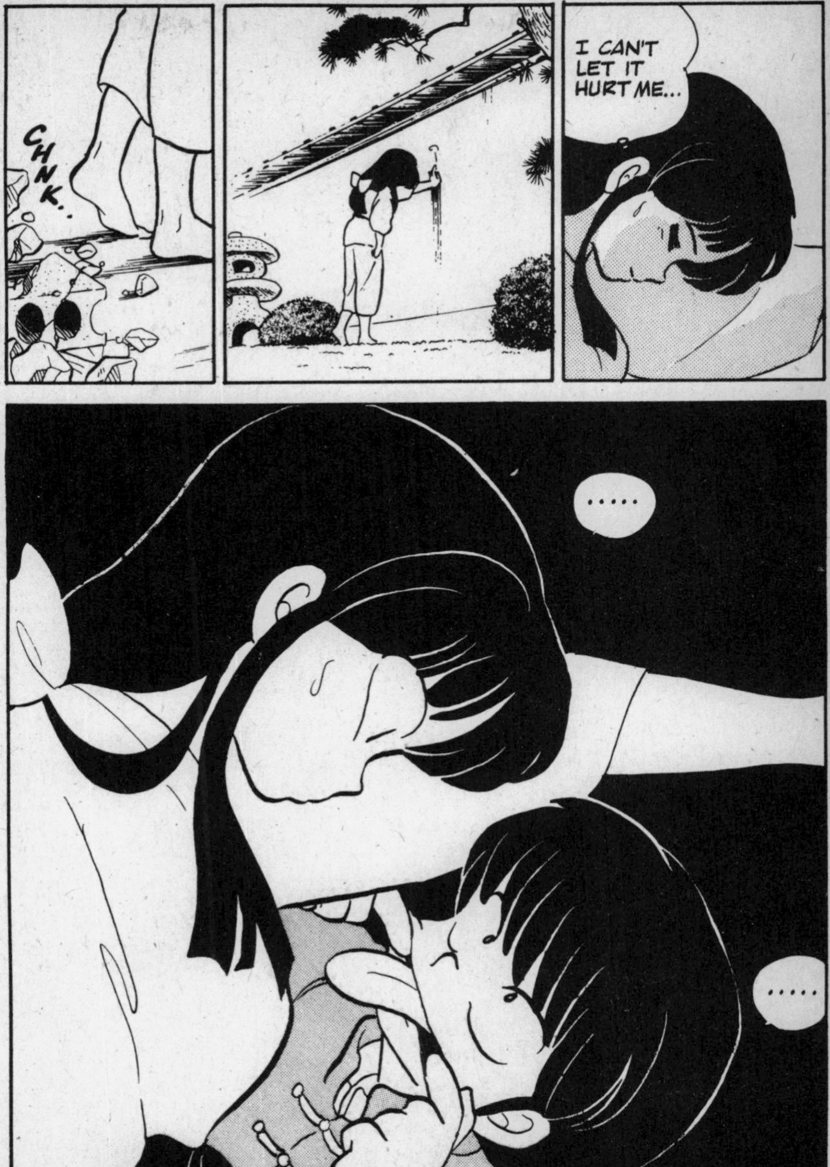
CHNK...
I CAN'T LET IT HURT ME...
......
......

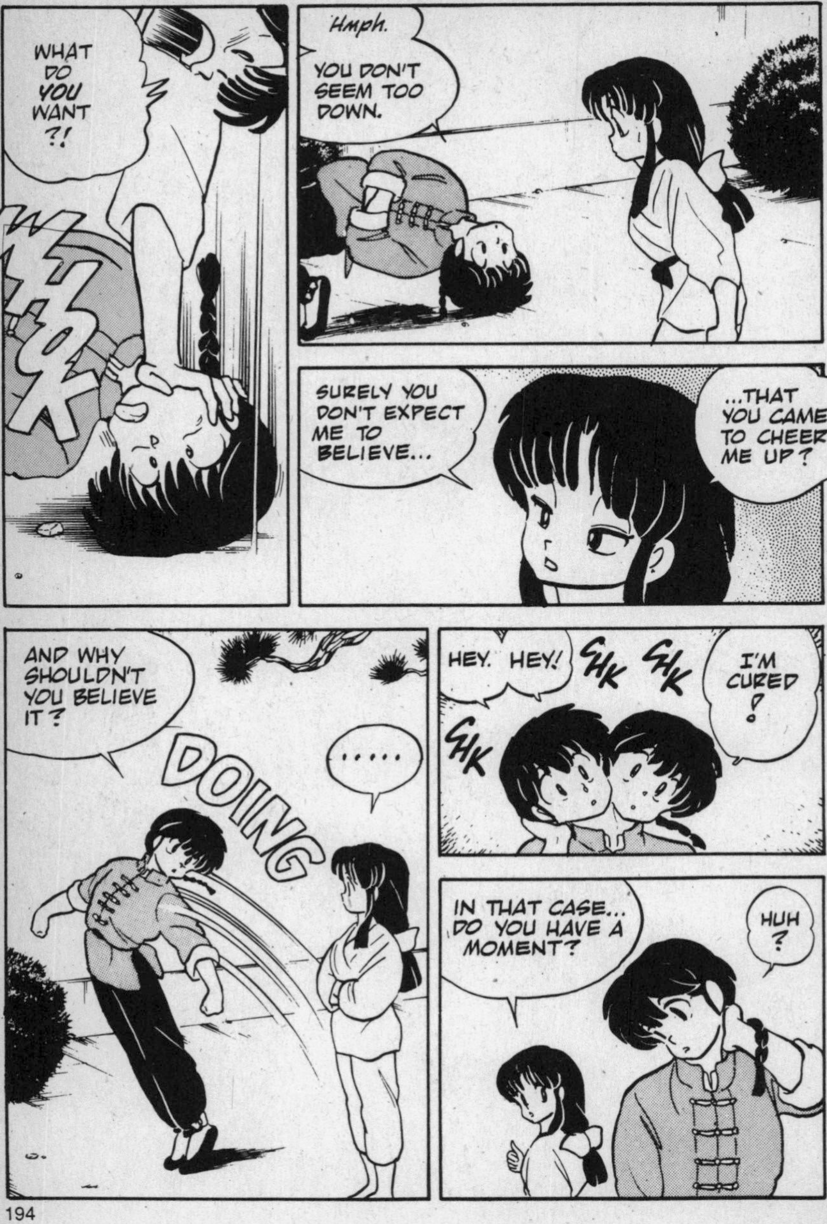

WHAT DO YOU WANT ?!
WOK
Hmph.
YOU DON'T SEEM TOO DOWN.
SURELY YOU DON'T EXPECT ME TO BELIEVE...
...THAT YOU CAME TO CHEER ME UP?
AND WHY SHOULDN'T YOU BELIEVE IT?
DOING
.....
HEY. HEY!
SHK SHK
SHK
I'M CURED!
IN THAT CASE... DO YOU HAVE A MOMENT?
HUH?

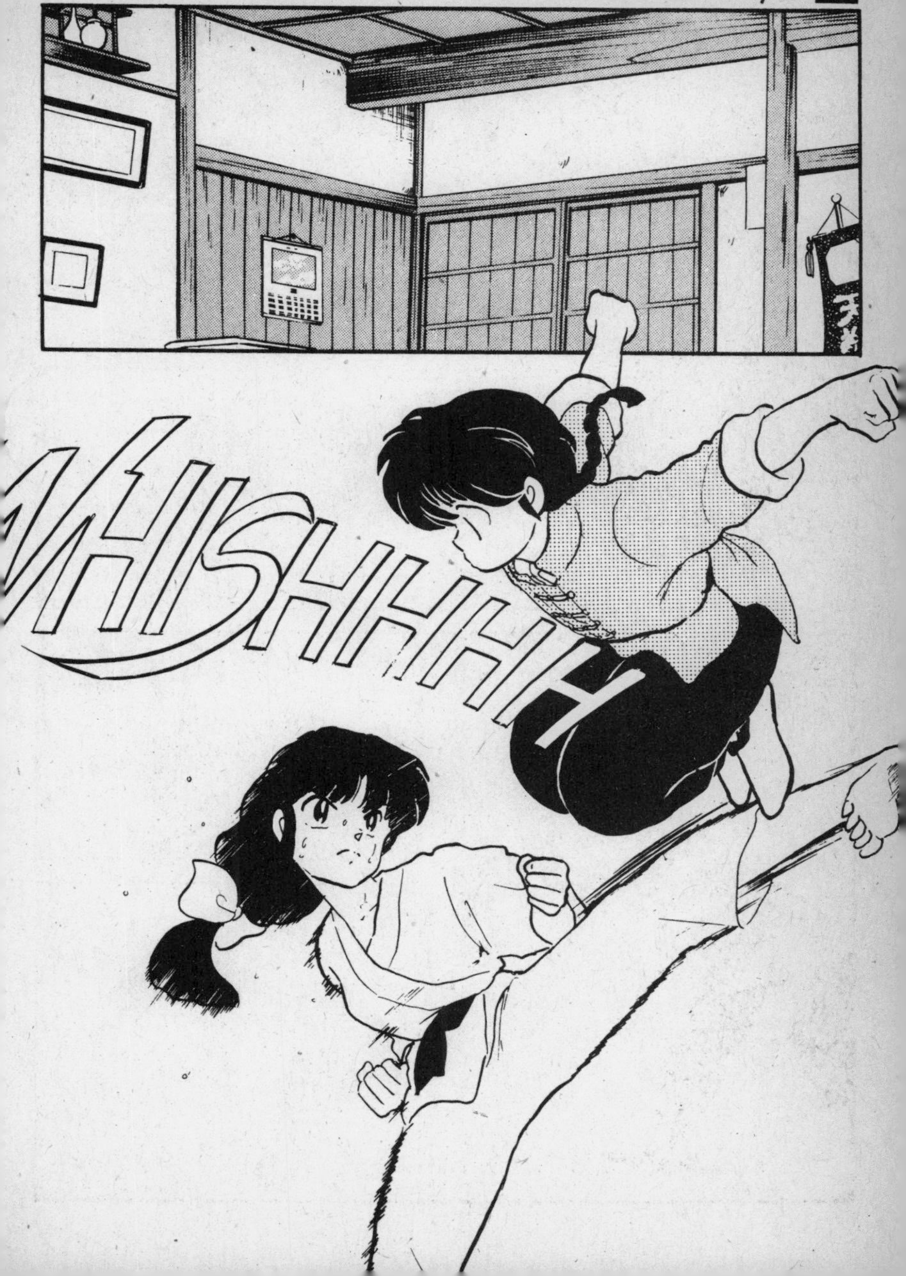
WHISHHHH

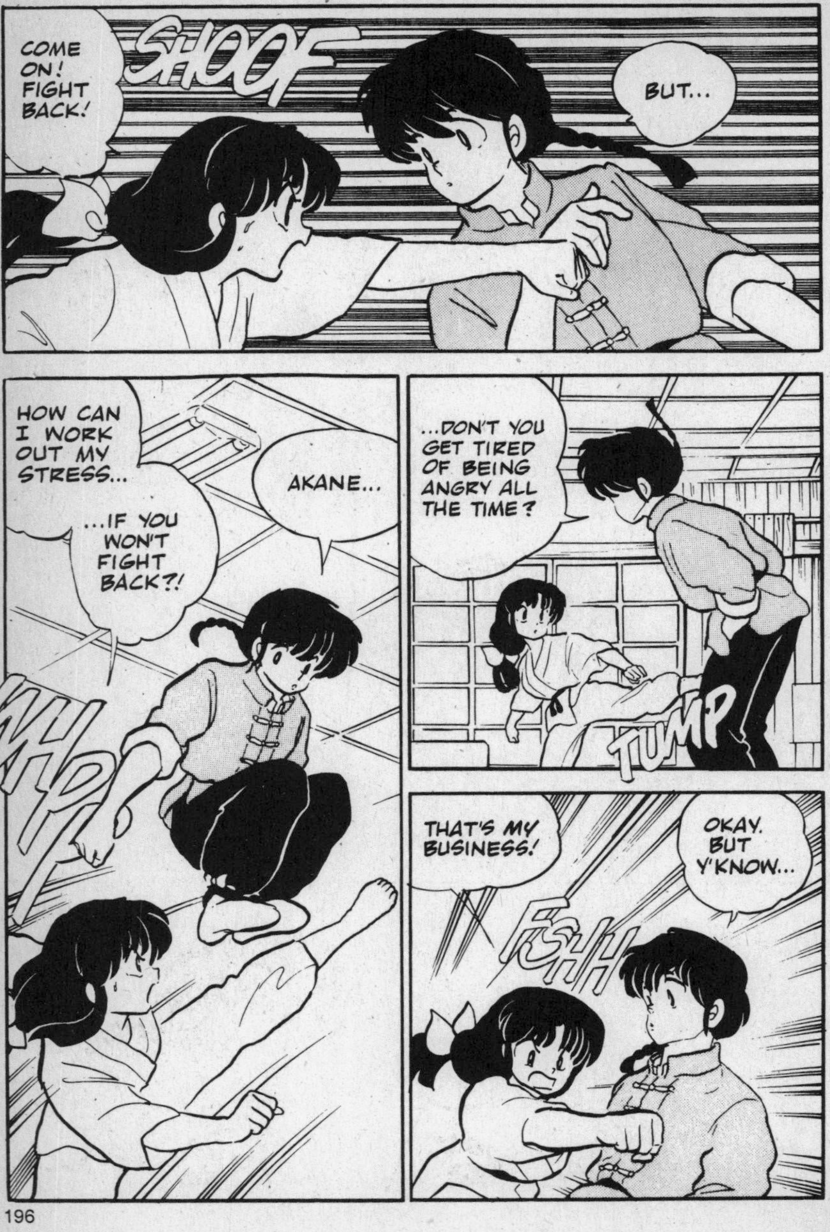
COME ON! FIGHT BACK!
SHOOF
BUT...
HOW CAN I WORK OUT MY STRESS...
...IF YOU WON'T FIGHT BACK?!
AKANE...
WHP
...DON'T YOU GET TIRED OF BEING ANGRY ALL THE TIME?
TUMP
THAT'S MY BUSINESS!
OKAY. BUT Y'KNOW...
FSHH

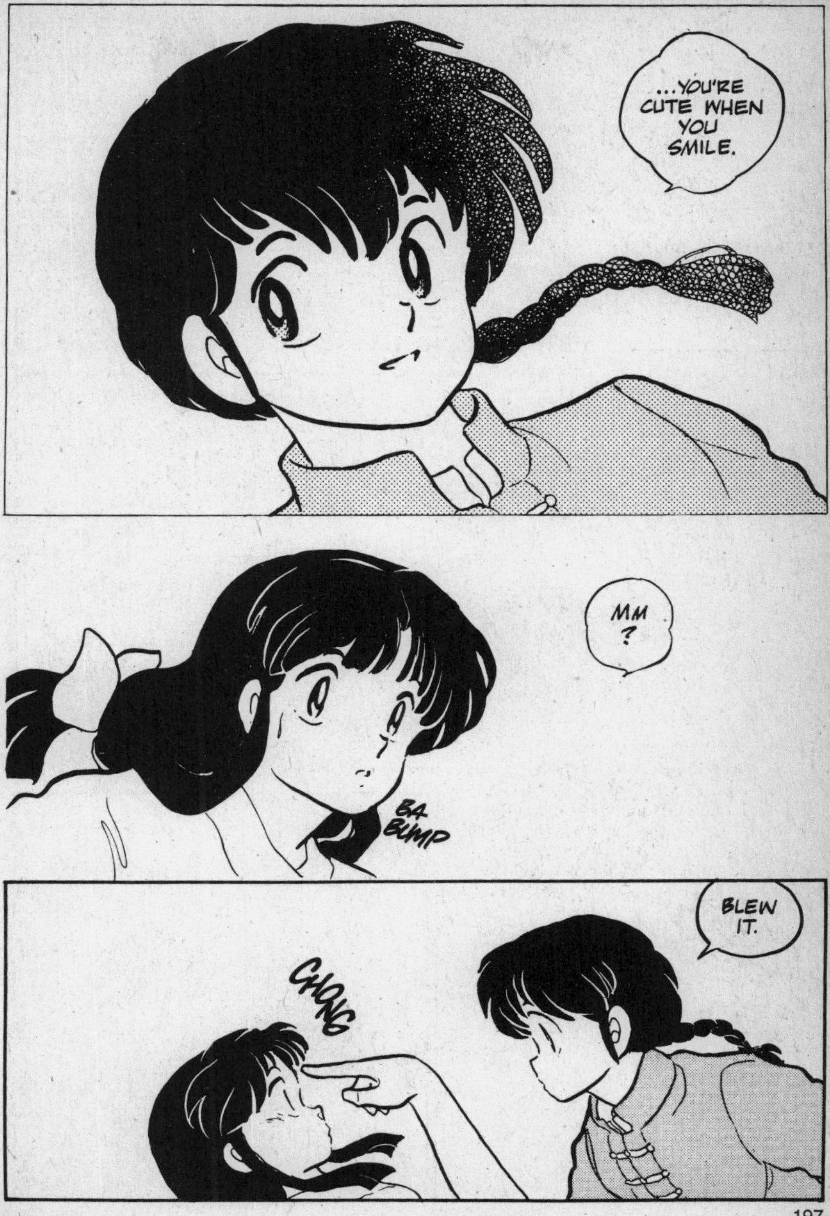
...YOU'RE CUTE WHEN YOU SMILE.
MM?
BA BUMP
CHONG
BLEW IT.

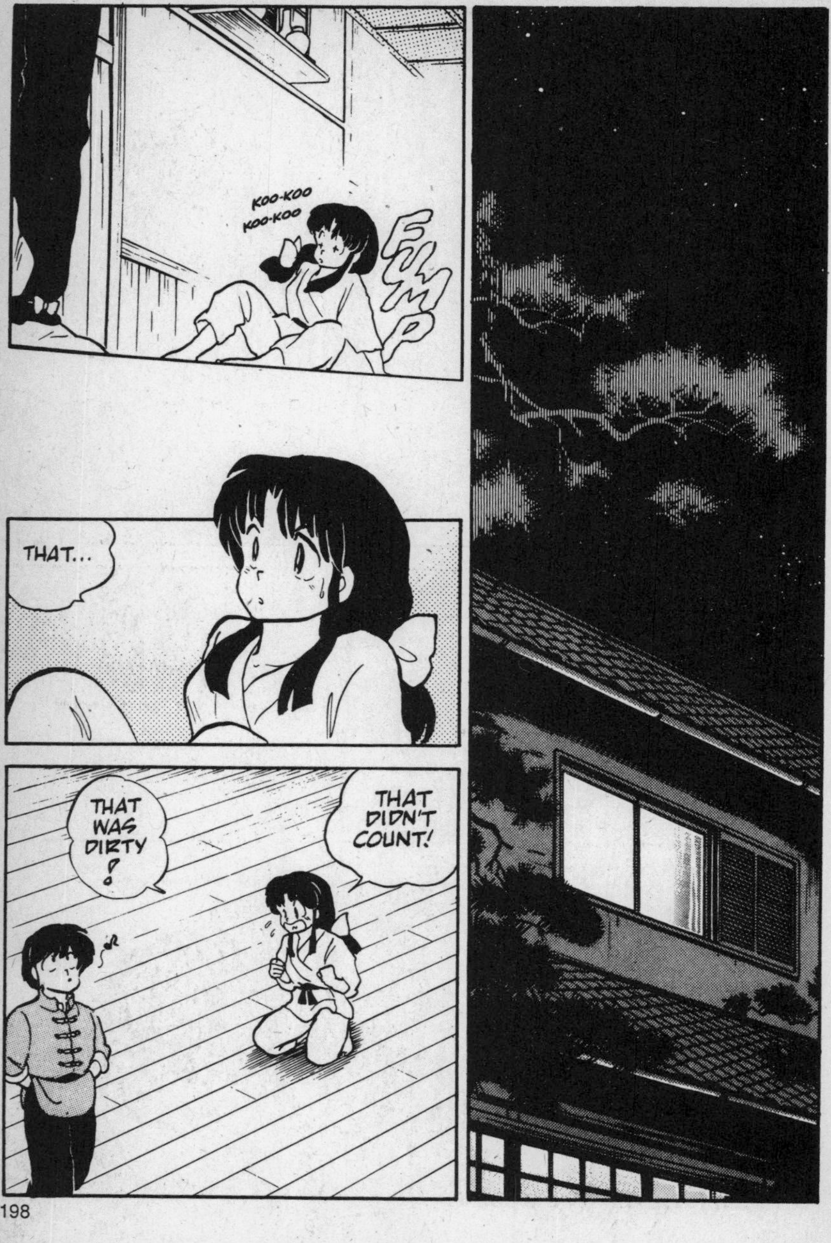
KOO-KOO
KOO-KOO
FUMP
THAT...
THAT WAS DIRTY!?
THAT DIDN'T COUNT!

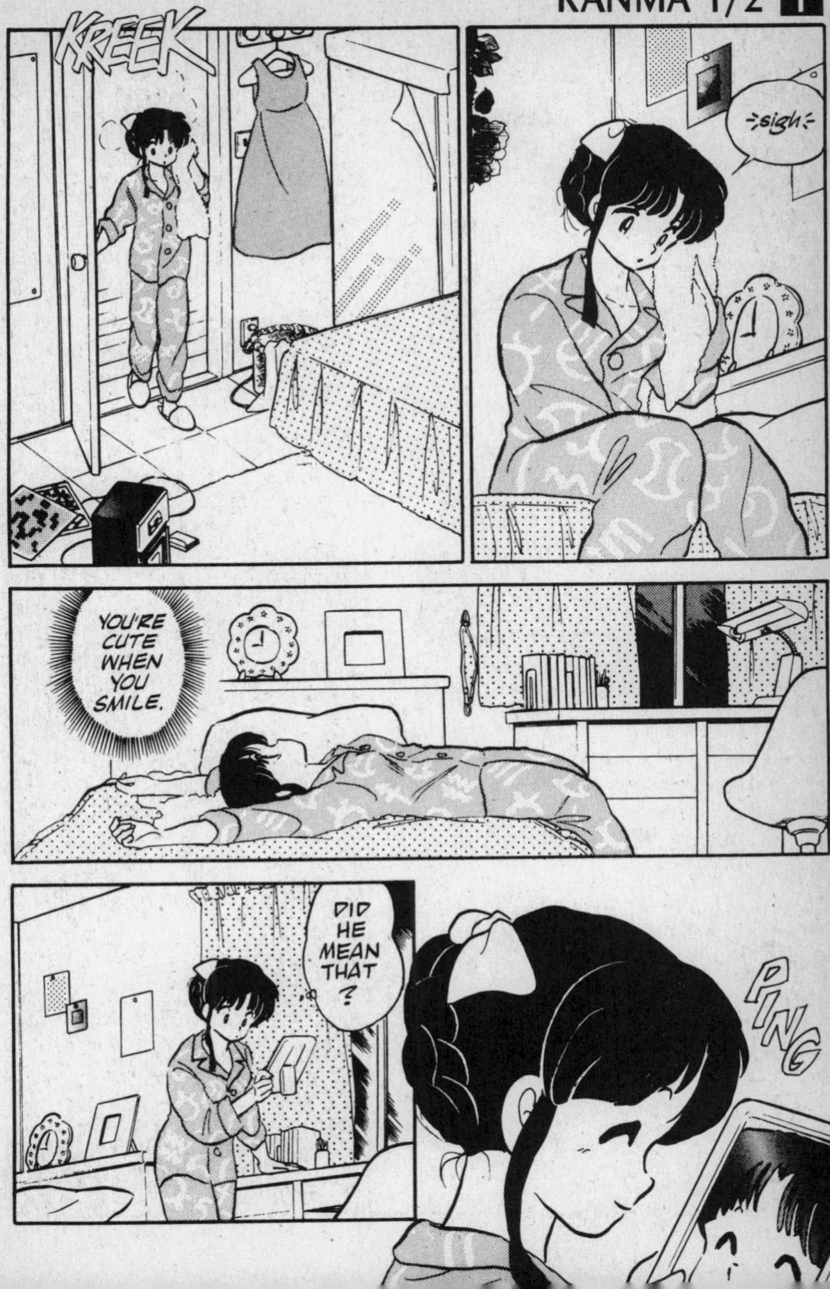
KREEK
sigh
YOU'RE CUTE WHEN YOU SMILE.
DID HE MEAN THAT?
PING

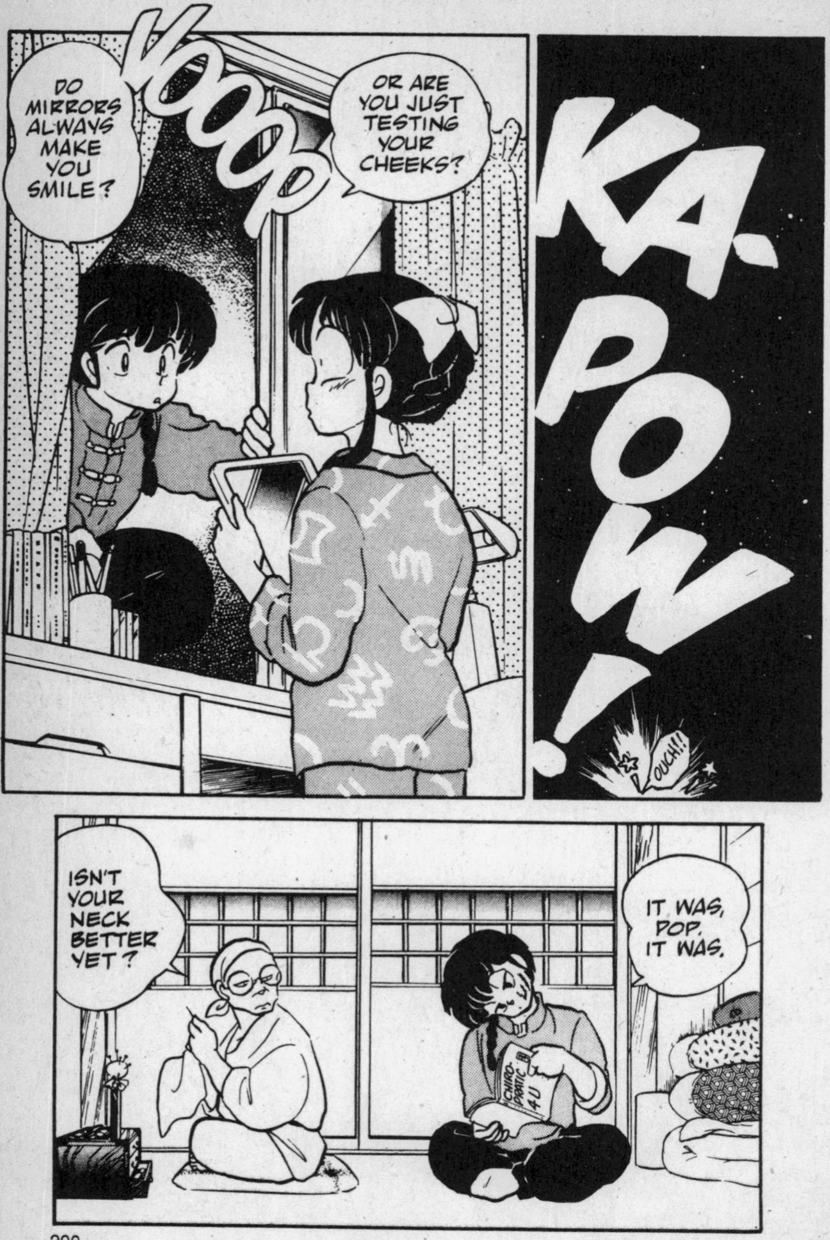
DO MIRRORS ALWAYS MAKE YOU SMILE?
VOOOP
OR ARE YOU JUST TESTING YOUR CHEEKS?
KA-POW!
OUCH!!
ISN'T YOUR NECK BETTER YET?
CHIRO-PRATIC 4 U
IT WAS, POP. IT WAS.

Part 10
THE HUNTER

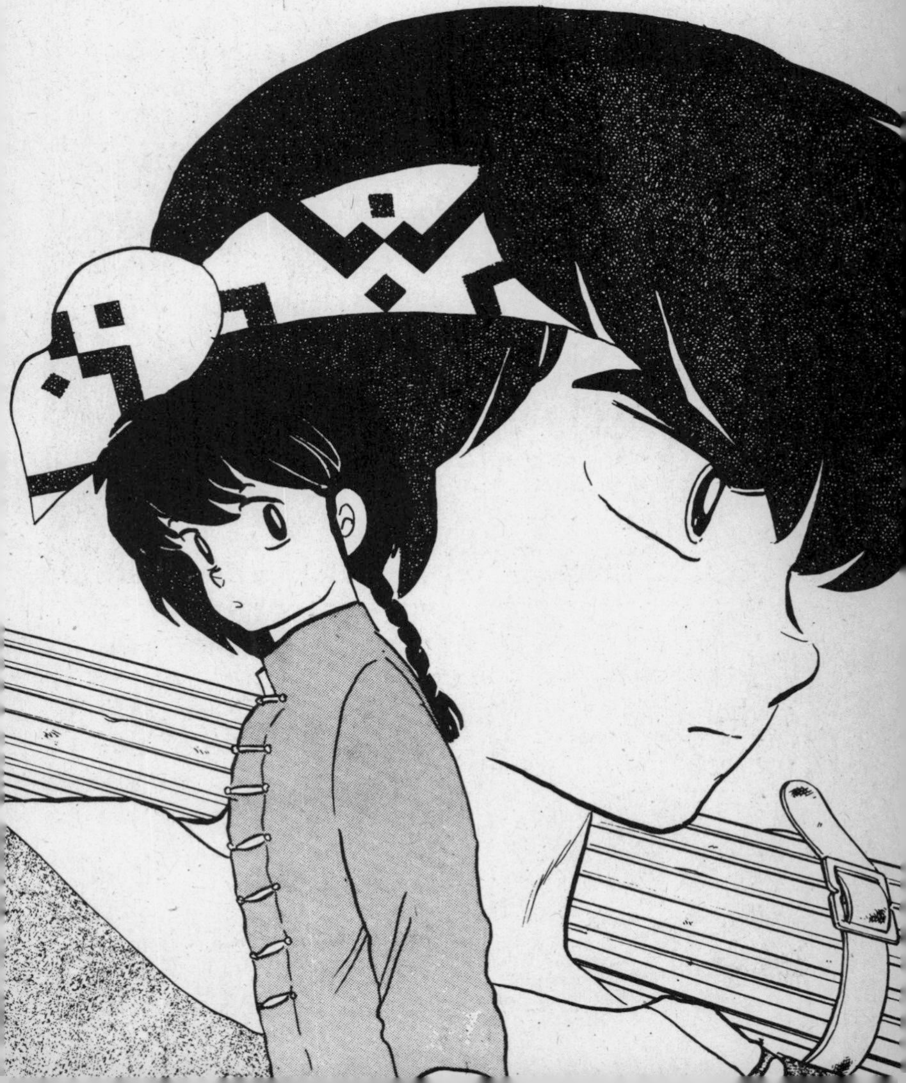

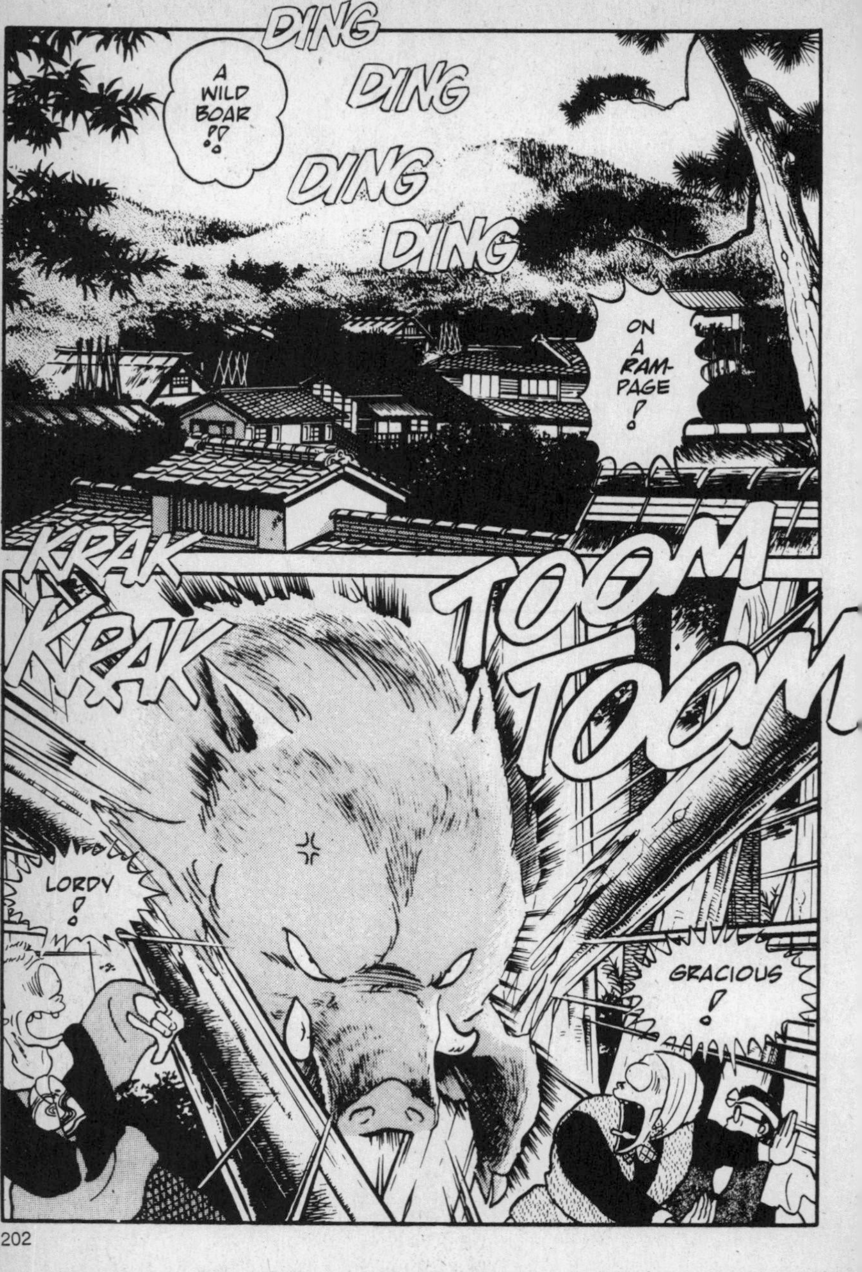
DING
DING
DING
DING
A WILD BOAR?!
ON A RAMPAGE!
KRAK KRAK
TOOM TOOM
LORDY!
GRACIOUS!

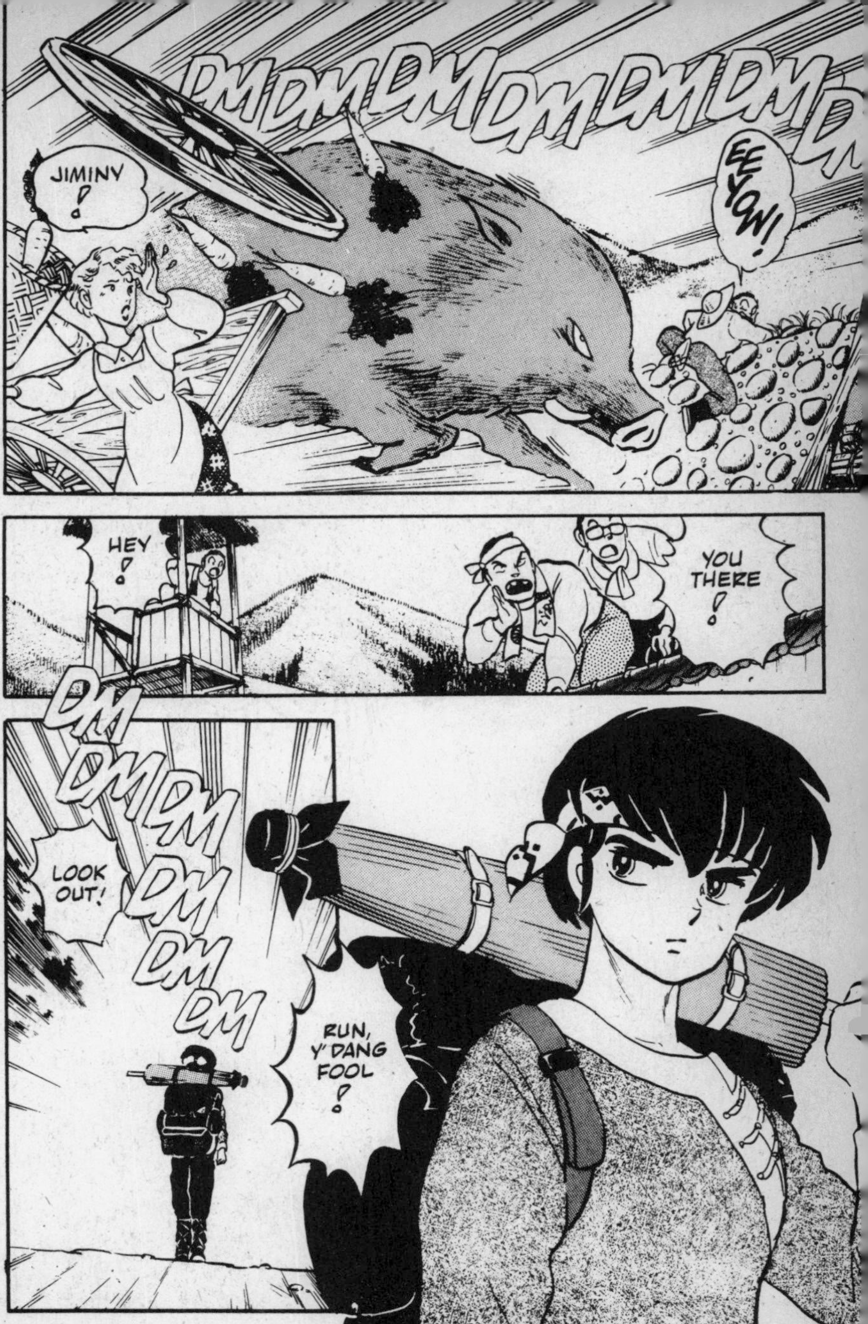
DMDMDMDMDMDMDMDMDM
EEYOW!
JIMINY!
YOU THERE!
HEY!
DM
DMDM
DM
DM
DM
LOOK OUT!
RUN, Y' DANG FOOL!

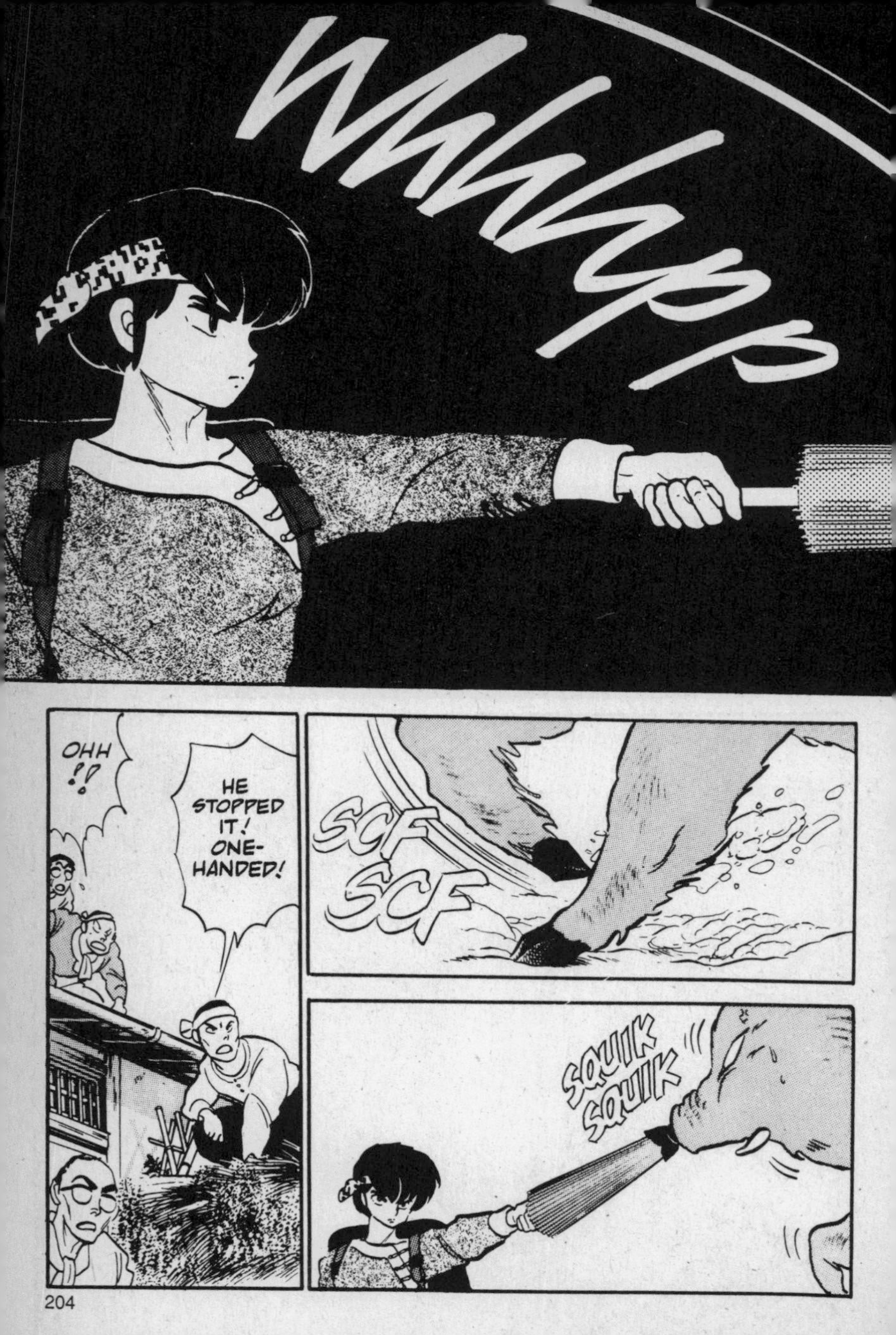
OHH !?
HE STOPPED IT! ONE-HANDED!
SCF
SCF
SQUIK
SQUIK

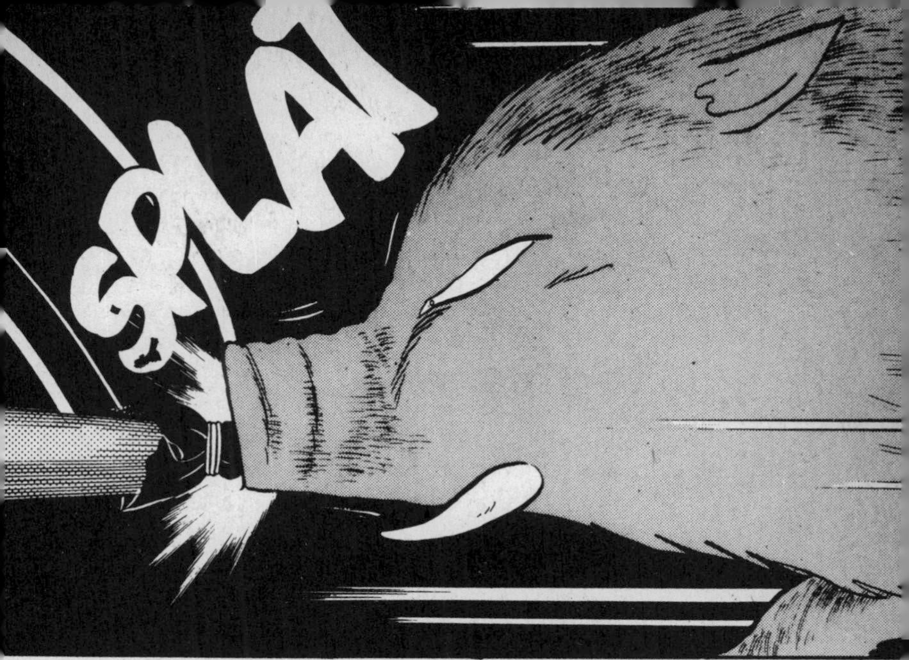
SPLAT
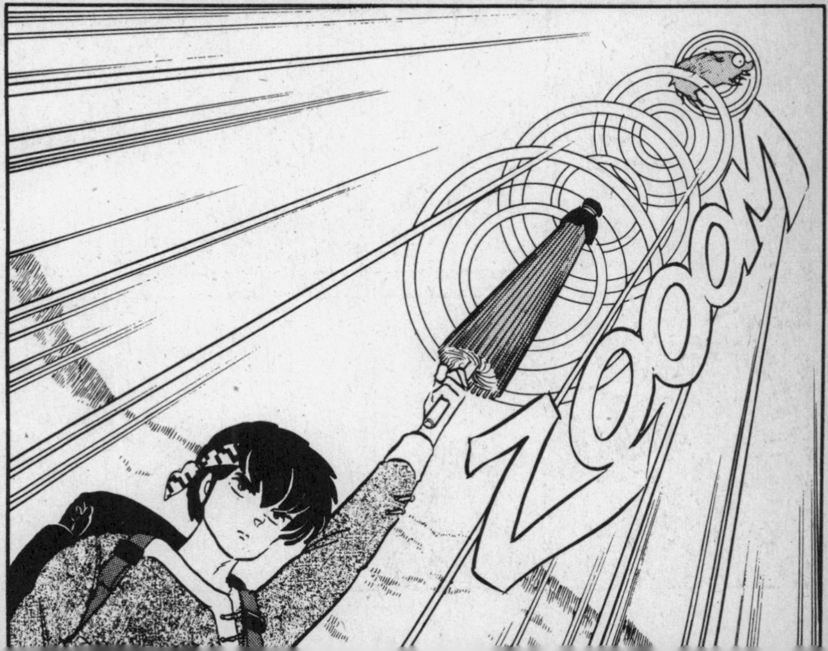
ZOOOOM

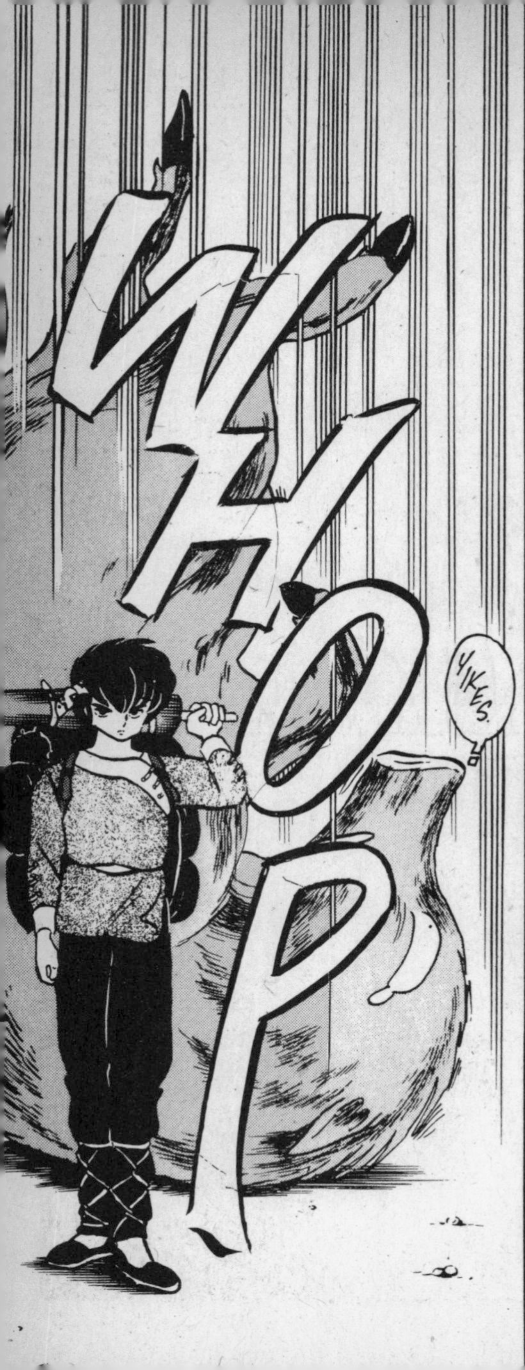
WHOP
YIKES!
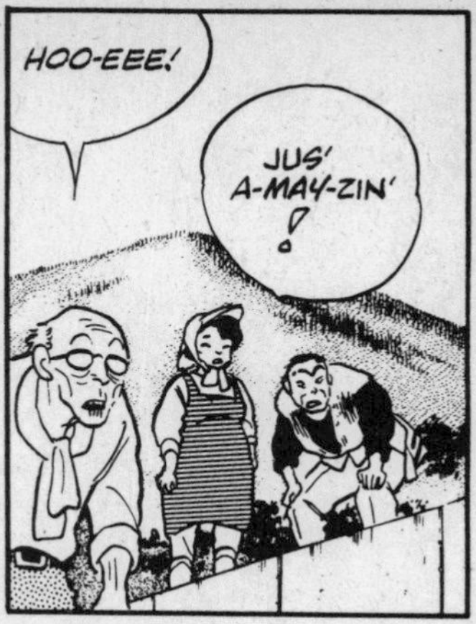
HOO-EEE!
JUS' A-MAY-ZIN'!
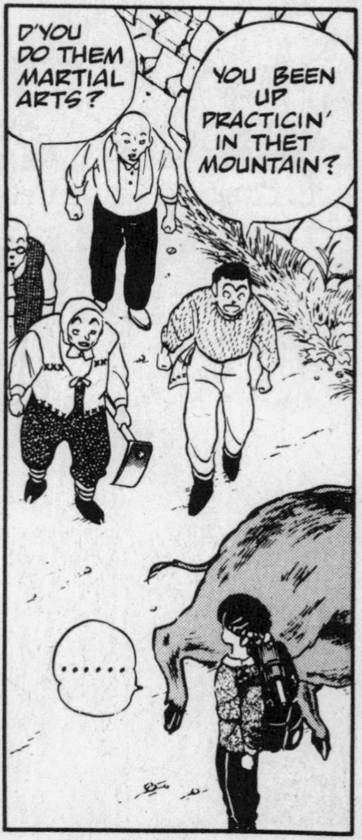
D'YOU DO THEM MARTIAL ARTS?
YOU BEEN UP PRACTICIN' IN THET MOUNTAIN?
......

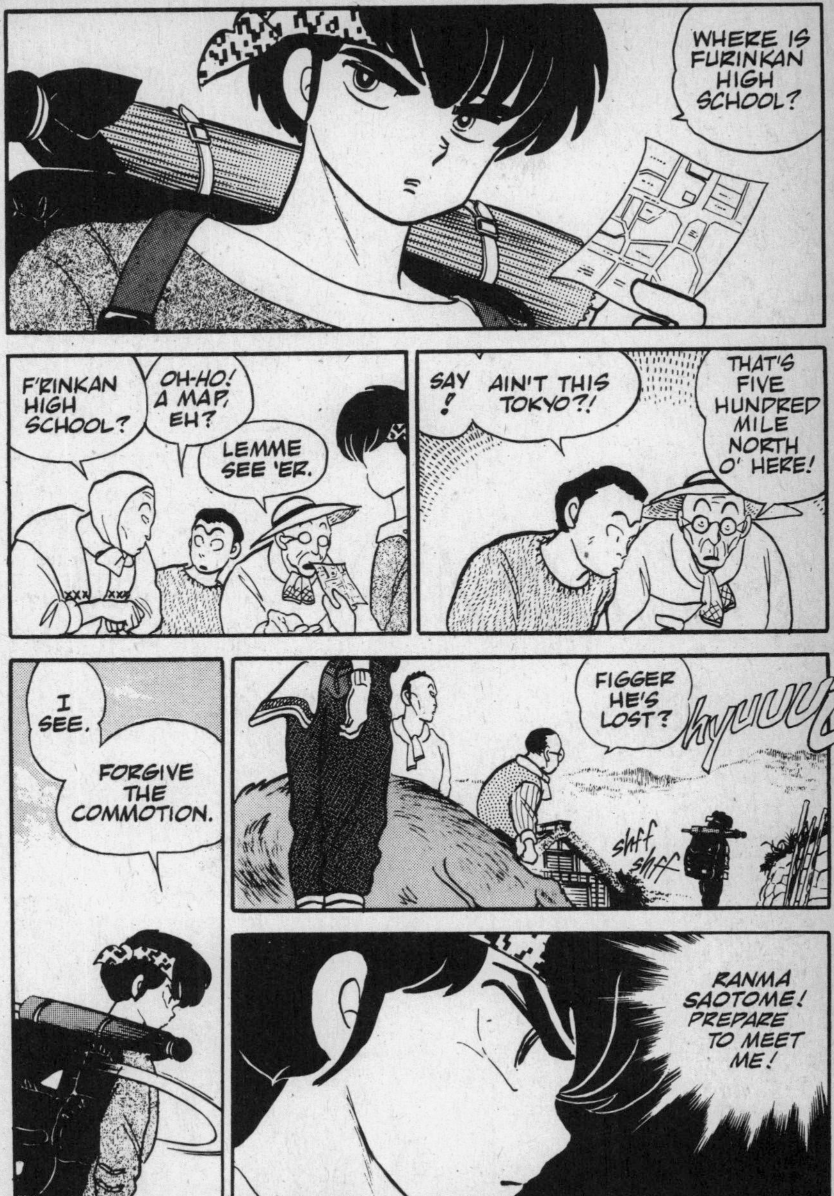
WHERE IS FURINKAN HIGH SCHOOL?
F'RINKAN HIGH SCHOOL?
OH-HO! A MAP, EH?
LEMME SEE 'ER.
SAY!
AIN'T THIS TOKYO?!
THAT'S FIVE HUNDRED MILE NORTH O' HERE!
I SEE.
FORGIVE THE COMMOTION.
FIGGER HE'S LOST?
hyuuu
shff shff
RANMA SAOTOME! PREPARE TO MEET ME!

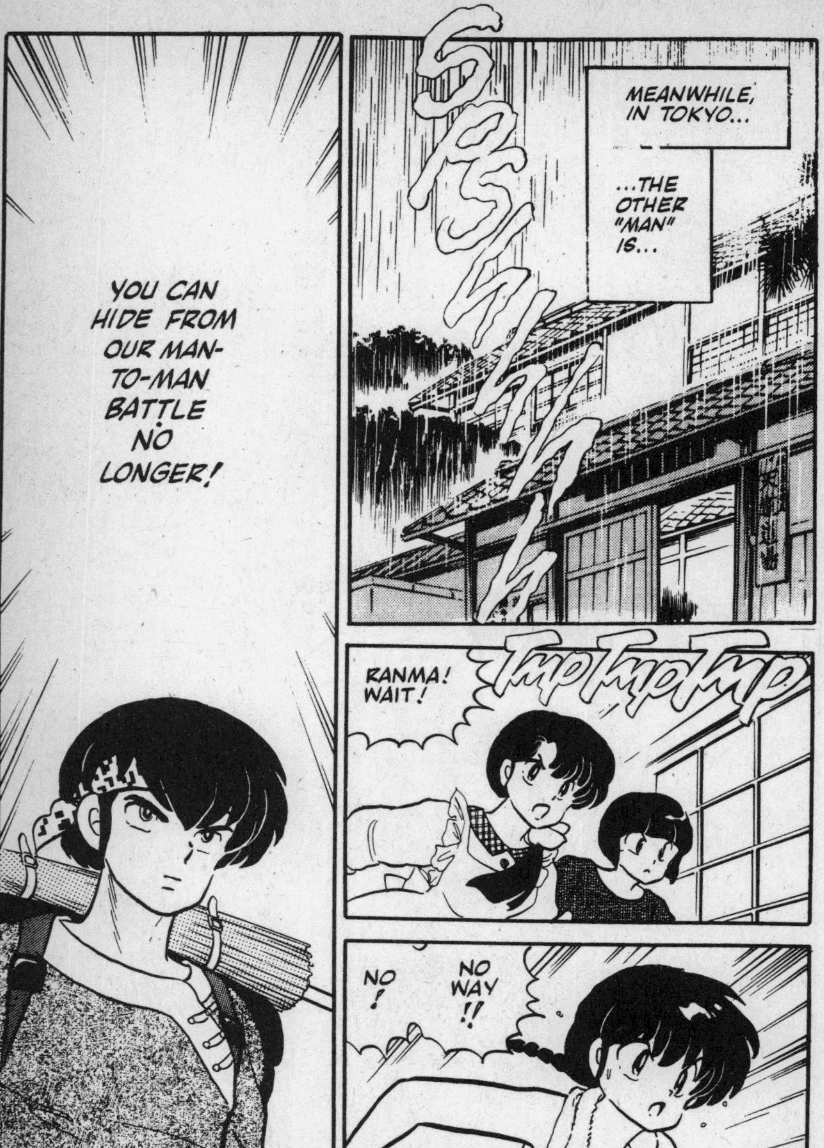

YOU CAN HIDE FROM OUR MAN-TO-MAN BATTLE NO LONGER!
MEANWHILE, IN TOKYO...
...THE OTHER "MAN" IS...
RANMA! WAIT!
TMP TMP TMP TMP
NO!
NO WAY!!

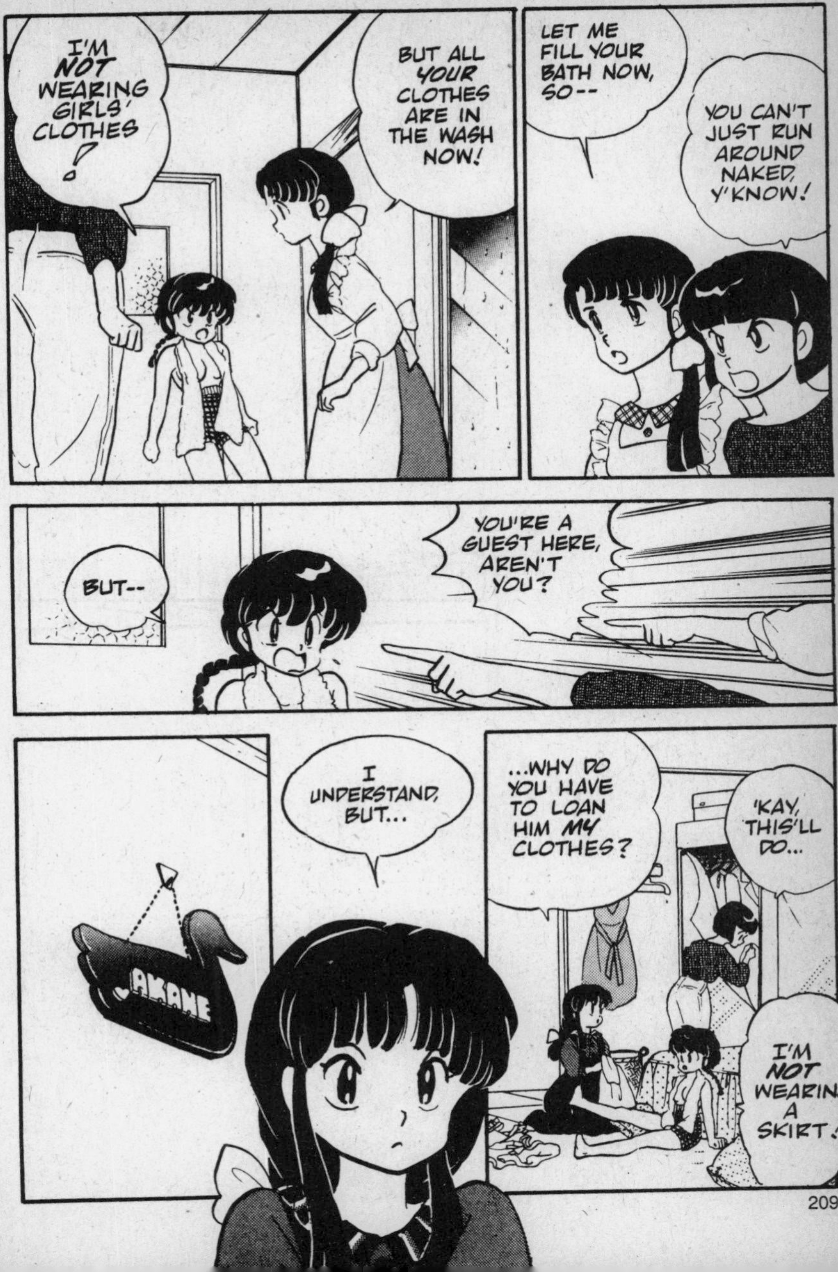
I'M NOT WEARING GIRLS' CLOTHES!
BUT ALL YOUR CLOTHES ARE IN THE WASH NOW!
LET ME FILL YOUR BATH NOW, SO--
YOU CAN'T JUST RUN AROUND NAKED, Y'KNOW!
BUT--
YOU'RE A GUEST HERE, AREN'T YOU?
AKANE
I UNDERSTAND, BUT...
...WHY DO YOU HAVE TO LOAN HIM MY CLOTHES?
'KAY, THIS'LL DO...
I'M NOT WEARING A SKIRT!

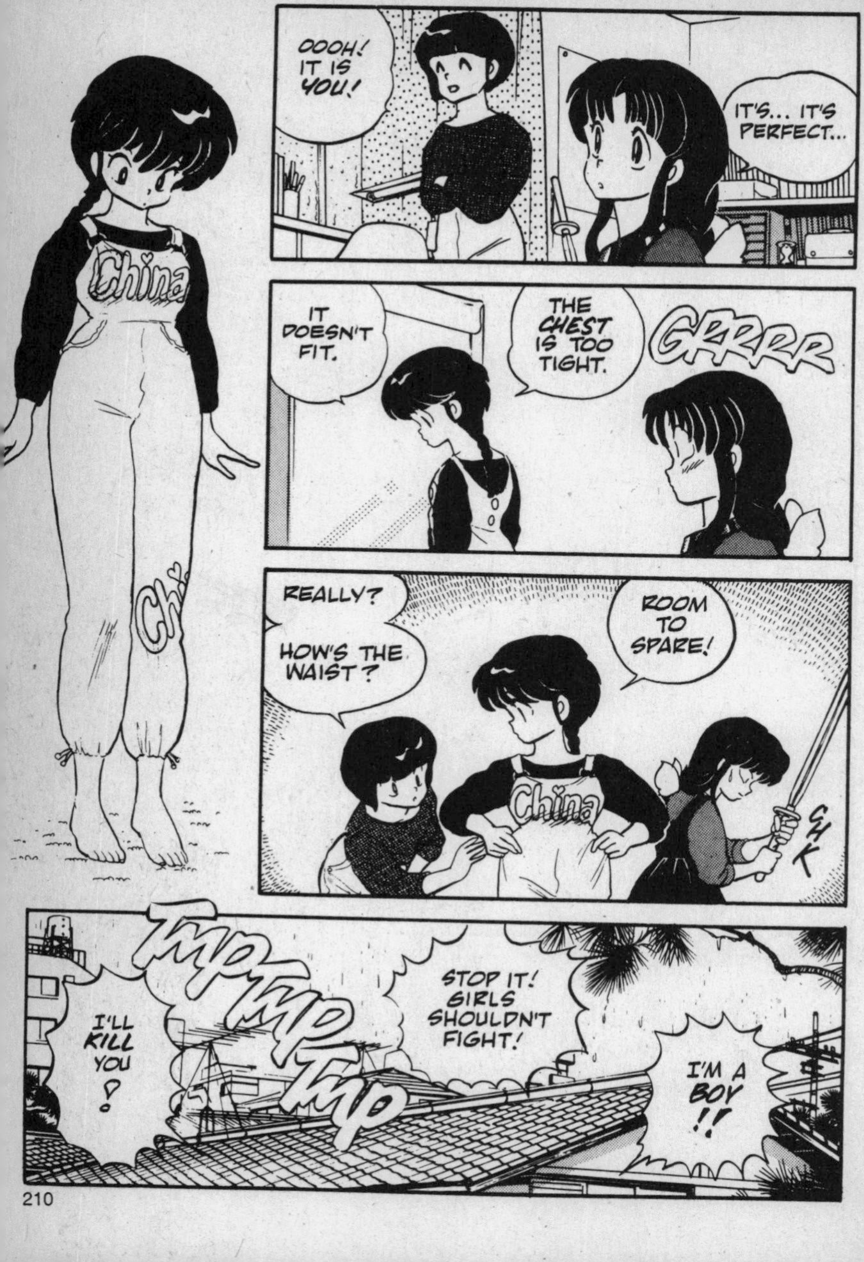
OOOH! IT IS YOU!
IT'S... IT'S PERFECT...
IT DOESN'T FIT.
THE CHEST IS TOO TIGHT.
GRRRR
REALLY?
HOW'S THE WAIST?
ROOM TO SPARE!
CHK
I'LL KILL YOU ?
Tmp Tmp Tmp Tmp
STOP IT! GIRLS SHOULDN'T FIGHT!
I'M A BOY !!

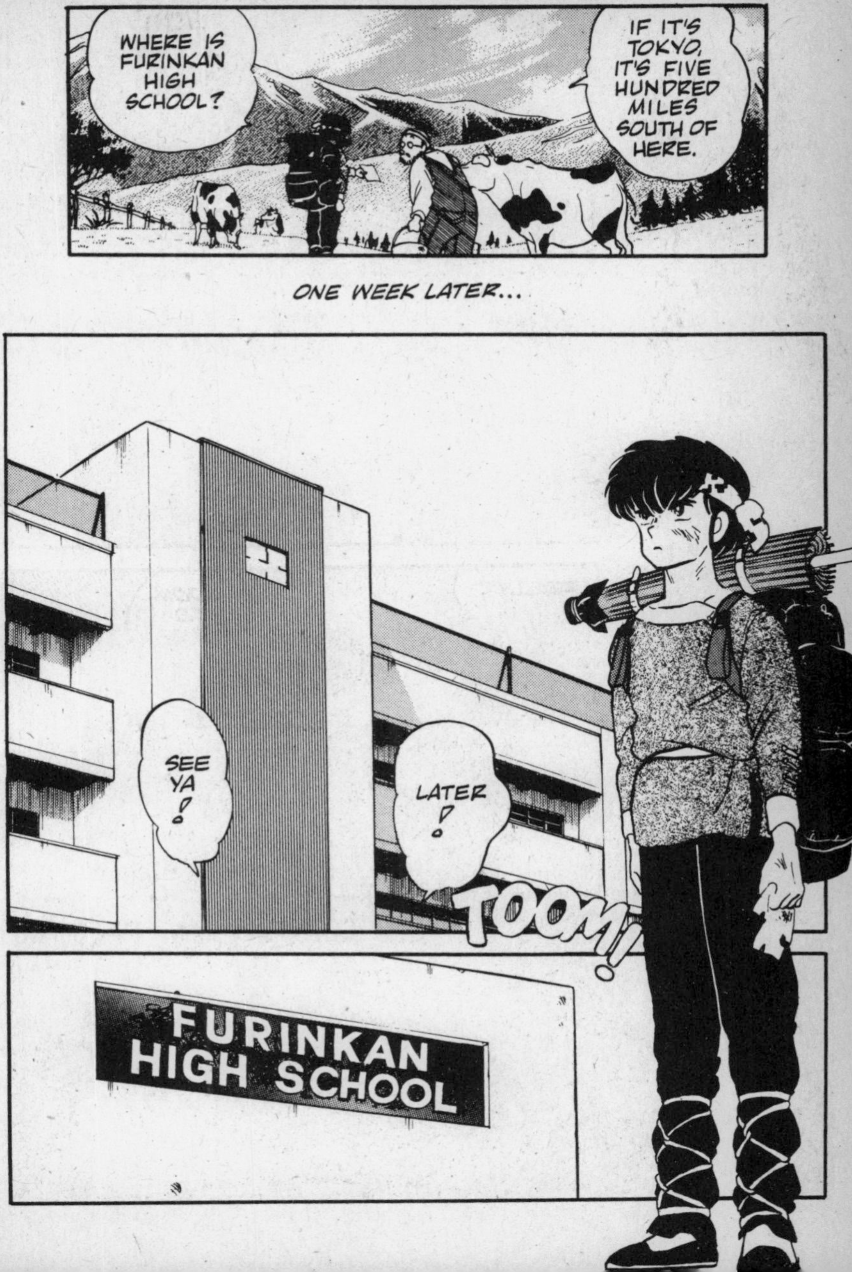
WHERE IS FURINKAN HIGH SCHOOL?
IF IT'S TOKYO, IT'S FIVE HUNDRED MILES SOUTH OF HERE.
ONE WEEK LATER...
SEE YA!
LATER!
TOOM!!
FURINKAN HIGH SCHOOL

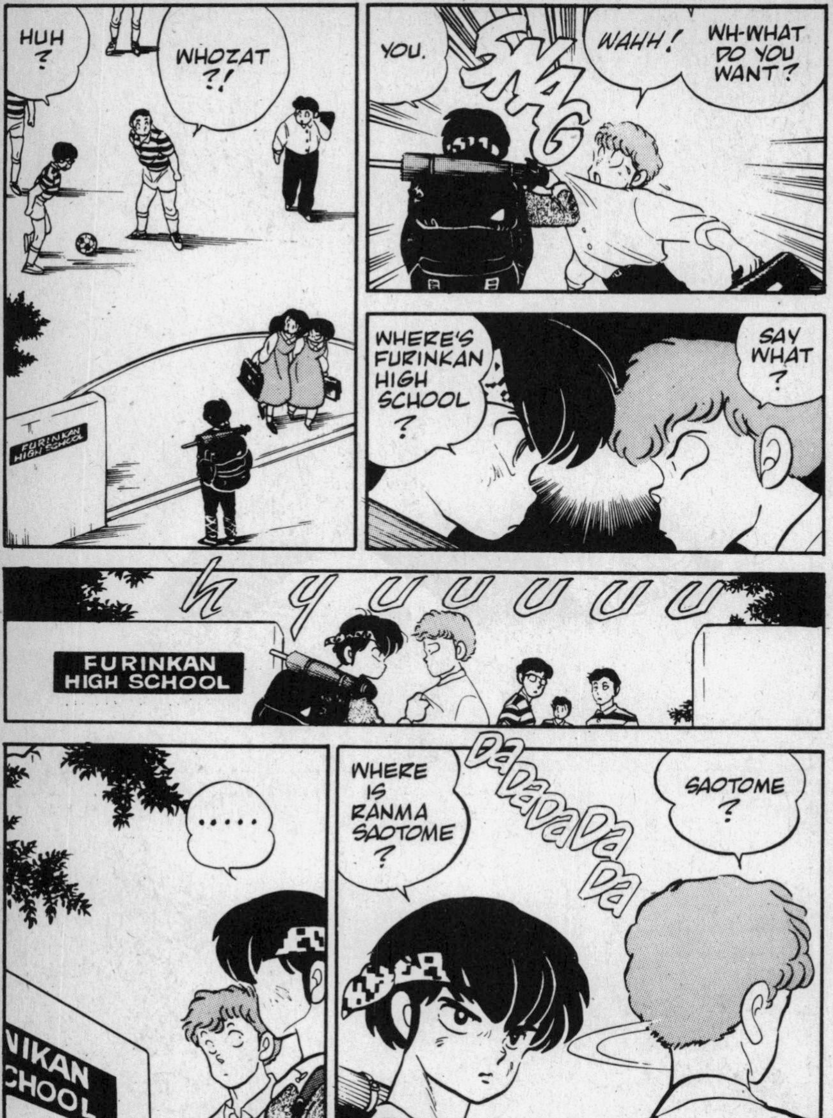
HUH ?
WHOZAT ?!
YOU.
SNAG
WAHH!
WH-WHAT DO YOU WANT?
FURINKAN HIGH SCHOOL
WHERE'S FURINKAN HIGH SCHOOL ?
SAY WHAT ?
h y u u u u u u u
FURINKAN HIGH SCHOOL
.....
NIKAN
CHOOL
WHERE IS RANMA SAOTOME ?
DA DA DA DA DA DA DA
SAOTOME ?

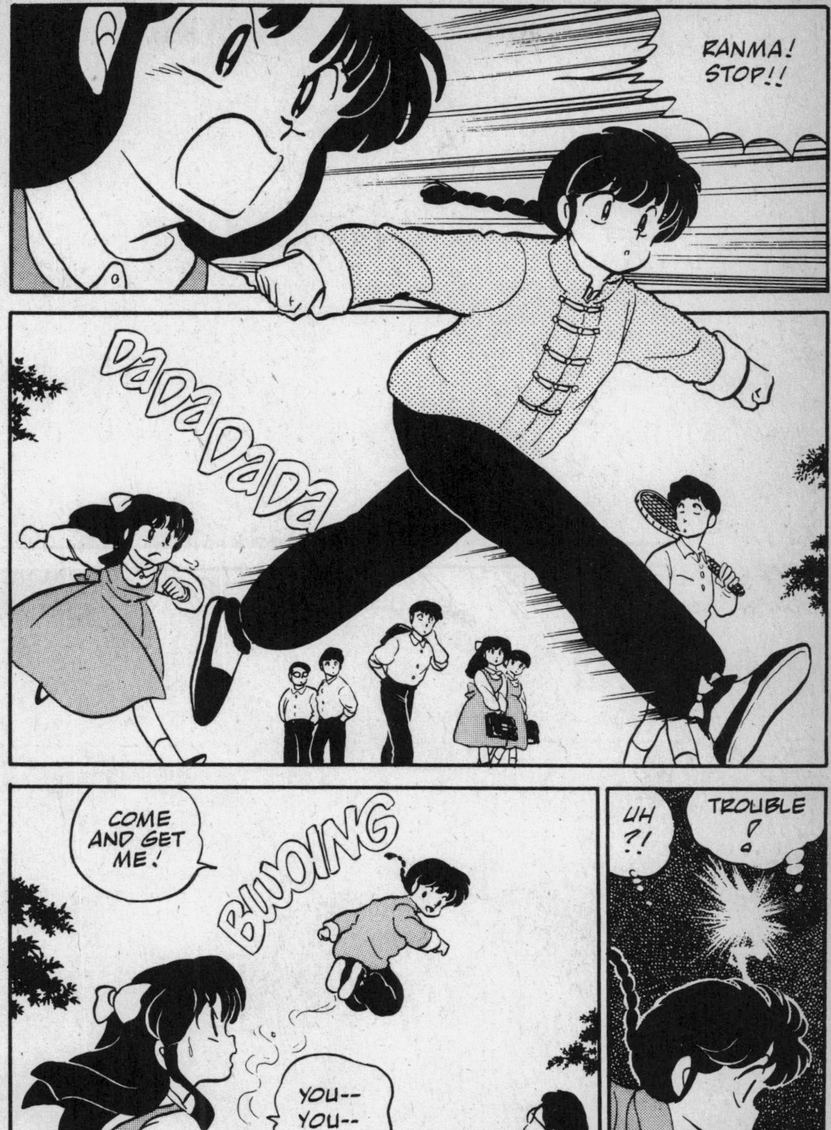
RANMA!
STOP!!
DADADADADA
COME AND GET ME!
BWOING
YOU-- YOU--
UH ?!
TROUBLE !

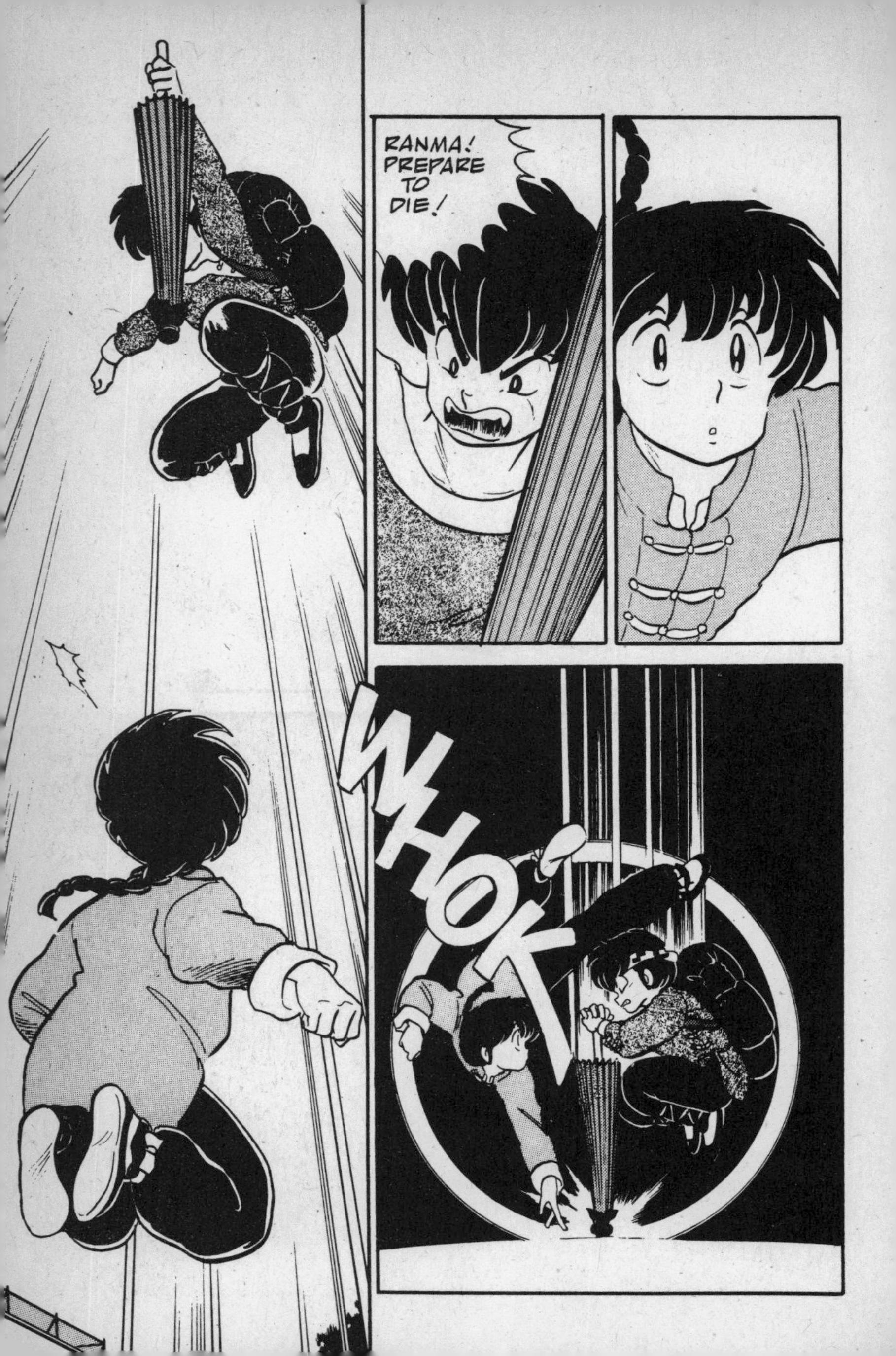
RANMA! PREPARE TO DIE!
WHOK

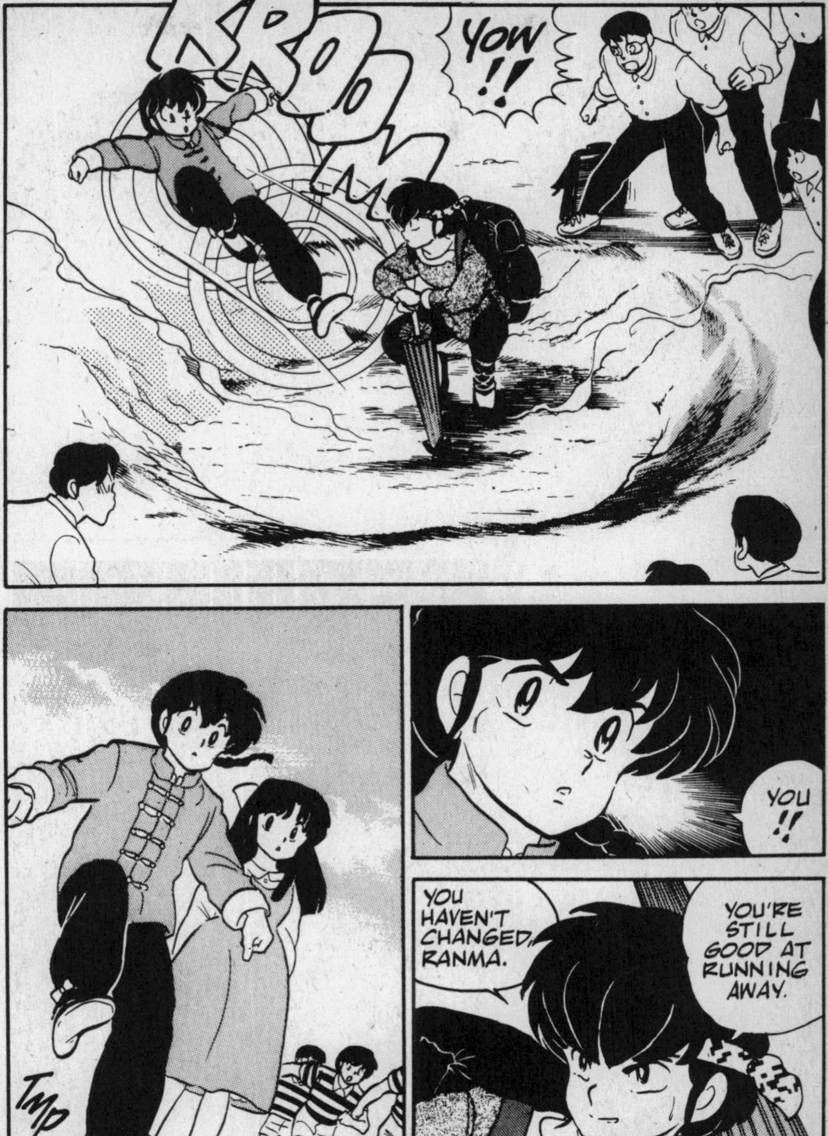
KROOOMM
YOW!!
Tmp
YOU!!
YOU HAVEN'T CHANGED, RANMA.
YOU'RE STILL GOOD AT RUNNING AWAY.

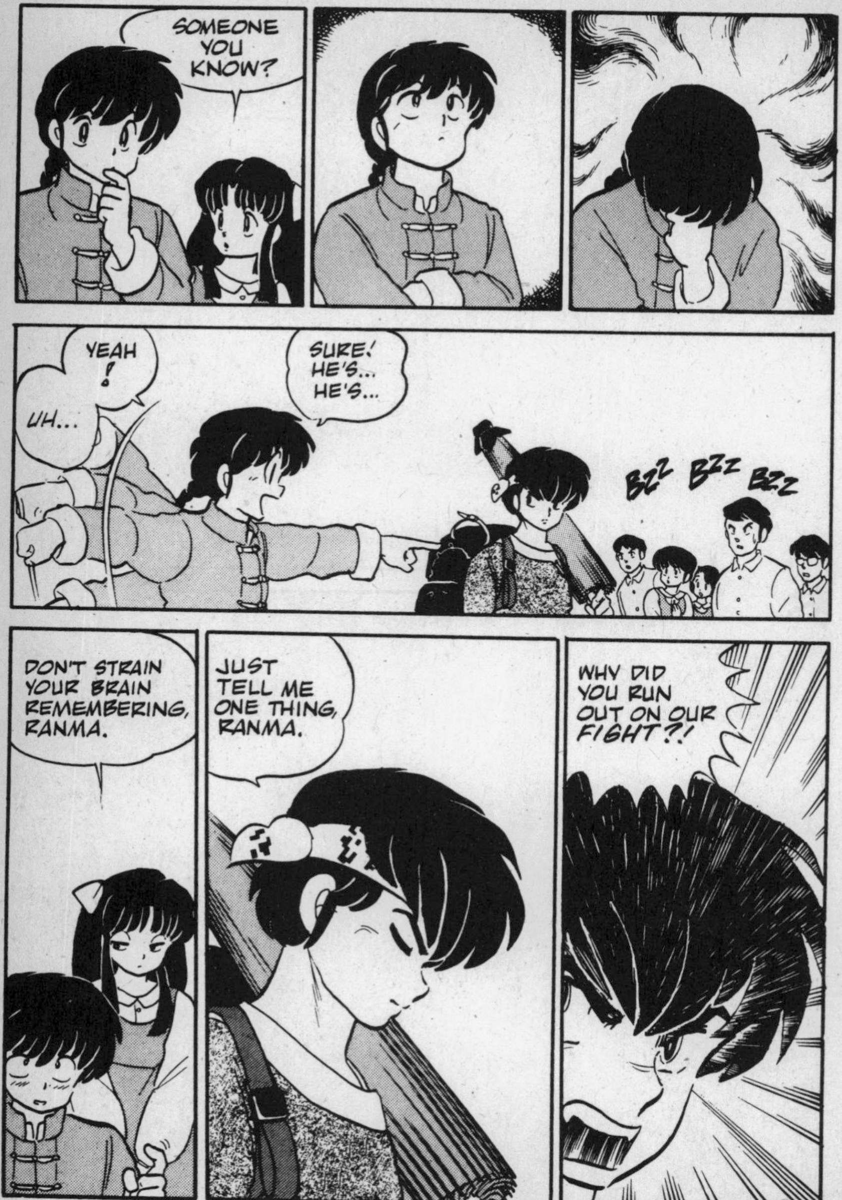
SOMEONE YOU KNOW?
YEAH!
UH...
SURE! HE'S... HE'S...
BZZ BZZ BZZ
DON'T STRAIN YOUR BRAIN REMEMBERING, RANMA.
JUST TELL ME ONE THING, RANMA.
WHY DID YOU RUN OUT ON OUR FIGHT?!

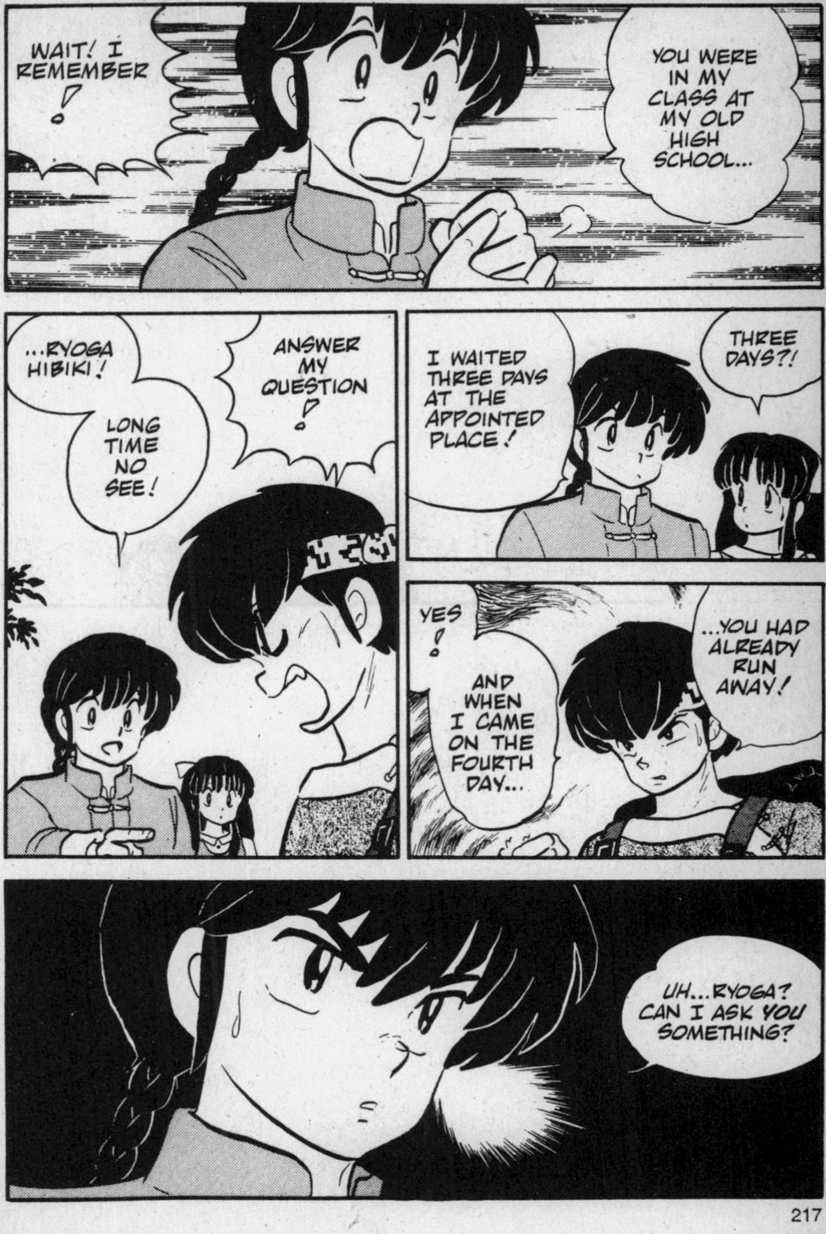
WAIT! I REMEMBER!
YOU WERE IN MY CLASS AT MY OLD HIGH SCHOOL...
...RYOGA HIBIKI!
LONG TIME NO SEE!
ANSWER MY QUESTION!
I WAITED THREE DAYS AT THE APPOINTED PLACE!
THREE DAYS?!
YES!
AND WHEN I CAME ON THE FOURTH DAY...
...YOU HAD ALREADY RUN AWAY!
UH...RYOGA? CAN I ASK YOU SOMETHING?

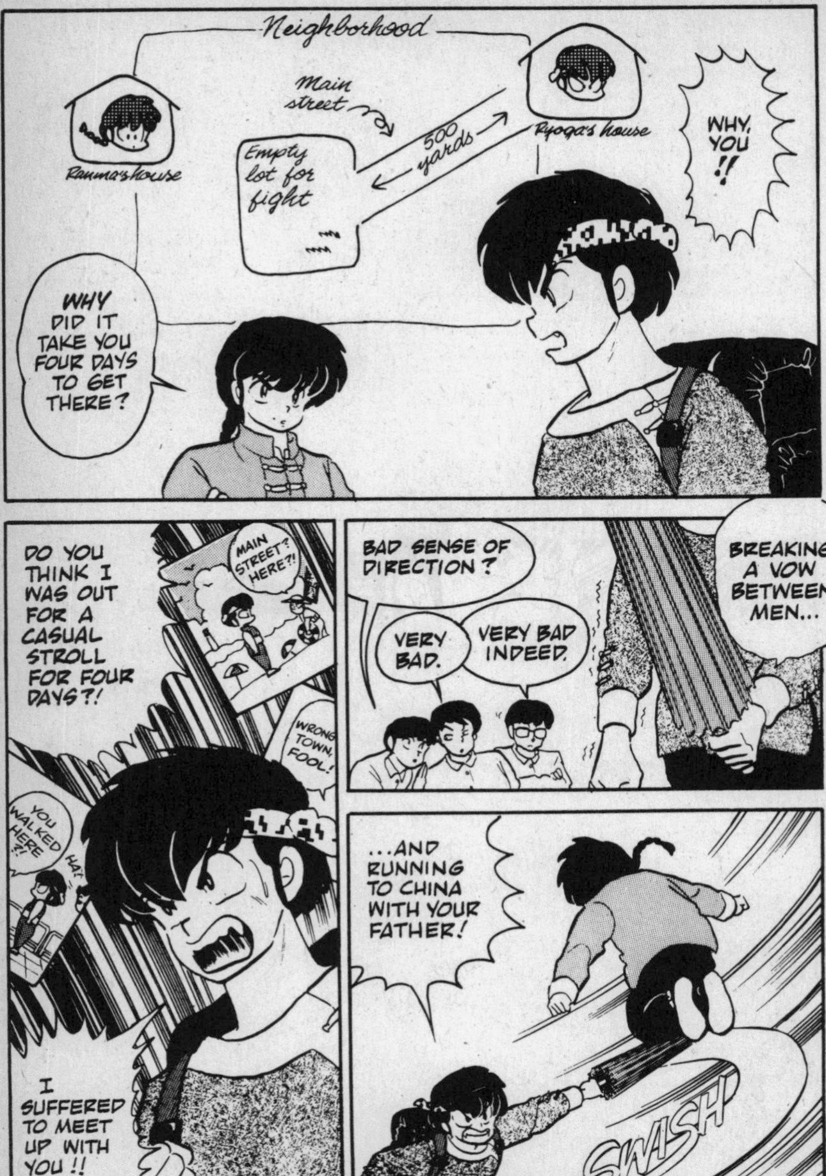
Neighborhood
Main street
Ranma's house
Empty lot for fight
500 yards
Ryoga's house
WHY DID IT TAKE YOU FOUR DAYS TO GET THERE?
WHY, YOU!!
DO YOU THINK I WAS OUT FOR A CASUAL STROLL FOR FOUR DAYS?!
MAIN STREET? HERE?!
WRONG TOWN, FOOL!
YOU WALKED HERE?!
HA!
I SUFFERED TO MEET UP WITH YOU!!
BAD SENSE OF DIRECTION?
VERY BAD.
VERY BAD INDEED.
BREAKING A VOW BETWEEN MEN...
...AND RUNNING TO CHINA WITH YOUR FATHER!
SWISH

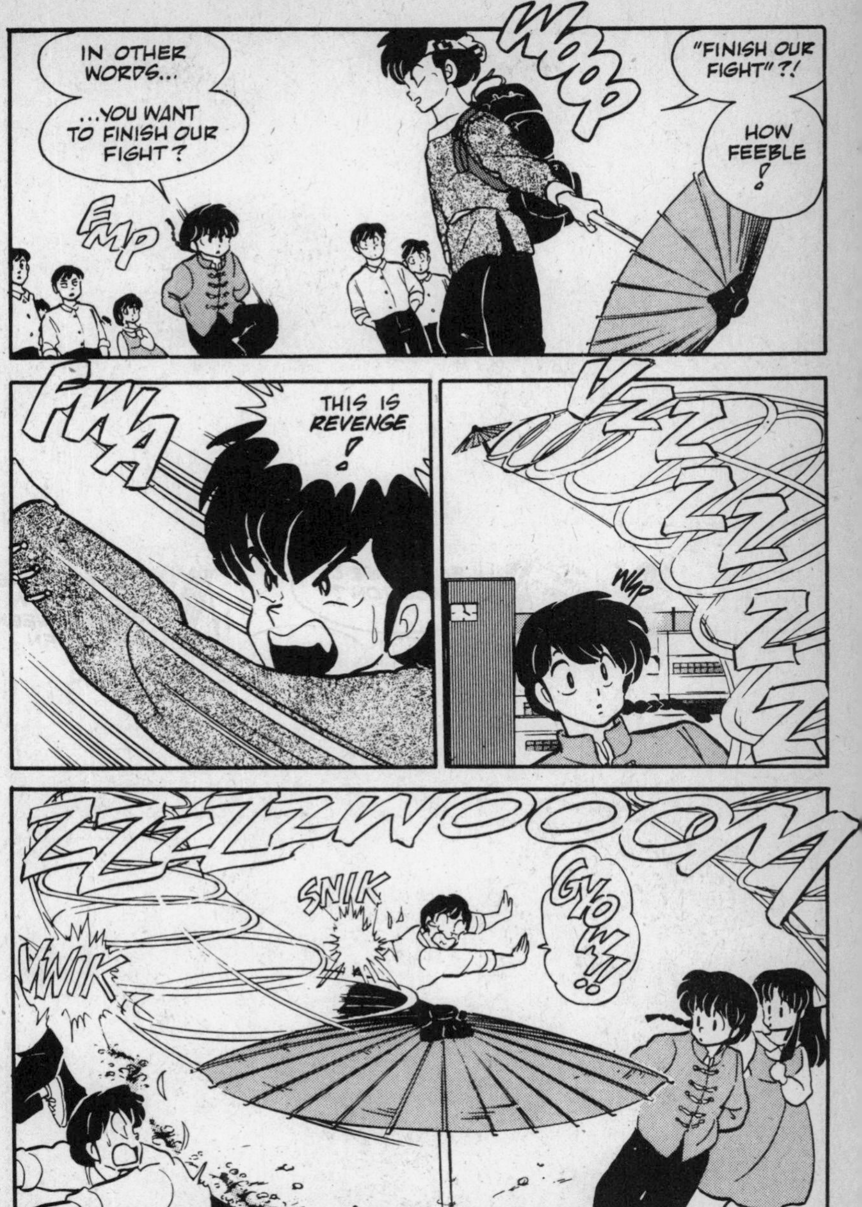
IN OTHER WORDS...
...YOU WANT TO FINISH OUR FIGHT?
FMP
WOOOP
"FINISH OUR FIGHT"?!
HOW FEEBLE!
FWA
THIS IS REVENGE!
VZZZZZZZ
WUP
ZZZZZWOOOOM
SNIK
GYOW!!
VWIK

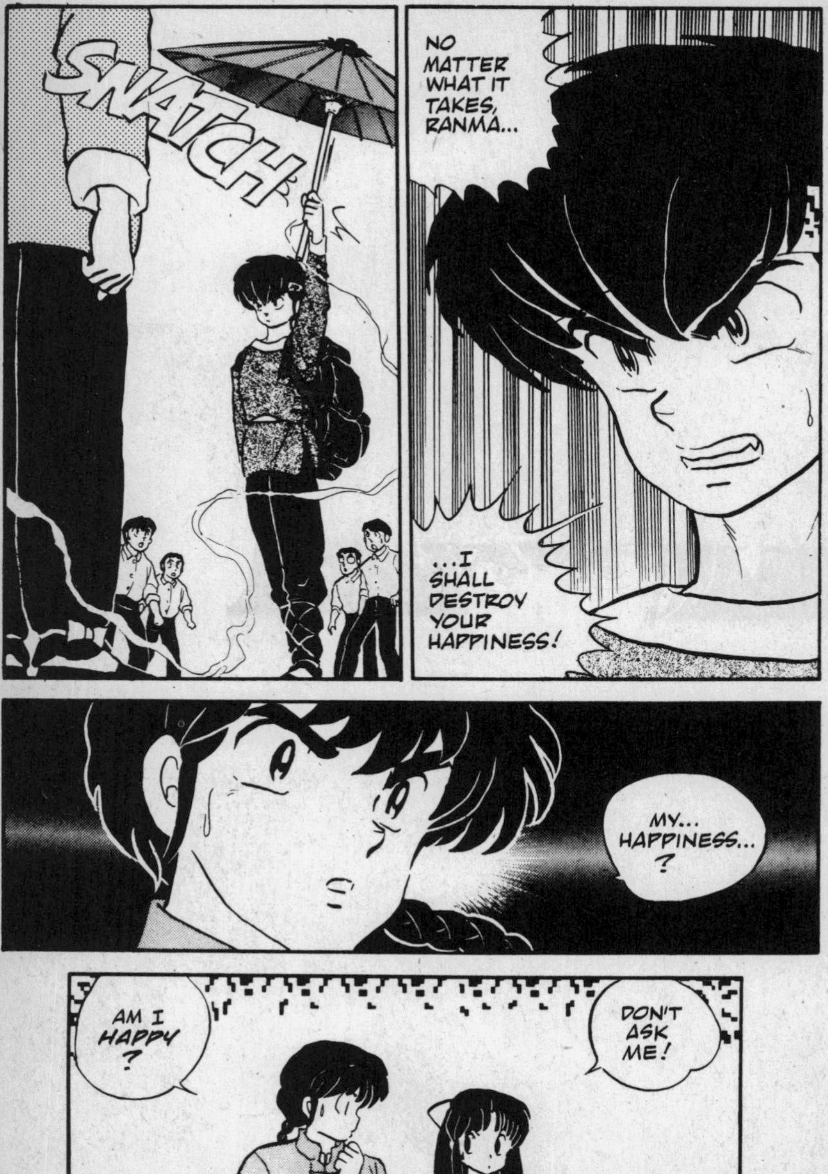
SNATCH
NO MATTER WHAT IT TAKES, RANMA...
...I SHALL DESTROY YOUR HAPPINESS!
MY... HAPPINESS... ?
AM I HAPPY ?
DON'T ASK ME!

Part 11
BREAD FEUD

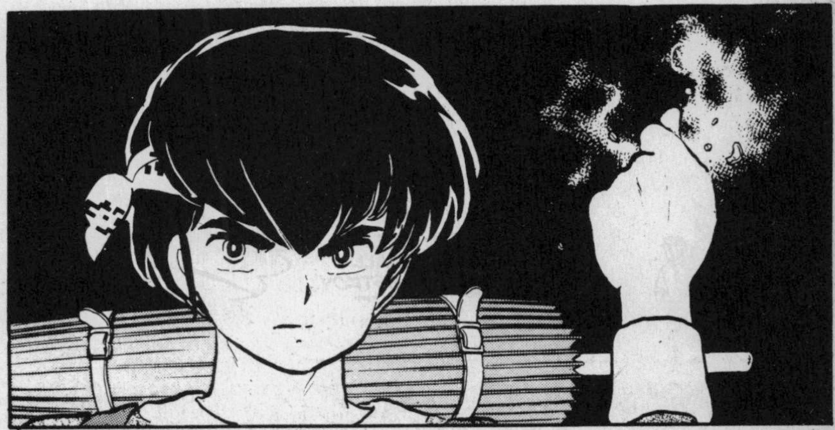

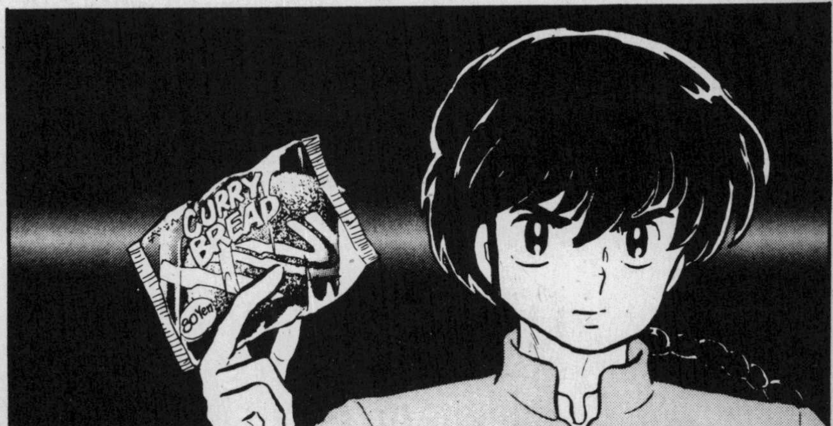
CURRY BREAD
80 Yen

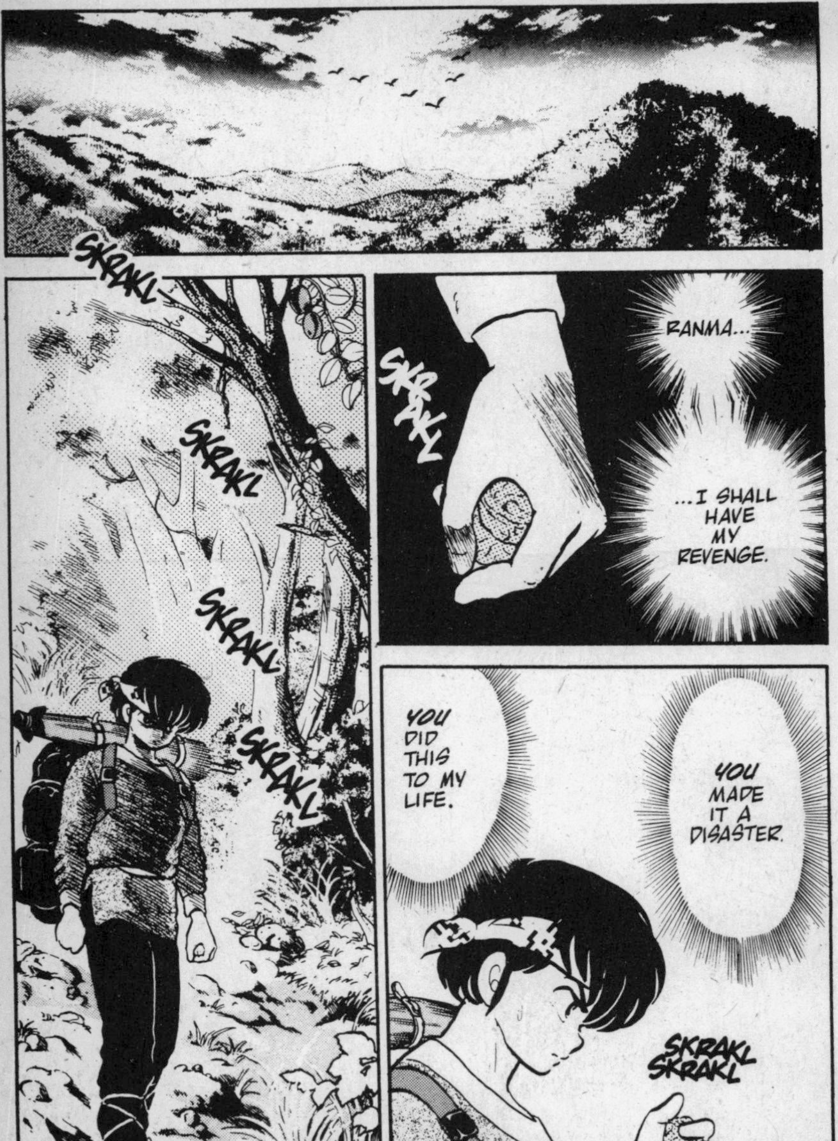
SKRAKL
SKRAKL
SKRAKL
SKRAKL
SKRAKL
RANMA...
...I SHALL HAVE MY REVENGE.
YOU DID THIS TO MY LIFE.
YOU MADE IT A DISASTER.
SKRAKL SKRAKL

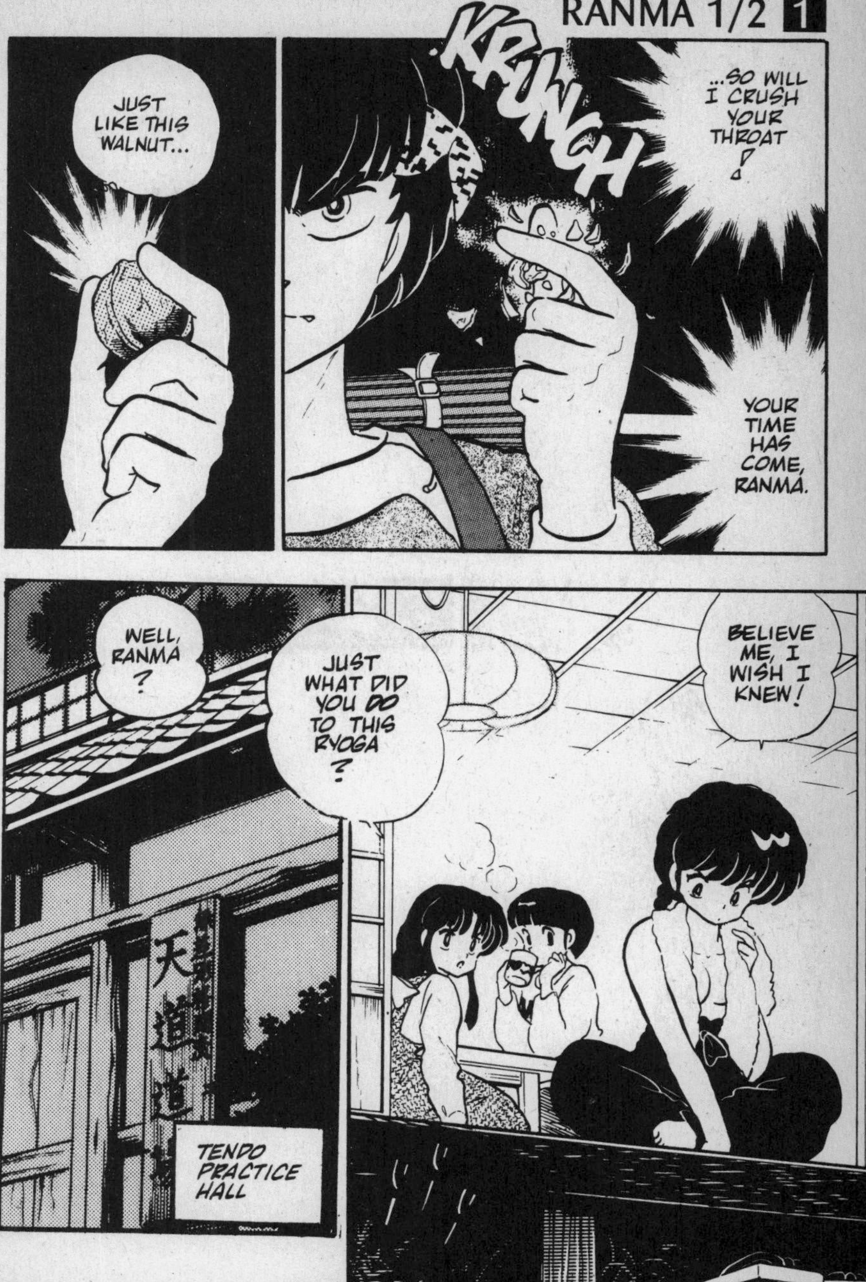
JUST LIKE THIS WALNUT...
KRUNCH
...SO WILL I CRUSH YOUR THROAT!
YOUR TIME HAS COME, RANMA.
WELL, RANMA?
TENDO PRACTICE HALL
JUST WHAT DID YOU DO TO THIS RYOGA?
BELIEVE ME, I WISH I KNEW!

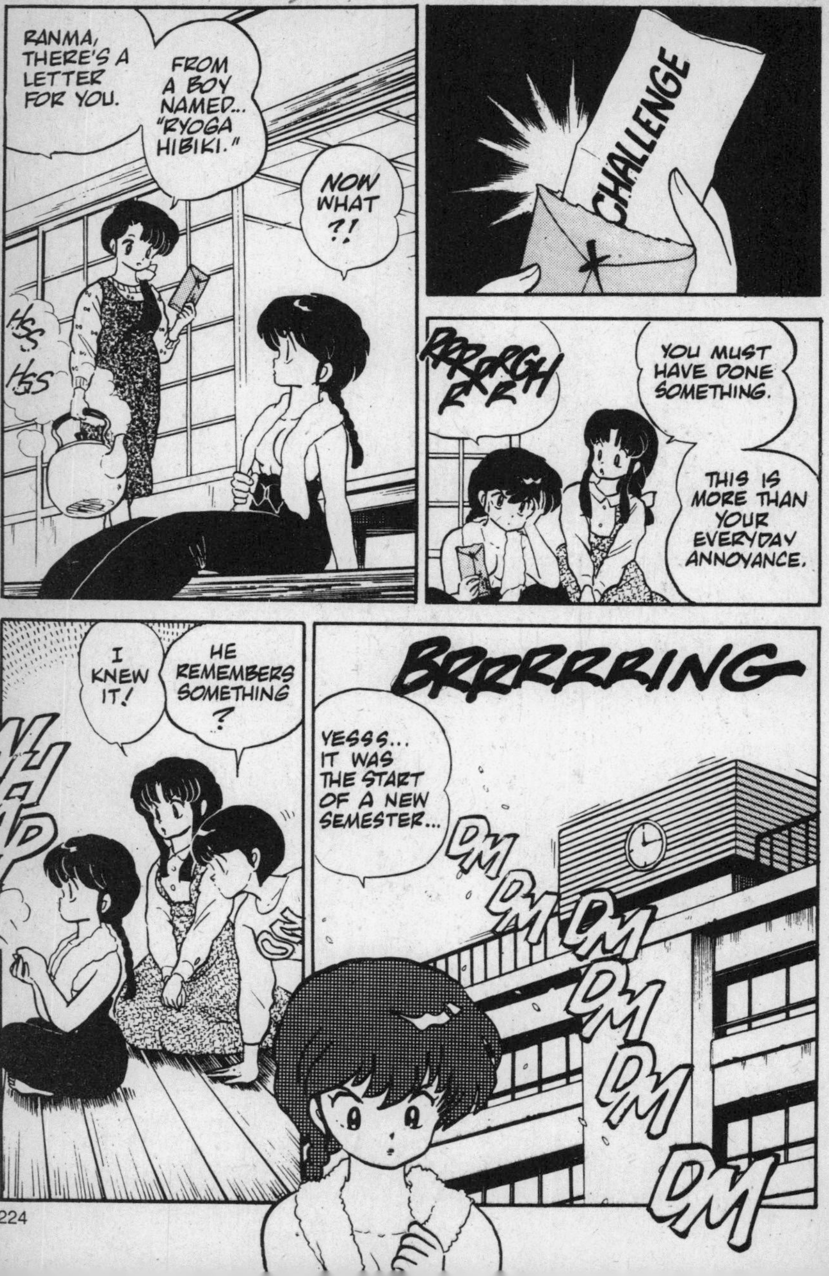
RANMA, THERE'S A LETTER FOR YOU.
FROM A BOY NAMED... "RYOGA HIBIKI."
NOW WHAT ?!
HSS HSS
CHALLENGE
BRRRRGH
YOU MUST HAVE DONE SOMETHING.
THIS IS MORE THAN YOUR EVERYDAY ANNOYANCE.
I KNEW IT!
HE REMEMBERS SOMETHING ?
WHAP
BRRRRRING
YESSS... IT WAS THE START OF A NEW SEMESTER...
DM DM DM DM DM DM DM DM DM

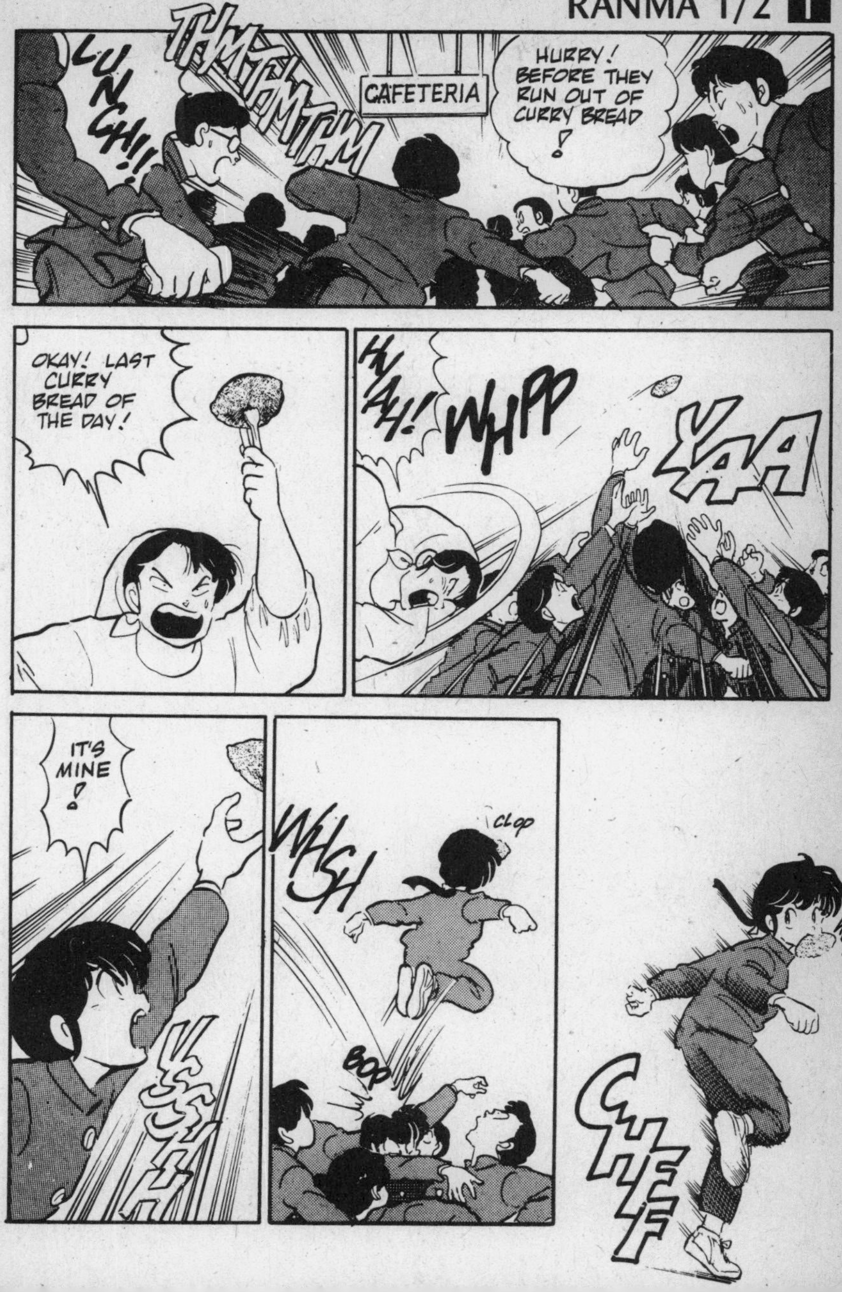
LUNCH!!!
THMTHMTHM
CAFETERIA
HURRY! BEFORE THEY RUN OUT OF CURRY BREAD!
OKAY! LAST CURRY BREAD OF THE DAY!
WHIPP
YAA
IT'S MINE!
WHSH
CLOP
BOP

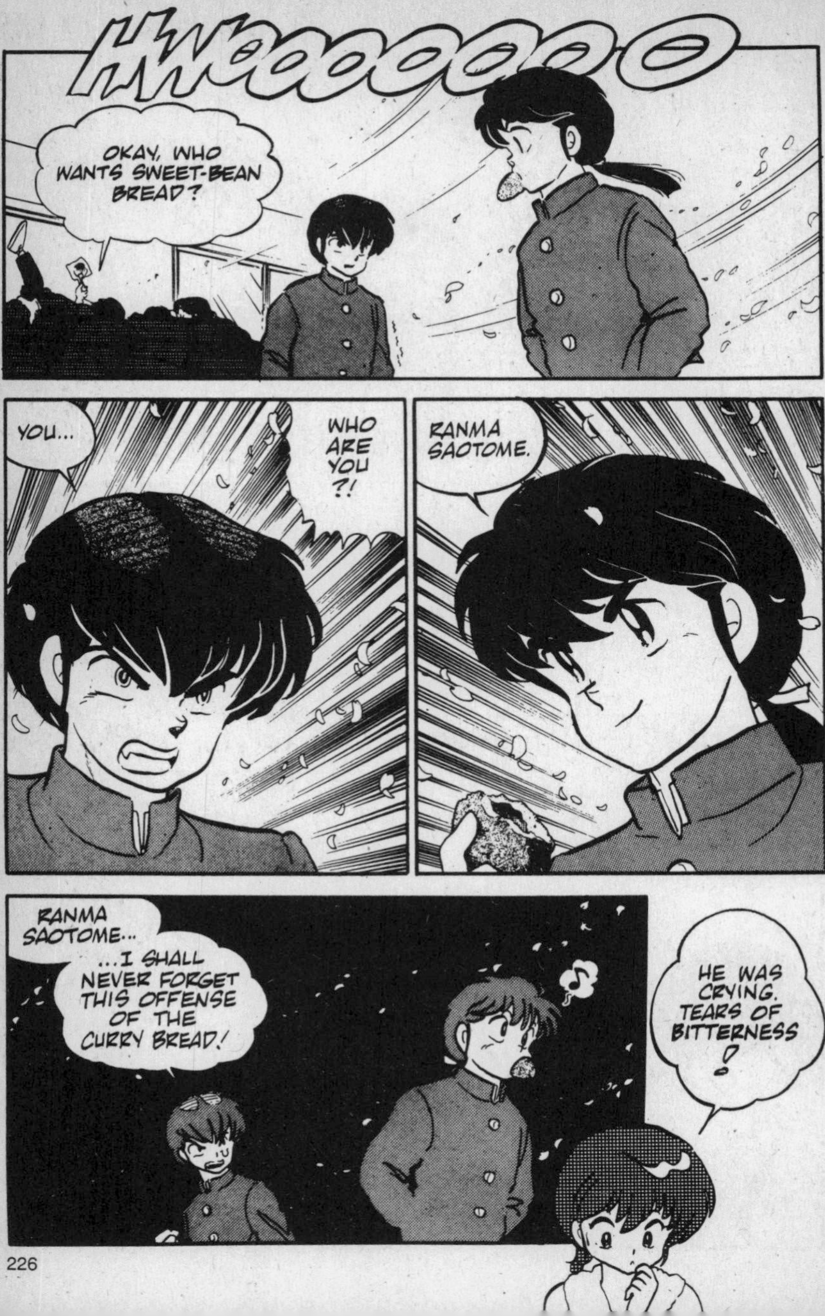
HWOOOOOOO
OKAY, WHO WANTS SWEET-BEAN BREAD?
YOU...
WHO ARE YOU?!
RANMA SAOTOME.
RANMA SAOTOME...
...I SHALL NEVER FORGET THIS OFFENSE OF THE CURRY BREAD!
HE WAS CRYING. TEARS OF BITTERNESS!

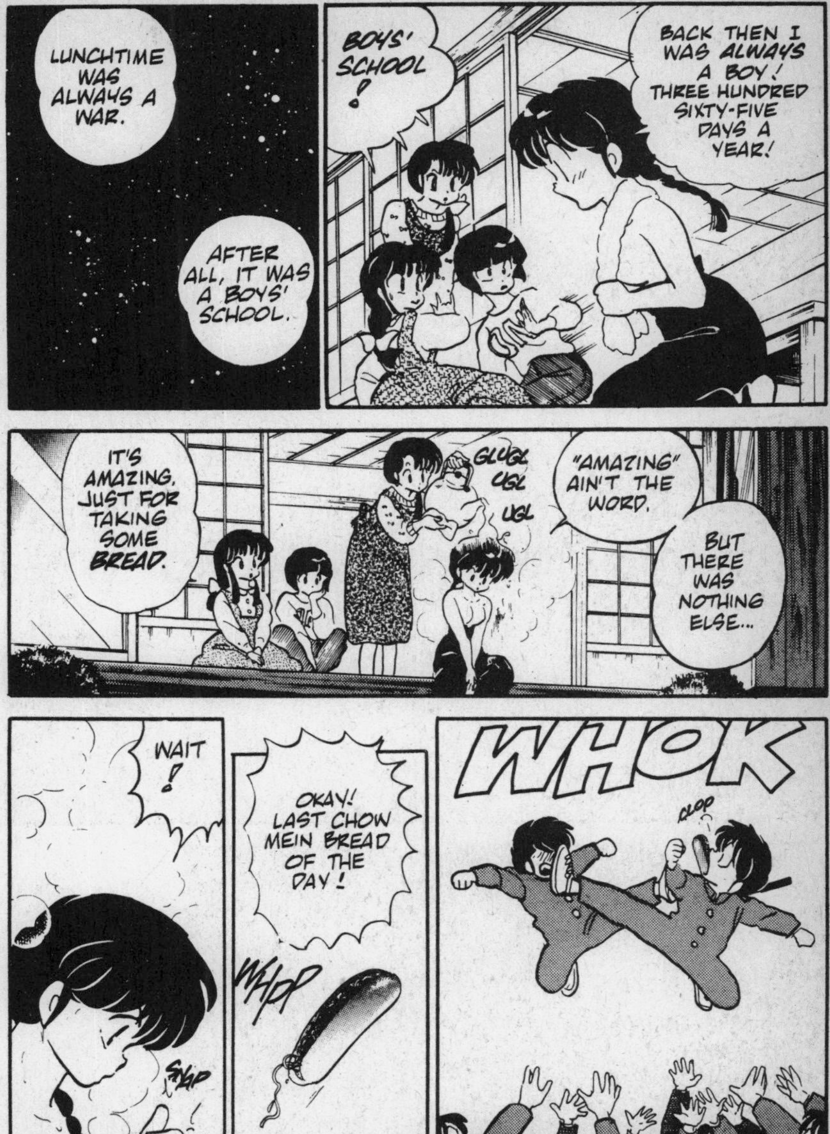
LUNCHTIME WAS ALWAYS A WAR.
AFTER ALL, IT WAS A BOYS' SCHOOL.
BOYS' SCHOOL!
BACK THEN I WAS ALWAYS A BOY! THREE HUNDRED SIXTY-FIVE DAYS A YEAR!
IT'S AMAZING, JUST FOR TAKING SOME BREAD.
GLUGL UGL
UGL
"AMAZING" AIN'T THE WORD.
BUT THERE WAS NOTHING ELSE...
WAIT!
OKAY! LAST CHOW MEIN BREAD OF THE DAY!
WHOK
CLOP

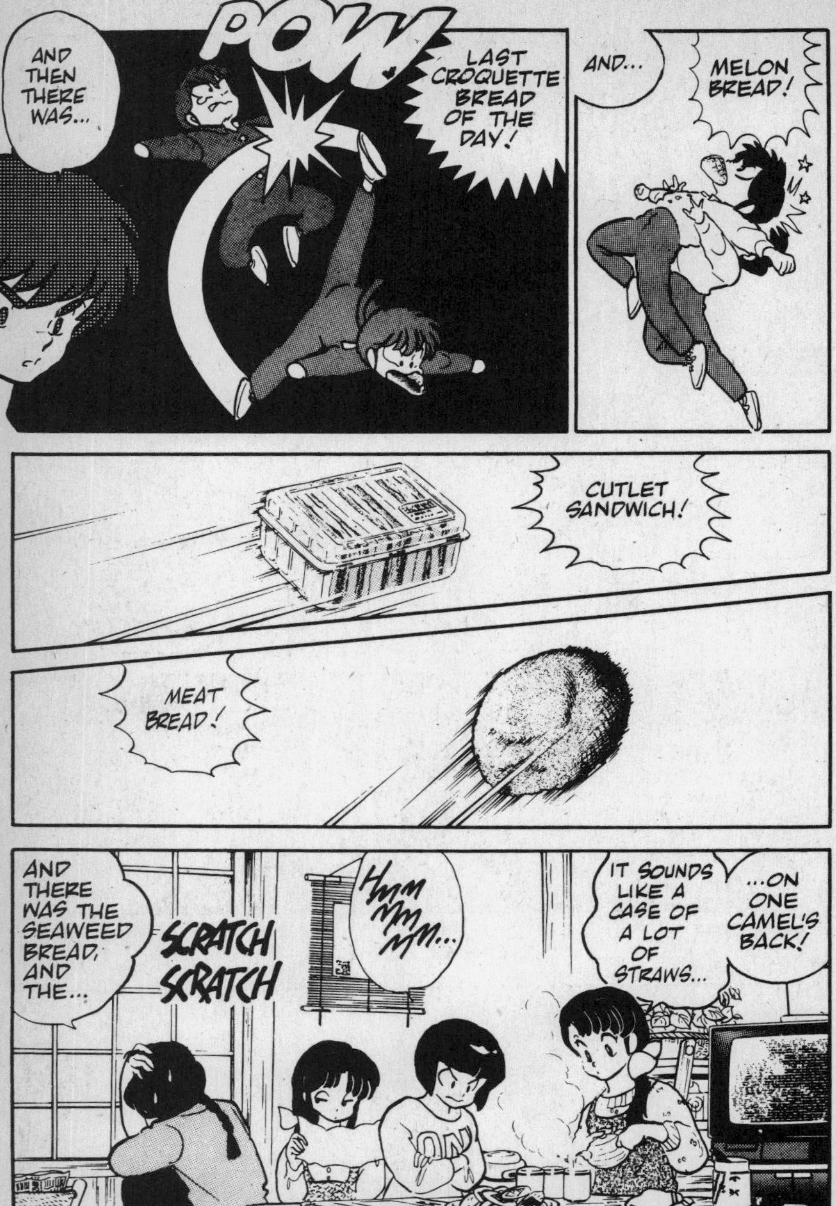
AND THEN THERE WAS...
POW
LAST CROQUETTE BREAD OF THE DAY!
AND...
MELON BREAD!
CUTLET SANDWICH!
MEAT BREAD!
AND THERE WAS THE SEAWEED BREAD, AND THE...
SCRATCH SCRATCH
HMM MM MM...
IT SOUNDS LIKE A CASE OF A LOT OF STRAWS...
...ON ONE CAMEL'S BACK!

HM?

UH... RANMA?

THE DATE OF YOUR SHOWDOWN WAS YESTERDAY!

NO PROBLEM.

THAT GUY'S GOT THE WORLD'S WORST SENSE OF DIRECTION.

RIGHT NOW HE'S PROBABLY ASKING SOMEBODY...

THEN IT'S *THIS* WAY TO TOKYO?

IT'S *THIS* WAY! *THIS* WAY!

WHY ARE YOU GOING THAT WAY?

ONE WEEK LATER...

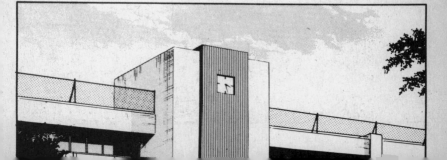

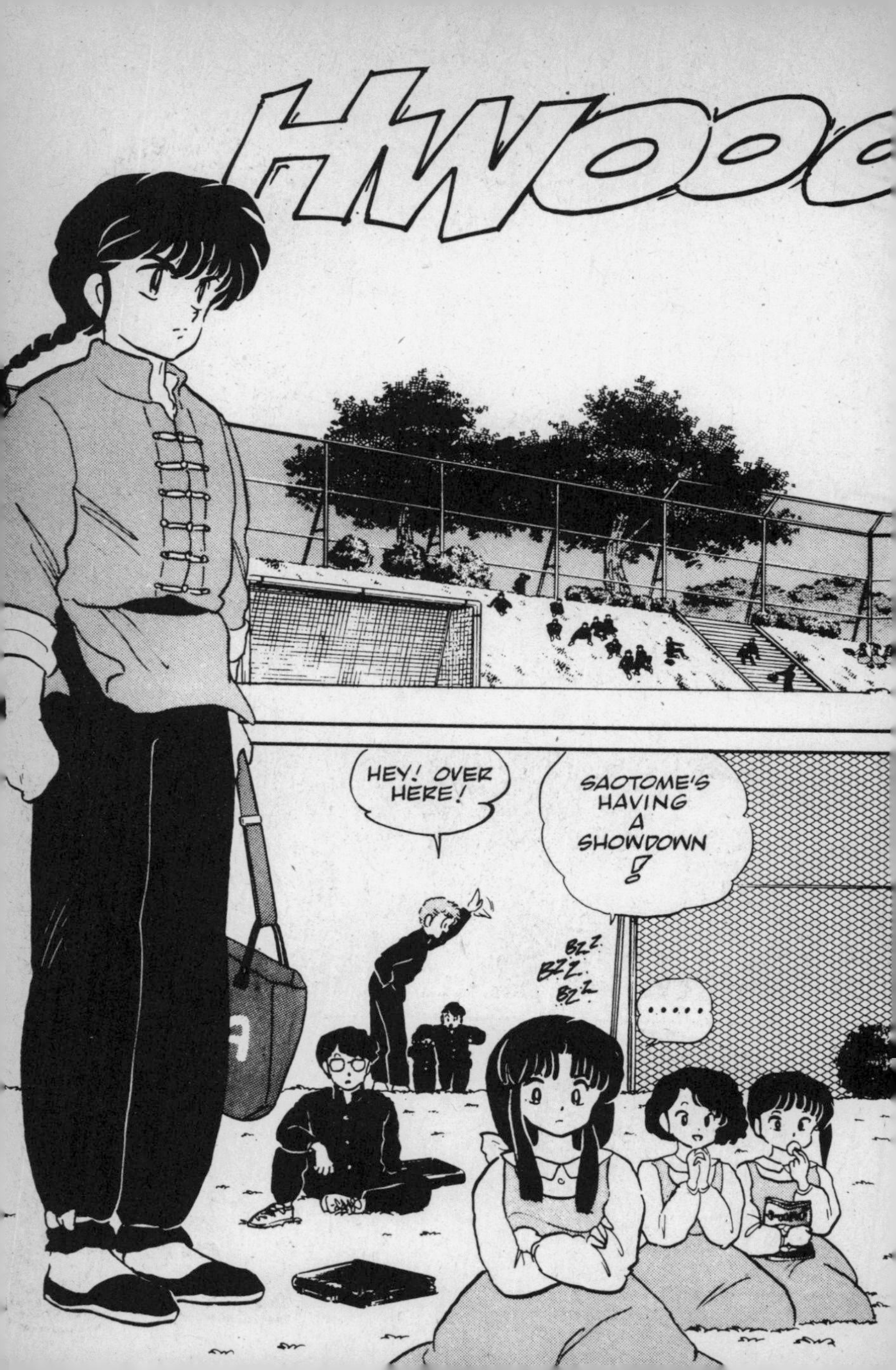
HWOOO
HEY! OVER HERE!
SAOTOME'S HAVING A SHOWDOWN!
BZZ BZZ BZZ
.....

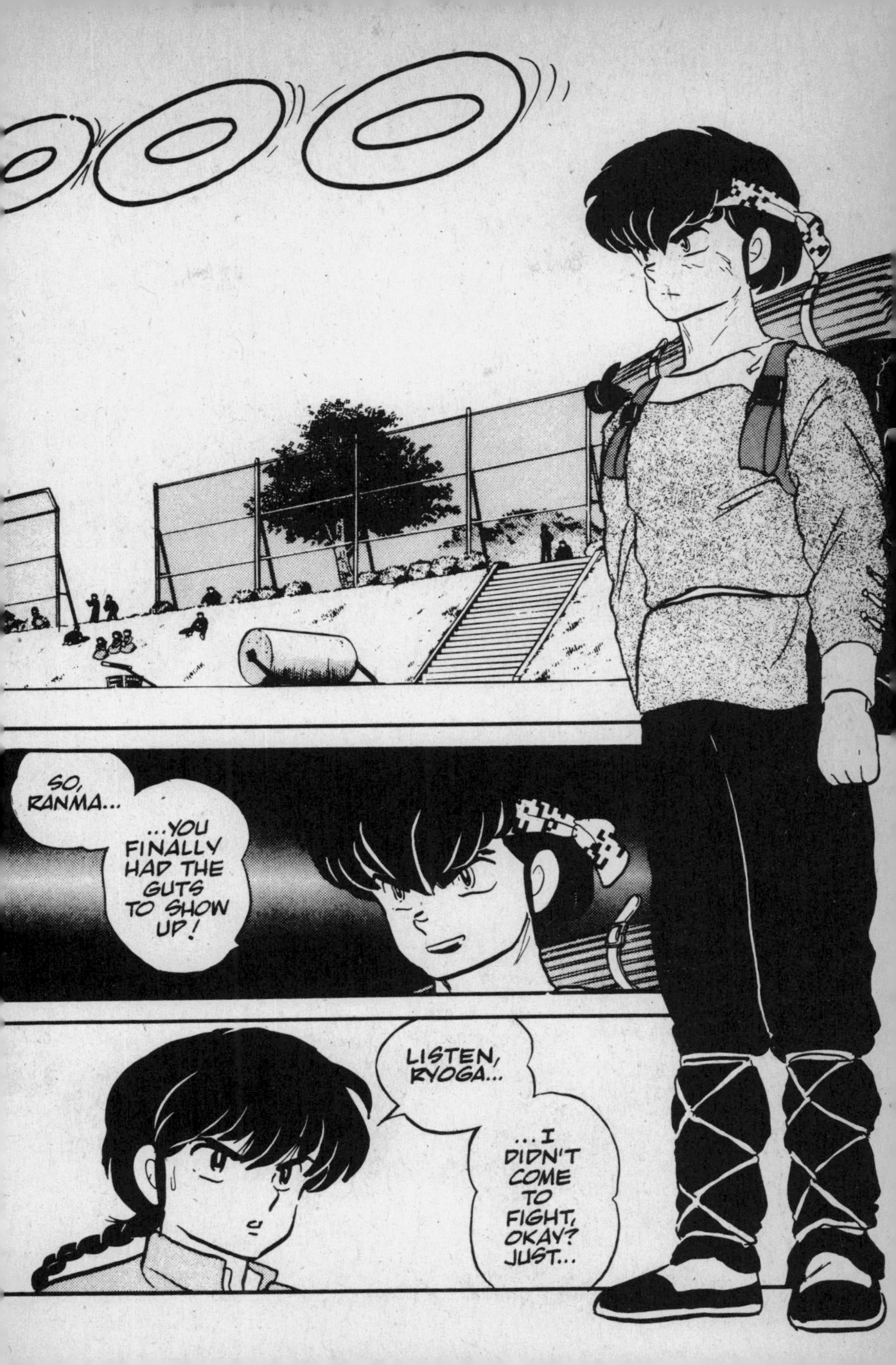
SO, RANMA...
...YOU FINALLY HAD THE GUTS TO SHOW UP!
LISTEN, RYOGA...
...I DIDN'T COME TO FIGHT, OKAY? JUST...

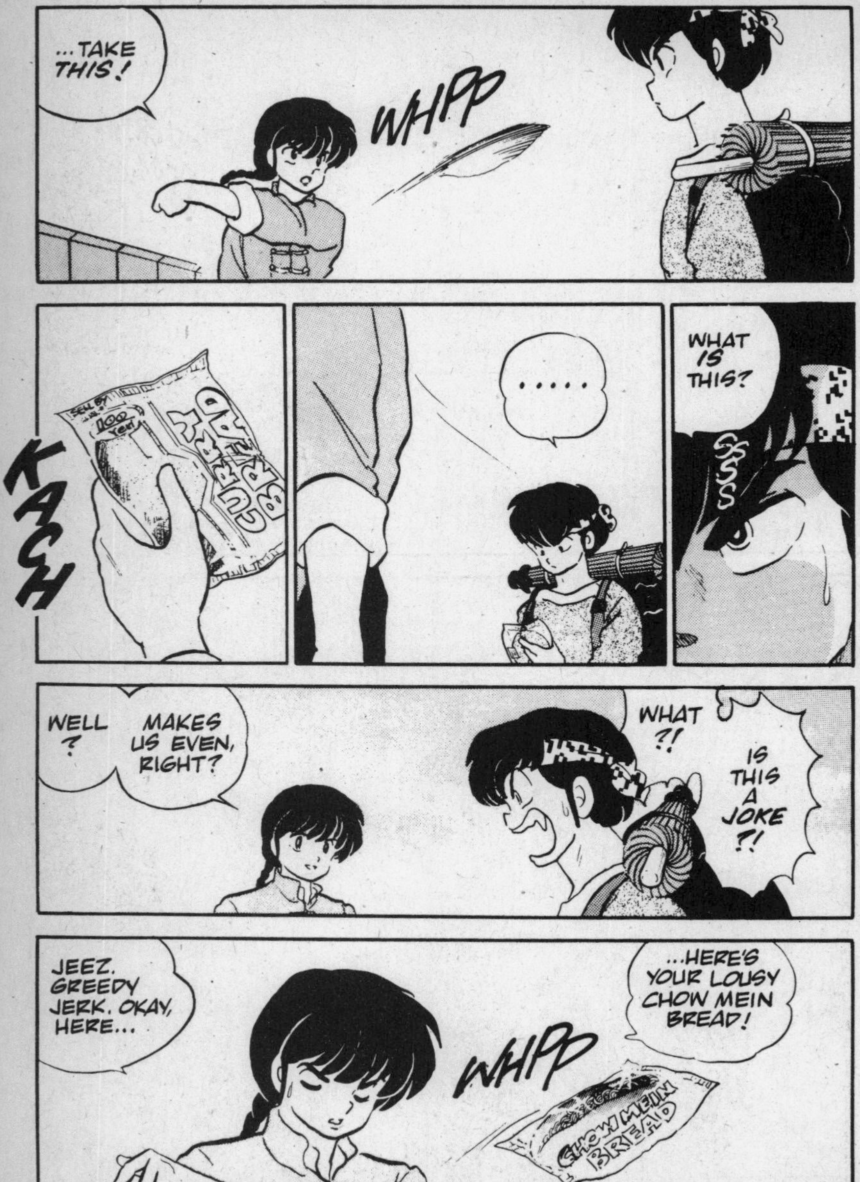
...TAKE THIS!
WHPP
KACH
SELL BY
100 Yen
CURRANT BREAD
.....
WHAT IS THIS?
GRSSS
WELL?
MAKES US EVEN, RIGHT?
WHAT?!
IS THIS A JOKE?!
JEEZ. GREEDY JERK. OKAY, HERE...
...HERE'S YOUR LOUSY CHOW MEIN BREAD!
WHPP
CHOW MEIN BREAD

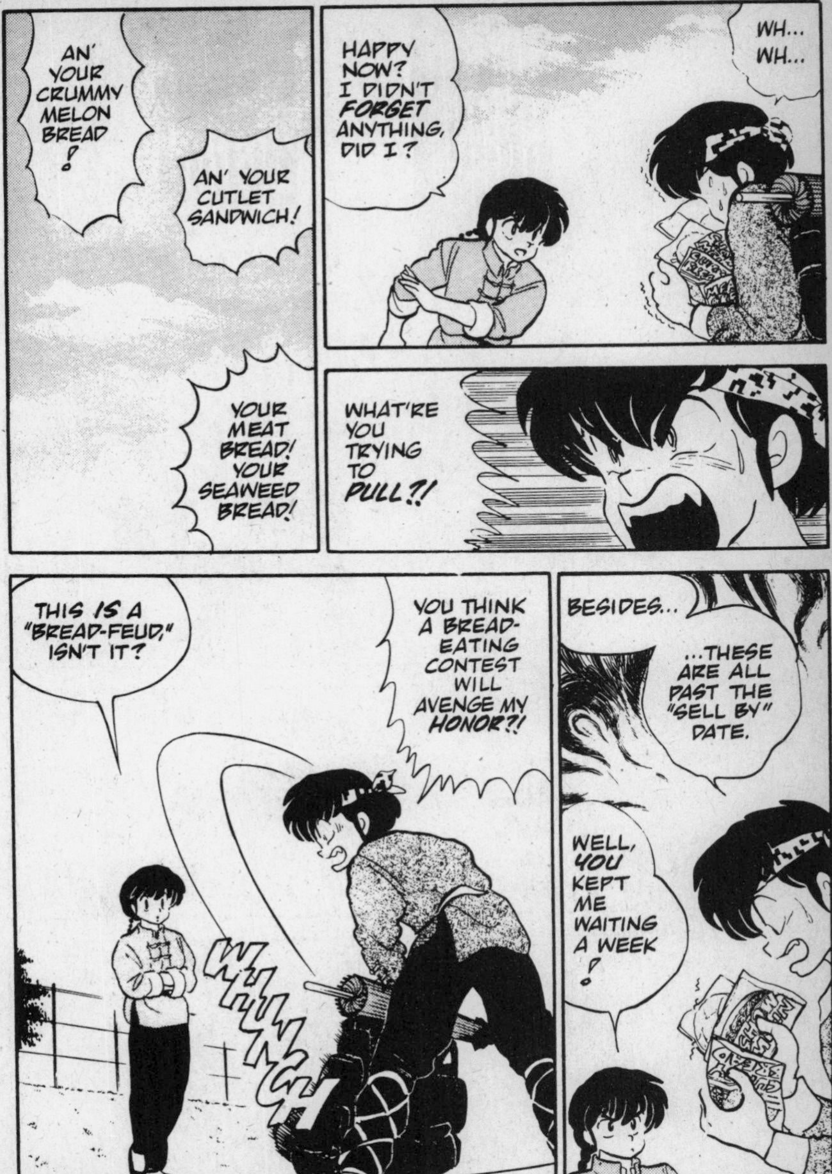
AN' YOUR CRUMMY MELON BREAD!
AN' YOUR CUTLET SANDWICH!
YOUR MEAT BREAD! YOUR SEAWEED BREAD!
HAPPY NOW? I DIDN'T FORGET ANYTHING, DID I?
WH... WH...
WHAT'RE YOU TRYING TO PULL?!
THIS IS A "BREAD-FEUD," ISN'T IT?
YOU THINK A BREAD-EATING CONTEST WILL AVENGE MY HONOR?!
BESIDES...
...THESE ARE ALL PAST THE "SELL BY" DATE.
WELL, YOU KEPT ME WAITING A WEEK!

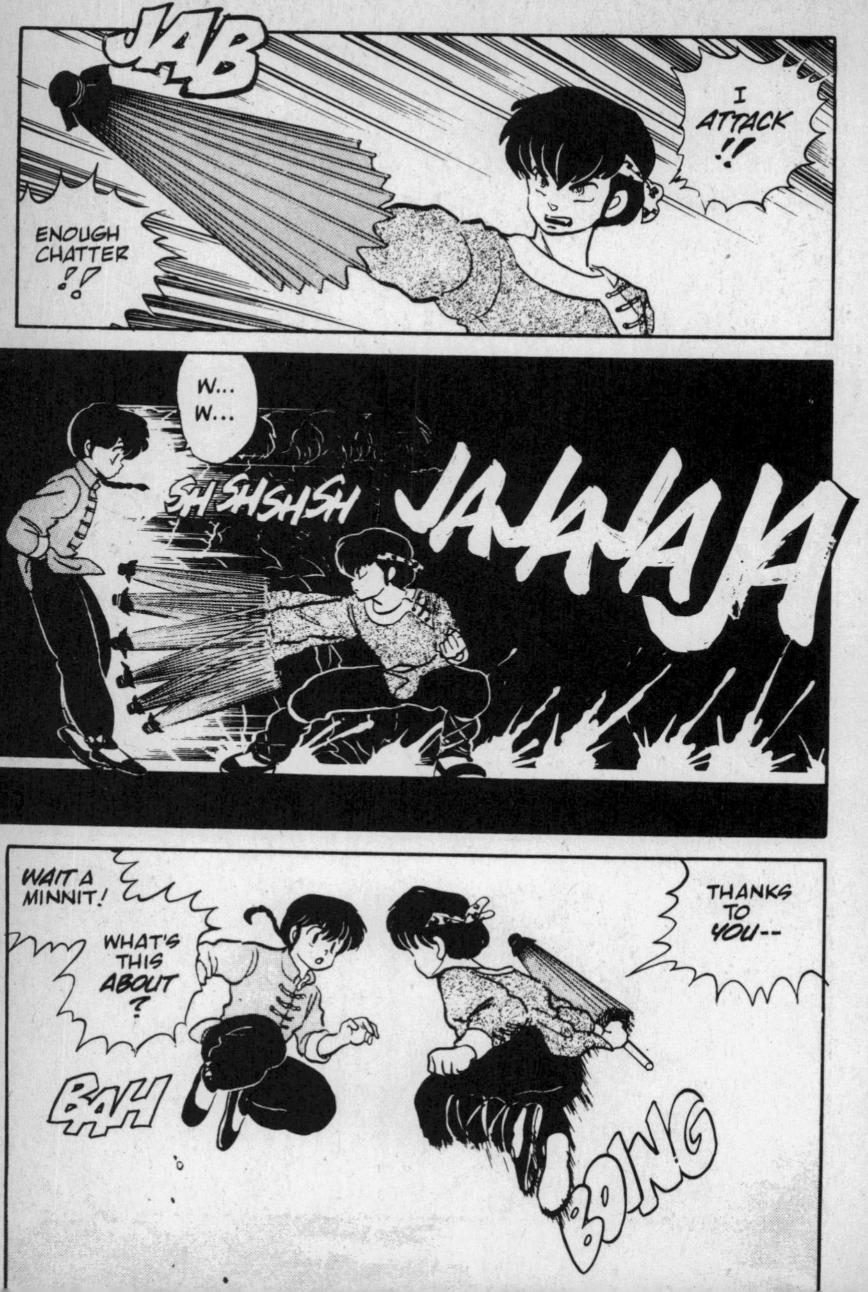
JAB
ENOUGH CHATTER !!
I ATTACK !!
W... W...
SH SHSHSH
JAJAJAJA
WAIT A MINNIT!
WHAT'S THIS ABOUT ?
BAH
THANKS TO YOU--
BOING

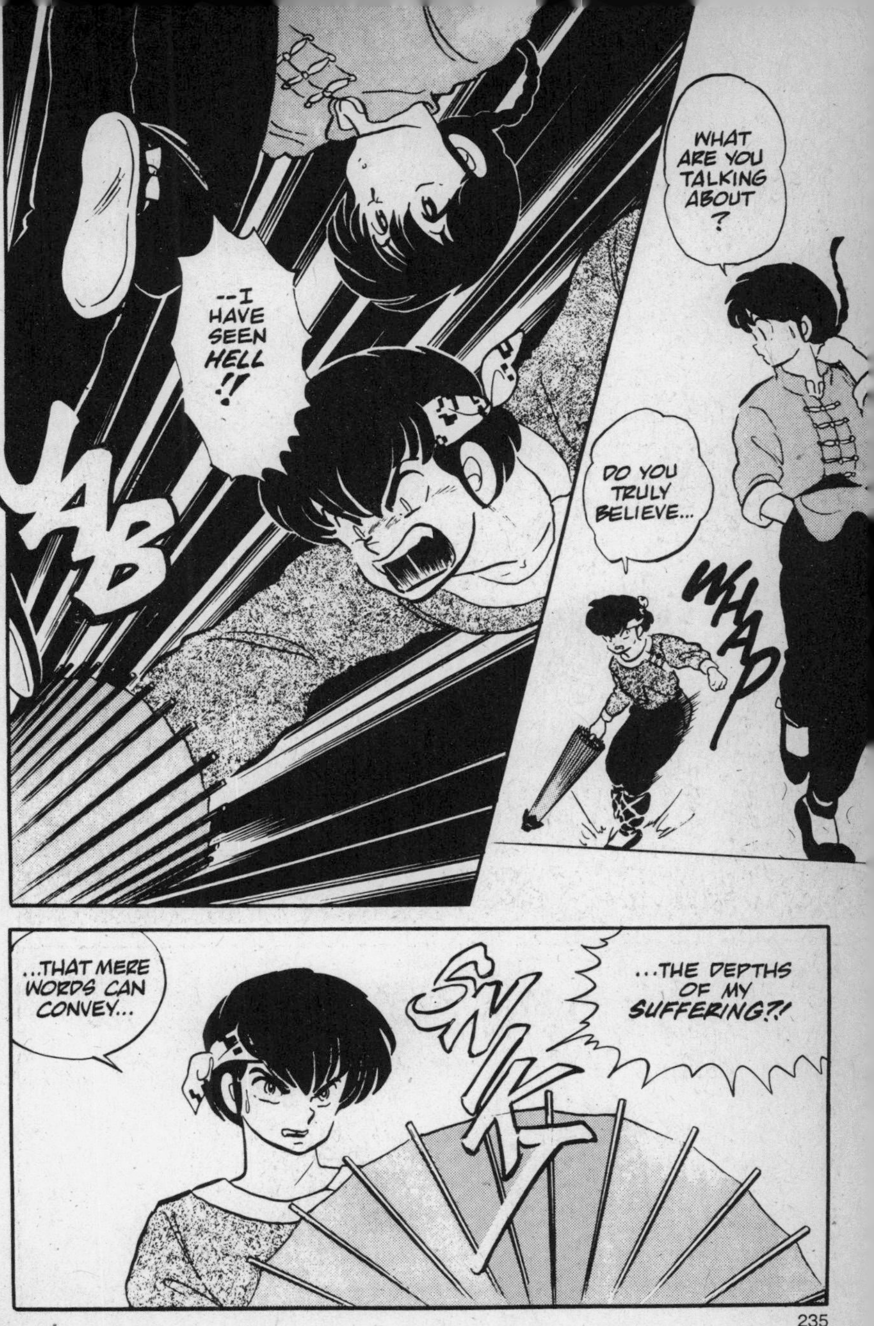
--I HAVE SEEN HELL!!
WHAT ARE YOU TALKING ABOUT?
DO YOU TRULY BELIEVE...
WHAP
...THAT MERE WORDS CAN CONVEY...
SNIK
...THE DEPTHS OF MY SUFFERING?!

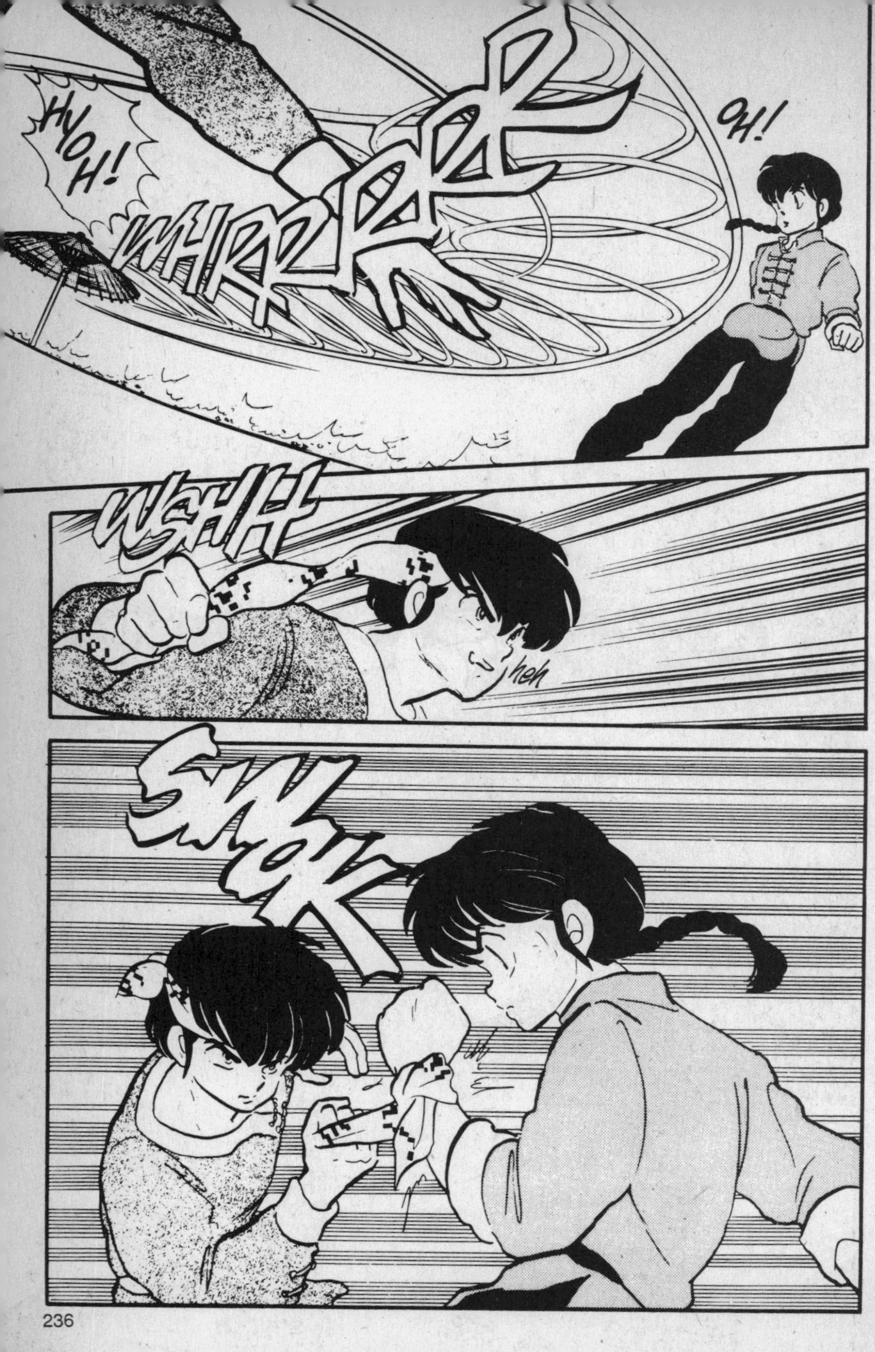
HYOH!
WHRRRR
OH!
WSHH
heh
SMOK

TELL ME SOMETHING...
THIS'LL KEEP YOU FROM RUNNING AWAY!
SHA...PUK
...HOW MANY BANDANAS ARE YOU WEARING?!
ZHA-
-WUK
WHRRRRR
YOU WON'T MAKE LIGHT OF THIS, SAOTOME!

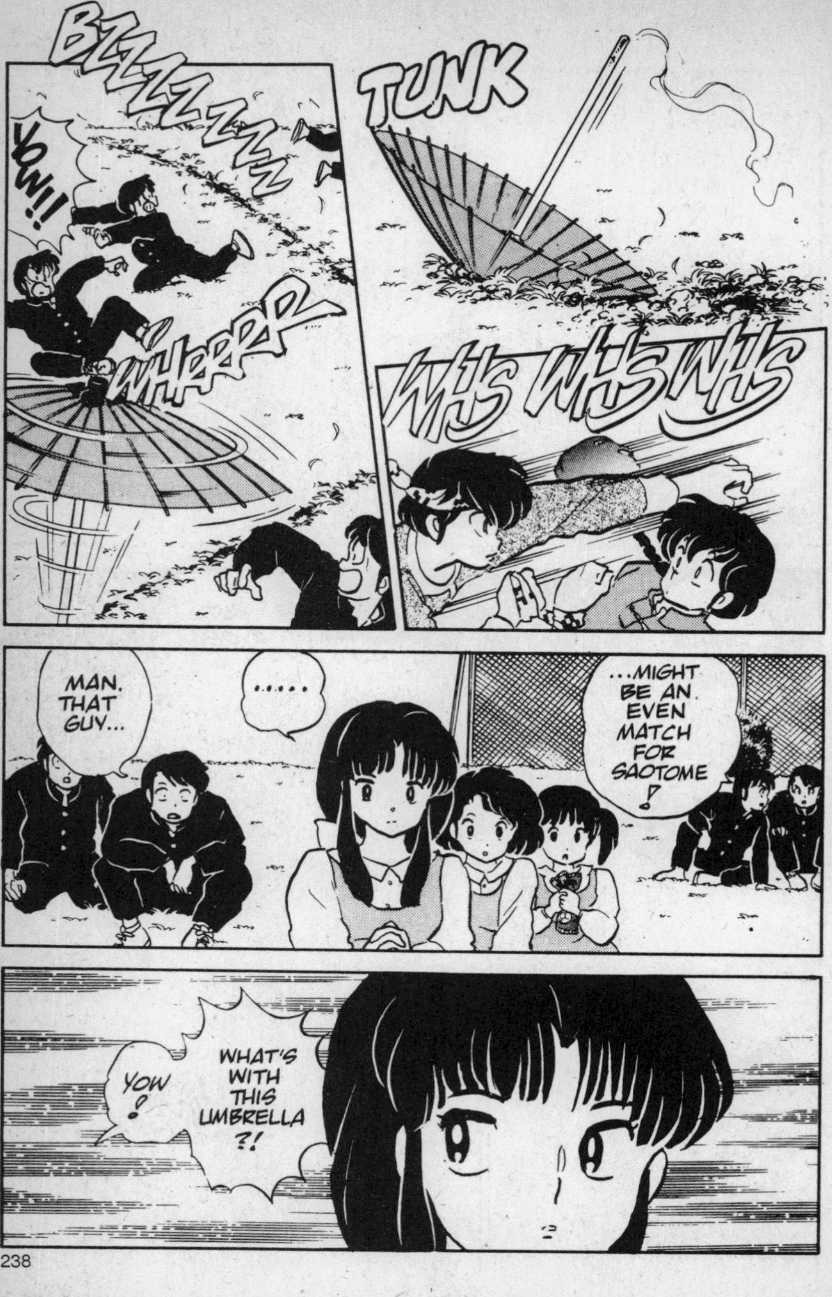

BZZZZZZZ
YOW!!!
WHRRRR
TUNK
WHS WHS WHS
MAN. THAT GUY...
.....
...MIGHT BE AN EVEN MATCH FOR SAOTOME!
YOW!
WHAT'S WITH THIS UMBRELLA?!

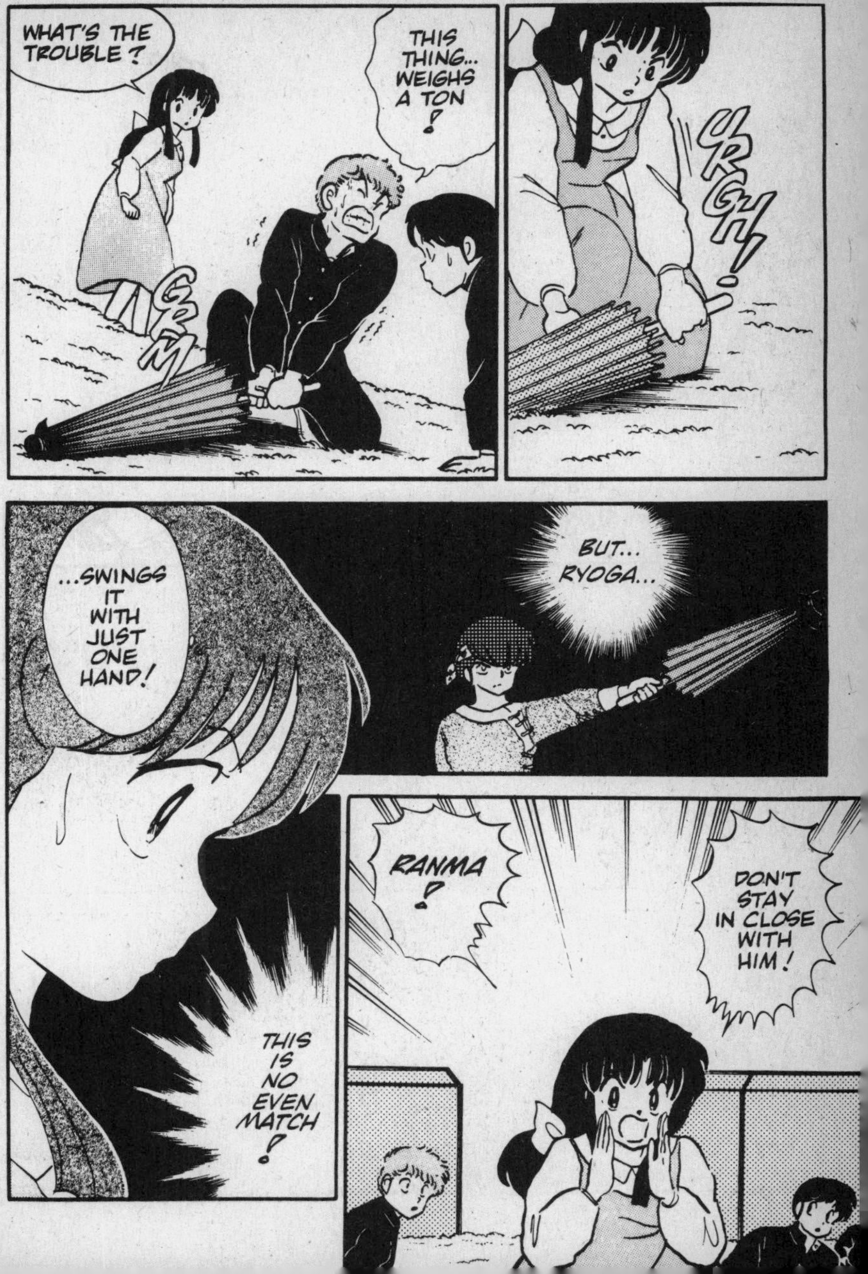
WHAT'S THE TROUBLE?
THIS THING... WEIGHS A TON!
GRNN
URGH!
BUT... RYOGA...
...SWINGS IT WITH JUST ONE HAND!
THIS IS NO EVEN MATCH!
RANMA!
DON'T STAY IN CLOSE WITH HIM!

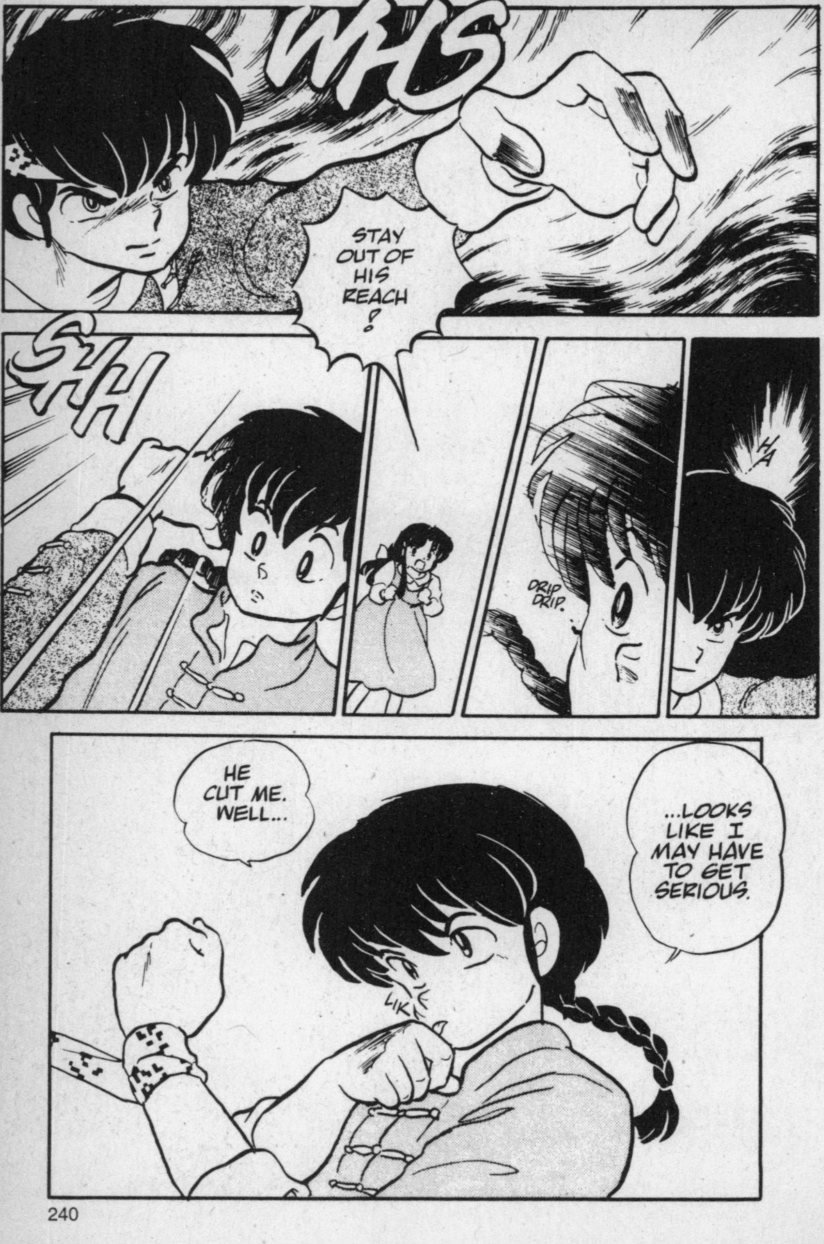
WHS
STAY OUT OF HIS REACH!
SHH
DRIP DRIP.
HA
HE CUT ME. WELL...
...LOOKS LIKE I MAY HAVE TO GET SERIOUS.
LIK

Part 12
SHOWDOWN

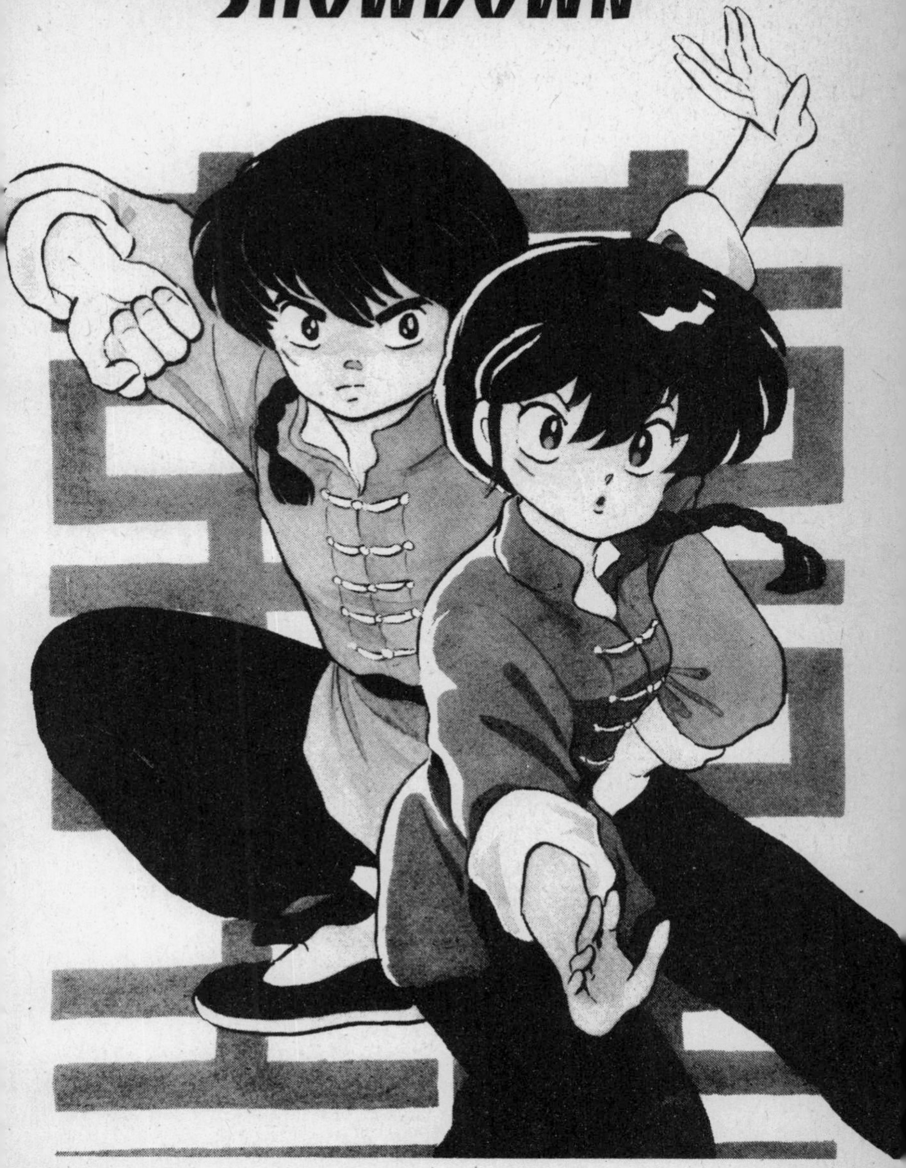

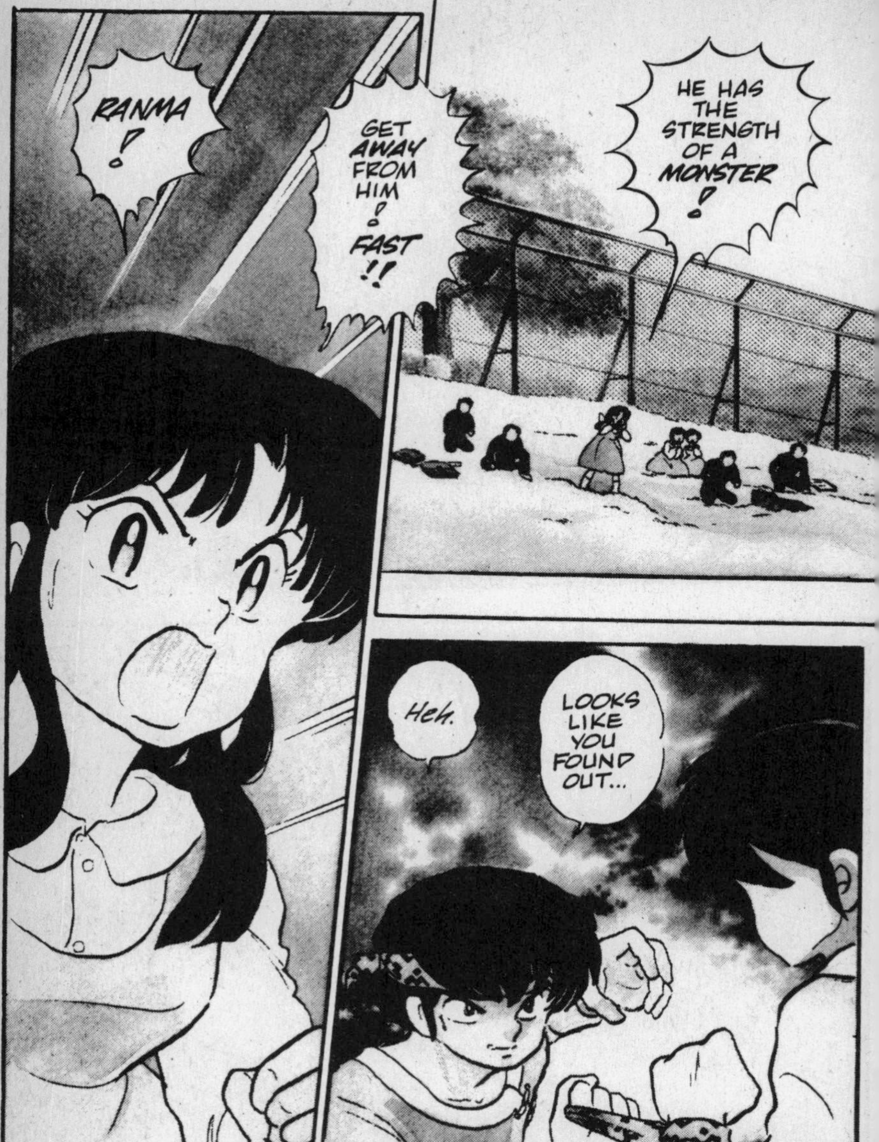
RANMA!
GET AWAY FROM HIM! FAST!!
HE HAS THE STRENGTH OF A MONSTER!
Heh.
LOOKS LIKE YOU FOUND OUT...

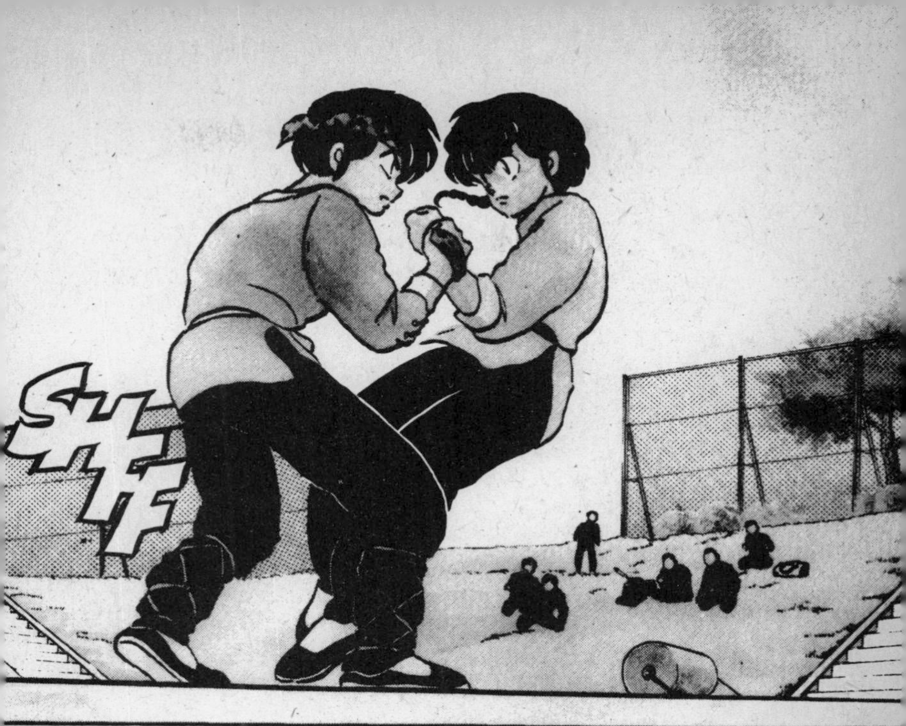
SHFF
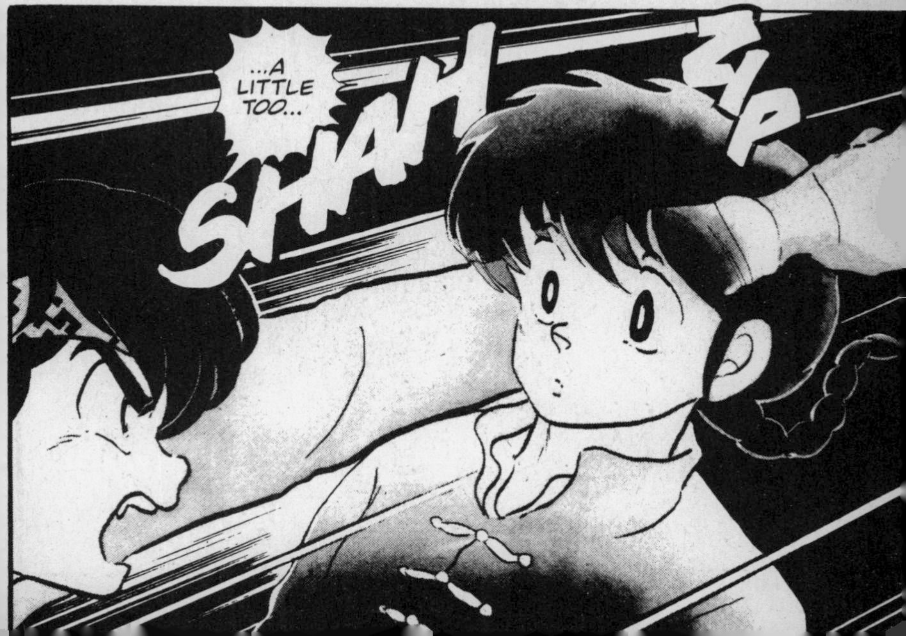
ZIP
SHAH
...A LITTLE TOO...

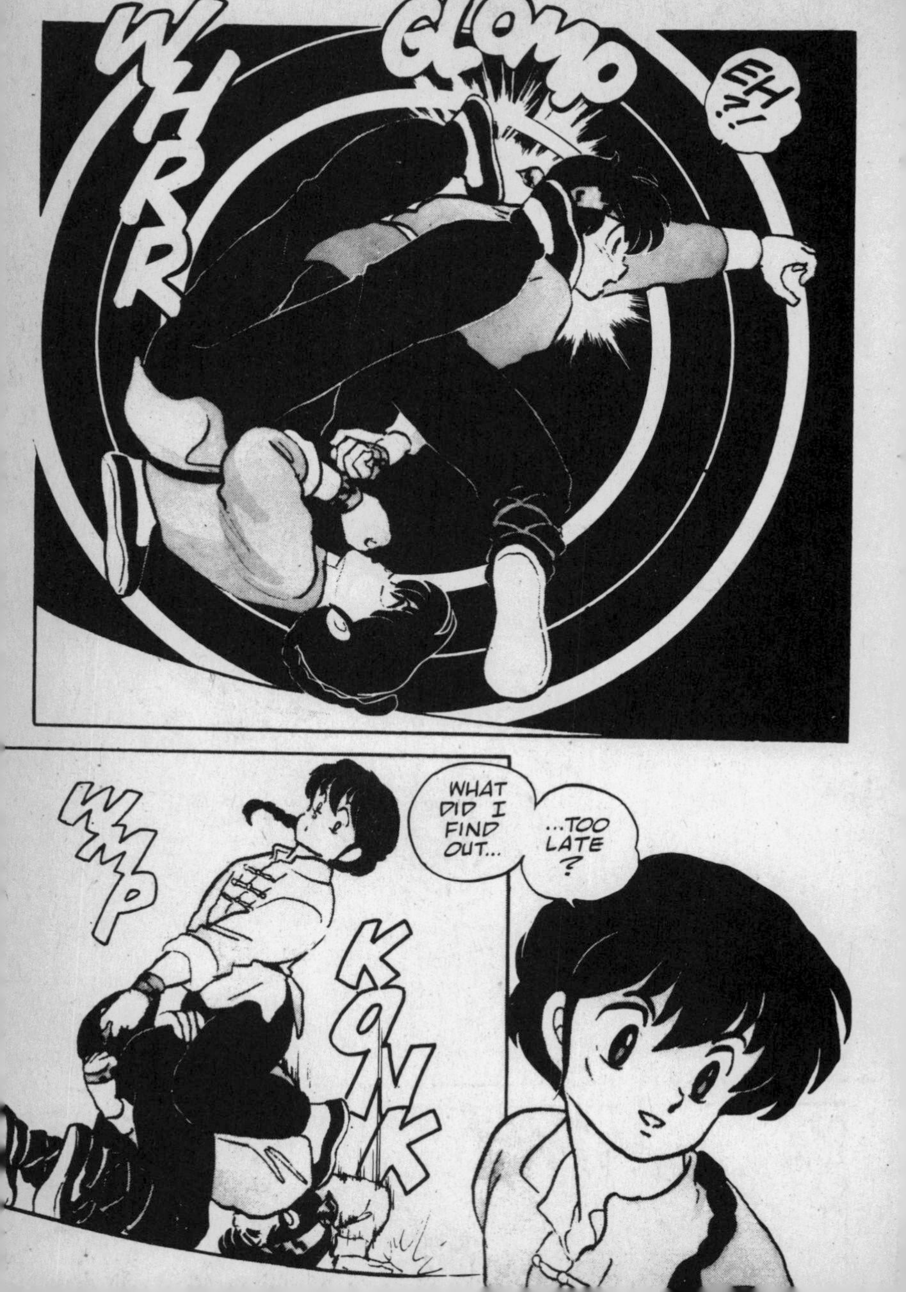
WHRR
GLOMP
EH?!
WMP
KONK
WHAT DID I FIND OUT...
...TOO LATE?

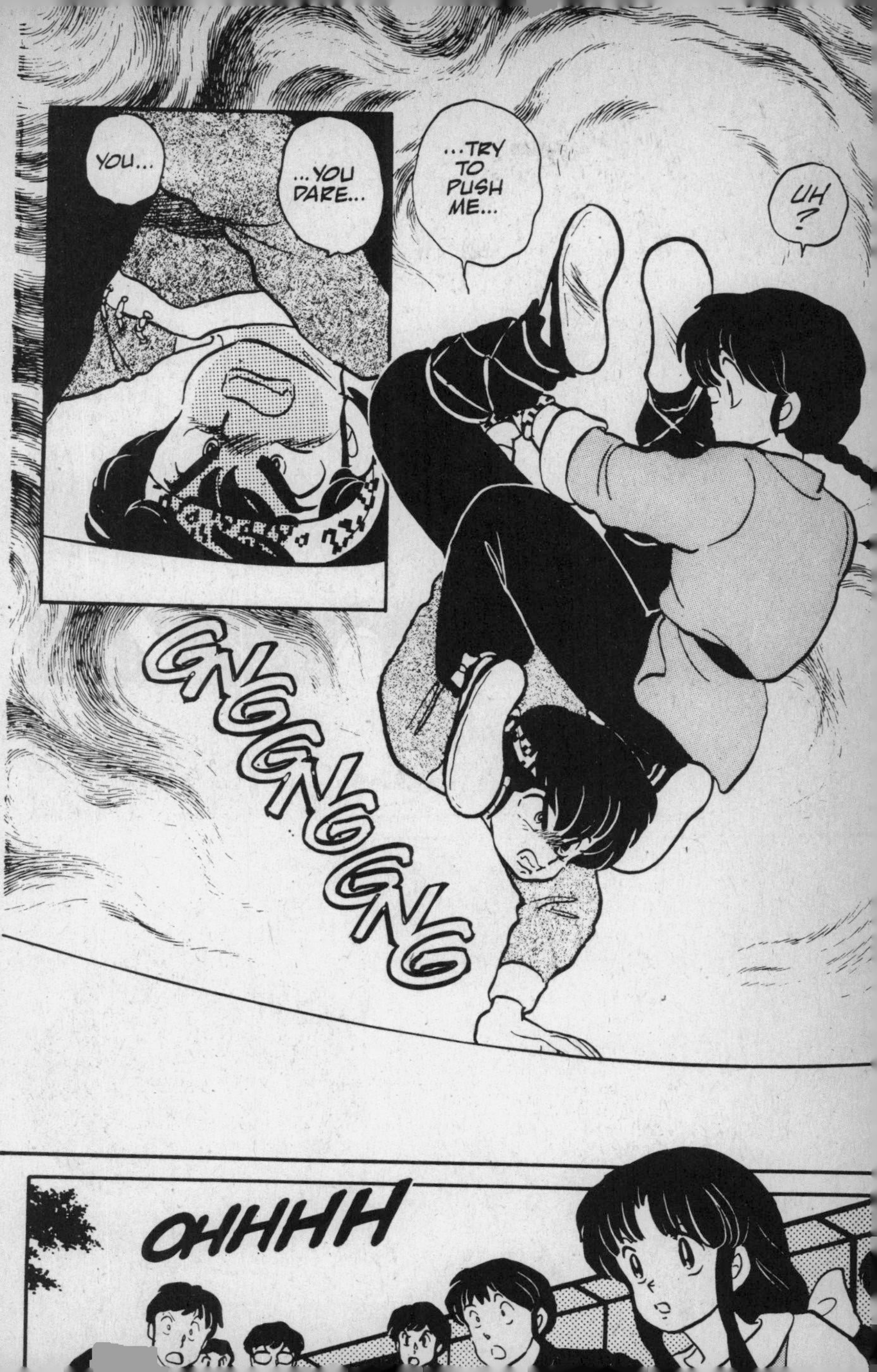
YOU...
...YOU DARE...
...TRY TO PUSH ME...
UH?
GNGNGNGNG
OHHHH

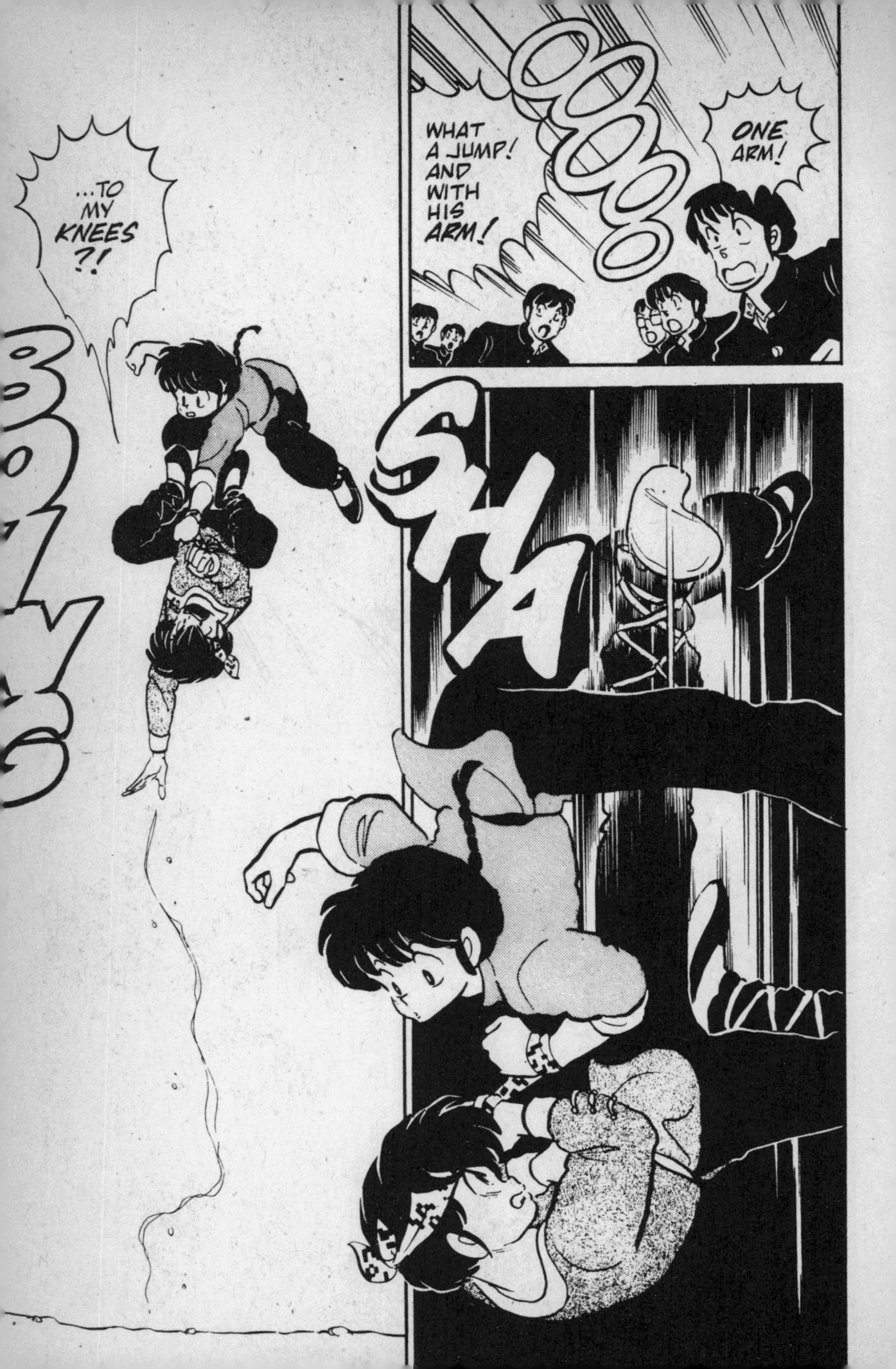
...TO MY KNEES ?!
BOING
WHAT A JUMP! AND WITH HIS ARM!
OOOOO
ONE ARM!
SHA

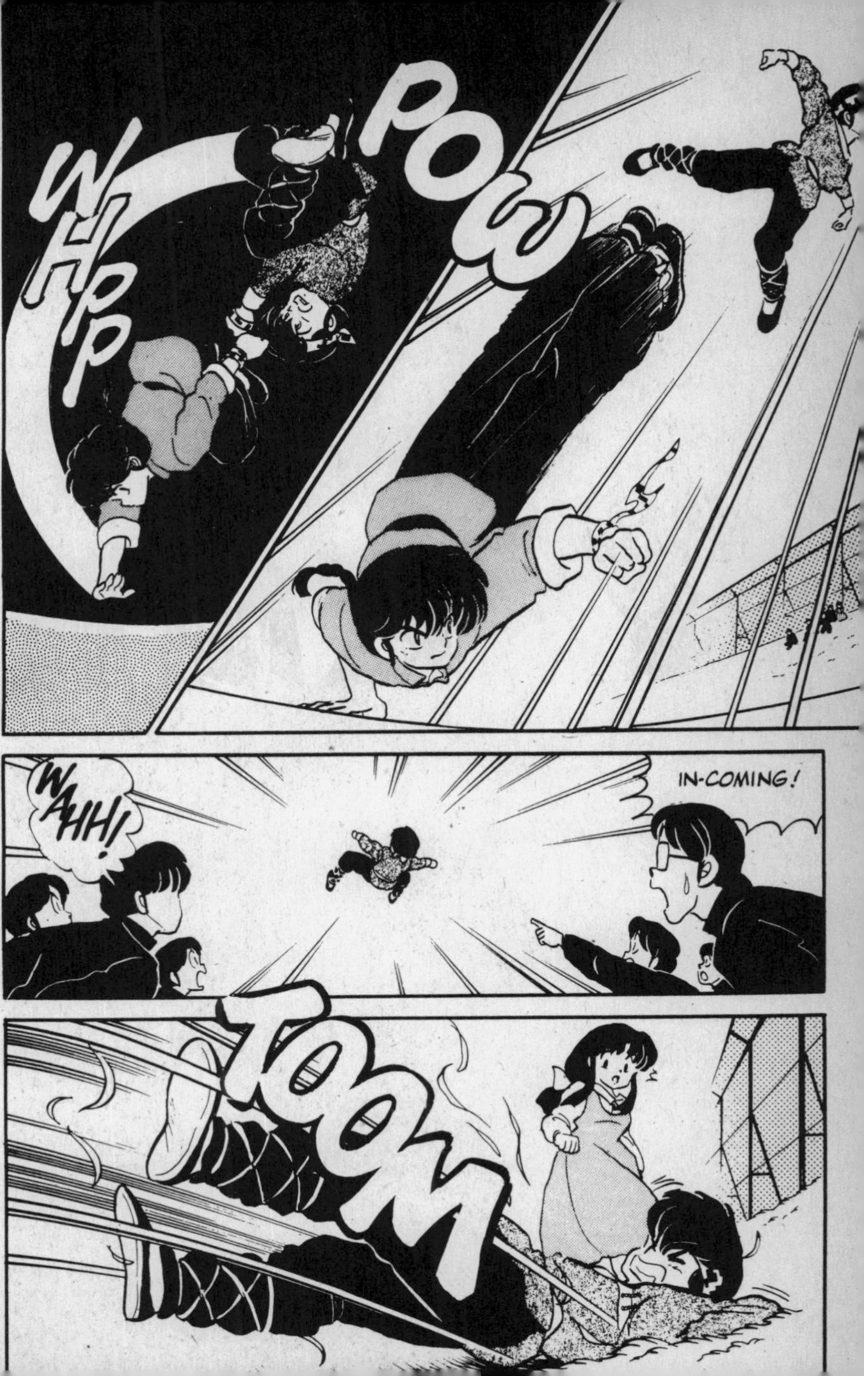
WHPP
POW
WAHH!
IN-COMING!
TOOM

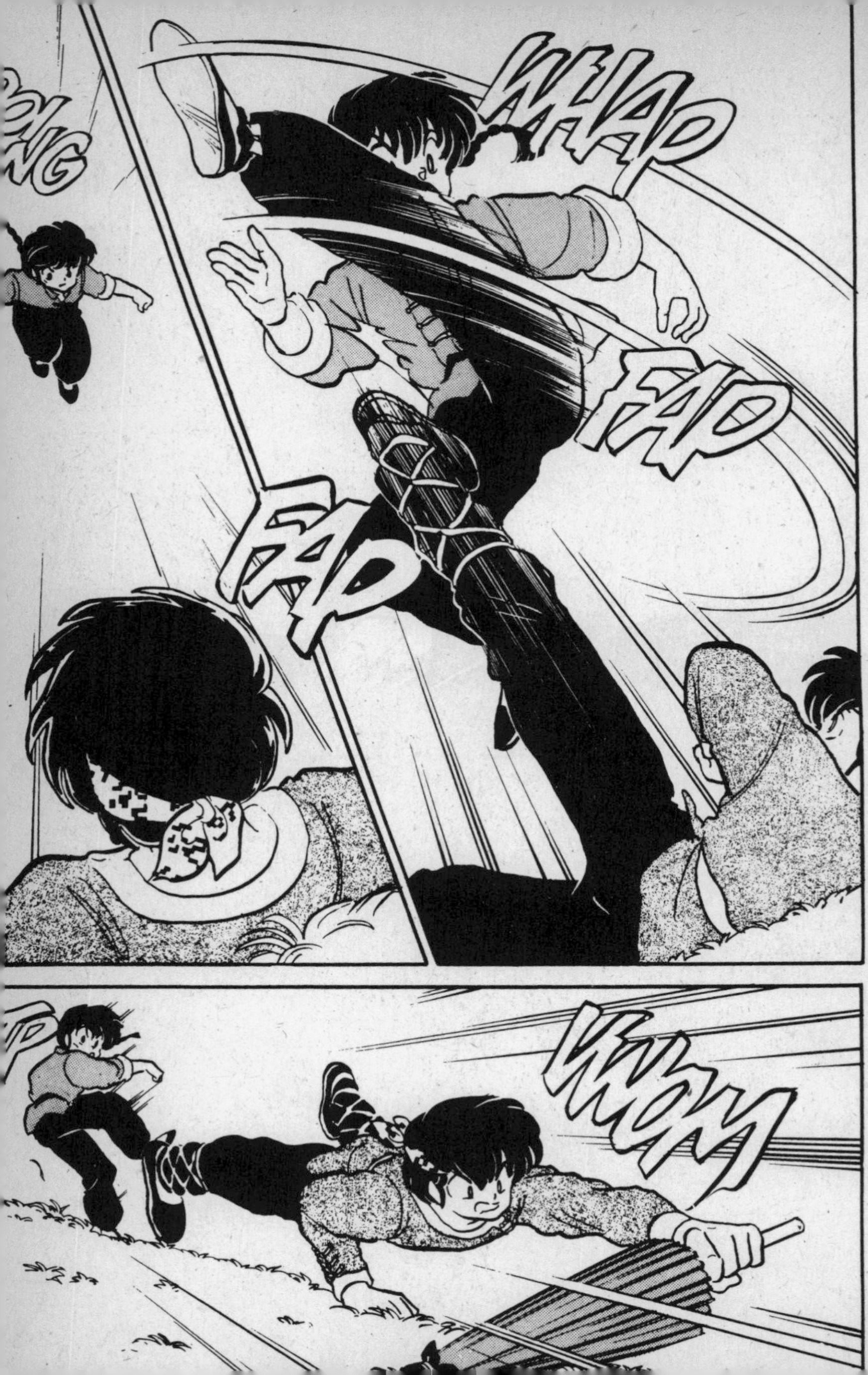

BOING
WHAP
FAP
FAP
VWOM

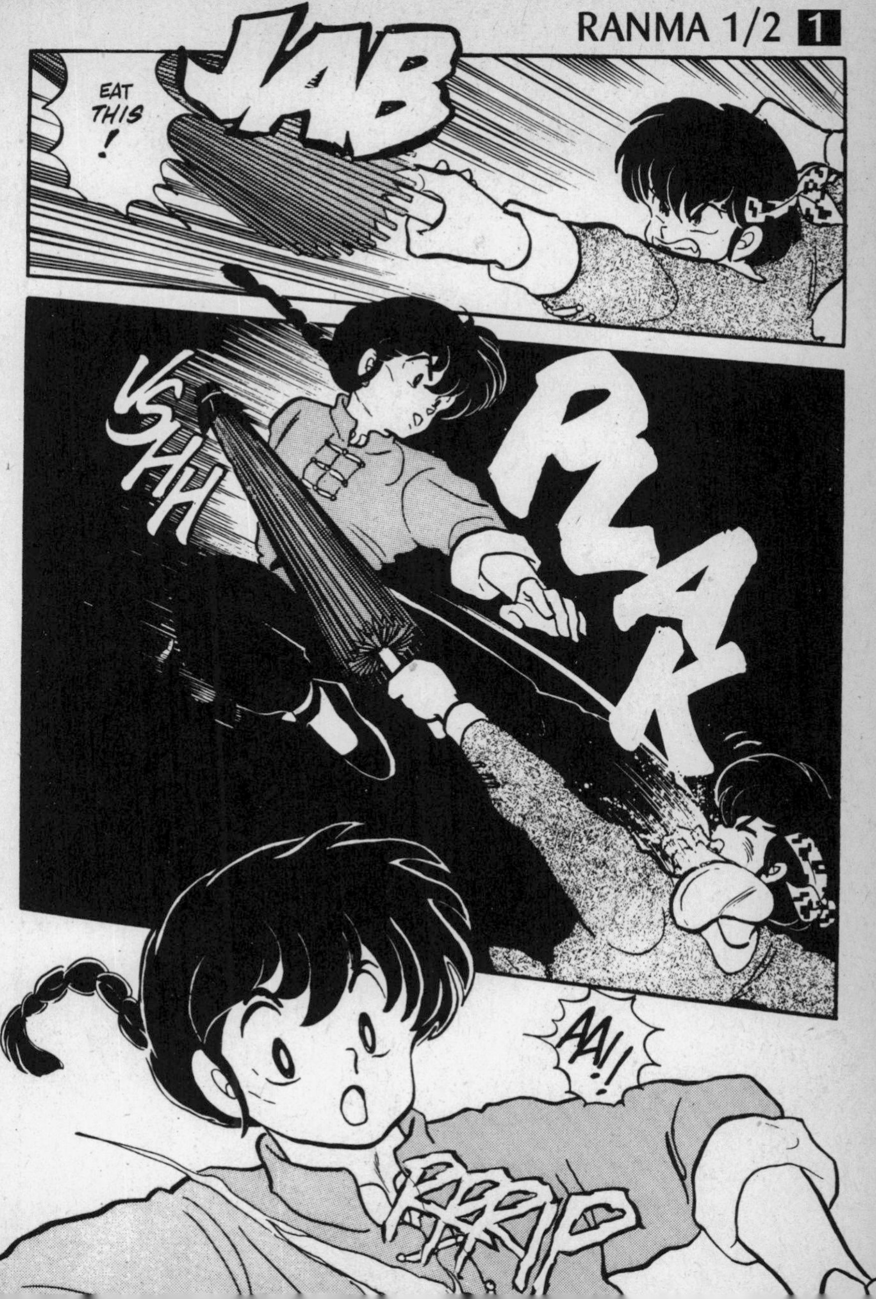
EAT THIS!
JAB
VSHHH
PLAK
AA!!

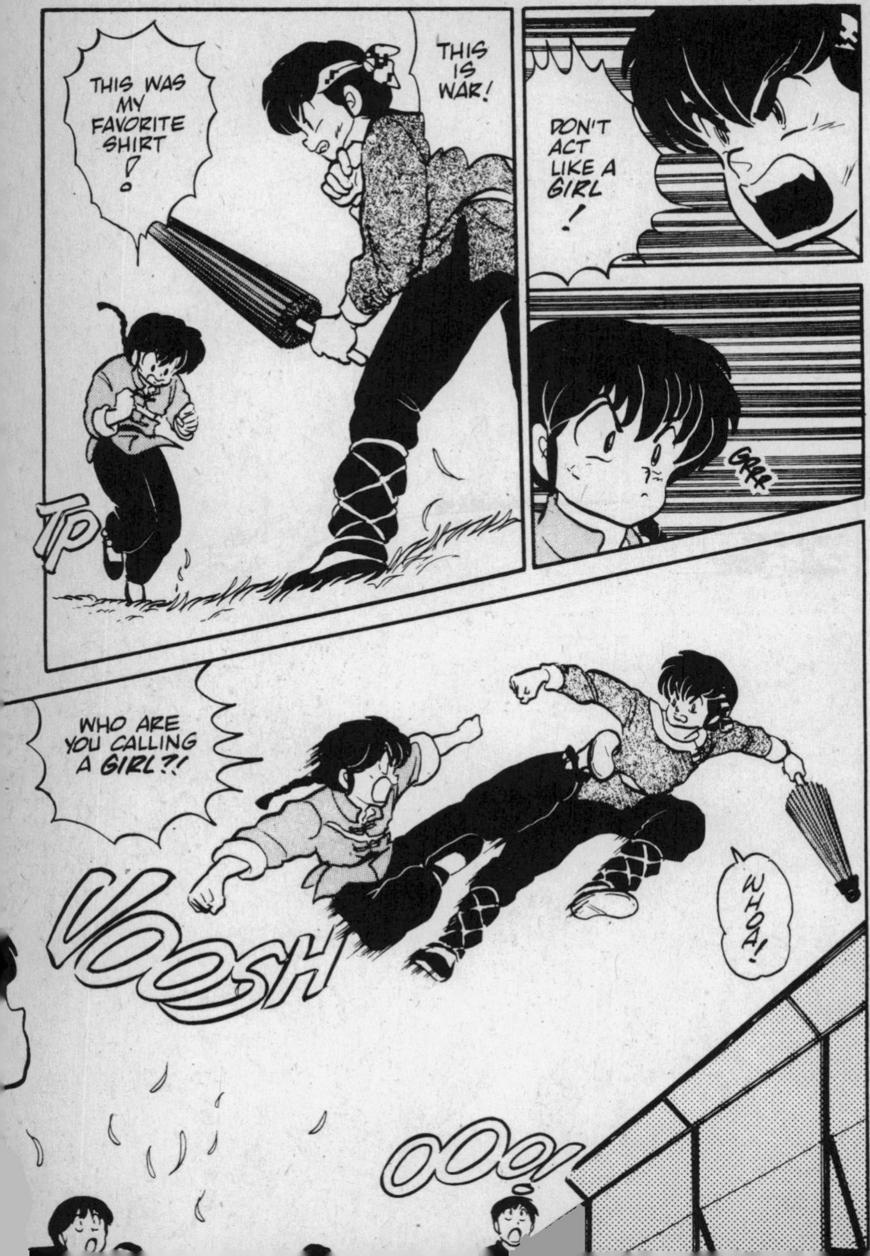
THIS WAS MY FAVORITE SHIRT!
THIS IS WAR!
TP
DON'T ACT LIKE A GIRL!
GRRR
WHO ARE YOU CALLING A GIRL?!
VOOSH
WHOA!
OOO!

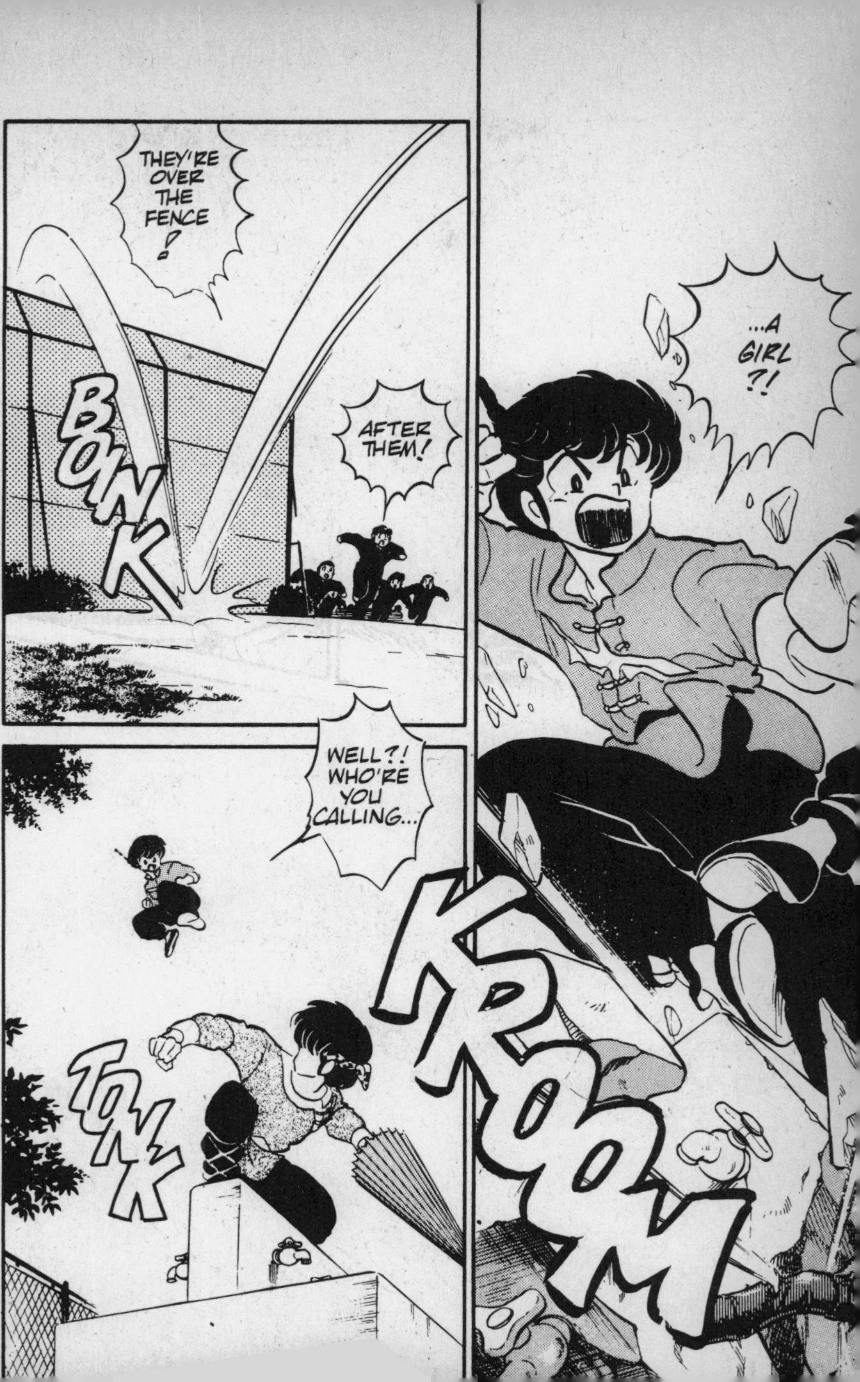
THEY'RE OVER THE FENCE!
BONK
AFTER THEM!
WELL?! WHO'RE YOU CALLING...
TONK
...A GIRL?!
KROOM

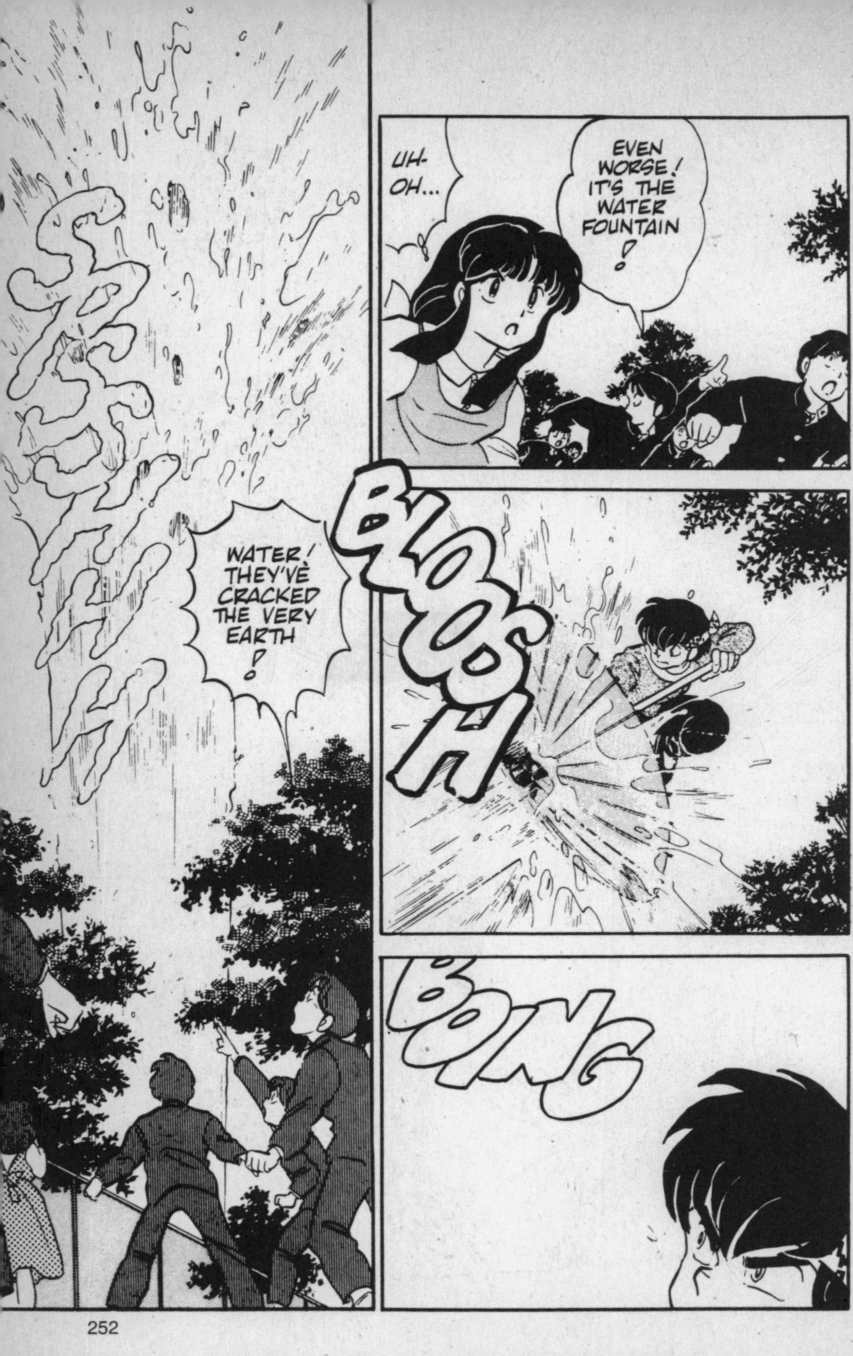
WATER! THEY'VE CRACKED THE VERY EARTH!
UH-OH...
EVEN WORSE! IT'S THE WATER FOUNTAIN!
BLOOSH
BOING

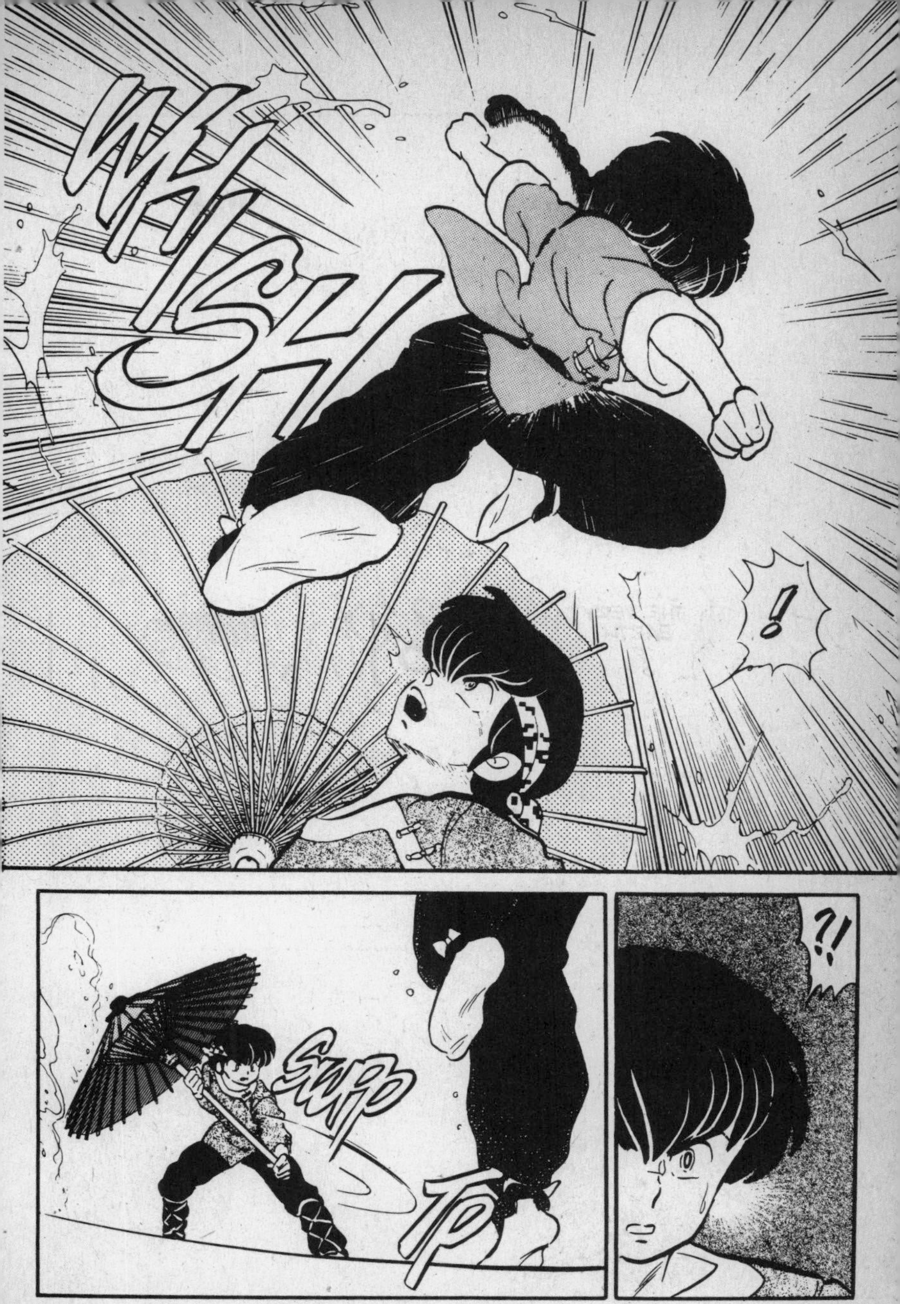
WHISH
!
Swip
Tp
?!

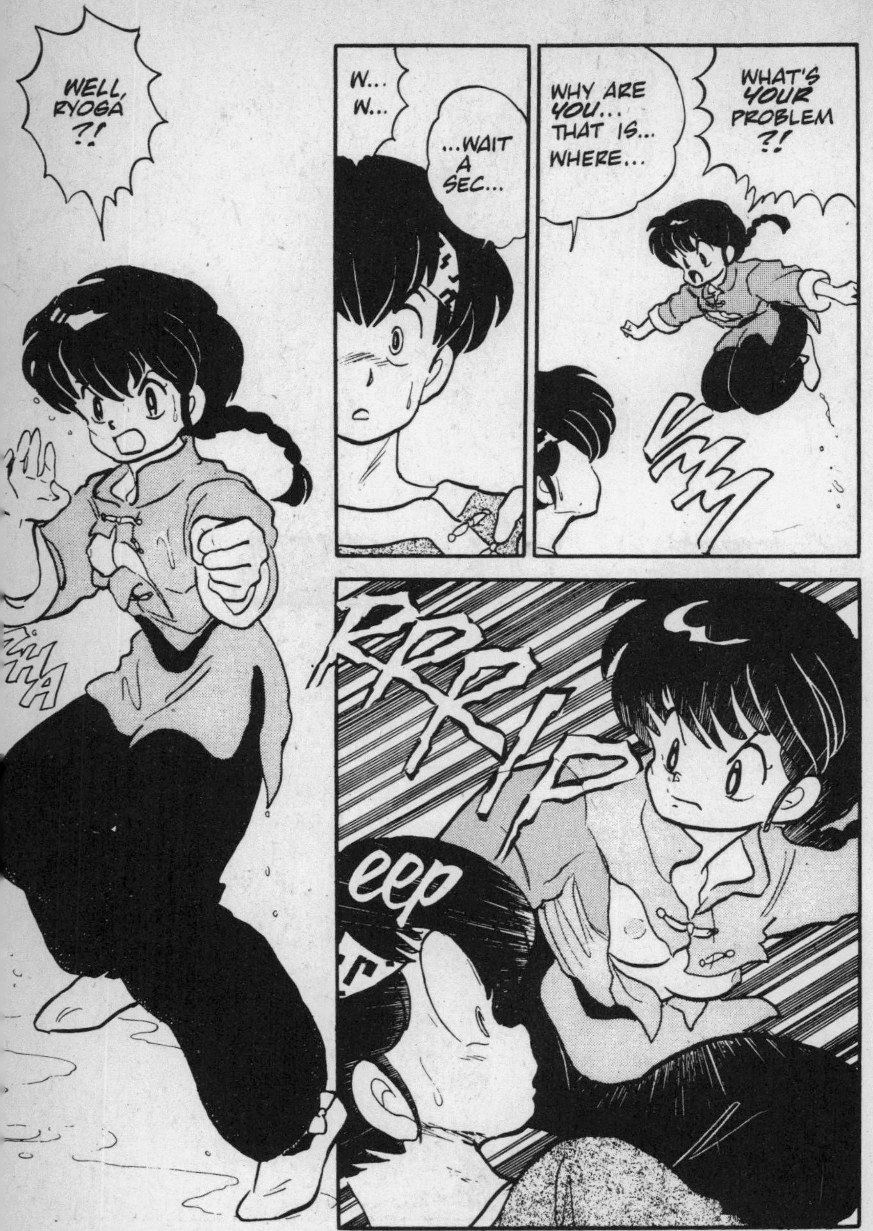

WELL, RYOGA ?!
W... W...
...WAIT A SEC...
WHY ARE YOU... THAT IS... WHERE...
WHAT'S YOUR PROBLEM ?!
RRRIP
eep

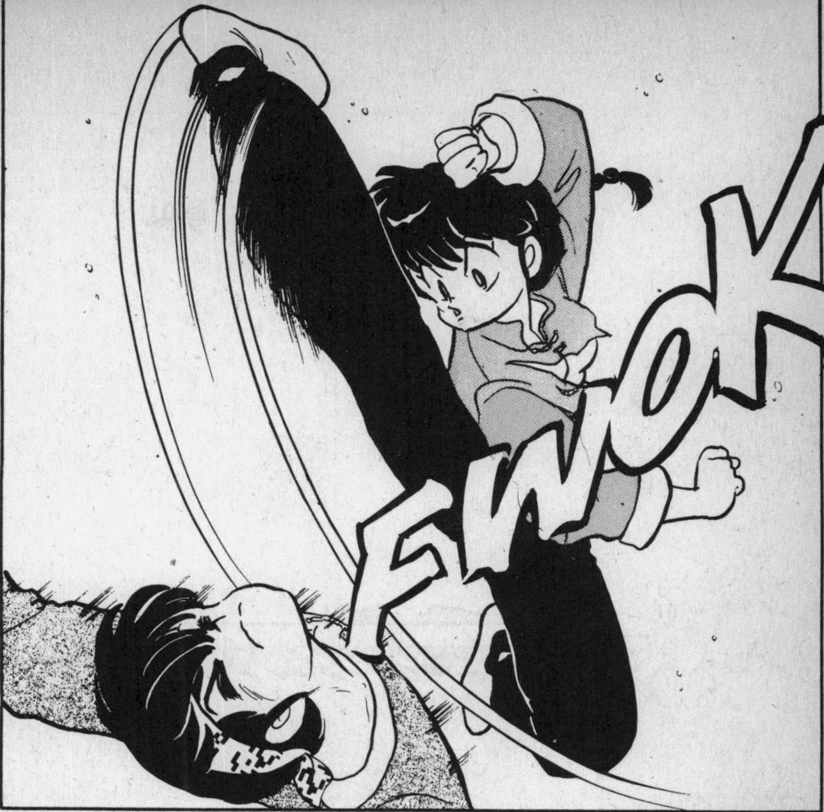
FWOK

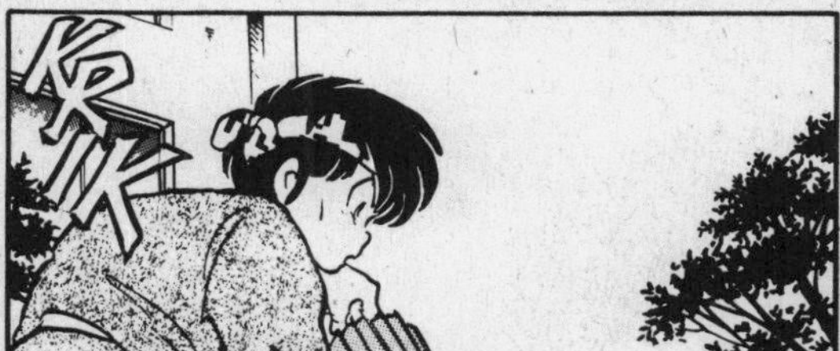
KRIK
TP

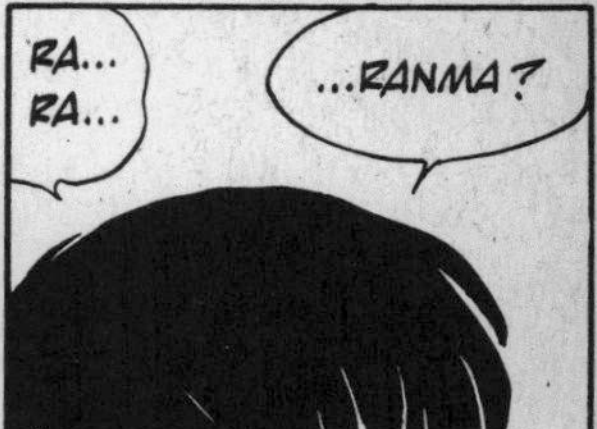
RA... RA...
...RANMA?

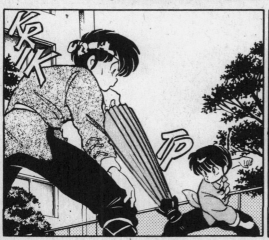

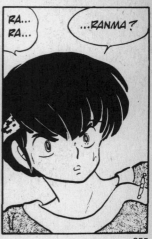

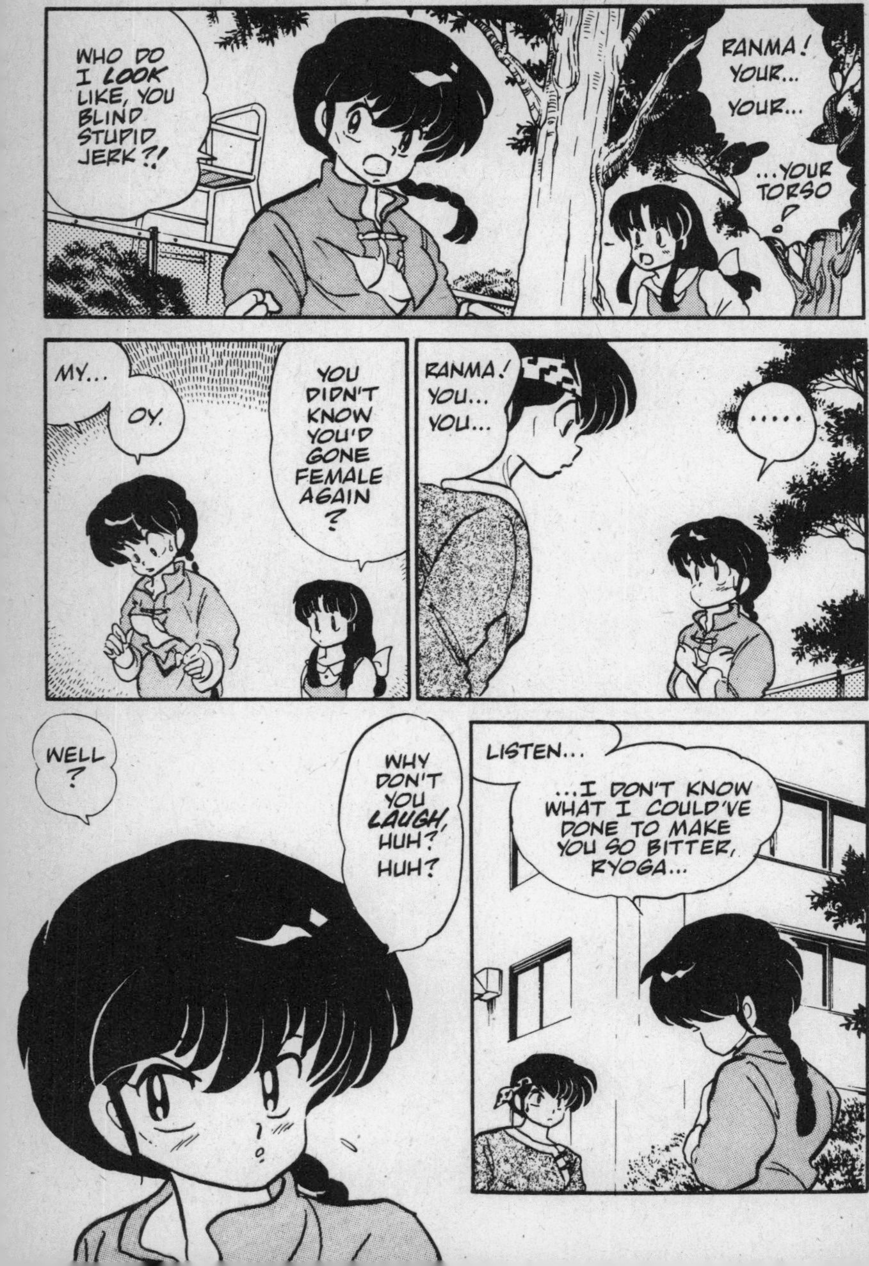
WHO DO I LOOK LIKE, YOU BLIND STUPID JERK?!
RANMA! YOUR... YOUR...
...YOUR TORSO?
MY...
OY.
YOU DIDN'T KNOW YOU'D GONE FEMALE AGAIN?
RANMA! YOU... YOU...
.....
WELL?
WHY DON'T YOU LAUGH, HUH? HUH?
LISTEN...
...I DON'T KNOW WHAT I COULD'VE DONE TO MAKE YOU SO BITTER, RYOGA...

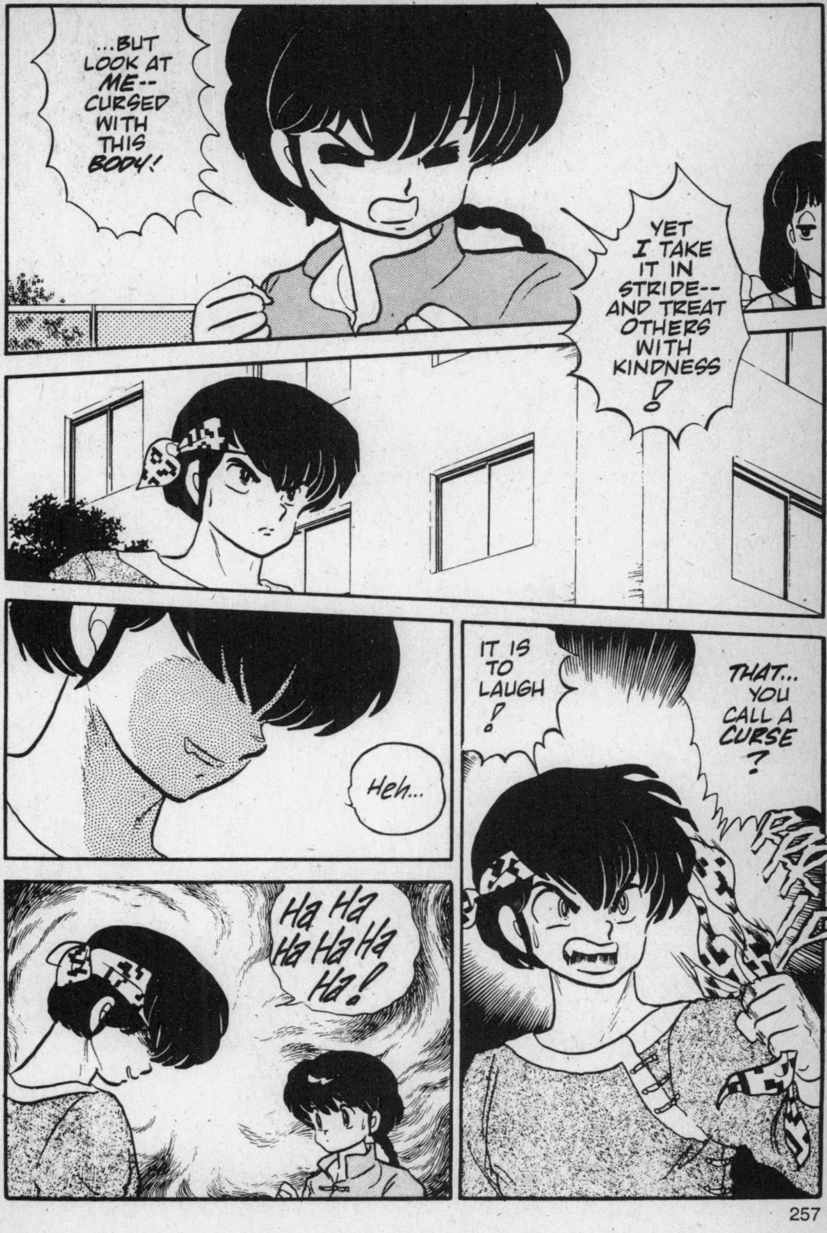
...BUT LOOK AT ME-- CURSED WITH THIS BODY!
YET I TAKE IT IN STRIDE-- AND TREAT OTHERS WITH KINDNESS!
Heh...
Ha Ha Ha Ha Ha Ha Ha!
IT IS TO LAUGH!
THAT... YOU CALL A CURSE?

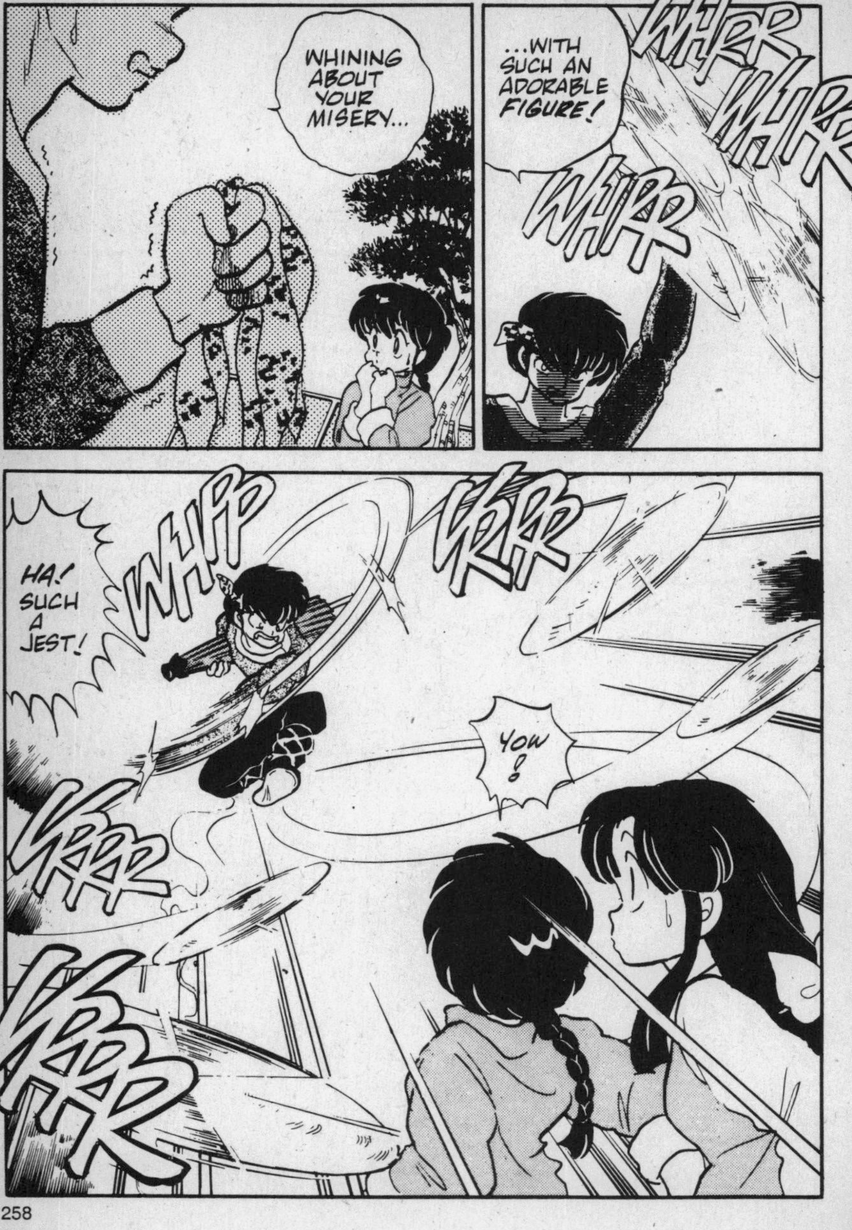
WHINING ABOUT YOUR MISERY...
...WITH SUCH AN ADORABLE FIGURE!
WHRR
WHRR
WHRR
HA! SUCH A JEST!
WHIP
VRRR
YOW!
VRRR
VRRR

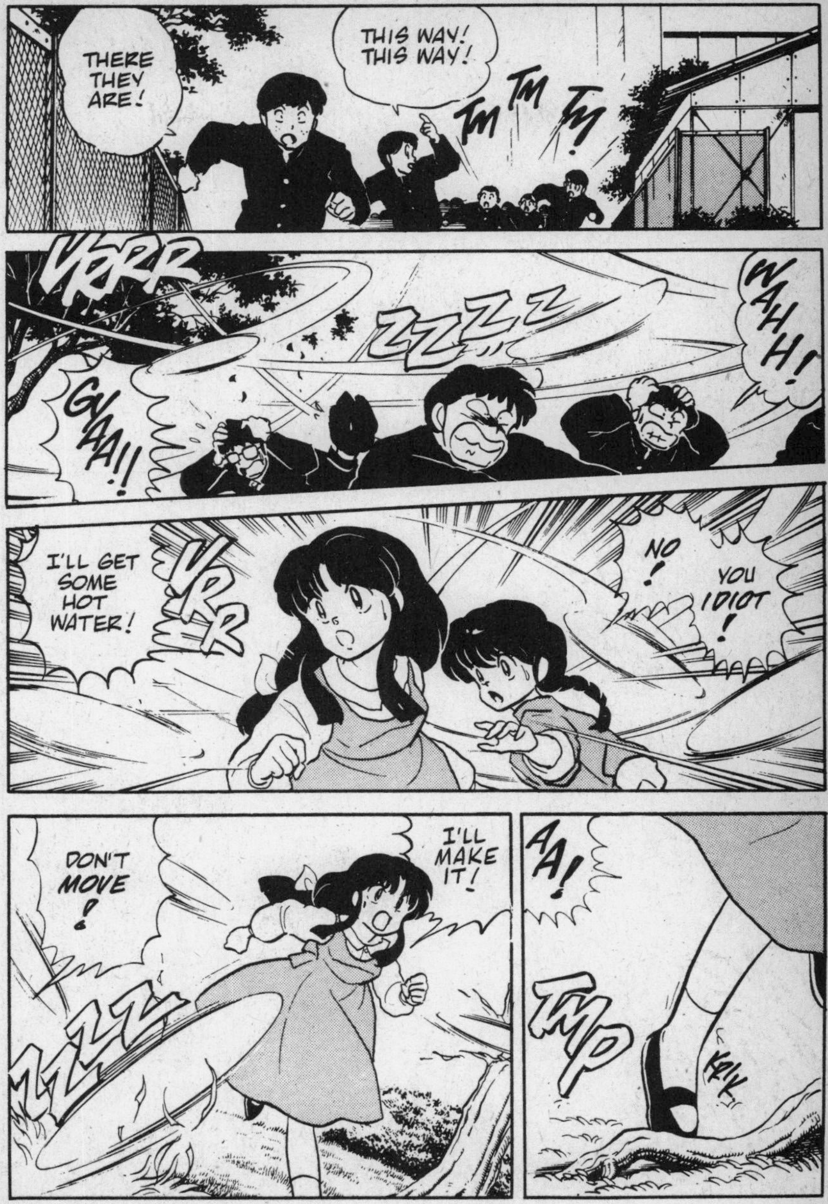
THERE THEY ARE!
THIS WAY! THIS WAY!
TM TM TM
VRRR
ZZZZZ
GUAAA!!
WAHHH!
I'LL GET SOME HOT WATER!
VRR
NO!
YOU IDIOT!
DON'T MOVE!
I'LL MAKE IT!
ZZZZZ
AA!
TMP
KRIK

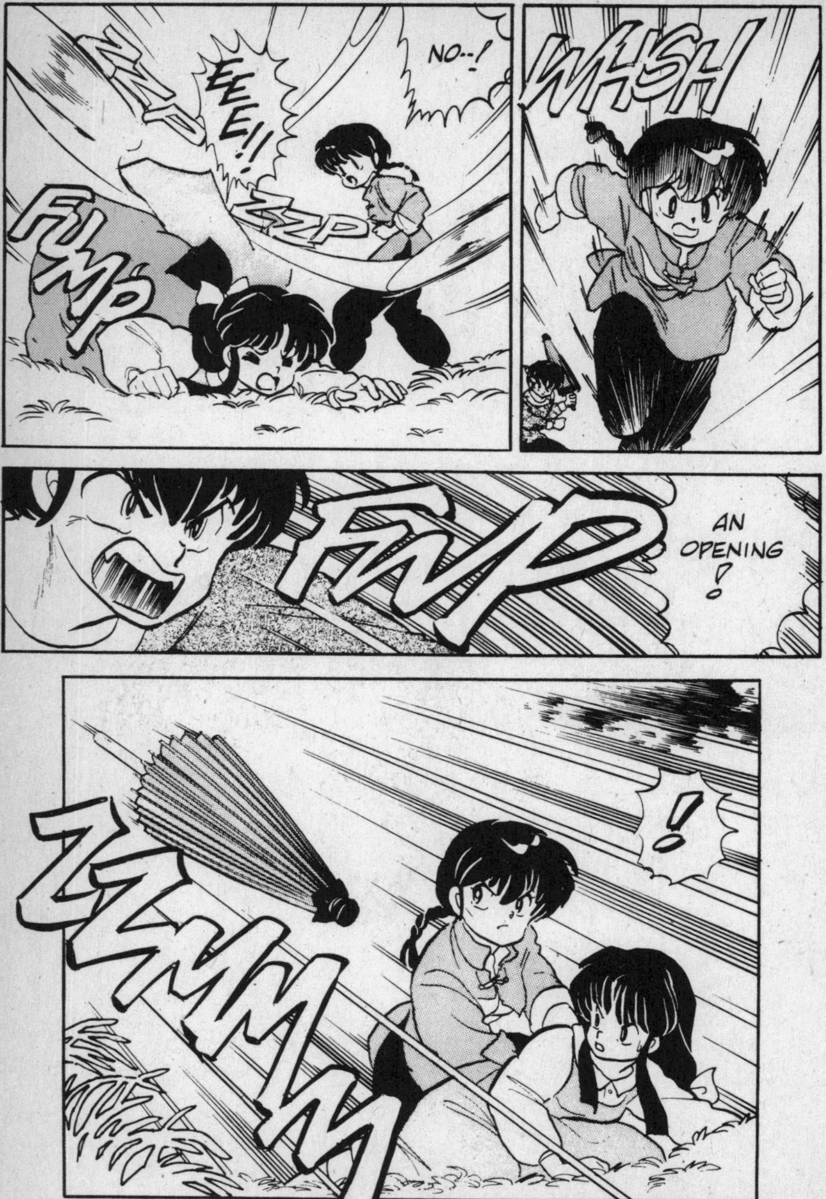
ZZZP
EEEE!!
NO--!
FUMP
ZZZP
WHSH
FWP
AN OPENING!?
ZUMMMM
!

Part 13
A BAD CUT

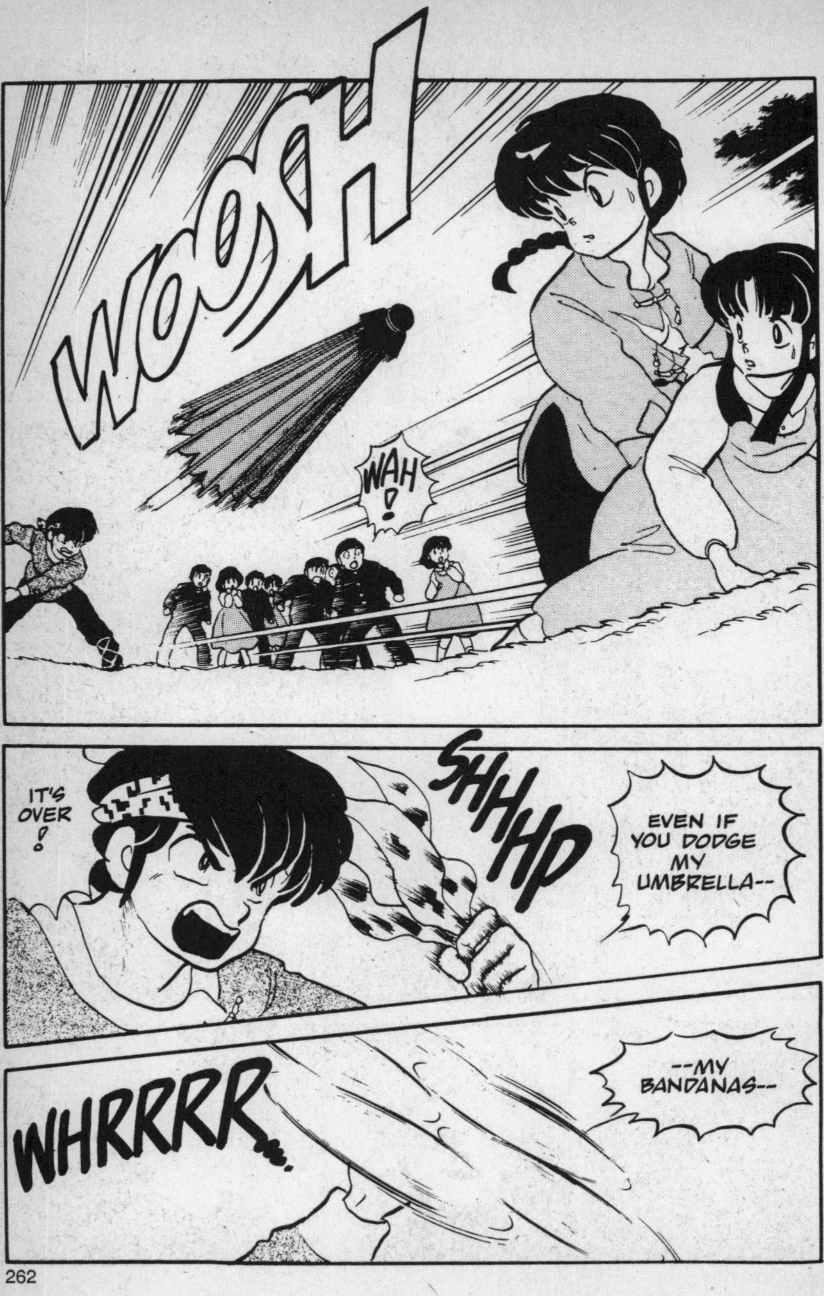
WOOSH
WAH!
IT'S OVER!
SHHHP
EVEN IF YOU DODGE MY UMBRELLA--
--MY BANDANAS--
WHRRRR...

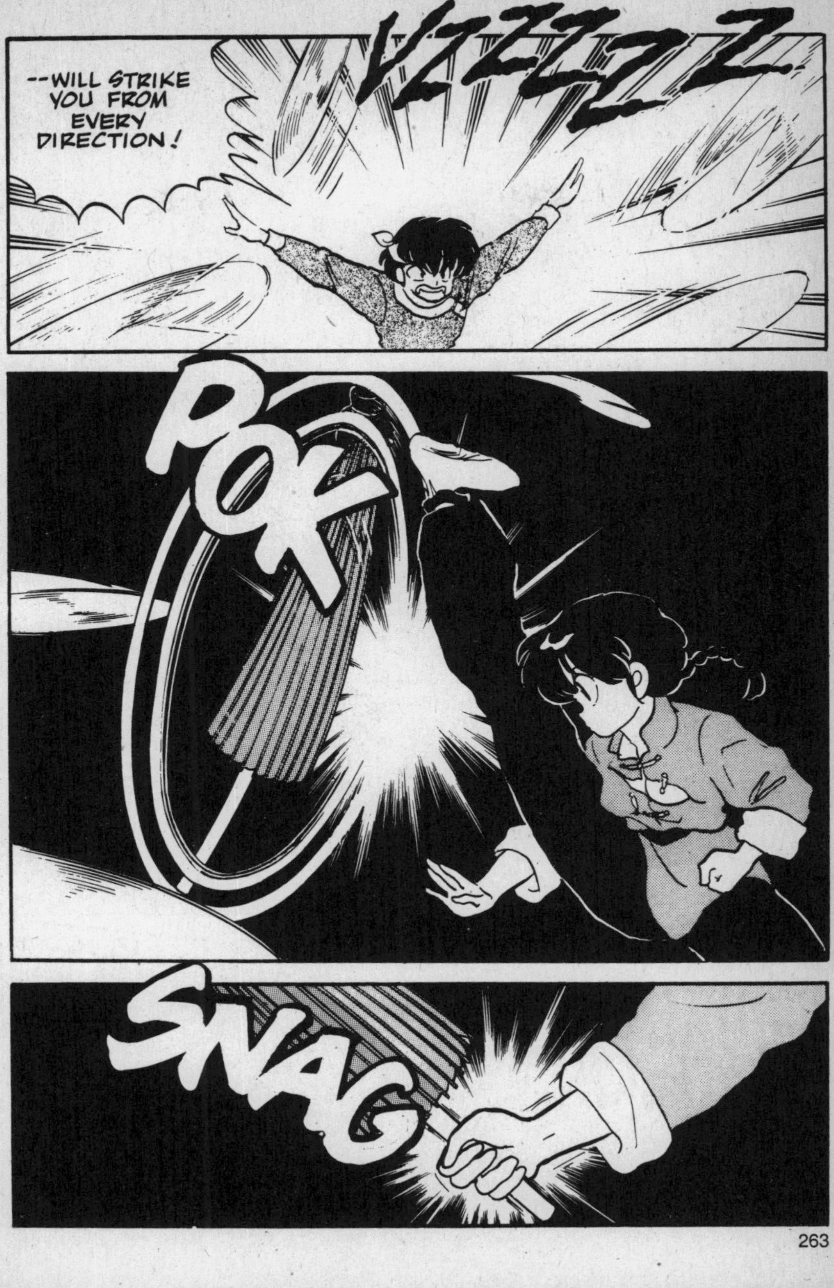
--WILL STRIKE YOU FROM EVERY DIRECTION!
VZZZZZ
POK
SNAG

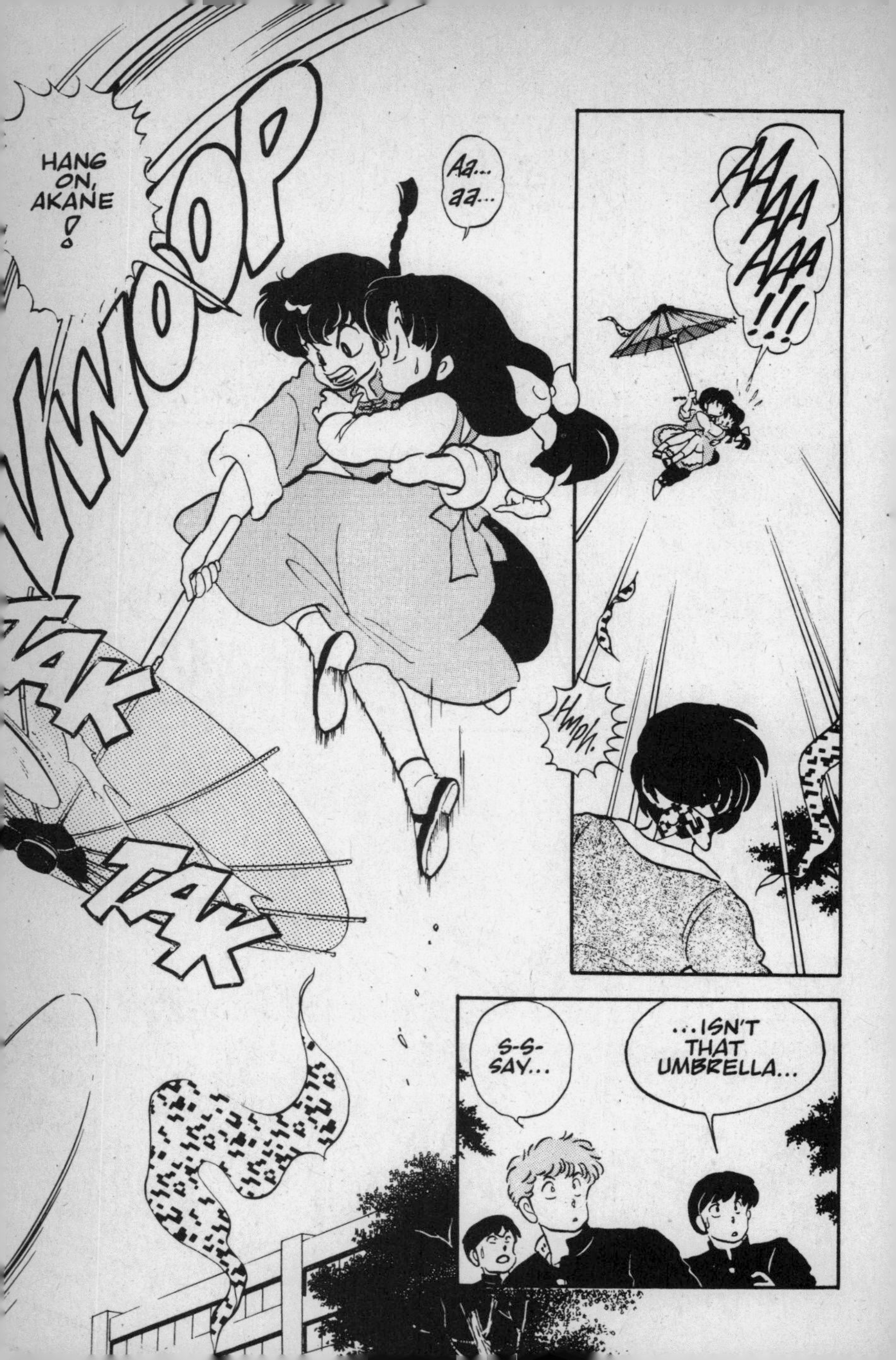
HANG ON, AKANE!
VWOOP
Aa... aa...
TAK
TAK
AAAAAAAA!!!
Hmph.
S-S-SAY...
...ISN'T THAT UMBRELLA...

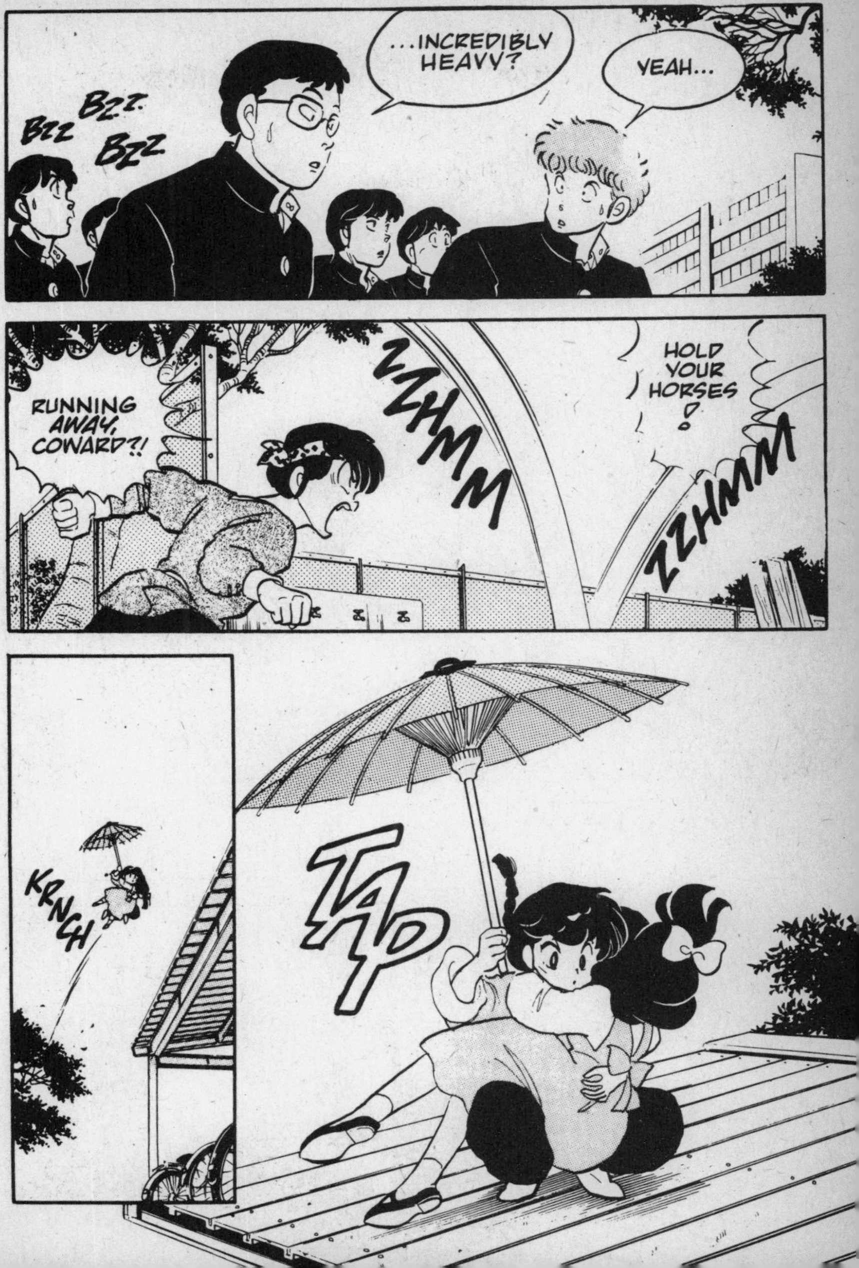
BZZ
BZZ.
BZZ.
...INCREDIBLY HEAVY?
YEAH...
RUNNING AWAY, COWARD?!
ZZHMMM
HOLD YOUR HORSES!
ZZHMMM
TAP
KRNCH

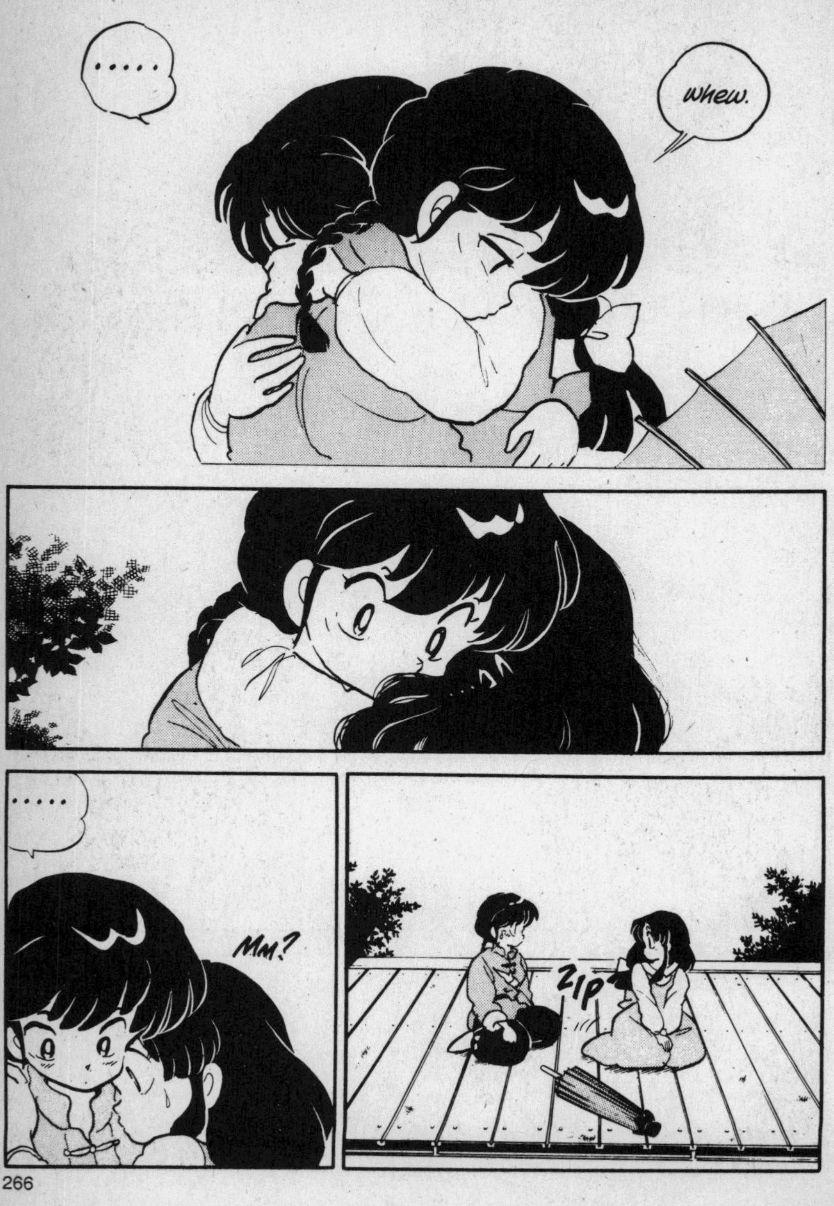
.....
whew.
.....
Mm?
ZIP

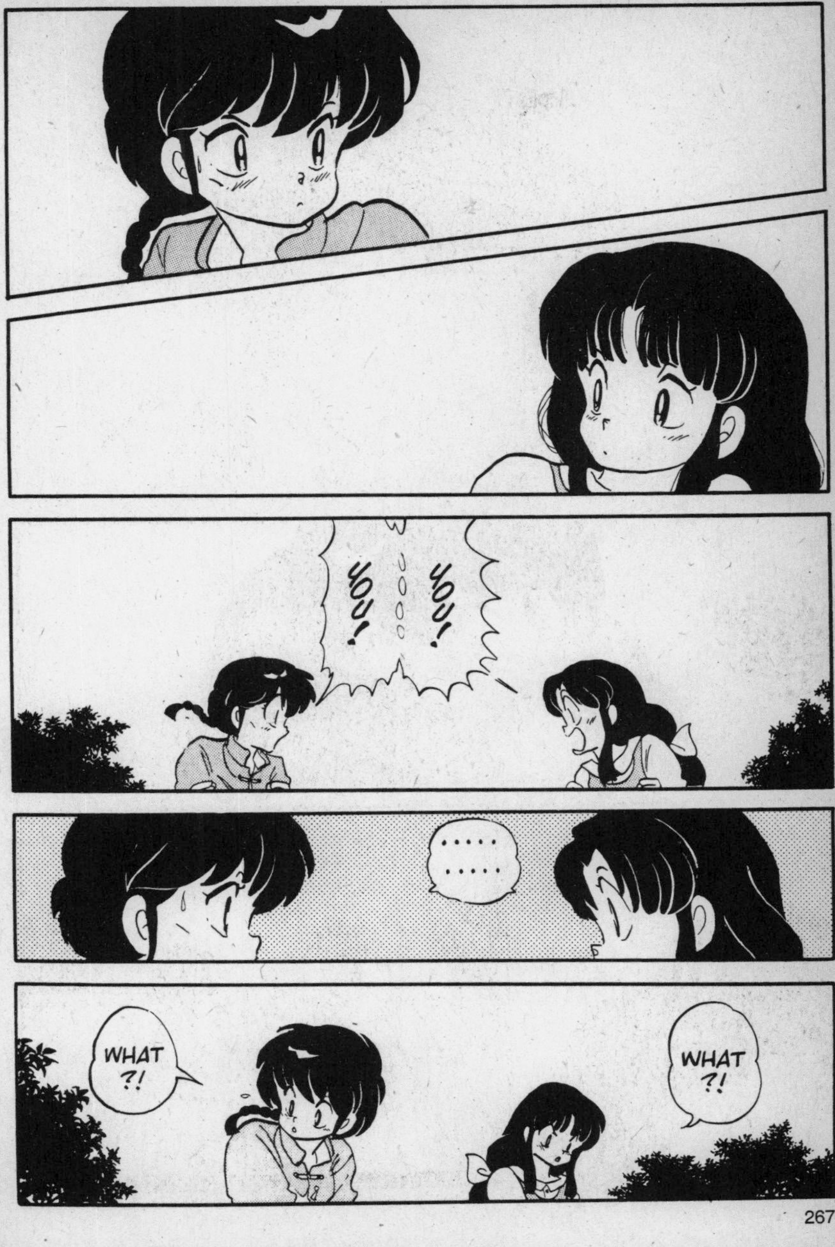
YOU!
OOOO
YOU!
......
......
WHAT ?!
WHAT ?!

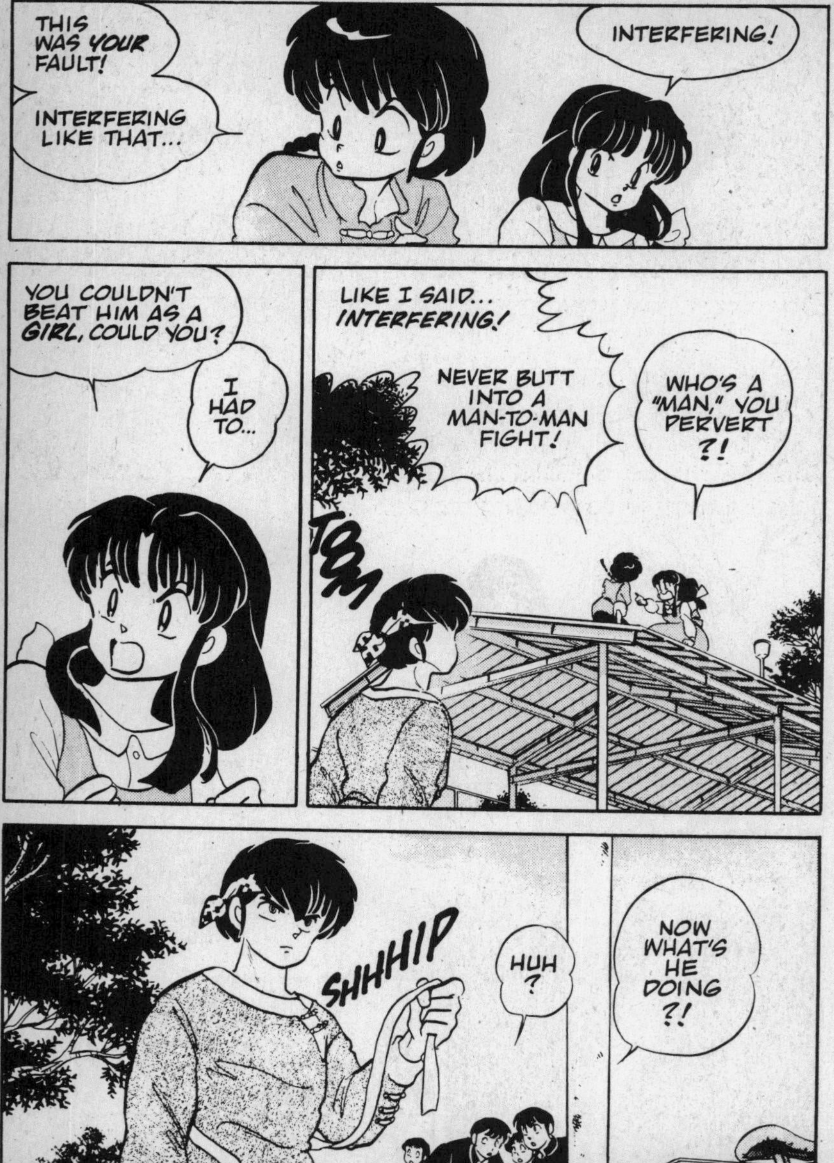
THIS WAS YOUR FAULT!
INTERFERING LIKE THAT...
INTERFERING!
YOU COULDN'T BEAT HIM AS A GIRL, COULD YOU?
I HAD TO...
LIKE I SAID... INTERFERING!
NEVER BUTT INTO A MAN-TO-MAN FIGHT!
WHO'S A "MAN," YOU PERVERT?!
TOM
SHHHIP
HUH?
NOW WHAT'S HE DOING?!

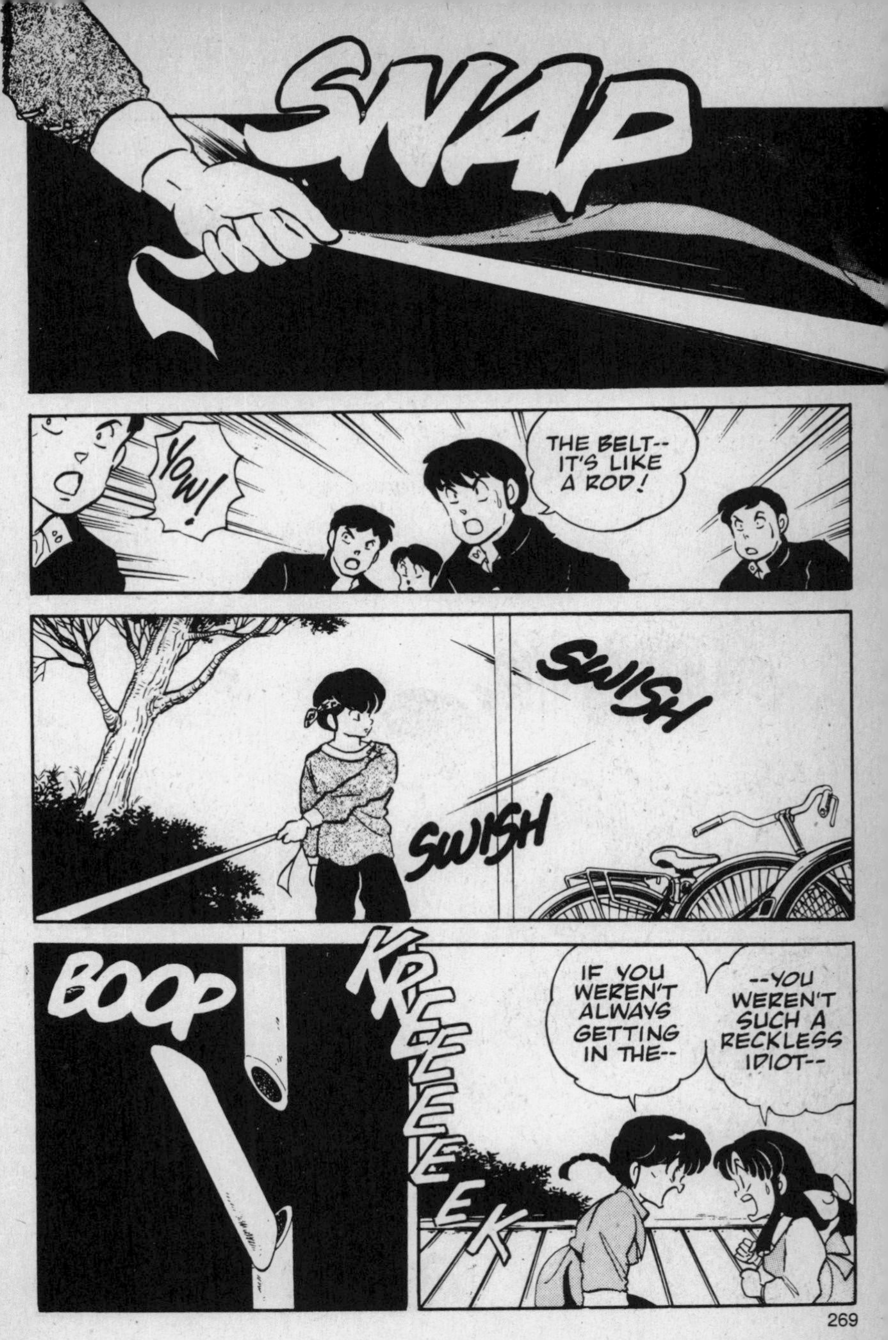
SNAP
YOW!
THE BELT-- IT'S LIKE A ROD!
SWISH
SWISH
BOOP
KREEEEEEK
IF YOU WEREN'T ALWAYS GETTING IN THE--
--YOU WEREN'T SUCH A RECKLESS IDIOT--

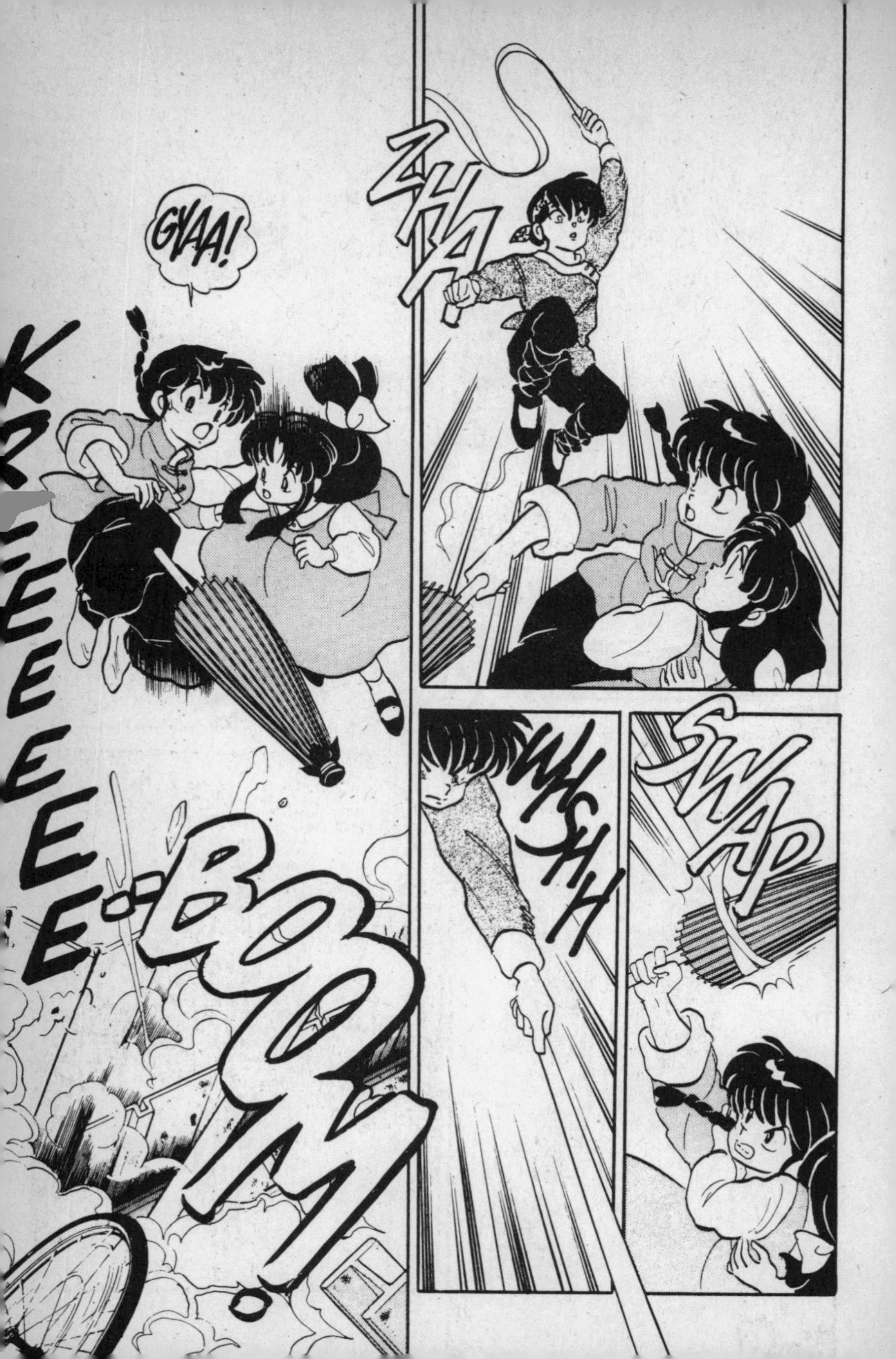
GYAA!
KREEEEEEE-BOOM!
ZHA
WHSHH
SWAP

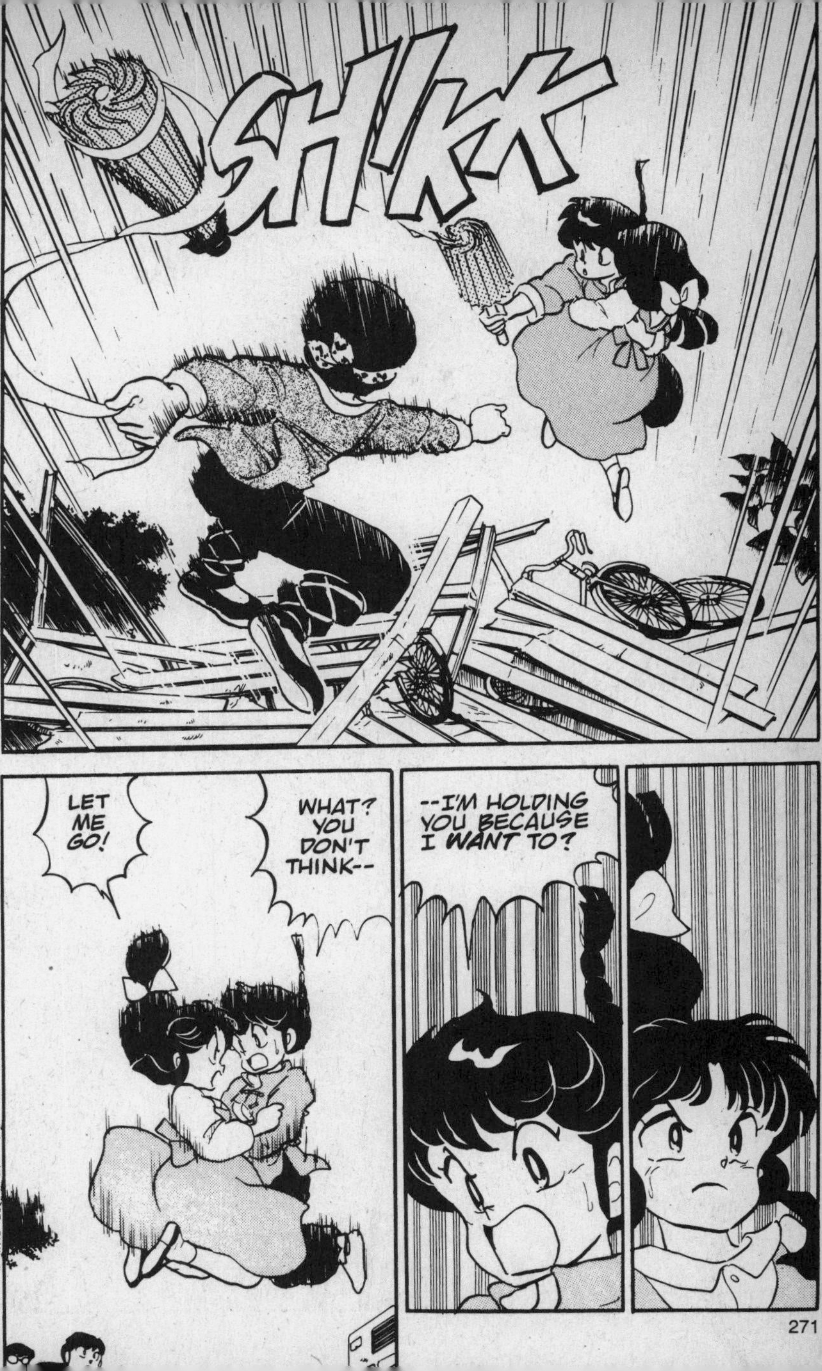
SHIKK
LET ME GO!
WHAT? YOU DON'T THINK--
--I'M HOLDING YOU BECAUSE I *WANT* TO?

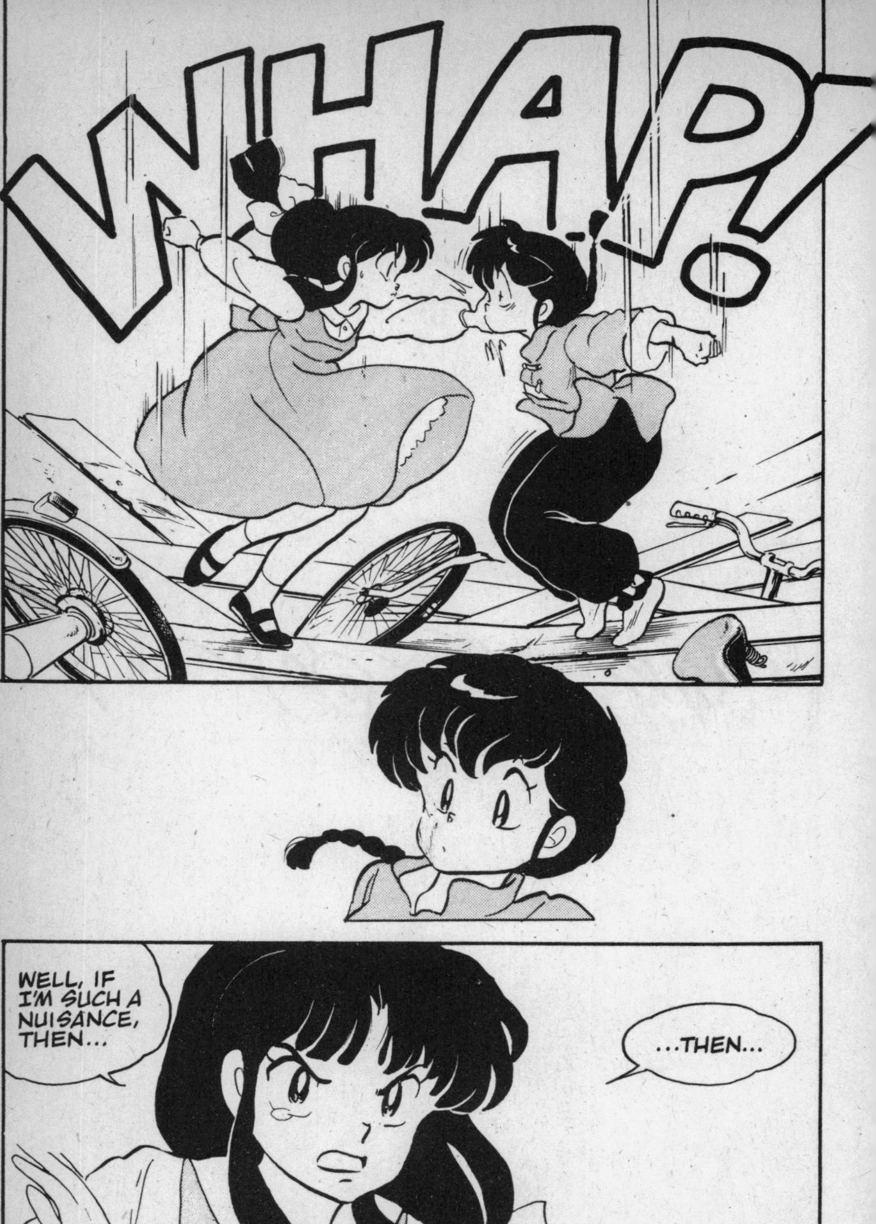
WHAP!
WELL, IF I'M SUCH A NUISANCE, THEN...
...THEN...

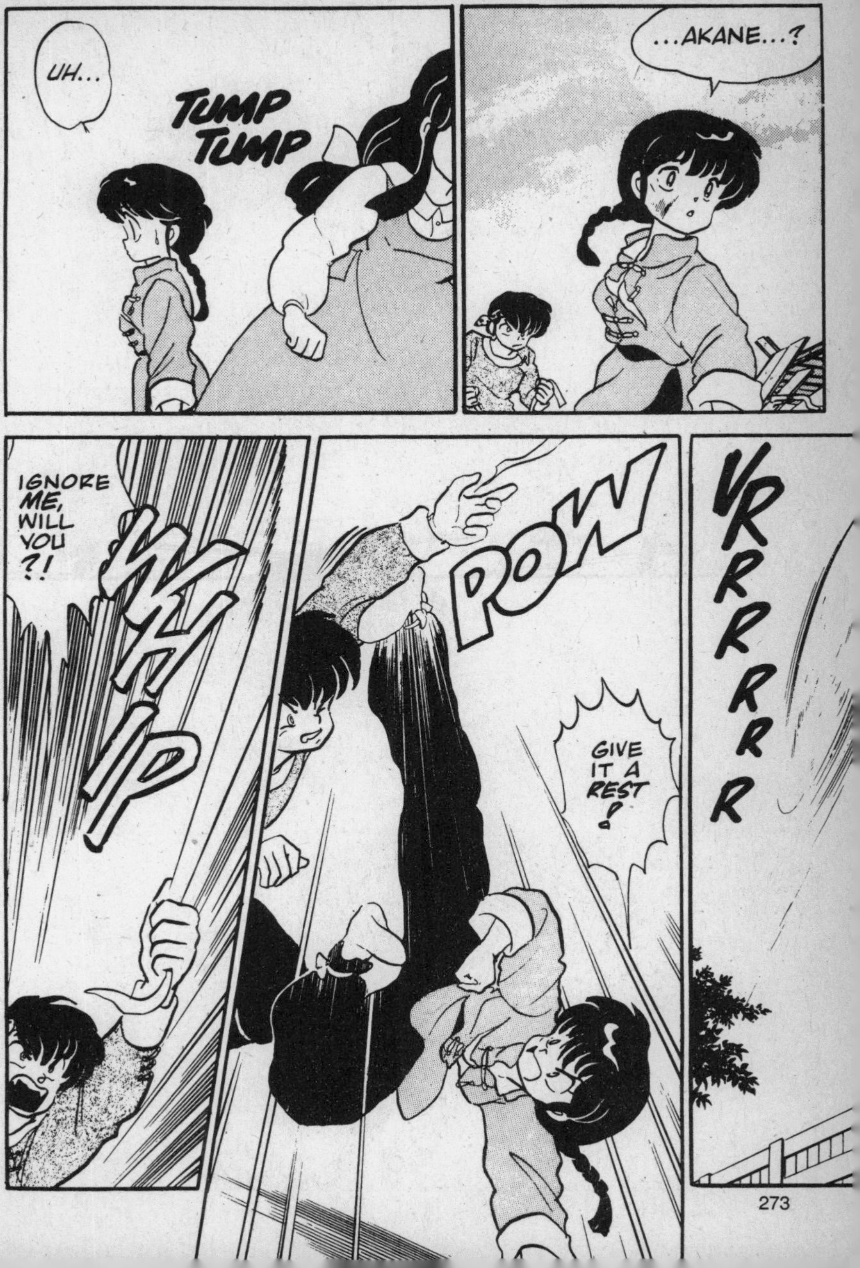
UH...
TUMP TUMP
...AKANE...?
IGNORE ME, WILL YOU ?!
WHIP
POW
GIVE IT A REST!
VRRRRRR

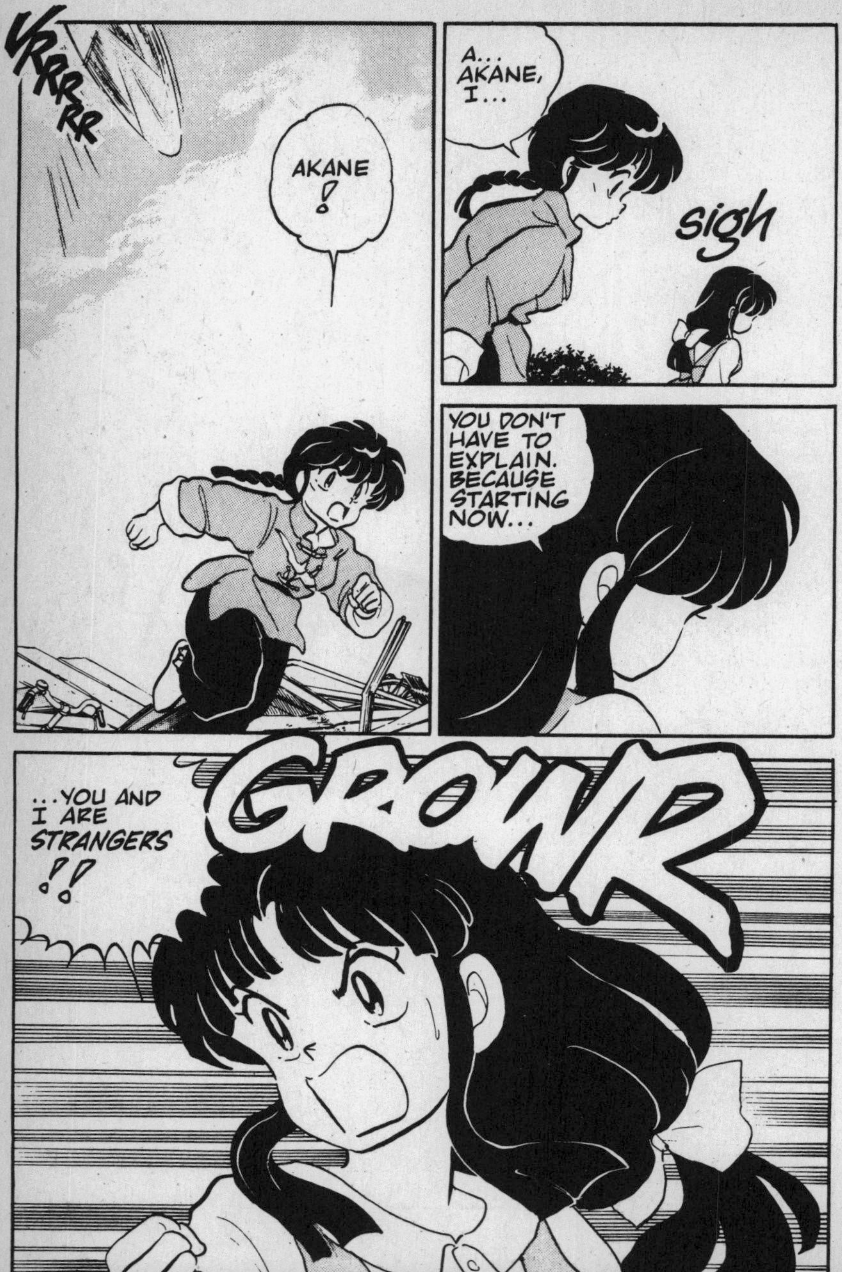
VRRRRR
AKANE!
A... AKANE, I...
sigh
YOU DON'T HAVE TO EXPLAIN. BECAUSE STARTING NOW...
...YOU AND I ARE STRANGERS!!
GROWR

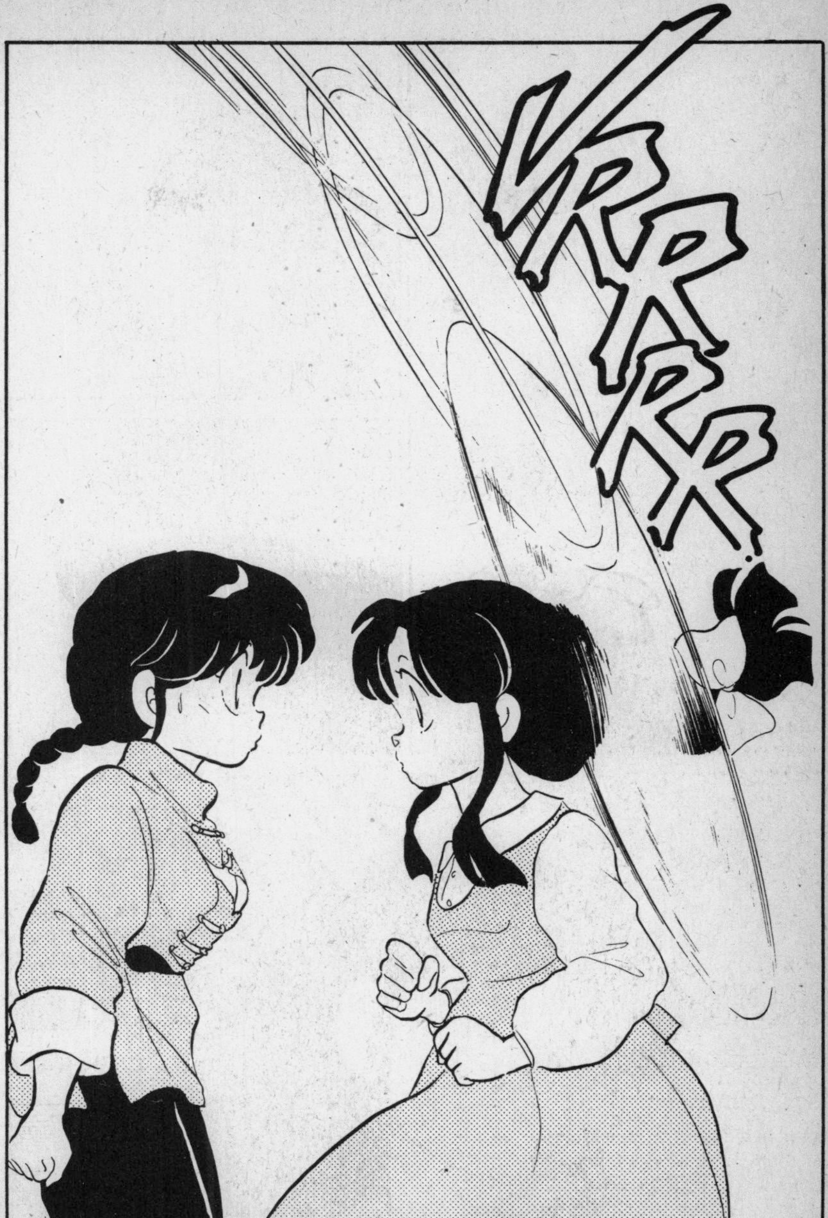
VRRRR

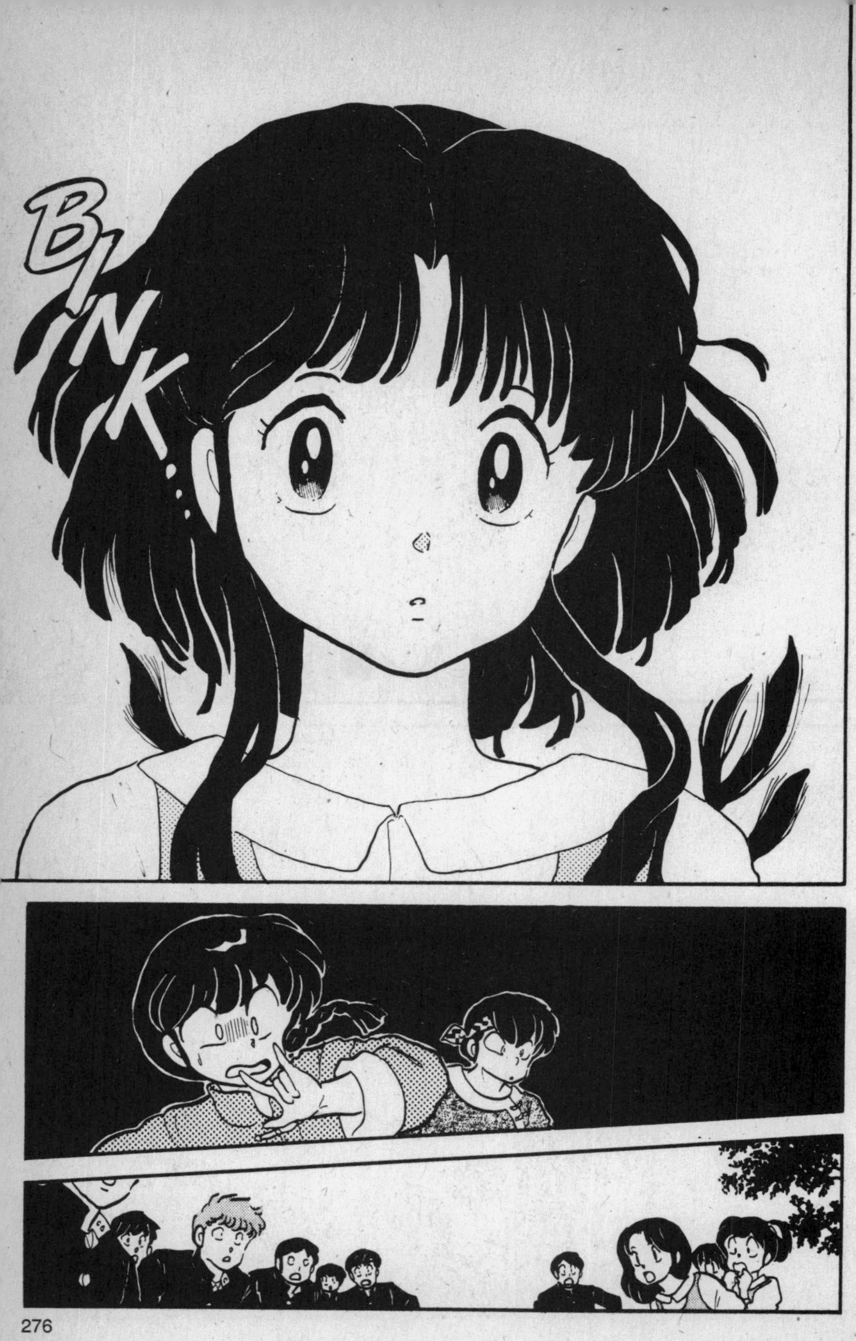
BLINK

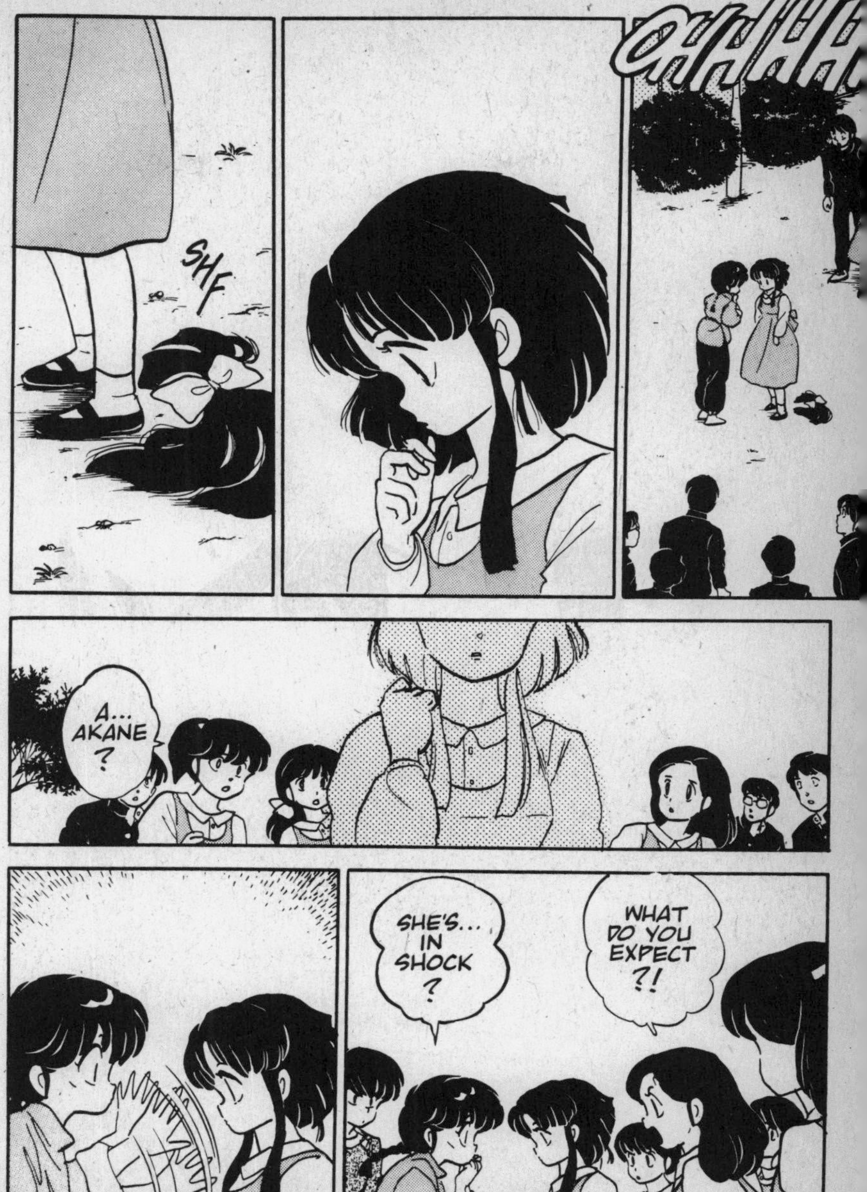
SHF
OHHHH
A... AKANE ?
SHE'S... IN SHOCK ?
WHAT DO YOU EXPECT ?!

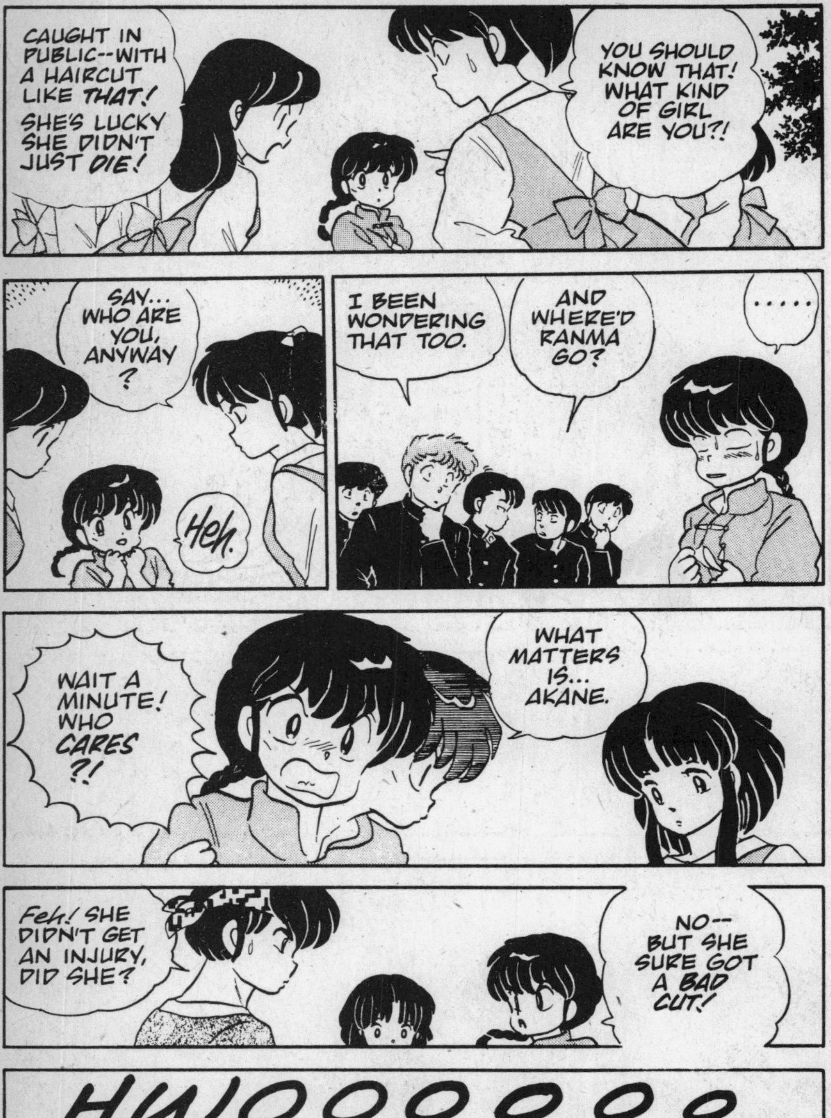

CAUGHT IN PUBLIC--WITH A HAIRCUT LIKE THAT! SHE'S LUCKY SHE DIDN'T JUST DIE!
YOU SHOULD KNOW THAT! WHAT KIND OF GIRL ARE YOU?!
SAY... WHO ARE YOU, ANYWAY ?
Heh.
I BEEN WONDERING THAT TOO.
AND WHERE'D RANMA GO?
.....
WAIT A MINUTE! WHO CARES ?!
WHAT MATTERS IS... AKANE.
Feh! SHE DIDN'T GET AN INJURY, DID SHE?
NO-- BUT SHE SURE GOT A BAD CUT!
HWOOOOOO

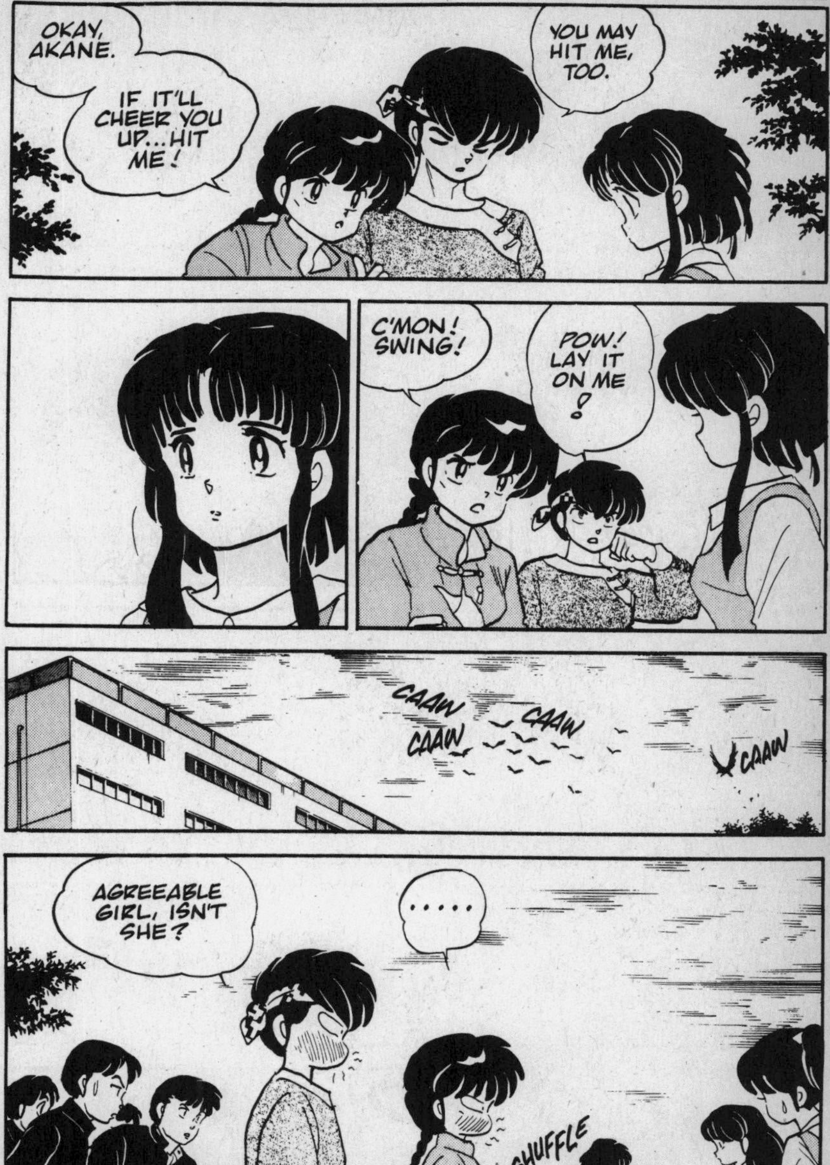
OKAY, AKANE.
IF IT'LL CHEER YOU UP...HIT ME!
YOU MAY HIT ME, TOO.
C'MON! SWING!
POW! LAY IT ON ME!
CAAW
CAAW
CAAW
CAAW
AGREEABLE GIRL, ISN'T SHE?
.....
SHUFFLE

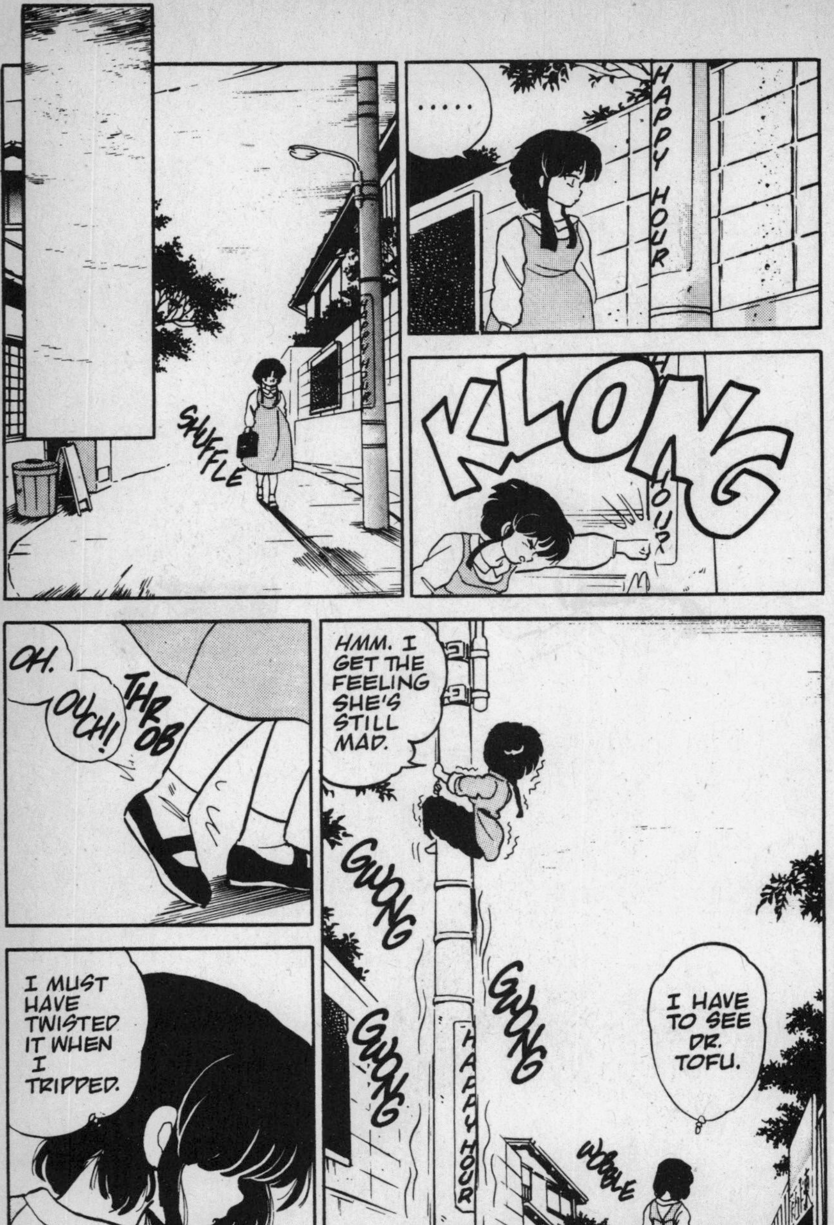
SHUFFLE
HAPPY HOUR
.....
HAPPY HOUR
KLONG
HOUR
OH.
OUCH!
THROB
I MUST HAVE TWISTED IT WHEN I TRIPPED.
HMM. I GET THE FEELING SHE'S STILL MAD.
GWONG
GWONG
GWONG
HAPPY HOUR
I HAVE TO SEE DR. TOFU.
WOBBLE

Part 14
WHO SAYS YOU'RE CUTE

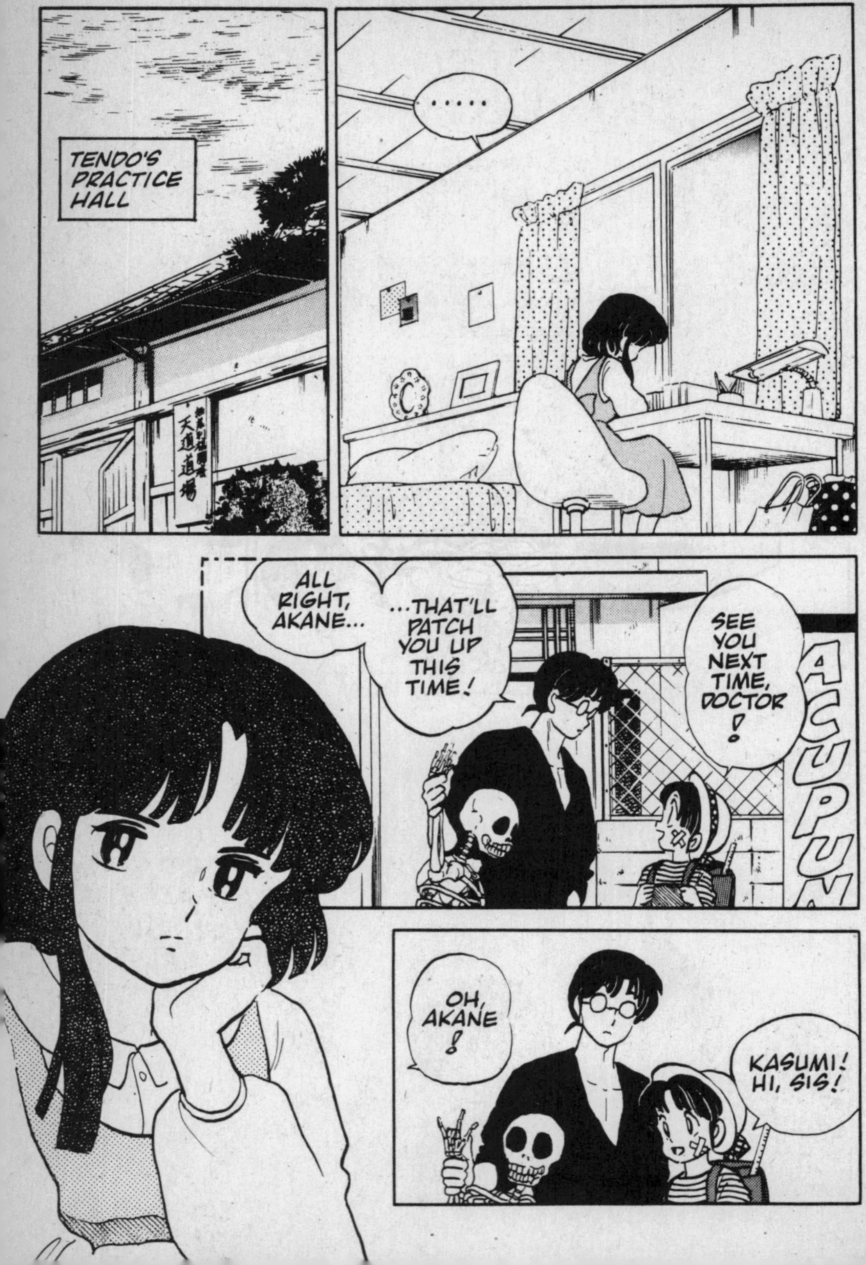
TENDO'S PRACTICE HALL
.....
ALL RIGHT, AKANE...
...THAT'LL PATCH YOU UP THIS TIME!
SEE YOU NEXT TIME, DOCTOR!
ACUPUN
OH, AKANE!
KASUMI! HI, SIS!

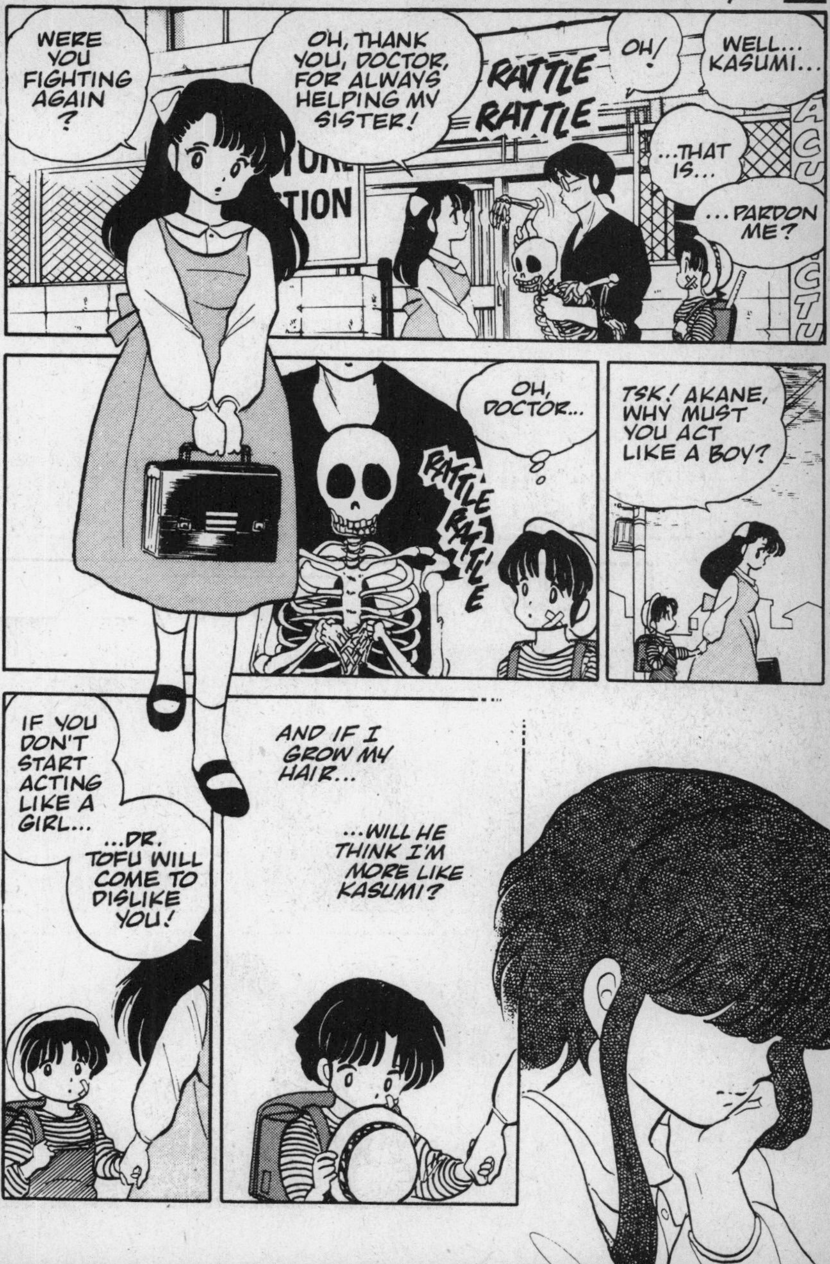
WERE YOU FIGHTING AGAIN?
OH, THANK YOU, DOCTOR, FOR ALWAYS HELPING MY SISTER!
RATTLE RATTLE
OH!
WELL... KASUMI...
...THAT IS...
...PARDON ME?
OH, DOCTOR...
RATTLE RATTLE
TSK! AKANE, WHY MUST YOU ACT LIKE A BOY?
IF YOU DON'T START ACTING LIKE A GIRL...
...DR. TOFU WILL COME TO DISLIKE YOU!
AND IF I GROW MY HAIR...
...WILL HE THINK I'M MORE LIKE KASUMI?

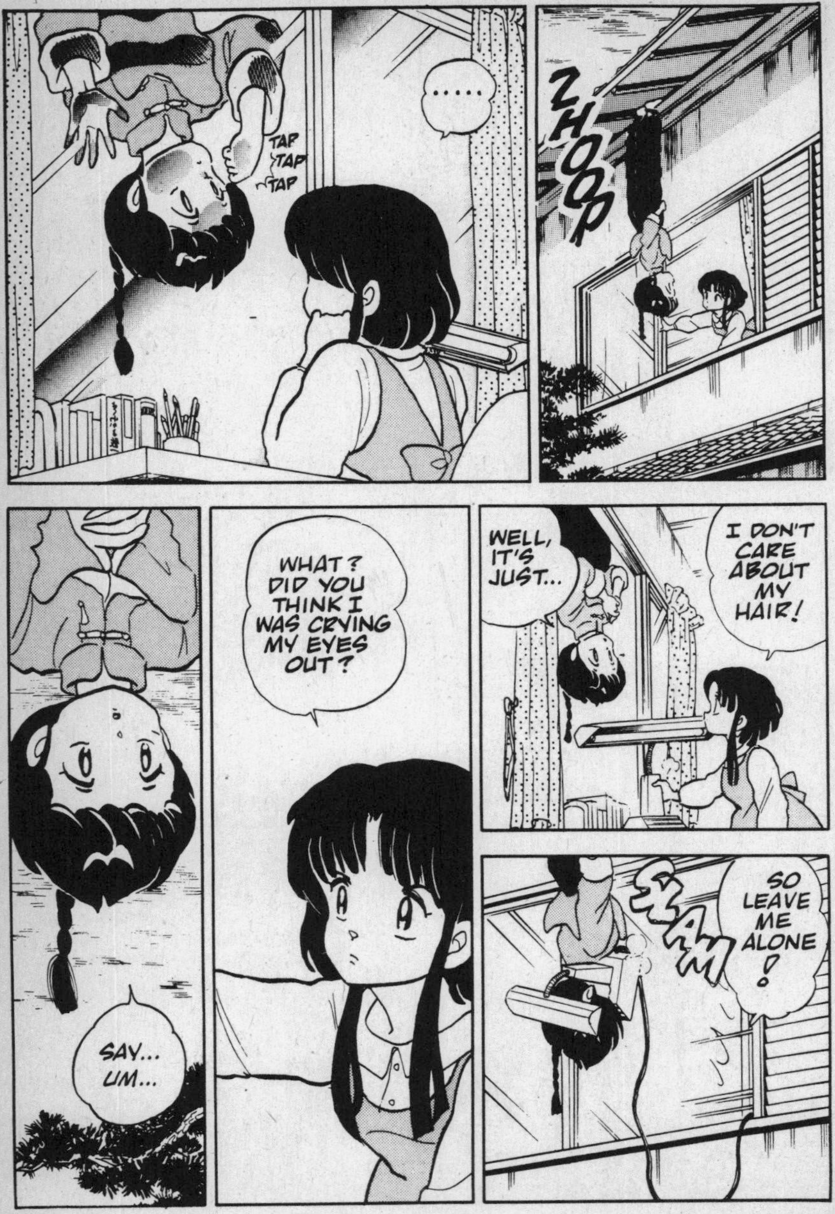
TAP
TAP
TAP
......
ZHOOP
SAY... UM...
WHAT? DID YOU THINK I WAS CRYING MY EYES OUT?
WELL, IT'S JUST...
I DON'T CARE ABOUT MY HAIR!
SLAM
SO LEAVE ME ALONE!

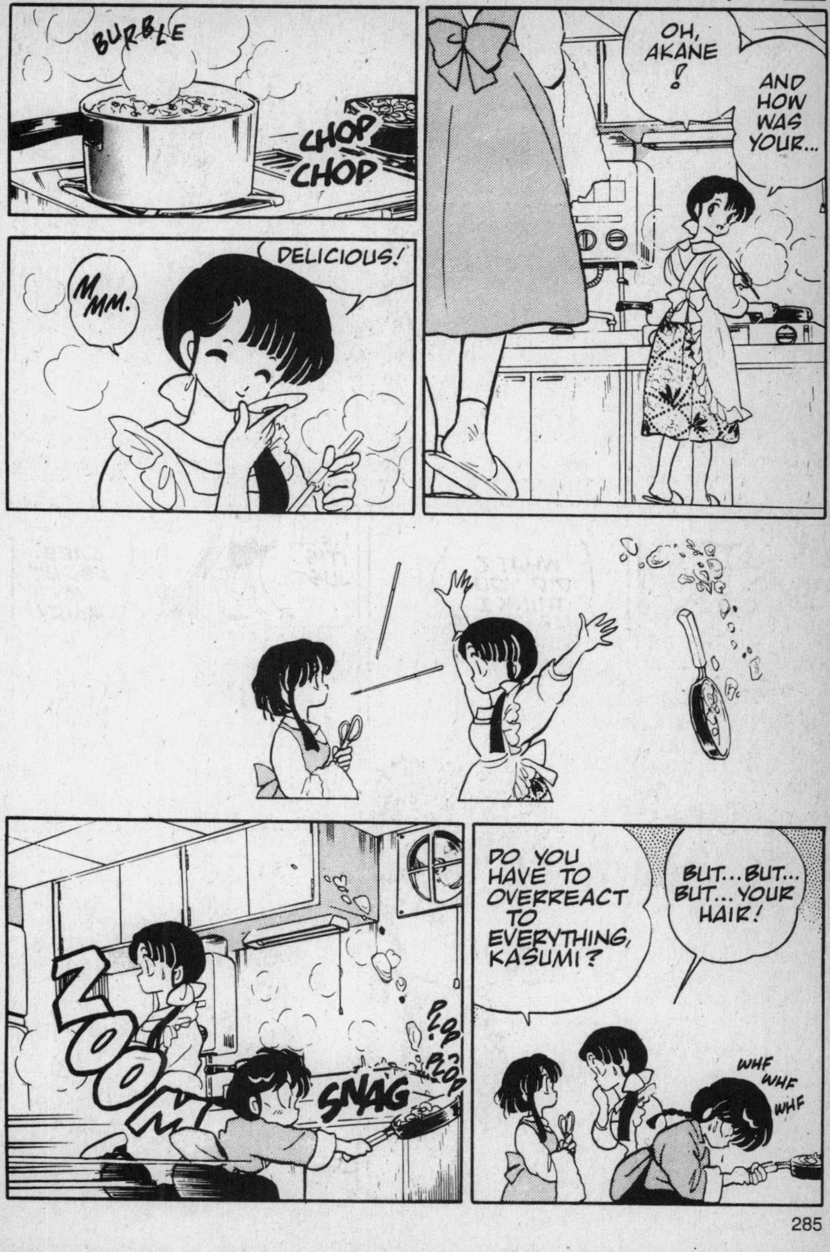
BURBLE
CHOP CHOP
M MM.
DELICIOUS!
OH, AKANE!
AND HOW WAS YOUR...
ZOOM
SNAG
PLOP PLOP
DO YOU HAVE TO OVERREACT TO EVERYTHING, KASUMI?
BUT... BUT... BUT... YOUR HAIR!
WHF WHF WHF

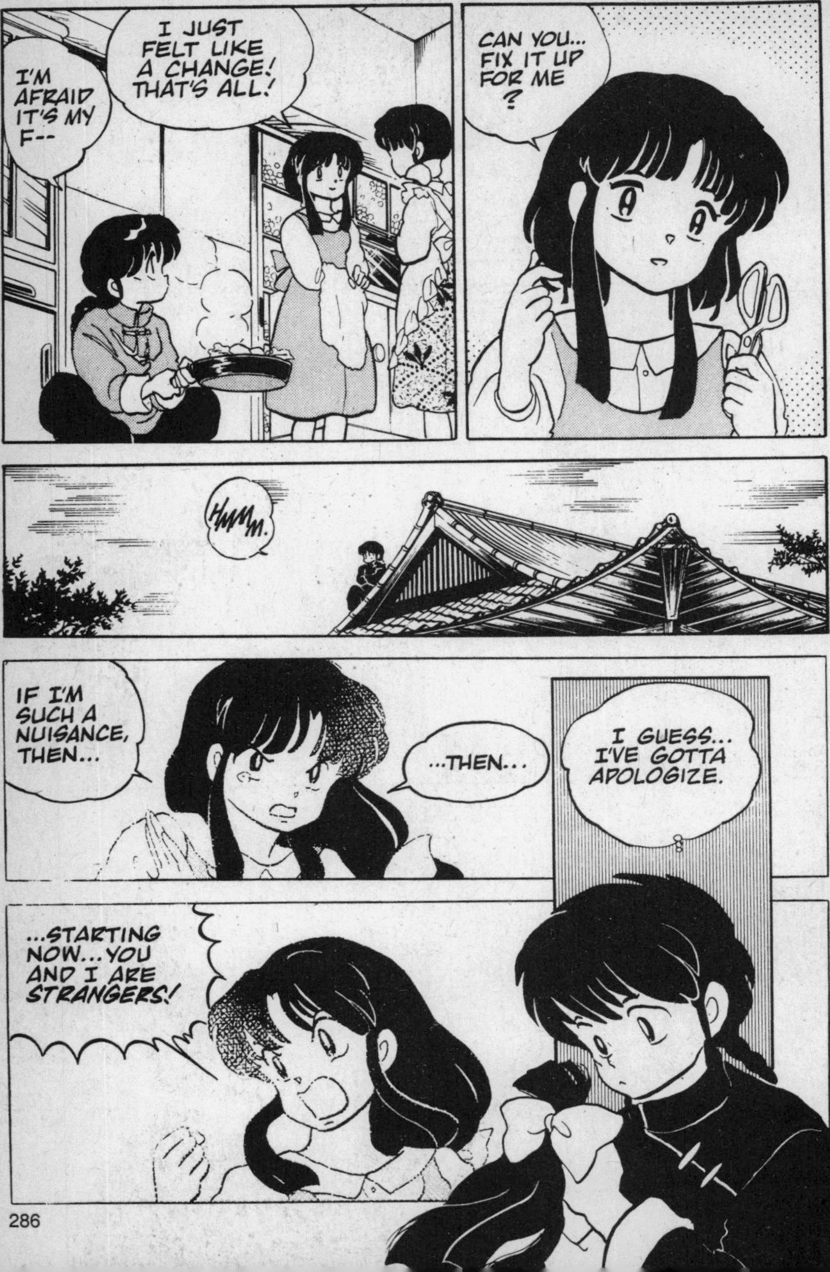
I'M AFRAID IT'S MY F--
I JUST FELT LIKE A CHANGE! THAT'S ALL!
CAN YOU... FIX IT UP FOR ME ?
HMMM.
IF I'M SUCH A NUISANCE, THEN...
...THEN...
I GUESS... I'VE GOTTA APOLOGIZE.
...STARTING NOW...YOU AND I ARE STRANGERS!

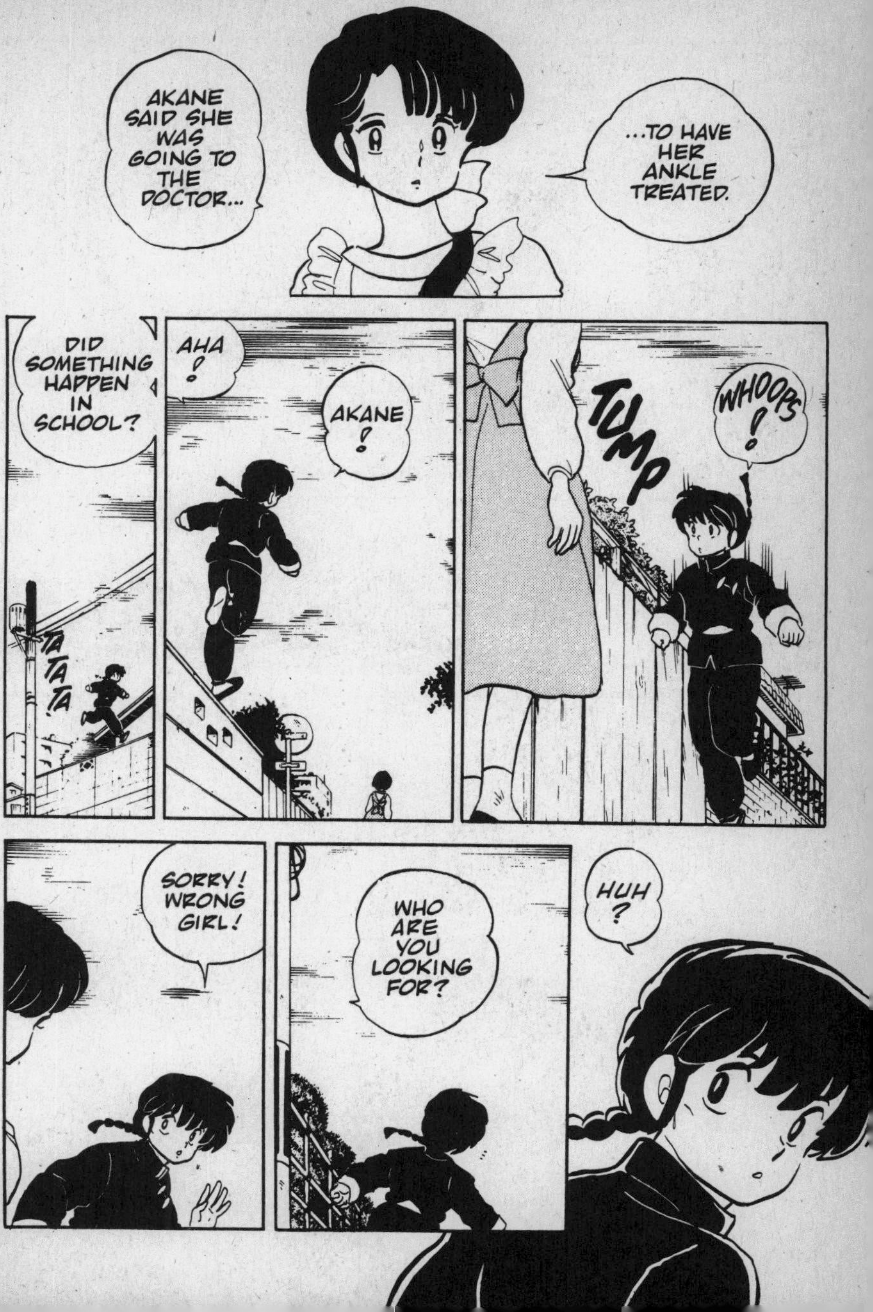
AKANE SAID SHE WAS GOING TO THE DOCTOR...
...TO HAVE HER ANKLE TREATED.
DID SOMETHING HAPPEN IN SCHOOL?
TATATA
AHA!
AKANE!
TUMP
WHOOPS!
SORRY! WRONG GIRL!
WHO ARE YOU LOOKING FOR?
HUH?

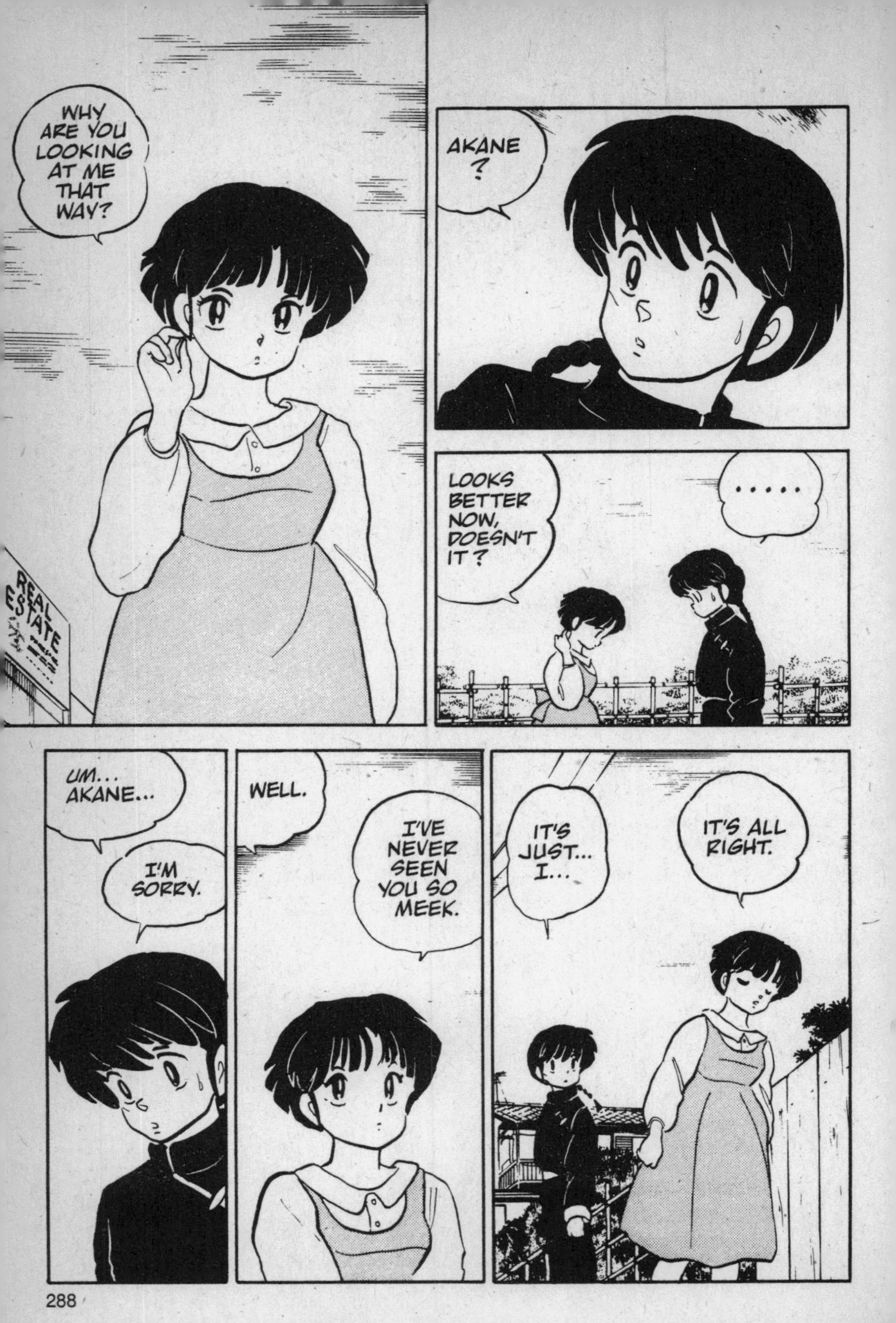
WHY ARE YOU LOOKING AT ME THAT WAY?
REAL ESTATE
AKANE?
LOOKS BETTER NOW, DOESN'T IT?
.....
UM... AKANE...
I'M SORRY.
WELL.
I'VE NEVER SEEN YOU SO MEEK.
IT'S JUST... I...
IT'S ALL RIGHT.

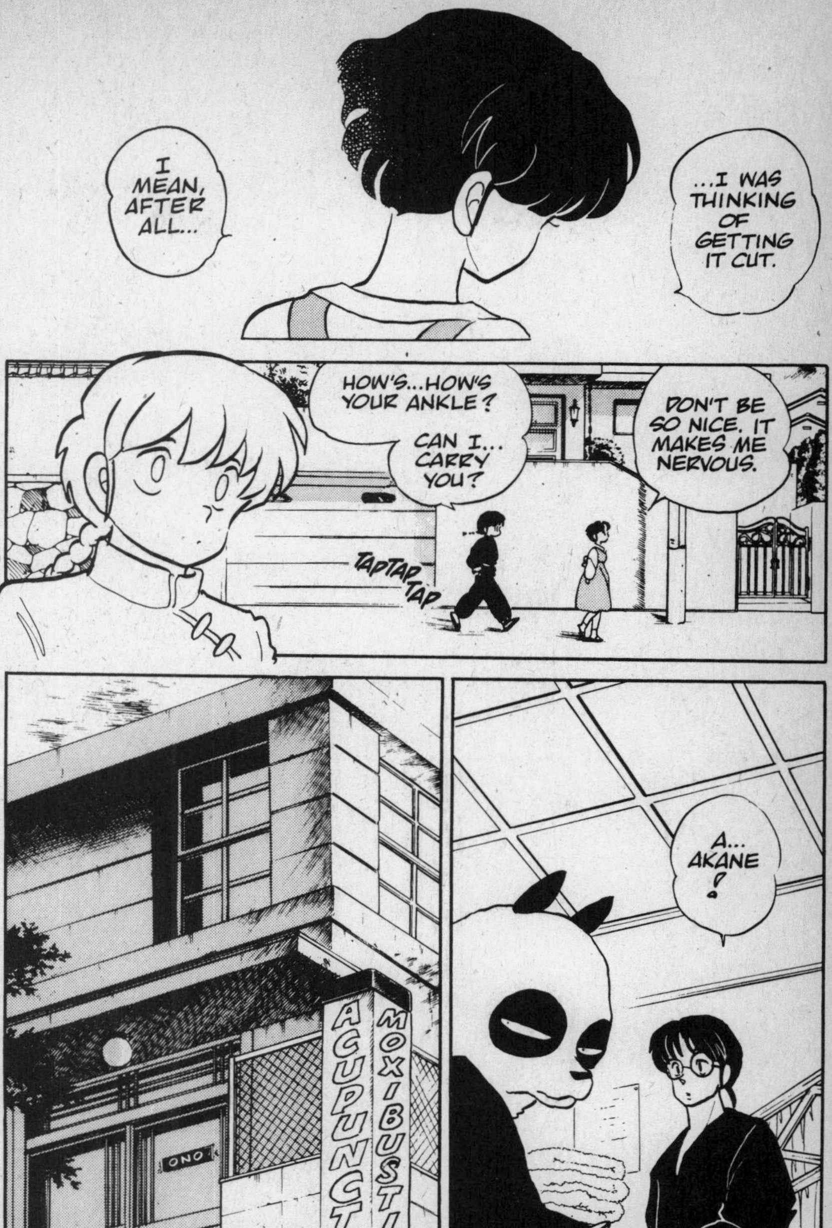
I MEAN, AFTER ALL...
...I WAS THINKING OF GETTING IT CUT.
HOW'S...HOW'S YOUR ANKLE?
CAN I... CARRY YOU?
DON'T BE SO NICE. IT MAKES ME NERVOUS.
TAPTAP TAP
ONO
ACUPUNCTU
MOXIBUSTIO
A... AKANE!

HELLO, DR. TOFU!

....

WELL, WELL. CUT IT SHORT AGAIN, EH?

MM-HM.

"AGAIN"?

LOOKS LIKE JUST A LIGHT SPRAIN.

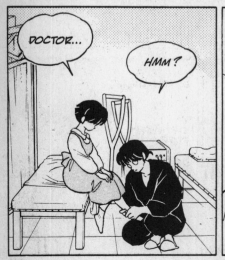

DOCTOR...

HMM?

DO YOU THINK IT... LOOKS GOOD?

OH, YES. IT'S VERY CUTE.

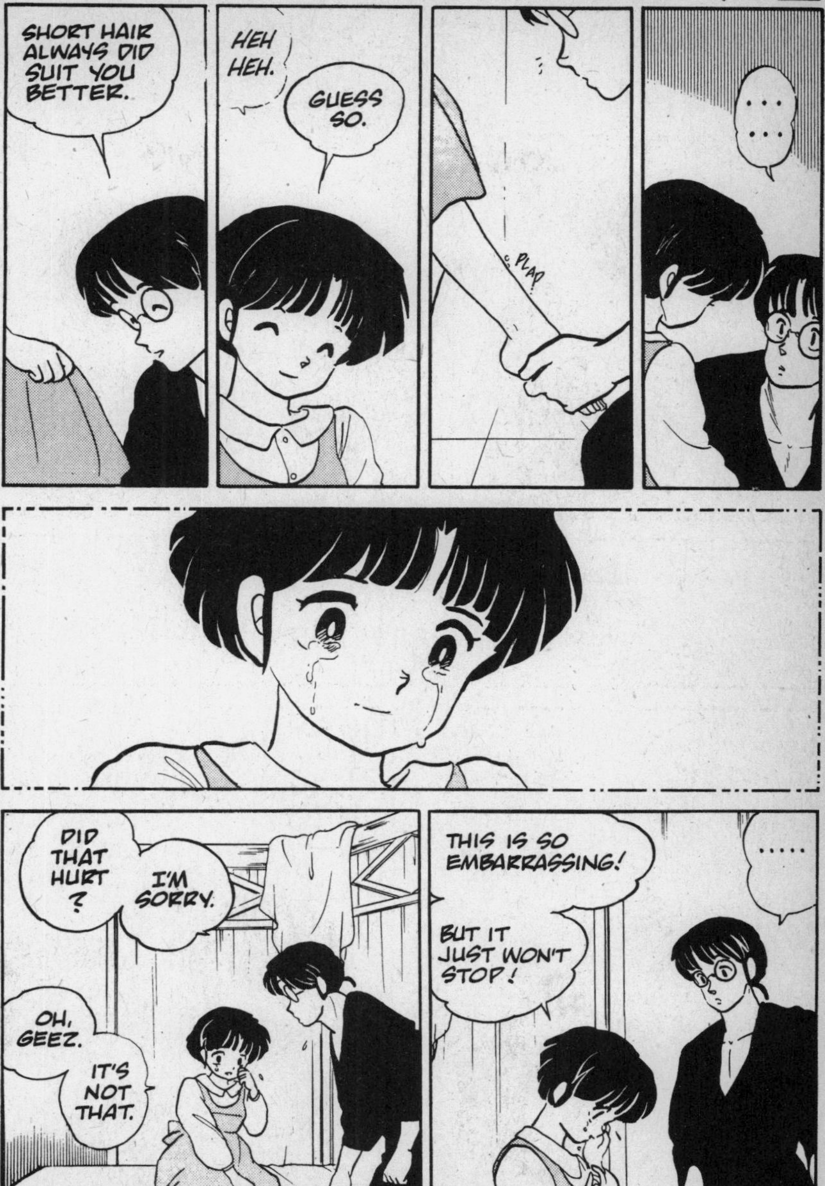
SHORT HAIR ALWAYS DID SUIT YOU BETTER.
HEH HEH.
GUESS SO.
PLAP
. . .
. . .
DID THAT HURT ?
I'M SORRY.
OH, GEEZ.
IT'S NOT THAT.
THIS IS SO EMBARRASSING!
BUT IT JUST WON'T STOP!
. . . . .

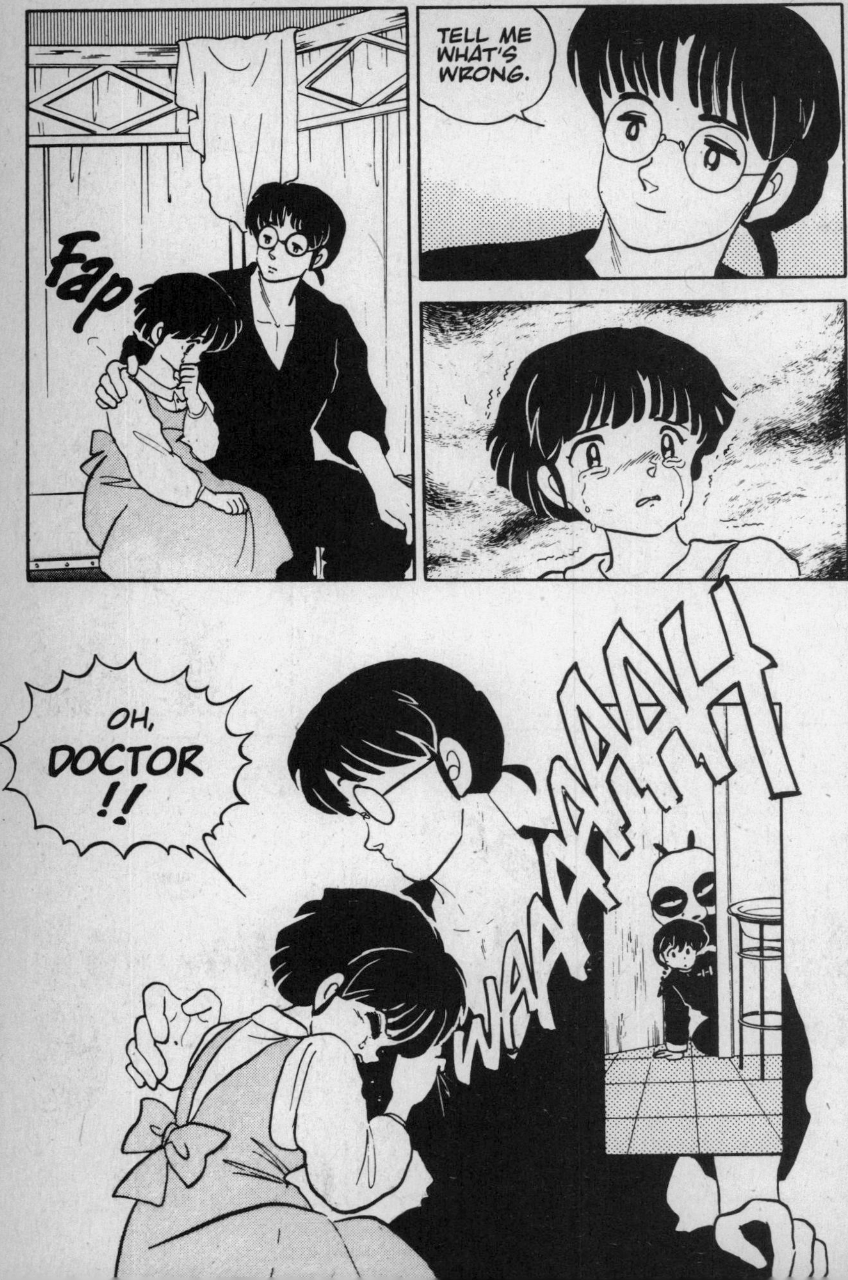
FAP
TELL ME WHAT'S WRONG.
OH, DOCTOR!!
WAAAAAAH

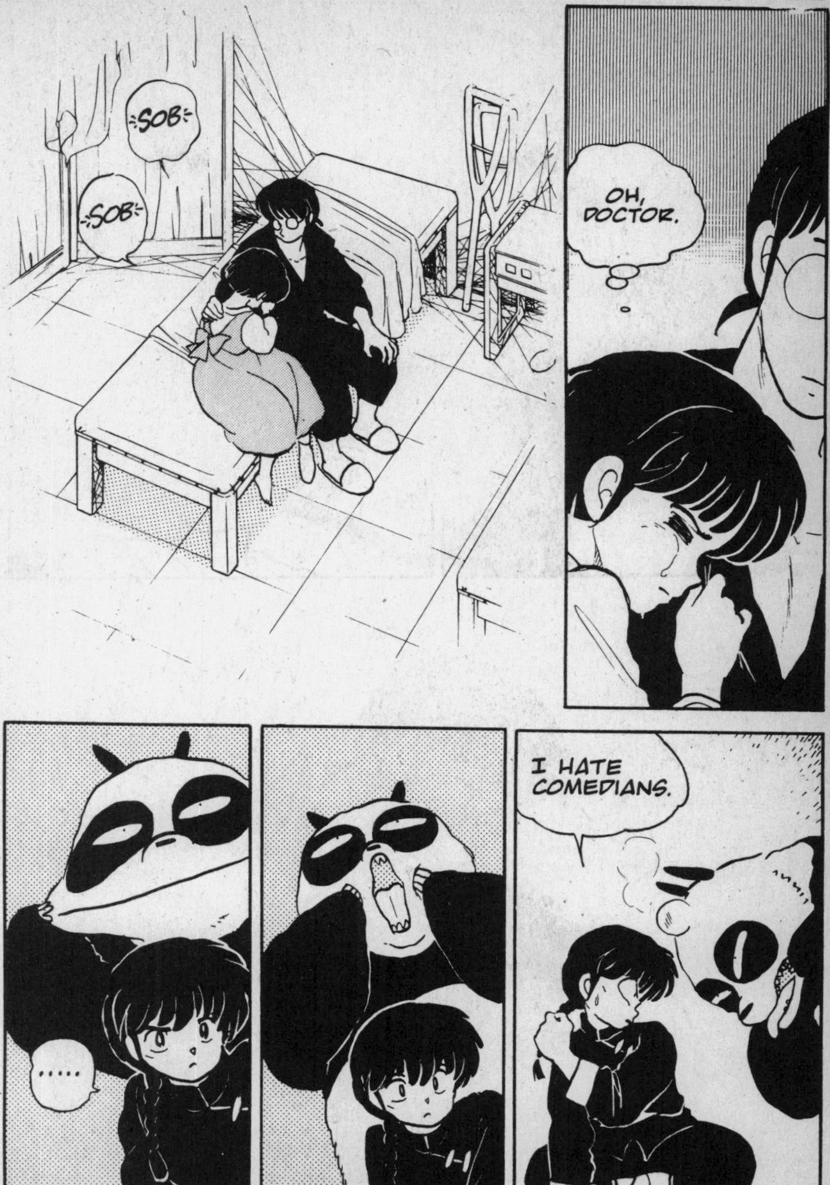
SOB
SOB
OH, DOCTOR.
.....
I HATE COMEDIANS.

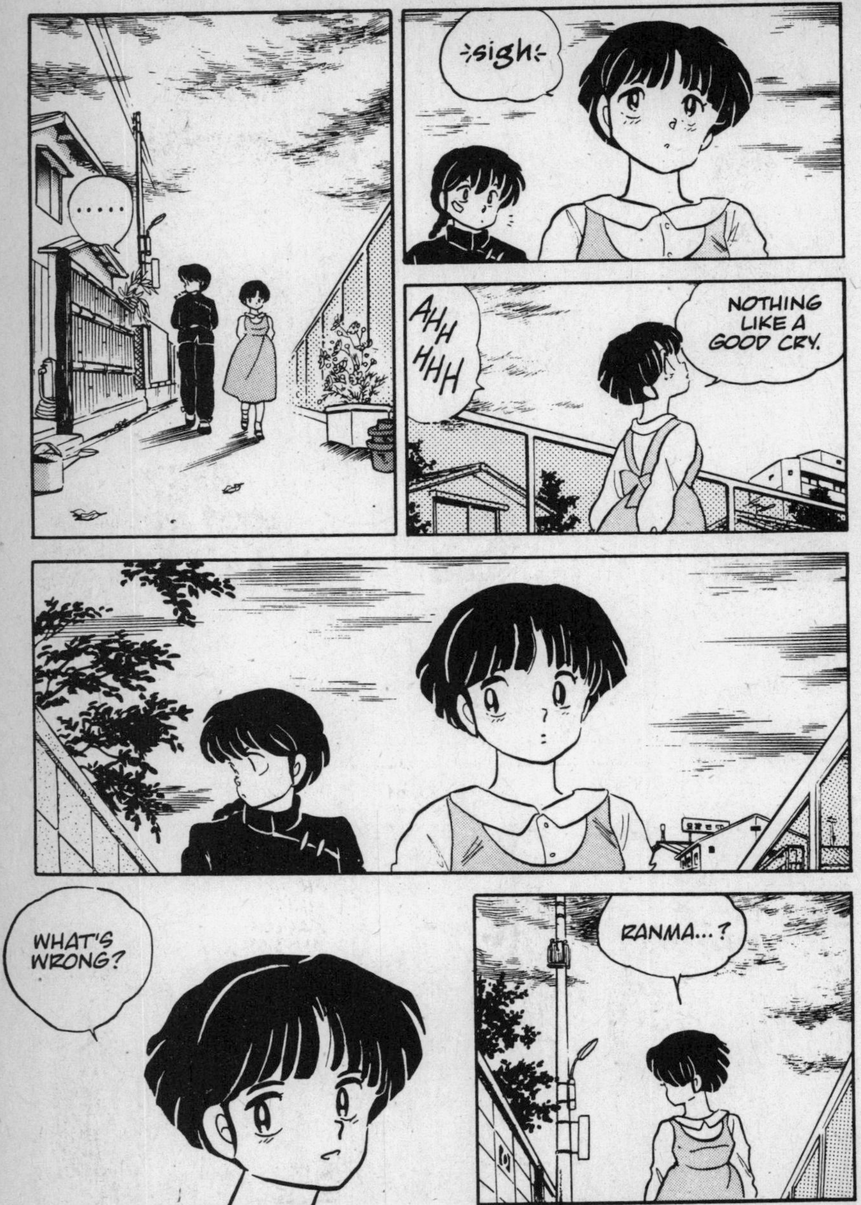
......
sigh
AHHHHH
NOTHING LIKE A GOOD CRY.
WHAT'S WRONG?
RANMA...?

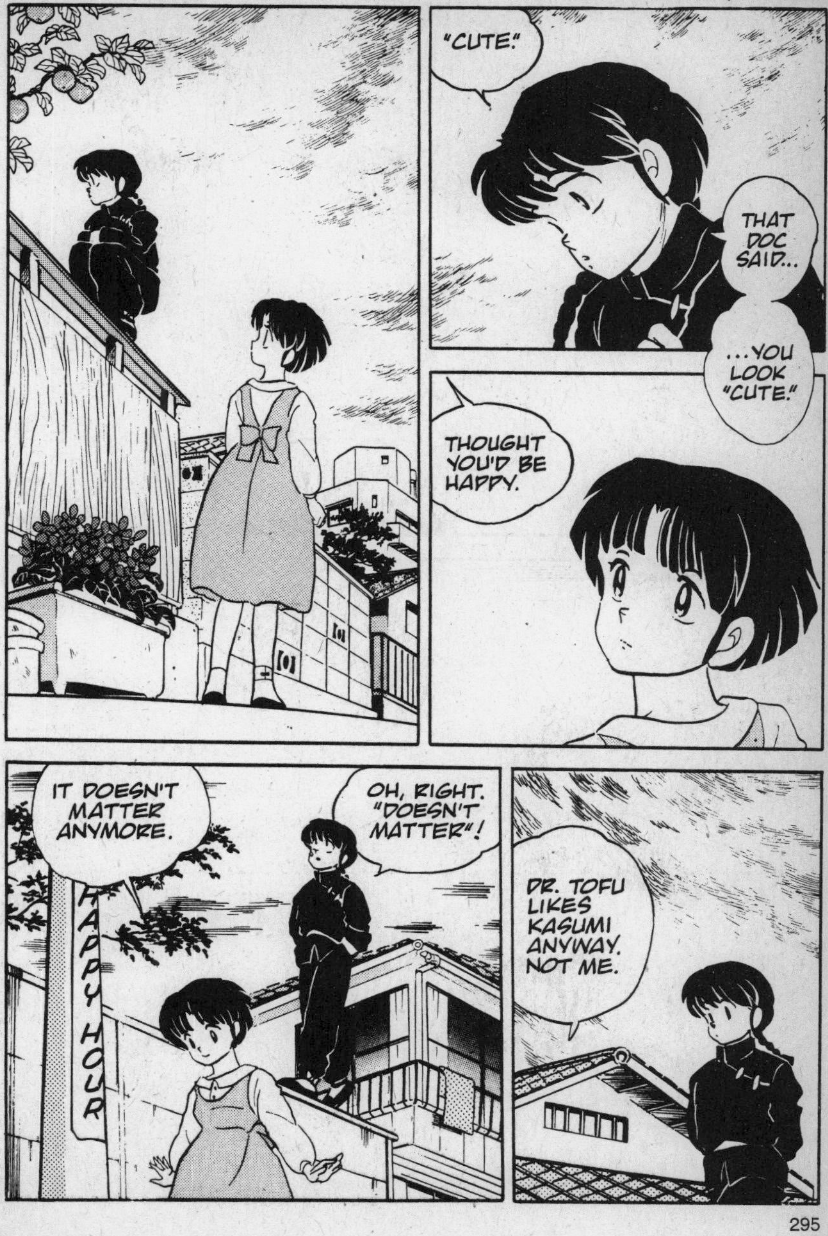
"CUTE."
THAT DOC SAID...
...YOU LOOK "CUTE."
THOUGHT YOU'D BE HAPPY.
IT DOESN'T MATTER ANYMORE.
HAPPY HOUR
OH, RIGHT. "DOESN'T MATTER"!
DR. TOFU LIKES KASUMI ANYWAY. NOT ME.

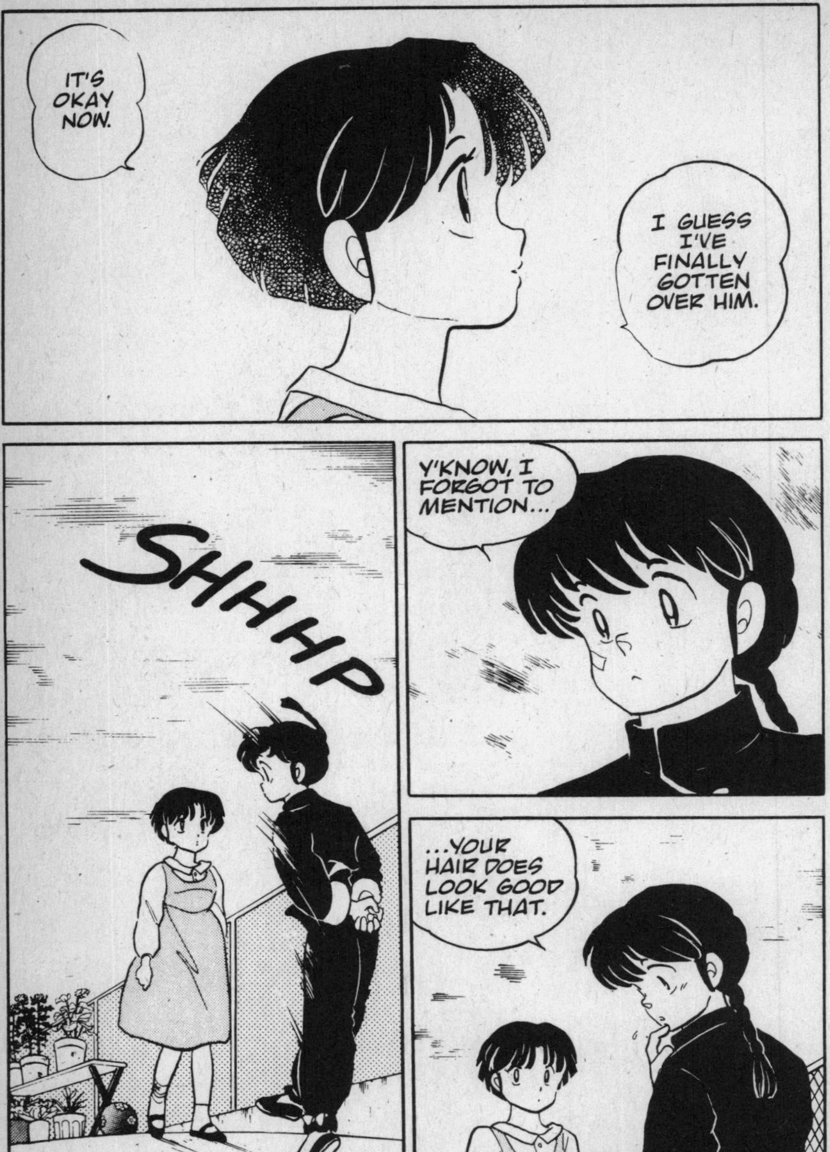
IT'S OKAY NOW.
I GUESS I'VE FINALLY GOTTEN OVER HIM.
SHHHP
Y'KNOW, I FORGOT TO MENTION...
...YOUR HAIR DOES LOOK GOOD LIKE THAT.

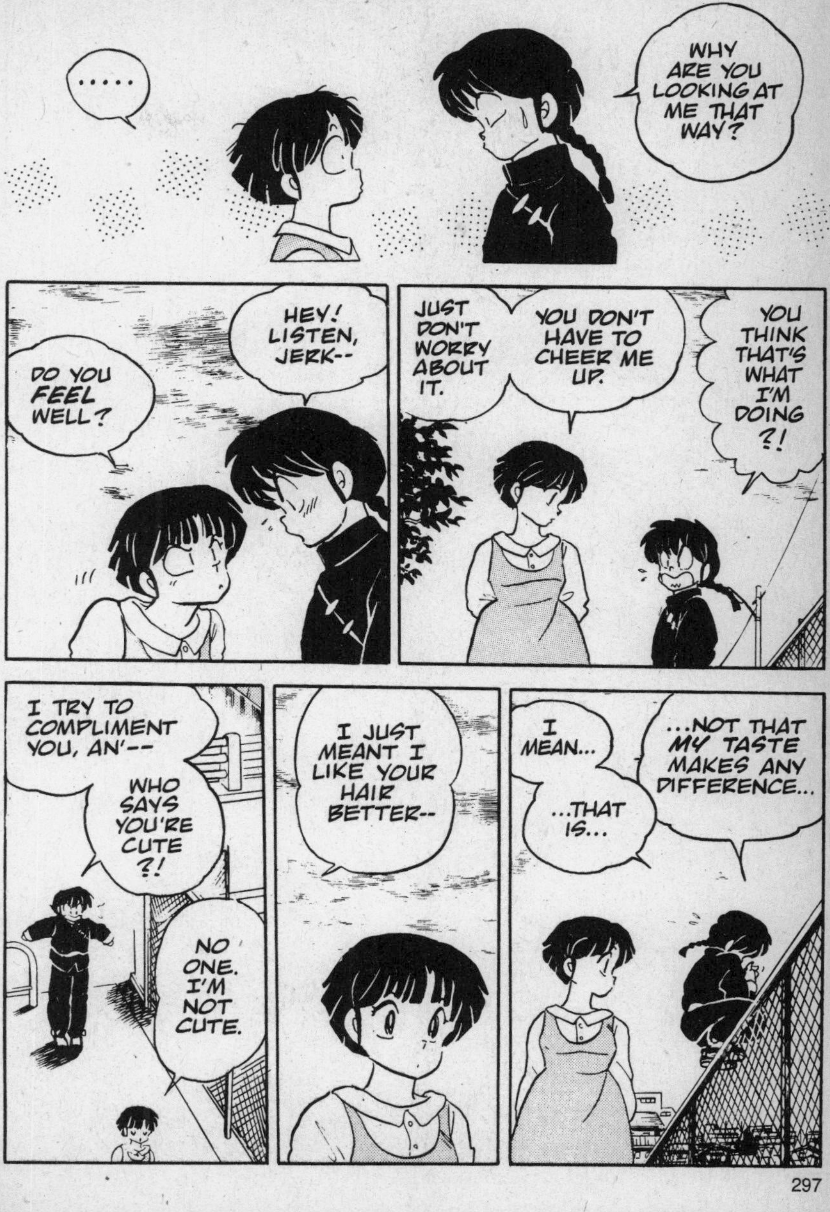
.....
WHY ARE YOU LOOKING AT ME THAT WAY?
DO YOU FEEL WELL?
HEY! LISTEN, JERK--
JUST DON'T WORRY ABOUT IT.
YOU DON'T HAVE TO CHEER ME UP.
YOU THINK THAT'S WHAT I'M DOING?!
I TRY TO COMPLIMENT YOU, AN'--
WHO SAYS YOU'RE CUTE?!
NO ONE. I'M NOT CUTE.
I JUST MEANT I LIKE YOUR HAIR BETTER--
I MEAN...
...THAT IS...
...NOT THAT MY TASTE MAKES ANY DIFFERENCE...

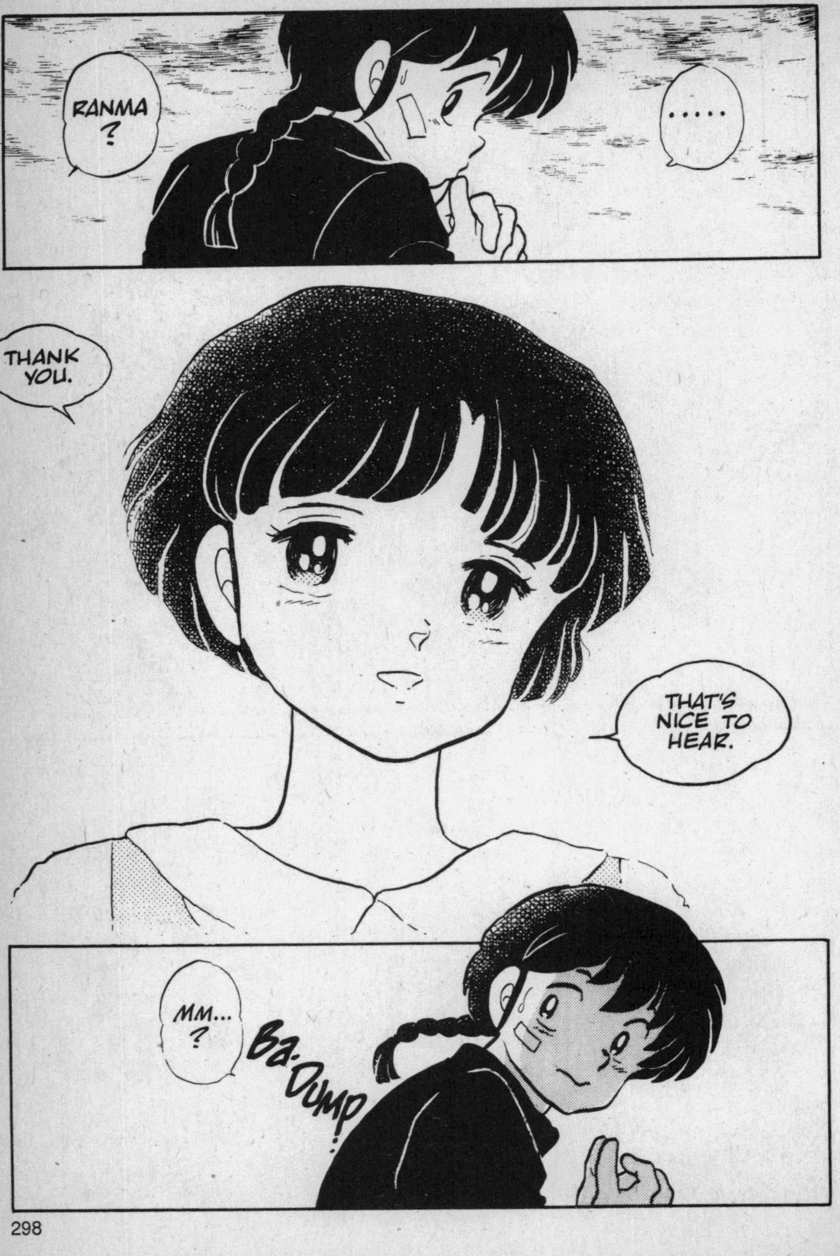
RANMA ?
.....
THANK YOU.
THAT'S NICE TO HEAR.
MM... ?
Ba-Dump!

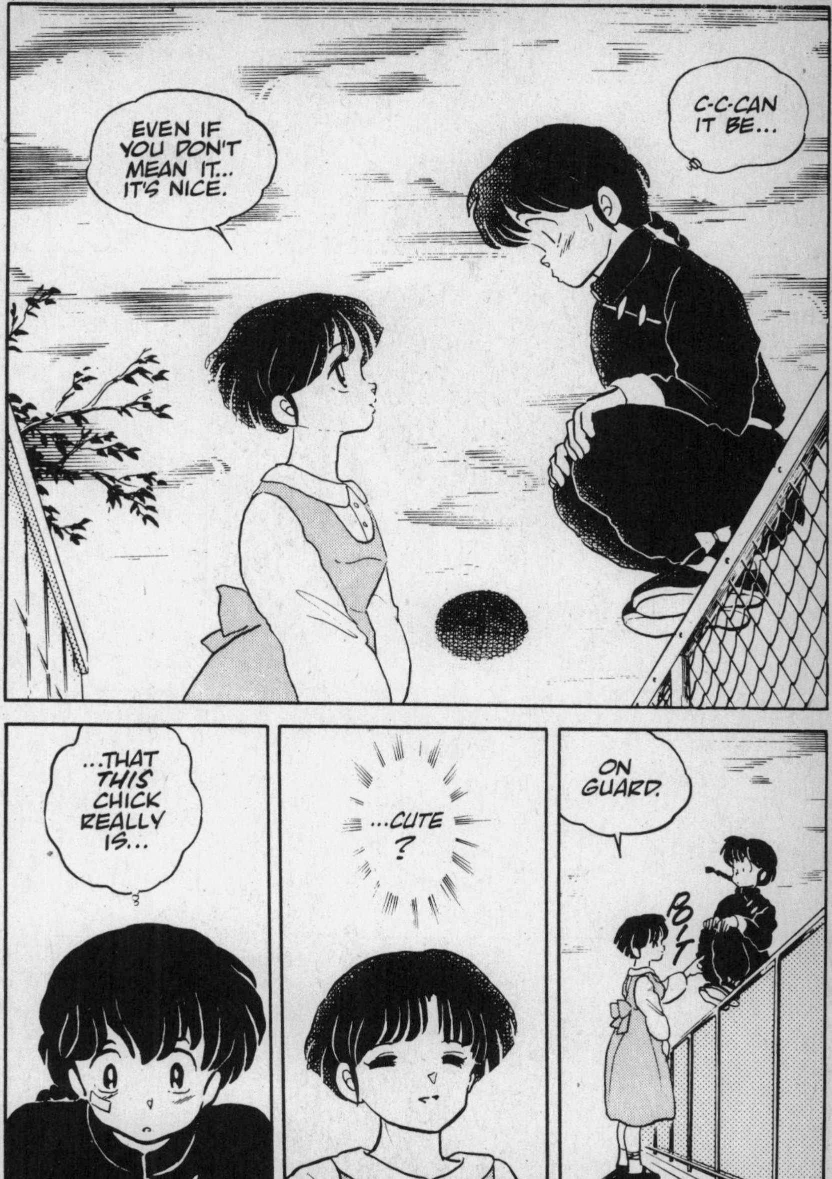
EVEN IF YOU DON'T MEAN IT... IT'S NICE.
C-C-CAN IT BE...
...THAT THIS CHICK REALLY IS...
...CUTE ?
ON GUARD.
POIT

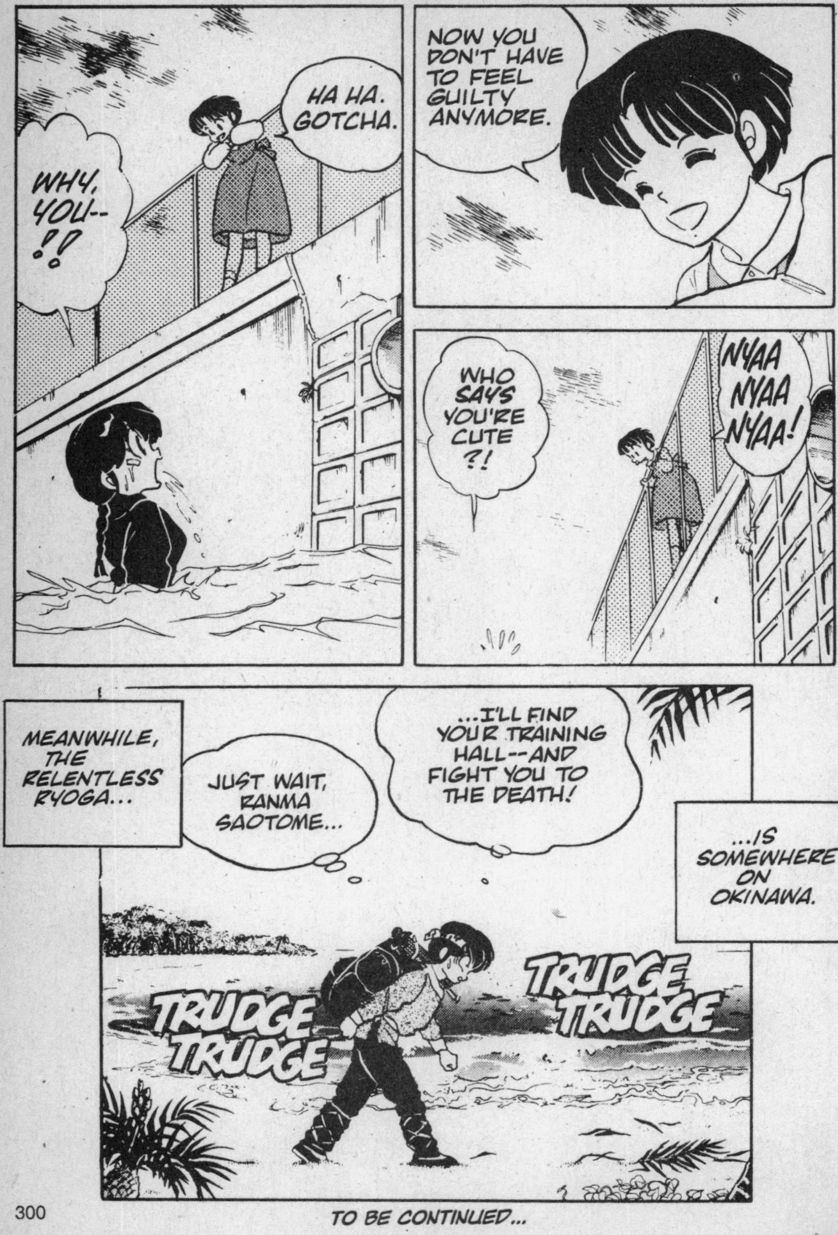

WHY, YOU-- !!
HA HA. GOTCHA.
NOW YOU DON'T HAVE TO FEEL GUILTY ANYMORE.
WHO SAYS YOU'RE CUTE ?!
NYAA NYAA NYAA!
MEANWHILE, THE RELENTLESS RYOGA...
JUST WAIT, RANMA SAOTOME...
...I'LL FIND YOUR TRAINING HALL--AND FIGHT YOU TO THE DEATH!
...IS SOMEWHERE ON OKINAWA.
TRUDGE TRUDGE
TRUDGE TRUDGE

TO BE CONTINUED...

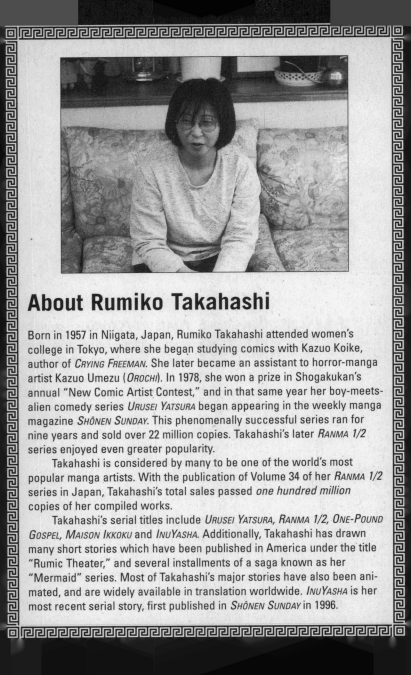

About Rumiko Takahashi

Born in 1957 in Niigata, Japan, Rumiko Takahashi attended women's college in Tokyo, where she began studying comics with Kazuo Koike, author of *CRYING FREEMAN*. She later became an assistant to horror-manga artist Kazuo Umezu (*OROCHI*). In 1978, she won a prize in Shogakukan's annual "New Comic Artist Contest," and in that same year her boy-meets-alien comedy series *URUSEI YATSURA* began appearing in the weekly manga magazine *SHÔNEN SUNDAY*. This phenomenally successful series ran for nine years and sold over 22 million copies. Takahashi's later *RANMA 1/2* series enjoyed even greater popularity.

Takahashi is considered by many to be one of the world's most popular manga artists. With the publication of Volume 34 of her *RANMA 1/2* series in Japan, Takahashi's total sales passed *one hundred million* copies of her compiled works.

Takahashi's serial titles include *URUSEI YATSURA, RANMA 1/2, ONE-POUND GOSPEL, MAISON IKKOKU* and *INUYASHA*. Additionally, Takahashi has drawn many short stories which have been published in America under the title "Rumic Theater," and several installments of a saga known as her "Mermaid" series. Most of Takahashi's major stories have also been animated, and are widely available in translation worldwide. *INUYASHA* is her most recent serial story, first published in *SHÔNEN SUNDAY* in 1996.

EDITOR'S RECOMMENDATIONS

d you like *RANMA 1/2?* Here's
at we recommend you try next:

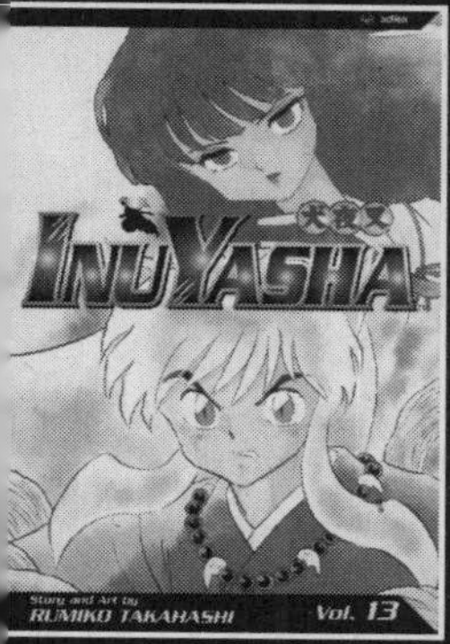
INUYASHA
RUMIKO TAKAHASHI
Vol. 13

INUYASHA is the manga serial Rumiko Takahashi began working on after she finished *RANMA 1/2*. It's a historical adventure set in ancient Japan, with romance, mystery, and horror elements.

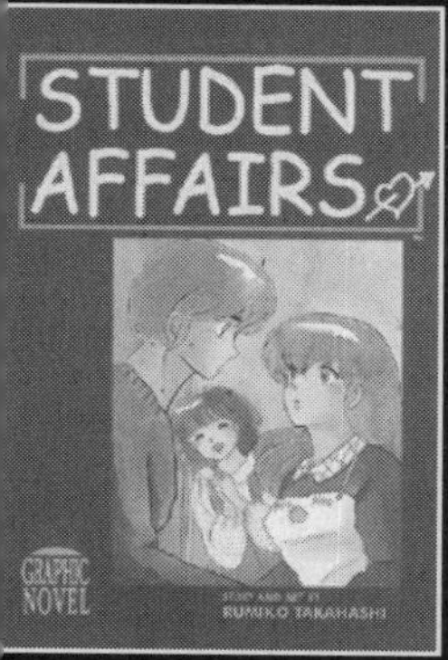
STUDENT AFFAIRS
GRAPHIC NOVEL
RUMIKO TAKAHASHI

MAISON IKKOKU is Takahashi's most romantic series. It's set in modern-day Japan, and traces the lives of the residents of a boarding house. It's intense, it's angsty, and it's one of the most absorbing manga romances ever written.

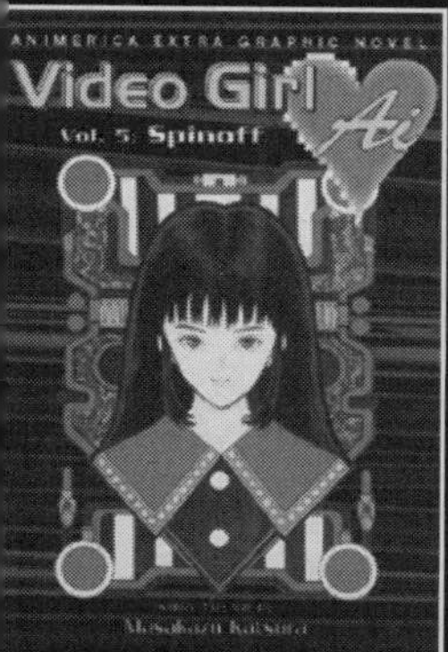
ANIMERICA EXTRA GRAPHIC NOVEL
Video Girl Ai
Vol. 5: Spinoff

VIDEO GIRL AI, by Masakazu Katsura, is a romance set in modern day Japan. Whereas *RANMA 1/2* deals with teen romances in a comedic way, *VIDEO GIRL AI* goes for angst, and masterfully explores the feelings of first love and loss. Katsura also draws some of the most beautiful women in manga!

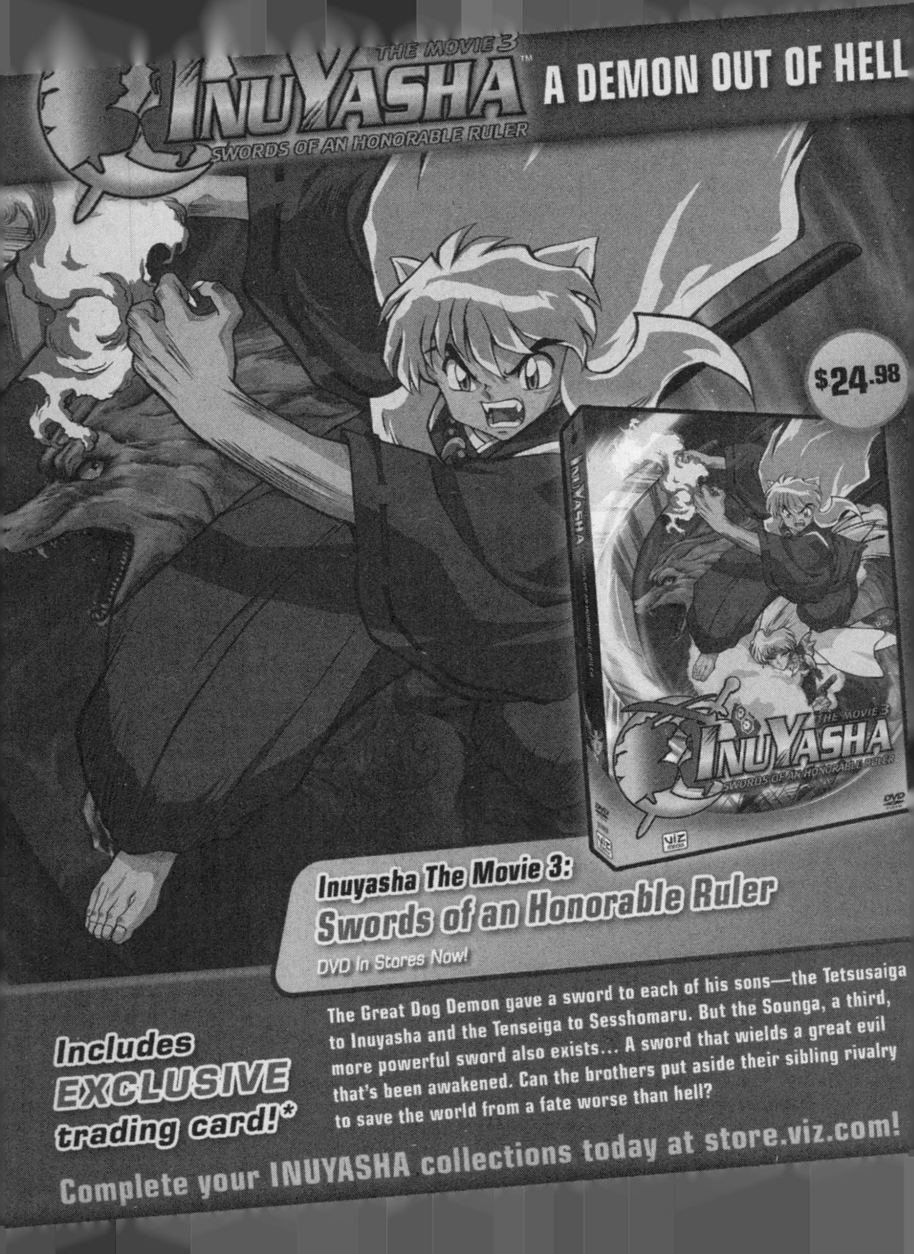
THE MOVIE 3
INUYASHA™
SWORDS OF AN HONORABLE RULER
A DEMON OUT OF HELL
$24.98
Inuyasha The Movie 3:
Swords of an Honorable Ruler
DVD In Stores Now!
The Great Dog Demon gave a sword to each of his sons—the Tetsusaiga
to Inuyasha and the Tenseiga to Sesshomaru. But the Sounga, a third,
more powerful sword also exists... A sword that wields a great evil
that's been awakened. Can the brothers put aside their sibling rivalry
to save the world from a fate worse than hell?
Includes EXCLUSIVE trading card!*
Complete your INUYASHA collections today at store.viz.com!

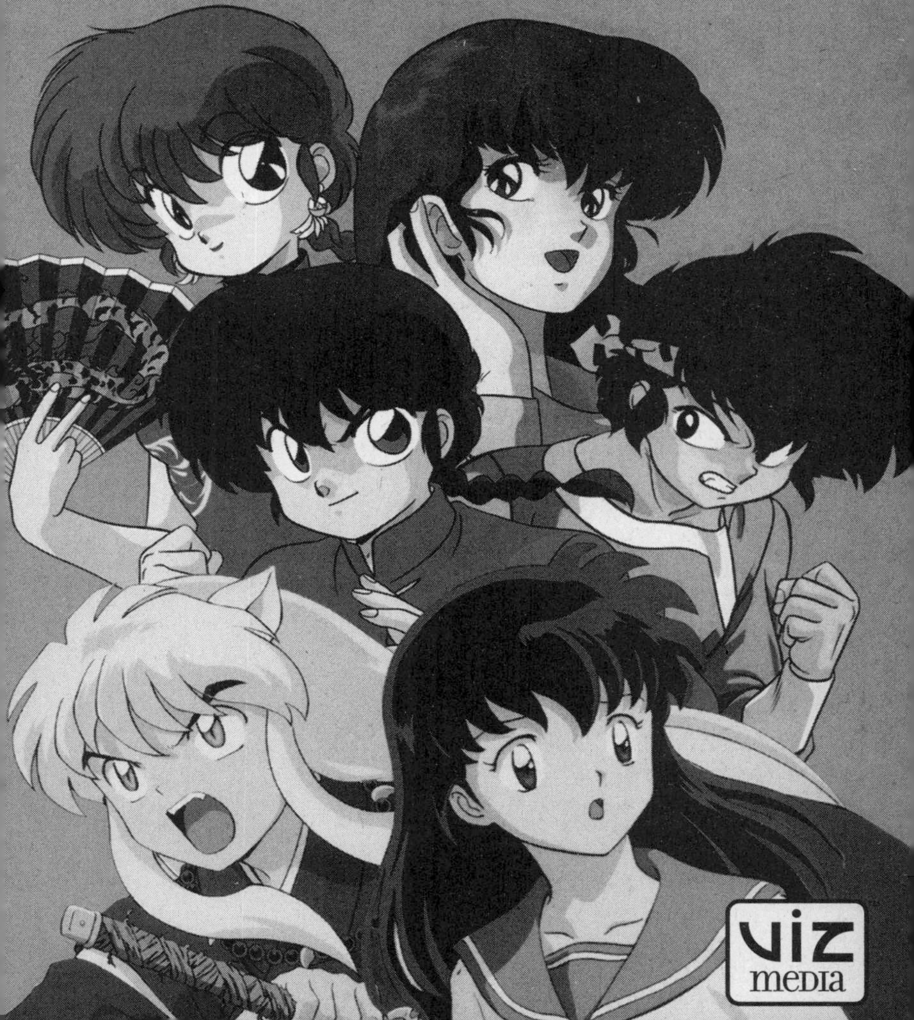

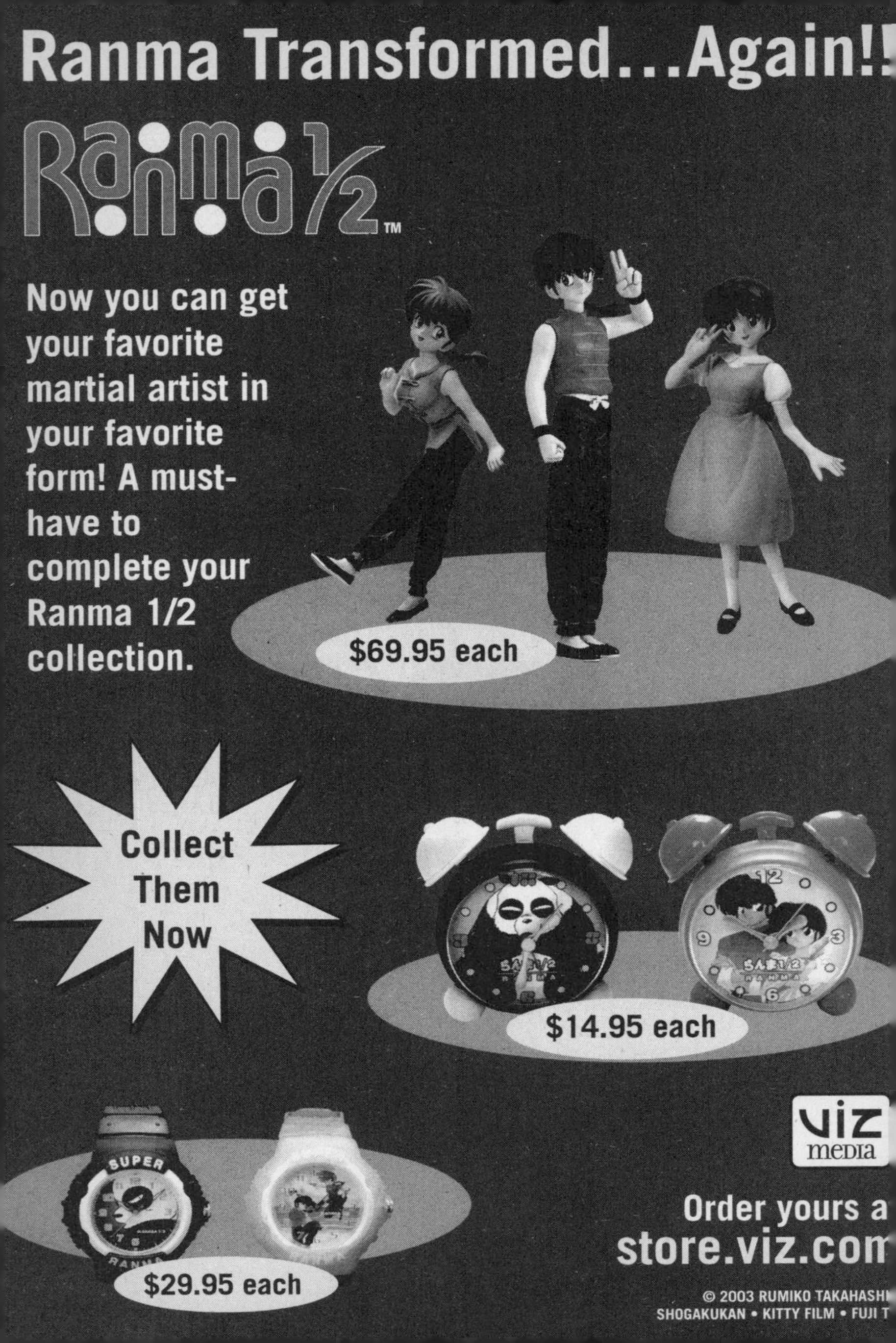
Ranma Transformed...Again!!
Ranma 1/2™
Now you can get your favorite martial artist in your favorite form! A must-have to complete your Ranma 1/2 collection.
$69.95 each
Collect Them Now
$14.95 each
$29.95 each
viz media
Order yours a
store.viz.com
© 2003 RUMIKO TAKAHASHI
SHOGAKUKAN • KITTY FILM • FUJI T

The Evolution of Science...
The Downfall of Man?

Based on the hit movie from Katsuhiro Otomo

STEAMBOY

Meet Ray Steam,
a resourceful
young inventor
whose father and
grandfather
have harnessed
the ultimate
energy source
that will transform
the world for
better or worse!

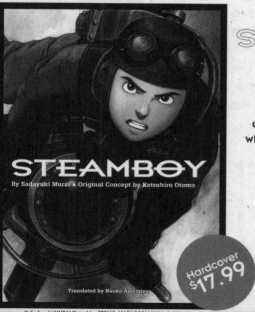

Their *Journey.*
Your **Adventure.**

Join Edward and Alphonse as they continue their quest for the Philosopher's Stone and a return to normalcy.

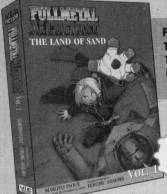

**Fullmetal Alchemist:
The Land of Sand**
The Elric brothers get their identity stolen. Now it's Alphonse and Edward vs. Alphonse and Edward: the ultimate alchemist smackdown!

$9.99
paperback

**Fullmetal Alchemist:
The Abducted Alchemist**
Alphonse and Edward get caught up in a string of terrorist bombings. Can they stop the reign of terror before they become suspects?

Full-length FULLMETAL ALCHEMIST novels now available.

Buy yours today at store.viz.com!

© Hiromu Arakawa, Makoto Inoue/SQUARE ENIX
Cover art subject to change.